D0883331
UNIVERSITY
LIBRARY

Teaching Elementary School Mathematics

FOURTH EDITION

Teaching Elementary School Mathematics

FOURTH EDITION

KLAAS KRAMER
State University College
Brockport, New York

Allyn and Bacon, Inc.
Boston, London, Sydney, Toronto

To Joan, Joanne, and Nick

Copyright © 1978, 1975, 1970, 1966 by Allyn and Bacon, Inc., 470 Atlantic Avenue, Boston, Massachusetts 02210. All rights reserved. Printed in the United States of America. No part of the material protected by this copyright notice may be reproduced or utilized in any form or by any means, electronic or mechanical, including photocopying, recording, or by any information storage and retrieval system, without written permission from the copyright owner.

Library of Congress Cataloging in Publication Data

Kramer, Klaas, 1916–
Teaching elementary school mathematics.

First ed. published in 1966 under title: The teaching of elementary school mathematics.
Includes bibliographies and index.
1. Mathematics—Study and teaching (Elementary)
I. Title.
QA135.5.K7 1978 372.7 77-28572
ISBN 0-205-06054-4

Contents

Preface

The fourth edition of *Teaching Elementary School Mathematics* has the same purpose as the previous three editions: to offer a program of instruction in mathematics for the elementary school. The program is based upon the author's many years of experience as a teacher of mathematics. The book is intended for use by elementary school teachers and by students preparing to teach mathematics in the elementary school.

Important characteristics of the program are:

1. Teachers are encouraged to use the inductive approach when introducing a process. This approach tends to stimulate class discussion and to encourage the pupils to form generalizations.
2. After the meaning of a process has been introduced, the necessity of supplying practice in using that process is stressed.
3. Promising ideas from new programs in elementary school mathematics have been incorporated.
4. A proper sequence of subject matter is suggested.
5. Number properties and patterns are emphasized.
6. Relationships between operations are stressed.
7. Systematic instruction in mental computation is emphasized and several examples are presented.
8. The need to respect individual differences is recognized. In many presentations of new processes various methods of solution are offered.

The book consists of three parts. Part I discusses past and present trends in the teaching of elementary school mathematics. Part II deals with topics in contemporary mathematics programs. It can serve as a review if the class has recently completed a course in mathematics. Part III presents content, methods, and materials for teaching mathematics. Skills tests are presented at the beginnings of Chapters 11–18 so that the student may determine whether or not he or she possesses prerequisite skills. If the student has difficulty with any of the computations in the skills tests, the deficiencies should be remedied before or during the study of the chapter. An answer key to the tests is provided at the end of the book.

In this fourth edition topics have been added, deleted, expanded, or condensed, and some research has been updated. The chapters entitled Geometry, Beginning Instruction in Mathematics, and The Metric System of Measures and Weights (SI) have been either rewritten or greatly expanded. And more activities for pupils have been introduced.

The author is indebted to Dr. Herbert F. Spitzer, formerly of the State University of Iowa, for stimulating his interest in the teaching of elementary school mathematics. Special thanks are also due to readers of the manuscript for several suggested improvements.

K.K.
Brockport, New York

I

Past and Present Trends

Basic Tenets and Trends 1

Advances in science have increased the body of mathematical knowledge and have led to a more extensive use of mathematics in technology and in daily life. More scientists and mathematicians are needed now than ever before. These developments have placed upon the institutions of learning a great responsibility to improve and accelerate the mathematics curriculum. The elementary school shares in this responsibility, for there the foundation of mathematics must be laid, its underlying principles taught, and a reasonable degree of skill in computation and problem solving developed.

Findings of experimental mathematics programs and research studies and discussions among educators, mathematicians, and psychologists have brought about changes in methods of teaching mathematics, in content offered, and in ways of dealing with individual differences. During the last few decades efforts have been made to improve basic methods of teaching by using new ideas concerning the learning process. At present, emphasis is placed on teaching the structure of mathematics, the development of thought patterns, and the forming of generalizations.

Additional topics such as geometry, probability, and statistics have been included in mathematics curriculum of the elementary school. Also, the increased use of the metric system of measures and weights makes its teaching mandatory.

In spite of all efforts to improve the teaching and learning of mathematics, pupil performance on nationally standardized tests has declined. As a result, recent critics of schools are calling for a "return to the basics." As stated elsewhere in this chapter, the expression "back to basics" may have different connotations for different people.

As an introduction to this volume's proposed program, Chapter 1 suggests some objectives for and characteristics of a desirable mathematics program in the elementary school, and identifies some trends in mathematics education.

LONG-RANGE GOALS

The history of arithmetic as a school subject—a survey of which is presented in Chapter 2—reveals that the aims of teaching mathematics have been undergoing continuous change. The disciplinary, utilitarian, mathematical, and social aims have each been dominant at various times. At present, the mathematical and social aspects of the subject are emphasized, and programs stressing mathematical understanding and social content are favored.

A statement of general purposes is a basic requirement for the construction of an elementary school curriculum and for the evaluation of teaching and learning. Several such statements can be found in professional books dealing with curriculum.

The Educational Policies Commission[1] emphasizes the fact that the general purpose, which runs through and strengthens all other purposes, is the development of the ability to think. The school must focus on this general purpose in teaching the fundamental processes.

General purposes should be developed into sets of clear objectives for each subject area. The school faculty should then agree on the desired outcomes for each grade level. A mathematics teacher should be acquainted with the scope and sequence of the mathematics the pupils[2] have studied in the preceding grades and will study in the following grades.

To assist the teacher in the formulation of objectives for mathematics instruction in the elementary school, the following long-range goals are suggested.

The pupil should acquire—

1. an *understanding* of the structure of the real number system, of basic geometric ideas, and of principles underlying the basic mathematical processes.
2. functional *knowledge* of quantitative terms and symbols; of graphs, scale drawings, charts, and tables; of simple geometric terms and figures; and of common measures.

---

1. Educational Policies Commission, National Education Association, *The Central Purpose of Education* (Washington, D.C.: The Association, 1961).

2. In this book, references to *pupils* mean male or female elementary school pupils; references to *students* mean male or female students of the teaching of elementary school mathematics—the readers of this book. Where the pronoun "he" is used, it is a contraction, for ease of reading, of "he or she." We have also used "he or she" and "child" in an effort to avoid sexist usage.

3. *skill* in:
   a. thinking critically—following and building patterns of organized thought;
   b. performing common written and mental computations with reasonable speed and accuracy;
   c. appraising the correctness of acquired results;
   d. applying acquired techniques intelligently in verbal problems, in other school subjects, and in daily life.
4. favorable *attitudes* toward mathematics and an awareness of the place and importance of mathematics in life.
5. *confidence* in his or her ability to reason independently.

BEHAVIORAL OBJECTIVES

Long-range goals serve as landmarks. They are important, but they are not sufficient. For each mathematics period the teacher has to plan teaching-learning strategies, depending upon the teacher's objectives, procedures, and evaluation techniques.

The trend is to express objectives in behavioral terms—in part a result of public demand for teacher accountability. Such objectives are being written by national, state, district, and school committees, by individual teachers, and by authors of text materials. The verbs "demonstrate," "show," "name," "state," "identify," "solve," "list," and "construct" are common terms in behavioral statements. Examine the following examples.

The pupil will

write a given number as a Roman numeral;

name the length of a given object;

construct a circle with a given radius;

apply the rule of compensation in subtraction;

identify a square.

In the numerous sets of behavioral or performance objectives that have been written, there is a great variation in specificity, content, and assessment.

Proponents of behavioral objectives claim that they help classroom teachers in planning instruction, make schools accountable for achieving their main goals, and can assist in individualizing instruction by keying the objectives to related topics in different textbooks.

Opponents don't like the triviality of many behavioral objectives and point to the danger that, if teachers will be satisfied when these requirements have been met, further possible learning will not be achieved and creativity will be discouraged.

The teacher's goals should include more than the development of mathematical skills, knowledge, and understanding; they should also include improving the pupil's attitudes toward the subject, building confidence, and motivating the pupil to go beyond the required tasks and to explore new ideas.

The National Advisory Committee on Mathematical Education (NACOME) concluded a discussion of the present trend to state mathematical competencies in behavioral terms as follows:[3]

> One of the unfortunate patterns in American response to educational innovation is a tendency to draw hard and fast battle lines between dichotomous positions. From both sides the debate over behavioral objectives and their uncritical application in mathematics instruction has taken on an "all or none" tone. The members of NACOME believe that the extreme and hard positions taken by some persons on each side of the debate are unhealthy and that both points of view lend valuable insight to the design, execution, and assessment of mathematics instruction. But we agree that implementation of an extremely narrow, overly-specific conception of behavioral objectives is a severe danger to mathematical education and we deplore much of what is current practice in producing more and more lists of low-level, narrow skills as the sole or major objectives of mathematical instruction. We challenge the uncritical acceptance of the engineering or management metaphors as the best models for educational practice.
>
> We urge all mathematics educators to tackle the task of developing and measuring attainment of the attitudes, problem solving, and critical thinking abilities traditionally judged so important in mathematics teaching. We urge similar experimentation with flexible curriculum structures that nonetheless convey to students the powerful unity of mathematical ideas and methods. And we urge that these mathematical ideas be offered in a variety of instructional modes until or unless sound research demonstrates (far more convincingly than evidence now available) superiority of particular methods.

CHARACTERISTICS OF A DESIRABLE PROGRAM

An elementary school mathematics program should possess the following characteristics:

I. *The pupil is guided to discover mathematical principles, patterns, and procedures.*

The best learning takes place when the pupils acquire a concept and find a procedure leading to the correct answer as a result of their being actively engaged in the learning process. The teacher's pertinent guide questions and interpretations assist the pupils in building and refining mathemat-

---

3. S. Hill et al., National Advisory Committee on Mathematical Education, *Overview and Analysis of School Mathematics Grades K–12* (Washington, D.C.: Conference Board of the Mathematical Sciences, 1975), p. 55.

ical concepts, in developing thought patterns, and in discovering relationships. Pupils are encouraged to think critically; to find, use, and test various methods of solution; and to prove their conclusions. New concepts are developed as an outgrowth of previous learnings. The process of learning, as well as the product, is emphasized. Thus, not only is the desire to arrive at a correct answer fostered, but a questioning attitude toward procedures and their critical evaluation is also encouraged. This method of teaching stimulates curiosity and elicits internal motivation. Although it is called the *discovery method,* the process is one of directed discovery. The time element and the ability of some pupils may make it impossible to adhere to this approach at all times. The teacher should strive to use the allotted time wisely and to guide the children as frequently as possible to the discovery of mathematical patterns, principles, rules, and relationships.

II. *Generalizations are formed inductively and applied deductively.* When a generalization is to be formed, the teacher presents a problem situation and invites the pupils to find the answer. The pupils attempt to do so by using concepts and knowledge already acquired. Then, in the class discussion, the processes are explored, patterns are identified, and the pupils are guided to form the generalization. This generalization is applied deductively in several exercises and word problems, and the pupils are encouraged to test the principle in more difficult cases.

III. *The pupil is guided through the necessary stages of development toward the formation of mathematical concepts. During this process, proper visual aids are used.*
Pupils should be provided with experiences that build a meaningful background for mathematical abstraction. In early number experiences, most children are led through the concrete and semiconcrete stages of development to the abstract stage.

Manipulative materials are used for the concrete stage. Physical experiences, such as working with the counting frame, the abacus, toy money, rods, and pegs, will be helpful for most pupils in the acquisition of mathematical concepts. For the semiconcrete stage, representations such as pictures, diagrams, dots, and marks are employed. During the abstract stage, the pupils work with mathematical symbols. Manipulation of materials by the children, representation of the situation on paper, and a gradual increase in the difficulty level of the stages offer even the below-average pupil the opportunity to learn to understand the process and to acquire the mathematical concepts involved. Because of the differences in mathematical maturity among children, some of them will not need to pursue the first stage of development identified above. On the other hand, there may be children for whom it will be difficult or even impossible to move to the abstract stage for a long time. It is the teacher's task to determine the degree of the child's maturity and to encourage him to work at a level that stimulates his continued progress.

IV. *Practice exercises are presented after the process to be mastered has been meaningfully explored.*
The abstract rote drill of several decades ago has been replaced by practice that aims at automatic mastery of facts the pupil understands and at anchoring skills he has explored meaningfully. The modern teacher recognizes the significance of such purposeful practice. He strives to make a process meaningful to the pupil and follows or accompanies this activity with sufficient number of practice exercises.

When assigning practice, the teacher should consider the following principles:

1. The pupil should understand what he is practicing, because:
   a. Processes that are understood require a minimum amount of practice to be mastered.
   b. Retention of processes is easier when those processes are understood.
   c. Forgotten skills seem to be more easily regained when the processes were originally understood.
   d. Meaningful work incites motivation to practice, since the pupil is more apt to see the need for the skill.
2. Practice should extend and consolidate understandings established by previous learning.
3. The pupil should be motivated to work the exercises and see a need for the practice.
4. Practice on the basic facts should aim at complete mastery.
5. Practice periods should be relatively short and should be scheduled frequently.
6. Practice should be carefully arranged so that mastered skills are reviewed in practice periods spaced by intervals that become gradually longer.
7. Practice on a skill should include different kinds of exercises so that monotony is avoided.
8. As a result of practice the pupil should develop confidence in his mathematical skill.

V. *In the selection of content, mathematical and social aims are considered.*
To satisfy the mathematical aim, content is selected that will build math-

ematical understanding. Expected outcomes include: an understanding of the structure of the real number system; an understanding of the fundamental operations; the discovery of principles, patterns, and relationships; the formulation of generalizations; and the ability to reason logically and think critically.

Content selected with the social aim in mind should serve to increase the pupils' proficiency in using mathematical knowledge in school and in daily life. For this purpose skills such as the following are stressed: written and mental computation; making change; estimating; measuring; problem solving; using quantitative terms; reading graphs, charts, tables, and scale drawings; and interpretating quantitative situations presented in newspapers, magazines, and books.

VI. *The program is mathematically correct and presents a sequential plan that is pedagogically sound.*
Good mathematics programs are built on unifying ideas, such as structure, operations, and generalizations. In these programs correct mathematical language is emphasized.

Since the acquisition of mathematical concepts is difficult for children, a sequential plan is followed in which the pupils are guided to form new abstractions by using knowledge and concepts they have already acquired. However, the logical sequence of the subject matter is not followed when it appears that, for psychological reasons, topics should be delayed.

VII. *The spiral plan is followed in the presentation of the content.*
The spiral plan calls for an organization of content in which learnings are maintained and extended at successive grade levels. This should result in a better mastery of skills and in refinement and extension of already established concepts.

The spiral type of content organization is illustrated in modern programs in which, for example, fractions are presented at each grade level. Whereas decades ago fractions were introduced in the intermediate grades, at present some simple concepts of fractional numbers are developed as early as Grade 1. In each successive grade the learnings are then reviewed and extended to include more difficult concepts.

VIII. *The program provides for individual differences.*
Analyses of test results reveal, as a rule, a wide range in intelligence and in level of achievement among pupils in the same grade. The range in ability in quantitative problem solving and in computation is usually quite wide and increases if good teaching and learning conditions prevail. This places on the teacher the responsibility of acquainting himself thoroughly

with the intellectual ability and mathematical achievement of each pupil and of planning his teaching and work assignments accordingly. A specified amount of practice may be too much for one pupil and not enough for another. Identification of each pupil's background, motivation, and ability is a most difficult and important task of the teacher. After a pupil's need has been determined, every effort should be made to meet it. In a good school each pupil is challenged to achieve as much as his ability allows.

Since individual instruction is impossible in the typical class of approximately thirty pupils, the teacher will have to select procedures for dealing with the problem from several available techniques. Such techniques include: ability grouping; assigning different amounts of practice; assigning different kinds of exercises; allowing different amounts of time; assigning contracts, as in the Dalton system; departmentalization; enrichment activities that pursue topics presented to the class in more depth or additional topics more advanced than those presented to the class; and remedial work for the slow learners.

IX. *Mathematical skills are used in quantitative problem situations that arise in class.*
Number situations emerge frequently from daily school activities and from the various school subjects. Money has to be counted, cost per pupil for a trip has to be estimated, results of drives have to be reported, tickets have to be sold, records have to be kept, etc. Various experiences that call for the use of mathematical skills are provided in the social studies, where, for example, maps have to be read, and in science, where such activities as the interpretation of statistics are often required. Such practical situations and applications make the pupils see the importance of mastering mathematical skills and offer opportunities for practice on meaningful materials. At each grade level, the resourceful teacher will identify situations in which quantitative problem solving is required and will use such situations to advantage.

X. *Proper motivational techniques are applied in order to arouse the child's interest in mathematics.*
The pupil learns best when his part in the learning process is an active one. Such an involvement is induced by motives, which are conditions that stimulate his activity. These motives incite him to pursue learnings. Thus, it is the task of the teacher to create an intellectual environment in the classroom conducive to development of proper motives.

The use of incentives that stimulate the child to perform in the desired way is called *motivation*. Motivation may be *extrinsic* or *intrinsic*.

In extrinsic motivation, external incentives or devices are applied to encourage the child to perform the task in order to attain some goal besides the mere completion of the assigned work. The child sees his activities as a means toward an end. Rewarding a pupil for good work or punishing him for poor work may stimulate him to meet the teacher's requirements. Rewards may consist of a high score, a prize, praise, prestige, etc. Punishment may also take several forms. In intrinsic motivation, the incentives are embodied in the task itself and the child has as his goal the fulfillment of the task to be performed. Such motives incite in the child the desire to study the subject for its own sake. The teacher's goal should be the development of intrinsic motivation.

Usually, extrinsic motives prevail originally. A child will start a task that has no appeal to him only because it has been assigned. In a wholesome learning environment, he should gradually begin to see the importance of the work he is doing, so that his motivation becomes intrinsic and he acquires a strong interest in the subject itself.

Many motivational techniques have been suggested for the teaching of elementary school mathematics. Such techniques include: arousing the pupil's interest in the content presented and stirring his curiosity; making the pupil see the importance of what he is doing and thereby feel the need for the work; conducting interviews with pupils for guidance purposes; teaching patterns of thought that the child can apply successfully; recognizing good work; reproving lack of effort; presenting enrichment activities, including games, puzzles, and mathematical tricks; allowing pupils to study programmed materials that fit their level of achievement; and using teaching aids, such as films, filmstrips, slides, bulletin boards, posters, clippings, pictures, and teaching machines. Several of these techniques will be described in the following chapters.

XI. *The effectiveness of teaching and learning is evaluated by using various methods and techniques, and identified weaknesses are removed.* In evaluating pupil progress in elementary school mathematics, the teacher first wants to appraise the degree of success of the teaching and learning processes in reaching specific goals of pupil development. The next step is to determine where improvement is needed.

After the interpretation of the data provided by measurement, the results are—ideally—put to use in these ways:

1. Weaknesses in the teaching procedures are removed.
2. Pupil deficiencies are remedied.
3. Pupils are informed of their progress so that proper motivation takes place.
4. Parents are supplied with information about their children's progress by written reports and by discussing these reports with them at regular intervals.

5. Pupils' records are kept up to date by entering all necessary information on the proper forms.

Traditionally, the scope of evaluation in arithmetic has been narrow. It has been concerned mainly with the pupils' speed and accuracy in computation and their skill in problem solving. At present, evaluation also seeks to determine the pupils' understanding of concepts and processes, their ability in applying skills, and their attitude toward the subject. In good programs an attempt is made to assess the children's skill in mental computation and their ability to decide whether the answer to a written computation makes sense.

Several methods and techniques are used in evaluating pupils' progress in elementary school mathematics. Both subjective appraisal and objective measurement are included in a good evaluation program. Because each of these methods has advantages and disadvantages, they should supplement each other.

When appraisal is made subjectively by using instruments that the teacher constructs, there is a strong tendency to consider the child's strengths and weaknesses and to evaluate the pupils' understandings, skills, knowledge, and attitudes according to what the teacher considers important. In doing this, the teacher may overlook or ignore important outcomes and may make premature and unreliable generalizations. When measures are arrived at objectively with instruments carefully constructed by experts, teacher bias is eliminated; however, there may be a tendency to treat the child as a number or a case, since local and personal conditions cannot be weighted proportionately.

By pooling information obtained from several sources and by applying different techniques, broad appraisal and narrow measurement are combined into a comprehensive program. Suggested techniques and methods include: (1) observation, (2) analysis of daily written work, (3) testing, and (4) interviewing.

THE "BACK-TO-BASICS" MOVEMENT

The National Assessment of Educational Progress (NAEP) conducted during the 1972–1973 school year an assessment in mathematics of nine-year-olds, thirteen-year-olds, seventeen-year-olds, and young adults. The results were not encouraging. Some of the findings of the survey are presented in the Selected Research section near the end of this chapter.

Mean scores on the mathematics part of the Scholastic Aptitude Test (SAT) taken by many high school students fell from 502 (on a range of 200–800) in the 1962–1963 school year to 472 in the 1974–1975 school year.

The decline in basic mathematical skills has caused a "back-to-basics" trend. A return to the basics does not have the same connotation for all who advocate it. Hopefully, not many critics will want to return to the exclusive rote-drill method and eliminate teaching for mathematical understanding.

Glennon[4] writes:

I believe that in the years immediately ahead we can stop reinventing the wheel and stop repeating the mistakes of our past. In tomorrow's school math program we will, I hope, find continued emphasis on sequential, systematic, and structured teaching using a variety of programs, working in settings of individualizing through small-group instruction in a socio-emotional climate reflecting the new humanism.

The National Council of Teachers of Mathematics issued the following position statement on basic skills:[5]

The National Council of Teachers of Mathematics is encouraged by the current public concern for universal competence in the basic computational skills. The Council supports strong school programs that promote computational competence within a good mathematics program, and we urge all teachers of mathematics to respond to this concern in positive ways.

We are deeply distressed, however, by the danger that the "back to basics" movement might eliminate teaching for mathematical understanding. It will do citizens no good to have the ability to compute if they do not know what computations to perform when they meet a problem. The use of the hand-held calculator emphasizes this need for understanding: one must know when to push what button.

Consider in this regard a disturbing result of one recent national examination. Students were asked to determine 70 percent of the 4,200 votes cast in an election. Almost half of the thirteen-year-olds and one out of five of the seventeen-year-olds applied the wrong arithmetic process. Some divided, some added, and some subtracted! Computational skills in isolation are not enough; the student must know *when* as well as *how* to multiply. We must address skills, but we must address them within a total mathematics program.

In a total mathematics program, students need more than arithmetic skill and understanding. They need to develop geometric intuition as an aid to problem solving. They must be able to interpret data. Without these and many other mathematical understandings, citizens are not mathematically functional.

Yes, let us stress basics, but let us stress them in the context of total mathematics instruction.

Hilton and Rising[6] expressed the following thoughts:

---

4. V.J. Glennon, "Mathematics: How Firm the Foundations?" *Phi Delta Kappan* (January, 1976), p. 305.

5. National Council of Teachers of Mathematics, *Newsletter,* (December, 1976).

6. P.H. Hilton and G.R. Rising, "Thoughts on the State of Mathematics Education Today," *The NIE Conference on Basic Mathematical Skills and Learning,* vol. II (Euclid, Ohio: National Institute of Education, 1975), p. 35.

> . . . we wish to emphasize that mathematics, however important, forms only a part of education. The SAT statistics, which have created so much furore recently, show quite clearly that the decline in arithmetical skills is simply a part of the general decline in the effectiveness of basic education. We must insist that it is not fair or reasonable to stigmatize mathematics education as if it were an isolated instance of educational failure. We believe that there will be a really significant improvement in the effectiveness of mathematics education only when the importance of education itself is once again recognized by all the constituencies that education serves; primary among these are the students themselves, their parents and their teachers. And, by the same token, mathematics education will only be effective when it, mathematics education itself, is recognized as important by all teachers regardless of their specialties.

The basics should indeed be stressed in the context of total mathematics instruction. In addition, ways and means of increasing the time allotted to mathematics in the elementary school should be found—to provide more opportunities both for meaningful computational practice designed to anchor acquired skills and for applying such skills in quantitative problem solving.

INDIVIDUALIZATION OF INSTRUCTION[7]

The concern to gear teaching and learning to the capability of each pupil has led to the development of programs in which instruction is individualized. One such program is the Individually Prescribed Instruction (IPI) project, which is briefly described in Chapter 3.

In a program that attempts to individualize instruction completely, the pupil takes diagnostic tests, works prescribed assignments, is post-tested, and, if the objectives have not been achieved, works additional prescribed assignments.

Criticisms of individualization of instruction include: (1) Interaction with the teacher and with other pupils—a valuable source of learning—is lacking. (2) All pupils work the same assignments and only the pace of learning differs. (3) The amount of record-keeping takes too much time.

A distinction should be made between individualization of instruction as described above and the techniques that teachers use to provide for individual differences, several of which were listed previously in this chapter.

---

7. For a presentation of patterns of instruction, the student is referred to: S. Hill et al., National Advisory Committee on Mathematical Education, *Overview and Analysis of School Mathematics Grades K–12* (Washington, D.C.: Conference Board of the Mathematical Sciences, 1975), chap. III.

SELECTED RESEARCH

During the 1972–1973 school year, the National Assessment of Educational Progress (NAEP) conducted an assessment in mathematics in order to provide data on Americans' mathematical skills and knowledge.[8] The assessment involved approximately 25,000 nine-year-olds, 30,000 thirteen-year-olds, 34,000 seventeen-year-olds, and 4,000 young adults of ages 26–35.

Some sample items and percentages of correct responses by age level are presented below.

	Age 9	Age 13	Age 17	Adult
1. Add: $\begin{array}{r} 38 \\ +19 \\ \hline \end{array}$				
Correct response:	79%	94%	97%	97%
2. Add: $\begin{array}{r} \$\ 3.09 \\ 10.00 \\ 9.14 \\ 5.10 \\ \hline \end{array}$				
Correct response:	40%	84%	92%	86%
3. Subtract: $\begin{array}{r} 36 \\ -19 \\ \hline \end{array}$				
Correct response:	55%	89%	92%	92%
4. Multiply: $\begin{array}{r} 38 \\ \times\ 9 \\ \hline \end{array}$				
Correct response:	25%	83%	88%	81%
5. Divide: $5\overline{)125}$				
Correct response:	15%	89%	93%	93%
6. Add: $\frac{1}{2} + \frac{1}{3} =$				
Correct response:		42%	66%	

8. *Math Fundamentals: Selected Results from the First National Assessment of Mathematics* (Denver: National Assessment of Educational Progress, 1975). Available from the Superintendent of Documents, U.S. Government Printing Office, Washington, D.C.

7. 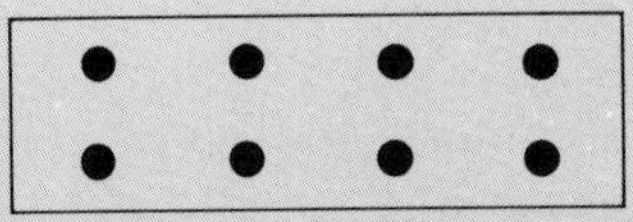

If one fourth of the dots on the above figure are removed, how many dots will be left?

	Age 9
Correct response:	21%

8. Mary took four spelling tests. Each test had 30 words. On the four tests she spelled correctly the following number of words:

25, 23, 27, and 24

Altogether, how many words did she MISS on all four tests?

	Age 9	Age 13
Correct response:	16%	60%

9. If John drives at an average speed of 50 miles an hour, how many hours will it take him to drive 275 miles?

	Age 9	Age 13	Age 17	Adult
Correct response:	6%	33%	64%	67%

EXERCISES

1. Give examples of ways in which creativity in mathematics can be fostered in children.
2. Explain the statement: The best learning takes place when the child takes an active part in the learning process.
3. Illustrate the use of the inductive and the deductive approach in elementary school mathematics.
4. On the basis of the characteristics of a desirable program as outlined in this chapter, describe some differences between contemporary elementary school mathematics programs and those in use at the time you were an elementary school pupil.
5. Explain the statement: The best motivation is intrinsic motivation.
6. Examine a set of behavioral objectives for a grade level that interests you. Select from the list those objectives which, in your opinion, identify trivial behaviors.
7. State and defend your opinion on the "back-to-basics" movement.
8. Report on the research study described in this chapter.

SOURCES FOR FURTHER READING

Biggs, E. E., and M. L. Hartung, "The Role of Experience in the Learning of Mathematics," *The Arithmetic Teacher,* May, 1971, pp. 278–295.

Brownell, W. A., "Meaning and Skill: Maintaining the Balance," *The Arithmetic Teacher,* October, 1956, pp. 129–136.

"Curriculum for the Elementary School (K–6)," *Goals for School Mathematics,* The Report of the Cambridge Conference on School Mathematics. Boston: Houghton Mifflin Company, 1973, pp. 31–41.

Edwards, E. L., Jr., E. D. Nichols, and G. H. Sharpe, "Mathematical Competencies and Skills Essential for Enlightened Citizens," *The Arithmetic Teacher,* November, 1972, pp. 601–607.

Fehr, H. F., "Modern Mathematics and Good Pedagogy," *The Arithmetic Teacher,* November, 1963, pp. 402–411.

Gronlund, N. E., *Stating Behavioral Objectives for Classroom Instruction.* New York: Macmillan Publishing Company, Inc., 1971.

Kersh, B. Y., "Learning by Discovery: Instructional Strategies," *The Arithmetic Teacher,* October, 1965, pp. 414–417.

Kline, M., *Why Johnny Can't Add: The Failure of the New Math.* New York: Vintage Books, 1974.

National Advisory Committee on Mathematical Education, *Overview and Analysis of School Mathematics Grades K–12.* Washington, D.C.: Conference Board of the Mathematical Sciences, 1975.

Nichols, E. D., "Are Behavioral Objectives the Answer?" *The Arithmetic Teacher,* October, 1972, pp. 418, 474–476.

Riedesel, C. A., *Guiding Discovery in Elementary School Mathematics,* 2nd ed. Englewood Cliffs: Prentice Hall, Inc., 1973, Chap. XVII.

Sund, R. B., and A. J. Picard, *Behavioral Objectives and Evaluation Measures: Science and Mathematics.* Columbus: Charles E. Merrill Publishing Company, 1972.

Suydam, M. N., *Evaluation in the Mathematics Classroom.* Columbus: ERIC Information Center for Science, Mathematics, and Environmental Education, 1974.

TenBrink, T. D., *Evaluation: A Practical Guide for Teachers.* New York: McGraw-Hill Book Company, 1974.

Walbesser, H. H., "Behavioral Objectives, A Cause Célèbre," *The Arithmetic Teacher,* October, 1972, pp. 418, 436–440.

Westcott, A. M., and J. A. Smith, *Creative Teaching of Mathematics in the Elementary School.* II. Boston: Allyn and Bacon, Inc., 1978.

Worthen, B. R., "A Study of Discovery and Expository Presentation: Implications for Teaching," *Journal of Teacher Education,* Summer, 1968, pp. 223–242.

Historical Antecedents of Current Mathematics Teaching

2

The place mathematics now occupies in the curriculum of the elementary school, the content taught, and the methods of presentation are a result of a gradual development of the subject, the differing and increased needs of society, and the findings of educators and psychologists concerning the way in which children learn. An examination of literature available on the history of mathematics as a school subject reveals gradual expansion of the content, changes in purposes of teaching the subject, and continuous improvement in method of presentation.[1]

BEGINNINGS

There are indications that as early as four or five thousand years ago a book on mathematics was written in Egypt, where the subject was studied by the priests and its main principles taught to children. The Babylonians made great advances in mathematics. Records and materials that have been discovered, such as tablets with mathematical data, bank accounts, and specimens of pupils' arithmetic work, point to a high level of mathematical achievement. The Greeks included mathematics in the requirements for a liberal education.

During the Middle Ages, arithmetic was included in the "Seven Liberal Arts," and it was taught in the church schools for religious purposes,

---

1. For much of the information contained in this chapter the author is indebted to Commissioner of Education, "Development of Arithmetic as a School Subject," bulletin no. 10 (Washington, D.C.: U.S. Government Printing Office, 1917).

such as the computation of the dates of religious holidays. The Hanseatic League, an organization founded in the thirteenth century to protect trade routes, was the cause of the establishment of "Rechen Schulen," special schools in which commercial arithmetic was taught.

During the Renaissance, several factors stimulated the expansion of mathematics. The invention of the art of printing aided the process of standardization of mathematical terms and symbols and helped the knowledge of mathematics to spread gradually. The increase in trade necessitated teaching the subject to more people. The replacement of the Roman system by the Hindu-Arabic system, which was finally accomplished in the sixteenth century, simplified calculation. Through all these influences, arithmetic gradually became established as one of the common school subjects. However, since the use of the Hindu-Arabic symbols made calculation simpler, the abacus was discarded, and throughout the following few centuries the teaching of arithmetic consisted primarily of having pupils copy examples, memorize rules, and

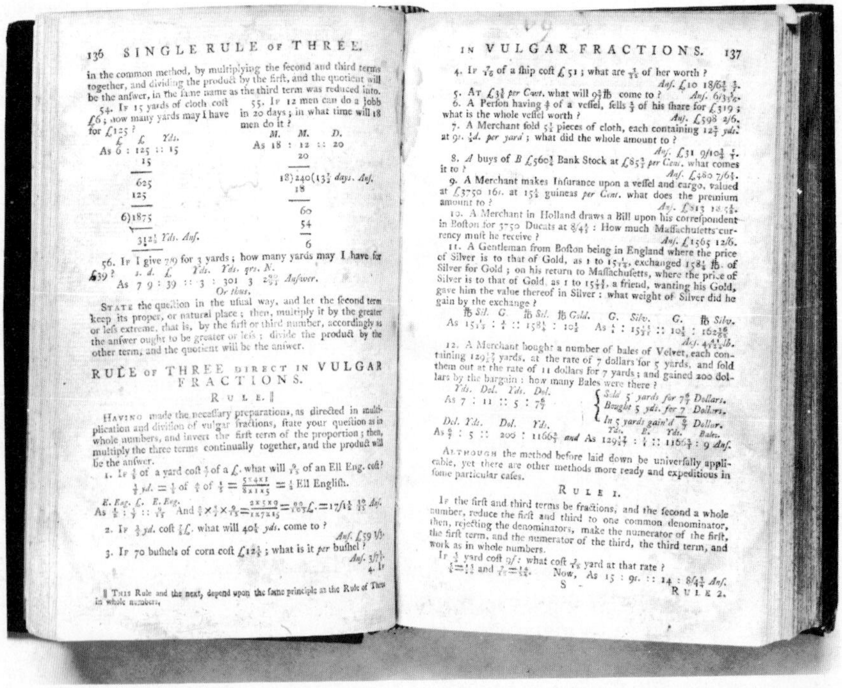

136 SINGLE RULE OF THREE.

in the common method, by multiplying the second and third terms together, and dividing the product by the first, and the quotient will be the answer, in the same name as the third term was reduced into.

54. If 15 yards of cloth cost £6; how many yards may I have for £125?

As 6 : 125 :: 15 — 312½ Yds. Ans.

55. If 12 men can do a jobb in 20 days; in what time will 18 men do it?

As 18 : 12 :: 20 — 18)240(13⅓ days. Ans.

56. If I give 7/9 for 3 yards; how many yards may I have for £39?

As 7 9 : 39 :: 3 : 301 3 $2\frac{90}{93}$ Answer.

Or thus.

State the question in the usual way, and let the second term keep its proper, or natural place; then, multiply it by the greater or less extreme, that is, by the first or third number, accordingly as the answer ought to be greater or less; divide the product by the other term, and the quotient will be the answer.

RULE OF THREE DIRECT IN VULGAR FRACTIONS.

RULE.‖

Having made the necessary preparations, as directed in multiplication and division of vulgar fractions, state your question as in whole numbers, and invert the first term of the proportion; then, multiply the three terms continually together, and the product will be the answer.

1. If ⅜ of a yard cost ⅖ of a £. what will $\frac{9}{15}$ of an Ell Eng. cost?

2. If ⅔ yd. cost ⅘ £. what will 40½ yds. come to? Ans. £59 1/3.

3. If 70 bushels of corn cost £12⅔; what is it per bushel? Ans. 3/7⅓.

‖ This Rule and the next, depend upon the same principle as the Rule of Three in whole numbers.

IN VULGAR FRACTIONS. 137

4. If $\frac{7}{16}$ of a ship cost £51; what are $\frac{5}{32}$ of her worth? Ans. £10 18/6¾ ⅐.

5. At £3⅞ per Cwt. what will 9½ ℔ come to? Ans. 6/3$\frac{5}{16}$.

6. A Person having ⅘ of a vessel, sells ⅔ of his share for £319; what is the whole vessel worth? Ans. £598 2/6.

7. A Merchant sold 5½ pieces of cloth, each containing 12⅔ yds. at 9s. ½d. per yard; what did the whole amount to? Ans. £31 9/10¾ ⅐.

8. A buys of B £560¾ Bank Stock at £85⅗ per Cent. what comes it to? Ans. £480 7/6¼.

9. A Merchant makes Insurance upon a vessel and cargo, valued at £3750 16s. at 15½ guineas per Cent. what does the premium amount to? Ans. £813 18.5½.

10. A Merchant in Holland draws a Bill upon his correspondent in Boston for 3750 Ducats at 8/4⅕: How much Massachusetts currency must he receive? Ans. £1565 12/6.

11. A Gentleman from Boston being in England where the price of Silver is to that of Gold, as 1 to 15$\frac{1}{12}$, exchanged 158¼ ℔. of Silver for Gold; on his return to Massachusetts, where the price of Silver is to that of Gold, as 1 to 15$\frac{1}{11}$, a friend, wanting his Gold, gave him the value thereof in Silver: what weight of Silver did he gain by the exchange?

12. A Merchant bought a number of bales of Velvet, each containing 129$\frac{17}{21}$ yards, at the rate of 7 dollars for 5 yards, and sold them out at the rate of 11 dollars for 7 yards; and gained 200 dollars by the bargain: how many Bales were there?

As 7 : 11 :: 5 : 7$\frac{6}{7}$

Sold 5 yards for 7$\frac{6}{7}$ Dollars.
Bought 5 yds. for 7 Dollars.
In 5 yards gain'd $\frac{6}{7}$ Dollar.

Although the method before laid down be universally applicable, yet there are other methods more ready and expeditious in some particular cases.

RULE 1.

If the first and third terms be fractions, and the second a whole number, reduce the first and third to one common denominator, then, rejecting the denominators, make the numerator of the first, the first term, and the numerator of the third, the third term, and work as in whole numbers.

If ⅗ yard cost 9/: what cost $\frac{7}{15}$ yard at that rate?

Now, As 15 : 9s. :: 14 : 8/4⅘ Ans.

S

RULE 2.

Two-page spread from *A New and Complete System of Arithmetic,* by Nicholas Pike, published in 1788 by John Mycall of Newburyport, Mass. Supplied through the courtesy of Esther Unkel.

juggle figures. Not until the eighteenth century were improvements made. Methods employing objects and pictures were used to make the fundamental processes more meaningful to children and to introduce arithmetic problems in a concrete way. The greatest influence on the method of teaching arithmetic was exerted by the Swiss educator Johann Heinrich Pestalozzi (1746–1827), who utilized objects in his teaching, insisted upon a clear understanding of arithmetical concepts before drill, introduced the subject as early as Grade 1, and emphasized the importance of mental arithmetic. Pestalozzi's influence reached as far as the United States.

ARITHMETIC AS A SCHOOL SUBJECT IN THE UNITED STATES

From the Beginnings of the Colonies to 1821

From the time that the colonies were founded, arithmetic was probably taught in many public schools to satisfy the need of the settlers for some knowledge of the subject in order to carry on their many activities in trade and commerce. During the middle of the eighteenth century, Benjamin Franklin encouraged the teaching of arithmetic because of its utility. By 1789, when the teaching of arithmetic was made obligatory in the states of Massachusetts and New Hampshire, colleges had begun to require the subject for entrance and arithmetic had become an essential part of the grammar school curriculum.

During this time, arithmetic textbooks were very scarce. It was an exception for a pupil to possess a book, and many teachers had only their own written copy. The child was provided with a blankbook or ciphering book, in which he daily wrote "sums," rules, and solutions. The master set the pupil a "sum," told him the rule for its solution without any explanation, and the child had to try to work the "sum" on scrap paper or on a slate. When it has been solved to the master's satisfaction, the pupil had to copy the solution into his ciphering book. If the pupil's answer did not agree with the one in the master's book, the child had to try again.

The earliest arithmetic books used in the colonies were of English authorship. The first American arithmetic textbook, published in 1729, was followed by several other arithmetic books. The most popular textbook was probably Nathan Daboll's *Schoolmaster's Assistant,* published in 1799, although several other texts were also widely used.

The arithmetic books of this period presented a large number of rules. The "sum" had to be solved by written computation, and exercises in mental arithmetic were not included. The order of instruction was from the abstract to the concrete. The children were instructed to begin by committing the rule to memory. Very little time was devoted to practice. The presentations were topical. Usually the topics "notation" and "numeration" were followed by the fundamental operations of addition, subtraction, multiplication, and division, in that order. Fractions were dealt with extensively in some books; in others they received only minor attention. Decimals were stressed after 1786, when federal money was established. Other topics included denominate numbers, the rule of three, barter, partnership, exchange, applications of percentage, progressions, permutations, longitude and time, mensuration, duodecimals, and puzzles.

From 1821 to 1892

Warren Colburn published his *First Lessons in Arithmetic on the Plan of Pestalozzi* in 1821. He is said to have exerted a greater influence than any other person upon the development of arithmetic as a school subject in the United States.

Pestalozzi held that the faculties or capacities of the child were developed naturally, but that man had to assist the development by using the materials and art of instruction employed by nature. To Pestalozzi, sense impressions were the foundation of all knowledge, and arithmetic was the most important means of giving mental training that would result in the power to form clear ideas. Thus, the elements of arithmetic had to be identified, and in the method of instruction a series of steps had to be formulated. When the elements of the subject were taught in the proper sequence, clear ideas would be formed. A clear idea of the number seven, for example, had to be acquired by counting seven objects. Children used their fingers, pebbles, or other objects to obtain the proper sense perceptions.

Several "tables" were devised by Pestalozzi to serve as aids. The units table consisted of ten rows of ten rectangles. Each rectangle in the first row had one vertical mark, each rectangle in the second row had two vertical marks, etc. Eight sets of exercises were to follow the presentations. One consisted of counting exercises; another involved expressing a number of units as twos, threes, fours, etc.

Pestalozzi attempted to analyze the process of the human mind psychologically and aimed at training the child's mental powers by using arithmetic exercises in which the subject had been reduced to its elements. During the first part of the training, no arithmetic symbols were presented, since clear number ideas and their relations were stressed. These were to be acquired by counting, expressing numbers in different ways, putting units together, and separating them. Such activities were meant to lead the child to the consciousness of "the real relations of things, which lie at the bottom of all calculation." Consequently, beginning arithmetic instruction was oral.

Colburn's indebtedness to Pestalozzi can be inferred from the original title of his arithmetic textbook. He was probably introduced to Pestalozzi's ideas during his college days and had the intelligence and courage to break with the method of instruction by which he had learned arithmetic.

His first book was intended for children five or six to eight or nine years old. This book was published later under the title *Colburn's First Lessons. Intellectual Arithmetic upon the Inductive Method of Instruction.* As his title indicates, Colburn departed from the deductive method. He had his pupils develop their own rules. His aim was twofold: to provide practical problems and to train the mind.

In the first part of his first book Colburn did not use arithmetic symbols. The numbers used were small enough that the answers to the problems could be computed without the use of paper and pencil. Consequently, the master had to be actively engaged in the teaching process and, instead of "setting a sum" for each individual pupil, he had to teach the class. Colburn used objects extensively; for example, he originally used the Pestalozzian tables. He omitted from his books several difficult topics that formed a part of the ciphering books, and he included exercises for drill.

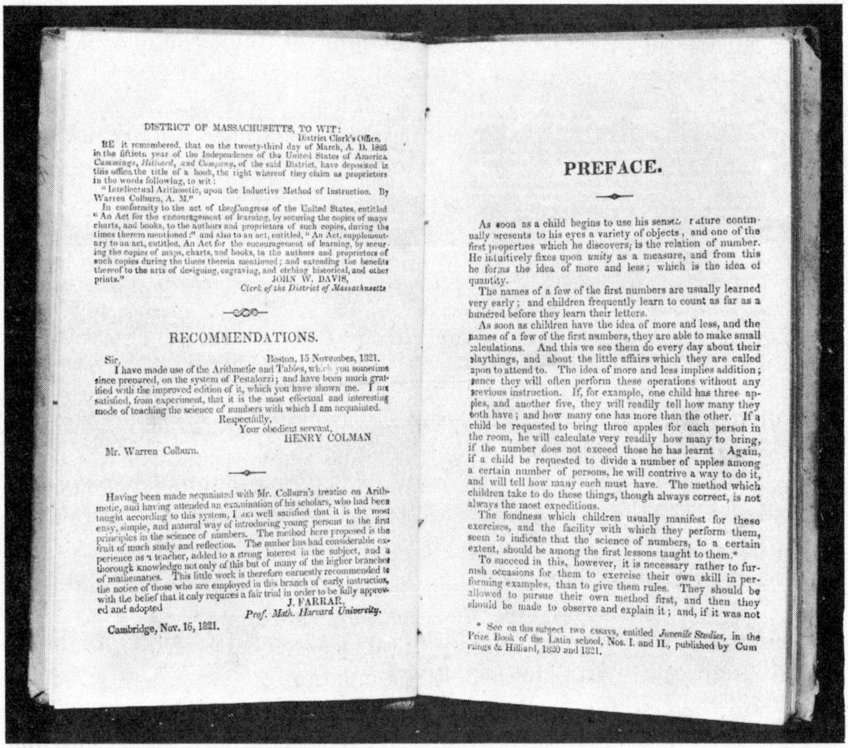

DISTRICT OF MASSACHUSETTS, TO WIT:

District Clerk's Office.

BE it remembered, that on the twenty-third day of March, A. D. 1826 in the fiftieth year of the Independence of the United States of America, *Cummings, Hilliard, and Company*, of the said District, have deposited in this office the title of a book, the right whereof they claim as proprietors in the words following, to wit:

"Intellectual Arithmetic, upon the Inductive Method of Instruction. By Warren Colburn, A. M."

In conformity to the act of the Congress of the United States, entitled "An Act for the encouragement of learning, by securing the copies of maps charts, and books, to the authors and proprietors of such copies, during the times therein mentioned:" and also to an act, entitled, "An Act, supplementary to an act, entitled, An Act for the encouragement of learning, by securing the copies of maps, charts, and books, to the authors and proprietors of such copies during the times therein mentioned; and extending the benefits thereof to the arts of designing, engraving, and etching historical, and other prints."

JOHN W. DAVIS,
Clerk of the District of Massachusetts

RECOMMENDATIONS.

Sir, Boston, 15 November, 1821.

I have made use of the Arithmetic and Tables, which you sometime since prepared, on the system of Pestalozzi; and have been much gratified with the improved edition of it, which you have shown me. I am satisfied, from experiment, that it is the most effectual and interesting mode of teaching the science of numbers with which I am acquainted.

Respectfully,
Your obedient servant,
HENRY COLMAN

Mr. Warren Colburn.

Having been made acquainted with Mr. Colburn's treatise on Arithmetic, and having attended an examination of his scholars, who had been taught according to this system, I am well satisfied that it is the most easy, simple, and natural way of introducing young persons to the first principles in the science of numbers. The method here proposed is the fruit of much study and reflection. The author has had considerable experience as a teacher, added to a strong interest in the subject, and a thorough knowledge not only of this but of many of the higher branches of mathematics. This little work is therefore earnestly recommended to the notice of those who are employed in this branch of early instruction, with the belief that it only requires a fair trial in order to be fully approved and adopted

J. FARRAR,
Prof. Math. Harvard University.

Cambridge, Nov. 16, 1821.

PREFACE.

As soon as a child begins to use his senses, nature continually presents to his eyes a variety of objects, and one of the first properties which he discovers, is the relation of number. He intuitively fixes upon *unity* as a measure, and from this he forms the idea of more and less; which is the idea of quantity.

The names of a few of the first numbers are usually learned very early; and children frequently learn to count as far as a hundred before they learn their letters.

As soon as children have the idea of more and less, and the names of a few of the first numbers, they are able to make small calculations. And this we see them do every day about their playthings, and about the little affairs which they are called upon to attend to. The idea of more and less implies addition; hence they will often perform these operations without any previous instruction. If, for example, one child has three apples, and another five, they will readily tell how many they both have; and how many one has more than the other. If a child be requested to bring three apples for each person in the room, he will calculate very readily how many to bring, if the number does not exceed those he has learnt. Again, if a child be requested to divide a number of apples among a certain number of persons, he will contrive a way to do it, and will tell how many each must have. The method which children take to do these things, though always correct, is not always the most expeditious.

The fondness which children usually manifest for these exercises, and the facility with which they perform them, seem to indicate that the science of numbers, to a certain extent, should be among the first lessons taught to them.*

To succeed in this, however, it is necessary rather to furnish occasions for them to exercise their own skill in performing examples, than to give them rules. They should be allowed to pursue their own method first, and then they should be made to observe and explain it; and, if it was not

* See on this subject two essays, entitled *Juvenile Studies*, in the Prize Book of the Latin school, Nos. I. and II., published by Cummings & Hilliard, 1820 and 1821.

Two-page spread from *Colburn's First Lessons. Intellectual Arithmetic upon the Inductive Method of Instruction,* by Warren Colburn, published in 1844 by William J. Reynolds of Boston. Supplied through the courtesy of Esther Unkel.

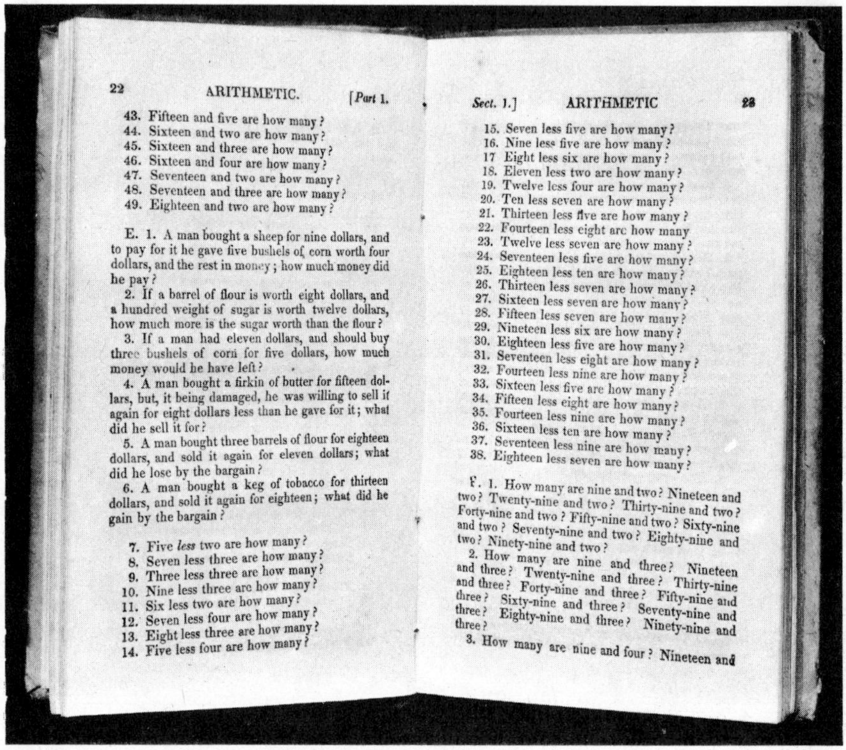

22 ARITHMETIC. [*Part* 1.

43. Fifteen and five are how many?
44. Sixteen and two are how many?
45. Sixteen and three are how many?
46. Sixteen and four are how many?
47. Seventeen and two are how many?
48. Seventeen and three are how many?
49. Eighteen and two are how many?

E. 1. A man bought a sheep for nine dollars, and to pay for it he gave five bushels of corn worth four dollars, and the rest in money; how much money did he pay?

2. If a barrel of flour is worth eight dollars, and a hundred weight of sugar is worth twelve dollars, how much more is the sugar worth than the flour?

3. If a man had eleven dollars, and should buy three bushels of corn for five dollars, how much money would he have left?

4. A man bought a firkin of butter for fifteen dollars, but, it being damaged, he was willing to sell it again for eight dollars less than he gave for it; what did he sell it for?

5. A man bought three barrels of flour for eighteen dollars, and sold it again for eleven dollars; what did he lose by the bargain?

6. A man bought a keg of tobacco for thirteen dollars, and sold it again for eighteen; what did he gain by the bargain?

7. Five *less* two are how many?
8. Seven less three are how many?
9. Three less three are how many?
10. Nine less three are how many?
11. Six less two are how many?
12. Seven less four are how many?
13. Eight less three are how many?
14. Five less four are how many?

Sect. 1.] ARITHMETIC 23

15. Seven less five are how many?
16. Nine less five are how many?
17 Eight less six are how many?
18. Eleven less two are how many?
19. Twelve less four are how many?
20. Ten less seven are how many?
21. Thirteen less five are how many?
22. Fourteen less eight are how many
23. Twelve less seven are how many?
24. Seventeen less five are how many?
25. Eighteen less ten are how many?
26. Thirteen less seven are how many?
27. Sixteen less seven are how many?
28. Fifteen less seven are how many?
29. Nineteen less six are how many?
30. Eighteen less five are how many?
31. Seventeen less eight are how many?
32. Fourteen less nine are how many?
33. Sixteen less five are how many?
34. Fifteen less eight are how many?
35. Fourteen less nine are how many?
36. Sixteen less ten are how many?
37. Seventeen less nine are how many?
38. Eighteen less seven are how many?

F. 1. How many are nine and two? Nineteen and two? Twenty-nine and two? Thirty-nine and two? Forty-nine and two? Fifty-nine and two? Sixty-nine and two? Seventy-nine and two? Eighty-nine and two? Ninety-nine and two?

2. How many are nine and three? Nineteen and three? Twenty-nine and three? Thirty-nine and three? Forty-nine and three? Fifty-nine and three? Sixty-nine and three? Seventy-nine and three? Eighty-nine and three? Ninety-nine and three?

3. How many are nine and four? Nineteen and

Another two-page spread from *Colburn's First Lessons. Intellectual Arithmetic upon the Inductive Method of Instruction,* by Warren Colburn, published in 1844 by William J. Reynolds of Boston. Supplied through the courtesy of Esther Unkel.

Colburn's second book, *The Sequel,* was intended for pupils who had completed his *First Lessons.*

Several arithmetic textbooks patterned after Colburn's books were published during the period from 1821 to 1857. Joseph Ray's series, dating from 1834, appears to have been very popular.

The period of Colburn's influence was followed by a static period. After 1857, arithmetic textbooks became deductive again. Rules were presented instead of developed, drill was stressed, and motivation was mostly the result of artificial incentives.

In 1870 the *German Grube method* was introduced in the United States. A new principle in this method was the simultaneous introduction of the four fundamental operations for each number before proceeding to the next number. The plan, called a *concentric circle plan,* was one in which, during the first year of school, the operations were presented for the numbers 1 to 10 and, for the next three years, for the numbers 10 to 100. The method, aiming at a complete mastery of the fundamentals and employing objects for concrete presentation, was thorough. However, since it carried illustrations to an extreme and dealt with the four fundamental operations simultaneously, it resulted in mechanical instruction and did not elicit much motivation. The method was criticized by John Dewey.

From 1892 to 1935

During the last decade of the nineteenth century, American educators became actively interested in the educational principles of the German philosopher and psychologist Johann Friedrich Herbart (1776–1841). Herbart developed the principle of *apperception,* according to which new experiences were interpreted and given meaning by means of old, existing ideas that were the result of past experiences. This principle is expressed by the phrase "teach the new in terms of the old."

The apperception theory opposed the long-dormant disciplinary concept of education. It emphasized the content of a subject. The greater the number of clear concepts formed in the child's mind, the better prepared he would be to cope with new situations. Thus, the mind was considered to be a storehouse in which ideas were accumulated for future help in meeting new situations.

Herbart's immediate aim in education was to develop in the child a "many-sided interest" by introducing him to many aspects of the external world. Consequently, the Herbartians emphasized history and literature as elementary school subjects and were therefore responsible for a reduction in the time allotted to arithmetic.

The Herbartian movement led to the inductive approach in the teaching of arithmetic. Every arithmetic topic was to be developed or rationalized, and the "why" of a process was to be explained. The general processes were derived by presenting the topics according to the Herbartian steps: (1) preparation, (2) presentation, (3) comparison or abstraction, and (4) generalization. The followers of Herbart distinguished five steps: (1) preparation—a review of related materials, (2) presentation—the presentation of the new materials, (3) comparison—an organization of the facts, (4) conclusion—a generalization from the old to the new facts, and (5) application—an application of the principles learned.

The influence of Herbart's theory was most pronounced in the United States in the 1890s. At the same time William James published his *Principles of Psychology,* in which he contradicted the existence of general transfer of training and denied that a general capacity—for example, the power to remember—could be trained by specific exercises. Consequently, the way in which arithmetic was taught in the public schools—

especially the great emphasis on memorization—and the generous amount of time allotted to the subject were severely criticized.

In 1893 the Committee of Ten recommended that obsolete topics be eliminated from the arithmetic curriculum. In line with Herbart's theory, the chairman of the committee stated that "the main end of mathematical teaching . . . is to store the mind with clear conceptions of things and their relations." The Committee of Fifteen recommended, in 1895, that arithmetic instruction begin in the second school year and that it end with the close of the sixth year. The committee also suggested that the practice of teaching two arithmetic lessons daily—a mental and a written lesson—be discontinued.

Another critic of educational theory and practice was John Dewey, who emphasized that the environment of the child provided many problems that were solved by number and number relations. Thus, according to Dewey, authors of arithmetic textbooks and teachers of the subject had to present situations that called for measurement and the relating of quantities. Soon after these views had been published, some arithmetic textbooks appeared that, according to the authors, were based on the ideas of Dewey. Since problems arising from practical situations were emphasized, the social value of arithmetic received more recognition.

At the turn of the century, the recommendations of the Committees of Ten and Fifteen attracted favorable attention, and elementary school arithmetic topics were screened. The *theory of social utility* was applied. This theory stressed the social phase of arithmetic instruction and aimed at including in the curriculum only those topics that served a real need in life. This movement reached its peak in 1920. Studies were conducted to determine what arithmetic topics were used by adults in their vocational activities and in daily life. Topics considered nonfunctional and therefore eliminated from the curriculum included square root, cube root, factors, fractions with large denominators, repeating decimals, proportions, and commercial arithmetic. Though the application of the social utility theory served some useful purposes, the theory was rightly criticized by educators who pointed out that the teaching of more arithmetic and the use of improved methods would result in an increased use of arithmetic in daily life.

In the meantime, the method of teaching arithmetic had been reconsidered. Results of experiments had indicated that there was no general transfer of learning. One of the psychologists who conducted experiments that showed there was no automatic transfer of learning was Edward L. Thorndike, who developed his *stimulus-response bond (S-R bond)* or *connectionist theory*. This association theory held that for every stimulus or situation there was a particular response and that these two were associated by a bond. For example, the stimulus 3×2 should elicit the response 6. The elements of complex learnings had to be isolated, taught, and mastered separately. Thus, the arithmetic skills were presented in sequential order, and the steps were analyzed. Thorndike's *law of exercise,* stating that repetition strengthens a bond, was applied, and skills were mastered by drill. Indeed, drill was used excessively to fix in the minds of the pupils the numerous arithmetic facts. Critics disliked the theory because it broke arithmetic into unrelated facts; they called it an atomistic theory. It was also called a mechanistic theory, since mechanical drill was emphasized and teaching for understanding was deemphasized.

During the 1920s, the *child study movement,* started by G. Stanley Hall in 1880, was quite popular. The proponents of this movement investigated the growth and development of children and claimed that the curriculum and instructional procedures should be the result of an understanding of the interests and needs of the children. This movement was a part of and gave impetus to the *progressive education movement,* which encouraged unit teaching, incidental learning, the teaching of arithmetic in activity programs, and arithmetic instruction as an integrated part of other school subjects. The proponents of the incidental method claimed that the various topics of arithmetic should be taught when the child showed an interest in them, since internal motivation was more important than the logical sequence of the subject. Therefore, in such programs, no specific time was set aside for the teaching of arithmetic, but topics were taught as the need arose.

The incidental theory met with valid criticisms. Though the best teaching is done when the pupils are internally motivated, the method did not produce the desired results. Serious gaps were discovered in the knowledge of the pupils, since not all topics that needed to be studied arose from problem situations. Moreover, the sequential nature of arithmetic did not lend itself to such an approach.

After 1935

Since 1935, the *Gestalt theory of learning* has exercised a great influence on the teaching of arithmetic in the United States. The theory was first presented in Germany by Max Wertheimer.

According to the Gestalt theory, the learning process is not built up of elements, nor is it a process of association, but it is a result of seeing the overall pattern or unity that gives meaning to all of the parts. The result is a configuration, or a Gestalt. When, by means of insight, the learner recognizes the interrelationship of elements and the overall relationship that exists between the parts and the whole, he has acquired a basic understanding. Learning is not exclusively an inductive process and does not proceed basically by trial and error, but it is a function of insight and maturation. The pupil must see the goals and must be motivated to learn, and the teacher has the responsibility for guiding the child toward seeing the goals and inciting him to learn.

The belief that memorization results in automatic transfer of learning is not accepted. The Gestaltists consider transfer of learning possible only when the learning to be transferred can be associated with the area to which transfer is desired. The need for functional subject matter is stressed, since greater transfer seems to occur when the teacher makes use of content that is meaningful to the child. From this it can be inferred that the Gestaltist is interested in arriving at general understandings or principles that will enable him to grasp the meanings of individual experiences or concrete facts.

In the *Tenth Yearbook of the National Council of Teachers of Mathematics,* published in 1935, the *meaning theory* was presented. During the following years it gradually became widely accepted. Based on Gestalt psychology, it maintains that children must understand the structure of the number system and be able to perform number operations meaningfully. When the meaning theory is properly applied, children are guided to develop procedures by applying what they have learned; they are encouraged to find rules inductively and to apply them deductively; they are urged to take part in class discussions where number relations and number principles are explored; and they are stimulated to apply their mathematical knowledge creatively and imaginatively in other school subjects and in daily life.

When the meaning theory was introduced, great emphasis was placed on the development of meaning in arithmetic, and there was no general agreement concerning the necessity for drill. At the present time, the need for practice after a meaningful introduction of a topic is recognized.

More recent contributions of learning theorists are presented in Chapter 3 of this volume, where ideas of Piaget, Bruner, Dienes, and Gagné are briefly described.

During the years of the Second World War some research pertaining to the level of achievement in arithmetic at secondary and college level showed that pupils lacked much skill and did not understand many important mathematical ideas. Brueckner[2] administered a 30-item test in the four fundamental operations and in percentage to seniors in more than twenty states in all parts of the country and found the median score to be 17.1, or 57 percent correct. In reporting on the results of a selective examination given to 4,200 entering freshmen at twenty-seven universities and colleges, Admiral Nimitz[3] stated that more than 50 percent of the pupils taking the examination were unable to pass the arithmetic reasoning test.

---

2. L. J. Brueckner, "Testing the Validity of Criticisms of the Schools," *Journal of Educational Research* (February, 1943), pp. 465–467.

3. Admiral C. W. Nimitz, in "The Importance of Mathematics in the War Effort," *The Mathematics Teacher* (February, 1942), pp. 88–89.

International studies designed to compare mathematics achievement of elementary school pupils in the United States and Europe were conducted during the second half of the 1950s by Buswell,[4] Tracy,[5] and Kramer.[6] In the three studies significant differences were found in favor of the English and the Dutch children tested.

The increased need for mathematics skills in society, the meager results of mathematics teaching, the consistency of sizable differences in favor of foreign pupils in mathematics achievement tests, and the Sputnik event in 1957 gave impetus to a movement to develop experimental mathematics programs. Financial aid for such programs was made available by the United States government and by various private foundations. Exploratory programs started in the late 1950s[7] included:

School Mathematics Study Group (SMSG). The SMSG produced a mathematics program for grades K–12, designed to guide pupils to a better understanding of the basic concepts and structure of mathematics. The program had more breadth and depth than previous programs and included new topics, emphasized principles of mathematics, and stressed precise language. The project was phased out in 1972. It appears that the SMSG has been the most influential of all experimental mathematics projects.

Madison Project. This program contained supplemental and enrichment materials that were to be used along with the regular mathematics program. Its purposes included building a sound background for future mathematics, stimulating creativity in children, and developing greater interest in mathematics. Many of the materials for elementary school children dealt with basic concepts of algebra and geometry. Concepts were introduced early; discovery of patterns was encouraged; the inductive approach was stressed; conversations and discussions were preferred to lectures; and games were used to assist the learning of mathematics.

An issue that invited widespread discussion concerned the goals for elementary school mathematics. During the summer of 1963, twenty-nine mathematicians and scientists met in Cambridge, Massachusetts to review school mathematics and to establish goals for mathematics educa-

---

4. G. T. Buswell, "A Comparison of Achievement in Arithmetic in England and Central California," *The Arithmetic Teacher* (February, 1958), pp. 1–9.

5. N. H. Tracy, "A Comparison of Test Results—North Carolina, California, and England," *The Arithmetic Teacher* (October, 1959), pp. 199–202.

6. K. Kramer, "Arithmetic Achievement in Iowa and The Netherlands," *The Elementary School Journal* (February, 1959), pp. 258–263.

7. A few additional programs are described briefly in Chapter 3.

tion. The conference resulted in the bulletin, *Goals for School Mathematics, The Report of the Cambridge Conference on School Mathematics,* commonly called "The Cambridge Report." It included proposals for mathematics curricula for the elementary school and the high school. If a pupil were to work through the proposed thirteen years of mathematics in Grades K–12, the pupil would be expected to have a level of training comparable to three years of top-level college training; in fact, the pupil would be expected to have the equivalent of two years of calculus and one semester each of modern algebra and probability theory. In the report it was suggested that the curriculum be brought into being over the next few decades, and it was stated that the expressed views were intended to serve as a basis for further discussion and experimentation. As could be expected, the report received both praise and criticism.[8]

In the 1960s, some reports were published that dealt with the training of elementary school mathematics teachers. The Committee on the Undergraduate Program in Mathematics (CUPM)—a committee of the Mathematical Association of America—recommended the following courses for college training of teachers of elementary school mathematics:[9]

a. One or two courses—depending upon the previous preparation of the student—in the structure of the real number system and its subsystems.
b. A course devoted to the basic concepts of algebra.
c. A course in informal geometry.

Another report on mathematical education of elementary teachers was presented by the Cambridge Conference on Teacher Training. The student is referred to the report and to an article by Morley in *The Arithmetic Teacher,* identified at the end of the chapter.

Especially during the past one or two decades, efforts have been made to improve the teaching and learning of mathematics by experimenting with alternate methods of instruction—not all of them new—and by using new approaches, techniques, and tools. A part of Chapter 3 deals with these topics.

---

8. M. H. Stone "Reviews and Evaluations," *The Mathematics Teacher,* ed. H. Tinnappel (April, 1965), pp. 353–360; I. Adler, "The Cambridge Conference Report: Blueprint or Fantasy?" *The Arithmetic Teacher* (March, 1966), pp. 179–186.

9. "Recommendations of the Mathematical Association of America for the Training of Mathematics Teachers," *American Mathematical Monthly* (December, 1960), pp. 982–992; CUPM, *Report Number 13* (April, 1966); CUPM, *Course Guides for the Training of Teachers of Elementary School Mathematics* (1968).

SELECTED RESEARCH

This study,[10] conducted during the second quarter of the 1960s, involved about 133,000 pupils in more than 5,300 schools in 12 countries. The mathematical achievement and attitudes of pupils were studied in these populations:

I. Thirteen-year-old pupils.
II. The grade group containing most thirteen-year-olds.
III. Mathematics pupils in their final year of high school.
IV. Nonmathematics pupils in their final year of high school.

The average test scores of the sample are presented in Table 2.1. The Roman numerals refer to the populations identified above.

Table 2.1

Test Scores of Four Populations

Country	*I*	*II*	*III*	*IV*
Australia	20	19	22	—
Belgium	28	30	35	24
England	19	24	35	21
Finland	24	26	25	23
France	18	21	33	26
Germany	—	25	29	28
Israel	—	32	36	—
Japan	31	31	31	25
The Netherlands	24	21	32	25
Scotland	19	22	26	21
Sweden	16	15	27	13
United States	16	18	14	8
Possible score	70	70	69	58

It was emphasized that the project was not designed to be an international test. Carnett[11] quotes one of the investigators as follows: "The object of the enterprise has been to discern more clearly the interrelationship between aspects of organization, curriculum and

10. T. Husén, ed., *International Study of Achievement in Mathematics* (New York: John Wiley & Sons, Inc., 1967).

11. G. S. Carnett, "Is Our Mathematics Inferior?" *The Mathematics Teacher* (October, 1967), p. 582.

teaching, and social factors, on the one hand, and mathematics performance on the other hand."

Carnett also notes that pupils in all the countries earned almost identical scores up to the end of the period of universal education when policies are used to select pupils for secondary institutions of learning.

The study has rightfully raised questions about the wisdom of a national policy of selective education as opposted to comprehensive education.[12] Indeed, in the United States, a much larger number of pupils are retained for a longer period of time than in other countries. For example, the study indicates that in the United States, 70 percent of the appropriate age group was enrolled in the last secondary school grade, whereas The Netherlands enrolled 8 percent.

Other findings of the study include:

1. The more homework that was assigned in a country, the higher the pupils' scores tended to be.
2. Schools that enrolled more than 800 pupils earned higher scores than smaller schools.
3. Boys performed better than girls.
4. Boys were more interested in mathematics than girls.

EXERCISES

1. Enumerate and explain different aims of arithmetic instruction that have been dominant in the past.
2. Describe the method by which arithmetic was taught and learned during the ciphering-book period.
3. In your opinion, what was the importance of Colburn's first arithmetic book?
4. Explain and illustrate the utilitarian aim of arithmetic instruction.
5. In an old arithmetic book, find some examples of arithmetic problems presented to train the mind.
6. Explain the principle expressed by "teach the new in terms of the old." How is it related to the apperception theory?
7. Explain the S-R bond theory in the teaching of arithmetic.

---

12. *Ibid,* p. 583.

8. Contrast the drill theory and the meaning theory.
9. How did the Herbartian movement in the United States bring about a reduction in time allotted to arithmetic?
10. Explain: The whole is more than the sum of the parts. Relate this statement to a theory discussed in this chapter.
11. State and defend your opinion concerning the quality of the training of elementary school mathematics teachers. Suggest improvements if you feel that they are needed.
12. Report on the research described in this chapter.

SOURCES FOR FURTHER READING

Burns, P. C., "Development of Elementary School Mathematics in the United States," *The Arithmetic Teacher,* May, 1970, pp. 428–437.

Ebel, R. L., ed., *Encyclopedia of Educational Research.* New York: Macmillan Publishing Company, Inc., 1969, pp. 766–777.

Educational Development Center, Inc., *Goals for Mathematical Education of Elementary School Teachers,* A Report of the Cambridge Conference on Teacher Training. Boston: Houghton Mifflin Company, 1967.

Educational Services Incorporated, *Goals for School Mathematics,* A Report of the Cambridge Conference on School Mathematics. Boston: Houghton Mifflin Company, 1963.

Fehr, H. F., "Theories of Learning Related to the Field of Mathematics," *The Learning of Mathematics, Its Theory and Practice, Twenty-first Yearbook.* Washington, D.C.: National Council of Teachers of Mathematics, 1953, Chap. I.

Grossman, A. S., "Mid-nineteenth Century Methods for the 1970s," *The Arithmetic Teacher,* April, 1971, pp. 230–233.

Monroe, W. S., *Development of Arithmetic as a School Subject,* Bulletin No. 10. Washington, D.C.: U.S. Government Printing Office, 1917.

Morley, A., "Goals for Mathematical Education of Elementary School Teachers," *The Arithmetic Teacher,* January, 1969, pp. 59–62.

National Council of Teachers of Mathematics, *A History of Mathematics Education in the United States and Canada, Thirty-second Yearbook.* Washington, D.C.: The Council, 1970.

Wilson, G. M., "The Social Utility Theory as Applied to Arithmetic, Its Research Basis, and Some of Its Applications," *Journal of Educational Research,* January, 1948, pp. 321–337.

The Search to Improve Instruction

3

During the past few decades a great deal of research has been conducted on the nature of learning and on how learning can be improved.

This chapter introduces the learning theorists Piaget, Bruner, Dienes, and Gagné. It also identifies some experimental mathematics projects that have been in the limelight for some time. Finally, it describes some approaches and techniques that are currently used in mathematics education in the elementary school.

LEARNING THEORISTS

Piaget

Jean Piaget, the leader of the Geneva School, has studied conceptual thinking in children for several decades. Though his findings have met with some criticism, they are so important that they should not be ignored by teachers of elementary-school mathematics. Several authors have interpreted his writings or have continued research in this area, and replications of his investigations generally corroborate his results.

Piaget distinguishes four stages in the development of concepts. The characteristics of these periods, as described by Piaget, are briefly presented below.[1]

1. *The sensori-motor stage,* from birth to two years of age. This is the period before the child begins to use language. The initial simple reflexes become gradually modified. There is behavior that can be called intelli-

1. J. Piaget, *The Child's Conception of Number,* trans. C. Gattegno and F. M. Hodgson (London: Routledge & Kegan Paul Ltd., 1961).

gent, but intelligence is not yet operational[2] in the sense that the child can imagine or think an act before carrying it out; the child's behavior rests largely on performing actions. If the child, when striking an object with a stick, happens to move the object in a certain direction, and because of this effect repeats the action, the child gives evidence of intelligent behavior, since the same result is anticipated. Transfer from observed effects to other situations is noticeable.

2. *The pre-operational stage,* from two to six or seven years of age. During this stage, the child begins to represent something by means of something else. Signs are beginning to be understood and language is acquired.

The pre-operational stage is characterized by an absence of knowledge of conservation, the fact that an object or relation remains unchanged even though there is a change in its perceivable features. Suppose a child is shown two rows of five beads each that are arranged as follows:

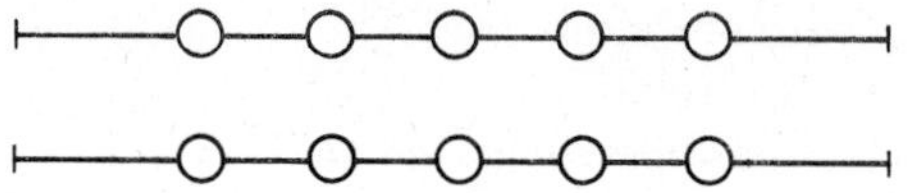

The pupil may agree that there are just as many beads in the top row as there are in the bottom row. Then the arrangement of the beads is changed to this pattern:

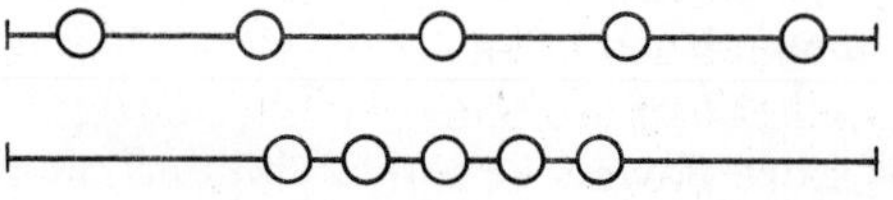

Now the child at this level may decide that there are more beads in the top row than there are in the bottom row. The child is unable to give reasons for the response, yet may insist that he or she is right and point out that the top row is longer. The pupil concentrates on one of the features of the situation and reports only what he or she perceives. The inability to understand that a quantity is conserved if its units are rearranged indicates that the child has not yet grasped the group meaning of number, the "fiveness" of five.

---

2. Operations are considered to be actions that can be internalized by the child. If a child carries out a physical manipulation symbolically and thus "thinks" the action, i.e., carries it out in his mind, it is said that he has *internalized* the action.

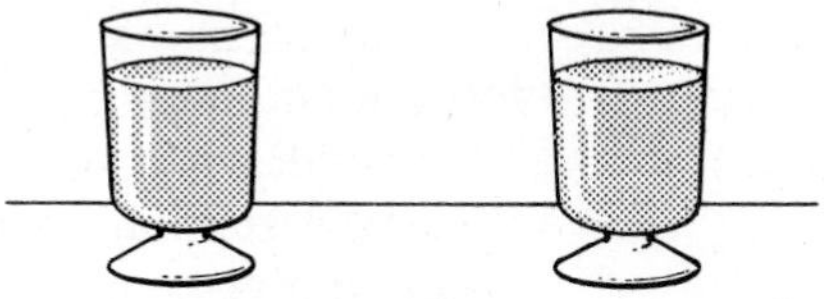

Figure 3.1

The same faulty reasoning may occur when the experiment is conducted with continuous quantities. For example, the child is shown two similar glasses of water, as in Figure 3.1.

The pupil may agree that the glasses contain the same amount of water. When all the water from one glass is poured into a taller, narrower glass, as in Figure 3.2, the child at this level may state that there is more water in the tall glass than in the wide glass and point to the water level.

In another experiment Piaget shows a child about twenty wooden beads, the majority of which are brown and the rest white. When the child is asked whether there are more brown beads or wooden beads, the typical answer is that there are more brown beads. Piaget feels that a child at this age fails to see the relationship of the part to the whole, does not realize that a subclass has been included, and seems to reason on the basis of either the whole or the part. According to Piaget, the ability to solve a problem of inclusion appears around the seventh or eighth year of age.

3. *The stage of concrete operations,* from six or seven to eleven or twelve years of age. During this stage the child becomes capable of classifying objects according to their similarities and differences. Piaget reports an example in which a child observes a bouquet of flowers; one-half are daisies and the other half are other flowers. The child can now decide whether there are more flowers or more daisies. Thus the pupil understands that the part is complementary to the rest and realizes that a subclass has been included. The one-to-one correspondence between elements of sets can now be seen, and the child becomes aware of conser-

Figure 3.2

vation of discontinuous and continuous quantities. The child can reverse his thinking: when presented with the situation described before when water was poured from a wide glass into a narrow, tall glass, he or she realizes that when the water is poured back into the original glass, the amount will be the same. Also, without performing the operation itself, the child understands that a rearrangement of a set of objects may be reversed again to undo that rearrangement. This ability will enable the pupil to understand that, for an operation such as $2 + 1 = 3$, there is another operation, $3 - 1 = 2$, that undoes the original operation. The child is also capable of seriation, which means that objects can be placed in a series according to their selected characteristics. For example, the child can place rods of varying lengths in order from the shortest to the longest, and can arrange objects according to their weights.

Piaget believes that the child has now mastered the prerequisites for the formation of the concept of number, since the child can classify objects and can put them in order of size. Now the child can learn to combine the operations of classification and seriation, and can see the unit both as an element in a class and as an element within a series. He or she can make a statement about the collection as a whole and can identify any individual item. For example, when counting three apples, the child arrives at the cardinal number 3 and can identify the position of each apple in the series.

4. *The stage of formal operations,* after eleven or twelve years of age. This is a period of great progress, since the child starts to reason on the basis of hypotheses or propositions and thus acquires a capacity for abstract thinking. Piaget quotes the following example. Children of different ages are asked to compare the hair colors of three girls: Edith is fairer than Susan; Edith is darker than Lilly; who is the darkest of the three? The thinking required to solve such a problem is more complicated than the operational thinking that can be applied to concrete operations, which, of course, deal with practical problems and concrete situations. At the stage of formal operations, concrete facts are no longer needed, and the child can make logical deductions from hypotheses. The pupil also begins to understand mathematical proportions in which two systems of reference are used at the same time.

Piaget, Inhelder, and Szeminska have conducted extensive research on the development of concepts associated with length and measurement. Some of their views and findings are presented in the following paragraphs.[3]

---

3. J. Piaget, B. Inhelder, and A. Szeminska, *The Child's Conception of Geometry,* trans. E. A. Lunzer (New York: Basic Books, Inc., 1960). Copyright Routledge & Kegan Paul Ltd.

Before the child can form the concept of measurement, he or she must learn conservation of distance and length.[4] The child must first understand that the distance between two objects remains unchanged if a third object is placed between them. He must also grasp the symmetrical character of distance: $AB = BA$. Such understanding should help to bring about the concept of conservation of length, and the child should discover that the length of an object does not change when the object is moved. Conservation of distance and length was observed in children of seven to eight years of age.

Other prerequisites for measurement are the realization that the whole is the sum of the component parts, and the understanding of the principles of substitution and iteration. Selected measurement units may have to be applied several times to the object or distance to be measured. The child of seven to eight years of age realizes the need for several measurements in locating points, and can subdivide line segments. When the child is eight to nine years old, he attains the concept of unit iteration.

With the assistance of the background information presented above, the student of education will be able to appreciate the following experiment reported by Piaget, Inhelder, and Szeminska.

The child is shown a model tower built on a table. The child then has to construct a similar tower on a table with a top higher or lower than the first one, and has to use blocks of a different size. The following observations were made:

1. The child up to about four and a half years of age makes comparisons only by visual transfer—that is, just by looking at the objects.
2. The child of about six years of age begins using bodily transfer—that is, using parts of the body, such as hands or arms, as a measuring instrument. For example, the child represents the height of the model tower by a distance between his or her hands, and then goes to the second tower to compare its height with that distance. Of course, the transferred length can hardly be kept constant.
3. The child of seven or eight years of age tends to use a measuring stick of the same length as or longer than the object to be measured. By doing this the principle that if $A = B$ and $B = C$, then $A = C$ is applied. If the measuring stick is longer than the object to be measured, the child marks the stick in order to transfer a constant length.
4. The child of eight or nine years of age becomes capable of operational measurement, since he or she can use a measuring stick that is shorter

---

4. *Distance* refers to the linear separation of objects or to "empty space"; *length* refers to the size of "filled space" or to objects as such.

than the object to be measured. The child realizes that the whole equals the sum of the component parts, and uses the principles of substitution and unit iteration by applying the selected unit repeatedly to the object to be measured. Then the child assigns a number to the object in terms of the selected unit of measure.

In an attempt to measure awareness of conservation of area, the same authors conducted the following experiment, illustrated in Figure 3.3. Two squares, a and b, are presented. The child realizes that the squares are congruent. Square b is divided into two congruent parts by means of a diagonal, and the parts are arranged perpendicularly to one another, as in c. Not until the child is seven or eight years old is there operational conservation of area. The child of eight to ten years of age can use the principle of unit iteration and thus repeatedly apply units of area—for example, a model of the square inch—when measuring a total area.

The results of the work of the Geneva School suggest that, in the maturation of basic mathematical concepts, the child moves through a developmental pattern of clearly defined stages. Piaget feels that although further research may show that the general rate of progress through the stages may be accelerated or retarded by cultural or other factors, the sequence of stages is invariant, because maturation takes this form. The assumption of this uniformity for all individuals has met with some criticism. Churchill[5] indicates that research conducted by other people resulted in findings that suggest there are factors that make for differences in

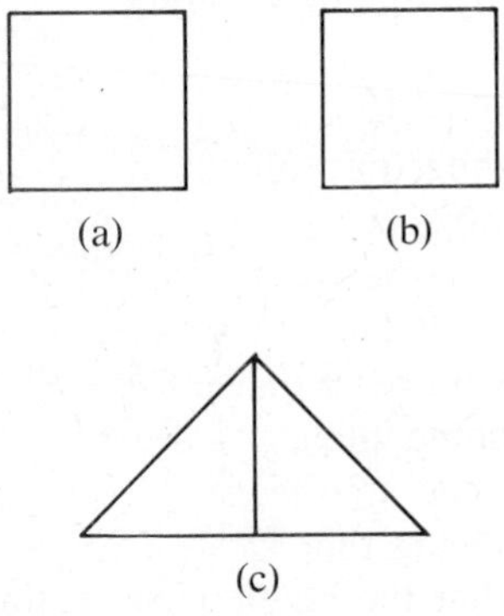

Figure 3.3

5. E. M. Churchill, *Counting and Measuring* (Toronto: University of Toronto Press, 1961), pp. 89–90.

individual development not revealed in Piaget's approach. It has been shown that a child can be at the stage of concrete operations in one test but not in another. Children may arrive at concepts partly as a result of logical reasoning and partly because of experience with manipulating objects.

Piaget's implication that the general rate of progress through the stages may vary with individuals and with societies and that it may be accelerated by certain factors[6] probably will not be contradicted by many psychologists and educators. Some research findings indicate that skillful instruction may change the age at which children attain a stage. Coxford[7] reports, for example, that instruction given to a limited sample of exceptionally bright children resulted in significant gains in stage placement. This possibility places upon the teacher the responsibility of creating an atmosphere in the classroom in which such acceleration is possible, even if not probable. The teacher's knowledge of the form that maturation takes and of the child's abilities and limitations should enable him or her to provide experiences that will assist the pupil in grasping basic mathematical concepts. The environment that the teacher creates should stimulate the child to participate in activities, manipulate, perform experiments, seek and verify his or her own answers, discover structures, and discuss problems with classmates. The development of such a questioning mind should be one of the teacher's main objectives.

Bruner

Jerome S. Bruner of Harvard University is an advocate of the learning-by-discovery theory. For Bruner, it is the method of learning, the process, that is most significant. His goal is discovery. Discovery does not necessarily result in something that is new to the learner; it is, rather, an internal reorganization of something that was already present in the person.

The child, according to Bruner, moves through three levels of understanding: the enactive, the iconic, and the symbolic. At the enactive level, the child manipulates objects. At the iconic level, the child thinks of objects and uses imagery. When he or she has reached the symbolic level, the child manipulates symbols and translates experience into language.

Bruner's hypothesis on readiness for learning is that any subject can be taught effectively in some intellectually honest form to any child at any stage of development. The statement has puzzled many and has been widely discussed. It appears that Bruner wants teachers to realize that they must determine what the child is ready for and then organize the

---

6. E. Duckworth, "Piaget Rediscovered," *The Arithmetic Teacher* (November, 1964), pp. 496–499.

7. A. F. Coxford, "The Effects of Instruction on the Stage Placement of Children in Piaget's Seriation Experiments," *The Arithmetic Teacher* (January, 1964), pp. 4–9.

subject matter accordingly. Depending upon the level at which the child can function, subject matter is to be presented on the symbolic, iconic, or enactive level.

Bruner is also concerned with the problem of how to improve learning. He presents four major matters that a theory of instruction should specify:

1. *Experiences that instill in the person a tendency toward learning.* The environment must be conducive to learning. The child has to experience success and confidence must be built.

2. *Knowledge that is structured in a way in which the child can grasp it.* When the learner grasps the structure of the subject, he or she understands it in a way that permits many other things to be related to it meaningfully. Therefore, to learn structure is to learn how things are related. Structure must be related to the status and the gift of the learner. Thus, the optimal structure of a body of knowledge is not absolute, but relative.

3. *The most effective sequences in which to present the materials to be learned.* Though sequences vary with the learner, as a rule they proceed from the enactive to the iconic to the symbolic level.

4. *The nature and pacing of rewards and punishments.* As learning progresses, there is a time when the learner should shift from immediate to deferred reward, from extrinsic to intrinsic reward.

Dienes Z. P. Dienes, who has worked in England, Australia, and Canada, has made a name in the United States especially with the teaching materials he has prepared. His approach to teaching mathematics is based on four principles of learning:

1. *The dynamic principle.* The child progresses from undirected play games in which the ingredients of the concept are available, to structured activities through which the concept should be grasped, to the practice stage during which the concept should be fixed and applied.

2. *The constructive principle.* Constructive thinking is developed before analytical thinking. Therefore, mathematical situations must be devised in which adventurous kinds of thinking can take place. Though a child may not be ready to make logical judgments, it is likely that he or she will be able to grasp an idea at the intuitive level. More mature analytical thinking seldom occurs before the child is twelve years old.

3. *The mathematical variability principle.* The relationship among the variables in a mathematical concept is constant; the variables themselves

Figure 3.4

vary. To help in the development of a concept, all possible variables should be made to vary while the concept is kept intact. For example, a square should be represented in different positions and in different sizes, as in Figure 3.4.

4. *The perceptual variability principle.* The perceptual representation should be varied while the conceptual structure remains constant. Thus, tasks should be provided that look different but have essentially the same conceptual structure. When parallelograms are drawn on paper, or laid out with rubber bands on a geoboard, or identified in a printed wallpaper pattern, the perceptual representation is varied, but the conceptual structure is the same. The common feature is the mathematical concept. Therefore, to grasp the concept, the child must see what the different representations have in common.

Gagné

Robert M. Gagné, of Florida State University, advocates the guided learning approach. Whereas Bruner stresses the process by which learning is acquired, Gagné is concerned with the product, or the behavior. His goal is learning and he is interested in what the child must know. He states in specific behavioral terms what he wants the child to be able to do.

Since Gagné wants to guide the child closely in learning experiences, the sequence followed is all-important to him. Pre-tests determine the level of the child. Then it is decided what subject matter must be presented, and a tight, sequential program is prescribed. The child is guided step by step. The child is to move from the lowest levels of development, simple learning, through concepts and principles, to the highest level, the solving of problems.

According to Gagné, a child is ready for a new concept when all the subconcepts that are prerequisite to that concept are mastered. Therefore, the structure of the presented materials is most significant. Understandably, his approach promotes programmed instruction.

MATHEMATICS PROJECTS FOR THE ELEMENTARY SCHOOL

In Chapter 2 some characteristics of the School Mathematics Study Group program and the Madison Project, both of which were planned in the late 1950s, were presented. In the following paragraphs some additional projects are briefly described.

Nuffield Mathematics Teaching Project

The Nuffield Project was started in the mid-1960s under the direction of Geoffry Matthews. The aim was to produce a contemporary course in mathematics for children from five to thirteen years of age. Pilot areas were established in England, Scotland, and Wales.

The project emphasizes learning by doing and quotes the old proverb:

> I hear, and I forget;
> I see, and I remember;
> I do, and I understand.

Small children work with real objects and are encouraged to find things out for themselves. It is assumed that such learning does not need much time for practice. Readily available materials are preferred to expensive devices.

The materials and ideas are presented in teachers' guides, which include examples of suggested work cards and samples of work done by children.

A great deal of the theory that underlies the project rests on Jean Piaget's experiments. The originators emphasize child-centered learning and stress the need for interactions of the children in exploring situations. The teacher has to create an environment in which active learning can occur and to assist children when needed. He or she listens, guides, asks relevant questions, and encourages discussions.

Individually Prescribed Instruction–Mathematics (IPI–Math)

The IPI-Math Project, planned in the late 1960s at the University of Pittsburg, is an individualized program. It is based on a sequence of many instructional objectives.

IPI–Math uses placement tests to assess the child's competency, to identify the child's level, and to determine what topics the child should study to meet the next learning goal. After assignments have been completed, results on post-tests indicate whether the pupil has attained the predetermined goal. If the child performs satisfactorily on a post-test, he or she starts working toward the next goal. If the pupil's score is below the acceptable level, he or she has the opportunity to receive more help and to do additional work in the same area.

Computer-Assisted Instruction (CAI)

Patrick Suppes of Stanford University has been engaged in research and development of computer-assisted instruction. Tutorial mathematics curricula and drill-and-practice materials have been used. It was reported that with computer-assisted instruction using drill-and-practice materials it took less time than it would have taken with the conventional classroom approach to attain at least the same results.[8]

---

8. P. Suppes and M. Morningstar, *Computer-assisted Instruction: The 1966–67 Stanford Arithmetic Program* (New York: Academic Press, Inc., 1969).

The National Council of Teachers of Mathematics issued the following position statement on computers in the classroom:[9]

NCTM's Instructional Affairs Committee recently prepared the following statement, which has been approved by the Board of Directors:

Although computers have become an essential tool of our society, their diverse and sustained effects on all of us are frequently overlooked. The astounding computational power of the computer has altered priorities in the mathematics curriculum with respect to both content and instructional practices. Improvements in computer technology continue to make computers, minicomputers, and programmable calculators increasingly accessible to greater numbers of students at reasonable cost.

An essential outcome of contemporary education is computer literacy. Every student should have firsthand experiences with both the capabilities and the limitations of computers through contemporary applications. Although the study of computers is intrinsically valuable, educators should also develop an awareness of the advantages of computers both in interdisciplinary problem solving and as an instructional aid. Educational decision makers, including classroom teachers, should seek to make computers readily available as an integral part of the educational program.

Space limitations make it impossible to describe additional promising experimental mathematics projects. The interested student is referred to *The Arithmetic Teacher* of May, 1972, pp. 391–395, for brief descriptions of other projects. Additional information is presented in the *Seventh Report of the International Clearinghouse on Science and Mathematics Curricular Developments,* which can be obtained from the Science Teaching Center, University of Maryland, College Park, Maryland, 20742.

APPROACHES, TECHNIQUES, AND TOOLS

Mathematics Activities and Laboratories

Mathematics activities have become increasingly popular in the curriculum. They are mostly used in structured curricula for purposes of enrichment, motivation, application of acquired skills, and provision for individual differences. There are also schools where the activity approach is used almost exclusively in an effort to provide a child-centered program. In such situations the children pursue the learnings that present themselves in the activities. Children do suggested things. Individual children or small groups of pupils discuss, explore, and solve problems in an atmosphere that stimulates curiosity and in a room that has a wealth of manipulative materials. The child keeps records of the results of investigations or presents oral reports.

Mathematics activities, laboratories, games, and puzzles are pre-

9. National Council of Teachers of Mathematics, *Newsletter,* (December, 1976).

sented in many contemporary mathematics series, supplementary materials, and kits. They are also often prepared by the classroom teacher—for example, on assignment cards from which the child can make a selection. In open classroom situations, where many pupils and several teachers often work together in the room and, consequently, the range in ability is great, a wide variety of activities and many mathematics resource books of different levels must be available. Materials range from teacher-made and inexpensive objects, such as counters, beads, charts, clay, counting frames, abaci, cubes, sand, containers, and rulers, to commercial models, structured materials, and expensive devices, such as balance scales, Cuisenaire rods, Stern blocks, Dienes multibase arithmetic blocks, logic blocks, computational devices, games, puzzles, kits, geoboards, and geometric models.

Tasks suggested on assignment cards vary from simple questions to elaborate laboratory activities. Questions may be closed or open. Some possible assignments are presented in the following paragraphs.

Closed Question. Get together with three of your friends. Put four chairs in a row. Find out in how many different ways the four of you can sit side by side.

Open Question. Guess how high a ball will bounce if you drop it from a height of two feet. Then do the activity and check your guess.

Measurement Activity.

1. Estimate how many paper clips you need to make a string of clips that just fits around the girth of your waist. (If you don't know what the word "girth" means, use a dictionary to find out.)
2. Make such a string and count the clips.
3. Find the difference between your estimate and the number of clips you needed.
4. Are paper clips always the same length? Find paper clips of different lengths. Now write a sentence that tells why a paper clip is not as good a unit of measure as an inch.
5. Measure your string of clips to find out how long the girth of your waist is in inches.
6. Find the length of the girth of your waist in centimeters.
7. If some other children have done the same activities, make a graph that shows the measure in inches for each child.

Geoboard Activity.

1. Construct the figures shown on the geoboard using rubber bands.

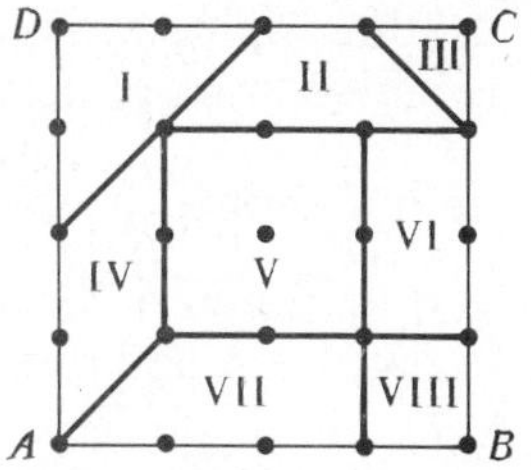

2. Find the area of the square *ABCD* in square units. (Note that on the geoboard the area of Figure VIII is one square unit.)
3. Find the area of each of the Figures I–VIII in square units.
4. If your answer in Exercise 2 is correct, how can you check your answers in Exercise 3?
5. Find as many special names as you can for the geometric figures in I–VIII.

Programmed Materials

In a programmed textbook, the material is presented in short sequential steps. The pupil studies the exposition, responds to questions, and checks answers by comparing them with the answers printed in the book. This technique of immediate self-correction leads to reinforcement of correct answers and correction of errors. In branching programs, the pupil who makes an error is directed to remedial work.

Programmed materials allow the pupil to work at his own rate and therefore assist the teacher in providing for individual differences. With this approach, the pupil does not have difficulty in making up work missed, a problem with the conventional approach.

Research has not shown the superiority of programmed materials over the conventional textbook, though there are indications that the use of programmed materials may save time. It is, however, realized that during class discussion learnings take place that cannot be measured by a paper-and-pencil test. Also, the monotony resulting from continous independent work and the reading problems that slow pupils encounter may have decreased the initial enthusiasm for the approach.

Programmed materials, if selected with care, appear to be useful for remedial instruction and for enrichment activities.

Structured Materials

Many devices have been constructed in an attempt to provide structured number experiences and to help children visualize number relations by using concrete models. These approaches usually provide some experimental play and then directed work with the materials, so that from the beginning the child is aided in abstracting number experiences. Of the variety of available materials, three apparatus are described briefly below. The Cuisenaire rods are presented in more detail in Chapter 10.

Stern Blocks. Catherine Stern's method is called "Structural Arithmetic." Stern was influenced by Max Wertheimer, the founder of Gestalt psychology.

Segmented unit blocks, each of a different color, represent the numbers 1 to 10. The blocks are placed into a variety of containers which serve different purposes.

The counting board has ten grooves of increasing length into which the unit blocks fit. Placing the blocks into the grooves is a self-corrective game.

The pattern boards, one for each of the numbers 1 to 10, are to be filled with the required number of cubes.

The unit box is used to match block pairs and to help the child form statements such as "the 6 needs 4 to make 10."

The number track on which the numerals 1 to 10 are painted can, for example, help the child discover that subtraction "undoes" what addition "does." For more advanced work, several sections of the number track can be joined.

Unifix. The Unifix is composed of cubes of various colors and trays. The units are plastic cubes that interlock so that the child can construct a rod that stands for a given number. Addition and subtraction can be represented by joining and removing units. A large rod can be broken into smaller pieces of equal length for fractional numbers.

Dienes Multibase Arithmetic Blocks. The purpose of Dienes multibase arithmetic blocks is to assist the child in abstracting mathematical concepts. They consist of:

units: small cubes, each representing 1;
longs: rods 10 units long, each representing 10;
flats: squares 10 units long and 10 units wide, each representing 100;
blocks: cubes 10 units long, wide, and high, each representing 1,000.

There are longs, flats, and blocks for different number bases. For example, for base three a long is 3 units, a flat is 9 units, and a block is 27 units.

The blocks can assist children in the development of the concept of place value, and operations can be made more meaningful with the materials. For example, the longs and units can be used in dividing 42 by 3:

$$
\begin{aligned}
42 &= 4 \text{ longs} + 2 \text{ units} \\
4 \text{ longs} + 2 \text{ units} &= 3 \text{ longs} + 1 \text{ long} + 2 \text{ units} \\
3 \text{ longs} + 1 \text{ long} + 2 \text{ units} &= 3 \text{ longs} + 12 \text{ units}
\end{aligned}
$$

Thus

$$
\begin{aligned}
42 \div 3 &= (30 + 12) \div 3 \\
(30 + 12) \div 3 &= (30 \div 3) + (12 \div 3) \\
(30 \div 3) + (12 \div 3) &= 10 + 4 \\
10 + 4 &= 14
\end{aligned}
$$

Media

Projection devices and audio materials are contributions of modern technology to education. Depending on the tool and the situation, they are used by large groups of pupils or by individual children. If properly used, such materials hold great promise for the improvement of mathematics instruction.

Films, Television, and Filmstrips. Though films have been produced on a variety of mathematical topics, they have not received widespread acceptance in the elementary school. The fact that often several concepts must be developed sequentially to cover a topic makes it difficult to meet the instructional objectives during the relatively short running time of a film. During the presentation, it is awkward to stop the film to answer questions. Films can probably be best used to review, to apply discussed concepts, to introduce topics dealing with the history of mathematics, and to present geometrical topics.

Jacobs and Bollenbacher[10] conducted a study to determine the effectiveness of teaching seventh-grade mathematics by television. The television method of instruction was found to be superior to the conventional methods for pupils of average ability, whereas pupils of high ability performed better with the conventional approach. It was suggested that television instruction was too slow for children of above-average ability.

Filmstrips can be shown at any speed desired. During the presentation, questions can be asked by the teacher and the pupils, and concepts can be carefully developed into conclusions. Topics such as patterns, geometry, and measurement can be presented especially effectively.

The Overhead Projector. The overhead projector is occasionally an effective substitute for the chalkboard. Previously prepared materials or commercial transparencies can be used repeatedly, thus saving time during the class period.

---

10. J. N. Jacobs and J. Bollenbacher, "Teaching Seventh-Grade Mathematics by Television," *The Mathematics Teacher* (November, 1960), pp. 543–547.

The Opaque Projector. The opaque projector has the advantage that a paper or a page from a book can be shown in its original colors and enlarged without being copied.

Audio Tapes. Audio tapes are especially useful for the slow learner who has reading difficulties, since the child receives oral information and directions. Word problems that are too difficult for a pupil to read but that can be understood and whose required computations can be performed can be solved by the pupil using casettes.

The Bulletin Board. The bulletin board is an inexpensive tool which, when presentations are properly prepared and not displayed too long, may motivate children to do additional investigation. The content may be selected by the teacher or may be the result of children's work supervised by the teacher. The board should be attractive, clear, and simple. It can be used for several purposes, such as introduction of a topic, reinforcement, enrichment, a display of samples of children's work, a display of graphs, charts, or tables.

Figure 3.5 depicts a possible bulletin board for a middle grade.

<u>Answer it</u>: If it takes 3 minutes to soft-boil 1 egg, how long does it take to soft-boil 12 eggs?

<u>Try it</u>: If you hold a mirror as shown, what word do you have?

T O 

<u>Guess it</u>: How many beans in the jar?
Write your name and your guess.

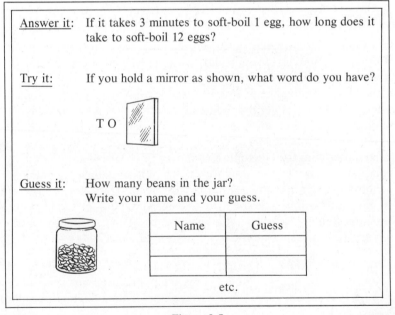

Name	Guess

etc.

Figure 3.5

The Minicalculator[11]

Recently a variety of literature dealing with the use of the minicalculator in the elementary school has been published. It is generally agreed that this tool can supplement and enrich the mathematics curriculum.

The calculator should be used properly so that pupils do not become dependent upon it. Pupils should acquire skill in performing common written and mental computations with reasonable speed and accuracy—a goal that should not be de-emphasized. Instead, the calculator should be used in controlled situations to reinforce such skills and to increase children's ability in estimation and verbal quantitative problem solving.

The minicalculator can be used in the elementary school for purposes that include those presented in the paragraphs that follow. Because of space limitations, the number of examples under each heading is restricted.

Checking Answers to Written Computations. If, for example, the product of the factors 24 and 25 has been computed, the pupil can use the calculator to check the answer by multiplying the factors or by dividing the obtained product by one of the factors.

Checking Answers to Mental Computations. The game "follow me" is played. In this game, children perform given operations mentally and write the last answer. For example, the teacher may say: start with 12, add 8, divide by 2, subtract 5, multiply by 4, add 10, divide by 5, write the

Even young children can use the minicalculator.

11. The student is referred to the November, 1976, issue of *The Arithmetic Teacher,* which focuses on the minicalculator.

last answer. Then the exercises are shown on the chalkboard or on a previously prepared transparency:

Start with 12 → + 8 → ÷ 2 → − 5 → × 4 → + 10 → ÷ 5 → ?

and the operations are performed on the calculator to check the answer.

Estimation and Verification. First estimate the sum of 32, 29, 58, and 63. To do this, the pupils round the numbers to multiples of ten and add the rounded numbers. Then the calculator is used to find the correct answer and the difference between the estimated answer and the correct sum is determined.

Demonstrating that Multiplication May be Used as a Short Form of Adding Equal Addends. The calculator is used to solve several sets of problems such as:

$$7 + 7 + 7 + 7 + 7 = \square \qquad 5 \times 7 = \square$$

Developing Understanding of Algorisms. First the pupil works, for example, a division problem on paper:

$$\begin{array}{r} 42 \\ 7\overline{)294} \\ \underline{28} \\ 14 \\ \underline{14} \\ 0 \end{array}$$

Then the teacher guides the child to check the answer by using the calculator. The checking process is recorded:

$$\begin{array}{r} 40 \times 7 = 280 \\ + \ 2 \times 7 = \ \ 14 \\ \hline 42 \times 7 = 294 \end{array}$$

Working Number Tricks. In this activity the directions are given by the teacher or by a pupil.

Directions:	*Example:*
Enter a number on the calculator	4
Add 10	4 + 10 = 14
Multiply by 2	2 × 14 = 28
Subtract 15	28 − 15 = 13
Multiply by 5	5 × 13 = 65
Subtract 25	65 − 25 = 40

The leader asks what the last answer is, divides it by 10, and tells the child that he or she started with the number 4.

Motivation. Most children are interested in problems such as the following if they may use a calculator. They can be asked to estimate the answer first.

> Imagine that you have a very, very long strip of paper that is one half millimeter thick. If you fold it once, the two parts together are 1 millimeter thick. If you fold it twice, the four parts form a stack that is 2 millimeters thick. Suppose you were able to fold the paper 27 times. Use a calculator to find how many millimeters, meters, or kilometers thick the stack of paper would be.

Finding and Continuing Patterns.

a. Use a calculator to find the answers:

$$11 - 2 = \square \qquad 1{,}111 - 112 = \square$$
$$111 - 12 = \square \qquad 11{,}111 - 1{,}112 = \square$$

b. Find the pattern.
c. Write the answers without computation:

$$111{,}111 - 11{,}112 = \square \qquad 11{,}111{,}111 - 1{,}111{,}112 = \square$$
$$1{,}111{,}111 - 111{,}112 = \square \qquad 111{,}111{,}111 - 11{,}111{,}112 = \square$$

Testing Number Properties. Children decide whether, for example, the distributive property of multiplication holds over subtraction by using the calculator to work sets of problems such as:

a. $7 \times 19 = \square$ and $(7 \times 20) - (7 \times 1) = \square$
b. $4 \times 28 = \square$ and $(4 \times 30) - (4 \times 2) = \square$
c. $6 \times 37 = \square$ and $(6 \times 40) - (6 \times 3) = \square$

Finding or Testing Rules for Divisibility. In lower grades children can use the calculator to divide several even numbers and odd numbers by 2, and decide upon a rule for divisibility by 2. In upper grades pupils can first determine whether, for example, the number 12,348 is divisible by 9 by dividing the sum of the digits by 9; then they can use the calculator to divide 12,348 by 9 in order to verify their conclusion.

Solving Word Problems. When pupils must solve verbal quantitative problems that require computations that the pupils have already mastered, a great deal of time is saved by allowing the children to use the calculator.

The time that is saved can be used to solve additional problems in order to improve the pupils' ability in this area.

Experiencing Calculator Pleasantries. First find the digits on the minicalculator which, when turned around, approach the form of letters. Then do the following activity:

> Use the calculator to determine whether these gains and losses at the end result in a gain or a loss: gain of $6,000, loss of $7,500, gain of $4,506, loss of $4,045, gain of $2,080, loss of $6,548. Then turn your calculator around and read whether your answer is correct. If the calculator does not show a sensible answer, try again.

It is the view of the National Advisory Committee on Mathematical Education (NACOME)[12] that for those pupils who have been unsuccessful in acquiring functional levels of arithmetic computation by the end of the eighth grade, pursuing these skills as a *sina qua non* through further programs seems neither productive nor humane. The committee feels that providing such pupils with electronic calculators to meet their arithmetic needs and allowing them to proceed to other mathematical experience in appropriately designed curricula is the wisest policy.

It will be realized that proper use of the calculator requires the ability to decide which operations must be performed. As Smith[13] remarks: "None of these calculators tell *when* to add, subtract, multiply, or divide. The calculator is designed to do only the keypuncher's bidding. Nor will the calculator tell whether or not an answer is reasonable. Estimation to judge the reasonableness of an answer will still require computational skill."

SELECTED RESEARCH

In this experiment[14] the results of teaching fourth-graders using programmed mathematics materials were compared with the results derived from use of materials presented in standard textbooks.

---

12. S. Hill et al., National Advisory Committee on Mathematical Education, *Overview and Analysis of School Mathematics Grades K-12*. (Washington, D.C.: Conference Board of the Mathematical Sciences, 1975), p. 25.

13. National Council of Teachers of Mathematics, "A Look at Mathematics Education Today," adapted from President E. P. Smith's address at the Annual Meeting, 26 April 1973, *The Arithmetic Teacher* (October, 1973), p. 505.

14. F. W. Banghart et al., "An Experimental Study of Programmed Versus Traditional Elementary School Mathematics," *The Arithmetic Teacher* (April, 1963), pp. 199–204.

The sample consisted of 195 children considered to be an acceptable cross section of fourth-graders in a large metropolitan area with respect to intelligence, achievement, and socioeconomic status.

The length of the daily periods for both the experimental and the control group was thirty to forty minutes. Experimental teachers were encouraged to supply needed additional drill. The pupils in the experimental group were allowed to progress through the programmed materials at their own rate, so that these children were relieved of the frustrations of trying to keep up with the faster pupils or of being detained by slower ones.

Of the investigators' tentative conclusions, the following are reported:

1. There is no indication in the study that children working with programmed materials achieve differently in arithmetic problem solving from those who work with conventional materials.
2. An important advantage of programmed materials is the freedom each child has to progress at his own rate.
3. Programmed materials are most effective when they are used to supplement classroom teaching.

EXERCISES

1. Describe the stages that Piaget distinguishes in the formation of concepts.
2. Describe an experiment conducted to determine if a child is aware of conservation of discontinuous quantities.
3. Compare Bruner's and Gagné's ideas on learning.
4. List some characteristics of the Nuffield Project.
5. List some characteristics of the IPI Math Project.
6. Write an open-ended mathematical question.
7. Construct a mathematics laboratory for a grade level you select.
8. Describe briefly the Stern blocks. If you can secure a set of these materials, perform some activities with them.
9. Explain how the Dienes blocks can assist in the development of the concept of place value.
10. Do you think that it is important to present mathematical concepts in proper sequence? Defend your opinion.
11. Visit a school and find out which approaches to learning and teaching mathematics are used and which media are available.

12. Explain how media can assist the child with reading difficulties.
13. Give your opinion on the use of films in the mathematics class.
14. Examine recent issues of *The Arithmetic Teacher.* Select and report on an article that suggests new approaches to teaching and learning. [*Note: The Arithmetic Teacher* is an official journal of the National Council of Teachers of Mathematics (NCTM).]
15. Try to determine why so many pupils show deficiencies in arithmetic at the end of their elementary school studies.
16. State and defend your opinion on the use of the hand-held calculator in the elementary school. Describe some purposes for which this tool can be used and provide examples.
17. Report on the research study described in this chapter.

SOURCES FOR FURTHER READING

Association of Teachers of Mathematics, *Notes on Mathematics in Primary Schools.* London: Cambridge University Press, 1969.

Biggs, E. E., and J. R. MacLean, *Freedom to Learn.* Don Mills, Ontario: Addison-Wesley (Canada), Ltd., 1969.

Bruner, J. S., *The Process of Education.* New York: Vintage Books (Random House), 1963.

Bruner, J. S., *Toward a Theory of Instruction.* New York: W. W. Norton & Company, Inc., 1968.

Buckeye, D. A., and J. L. Ginther, *Creative Mathematics.* San Francisco: Canfield Press (Harper & Row), 1971.

Churchill, E. M., *Counting and Measuring.* Toronto: University of Toronto Press, 1961.

Copeland, R. W., *How Children Learn Mathematics,* 2nd ed. New York: Macmillan Publishing Company, Inc., 1974, Chaps. II–V.

Copeland, R. W., *Mathematics and the Elementary School Teacher,* 2nd ed. Philadelphia: W. B. Saunders Company, 1972, Chaps. II, XI.

Dienes, Z. P., *Building Up Mathematics.* London: Hutchinson Educational Ltd., 1960, Chaps. I–III.

Dienes, Z. P., "Multi-base Arithmetic," *Grade Teacher,* April, 1962, pp. 56, 97–100.

Duckworth, E., "Piaget Rediscovered," *The Arithmetic Teacher.* November, 1964, pp. 496–499.

Dumas, E., and C. W. Schminke, *Math Activities for Child Involvement,* 2nd ed. Boston: Allyn and Bacon, Inc., 1977.

Ewbank, W. A., "The Mathematics Laboratory: What? Why? When? How?" *The Arithmetic Teacher,* December, 1971, pp. 559–564.

Fehr, H. F., "Sense and Nonsense in the Teaching of Mathematics," *The Arithmetic Teacher,* February, 1966, pp. 83–91.

Friesen, C. D., "Check Your Calculator Computations," *The Arithmetic Teacher,* December, 1976, p. 660.

Gagné, R. M., *The Conditions of Learning.* New York: Holt, Rinehart and Winston, Inc., 1965.

Glennon, V. J., "Mathematics: How Firm the Foundations?" *Phi Delta Kappan,* January, 1976, pp. 302–305.

Henderson, G. L., "Individualized Instruction: Sweet in Theory, Sour in Practice," *The Arithmetic Teacher,* January, 1972, pp. 17–22.

Inskeep, J. E., Jr., "Building a Case for the Application of Piaget's Theory and Research in the Classroom," *The Arithmetic Teacher,* April, 1972, pp. 255–260.

Iowa Council of Teachers of Mathematics, *The Hand-Held Calculator.* Cedar Falls: The Council, 1976.

Kidd, K. P., S. S. Myers, and D. M. Cilley. *The Laboratory Approach to Mathematics.* Chicago: Science Research Associates, Inc., 1970.

Lipson, J. I., "Hidden Strengths of Conventional Instruction," *The Arithmetic Teacher,* January, 1976, pp. 11–15.

Lipson, J. I., "I.P.I. Math—An Example of What's Right and Wrong with Individualized Modular Program," *Learning,* March, 1974, p. 60.

National Advisory Committee on Mathematical Education, *Overview and Analysis of School Mathematics Grades K–12.* Washington, D.C.: Conference Board of the Mathematical Sciences, 1975.

National Council of Teachers of Mathematics, *Instructional Aids in Mathematics, Thirty-fourth Yearbook.* Washington, D.C.: The Council, 1973.

National Council of Teachers of Mathematics, *The Slow Learner in Mathematics, Thirty-fifth Yearbook.* Washington, D.C.: The Council, 1972, Chaps. III, VII, VIII, XI.

Pagni, D. L., "The Computer Motivates Improvement in Computational Skills," *The Arithmetic Teacher,* February, 1971, pp. 109–112.

Piaget, J., *The Child's Conception of Number.* Translated by C. Gattegno and F. M. Hodgson. London: Routledge & Kegan Paul Ltd., 1961.

Piaget, J., "How Children Form Mathematical Concepts," *Scientific American,* November, 1953, pp. 74–79.

Piaget, J., "The Stages of Intellectual Development of the Child," *Bulletin of the Menninger Clinic,* May, 1962, pp. 120–128.

Piaget, J., B. Inhelder, and A. Szeminska, *The Child's Conception of Geometry.* Translated by E. A. Lunzer. New York: Basic Books, Inc., Publishers, 1960.

Rosskopf, M. F., "Piagetian Research and the School Mathematics Program," *The Arithmetic Teacher,* April, 1972, pp. 309–314.

Shulman, L. S., "Perspectives on the Psychology of Learning and the Teaching of Mathematics," in W. R. Houston (ed.), *Improving Mathematics Education for Elementary School Teachers,* A Conference Report Sponsored by The Science and Mathematics Teaching Center of Michigan State University and The National Science Foundation, 1967, pp. 23–37.

Stern, C., and M. B. Stern, *Children Discover Arithmetic: An Introduction to Structural Arithmetic.* New York: Harper & Row, Publishers, 1971.

Underhill, R. G., *Teaching Elementary School Mathematics.* Columbus: Charles E. Merrill Publishing Company, 1972, Chaps. I–III.

Weaver, J. F., "Some Concerns about the Application of Piaget's Theory and Research to Mathematical Learning and Instruction," *The Arithmetic Teacher,* April, 1972, pp. 263–270.

Williams, J. D., *Teaching Technique in Primary Maths.* London: National Foundation for Educational Research in England and Wales, 1971.

II

Topics in Contemporary Elementary School Mathematics

4 *Numbers, Numerals, and Notation Systems*

The number system we use today is the result of continuous development. From simple record keeping, man moved first toward the use of numbers in counting objects. Then the number system was gradually extended to include other number systems. In this chapter the development of number ideas is briefly traced, frequently used terms are explained, important properties of the whole numbers are identified, and notation systems (systems of writing numbers) are presented.

THE DEVELOPMENT OF NUMBER IDEAS[1]

Early man had little use for numbers. He took care of his own needs and was quite independent of the services of others. His challenge was to adjust to his environment. Consequently, he had to become aware of the relationships in space and the sequences in time. While observing the natural phenomena, he gradually learned to ascribe patterns to them. His periods of rest and work were determined by the rising and setting of the sun. The times of harvest appeared to have certain characteristics. There seemed to be a correlation between the phases of the moon and the height of the tides. The position of the sun in the sky had something to do with the temperature. The movements and phases of the moon were regular, and so were the apparent movements of the sun.

Man began to record the days as they passed, the phases of the moon

1. The student is referred to E. M. Churchill, *Counting and Measuring* (Toronto: University of Toronto Press, 1961).

as it waxed and waned, and the position of the sun as it seemed to change. He found patterns of relationship and definite sequences of time.

The first recording of the passing of time may have been done by putting a rock or a pebble at an isolated place for each day that passed. A record of the total time passed was then available.

There were other records used by early man. He may have kept a record of the number of sheep he owned by putting as many pebbles in a bag as he had sheep, one pebble for each sheep. When, at night, he wanted to determine whether all his sheep were in, he would match the pebbles and the sheep. There was supposed to be a *one-to-one-correspondence* between the pebbles and the sheep, which means that there was one and only one pebble for each sheep and one and only one sheep for each pebble. Thus it could be determined by the matching process whether all the sheep were in.

As time passed, man began to assign specific names to small groups. Originally, descriptive names were used for such small collections. There was not just one universal word to denote any set[2] of two, but different names were used to represent different objects. Number was considered a quality of specific things. In our language we have retained residues of this system in the form of words such as couple, twin, brace, team, yoke, etc. Large collections did not have to be called by specific names, since words meaning heap, lot, and flock were sufficient for communication.

Another technique was to match model groups against groups under consideration. A pair of wings or a pair of ears could represent a group of two; for three a clover leaf could be used, for four the legs of a deer, for five the fingers of one hand, and for ten the fingers of both hands. However, as culture advanced, this technique became insufficient; larger numbers had to be represented more efficiently. Man began to employ the tallying technique more extensively, probably by using the fingers of both hands and the toes of both feet, by making marks on a tree or on another object, or by putting aside pebbles, grains, etc. In doing this, he gradually created words and *numerals* to express numbers. Certainly the realization that two pebbles, two men, two hills, and two birds have an attribute or property in common—the *number* of each of these sets—represents a high level of abstraction.

The use of tallies or other figures to represent larger numbers soon became unwieldy, and man began to see a need for grouping to express and record larger numbers conveniently. In the Hindu-Arabic system which we use, the numbers are grouped by tens. It is assumed that ten

---

2. A *set* may be described as a collection of concrete or abstract entities. (Sets are introduced in Chapter 5.)

was selected as the *base,* or the first collection in the system, because we have ten fingers. Other bases have been used at different times in different parts of the world. Base two was probably developed from the technique of comparing quantities with model groups of two. Base five was selected because we have five fingers on one hand. Base twelve had its origin in the fact that there are twelve moons in a year. Base twenty, which was used by the Mayas, was adopted, we assume, because man has a total of twenty fingers and toes. Base sixty was used by the Babylonians.

TERMS[3]

A *number*[4] is an abstract idea. It is a property or an attribute common to all members of a collection of paired groups. For example, a group of two triangles, a group of two circles, and a group of two squares have the number property two in common. These groups can be *matched* and their members can be placed in one-to-one correspondence, as in Figure 4.1.

A *numeral* is a symbol for a number. Various symbols may represent the same number. For example, the number of the fingers on one hand may be named by the symbols 5, V, 3 + 2, 5 × 1, and five.

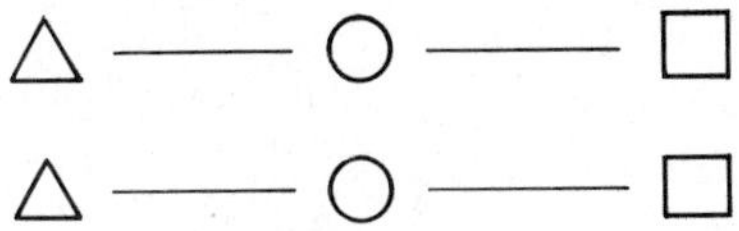

Figure 4.1

The purpose of the *cardinal* use of number is to indicate how many objects are considered.

Example

There are *five* books.

The purpose of the *ordinal* use of number is to identify the place that the object under consideration occupies in a series.

Example

The *fourth* book in the pile is mine.

The numbers that man used originally and that the child learns first are

---

3. Explanations or illustrations of terms and expressions are presented in the glossary in the back of this book.

4. In the interest of easy communication with the reader, in this volume the term *number* will be used frequently according to popular usage. For example, the term *two-digit number* will be used, rather than *number expressed by a two-digit numeral.*

often called *natural numbers*. The set of natural numbers is expressed as {1, 2, 3, · · · }.[5] Since the numbers are used in the counting series, they are also called *counting numbers*.

The set of numbers expressed as {0, 1, 2, 3, · · · } we shall call the set of *whole numbers:*

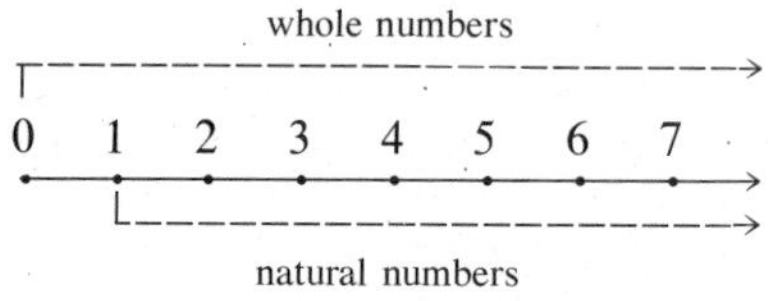

Numbers greater than zero are called *positive numbers*. When man had a need for expressing numbers less than zero, he invented *negative numbers*. The numerals for these numbers are preceded by a negative sign, as in $^-5$. Pairs of numbers such as $^+1$ and $^-1$, $^+3$ and $^-3$, $^+5$ and $^-5$ are *additive inverses,* since their sums equal 0.

The whole numbers and their additive inverses are called *integers*. The set of integers is expressed as {· · ·, $^-3$, $^-2$, $^-1$, 0, $^+1$, $^+2$, $^+3$, · · ·}.

The need to describe parts of a unit or of a group required the extension of the number system, and so fractional numbers were identified. The resulting new number system was called the system of *rational numbers*. Examples of rational numbers are $\frac{1}{2}$, $\frac{3}{4}$, $\frac{5}{2}$, $1\frac{1}{10}$, and 3.5. Integers are included in the set of rational numbers ($5 = \frac{5}{1}$; $^-3 = \frac{^-3}{1}$).

A number that cannot be expressed as the quotient of an integer and a nonzero integer is called an *irrational number*. In elementary school the irrational number represented by the symbol π (pi) is introduced in connection with circles.

The *real numbers* consist of both the rational and the irrational numbers.

SOME IMPORTANT PROPERTIES OF WHOLE NUMBERS

The basic properties of whole numbers are:

1. *Commutative property of addition*. In adding two whole numbers, the order of the addends can be changed without affecting the sum. Thus, if a and b are whole numbers, then $a + b = b + a$.

---

5. This expression is read "the set whose members are 1, 2, 3, and so on infinitely." The names of the elements of the set are listed between braces. The three dots denote that there is an endless number of elements.

Example

$$2 + 3 = 5 \text{ and } 3 + 2 = 5$$

$2 + 3 = 3 + 2$

The property can be illustrated on the number line:

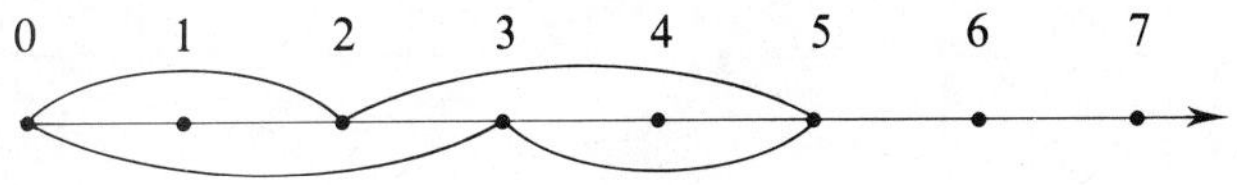

Note: Children must understand that the spaces along the number line are counted—from 0 to 1, from 1 to 2, etc.—and not the marked points on the line.

2. *Commutative property of multiplication.* In multiplying two whole numbers, the order of the factors can be changed without affecting the product. Thus, if a and b are whole numbers, then $a \times b = b \times a$.

Example

$$2 \times 3 = 6 \text{ and } 3 \times 2 = 6$$

$2 \times 3 = 3 \times 2$

The following diagram will assist children to understand the property:

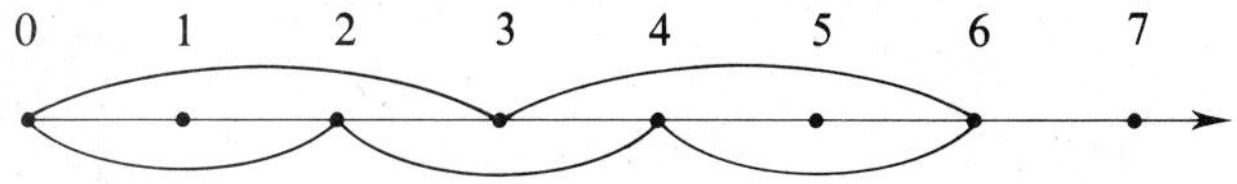

3. *Associative property of addition.* In adding more than two whole numbers, the way in which the addends are grouped does not affect the sum. Thus, if a, b, and c are whole numbers, then $(a + b) + c = a + (b + c)$.

Example

$$(2 + 3) + 4 = 5 + 4 \quad \text{and} \quad 2 + (3 + 4) = 2 + 7$$
$$= 9 \qquad\qquad\qquad\qquad = 9$$

$(2 + 3) + 4 = 2 + (3 + 4)$

Again, the number line can be used to illustrate the property:

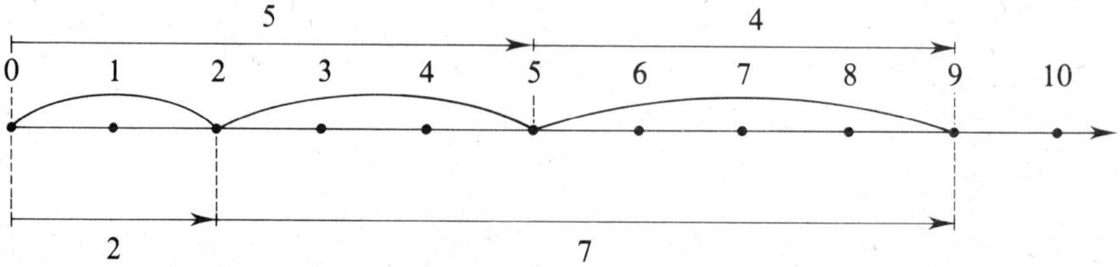

4. *Associative property of multiplication.* In multiplying more than two whole numbers, the way in which the factors are grouped does not affect the product. Thus, if a, b, and c are whole numbers, then $(a \times b) \times c = a \times (b \times c)$.

Example

$$(2 \times 3) \times 4 = 6 \times 4 = 24 \quad \text{and} \quad 2 \times (3 \times 4) = 2 \times 12 = 24$$

$$(2 \times 3) \times 4 = 2 \times (3 \times 4)$$

5. *Distributive property of multiplication with respect to addition.* When the sum of two whole numbers is to be multiplied by a given number, it is proper to multiply each addend by the given number and to add the products. Thus, if a, b, and c are whole numbers, then $a \times (b + c) = (a \times b) + (a \times c)$.

Example 1

$$3 \times (4 + 5) = (3 \times 4) + (3 \times 5) = 12 + 15 = 27$$

An application of this property follows.

Example 2

Examine this presentation:

$$\begin{aligned} 3 \times 12 &= 3 \times (10 + 2) \\ &= (3 \times 10) + (3 \times 2) \\ &= 30 + 6 \\ &= 36 \end{aligned}$$

In the second step a product is renamed as the sum of two products:

$$3 \times (10 + 2) = (3 \times 10) + (3 \times 2)$$

The property can be illustrated by using an array of dots:

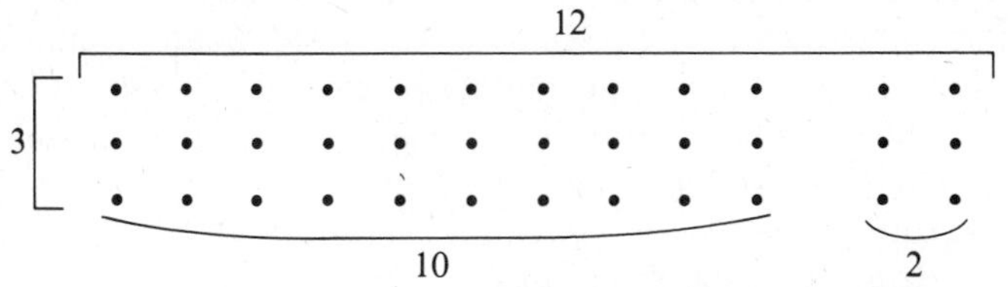

6. *Closure property of addition.* The result of the addition of any two whole numbers is a whole number. We say that the set of whole numbers is closed with respect to addition. Thus, if a and b are whole numbers, then $a + b$ is a whole number.

Example

$7 + 9 = 16.$

7. *Closure property of multiplication.* The result of the multiplication of any two whole numbers is a whole number. We say that the set of whole numbers is closed with respect to multiplication. Thus, if a and b are whole numbers, then $a \times b$ is a whole number.

Example

$7 \times 9 = 63.$

8. *Identity element for addition.* If zero is added to any whole number, the result is the same number. Zero is the identity element for addition. Thus, if a is a whole number, then $a + 0 = a$.

Example

$6 + 0 = 6.$

9. *Identity element for multiplication.* If any whole number is multiplied by 1, the result is the same number. One is the identity element for multiplication. Thus, if a is a whole number, then $1 \times a = a$.

Example

$1 \times 6 = 6.$

10. *Property of order.* For any whole numbers a and b, one and only one of the following three relationships exists: $a = b$, $a > b$, $a < b$. (The symbol $>$ means "is greater than"; the symbol $<$ means "is less than.")

Examples

If $a = 5$ and $b = 5$, then $a = b$.
If $a = 5$ and $b = 6$, then $a < b$.
If $a = 5$ and $b = 4$, then $a > b$.

THE HINDU-ARABIC SYSTEM OF NOTATION

The elements of our system of notation—the Hindu-Arabic system—were probably invented in India by the Hindus and transmitted to Europe by the Arabs. The earliest examples of the system date from a few centuries before Christ. At that time neither positional value nor the zero was used. Several centuries later positional value was employed and the zero was invented. The Arabic people used the system and probably introduced it to Europeans. By the sixteenth century the Hindu-Arabic system of notation was well established in Europe.

Characteristics of Our Notation System

The characteristics of our notation system are:

1. *It has place value or positional value.* The positional value of a digit in a numeral depends on the place it occupies in the numeral. In 32, the 3 has a face value of 3 and a positional value of 30, since it represents three tens. In 321, the 3 has a face value of 3 and a positional value of 300, since it represents three hundreds. In 3,210, the 3 has a face value of 3 and a positional value of 3,000, since it represents three thousands. Thus, in the decimal system, the positional value of a digit increases tenfold in each successive place to the left. Figure 4.2 illustrates the principle of place value.

2. *It has a base of ten.* The base is the basic counting group or the first collection in the number series. Collections less than ten are represented by the digits through 9. When a collection of ten is to be represented by a numeral, a 1 is put in the tens place and a 0 in the ones place. Thus 10 is the first collection in the series. When ten groups of ten are to be represented by a numeral, a 1 is put in the hundreds place, a 0 in the tens place, and a 0 in the ones place. Because of the grouping by tens and powers of ten, our system is called a *decimal system*. The word *decimal* is derived from the Latin *decem,* which means ten.

The role of ten and the powers of ten in the system is clearly illustrated by exponential notation. For example, $10{,}000 = 10^4$ (ten to the fourth power), $1{,}000 = 10^3$ (ten to the third power, or ten cubed), and $100 = 10^2$ (ten to the second power, or ten squared). In 10^3, the *exponent* (the superscript) indicates the number of times the *base* (10) is used as a factor: $10^3 = 10 \times 10 \times 10 = 1{,}000$. It should be noted that any nonzero number raised to the zero power is equal to 1. Thus $10^0 = 1$. (Consider: $10^2 \div 10^2 = 100 \div 100 = 1$ and $10^2 \div 10^2 = 10^{2-2} = 10^0$.)

3. *Ten symbols are used: 1, 2, 3, 4, 5, 6, 7, 8, 9 and 0.* A natural number can be expressed as a numeral by using one or more of these ten symbols. A zero in a numeral indicates that there is no quantity for the power of ten for which it holds the place.

hundred thousand	ten thousand	thousand	hundred	ten	one
100,000	10,000	1,000	100	10	1
10^5	10^4	10^3	10^2	10^1	10^0
2	2	2	2	2	2

$$2 \times 10^5 = 200,000$$
$$2 \times 10^4 = 20,000$$
$$2 \times 10^3 = 2,000$$
$$2 \times 10^2 = 200$$
$$2 \times 10^1 = 20$$
$$2 \times 10^0 = 2$$
$$\overline{222,222}$$

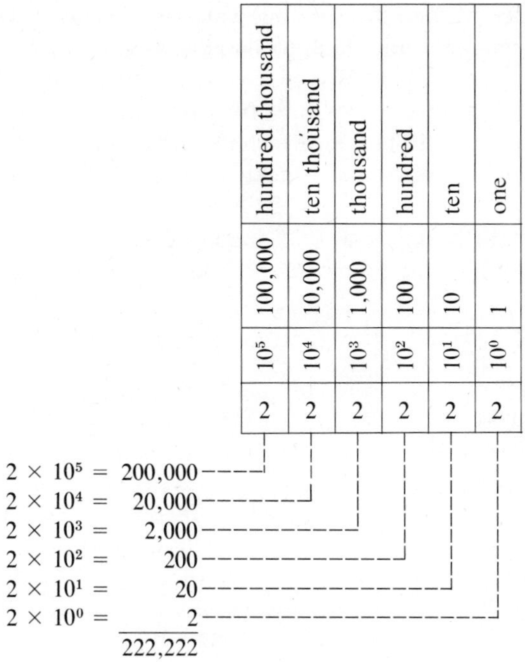

Figure 4.2

4. *It has the additive property.* Figure 4.2 shows that 222,222 = 200,000 + 20,000 + 2,000 + 200 + 20 + 2.

Numeration

Numeration is the art of expressing numbers by words and of reading numerals.

The number names through ten are independent of one another. Since—in the Hindu-Arabic system—numbers are grouped by powers of ten, man conveniently expresses larger numbers with the help of number names expressing smaller numbers.

Eleven and twelve come from words meaning "one left" and "two left" (after ten). Thirteen means "three and ten." It is not difficult to decide the origin of the number names fourteen, fifteen, etc. Similarly, twenty, thirty, forty, etc. mean two tens, three tens, four tens, etc.

The characteristic of positional value in our notation system simplifies the reading of numerals. Each digit in a numeral has both face value and positional value. The positional value of a digit increases tenfold in each successive place to the left. The face value is constant. This is shown in the following example, in which 6,666 is written in expanded notation:

$$\begin{aligned} 6{,}666 &= (6 \times 10^3) + (6 \times 10^2) + (6 \times 10^1) + (6 \times 10^0) \\ &= (6 \times 1{,}000) + (6 \times 100) + (6 \times 10) + (6 \times 1) \\ &= 6{,}000 + 600 + 60 + 6 \end{aligned}$$

The numeral 6,666 is read "six thousand six hundred sixty-six."

The word "and" should be reserved for the decimal point when reading a numeral.

Examples

406 four hundred six.
46.6 forty-six and six tenths.

The set of natural numbers is endless. Sometimes very large numerals must be read. Since it would require some time to determine what the digits stand for in large numerals such as 20594781, the digits are grouped into periods of three digits each. In the United States, these periods are set off by commas. The numeral above is therefore written as 20,594,781. It should be noted that the grouping into periods starts at the right and that, therefore, the period at the extreme left in the numeral above has only two digits.

Each period has a name: ones period, thousands period, millions period, etc. The periods are subdivided, as shown in Figure 4.3. Many more successive periods have been named, and, of course, more names can be devised when needed. Some period names with the required number of zeros are presented in Table 4.1.

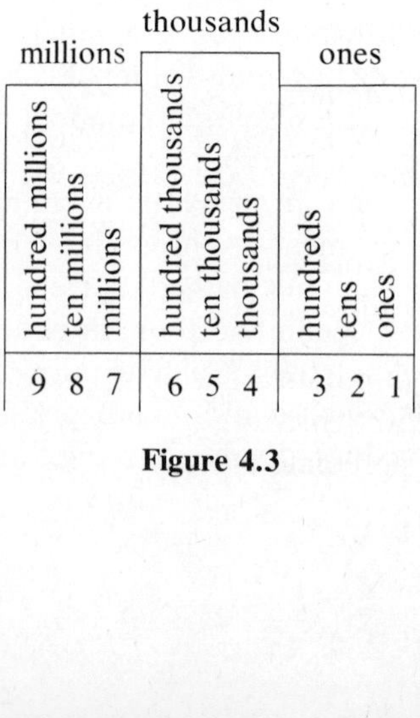
thousands
millions
ones
hundred millions
ten millions
millions
hundred thousands
ten thousands
thousands
hundreds
tens
ones
9 8 7
6 5 4
3 2 1

Figure 4.3

Table 4.1

Name	*Number of Zeros*
thousand	3
million	6
billion	9
trillion	12
quadrillion	15

The American and French systems differ from the English and German systems in the writing of large numbers. In the English-German system, a billion is a million millions, a trillion is a billion billions, a quadrillion is a trillion trillions, etc. The English-German system is the original. The French changed it, and other countries, including the United States, adopted the change.

THE ROMAN SYSTEM

Roman numerals are still being used for special purposes. They are often used on clock faces, tombstones, and cornerstones, and may be employed to express chapter numbers, volume numbers, and dates.

The Hindu-Arabic and the Roman systems have the same number base, but differ in notation.

The Roman system employs seven capital letters as symbols to express numbers: I = 1, V = 5, X = 10, L = 50, C = 100, D = 500, and M = 1,000. It should be noted that these symbols stand for 1, 10, 100, 1,000, and for the numbers that are, in each case, one half the next power of ten.

Observe these principles in the system:

1. *The principle of repetition.* For example, in XXX the X is repeated three times and the meaning of XXX is 30. Only the symbols I, X, C, and M are repeated.

2. *The principle of addition.* XI means 10 + 1. The symbols are written in order of increasing numerical value.

3. *The principle of subtraction.* This principle results in the use of fewer symbols. Instead of IIII, IV is written, with the understanding that, when a symbol of smaller value precedes a symbol of larger value, the smaller value must be subtracted from the larger. Only the symbols I, X, and C may precede a symbol expressing a larger numeral, and not more than one symbol is used at a time.

The Roman system of notation has many shortcomings compared with our system. The ease with which we can perform the fundamental operations should make us appreciate our system.

THE EGYPTIAN SYSTEM

About 5000 years ago the Egyptians employed a system, depicted in Table 4.2, in which representations of common objects were used to stand for powers of ten.

In the Egyptian system, the principles of addition and repetition were used. Thus, any symbol could be used nine times, and for the tenth one, another symbol was employed.

Examples

4: 

43: 

586: 

2035: 

Table 4.2

Object Represented	*Numeral*	*Hindu-Arabic Equivalent*
Staff or vertical stroke	|	1
Heel bone or arch	∩	10
Scroll or coiled rope		100
Lotus plant		1,000
Bent finger		10,000
Burbot (fish)		100,000
Man in astonishment		1,000,000

BASES OTHER THAN TEN

The decimal scale we use requires ten symbols. Grouping is done by tens and by powers of ten. When expressing a number as a numeral, we record the ones, tens, hundreds, thousands, etc., each in their assigned places according to the principle of place value. Each digit represents a power of ten.

Example

$$1{,}325 = (1 \times 10^3) + (3 \times 10^2) + (2 \times 10^1) + (5 \times 10^0)$$
$$= (1 \times 1{,}000) + (3 \times 100) + (2 \times 10) + (5 \times 1)$$

When 3 is to be added to 9, we have to regroup. First 1 is added to form 1 ten, and then we add 2 more: $9 + 3 = 9 + (1 + 2) = (9 + 1) + 2 = 10 + 2 = 12$. The result is 1 group of ten and 2 ones.

Base Five

In base five, grouping is done by fives and powers of five. Therefore, each digit in a numeral written to base five is a power of five.

Only five symbols are needed in base five: 0, 1, 2, 3, and 4.

In base five, the numeral 10 means 1 group of five and 0 ones:

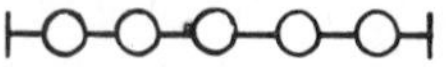

In base five, the numeral 11 means 1 group of five and 1 one:

In base five, the numeral 12 means 1 group of five and 2 ones:

In base five, the numeral 24 means 2 groups of five and 4 ones:

The sets of beads pictured below are counted in base five:

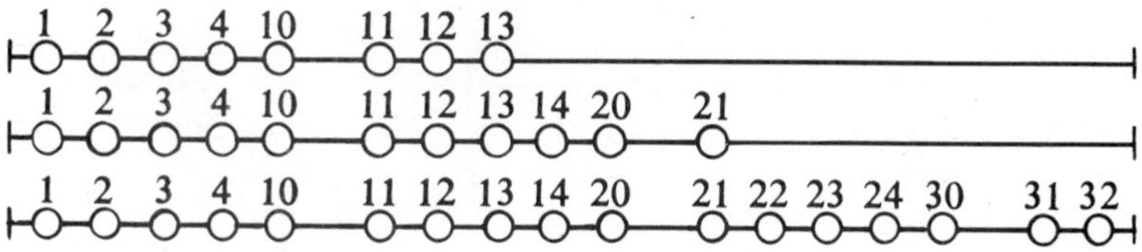

The following number line is accompanied by two scales of notation: one in base five, and one in base ten.

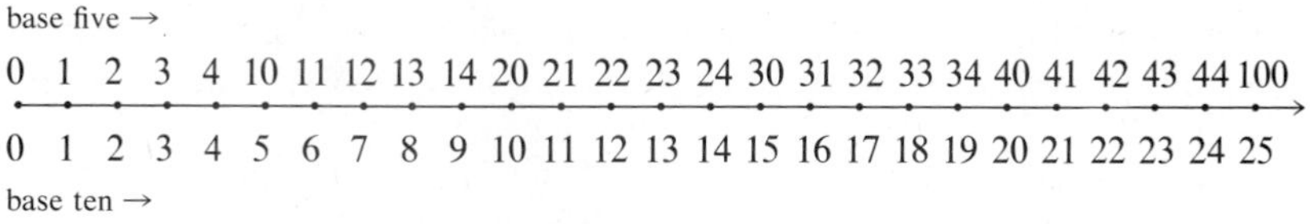

Example 1[6]

The numeral 12_{five} (read as "one, two, base five") means 1 group of five and 2 ones. Therefore, $12_{five} = 7_{ten}$.

---

6. The base is indicated by the subscript. Since there is no 5 in the number base under consideration, an expression such as 1×5^1—as used in the second example—would be better written as $1 \times 10^1{}_{five}$. However, in the interest of easy communication with the reader, the presented notation is used.

Example 2

$$\begin{aligned}4312_{\text{five}} &= (4 \times 5^3) + (3 \times 5^2) + (1 \times 5^1) + (2 \times 5^0)\\ &= (4 \times 125) + (3 \times 25) + (1 \times 5) + (2 \times 1)\\ &= 500 + 75 + 5 + 2\\ &= 582_{\text{ten}}\end{aligned}$$

This problem can also be worked as follows:

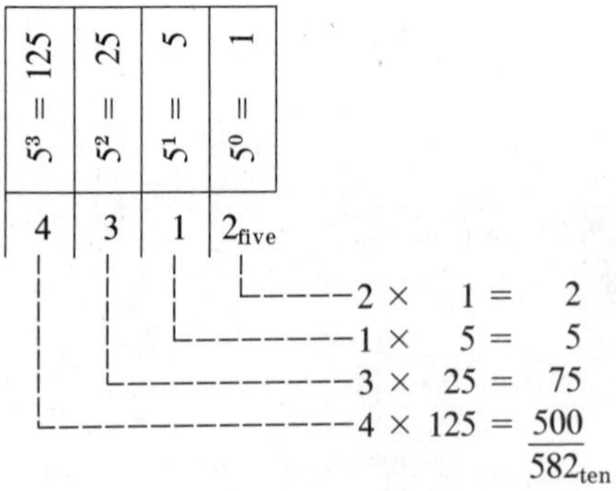

When a numeral in base ten is changed to a numeral in base five, we regroup by fives and by powers of five. It can be read from the number line above that $9_{\text{ten}} = 14_{\text{five}}$. By drawing arrows on the number line it can be demonstrated that 9 ones equal 1 five and 4 ones.

Example 3

Change 362_{ten} to base five.

Solution: In base five, the positional value of the successive digits starting from the right is a multiple of: one, five, five × five, five × five × five, etc. In base ten: 5^0 = one = 1; 5^1 = five = 5; 5^2 = twenty-five = 25; 5^3 = one hundred twenty-five = 125; etc.

It can be determined by division how many 125s, 25s, 5s, and 1s there are in 362_{ten}. An easy way to perform this division is shown below.

$$\begin{array}{rl} 362 & \div\ 125 = 2\\ \underline{250} & \\ 112 & \div\ \ 25 = 4\\ \underline{100} & \\ 12 & \div\ \ \ 5 = 2\\ \underline{10} & \\ 2 & \end{array}$$

Thus, in 362_{ten} there are two 5^3s, four 5^2s, two 5^1s, and two 5^0s. Therefore, $362_{\text{ten}} = 2422_{\text{five}}$. The answer can be checked by changing it back to base ten:

$5^3 = 125$	$5^2 = 25$	$5^1 = 5$	$5^0 = 1$
2	4	2	2_{five}

$$
\begin{aligned}
2 \times 1 &= 2 \\
2 \times 5 &= 10 \\
4 \times 25 &= 100 \\
2 \times 125 &= \underline{250} \\
& 362_{ten}
\end{aligned}
$$

Base Two

In base two (the binary base) grouping is done by twos and powers of two. Only two symbols are needed: 0 and 1. In base two, the numeral 10 means 1 group of two and no ones. The following number line compares the scales of notation in base two and in base ten.

base two →	0	1	10	11	100	101	110	111	1000	1001	1010	1011	1100
base ten →	0	1	2	3	4	5	6	7	8	9	10	11	12

Example 1

$10101_{two} = \underline{\qquad\qquad}_{ten}$.

Solution:

$$
\begin{aligned}
10101_{two} &= (1 \times 2^4) + (0 \times 2^3) + (1 \times 2^2) + (0 \times 2^1) + (1 \times 2^0) \\
&= (1 \times 16) + (0 \times 8) + (1 \times 4) + (0 \times 2) + (1 \times 1) \\
&= 16 + 0 + 4 + 0 + 1 \\
&= 21_{ten}
\end{aligned}
$$

Example 2

$27_{ten} = \underline{\qquad\qquad}_{two}$.

Solution: In base two, the positional value of the successive digits starting at the right is a multiple of: one, two, two × two, two × two × two, two × two × two × two, etc. In base ten: $2^0 = 1$; $2^1 = 2$; $2^2 = 2 \times 2 = 4$; $2^3 = 2 \times 2 \times 2 = 8$; $2^4 = 2 \times 2 \times 2 \times 2 = 16$; etc. The number of each of these powers of two in 27_{ten} is again determined by division.

$$
\begin{array}{l}
27 \div 16 = 1 \\
\underline{16} \\
11 \div \ 8 = 1 \\
\underline{\ 8} \\
\ 3 \div \ 4 = 0 \\
\underline{\ 0} \\
\ 3 \div \ 2 = 1 \\
\underline{\ 2} \\
\ 1
\end{array}
$$

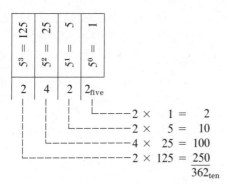

In 27_{ten} there is one 2^4, one 2^3, zero 2^2s, one 2^1, and one 2^0. Therefore, $27_{\text{ten}} = 11011_{\text{two}}$. The answer can be checked by changing it back to base ten.

Base Twelve In base twelve (the duodecimal base) grouping is done by twelves and powers of twelve. Twelve symbols are needed. If the two extra symbols were called a and b, there would be these symbols: 0, 1, 2, 3, 4, 5, 6, 7, 8, 9, a, and b. In base twelve, the numeral 10 means 1 group of twelve and no ones.

Example 1

$39_{\text{twelve}} = \underline{\hspace{2cm}}_{\text{ten}}$.

Solution: $\begin{aligned} 39_{\text{twelve}} &= (3 \times 12^1) + (9 \times 12^0) \\ &= (3 \times 12) + (9 \times 1) \\ &= 36 + 9 \\ &= 45_{\text{ten}} \end{aligned}$

Example 2

$37_{\text{ten}} = \underline{\hspace{2cm}}_{\text{twelve}}$.

Solution: $37 \div 12 = 3$

$\dfrac{36}{\overline{1}}$

In 37_{ten} there are 3 twelves and 1 one. Therefore, $37_{\text{ten}} = 31_{\text{twelve}}$. The answer should be checked by changing it back to base ten.

SOME SIMPLE OPERATIONS IN BASES OTHER THAN TEN

Example 1

$13_{\text{four}} + 12_{\text{four}} = \underline{\hspace{2cm}}_{\text{four}}$.

Solution:

0 1 2 3 10 11 12 13 20 21 22 23 30 31

$13_{\text{four}} + 12_{\text{four}} = 31_{\text{four}}$

Example 2

$32_{\text{seven}} - 16_{\text{seven}} = \underline{\hspace{2cm}}_{\text{seven}}$.

Solution:

0 1 2 3 4 5 6 10 11 12 13 14 15 16 20 21 22 23 24 25 26 30 31 32

$32_{\text{seven}} - 16_{\text{seven}} = 13_{\text{seven}}$

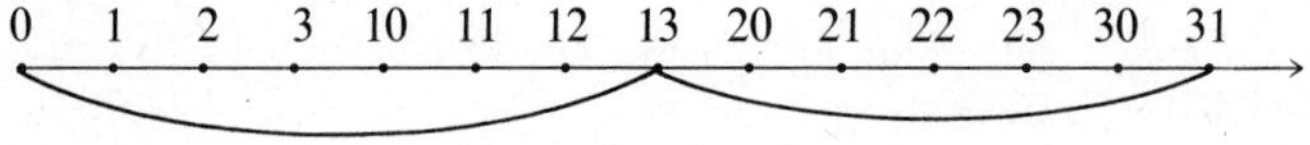

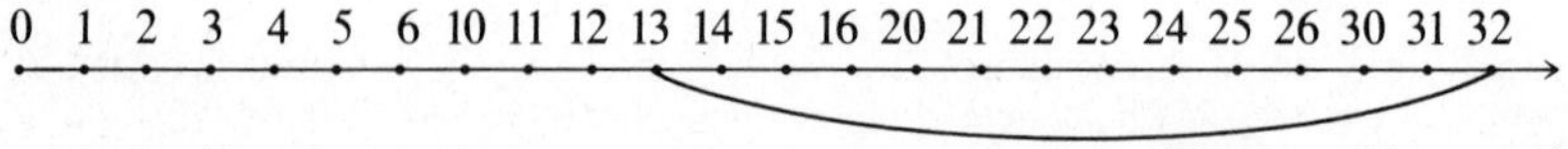

Example 3

$3 \times 4 = \underline{\qquad\qquad}_{\text{five}}.$

<u>Number question</u>: 3 fours is how much in base five?

Solution:

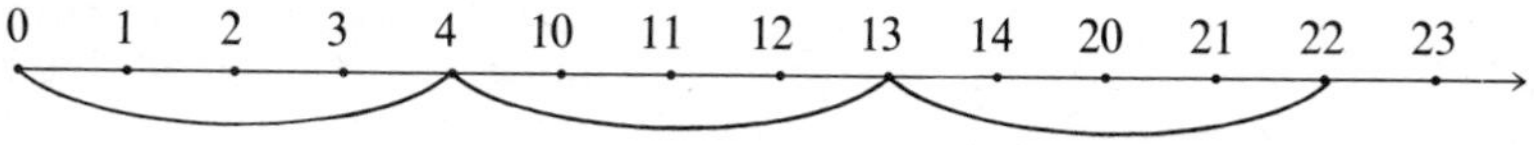

$3 \times 4 = 22_{\text{five}}$

Example 4

$33_{\text{four}} \div 3 = \underline{\qquad\qquad}_{\text{four}}.$

<u>Number question</u>: How many threes are there in 33_{four}?

Solution:

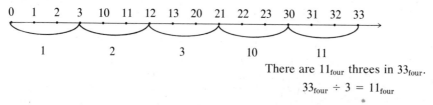

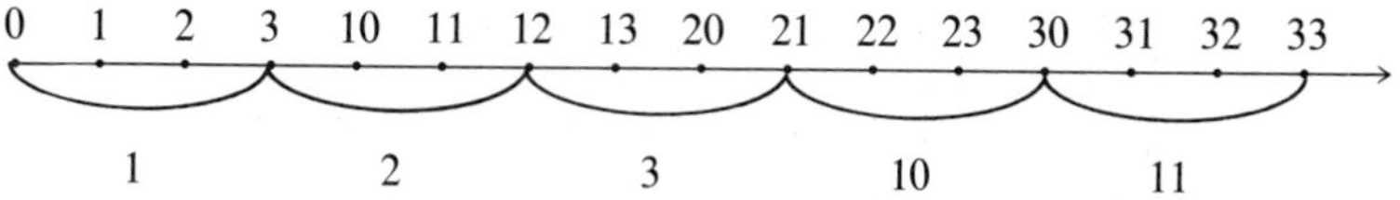

There are 11_{four} threes in 33_{four}.

$33_{\text{four}} \div 3 = 11_{\text{four}}$

SELECTED RESEARCH

The purpose of this study[7] was to determine the effect of studying nondecimal systems of numeration and of studying only base ten on fourth-graders' understanding of the decimal system and place-value systems in general.

Of the four classes that participated in the experiment, one class served as the control group and received no instruction in numeration, one studied only decimal numeration, one studied bases three, five, and ten, and one studied bases three, five, six, ten, and twelve.

All instruction was given by the same investigator. The three experimental programs provided experience with the same concepts and generalizations; only the base systems illustrating the concepts and generalizations varied with the group. The groups used the same textbook and the same aids.

---

7. R. C. Diedrick and V. J. Glennon, "The Effects of Studying Decimal and Nondecimal Numeration Systems on Mathematical Understanding, Retention, and Transfer," *Journal for Research in Mathematics Education,* vol. 1, no. 3 (May, 1970), pp. 162–172.

Instruction was carried on for nine consecutive schooldays and lasted thirty minutes per day. A pre-test, a post-test, and a retention test (six weeks after the post-test) were administered.

Of the findings and conclusions the following are presented:

1. Concerning the level of understanding of the decimal system of numeration:
   a. The three experimental groups studying numeration (one, three, or five place-value systems) performed, on the whole, better than the control group.
   b. A study of the decimal system alone is as effective as a corresponding study of nondecimal numeration.
2. Concerning level of understanding of place-value systems in general:
   a. A study of numeration is effective in promoting understanding of place-value systems in general.
   b. A study of nondecimal numeration is more effective than a study of the decimal system alone.

In discussing the study, the investigators remarked:

> If one wishes to foster, at fourth-grade level, understanding of the decimal system, the available evidence suggests that only the decimal system need be taught. Also, if one wishes to foster understanding of both decimal and nondecimal systems, the implication is that both decimal and nondecimal systems should be taught.

SELECTED ACTIVITIES FOR PUPILS

1. Developing the concept of one-to-one correspondence.

Example

Is there a flag for each boy? From each boy draw a line to a different flag.

2. Assigning a cardinal number to a set.

   Example

   Draw a line around the numeral that tells how many trees there are.

   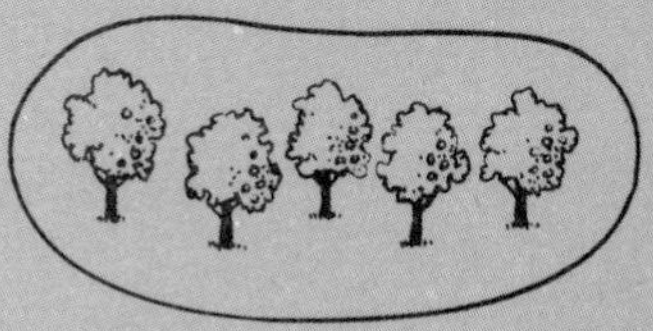

   4 5 6 7

3. Determining the ordinal number of a specific object in a series.

   Example

   Mark the third boy in the row.

4. Developing the idea that a number has many names.

   Example

   The same number is expressed by 6, 𝍸 |, 5 +1, ________, ________, and ________.

5. Assigning positional value to a digit.

   Example

   In 21, the 2 represents ________.

6. Expressing a number in expanded notation.

   Examples

   26 = 20 + ________.
   325 = ________ + ________ + ________.

7. Using number properties.

   Example 1

   5 + 7 = 7 + □. Complete the sentence and show it on the number line.

   Example 2

   Solve 78 ÷ 6 = □ by renaming and using the distributive property of division over addition.

Example 3

Solve $6 \times 19 = \square$ by renaming and using the distributive property of multiplication over subtraction.

Example 4

Complete:

$$\begin{aligned} 3 \times 24 &= 3 \times (20 + \square) \\ &= (3 \times 20) + (3 \times \square) \\ &= \bigcirc + \triangle \\ &= \hexagon \end{aligned}$$

8. Working exercises preparatory to learning to use bases other than ten.

Example

If you have 37 pennies, you can exchange them for ________ quarter, ________ nickels, and ________ pennies.

9. Working with Roman numerals.

Example

Write =, >, or < to make a true statement.

XL ○ 40	XIX ○ 20	10 + 6 ○ XVI
XC ○ 100	XXX ○ XXVI	MD ○ 500

10. Using exponents.

Example

Write the exponent that makes the sentence true: $5^{\square} = 16 + 9$.

11. Working with digits.

Example 1

How many times do you use the digit 1 to number the pages of a 123-page book?

Example 2

Ted knows all the digits of Ron's telephone number except the last right-hand digit. What is the greatest number of wrong numbers that Ted might dial before he gets Ron's residence?

12. Expressing the largest and the smallest number possible with a given set of digits.

Example

Write the largest and the smallest number possible—not using exponents—with the digits 2, 5, 6, and 9, and find the difference between the two numbers.

13. Studying ancient systems of notation, such as the Roman system.

Example

Find places where Roman numerals are used and translate these numerals into Hindu-Arabic numerals.

14. Finding out the meaning of terms.

Example

Use a dictionary to find out what the terms "googol" and "googolplex" mean.

15. Making a counting frame in a base other than ten.
The illustration shows a counting frame in base four. Base four uses four digits: 0, 1, 2, 3. How many digits are used in base five? Which ones? Complete the drawing of the counting frame in base five.

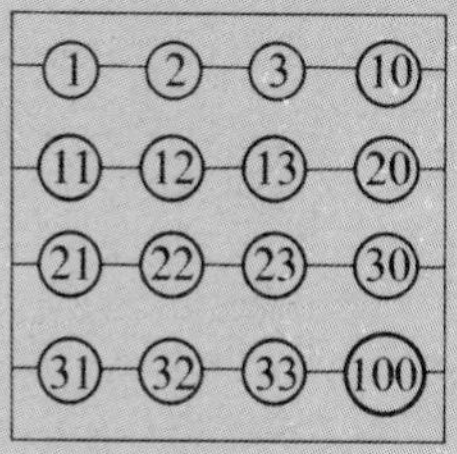

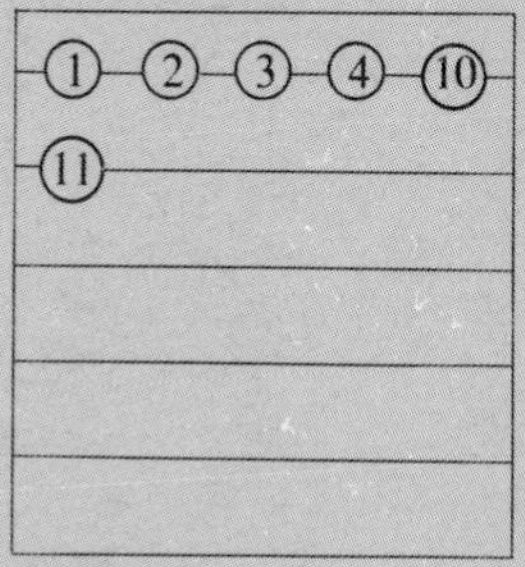

16. Playing a game in the binary base.
In this game four cards are used:

a		*b*		*c*		*d*	
1	9	2	10	4	12	8	12
3	11	3	11	5	13	9	13
5	13	6	14	6	14	10	14
7	15	7	15	7	15	11	15

Directions:

a. A person selects a number from 1 to 15. He does not say which number he has chosen.
b. He tells you on which card(s) the number is expressed. (It may be on one card, two cards, three cards, or all cards.)
c. You tell him his number.

Examples

If the selected number is—
1, it appears only on card *a*, and you take the first number shown on *a*;
2, it appears only on *b*, and you take the first number shown on *b*;
3, it appears only on *a* and *b*, and you add the first numbers shown on *a* and *b*;
13, it appears on *a*, *c*, and *d* and you add the first numbers shown on these cards;
15, it appears on all cards and you add 1, 2, 4, and 8.

Study the numbers expressed on the cards. Then explain why the game works.

Hint: Note the first number on the cards: $1 = 2^0$, $2 = 2^1$, $4 = 2^2$, $8 = 2^3$.

Make a set of cards with numbers through 31. Then play the game again. Since 31 includes 16 (2^4) but not 32 (2^5), you will need five cards. To get you started, let's consider a few numbers:
$16 = 2^4$ and appears only on card *e*.
$17 = 16 + 1$ and appears on *a* and *e*.
$18 = 16 + 2$ and appears on *b* and *e*.
$25 = 16 + 8 + 1$ and appears on *a*, *d*, and *e*.
$31 = 16 + 8 + 4 + 2 + 1$ and appears on all cards.

EXERCISES

1. Explain the difference between a number and a numeral.
2. Determine whether the use of the numbers in the following statements is cardinal or ordinal:
   a. There are 25 students present.
   b. Monday is the 2nd day of the week.
   c. Find page 9.
3. List the characteristics of the Hindu-Arabic system of notation.
4. What is the difference between face value and positional value?
5. What positional value does each digit in the numeral 12,345 represent?
6. List the properties of whole numbers presented in this chapter and give an example of each.

7. Decide which properties are used in the following examples:
 a. $91 \div 7 = (70 + 21) \div 7 = (70 \div 7) + (21 \div 7) = 10 + 3 = 13$
 b. $6 \times 19 = 6 \times (20 - 1) = (6 \times 20) - (6 \times 1) = 120 - 6 = 114$
 c. $95 \div 5 = (100 - 5) \div 5 = (100 \div 5) - (5 \div 5) = 20 - 1 = 19$

8. Explain the difference between numeration and notation.

9. List and give examples of the principles of the Roman system of notation.

10. a. Complete the following grids:

10^3	10^2	10^1	10^0
1,000			1

8^3	8^2	8^1	8^0
	64		1

2^3	2^2	2^1	2^0

 b. What generalization can you make about raising a nonzero number to the zero power?

11. Work the following problems:

$32_{\text{five}} = \underline{\hspace{2cm}}_{\text{ten}}$ $904_{\text{ten}} = \underline{\hspace{2cm}}_{\text{eight}}$

$131_{\text{four}} = \underline{\hspace{2cm}}_{\text{ten}}$ $37_{\text{ten}} = \underline{\hspace{2cm}}_{\text{two}}$

$723_{\text{eight}} = \underline{\hspace{2cm}}_{\text{ten}}$ $7 + 4 = \underline{\hspace{2cm}}_{\text{eight}}$

$1,011_{\text{two}} = \underline{\hspace{2cm}}_{\text{ten}}$ $13_{\text{five}} - 4 = \underline{\hspace{2cm}}_{\text{five}}$

$28_{\text{ten}} = \underline{\hspace{2cm}}_{\text{five}}$ $3 \times 3 = \underline{\hspace{2cm}}_{\text{four}}$

$129_{\text{ten}} = \underline{\hspace{2cm}}_{\text{four}}$ $20_{\text{five}} \div 2 = \underline{\hspace{2cm}}_{\text{five}}$

12. Write a brief outline of a lesson designed to introduce base five to children in an intermediate grade.

13. Explain and illustrate how you would teach the commutative property to Grade 2.

14. Give an example of the distributive property of division with respect to addition.

15. Work several examples to determine whether the distributive property of multiplication holds over subtraction.

16. Work several examples to determine whether the distributive property of division holds over subtraction.

17. Report on the research described in this chapter.

SOURCES FOR FURTHER READING

D'Augustine, C. H., *Multiple Methods of Teaching Mathematics in the Elementary School,* 2nd ed. New York: Harper & Row, Publishers, 1973, Chap. XIII.

Churchill, E. M., *Counting and Measuring*. Toronto: University of Toronto Press, 1961, Chaps. II, III.

Heddens, J. W., *Today's Mathematics*, 3d ed. Chicago: Science Research Associates, Inc., 1974, Units IV-VI, IX.

Ikeda, H., and M. Ando, "Introduction to the Numeration of Two-place Numbers," *The Arithmetic Teacher*, April, 1969, pp. 247–251.

Johnson, D. A., and W. H. Glenn, *Understanding Numeration Systems*. St. Louis: Webster Publishing Company (McGraw-Hill), 1960.

Kennedy, L. M., *Guiding Children to Mathematical Discovery*, 2nd ed. Belmont, California: Wadsworth Publishing Company, Inc., 1975, Chap. V.

National Council of Teachers of Mathematics, *Topics in Mathematics, Twenty-ninth Yearbook*. Washington, D.C.: The Council, 1964, Bklts. 2, 3.

Niman, J., "A Game Introduction to the Binary Numeration System," *The Arithmetic Teacher*, December, 1971, pp. 600–601.

Oosse, W. J., "Properties of Operations: A Meaningful Study," *The Arithmetic Teacher*, April, 1969, pp. 271–275.

Schminke, C. W., N. Maertens, and W. R. Arnold, *Teaching the Child Mathematics*. Hinsdale, Illinois: The Dryden Press, Inc., 1973, Chap. XI.

Smith, T., *Number*. Oxford: Basil Blackwell, 1960, Chap. VI.

Wolfers, E. P., "The Original Counting Systems of Papua and New Guinea," *The Arithmetic Teacher*, February, 1971, pp. 77–83.

Ziesche, S. S., "Understanding Place Value," *The Arithmetic Teacher*, December, 1970, pp. 683–684.

Sets 5

The concept of set is not new. In any primary grade the children work with sets, join groups, and remove elements from a given collection. Everyone is acquainted with such expressions as a pair of shoes, a team of horses, a set of dishes, and a herd of cattle.

Many mathematicians want to introduce set concepts and terminology in the elementary school in order to assist the child in his formation of proper number concepts and to guide him toward more precise mathematical language. It is expected that the child will be able to build advanced mathematical concepts more easily at a later level once simple concepts of sets are acquired in the elementary grades. Consequently, many programs for the elementary school claim to introduce basic ideas of sets, simple set operations, and important terminology. Ideally, the rapid learner is then introduced to more difficult operations and to more complicated terms and symbols.

In this chapter, simple set concepts, terms, and symbols are presented to acquaint the student with much of the content introduced in contemporary programs for the elementary school. This does not mean that the author recommends that all of this subject matter be introduced to all elementary school pupils. Similarly, the selected activities for pupils that appear at the end of the chapter are intended only to be illustrations of activities presented in various modern programs. More study and research is needed to determine which set concepts, terms, and symbols can be efficiently taught and used in the elementary school and to decide the grade level at which these concepts should be presented.

SETS DESCRIBED

A set may be described as a collection of concrete or abstract entities. It may consist of a collection of objects, persons, animals, letters, etc. The items which make up a set are called *members* or *elements* of the set.

Examples of sets are a family, a class, a team of basketball players, and the numbers greater than 10 and less than 20.

A mathematical set is a collection that is *well defined.* This means that the decision as to whether or not an object is a member of a set cannot be left to personal opinion. For example, "the set of nice girls in this class" cannot be considered to be a well-defined set.

A capital letter is usually used to designate a set. A set is tabulated as follows: $A = \{1, 3, 5, 7, 9\}$. This sentence is read "A is the set whose members are 1, 3, 5, 7, 9," or "A is the set of odd numbers from 1 through 9." Note that the names of the elements of the set are listed between braces. Elementary school pupils often draw a ring around the pictured elements of a set instead of using braces. A set whose elements are a house and a tree can be pictured as in Figure 5.1.

Set A
or

Figure 5.1

The cardinal number of a set tells us how many elements are contained in the set. If $A = \{\square, \triangle, \bigcirc\}$, we say that its cardinal number is 3. This may be expressed as $n(A) = 3$, which is read "The number of set A is 3." If $B = \{a, b, c, d, e\}$, we say that its cardinal number is 5, and we write $n(B) = 5$.

THE EMPTY SET

The *empty set* has no members at all. For example, there are no members in the set made up of the states of our country whose names begin with the letter Z. The empty set is also called the *null set.* The symbol for the empty set is $\varnothing$. The empty set may be represented as in Figure 5.2. The cardinal number of set A is zero. Thus $n(A) = 0$.

Set A

$A = \{\ \}$ or $A = \varnothing$ or

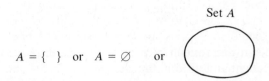

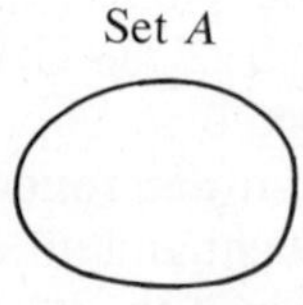

Figure 5.2

FINITE SETS

If the number of elements in a set is limited, the set is called a *finite set*. Some finite sets have so many elements, however, that to tabulate their names would be impractical. Generally, such sets have some pattern to their elements and, once this pattern has been indicated, three dots are used to denote continuation of the pattern, with the last element named to identify the end of the pattern. Thus $N = \{2, 4, 6, \cdots, 40\}$ represents the set of even integers from 2 through 40.

INFINITE SETS

If a set is not finite, it is an *infinite set*. In ordinary language it is said that the number of members in an infinite set is endless. Examples of infinite sets are the set of natural numbers, the set of even numbers, and the set of points on a line.

The set of natural numbers is expressed as follows: $N = \{1, 2, 3, \cdots\}$. This sentence may be read "the set of natural numbers 1, 2, 3, and so on infinitely."

EQUAL OR IDENTICAL SETS

If A and B are sets that have precisely the same members, then A and B are said to be *equal* or *identical sets*. If A and B are equal sets, then every element of A is an element of B, and vice versa. We write $A = B$. In a list of elements of a set, each object should be named once and only once. The order in which the elements are listed is immaterial.

Example 1

Let A represent all the books in John's library, and let B represent all the arithmetic books John has. John has only arithmetic books.

A = {the books in John's library}
B = {John's arithmetic books}
$A = B$

Example 2

Let A represent all the odd numbers between 2 and 8, and let B represent all the prime numbers between 2 and 8.

$$A = \{3, 5, 7\}$$
$$B = \{3, 5, 7\}$$
$$A = B$$

If two sets C and D are not equal, we write: $C \neq D$.

EQUIVALENT SETS

If the elements in one set can be placed in a one-to-one correspondence with another set (that is, if for each member of one set there is one and only one member of the other set, and vice versa), the sets are said to be *equivalent sets*.

Example

A = {boy, girl}
B = {flag, balloon}

A is equivalent to B, since the two sets can be *matched*. This means that the members of the sets can be placed in a one-to-one correspondence as follows:

A = {boy, girl}
↕ ↕
B = {flag, balloon}

or

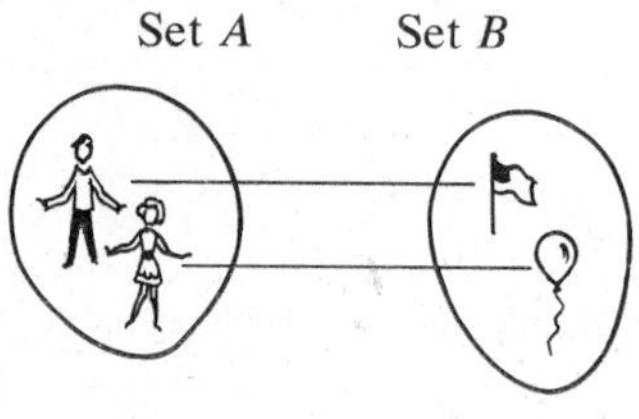

We write $A \leftrightarrow B$.

Two equal sets are always equivalent, since they can be matched. If A = {3, 5, 7} and B = {5, 3, 7}, then A and B are equal and equivalent.

However, two equivalent sets are not necessarily equal. If C = {Dick, Tom, Harry} and D = {train, car, bus}, then C and D are equivalent, since there is a one-to-one correspondence between elements of the sets. But C and D are not equal, since all members are not common to both sets.

If two sets E and F are not equivalent, we write: $E \not\leftrightarrow F$.

THE UNIVERSAL SET AND SUBSETS

Consider the following cases.

Example 1

U = {all people in New York City}
A = {all men in New York City}

This universal set and the subset can be represented in a diagram:

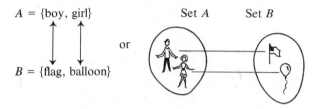

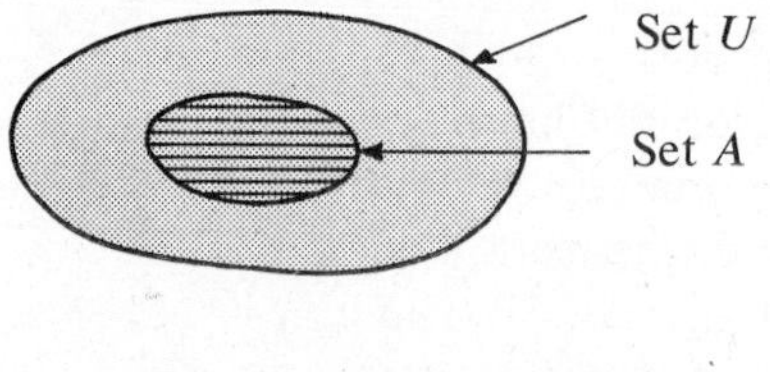

Set A is contained in set U and is called a *subset* of the universal set U. We write $A \subset U$. This sentence is read "A is a subset of U." The specified set from which subsets are derived is called the *universe* or the *universal set*. Examples of other subsets that can be drawn from the universe expressed above are the set of all women in New York City, the set of all men above 20 years of age in New York City, etc. Hence, a subset of a set U is any set whose members are members of U. Observe that the empty set is also a subset of the universal set. Note, furthermore, that a set is a subset of itself.

Example 2

Set $C = \{1, 2, 3\}$. Subsets of C are:

{1} {1, 2} {1, 2, 3} { }
{2} {2, 3}
{3} {1, 3}

Set C has 8 subsets.

A set with 3 elements has $2^3 = 8$ subsets.
A set with 4 elements has $2^4 = 16$ subsets.
A set with n elements has 2^n subsets.

OPERATIONS ON SETS

The two operations commonly performed on sets are union and intersection.

Union

The *union* of two sets is the set whose members belong to one set, the other set, or both sets.

Example

$A = \{1, 3, 4, 6\}$
$B = \{3, 6, 8, 9\}$

The set consisting of the members that are either A or B or in both is {1, 3, 4, 6, 8, 9}. We write $A \cup B = \{1, 3, 4, 6, 8, 9\}$, and we say: "$A$ union B is the set whose members are 1, 3, 4, 6, 8, 9."

The union of two sets is not the same operation as the addition of two numbers in arithmetic. In the example above, the union of A and B does not result in 8 elements but in 6, since A and B have two elements in common, whose names are not to be included twice in the tabulation. However, if A and B do not have any elements in common, the sets are *disjoint* sets, and the number of elements in the union of A and B is the sum of the number of elements in A and B. Thus if $A = \{1, 2, 3\}$ and $B = \{4, 5\}$, then $A \cup B = \{1, 2, 3, 4, 5\}$. The cardinal number of A is 3, and the cardinal number of B is 2. The cardinal number of the union of the sets is 5, and we write $n(A \cup B) = 5$.

Intersection

The *intersection* of two sets is the set that contains the members common to both sets. Hence, the new set consists only of the elements common to the original sets.

Example

$A = \{1, 3, 5, 7, 9\}$
$B = \{5, 7, 9, 11, 13\}$

The set consisting of the members that are in both set A and set B is $\{5, 7, 9\}$. We write $A \cap B = \{5, 7, 9\}$, and we say: "A intersection B is the set whose members are 5, 7, 9."

As stated before, if the intersection of two sets consists of no members and is therefore the empty set, the two sets are *disjoint* sets.

VENN DIAGRAMS Relations between sets and operations on sets can be shown graphically by the use of Venn diagrams. In a *Venn diagram,* a picture of a rectangle usually represents the universal set, and pictures of circles represent subsets. However, other shapes may also be used.

Example 1

In the following example, U = the set of all pupils of Lincoln School.

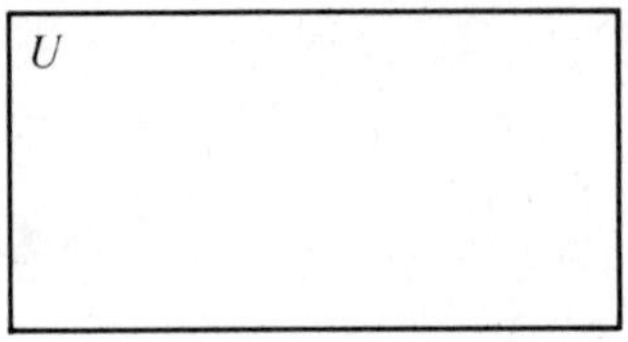

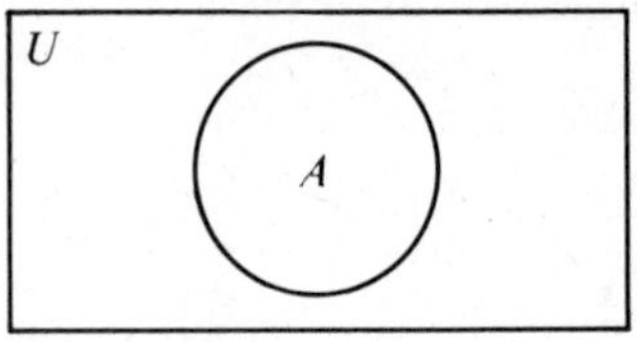

A = the set of all boys in Grade 6 of Lincoln School.
Set A is a subset of the universe U.

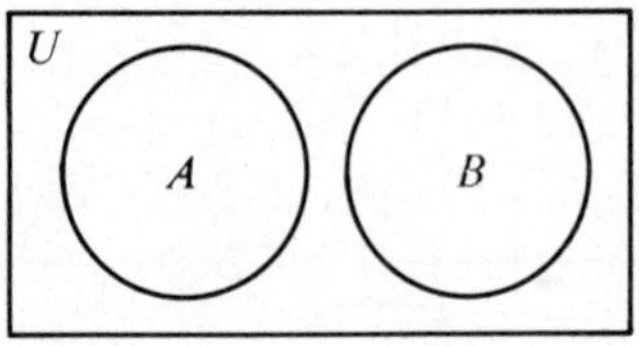

A = the set of all boys in Grade 6 of Lincoln School.
B = the set of all girls in Grade 6 of Lincoln School.
Set A and set B are both subsets of the universe U.
The intersection of set A and set B is the empty set.
Set A is disjoint from set B.

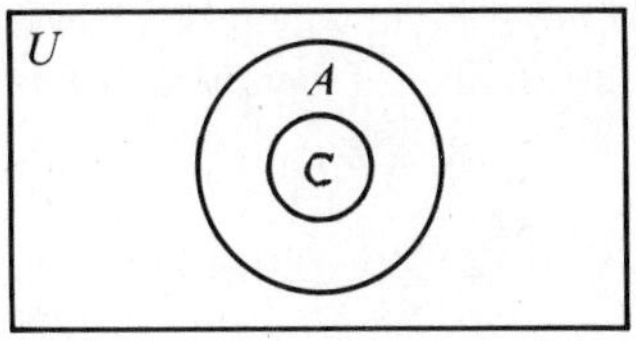

A = the set of all boys in Grade 6 of Lincoln School.
C = the set of all boys in Grade 6 of Lincoln School who are members of the choir.
Set A is a subset of the universe U.
Set C is a subset of set A.

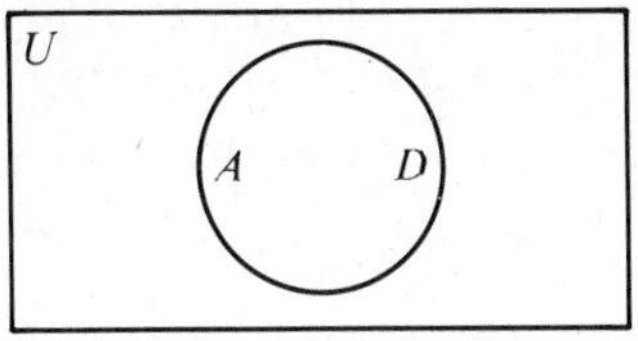

A = the set of all boys in Grade 6 of Lincoln School.
D = the set of all boys in Grade 6 who take physical education.

Set A is equal to set D or coincides with set D, because all the boys in Grade 6 take physical education.

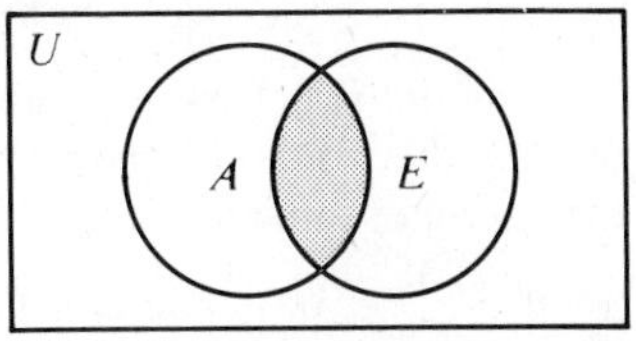

A = the set of all boys in Grade 6 of Lincoln School.
E = the set of all boys in Lincoln School who are members of the choir.
The intersection of A and E is not empty. The shaded part of the circles represents the intersection, and its members are the boys who are pupils of Grade 6 and who are also members of the choir.

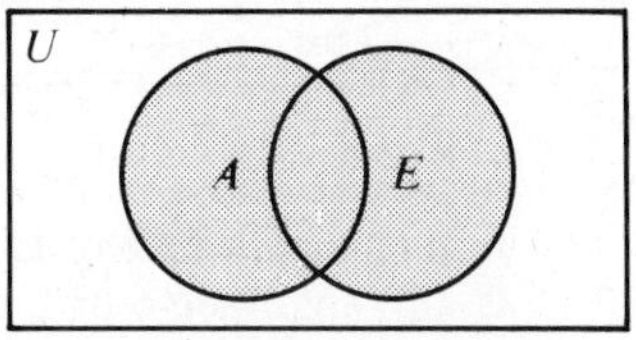

A = the set of all boys in Grade 6 of Lincoln School.
E = the set of all boys in Lincoln School who are members of the choir.

The union of set A and set E is shown in the diagram. The sum of the number of members in A and the number of members in E is larger than the number of members in $A \cup E$.

Example 2

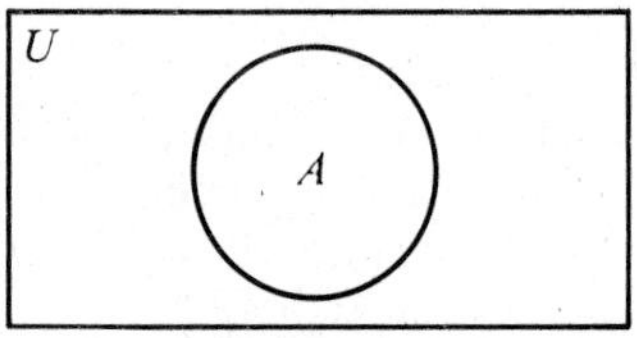

$U = \{1, 2, 3, \cdots\}$ (U is the set of natural numbers).
$A = \{2, 4, 6, \cdots\}$ (A is the set of even numbers).
A is a subset of U.

Example 3

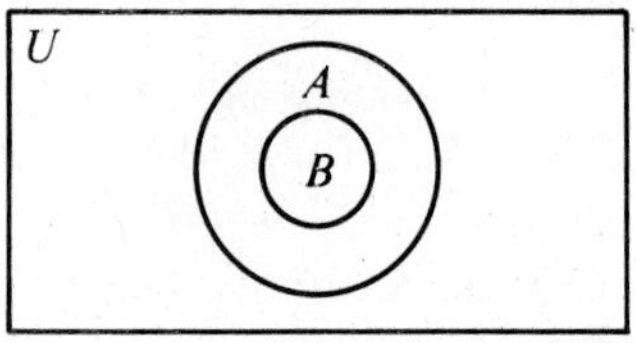

$U = \{1, 2, 3, \cdots\}$ (U is the set of natural numbers).
$A = \{2, 3, 4, 5, 6\}$ (A is the set whose members are 2, 3, 4, 5, 6).
$B = \{3, 4\}$ (B is the set whose members are 3, 4).
B is a subset of A.

Example 4

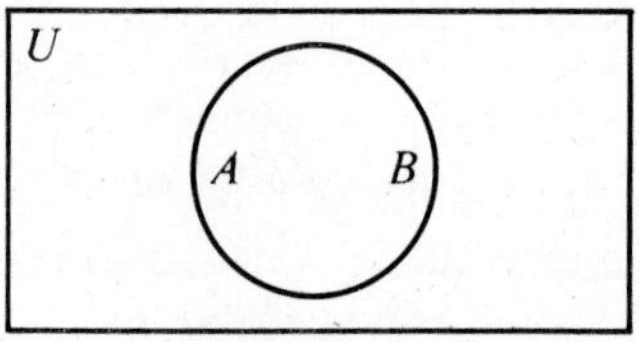

$U = \{2, 3, 4, 5, 6, 7, 8\}$ (U is the set whose members are 2, 3, 4, 5, 6, 7, 8).
$A = \{3, 5, 7\}$ (A is the set whose members are the odd numbers between 2 and 8).
$B = \{3, 5, 7\}$ (B is the set whose members are the prime numbers between 2 and 8).
A coincides with B, or A equals B.

Example 5

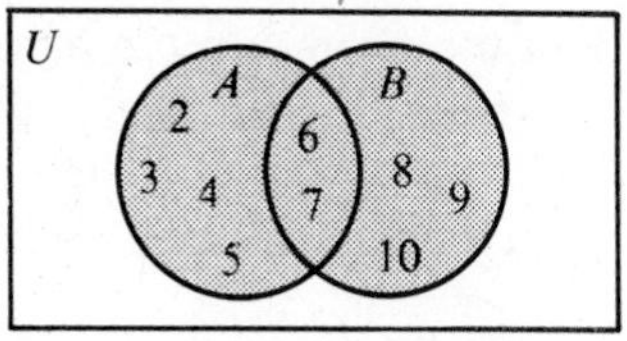

$U = \{1, 2, 3, \cdots\}$ (U is the set of natural numbers).
$A = \{2, 3, 4, 5, 6, 7\}$ (A is the set whose members are 2, 3, 4, 5, 6, 7).
$B = \{6, 7, 8, 9, 10\}$ (B is the set whose members are 6, 7, 8, 9, 10).
$A \cup B = \{2, 3, 4, 5, 6, 7, 8, 9, 10\}$ (A union B is the set whose members are 2, 3, 4, 5, 6, 7, 8, 9, 10).

Example 6

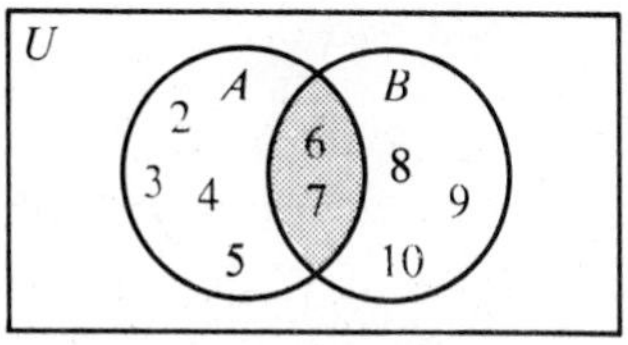

$U = \{1, 2, 3, \cdots\}$ (U is the set of natural numbers).
$A = \{2, 3, 4, 5, 6, 7\}$ (A is the set whose members are 2, 3, 4, 5, 6, 7).
$B = \{6, 7, 8, 9, 10\}$ (B is the set whose members are 6, 7, 8, 9, 10).
$A \cap B = \{6, 7\}$ (A intersection B is the set whose members are 6, 7).

Example 7

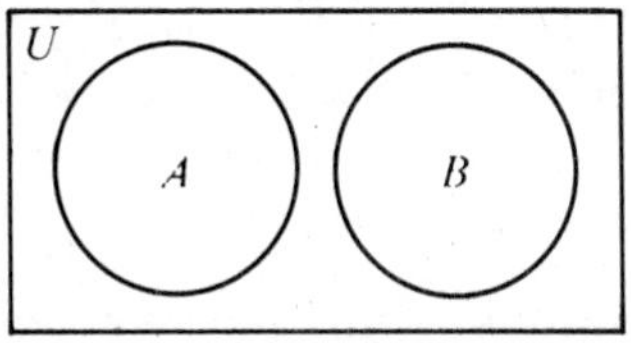

$U = \{1, 2, 3, \cdots\}$ (U is the set of natural numbers).
$A = \{2, 3, 4, 5\}$ (A is the set whose members are 2, 3, 4, 5).
$B = \{8, 9, 10\}$ (B is the set whose members are 8, 9, 10).
A and B are disjoint sets.

SOLVING PROBLEMS BY USING SETS

Of the junior class of Grant High School,

7 girls are in the choir
9 girls are in the band
10 girls are in the orchestra

Of these girls,

1 girl is only in the choir and the band
1 girl is only in the choir and the orchestra
2 girls are only in the band and the orchestra
2 girls are in the band, the choir, and the orchestra

How many girls take one or more of the three musical activities? (*Note:* In the Venn diagram below, the numerals used represent cardinal numbers and not elements. Thus, for example, 3 in part *A* refers to 3 girls.)

Three intersecting circles are drawn, each circular region representing one musical activity. (Thus sets *A, B,* and *C* are each represented by a circular region.) *U* = the set of girls in the junior class of Grant High School; *A* = choir; *B* = band; *C* = orchestra; *W* = choir and band; *X* = choir and orchestra; *Y* = band and orchestra; *Z* = choir, band, and orchestra.

1. Two girls take choir, band, and orchestra. Write 2 in region *Z*.
2. One girl takes choir and band. Write 1 in region *W*.
3. One girl takes choir and orchestra. Write 1 in region *X*.
4. Two girls take band and orchestra. Write 2 in region *Y*.
5. Since 7 girls take choir and 4 of them are in one or more other activities, 3 girls take only choir. Write 3 in circle *A*.
6. Nine girls take band and 5 of them are in one or more other activities. Write 4 in circle *B*.
7. Ten girls take orchestra and 5 of them are in one or more other activities. Write 5 in circle *C*.

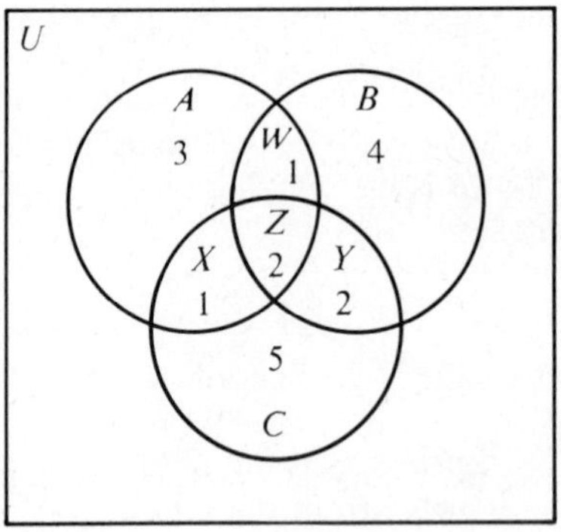

8. Now it can be determined how many girls take one or more of the musical activities:

3 girls take only choir
4 girls take only band
5 girls take only orchestra
1 girl takes only choir and band
1 girl takes only choir and orchestra
2 girls take only band and orchestra
2 girls take choir, band, and orchestra
18 girls take one or more musical activities

Thus $n(A \cup B \cup C) = 18$.

SELECTED RESEARCH

The aim of this investigation[1] was to measure first-graders' knowledge of equality and inequality and to test their understanding of the concept of subsets and of the number properties of sets.

A randomly selected sample of 220 first-graders was tested by cooperating teachers in the beginning of the year before formal work in arithmetic had begun. The test was a paper-and-pencil test of 27 items: seven items dealing with equality (two subtests, A and B), four with ordinal numbers, seven with sets and subsets (three subtests, A, B, and C), and nine with number properties of sets (two subtests, A and B). A child got credit for a subtest only if he or she marked all the items correctly. The test items were verbal problems presented orally.

The results of the study showed that the pupils in the sample knew less about number concepts than might have been supposed. About one-half of the subjects passed part A of the test of equality concepts, the test of ordinal numbers, part A of the test of knowledge of subsets, and the two subtests of number properties of sets. The percent of correct responses on the other subtests was between 10 percent and 20 percent.

The investigator suggested that the findings indicate that first-grade teachers need to give serious attention to developing concepts of equality and number properties of sets.

---

1. E. E. Holmes, "First Graders' Number Concepts," *The Arithmetic Teacher* (April, 1963), pp. 195–196.

SELECTED ACTIVITIES FOR PUPILS

1. Assigning a cardinal number to a set.

   Example

   How many trees are there in the set?

2. Developing the concept of equivalent sets.

   Example

   How many boys are there in set *A*? In set *B* there should be as many boats as there are boys in set *A*. Draw the boats.

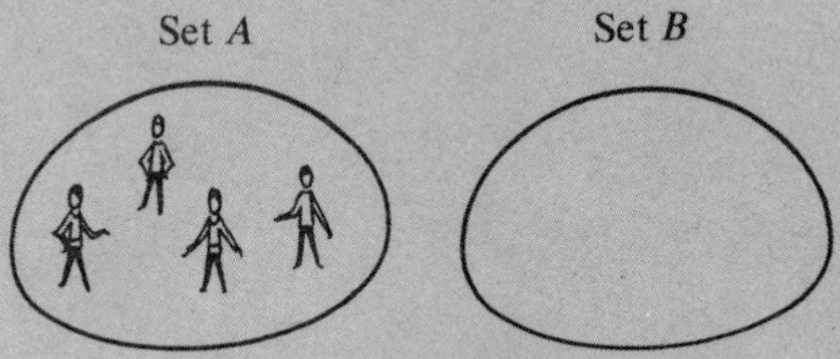

3. Listing the members of a set.

   Example

   List the members of the set of whole numbers greater than 5 and less than 10.

4. Describing sets.

   Example

   Describe set *A* in words.

   $A = \{10, 11, 12, 13, 14\}$

5. Listing subsets.

   Example

   Find all possible subsets of set *A*.

A = {John, Bill, Tom}

6. Forming the union of two sets.

   Example

   If A = {⬡, ○} and B = {⬡, △, □}, then $A \cup B$ = ________.

7. Forming the intersection of two sets.

   Example

   If A = {⬡, □} and B = {△, ⬡}, then $A \cap B$ = ________.

8. Describing disjoint sets.

   Example

   If $A \cup B$ = {1, 2, 3, 4}, describe a pair of disjoint sets that could have formed this union.

9. Working with Venn diagrams.

   Example 1

   a. Write the factors of 12.
   b. Write the factors of 30.
   c. Write the common factors of 12 and 30.
   d. Draw the Venn diagram shown.

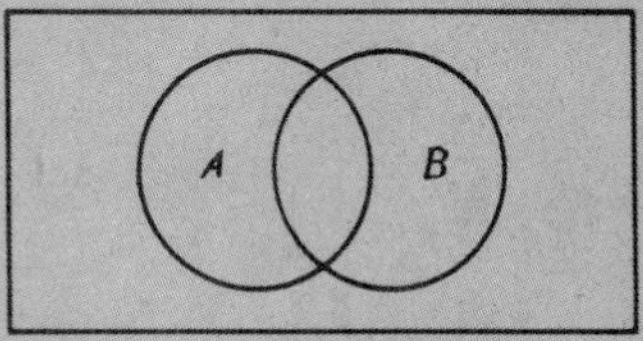

   e. Put the factors of 12 in A and the factors of 30 in B so that only the common factors are expressed in the intersection (the part that belongs to both A and B).
   f. Write the largest number that is a factor of both 12 and 30.

   Example 2

   a. Write the multiples of 2 that are less than 25.
   b. Write the multiples of 3 that are less than 25.
   c. Write the common multiples of 2 and 3 that are less than 25.
   d. Draw a Venn diagram as in Example 1.
   e. Put the multiples of 2 that are less than 25 in A, and put the multiples of 3 that are less than 25 in B so that only the common multiples are expressed in the intersection.
   f. Write the smallest number that is divisible by both 2 and 3.

Example 3

In the sixth grade of Jefferson School there are three clubs, the coin collectors club, the stamp collectors club, and the rock collectors club.

18 pupils are members of the coin collectors club.
16 pupils are members of the stamp collectors club.
15 pupils are members of the rock collectors club.

Of these pupils:

5 pupils are only members of the coin collectors club and the stamp collectors club.
3 pupils are only members of the coin collectors club and the rock collectors club.
4 pupils are only members of the stamp collectors club and the rock collectors club.
6 pupils are members of the coin collectors club, the stamp collectors club, and the rock collectors club.

How many pupils are members of one or more of these three clubs?

EXERCISES

1. Tabulate the set of even numbers greater than 15 and less than 24.
2. Tabulate the set of natural numbers less than 70 that are evenly divisible by 5.
3. Tabulate the set of factors of 21.
4. Read this sentence: $N = \{1, 2, 3, \cdots, 50\}$.
5. Tabulate the set of even numbers.
6. Determine the number of elements in this set:
   $A = \{\text{all the students in your class}\}$
7. $A = \{1, 3, 5, 7\}$ $\quad B \ \{5, 7, 9, 11\}$
   Is A equal to B? $\quad$ Is A equivalent to B?
8. $D = \{e, f, g\}$ $\quad E = \{h, i, j\}$
   True or false: $D = E$ $\quad D \neq E$ $\quad D \leftrightarrow E$ $\quad D \not\leftrightarrow E$
9. How many subsets can be derived from a set containing five elements?
10. $A = \{1, 3, 5\}$ $\quad B = \{5, 7, 9\}$
    $A \cup B =$ $\quad A \cap B =$
11. $C = \{a, b\}$ $\quad D = \{b, c, d\}$ $\quad E = \{d\}$
    $C \cup D =$ $\quad D \cup E =$ $\quad C \cup E =$
    $C \cap D =$ $\quad C \cap E =$ $\quad D \cap E =$
12. $A = \{7, 8, 9, 10\}$ $\quad B = \{9, 10, 11, 12\}$
    $A \cup B =$ $\quad A \cap B =$
    Draw Venn diagrams to illustrate these relations.

13. Decide whether these sets are finite or infinite:
    a. The set of natural numbers.
    b. The set of fractional numbers.
    c. The set of books in your library.
14. A is the set whose members are the prime numbers greater than 5 and less than 23. $n(A) =$
15. Read these sentences:
    $A \cup B = \{7, 9, 10\}$
    $C \cap D = \{4, 5\}$
    $A \leftrightarrow B$
    $A \not\leftrightarrow C$
    $C \neq D$
    $n(E) = 6$

SOURCES FOR FURTHER READING

Heddens, J. W., *Today's Mathematics,* 3d ed. Chicago: Science Research Associates, Inc., 1974, Unit II.

Johnson, D. A., and W. H. Glenn, *Sets, Sentences and Operations*. St. Louis: Webster Publishing Company (McGraw-Hill), 1960.

Mueller, F. J., and A. M. Hach, *Mathematics Enrichment*. New York: Harcourt, Brace Jovanovich, Inc., 1963, Book E, Unit IV.

National Council of Teachers of Mathematics, *Topics in Mathematics, Twenty-ninth Yearbook*. Washington, D.C.: The Council, 1964, Bklt. 1.

Sanders, W. J., "Equivalence and Equality," *The Arithmetic Teacher,* April, 1969, pp. 317–322.

Spitzer, H. F., *Teaching Elementary School Mathematics*. Boston: Houghton Mifflin Company, 1967, Chap. II.

Steinberg, Z., "Will the Set of Children . . . ?" *The Arithmetic Teacher,* February, 1971, pp. 105–108.

Vaughan, H. E., "What Sets Are Not," *The Arithmetic Teacher,* January, 1970, pp. 55–60.

Factors and Multiples 6

One of the main objectives in the teaching of mathematics is the development of an understanding of the structure of numbers. To become effective in computational procedures, the child must acquire skill in expressing given numbers as products of factors and prime factors and in finding multiples of given numbers.

In this chapter the natural numbers will be examined and various groups or sets of natural numbers will be classified according to distinctive properties they possess. Relationships between given numbers and their integral factors or parts will be illustrated, and factorization of natural numbers will be introduced.

FACTORS

The numbers that are multiplied to form a product are *factors* or *divisors* of that product. Thus, in $3 \times 4 = 12$, 3 and 4 are factors of the product 12. Since 12 has several factors, it may be expressed in various ways:

$$\begin{aligned} 12 = 1 \times 12 = 2 \times 6 &= 3 \times 4 \\ &= 4 \times 3 = 6 \times 2 = 12 \times 1 \end{aligned}$$

MULTIPLES

A *multiple* of a number is any number of which the given number is a factor. Thus a multiple of a number can be divided by the given number without leaving a remainder. For example, in $3 \times 4 = 12$, 12 is a multiple of 4, since 4 is a factor of 12. Four, of course, has an infinite number of multiples: 4, 8, 12, 16, 20, $\cdots$.

EVEN AND ODD NUMBERS

A natural number is either an even or an odd number.

Even numbers are numbers that are evenly divisible by 2. The set of even natural numbers is expressed as $\{2, 4, 6, \cdots\}$. Since any even number has 2 as a factor, it may be represented by $2 \times n$, where n is a natural number.

Examples

$2 = 2 \times 1$; $24 = 2 \times 12$; $36 = 2 \times 18$.

Odd numbers are numbers that, when divided by 2, leave a remainder of 1. They do not have the factor 2. The set of odd numbers is expressed as $\{1, 3, 5, \cdots\}$. Any odd number may be represented by $(2 \times n) - 1$, in which n is a natural number.

Examples

$3 = (2 \times 2) - 1$; $21 = (2 \times 11) - 1$.

Thus, any odd number is equal to an even number minus one.

PRIMES AND COMPOSITES

There are three classes of natural numbers:

1. The number 1.
2. The numbers greater than 1 that have exactly two factors: the number itself and 1.

   Examples

   The factors of 2 are 2 and 1;
   the factors of 5 are 5 and 1.

   These numbers are called *prime numbers* or *primes*.
3. The numbers that have factors other than the number itself and 1.

   Examples

   The factors of 4 are 1, 2, and 4;
   the factors of 10 are 1, 2, 5, and 10.

   These numbers are called *composite numbers* or *composites*.

The number 1 is neither prime nor composite, but is a unique or special number. It is a factor of every natural number.

Prime numbers are isolated in a simple way by using a method called the *Sieve of Eratosthenes*. In order to determine the prime numbers less than 25, the numbers from 2 to 25 are listed:

2	3	4	5	6	7	8	9	10	11	12	13
14	15	16	17	18	19	20	21	22	23	24	25

Then this procedure is followed:

1. The first prime number (2) is circled.
2. All the multiples of 2 are crossed out.
3. The prime number 3 is circled.
4. All the multiples of 3 are crossed out.
5. The prime number 5 is circled.
6. All the multiples of 5 are crossed out.

In order to find the primes between 2 and 25, we have to carry the process only to 5 and its multiples. The student should ascertain that the identification of multiples of primes greater than 5 is a duplication of the process.

Eratosthenes, a Greek who lived a few centuries before Christ, used this method. He probably cut holes in a parchment scroll instead of crossing out the figures; his paper ended up looking like a sieve.

TESTS FOR DIVISIBILITY

The teacher of modern elementary school mathematics will have to apply important tests for divisibility frequently—for example, when numbers must be factored. Some of the rules and their explanations are presented below.

1. *A number is divisible by 2 if and only if the number represented by the right-hand digit is divisible by 2.*

Examples

18; 150; 2,478 are divisible by 2.

Explanation: 2,478 = 2,470 + 8 or 247 × 10 + 8. Since 2 is a factor of 10, any multiple of 10 is divisible by 2. Hence, when determining whether a number is divisible by 2, we need only be concerned with whether the unit digit is divisible by 2.

2. *A number is divisible by 3 if and only if the sum of its digits is divisible by 3.*

Examples

12 is divisible by 3, since the sum of the digits (1 + 2 = 3) is divisible by 3. 2,403 is divisible by 3, since the sum of the digits (2 + 4 + 0 + 3 = 9) is divisible by 3.

Explanation: Any power of 10, when divided by 3, yields 1 as remainder, as shown below.

$$\begin{aligned} 111 &= 100 + 10 + 1 \\ &= (99 + 1) + (9 + 1) + 1 \\ &= 99 + 9 + 1 + 1 + 1. \end{aligned}$$

Since 99 + 9 is a multiple of 3, it follows that 111 equals a multiple of 3 plus the sum of the digits.

In 7,641, the 7 represents 7,000 or $(7 \times 999) + (7 \times 1)$,
the 6 represents 600 or $(6 \times 99) + (6 \times 1)$,
the 4 represents 40 or $(4 \times 9) + (4 \times 1)$,
the 1 represents 1.

$$\begin{aligned} \text{Hence, } 7{,}641 &= (7 \times 999) + (7 \times 1) + (6 \times 99) + 6 \times 1) + (4 \times 9) \times (4 \times 1) + 1 \\ &= (7 \times 999) + (6 \times 99) + (4 \times 9) + (7 \times 1) + (6 \times 1) + (4 \times 1) + 1 \\ &= (7 \times 999) + (6 \times 99) + (4 \times 9) + 7 + 6 + 4 + 1 \end{aligned}$$

Since 7 + 6 + 4 + 1 = 18 is divisible by 3, the number 7,641 is also divisible by 3.

Note: If 999 is evenly divisible by 3, then 7×999 is also evenly divisible by 3, since a factor of a number is also a factor of any of its multiples.

3. *A number is divisible by 4 if and only if the number represented by the two right-hand digits is divisible by 4.*

Examples

124; 3,428; 159,080 are divisible by 4.

Explanation: 3,428 = 3,400 + 28. Since 4 is a factor of 100, any multiple of 100 is divisible by 4. Hence, when determining whether a number is divisible by 4, we need only be concerned with whether the number represented by the two right-hand digits is divisible by 4.

4. *A number is divisible by 5 if and only it it ends in 5 or 0.*

Examples

75; 130; 2,435; 7,940 are divisible by 5.

Explanation: 2,435 = 2,430 + 5. Since 5 is a factor of 10, any multiple of 10 is divisible by 5. Hence, when determining whether a number is divisible by 5, we need only be concerned with whether the units digit is divisible by 5.

5. *A number is divisible by 6 if and only if it is divisible by 2 and by 3.*

Examples

48; 144; 2,316; 17,994 are divisible by 6.

Explanation: $6 = 2 \times 3$, and 2 and 3 are primes and have only 1 as a common factor.

6. *A test for divisibility by 7 will be illustrated by examples.*

Example 1

Is 368 divisible by 7?

$$\begin{array}{r|l} 36 & 8 \\ -16 & \\ \hline 20 & \end{array}$$

a. Isolate the digit in the ones place.
b. Multiply the number expressed in the ones place by 2 and subtract the product from the number expressed by remaining digits.
c. Since 20 is not a multiple of seven, 368 is not divisible by 7.

Example 2

Is 511 divisible by 7?

Test: $51 - 2 = 49$. Since 49 is a multiple of 7, we conclude that 511 is divisible by 7.

Example 3

Is 3,192 divisible by 7?

Note: If the first remainder is a number expressed by more than two digits, the process is continued until a remainder of less than 100 is obtained.

Test: $319 - 4 = 315$ and $31 - 10 = 21$. Since 21 is a multiple of 7, we conclude that 3,192 is divisible by 7.

Explanation: Let a stand for the digit in the ones place. It is doubled, written in the tens place and, if needed, in the hundreds place and subtracted from the original number. This reduces the original number by $20a$. Also, the ones digit is not considered any more so that the original number is reduced by $21a$. Since $21a$ (which is a multiple of 7) is subtracted, we need only be concerned with whether the remaining number is a multiple of 7. Consider again one of the examples:

$$\begin{array}{r|l} 51 & 1 \\ -\ 2 & \\ \hline 49 & \end{array}$$

49 stands for 490. Since 7 is a factor of 49, it is also a factor of 490, which is a multiple of 49.

7. *A number is divisible by 8 if and only if the number represented by the three right-hand digits is divisible by 8.*

Examples

1,800; 4,408; 73,960 are divisible by 8.

Explanation: $73{,}960 = 73{,}000 + 960$. Since 8 is a factor of 1,000, any multiple of 1,000 is divisible by 8. Hence, when determining whether a number is divisible by 8, we need only be concerned with whether the number represented by the three right-hand digits is divisible by 8.

8. *A number is divisible by 9 if and only if the sum of its digits is divisible by 9.*

Examples

18,279; 4,563; 19,467 are divisible by 9.

Explanation: Any power of ten when divided by 9 gives 1 as remainder. The explanation is similar to that for the rule of divisibility for 3.

9. *A number is divisible by 10 if and only if it ends in 0.*

Examples

60; 150; 2,560; 94,300 are divisible by 10.

10. *A number is divisible by 12 if and only if it is divisible by 3 and by 4.*

Examples

1,788; 4,044; 35,220 are divisible by 12.

Explanation: $12 = 3 \times 4$, and 3 and 4 have only 1 as a common factor.

Students who understand the rules of divisibility for 2, 4, and 8 will be able to formulate the rule of divisibility for 16. Similarly, if the rules of divisibility for 6 and for 12 are understood, it will not be difficult to formulate and explain the rule of divisibility for 15.

FACTORIZATION

If a composite number is expressed as a product of prime numbers, these numbers are called the *prime factors* of the number. In such a case, exponential notation may be used to advantage, as in the following examples.

Examples

$$9 = 3 \times 3 = 3^2$$
$$8 = 2 \times 2 \times 2 = 2^3$$
$$625 = 5 \times 5 \times 5 \times 5 = 5^4$$

The *Fundamental Theorem of Arithmetic* tells us that a composite number can be expressed as a product of primes in a unique way. Such prime factorization is unique in the sense that—apart from the order of the factors—one and only one set of primes can be used.

Examples

Six can be expressed in prime factors only as 2×3; 40 can be expressed in prime factors only as $2 \times 2 \times 2 \times 5$.

When the prime factors of a number are to be determined, it is advisable to follow a specific procedure. A method is illustrated below.

Example

Resolve 1,260 into prime factors.

Solution: The number is divided by prime numbers in order of size, starting with the smallest prime number, as follows:

1,260 is divisible by 2	2) 1260
630 is divisible by 2	2) 630
315 is divisible by 3	3) 315
105 is divisible by 3	3) 105
35 is divisible by 5	5) 35
7 is a prime number	7

$$1{,}260 = 2 \times 2 \times 3 \times 3 \times 5 \times 7 = 2^2 \times 3^2 \times 5 \times 7$$

A factor tree can also be used to express a number as a product of its primes:

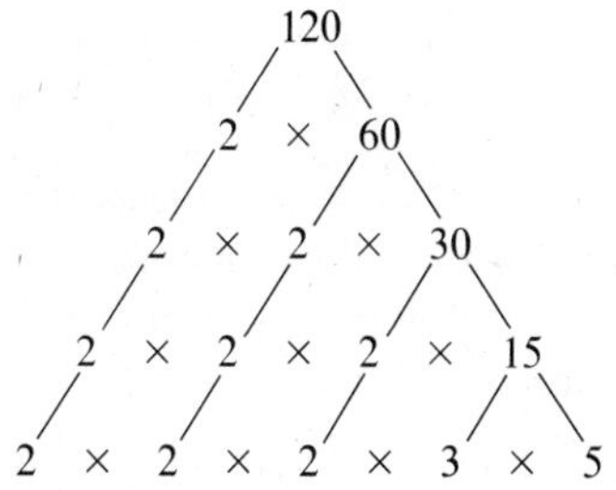

GREATEST COMMON DIVISOR

The *greatest common divisor* (GCD) of two or more numbers is the largest of all the common divisors of the numbers. The greatest common divisor is also called the *highest common factor* (HCF).

Example 1

Find the greatest common divisor of 72 and 90.

Solution: First 72 and 90 are resolved into prime factors:

2) 72	2) 90
2) 36	3) 45
2) 18	3) 15
3) 9	5
3	

$$72 = 2^3 \times 3^2$$
$$90 = 2 \times 3^2 \times 5$$

To find the greatest common divisor of 72 and 90, the common factors, each with the smallest exponent, are selected. These are 2 and 3^2. The greatest common divisor of 72 and 90 is, therefore, the product of these factors: $2 \times 3^2 = 18$. Eighteen is the largest number that evenly divides 72 and 90.

Example 2

Find the greatest common divisor of 36, 48, and 108.

Solution:

$$
\begin{array}{rrr}
2\underline{)\,36} & 2\underline{)\,48} & 2\underline{)\,108} \\
2\underline{)\,18} & 2\underline{)\,24} & 2\underline{)\,54} \\
3\underline{)\,9} & 2\underline{)\,12} & 3\underline{)\,27} \\
3 & 2\underline{)\,6} & 3\underline{)\,9} \\
 & 3 & 3
\end{array}
$$

$$
\begin{aligned}
36 &= 2^2 \times 3^2 \\
48 &= 2^4 \times 3 \\
108 &= 2^2 \times 3^3
\end{aligned}
$$

The GCD of 36, 48, and 108 is $2^2 \times 3 = 12$. Twelve is the largest number that evenly divides 36, 48, and 108.

A fraction can be renamed in lowest terms by dividing the numerator and the denominator by their greatest common divisor. Thus a fraction is expressed in lowest terms when the greatest common divisor of its numerator and denominator is 1.

Example

Rename the fraction $\frac{525}{630}$ in its lowest terms.

Solution: The greatest common divisor of two numbers is the largest of all the common divisors of the numbers. Hence, the greatest common divisor of 525 and 630 has to be determined.

$$
\begin{array}{rr}
3\underline{)\,525} & 2\underline{)\,630} \\
5\underline{)\,175} & 3\underline{)\,315} \\
5\underline{)\,35} & 3\underline{)\,105} \\
7 & 5\underline{)\,35} \\
 & 7
\end{array}
$$

$$
\begin{aligned}
525 &= 3 \times 5^2 \times 7 \\
630 &= 2 \times 3^2 \times 5 \times 7
\end{aligned}
$$

GCD is $3 \times 5 \times 7 = 105$.
Now it has been determined that the largest of all the common divisors of 525 and 630 is 105. Therefore, both the numerator and the denominator of the fraction $\frac{525}{630}$ are divided by 105:

$$\frac{525}{630} = \frac{525 \div 105}{630 \div 105} = \frac{5}{6}$$

LEAST COMMON MULTIPLE

The *least (lowest) common multiple* (LCM) of two or more numbers is the smallest number that is evenly divisible by each of these numbers.

Example 1

Find the least common multiple of 15 and 18.

Solution: The numbers are first resolved into prime factors:

$$15 = 3 \times 5$$
$$18 = 2 \times 3^2$$

To find the least common multiple of 15 and 18, all the different factors, each with the highest exponent, are selected. These are 2, 3^2, and 5. The least common multiple of 15 and 18 is the product of these factors:

$$2 \times 3^2 \times 5 = 90$$

Example 2

Find the least common multiple of 72, 150, and 200.

Solution:

2) 72	2) 150	2) 200
2) 36	3) 75	2) 100
2) 18	5) 25	2) 50
3) 9	5	5) 25
3		5

$$72 = 2^3 \times 3^2$$
$$150 = 2 \times 3 \times 5^2$$
$$200 = 2^3 \times 5^2$$

To find the least common multiple of 72, 150, and 200, we select all the different factors, each with the highest exponent. These are 2^3, 3^2, and 5^2. The least common multiple of 72, 150, and 200 is the product of these factors:

$$2^3 \times 3^2 \times 5^2 = 1{,}800$$

Why are all the different factors, each with the highest exponent, a necessary and sufficient set of factors to make up the least common multiple? The LCM must contain 72, which equals $2^3 \times 3^2$; also 150, which equals $2 \times 3 \times 5^2$; and 200, which equals $2^3 \times 5^2$. Hence, the LCM will contain all the different factors, each with the highest exponent. The different factors are 2, 3, and 5. These factors are represented in the three numbers more than once. If the factor 2^3 is included, then the factor 2 is also included. Consequently, it is sufficient to select the factors with the highest exponent.

The LCM is used in addition and subtraction with unlike fractions. The smallest common denominator of two or more fractions is the LCM of the denominators of the fractions.

Example

Add $\frac{2}{15}$, $\frac{1}{12}$, and $\frac{3}{50}$.

Solution: The first step is to resolve 15, 12, and 50 into prime factors:

$3\overline{)15}$	$2\overline{)12}$	$2\overline{)50}$
5	$2\overline{)\ 6}$	$5\overline{)25}$
	3	5

$$15 = 3 \times 5$$
$$12 = 2^2 \times 3$$
$$50 = 2 \times 5^2$$

Then the LCM of 15, 12, and 50 can be found. The LCM of these numbers is $2^2 \times 3 \times 5^2 = 300$. Hence, the smallest common denominator of $\frac{2}{15}$, $\frac{1}{12}$, and $\frac{3}{50}$ is 300. Finally, $\frac{2}{15}$, $\frac{1}{12}$, and $\frac{3}{50}$ are renamed as fractions with a denominator of 300, and the addition is performed:

$$\frac{2}{15} + \frac{1}{12} + \frac{3}{50} = \frac{40}{300} + \frac{25}{300} + \frac{18}{300} = \frac{83}{300}$$

SELECTED RESEARCH

The purpose of this study[1] was to compare the results of two methods for using visual-tactual devices to teach exponents and nondecimal bases to pupils nine to eleven years old.

Method I. Pupils manipulate visual-tactual aids.
Method II. Pupils observe and tell the teacher how to manipulate the aids.

Seven teachers taught twenty-one lessons to their fourth grades, following specified structured lesson plans. In each class the pupils were randomly assigned to one of the two methods. A test was administered immediately after the last lesson and also after a four-week period to measure retention.

1. C. R. Trueblood, "A Comparison of Two Techniques for Using Visual-Tactual Devices to Teach Exponents and Nondecimal Bases in Elementary School Mathematics," *The Arithmetic Teacher* (April, 1970), pp. 338–340.

The results indicated:

1. Pupils in Method II earned higher scores on the immediate post-test than those taught by Method I, but the difference was marginally significant ($P = .10$).
2. Though both methods resulted in a high degree of retention, pupils taught by Method II did not retain significantly more than those taught by Method I.
3. Exponential nondecimal base test scores had a high positive correlation with mental age.

In the discussion of the results, the investigator pointed out that the findings suggest that pupils ages nine to eleven have already passed the stage where incoming information is organized best from tactual sources and have entered a later stage where visual and auditory sources are as useful as tactual sources for gaining information. It was also pointed out that the different patterns of teacher–pupil interaction might have influenced results. Finally, the observation was made that the method familiar to most teachers is quite different from Method I.

SELECTED ACTIVITIES FOR PUPILS

1. Finding patterns.

Example 1

Try different numbers for △ and complete the sentences.

What can you tell about the □s?
What can you tell about the ○s?

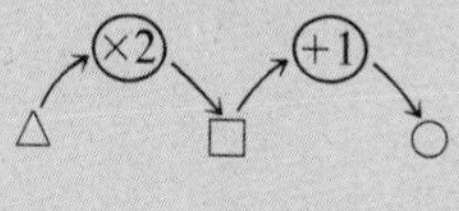

Example 2

Complete. Then circle the odd-numbered products.

×	1	2	3	4
1	1			
2				
3				
4		8		

Write odd or even:

Odd times odd is ________.

Even times even is ________.

Even times odd is ________.

Odd times even is ________.

Example 3

1 3 6 10

1, 3, 6, and 10 are triangular numbers. Write the next three triangular numbers. Use dots to show the triangles.

2. Finding prime factors.

Example

Complete the following factor tree.

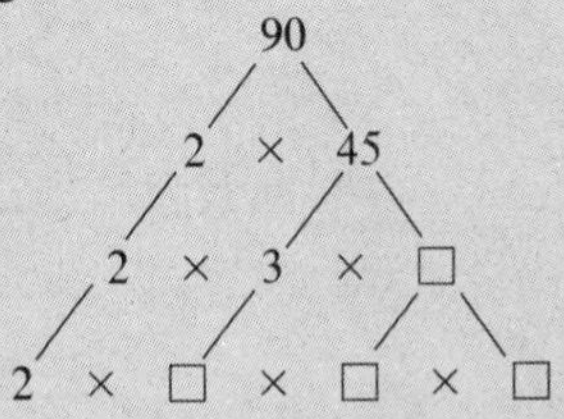

3. Finding the least common multiple of two numbers.

Example 1

I have more than 1 and fewer than 15 pennies in each hand. I have the same number of pennies in each hand. If I group the pennies in my left hand in sets of 3, I have none left. If I group the pennies in my right hand in sets of 4, I have none left. How many pennies do I have in each hand?

Example 2

Neal has invited 23 friends to his party. Each one will get a bun with a hot dog. Ned buys buns in packages of 8 and hot dogs in packages of 6. How many packages of buns and how many packages of hot dogs does Neal need to buy?

4. Isolating primes and multiples.

Example

I am thinking of a number greater than 10 and less than 20. The number is not prime. It is not a multiple of 3. It is not a multiple of 4. What is the number?

5. Using blocks to find factors.

Example

Get 12 blocks. Arrange them in sets of the same number in as many ways as you can. (One group of 12 counts.) Now say what the factors of 12 are.

6. Finding prime numbers.

Example

Write each number as the sum of two prime numbers: 5, 8, 9, 10, 12.

7. Using exponents.

Example

Write the exponent that makes the following a true statement:

$250 = 2 \times 5^{\square}$.

8. Finding patterns.

Example 1

Continue this pattern.

$$2^2 = 4 = 1 + 3$$
$$3^2 = 9 = 1 + 3 + 5$$
$$4^2 = 16 = 1 + 3 + 5 + 7$$
$$5^2 = 25 = 1 + 3 + 5 + 7 + 9$$

Example 2

Complete and continue the pattern.

$1 = 1^2$
$1 + 2 + 1 = 4 = 2^2$
$1 + 2 + 3 + 2 + 1 =$ ______ $=$ ______
$1 + 2 + 3 + 4 + 3 + 2 + 1 =$ ______ $=$ ______

Example 3

Study the presentation, then write the answers to the questions.

$1{,}001 \times 171 =$
$1{,}001 \times 808 =$
$1{,}001 \times 345 =$
$1{,}001 \times 999 =$

$$\begin{array}{r} 432 \\ \times\ 1001 \\ \hline 432 \\ 432 \\ \hline 432432 \end{array}$$

Example 4

a. Write any three-digit number. 201
b. Repeat the digits once. 201,201
c. Divide the number in (b) by 7. $201{,}201 \div 7 = 28{,}743$
d. Divide the quotient in (c) by 11. $28{,}743 \div 11 = 2{,}613$
e. Divide the quotient in (d) by 13. $2{,}613 \div 13 = 201$
f. Compare the final quotient with the number in (a).

g. Follow the same procedure with two other three-digit numbers.
h. Explain why the numbers in (a) and (e) are the same.

9. Working with Venn diagrams.

Example 1

a. Write the set of all factors of 60. Call it Set A.
b. Write the set of all factors of 140. Call it Set B.
c. The intersection of Set A and Set B contains the common factors of the two sets.
d. Write the factors of the numbers 60 and 140 in the diagram. A common factor is written only once.

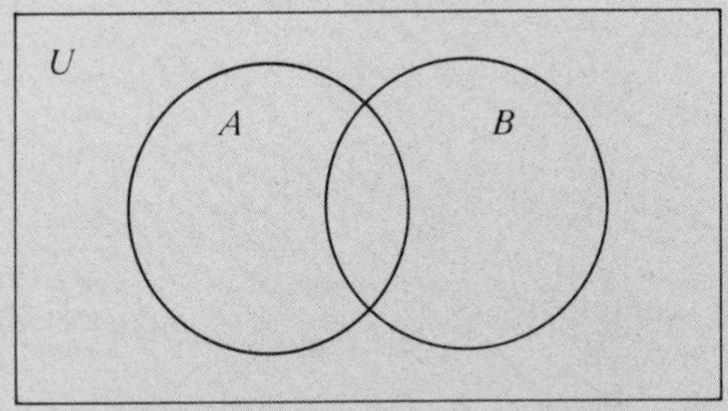

e. What is the greatest common factor of 60 and 140?

Example 2

a. Write the set of multiples of 3, less than 40, starting with 3. Call it Set A.
b. Write the set of multiples of 4, less than 40, starting with 4. Call it Set B.
c. Write the set of common multiples of 3 and 4, less than 40.
d. Write the multiples of the numbers 3 and 4, less than 40, in a Venn diagram as shown in Example 1.
e. What is the least common multiple of 3 and 4?

10. Identifying multiples of given numbers.

Example

In the array that is presented below numbers are expressed within squares. In this activity, a side or a diagonal of the square in which a number is expressed has to be traced or drawn with a colored pencil according to the directions. The sides or diagonals to be marked are identified by letters in the illustrated enlarged square.

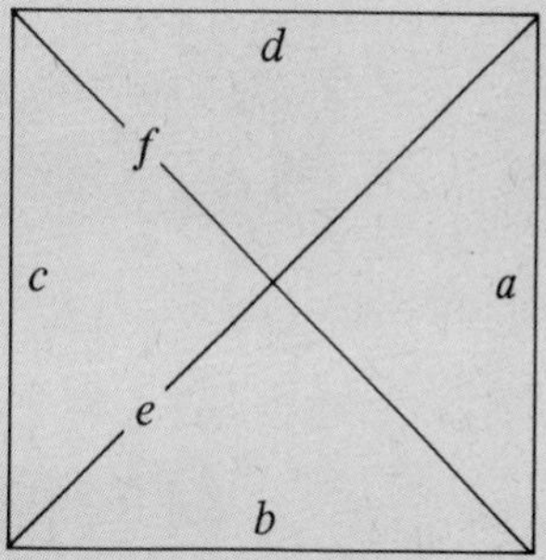

If the number is a multiple of—
2, draw diagonal *e*.
7, draw diagonal *f*.
9, trace side *a* of the square.
11, trace side *d* of the square.
13, trace side *b* of the square.
17, trace side *c* of the square.
What letters did you get?
If you did not get a message that you are right, you must be wrong!

64	121	49		51	128
17		45	27	16	
7	39	32	81	35	

11. Discovering patterns in a calendar.

S	M	T	W	TH	F	S
1	2	3	4	5	6	7
8	9	10	11	12	13	14
15	16	17	18	19	20	21
22	23	24	25	26	27	28
29	30	31				

Example 1

Cut from an index card, a rectangle of a size that, if put on the calendar, a 2 × 2 array of numbers (but no more) will show:

9	10
16	17

Note that the sum of the numbers in one diagonal is 26 and that the sum in the other diagonal is also 26.
Try it with other 2 × 2 arrays of numbers.

Example 2

Cut a square that will expose a 3 × 3 array of numbers. Check if the sum of the numbers in both diagonals is the same.

Example 3

Try the same activity with a 4 × 4 array of numbers.

12. Al is between 4 and 20 years old. The number that expresses his age is not a multiple of 2, it is not a multiple of 5, and it is not a prime number. How old is Al?

EXERCISES

1. Supply the integral factors of:

   24, 40, 75, 65, 100.

2. Express each number as a product of two factors in every possible way.

   20, 24, 65, 50, 60

3. How many even numbers are greater than 20 and less than 45?
4. Supply five multiples of 7.
5. Decide whether each of the numbers expressed below is a prime number or a composite number.

   16, 11, 23, 41, 74, 99, 3. 13, 37, 52

6. Test each of the numbers expressed below for divisibility by 2, 3, 4, 5, 6, 8, and 10.

   312; 927; 14,928; 64,500; 134,880

7. Test the numbers 588 and 2,261 for divisibility by 7.

8. Resolve into prime factors:

$$252, \quad 540, \quad 375, \quad 3{,}150, \quad 2{,}112.$$

9. Determine the smallest common denominator of these fractions:

$$\tfrac{1}{3}, \tfrac{2}{5}, \tfrac{7}{15}, \text{ and } \tfrac{9}{10}.$$

10. Find the LCM of 12, 21, and 50.
11. Find the GCD of 14, 21, and 49.
12. Find both the GCD and the LCM of 30 and 54.
13. Write this expression in a shorter form by using exponents:

$$2 \times 2 \times 3 \times 3 \times 5 \times 5 \times 5.$$

SOURCES FOR FURTHER READING

D'Augustine, C. H., *Multiple Methods of Teaching Mathematics in the Elementary School,* 2nd ed. New York: Harper & Row, Publishers, 1973, Chap. XV.

Davies, R. A., "Low Achiever Lesson in Primes," *The Arithmetic Teacher,* April 1969, pp. 529–532.

Dubish, R., "The Sieve of Eratosthenes," *The Arithmetic Teacher,* April, 1971, pp. 236–237.

Erb, C. A., "What Do You See?—A Discovery Approach to Prime Numbers," *The Arithmetic Teacher,* April, 1975, pp. 272–273.

Heddens, J. W., *Today's Mathematics,* 3d ed. Chicago: Science Research Associates, Inc., 1974, Unit XI.

Holdan, G., "Prime: A Drill in the Recognition of Prime and Composite Numbers," *The Arithmetic Teacher,* February, 1969, pp. 149–151.

Kennedy, L. M., *Guiding Children to Mathematical Discovery,* 2nd ed. Belmont, California: Wadsworth Publishing Company, Inc., 1975, Chap. X.

National Council of Teachers of Mathematics, *Topics in Mathematics, Twenty-ninth Yearbook.* Washington, D.C.: The Council, 1964, Bklt. 5.

Rasof, E., "The Fundamental Principle of Counting, Tree Diagrams, and the Number of Divisors of a Number (the Nu-Function)," *The Arithmetic Teacher,* April, 1969, pp. 308–310.

Schminke, C. W., N. Maertens, and W. R. Arnold, *Teaching the Child Mathematics*. Hinsdale, Illinois: The Dryden Press, Inc., 1973, Chap. XII.

Smith, F., "Divisibility Rules for the First Fifteen Primes," *The Arithmetic Teacher,* February, 1971, pp. 85–87.

Unenge, J., "A Crossnumber Game with Factors," *The Arithmetic Teacher,* May, 1975, pp. 426–428.

Mathematical Sentences 7

A sentence is a group of words that tells or asks something by itself. The words, spoken or written, are symbols that stand for ideas. In a mathematical sentence mathematical symbols express mathematical ideas concisely. For example, instead of expressing the distributive property of multiplication with respect to addition in printed words, the mathematical sentence $a \times (b + c) = (a \times b) + (a \times c)$ (presented in Chapter 4) expresses the idea concisely in comparatively few symbols.

If a mathematical sentence states something, as in $3 + 2 = 5$ or in $3 + 2 = 4$, it is a *statement* that is true or that is false, and it is called a *closed sentence*. If it asks something, as in $3 + \square = 5$, it contains an unknown, and is called an *open sentence*.

By itself, $3 + 2$ is not a sentence, since it alone does not state or ask anything—instead, it is called a *mathematical phrase* or *expression*.

SYMBOLS

A mathematical sentence may contain several kinds of symbols: symbols to express the objects under consideration, symbols of operation, symbols of relation or comparison, and punctuation symbols.

1. The symbols that express the *objects* on which the operation is performed may represent numbers or sets.

   Examples

   $4 + 3 = 7$;
   $\{3, 4\} \cup \{5, 6\} = \{3, 4, 5, 6\}$.

2. The most frequently used symbols indicating *operations* that must be performed are found in Table 7.1.

Table 7.1

Symbol	*Operation*	*Example*
+	addition	$3 + 2 = 5$
−	subtraction	$5 - 2 = 3$
×	multiplication	$3 \times 2 = 6$
÷	division	$6 \div 2 = 3$
∪	union	$\{\triangle, \bigcirc\} \cup \{\square\} = \{\triangle, \bigcirc, \square\}$
∩	intersection	$\{\triangle, \bigcirc, \square\} \cap \{\square, \bigcirc\} = \{\bigcirc\}$

When more than one number operation is indicated, it is essential to know the order in which they must be performed. When there is any danger of misrepresentation, parentheses, brackets, and braces (shown in Table 7.3) are used to designate the required order of operations. Operations indicated within parentheses are usually performed first, then those indicated within brackets, and finally those indicated within braces.

$$\begin{aligned} 125 - \{80 \div [2 \times (15 - 5)]\} &= 125 - [80 \div (2 \times 10)] \\ &= 125 - (80 \div 20) \\ &= 125 - 4 \\ &= 121 \end{aligned}$$

3. Important *relation* symbols are found in Table 7.2.
4. *Punctuation* symbols are found in Table 7.3.

Table 7.2

Symbol	*Meaning*	*Example*
=	is equal to	$3 + 2 = 5$
≠	is not equal to	$3 + 2 \neq 6$
>	is greater than	$3 > 2$
<	is less than	$3 < 4$
⊂	is a subset of	If $A = \{1, 2, 3\}$ and $B = \{1, 2\}$, then $B \subset A$.
↔	is equivalent to	If $C = \{1, 2, 3\}$ and $D = \{4, 5, 6\}$, then $C \leftrightarrow D$.
↮	is not equivalent to	If $E = \{8\}$ and $F = \{9, 10\}$, then $E \nleftrightarrow F$.

Table 7.3

Symbol	*Name*	*Example*
( )	parentheses	$4 \times (2 + 3) = 20$
[ ]	brackets	$60 \div [4 \times (2 + 3)] = 3$
{ }	braces	$100 - \{40 \div [4 \times (2 + 3)]\} = 98$
.	decimal point	4.5
,	comma	35,984

STATEMENTS

An *equation* is a sentence that asserts an equality between two expressions. The symbol = is used to express an equality.

Example

$5 + 2 = 7.$

The expressions to the left and the right of the equal sign are the *members* of the equation.

An *inequality* states that two expressions are unequal. An inequality may be expressed by the symbol $\neq$, $>$, or $<$.

Examples

$5 + 2 \neq 8$; $5 + 2 \neq 6$;
$5 + 2 < 8$; $5 + 2 > 6$.

A *closed sentence* is a statement that is true or a statement that is false.

Examples

$5 + 2 = 7$ is a true statement.
$5 + 2 = 6$ is a false statement.
$5 + 2 \neq 6$ is a true statement.
$5 + 2 \neq 7$ is a false statement.
$5 + 2 > 6$ is a true statement.
$5 + 2 < 7$ is a false statement.

OPEN SENTENCES

An open sentence contains a symbol for an unknown and cannot be said to be either true or false. For example, the equation $3 + n = 5$ is an open sentence in which n holds the place for a numeral. Instead of a letter, a question mark, an empty space, or a frame such as □, △, or ○ is often used in the elementary school. Though, strictly speaking, $5 + 3 = \quad$ is not a sentence, it is understood that the empty space serves the same purpose as the symbols just presented.

If, in $4 + n = 7$ or in $4 + \square = 7$, the letter or the frame is replaced by 3, the sentence is closed and *the condition is satisfied,* because the statement $4 + 3 = 7$ is a true statement. If, in $4 + n = 7$, the unknown n is replaced by 5, the sentence is closed, but the condition is not satisfied, because $4 + 5 = 7$ is a false statement.

The *solution* of the sentences $2n = 8$, $1 + n = 5$, and $5 - n = 1$ is 4. Equations that have the same solution are called *equivalent equations*.

When solving an equation these principles may be used:

1. An equivalent equation is obtained if both members of a given equation are increased or decreased by the same number.
2. An equivalent equation is obtained if both members of a given equation are multiplied or divided by the same nonzero number.

Example 1

Solve $n + 2 = 7$.

Solution: Subtract 2 from both members of the equation:

$$n + 2 - 2 = 7 - 2$$
$$n = 5$$

The sentence can be pictured on the number line:

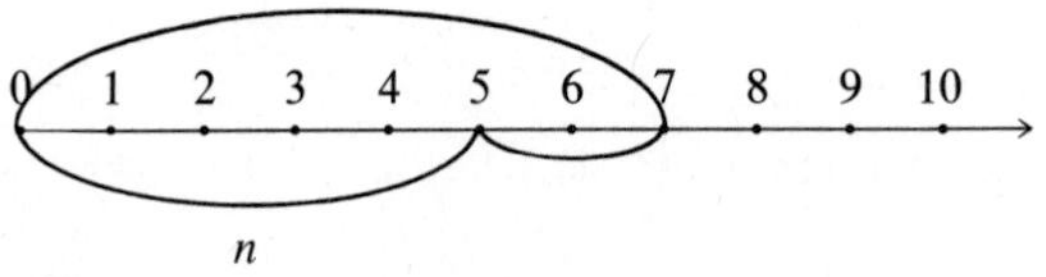

Example 2

Solve $n - 3 = 5$.

Solution: Add 3 to both members of the equation:

$$n - 3 + 3 = 5 + 3$$
$$n = 8$$

Illustration of the sentence on the number line:

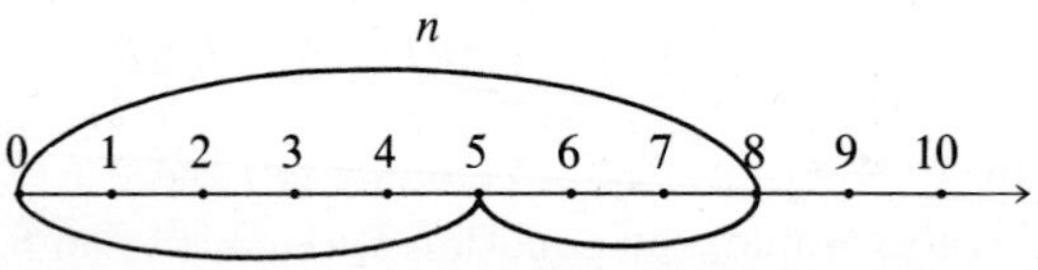

Example 3

Solve $3n = 12$.

Solution: Divide both members of the equation by 3:

$$3n \div 3 = 12 \div 3$$
$$n = 4$$

Illustration of the sentence on the number line:

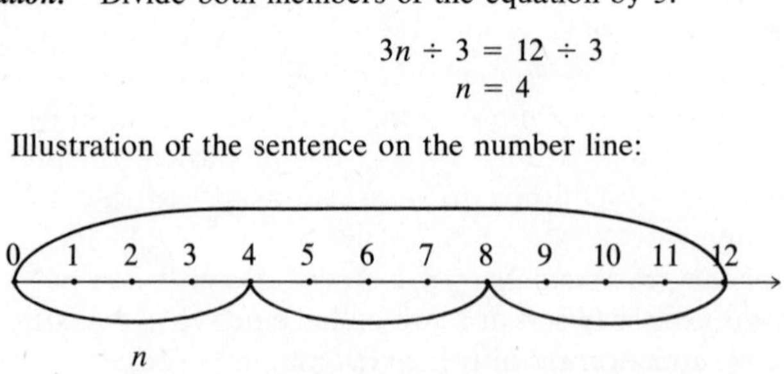

Example 4

Solve $n \div 5 = 2$.

Solution: Multiply both members of the equation by 5:

$$5 \times (n \div 5) = 5 \times 2$$
$$n = 10$$

Illustration on the number line:

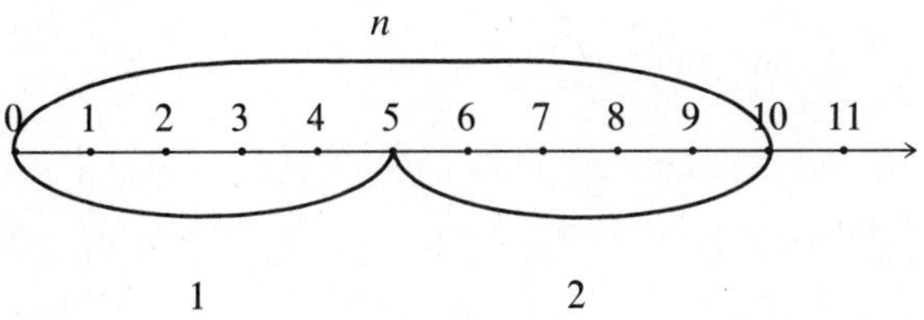

Example 5

Solve $2n + 5 = 13$.

Solution:

Step 1: Subtract 5 from both members of the equation:

$$2n + 5 - 5 = 13 - 5$$
$$2n = 8$$

Step 2: Divide both members of the equation by 2:

$$2n \div 2 = 8 \div 2$$
$$n = 4$$

Illustration on the number line:

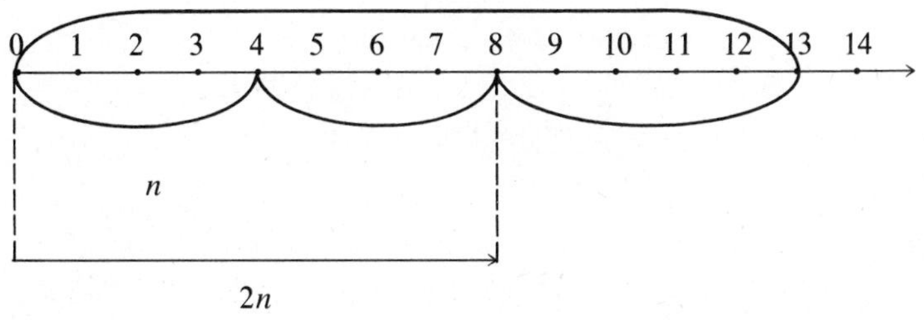

MATHEMATICAL PHRASES

In the introduction to this chapter it was stated that $3 + 2$ is not a sentence, because it does not tell or ask something by itself. It was called a *mathematical phrase* or *expression*.

Certain word phrases can be translated into mathematical phrases, such as those in Table 7.4.

Table 7.4

Word Phrase	*Mathematical Phrase*
Seven plus two	$7 + 2$
Four times three	4×3
A certain number increased by seven	$n + 7$
A certain number decreased by five	$n - 5$
Six subtracted from a certain number	$n - 6$
Seven times a certain number	$7n$
A certain number divided by two	$\frac{n}{2}$ or $n \div 2$
Three times the difference between eight and six	$3 \times (8 - 6)$

SOLVING PROBLEMS When solving a verbal problem, one must read the problem carefully in order to decide what is given and what is asked. Then the situation is expressed in an open mathematical sentence or equation in which the unknown is represented by a letter or a frame. Finally the equation is solved.

Example 1

Five more than 3 times a certain number is 17. What is the number?

Mathematical sentence: $3n + 5 = 17$.

Solution:

Step 1: Subtract 5 from both members of the equation:

$$3n + 5 - 5 = 17 - 5$$
$$3n = 12$$

Step 2: Divide both members of the equation by 3:

$$3n \div 3 = 12 \div 3$$
$$n = 4$$

The number is 4.

Check: $3 \times 4 + 5 = 12 + 5 = 17$.

Example 2

Tom and Ray each have a coin collection. Ray has 6 more than 3 times as many coins as Tom. If Ray has 126 coins, how many coins does Tom have?

Mathematical sentence: $3n + 6 = 126$.

Solution:

Step 1: Subtract 6 from both members of the equation:

$$3n + 6 - 6 = 126 - 6$$
$$3n = 120$$

Step 2: Divide both members of the equation by 3:

$$3n \div 3 = 120 \div 3$$
$$n = 40$$

Tom has 40 coins.

Check: $3 \times 40 + 6 = 120 + 6 = 126$.

REPLACEMENT SETS AND SOLUTION SETS

In the open sentences $3 + n < 9$ and $3 + \square < 9$ (where n and $\square$ stand for any member of the set of natural numbers), the symbols n and $\square$ can be replaced by any natural number. Other letters and frames may also be used as placeholders.

The specified set from which the substitution can be made, in this case the set of natural numbers, is called the *replacement set,* the *domain,* or the *universe* (U). The replacement of n in $3 + n < 9$ by a member of the set of natural numbers does not always result in a true statement. For example, $3 + 6 < 9$ is a false statement. In the example under consideration, we can only arrive at a true statement by replacing n by 1, 2, 3, 4, or 5. The set containing the members that, when substituted for n, satisfy the condition and make the statement true is called the *solution set* or the *truth set* of the sentence. Thus, in the above example, the solution set is $\{1, 2, 3, 4, 5\}$.

Example 1

$U = \{1, 2, 3, \cdots\}$. Find the solution set of $3 + n = 4$.

Solution: The only member of the replacement set or universe that, by replacing n, causes the statement to be true and therefore satisfies the condition for n in $3 + n = 4$ is 1, since $3 + 1 = 4$. The solution set is $\{1\}$.

Example 2

$U = \{3, 4, 5, 6, 7, 8, 9, 10\}$. Find the solution set for $\square - 3 > 4$.

Solution set: $\{8, 9, 10\}$.

Example 3

$U = \{1, 2, 3, \cdots\}$. Find the solution set for $n < 7$.

Solution set: $\{1, 2, 3, 4, 5, 6\}$. The replacement of n by any member of the solution set $\{1, 2, 3, 4, 5, 6\}$ makes the sentence $n < 7$ true and satisfies the condition.

Another way of writing $n < 7$ is $\{n|n < 7\}$. This is read "the set whose members are all natural numbers n that satisfy the condition that n be less than 7." The expression $\{n| \}$ is called the *set-builder*.

Example 4

Write the following expression using the set-builder, and find the solution set: the set of all natural numbers greater than 5.

Solution set: $\{6, 7, 8, \cdots\}$. The expression is written with the set-builder as $\{n|n > 5\}$; this is read "the set whose members are all natural numbers n that satisfy the condition that n be greater than 5."

TRANSLATING A GIVEN PROBLEM SITUATION INTO A MATHEMATICAL SENTENCE

Pupils should develop skill in translating the situation presented in a verbal problem into a number question or an open mathematical sentence. To construct such a sentence, the pupil must analyze the situation, isolate the pertinent facts, state the question, and identify the needed mathematical symbols. The pupil must further determine the relationship between the facts and the unknown and arrange the symbols in the form of a mathematical sentence.

1. Betty had 8 flowers. She picked 5 more. How many flowers did Betty then have in all?

   Mathematical sentence: $8 + 5 = \square$.

2. Ann had 7 flowers. After she picked some more, she had 12 flowers. How many flowers did Ann pick?

   Mathematical sentence: $7 + \square = 12$.

3. After Tim received 3 marbles, he had a total of 11 marbles. How many marbles did Tim have to begin with?

   Mathematical sentence: $\square + 3 = 11$.

4. Three of the 12 teachers in Lincoln School are men. How many women teachers are there in Lincoln School?

   Mathematical sentence: $12 = 3 + \square$.

5. Ann gave 7 of her 13 picture cards to her sister. How many cards did Ann have left?

   Mathematical sentence: $13 - 7 = \square$.

6. After Larry gave some of his 15 baseball cards to his friend, he had 9 cards left. How many cards did Larry give to his friend?

   Mathematical sentence: $15 - \square = 9$.

7. After Lois spent 8¢ she had 7¢ left. How much money did Lois have to begin with?

   <u>*Mathematical sentence:*</u> $\square - 8 = 7$.

8. How many days equal 3 weeks?

   <u>*Mathematical sentence:*</u> $3 \times 7 = \square$.

9. Mother bought 5 boxes of apples. If she bought a total of 20 apples, and there was the same number of apples in each box, how many apples were in each box?

   <u>*Mathematical sentence:*</u> $5 \times \square = 20$.

10. Linda bought some packages of chocolate bars. There were 5 bars in each package. If Linda bought 15 bars in all, how many packages did she buy?

    <u>*Mathematical sentence:*</u> $\square \times 5 = 15$.

11. There are 45 chairs in a room. The chairs are placed in rows of 9 chairs each. How many rows of chairs are there?

    <u>*Mathematical sentence:*</u> $45 = \square \times 9$.

12. How many committees of 5 children each can be formed from a group of 15 children?

    <u>*Mathematical sentence:*</u> $15 \div 5 = \square$.

13. Mrs. Bird divided 12 cupcakes equally among some girls. If each girl got 3 cupcakes, how many girls were there?

    <u>*Mathematical sentence:*</u> $12 \div \square = 3$.

14. A number of pictures were equally divided among 5 girls. If each girl got 3 pictures, how many pictures were there?

    <u>*Mathematical sentence:*</u> $\square \div 5 = 3$.

In the following example a two-step verbal problem is presented. The answer to the problem is obtained by performing the necessary operations in a specific order which must be expressed in the mathematical sentence.

15. Tony bought a composition book for 25¢ and a pen for 35¢. He gave the clerk a one-dollar bill. How much change did Tony receive?

    <u>*Mathematical sentence:*</u> $100 - (25 + 35) = \square$.

16. After Jim received 2 marbles, he had fewer than 8 marbles. How many marbles could Jim have had before he got the 2 marbles?

    Mathematical sentence: $n + 2 < 8$ or $\square + 2 < 8$.

SELECTED RESEARCH

This comparative study[1] was carried out in the Pueblo, Colorado, public schools over a 30-week period of the year 1963–64. All fifth-grade classes participated in the study. Because of differences in school organization, it was decided to make the school the sampling unit. Schools were randomly assigned to the experimental and control groups, 15 in each group. The experimental group was composed of 33 classes and 843 pupils; the control group was composed of 35 classes and 881 pupils.

There was no change in the instruction of the control classes; experimental classes had twenty minutes of mental computation activities three days a week during their regular arithmetic class period. (*Note:* The total time allotted for arithmetic was the *same* in the two groups.) Activities pertaining to mental computation were scheduled for the experimental group as follows: Mondays and Wednesdays, presentation of lessons according to the directions in the instructional manual; Fridays, completion of practice problems in mental computation booklets. Experimental pupils covered one lesson a week.

The 100-item test constructed by the author was administered in all classes in October and May, before and after the experimental classes had used the mental computation materials. Pre-test and post-test school means were computed for raw scores, and an analysis of covariance was made, pre-test means being used as adjusting or controlling variables for the post-test means. The results are presented in Table 7.5.

The data indicated that pupils whose arithmetic instruction was supplemented by mental computation materials made statistically significant gains[2] over control pupils. Experimental pupils worked more problems correctly both within the 25-minute time period and when no time limit was imposed.

The California Arithmetic Test (Form Y) was also administered to

---

1. J. F. Payne, "An Experimental Study on the Effectiveness of Instruction in Mental Computation in Grade V," unpublished Ed.D. thesis, (Greeley: Colorado State College, 1965). From K. Kramer, *Mental Computation, Books A–F, Teacher's Guide* (Chicago: Science Research Associates, Inc., © 1965), pp. xvii, xviii. Reprinted by permission of the publisher.
2. The .01 level of significance was used.

both groups before and after the experimental classes had used the mental computation materials. It was important to determine whether time taken from the regular arithmetic class period for mental computation training would have an adverse effect on the experimental group's performance on regular paper-and-pencil achievement tests. Analysis of covariance of pre-test and post-test school means yielded no significant difference between the two groups.[3]

Table 7.5

Raw Score Means and Differences between Means Obtained by 1,724 Subjects in Fifth-Grade Experimental and Control Groups on a Test of Mental Computation

Group	*Raw Score Means*			*Raw Score Means*		
	Pre-test (timed)	*Post-test (timed)*	*Difference**	*Pre-test (untimed)*	*Post-test (untimed)*	*Difference**
Experimental	32	78	15†	47	83	10†
Control	35	63		52	73	

* Experimental post-test mean—control post-test mean.
† Significant at .01 level.

These data demonstrate that, in the population studied, pupils who used the mental computation materials without increasing the total amount of time spent on arithmetic improved their accuracy and increased their speed in mental computation. Moreover, no difference between these experimental pupils and control groups was found in performance on a standardized paper-and-pencil arithmetic achievement test, even though time was taken from the arithmetic class period of the experimental pupils for special instruction in mental computation.

SELECTED ACTIVITIES FOR PUPILS

1. Deciding whether a statement is true or false.

Example

True or false:

$7 \times 9 < 50$ $\quad 30 \div 6 > 3 \times 2$
$25 - 9 = 15$ $\quad 5 + 7 \neq 12$

---

3. The .05 level of significance was used.

2. Selecting the proper operation symbol.

   Example

   Write +, −, ×, or ÷ in each of the circles to make the sentence true.

   6 ○ 3 = 18   25 ○ 15 = 10
   9 ○ 3 = 12   25 ○ 5 = 5

3. Constructing mathematical sentences to fit a picture situation.

   Example

   Write as many mathematical sentences as you can to go with this picture.

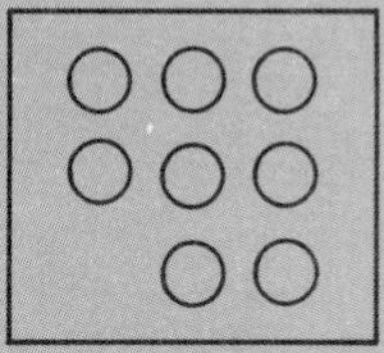

   Possible solutions:

   $6 + 2 = 8$
   $8 - 2 = 6$
   $(2 \times 3) + 2 = 8$

4. Constructing a mathematical sentence that fits a given word problem.

   Example

   Write a mathematical sentence that fits the following word problem. Ted had some marbles. After he lost 7 of them, he had 20 marbles left. How many marbles did Ted have in the beginning?

5. Constructing a word problem to fit a given mathematical sentence.

   Example

   Write a word problem that fits this mathematical sentence: $(5 \times 3) + 2 = 17$.

6. Changing a false statement into a true statement.

   Example

   Make the statement $7 + 5 = 13$ true in different ways, changing only one numeral or relation symbol each time.

7. Replacing frames with numerals.

Example

$U = \{1, 2, 3, \cdots\}$.

$15 + \triangle = 23$ $\quad \square + \square = 4$ $\quad \square + \bigcirc = 5$

$3 \times 12 = (3 \times \square) + (3 \times \bigcirc) = 36$

$5 \times 7 + 3 = \triangledown$ $\quad \square \times 3 < 10$

8. Using letters for numerals.

Example

If $15 - 2n = 7$, then $n =$ ______.

9. Deciding whether a given sentence expresses an inequality.

Example

Underline each sentence that expresses an inequality.

$26 + 9 = 35$ $\quad 6 \times 4 + 10 > 30$

$45 + 15 \neq 55$ $\quad 8 \div 4 + 3 < 8$

10. Using relation symbols.

Example

Construct several mathematical sentences using the symbols $=$, $\neq$, $>$, and $<$.

11. Using punctuation symbols.

Example

Perform the indicated operations and explain why you obtained different solutions. You may want to use the number line.

$(5 \times 3) + 2 = \square$

$5 \times (3 + 2) = \square$

12. Making a statement true by changing a symbol.

Example 1

Make each statement true by changing one operation symbol.

$7 + 8 - 4 = 19$ $\quad (6 + 7) + 8 = 50$

$(5 + 0) \times 8 = 0$ $\quad (9 \times 4) \div 2 = 34$

$(0 \div 4) - 4 = 4$ $\quad (18 \times 3) + 17 = 23$

Example 2

Make each statement true by changing the relation symbol.

$(8 \times 12) + 4 > 100$ $\quad 100 - 25 - 16 - 8 = 53$

$19 + 19 - 9 = 30$ $\quad (6 \times 7 \times 2) - 14 > 70$

$(72 \div 8) \times 3 < 25$ $\quad (70 - 20 - 5) \div 9 = 9$

13. Making number sentences by using given numbers.

Example

If the numbers 20, 10, and 5 are used, number sentences are made such as the following:

$(20 \div 10) \times 5 = 10$ $\quad$ $(5 \div 5) + 10 = 11$

14. Using the same four digits to construct number sentences with different sums.

Example

$0 = (2 + 2) - (2 + 2)$
$1 = (2 \div 2) \times (2 \div 2)$
$2 = (2 \div 2) + (2 \div 2)$
$3 = (2 \times 2) - (2 \div 2)$

Try to find sums of 4 through 10 by using four 2s. You may also use other symbols; for example, the decimal point. Also use four 4s to form number sentences with sums from 0 through 10.

15. Building a pattern.

Example

Complete and continue the pattern.

$(1 \times 9) + 1 = 10$
$(2 \times 9) + 2 = \square$
$(3 \times 9) + 3 = \square$
____
____
____

16. Writing number sentences.

Example

Write several number sentences that are suggested by the model.

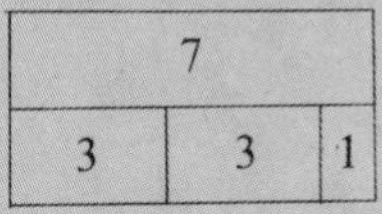

Possible sentences:

$3 + 3 + 1 = 7$ $\quad$ $(7 - 1) \div 2 = 3$
$7 - 1 = 2 \times 3$ $\quad$ $7 \div 3 = 2$, remainder 1
$(2 \times 3) + 1 = 7$ $\quad$ $\frac{3}{7} + \frac{3}{7} + \frac{1}{7} = 1$

17. Finding sets of coins that can be used to pay a given debt.

Example

A debt of 27 cents can be paid by using, for example, 1 quarter and 2 pennies. Find all the possible combinations of coins with a total value of 27 cents.

18. Finding combinations of scores to get a given total score.

Example

Suppose you are throwing darts at a dartboard with possible scores as shown. Write several combinations of scores to get the total score indicated below. Of course, you may hit the same section more than once.

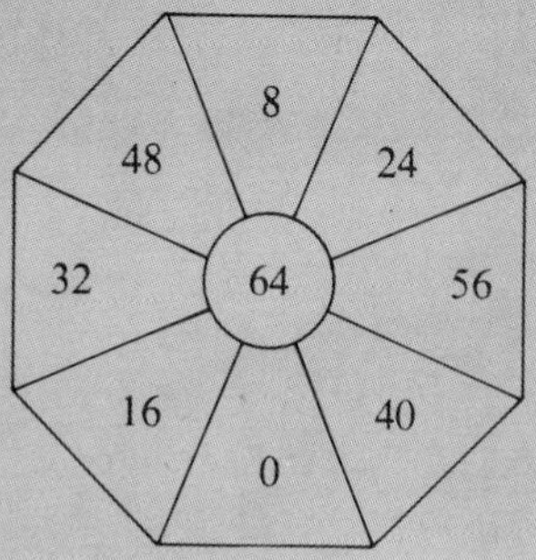

Total Score	*Number of Darts Thrown*	*Combinations*
56	2	56 + 0; 48 + 8; 40 + 16; 32 + 24
32	3	
8	3	
96	3	
40	4	
128	4	
256	8	

19. Making equations.

Example 1

The drawings show that 1 dime balances with 4 thumbtacks, and that 1 thumbtack balances with 4 pins.

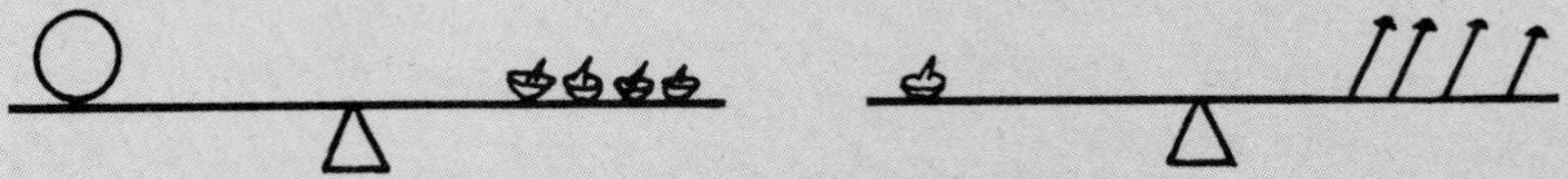

We conclude that 1 dime balances with 16 pins.
We can write: $1d = 4t$, $1t = 4p$, $1d = 16p$.
Write the numeral that expresses the number of indicated objects needed to balance the scale.

$2d$ _____ $\square\,t$ $1d + 2t + 2p$ _____ $3t + \square\,p$

$1d + 16p$ _____ $\square\,t$ $8t + 64p$ _____ $\square\,d$

$1t + 3p$ _____ $\square\,p$ $\square\,d + \square\,t$ _____ $24p$

$3d + 2t$ _____ $\square\,p$ $\square\,d + \square\,t$ _____ $6t$

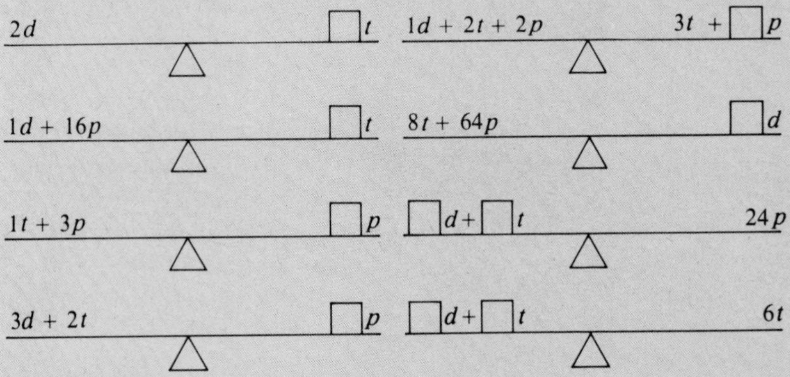

Example 2

If $1a = 2b$, then $2a = 2 \times 2b$, or $4b$.

Complete:

$1a = 3b$	$2c = 5d$	$7e = 10f$
$5a = _b$	$4c = _d$	$21e = _f$
$3b = _a$	$10d = _c$	$40f = _e$
$_b = 4a$	$_d = 10c$	$_f = 70e$

EXERCISES

1. Replace each frame by the symbol =, >, or < to make the sentence true.

   $7 \times 12 \square 4 \times 21$ $15 \times 121 \square 121 \times 15$
   $91 \div 7 \square 55 \div 5$ $96 \div 8 \square 3 \times 4$
   $11 \times 22 \square 6 \times 41$ $174 + 241 \square 241 + 174$

2. Which of these sentences express an inequality?

   $7 \times 9 = 63$ $319 + 11 = 11 + 319$ $8 \times 21 > 160$
   $47 + 36 \neq 100$ $98 \div 7 \neq 13$ $100 - 73 < 31$

3. Give examples of open and closed mathematical sentences.
4. Complete these sentences so that each expresses a true statement.

   $127 + \underline{\qquad} = 135$ $6 \times 23 = \underline{\qquad}$ $95 \div \underline{\qquad} = 19$
   $243 - \underline{\qquad} = 129$ $9 \times \underline{\qquad} = 126$ $\underline{\qquad} \div 7 = 15$

5. Solve:

   $2n + 9 = 31$ $7n - 10 = 74$ $3n - 6 = 9$
   $\frac{n}{7} - 2 = 3$ $5n + 12 = 57$ $9n + 13 = 148$

6. Translate these word phrases into mathematical phrases:
   a. A certain number divided by nine.
   b. Four times the sum of ten and fifteen.
   c. Nine less than three times a certain number.
7. Eleven times what number is 132?
8. Bill has a total of 29 dimes and quarters. If Bill has 5 more dimes than quarters, how many of each does he have?
9. $U = \{1, 2, 3, \cdots, 10\}$.

	Solution set:
$7 + \square = 10$	_______
$n < 6$	_______
$n + 3 < 6$	_______

10. Read this expression: $\{n | n + 2 > 5\}$. The universe is the set of natural numbers.

SOURCES FOR FURTHER READING

Heddens, J. W., *Today's Mathematics,* 3d ed. Chicago: Science Research Associates, Inc., 1974, Unit X.

Johnson, D. A., and W. A. Glenn, *Sets, Sentences, and Operations.* St. Louis: Webster Publishing Company (McGraw-Hill), 1960.

Kessler, B. M., "Sue's Secret Mathematics: One Child's View of Finite Differences," *The Arithmetic Teacher,* May, 1971, pp. 297–300.

National Council of Teachers of Mathematics, *Topics in Mathematics, Twenty-ninth Yearbook.* Washington, D,C.: The Council, 1964, Bklt. 8.

Page, D. A., "Do Something About Estimation!" *Updating Mathematics,* Vol. 2, No. 8. New London, Conn.: Croft Educational Services, April, 1960.

Swart, W. L., "Secret Number Sentence," *The Arithmetic Teacher,* February, 1969, pp. 113–114.

Geometry 8

Geometry is a branch of mathematics. The word literally means "land measurement." Geometric ideas were developed by early man when he observed and compared different shapes in his environment and when he was faced with the problem of measuring land. These ideas were gradually developed and organized into an orderly and logical pattern.

In recent elementary school mathematics programs, more geometry is being introduced than in traditional programs. In primary and intermediate grades, informal geometry is emphasized. In informal geometry, properties of geometric figures are studied by inductive reasoning through measurement and experimentation. Formal geometry, in which deductive reasoning is employed to lead to logical proofs, is dealt with predominantly in the secondary school.

The emphasis on the inductive approach to geometry at the elementary school level does not exclude deductive reasoning, however. When concepts have been formed intuitively by experimentation and direct comparison of concrete materials, the generalizations formed should be used deductively in problem solving. The pupils will become better prepared for deductive reasoning as they accumulate more concepts and as the concepts become more refined.

Opinions concerning the scope and sequence of geometry topics in the elementary school differ. However, there seems to be an agreement that the geometry program should be kept informal and allow for much exploration on the part of the pupil.[1]

The content and activities that follow are intended to be one source from which the teacher can gather ideas to be used in constructing a geometry program in the sequence that he or she prefers or that is prescribed by the local school curriculum.

Framed illustrations with simple language—dealing only with basic concepts—accompany several presentations in order to assist the teacher in presenting the topics in a meaningful way and in preparing bulletin boards and overhead transparencies. It will not be difficult to construct additional questions and activities as needed.

POINTS Sets of points have been called the building blocks of geometry. A line is a set of points, a plane is a set of points, and space is the set of all points. A point, a line, and a plane are subsets of geometric space.

A *geometric point* is an idea. It does not exist in a physical sense; it has no dimension. A point is represented on paper by a dot and named by a capital letter. In Figure 8.1, four points have been named.

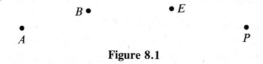

Figure 8.1

When children understand that a point has no dimension, they will realize that the smallest dot is the best representation of a point.

You cannot see a point.

A dot represents a point.

The smallest dot is the best representation of a point.

1. L. G. Callahan and V. J. Glennon, *Elementary School Mathematics: A Guide to Current Research,* 4th ed. (Washington, D.C.: Association for Supervision and Curriculum Development, 1975), p. 40.

LINES AND CURVES

A *line* is also a mathematical idea, and is thought of as an infinite set of points. It has one dimension: length. In geometry the term "line" is understood to mean a straight line. The representation of a line on paper can be made with a straightedge and a pencil. Figure 8.2 shows symbols that represent lines. The arrowheads indicate that a line extends in opposite directions and that it has no end.

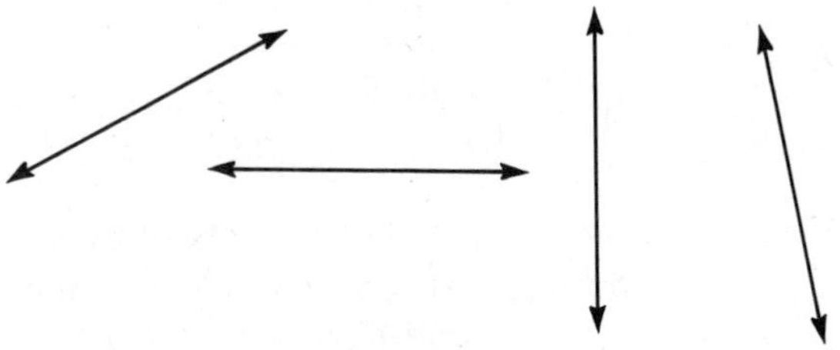

Figure 8.2

The direction and location of a line are determined by two different points on the line. Figure 8.3 depicts a line determined by the points *A* and *B*. This line is named by the symbol $\overleftrightarrow{AB}$. $\overleftrightarrow{AB}$ is read "line *AB*." It should

A
B

Figure 8.3

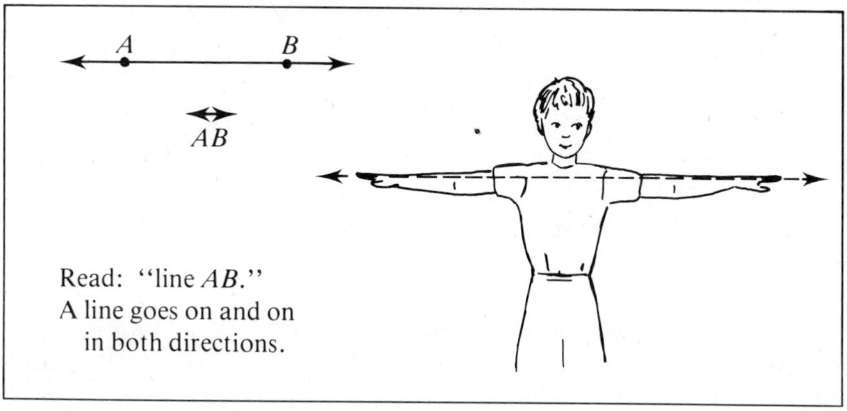
A
B
$\overleftrightarrow{AB}$
Read: "line *AB*."
A line goes on and on in both directions.

be realized that the symbol $\overleftrightarrow{AB}$ indicates that the line under consideration passes through points A and B and that it extends indefinitely.

Points that are in the same line are called *collinear* points. In Figure 8.4, points A, B, and C are collinear. Point B is said to be *between* point A and point C. Point D is not contained in $\overleftrightarrow{AB}$ and therefore is not between point A and point B.

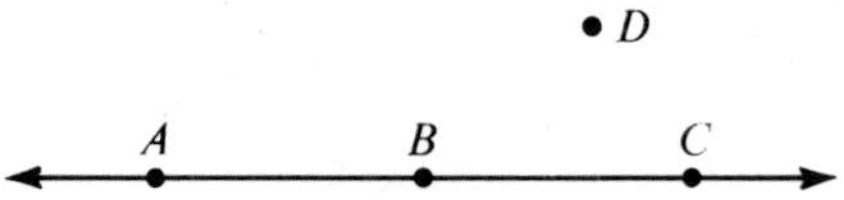

Figure 8.4

A line segment is a set of points whose members are two given points and all points on the line between these two points. The line segment from point A to point B inclusive in Figure 8.5 is identified by the symbol $\overline{AB}$. We read $\overline{AB}$ as "line segment AB." A line segment is finite in length. The *endpoints* of the line segment are points A and B.

Figure 8.5

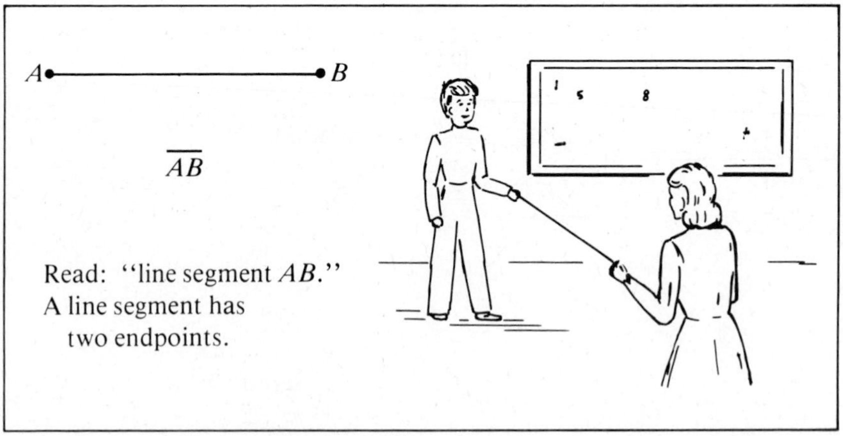

Line segments that have the same length are *congruent* segments. The symbol $\cong$ is used to express the idea of congruence. $\overline{AB} \cong \overline{CD}$ is read "line segment AB is congruent to line segment CD."

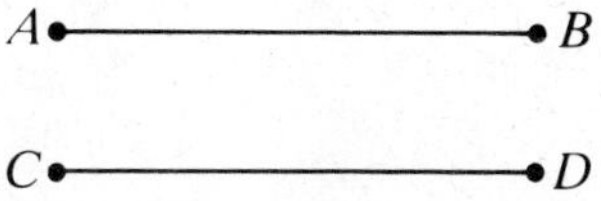

$\overline{AB} \cong \overline{CD}$

Read: "line segment *AB* is congruent to line segment *CD*."
Congruent line segments have the same length.

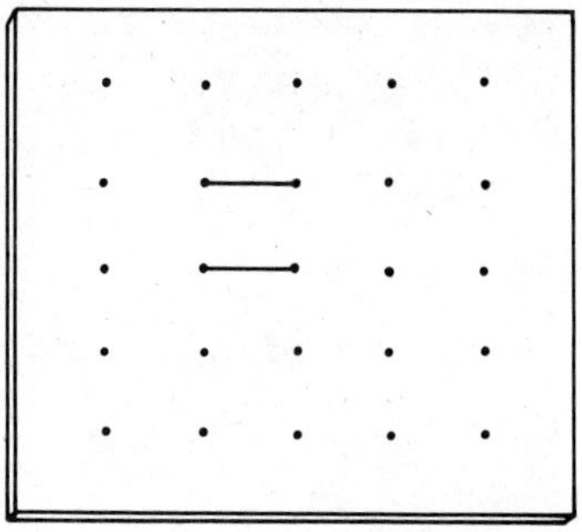

A set of points containing the point of origin and all the points on the line extending in one direction from that point is called a *ray*. Figure 8.6(a) represents a ray. A ray has a point of *origin* and goes on and on in one direction as indicated by the arrowhead. In Figure 8.6(b) two rays are

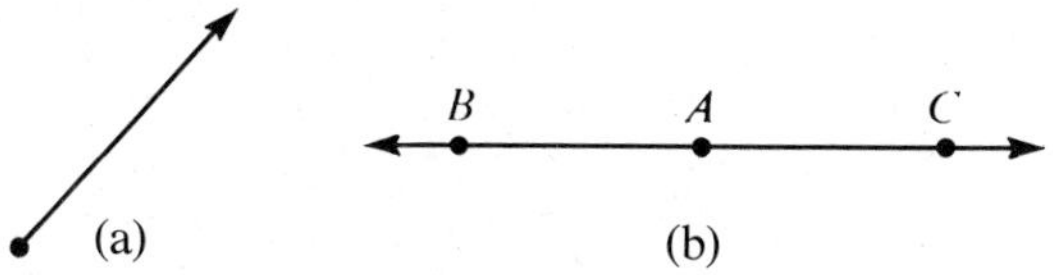

Figure 8.6

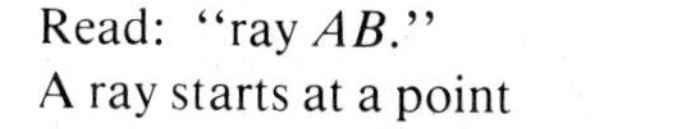

$\overrightarrow{AB}$

Read: "ray *AB*."
A ray starts at a point and goes on and on in one direction.

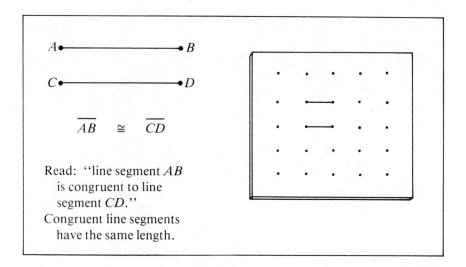

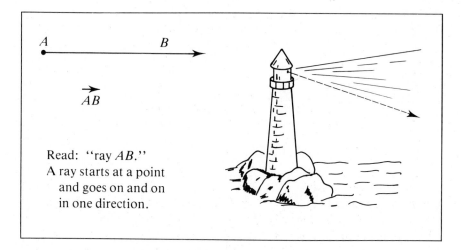

Symbols, symbols, all around.

pictured: ray *AB* and ray *AC* ($\overrightarrow{AB}$ and $\overrightarrow{AC}$). Point A is the origin of both rays; thus the intersection of $\overrightarrow{AB}$ and $\overrightarrow{AC}$ is point *A*.

A *curve* is thought of as a continuous set of points passed through in going from one point to another. A curve, like a point, is an idea and cannot be seen. Curves can be represented on paper. In Figure 8.7 several curves are illustrated.

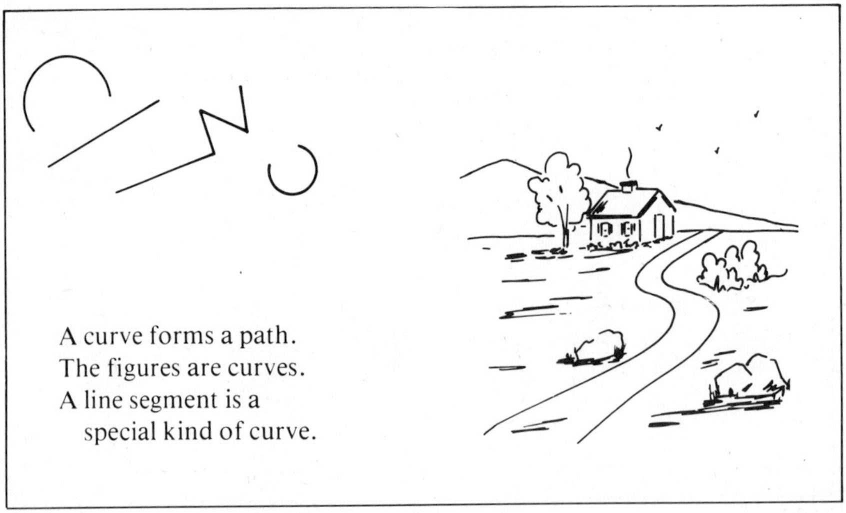

A curve forms a path.
The figures are curves.
A line segment is a
special kind of curve.

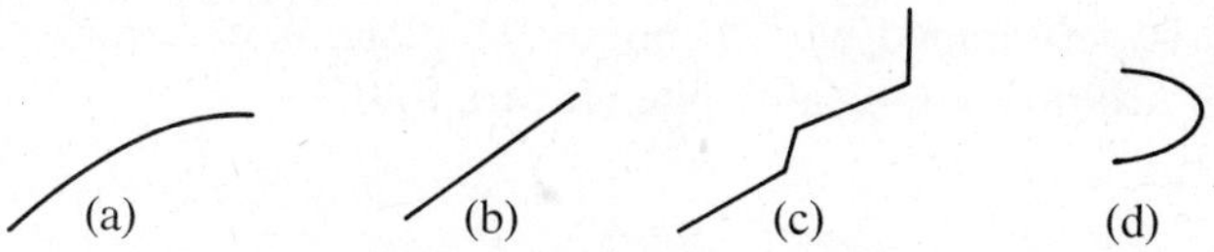

Figure 8.7

It should be noted that Figure 8.7(b), which is an illustration of a line segment, also represents a curve. A line segment is said to be a special kind of curve. Figure 8.7(c) represents a broken-line curve.

PLANES

A *plane* is another mathematical idea. It is a set of points that can be thought of as a flat surface, such as an extended table top. A plane contains an infinite set of points and an infinite set of lines, and is unlimited in extent, as indicated by the arrows in Figure 8.8.

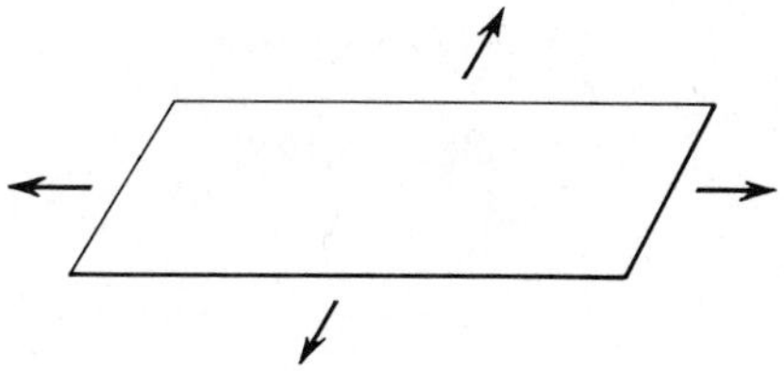

Figure 8.8

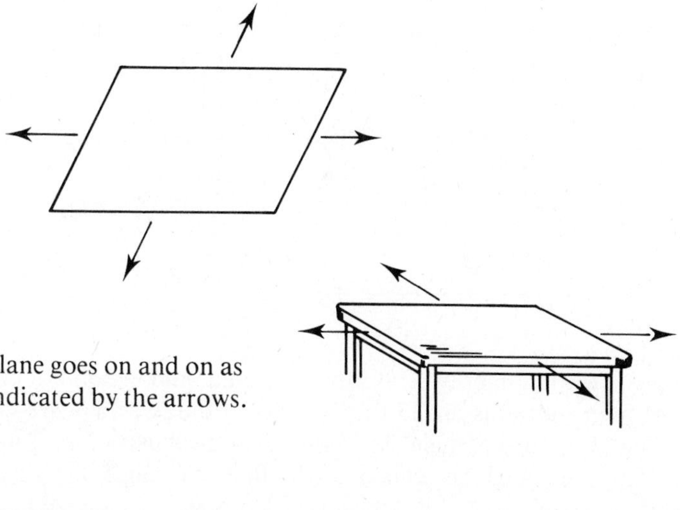

A plane goes on and on as indicated by the arrows.

A line is determined by two points. A plane is determined by three points that are not in the same line (Figure 8.9).

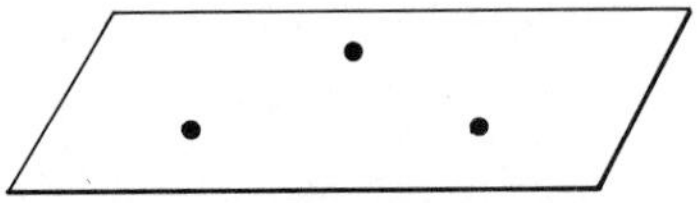

Figure 8.9

Lines that are in the same plane but have no point in common are called *parallel lines*. An illustration of two parallel lines is shown in Figure 8.10. Since parallel lines have no point in common, the intersection of such lines is the empty set.

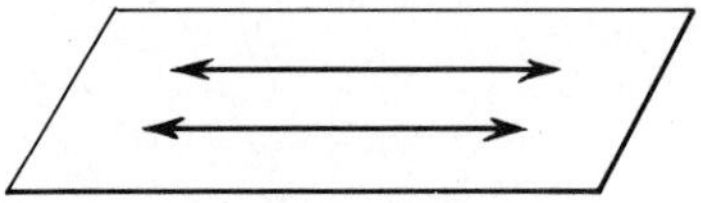

Figure 8.10

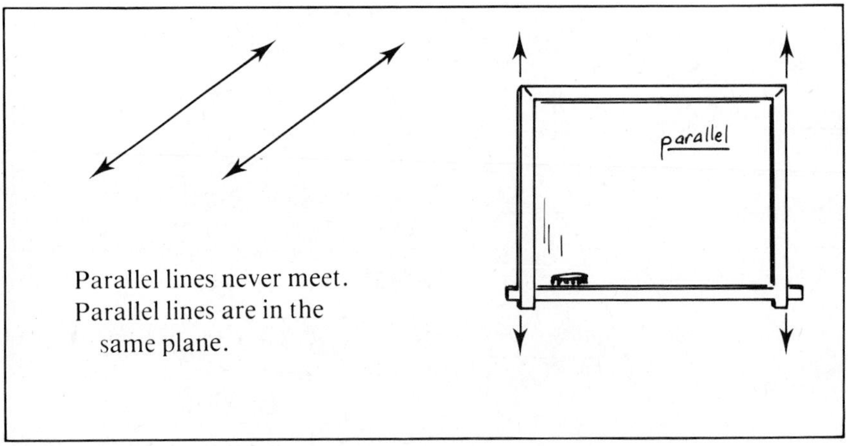
Parallel lines never meet.
Parallel lines are in the same plane.
parallel

ANGLES An angle is the union of two rays that have a common point of origin. The point of intersection is called the *vertex* and the two rays are commonly called the *sides* of the angle. In Figure 8.11 an illustration of an angle is presented. This angle is called angle *BAC* or angle *CAB* ($\angle BAC$ or

∠CAB). The letter A names the vertex of the angle. The angle may also be called angle A(∠A).

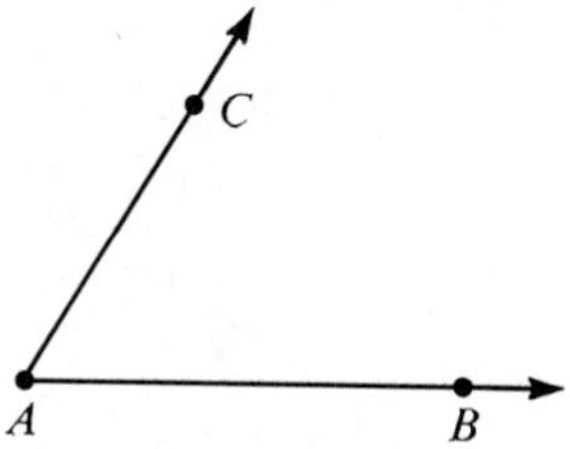

Figure 8.11

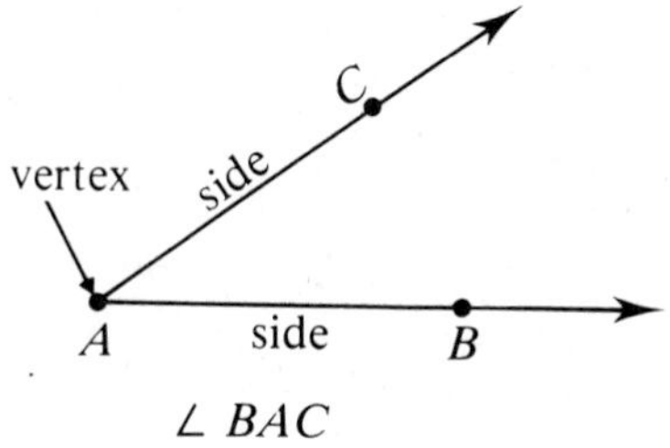

Read: "angle BAC."
An angle has two rays
or sides and a *vertex*.

An angle has an *interior,* or inside, and an *exterior,* or outside. In Figure 8.12, the interior of ∠CAB has been shaded.

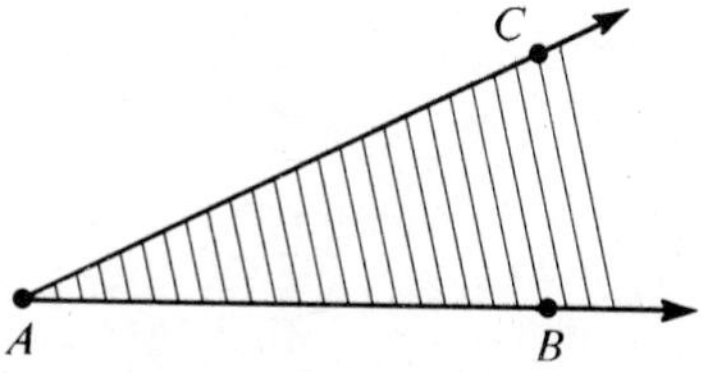

Figure 8.12

Figure 8.13 illustrates two angles in the same plane that have a common vertex A and a common side $\overrightarrow{AC}$ between them. $\angle BAC$ and $\angle CAD$ are called *adjacent angles*.

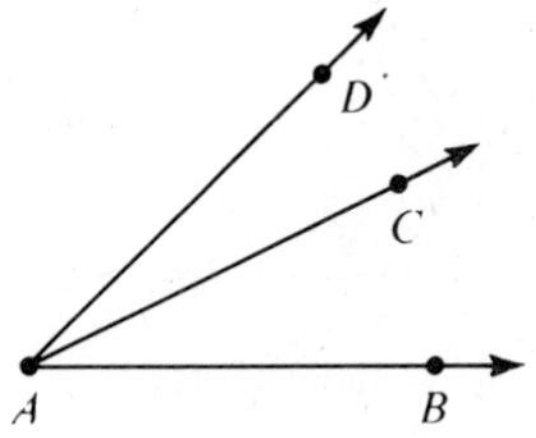

Figure 8.13

If $\overrightarrow{AC}$ in Figure 8.14 were to rotate from the original position $\overrightarrow{AB}$ in the direction of the arrow until it met $\overrightarrow{AB}$, it would have made a complete rotation. For measurement purposes, a complete rotation is divided into 360 equal parts, each part of which is called a *unit angle*. The measure of a unit angle in degrees is 1, and the measure of a complete rotation in degrees is 360. The symbol for degree is °.

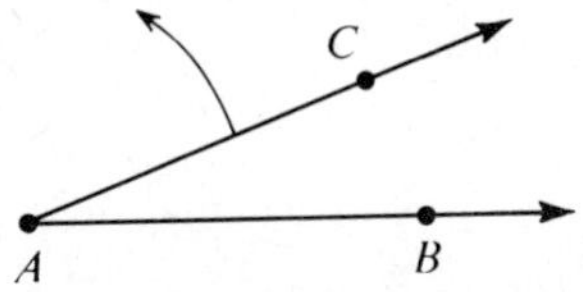

Figure 8.14

Figure 8.15 represents two angles in the same plane that have one common side, a common vertex, and sides (AB and AD) that form a line. The sum of the measures of $\angle DAC$ and $\angle BAC$ is 180°, and such angles are

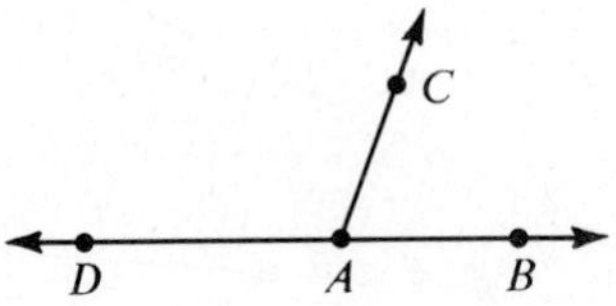

Figure 8.15

called *supplementary angles*. $\angle DAC$ is the supplement of $\angle BAC$ and $\angle BAC$ is the supplement of $\angle DAC$.

$\angle DAC$ and $\angle BAC$ in Figure 8.16 have the same measure, and angles that have the same measure are called *congruent angles*. In this example, each angle has a measure of 90°. An angle that has a measure of 90° is called a *right angle*.

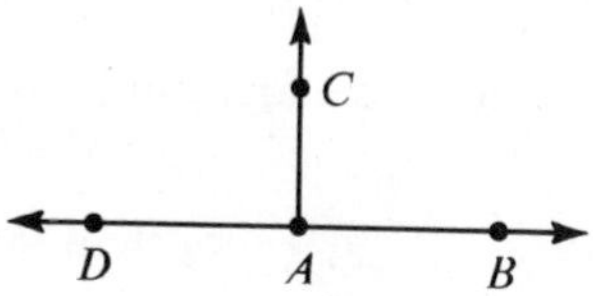

Figure 8.16

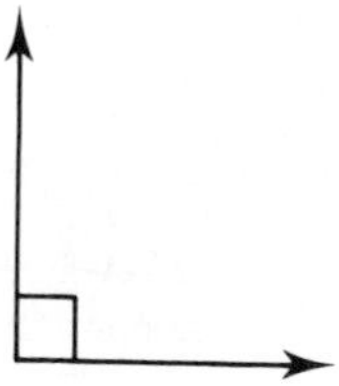

The figure shows a square corner.
The box fits in a square corner.
The square corner is a right angle.
The symbol ┐ tells that the angle is a right angle.

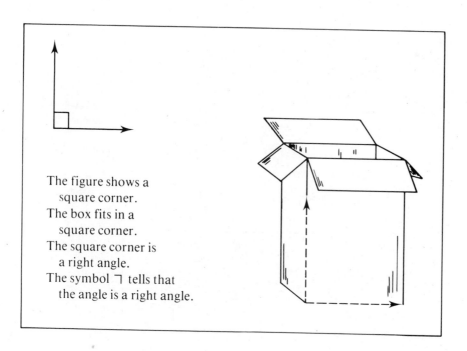

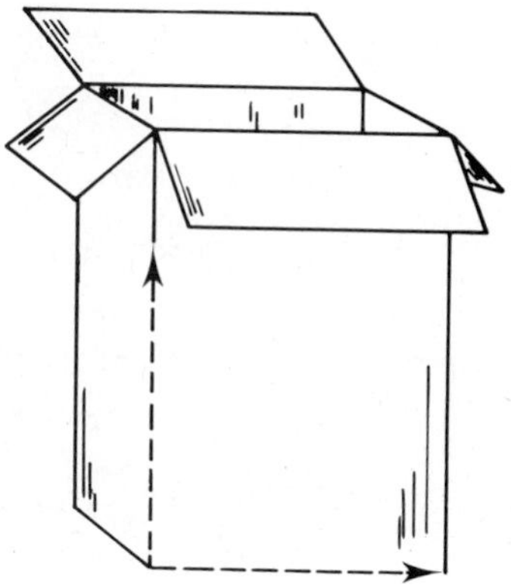

Two lines that intersect at right angles are *perpendicular lines*. In Figure 8.17, $\overleftrightarrow{AB}$ and $\overleftrightarrow{CD}$ are perpendicular lines.

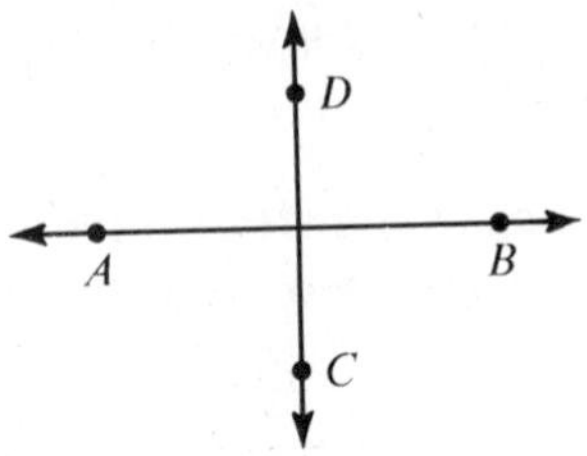

Figure 8.17

Examples of various angles are shown in Figure 8.18; their measures are given below.

An *acute angle* is greater than 0° and less than 90°.
A *right angle* is 90°.
An *obtuse angle* is greater than 90° and less than 180°.
A *straight angle* is 180°.

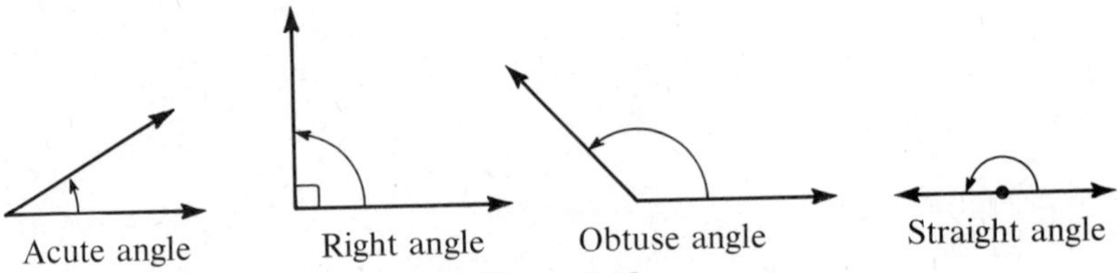

Figure 8.18

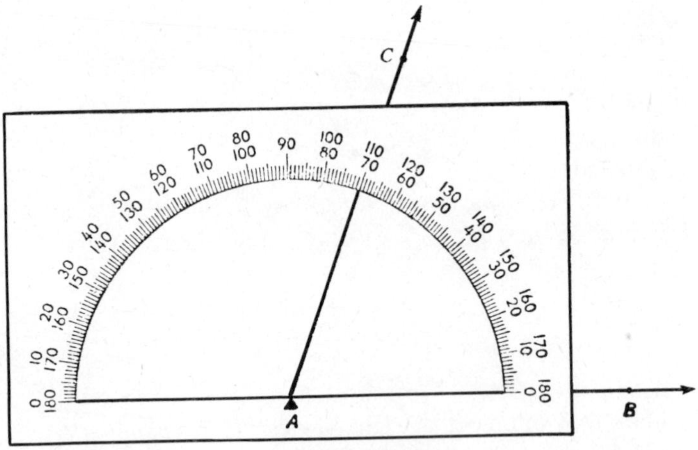

Figure 8.19

The measure of an angle may be found by using a protractor. A protractor is pictured in Figure 8.19.

SIMPLE CLOSED CURVES

A *simple closed curve* is a curve that returns to the point where it started without crossing itself. Figure 8.20 represents illustrations of some simple closed curves.

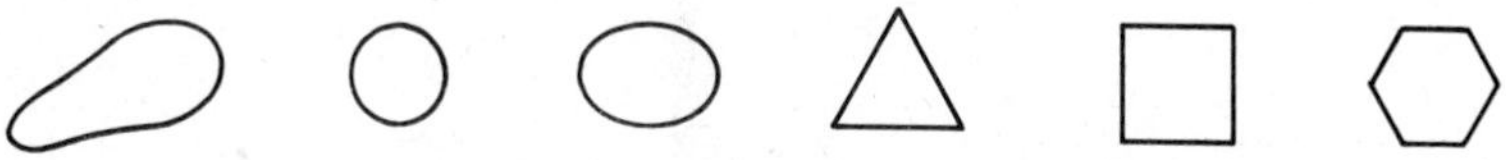

Figure 8.20

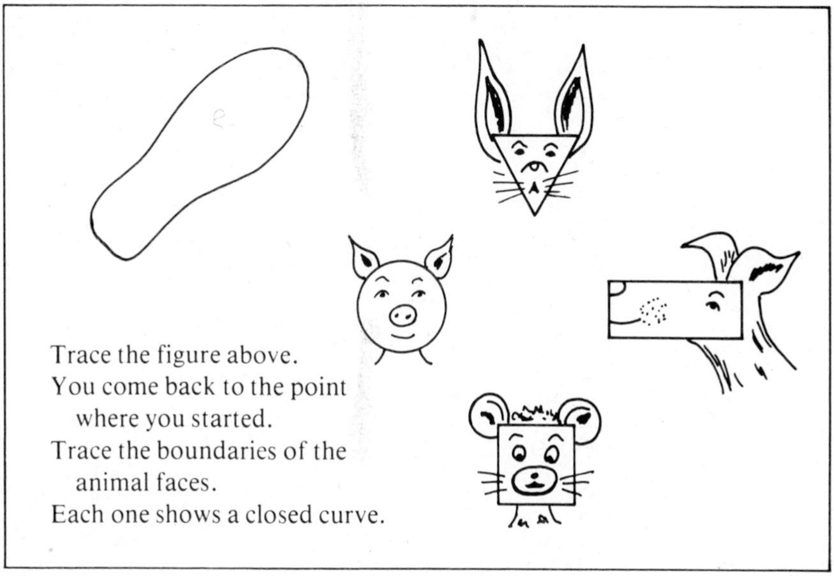

Trace the figure above.
You come back to the point where you started.
Trace the boundaries of the animal faces.
Each one shows a closed curve.

A simple closed curve divides a plane into the *interior* and the *exterior* of the simple closed curve. The simple closed curve itself is the boundary of these regions (Figure 8.21).

Figure 8.21

Polygons A *polygon* is a simple closed curve that is the union of line segments which are called sides. All the plane figures in Figure 8.22 are illustrations of polygons.

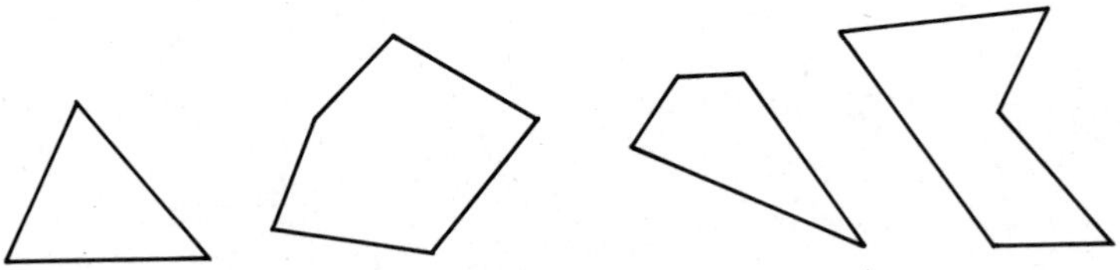

Figure 8.22

Each figure is a closed curve.
Each figure has more than two sides
and more than two angles.
Each figure is a polygon.
Poly means many.
Polygon means many angles.
Find the number of sides of
the polygons in the picture.

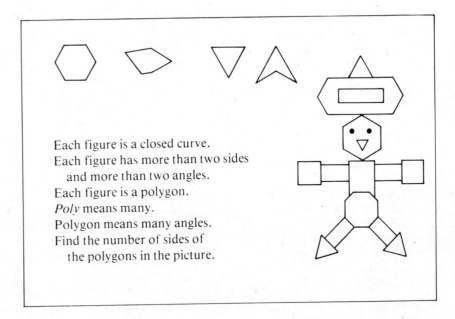

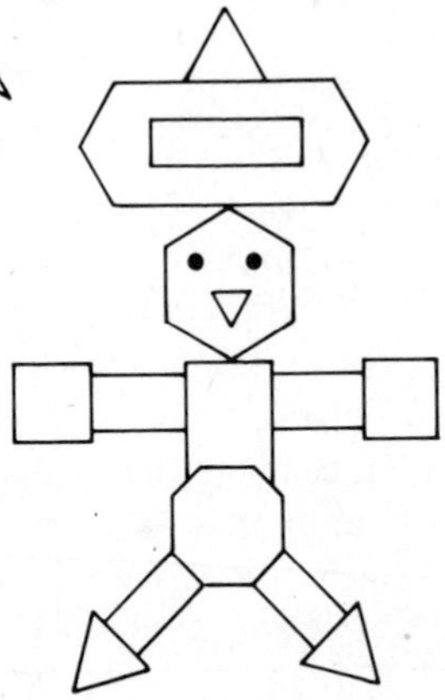

There are several kinds of polygons. A *triangle* is a three-sided polygon. A *quadrilateral* has four sides. A *pentagon* has five sides. A *hexagon* has six sides. An *octagon* has eight sides.

Two vertices that have a common side between them are called *adjacent* vertices. A line segment that connects two nonadjacent vertices of a

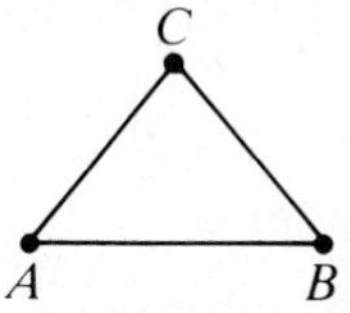

$\triangle$ *ABC*

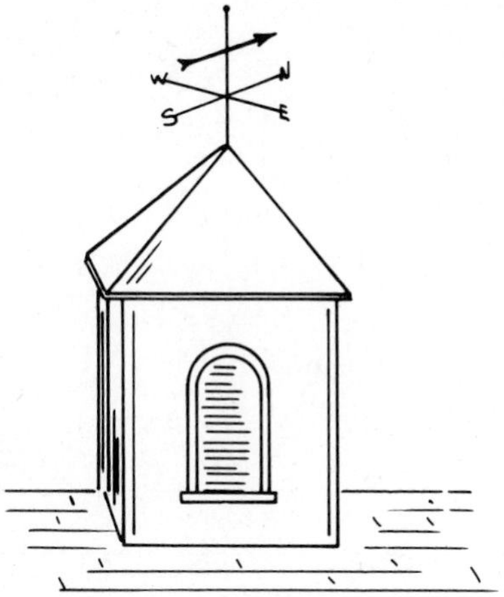

Read: "triangle *ABC*."
The polygon has 3 sides
and 3 angles.
It is a triangle.
Tri means three.
Find triangles in the picture.

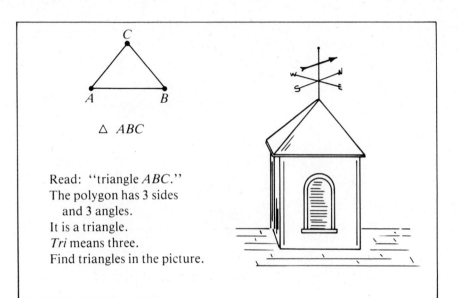

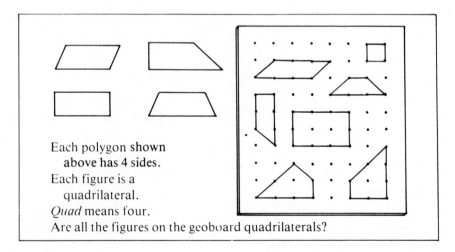

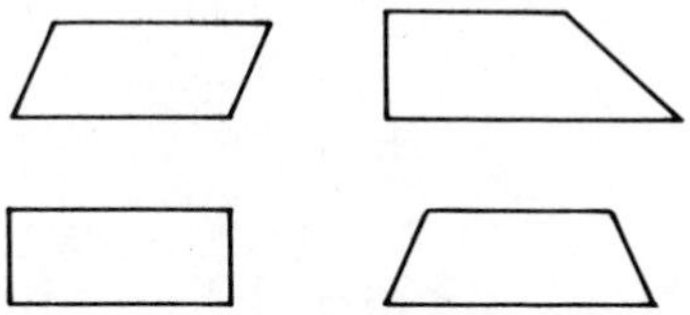

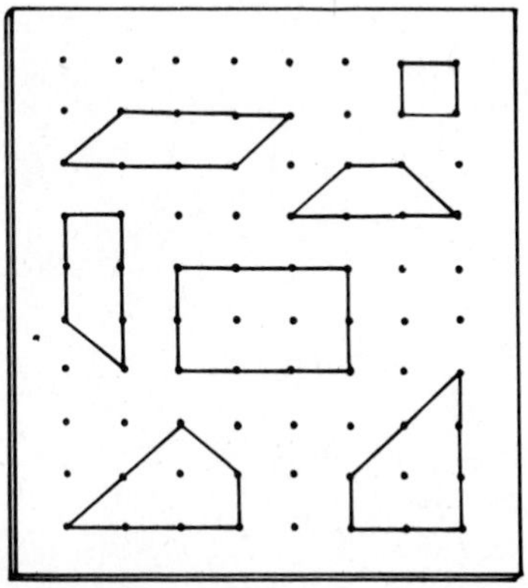

Each polygon shown
above has 4 sides.
Each figure is a
quadrilateral.
Quad means four.
Are all the figures on the geoboard quadrilaterals?

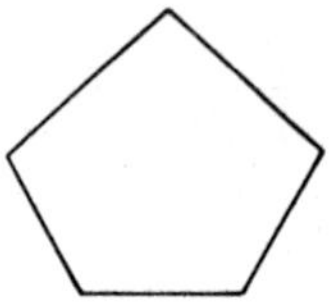

The polygon has 5
sides.
It is a pentagon.
Pent means five.

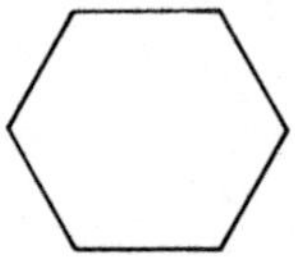

The polygon has 6
sides.
It is a hexagon.
Hex means six.

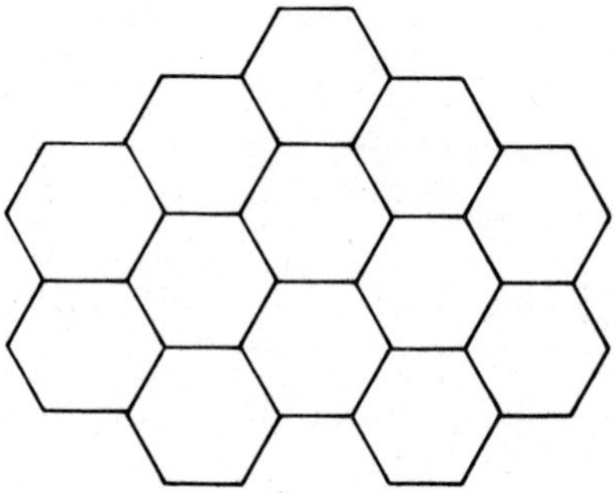

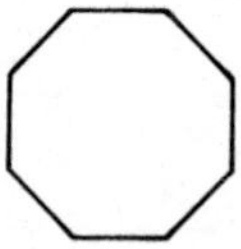

The polygon has 8
sides.
It is an octagon.
Oct means eight.

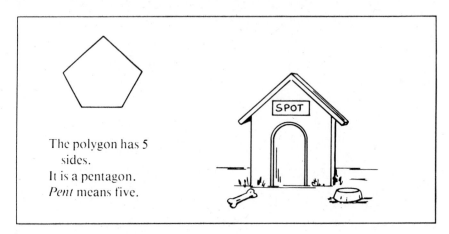

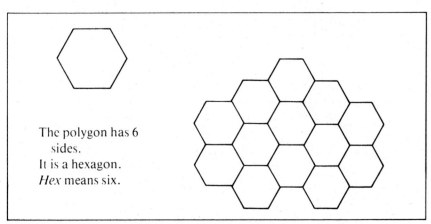

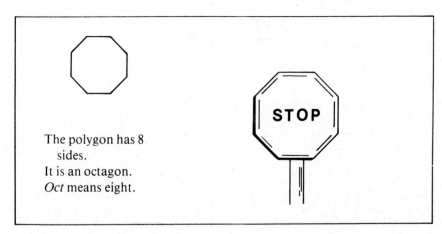

polygon is called a *diagonal* of the polygon. In Figure 8.23, diagonal *EB* connects the two nonadjacent vertices *E* and *B*. The plane figure represented in Figure 8.23 has five vertices (*A*, *B*, *C*, *D*, and *E*) and five sides (*AB*, *BC*, *CD*, *DE*, and *EA*). The figure is called pentagon *ABCDE*.

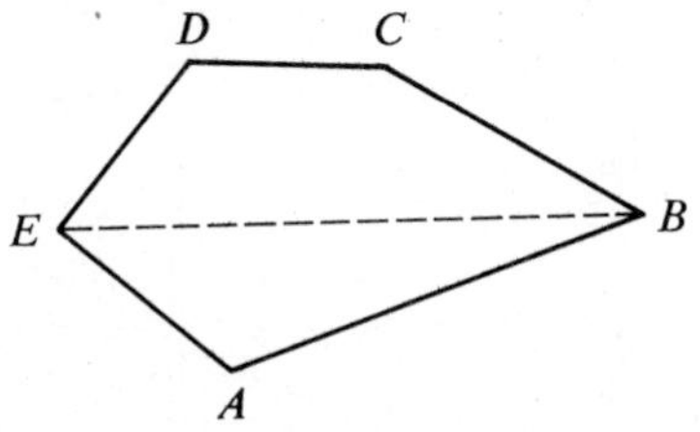

Figure 8.23

There are several special kinds of quadrilaterals. All the illustrations in Figure 8.24 represent quadrilaterals.

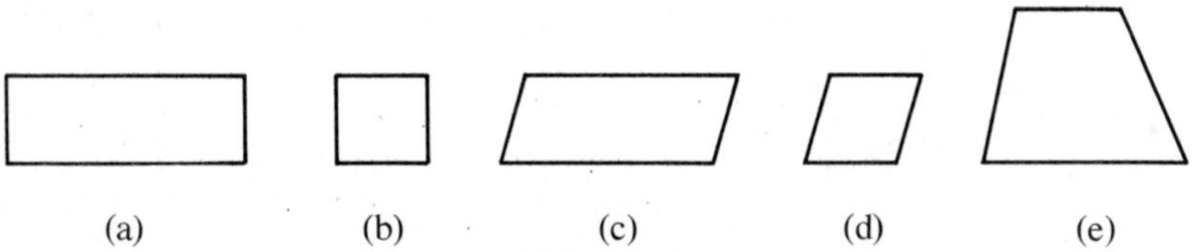

Figure 8.24

In Figure 8.24(a), all four angles are right angles. This quadrilateral is called a *rectangle*.

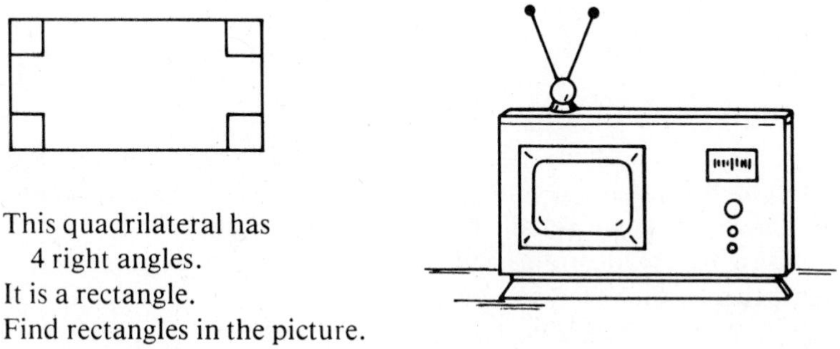

This quadrilateral has
4 right angles.
It is a rectangle.
Find rectangles in the picture.

A special type of rectangle is one with four congruent sides as in Figure 8.24(b). This type is called a *square*.

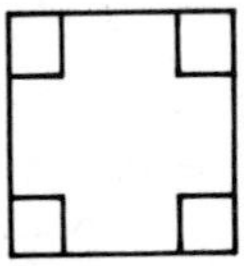

The rectangle has 4
congruent sides.
It is a square.
Find squares in the picture.

Figure 8.24(c) is an illustration of a *parallelogram*. In a parallelogram the pairs of opposite sides are parallel. Notice that a rectangle is a parallelogram. If the four sides of a parallelogram are congruent, the figure is called a *rhombus*. Thus a square is a rhombus, but not all rhombuses are squares. A rhombus that is not a square is shown in Figure 8.24(d).

Figure 8.24(e) represents a *trapezoid*. A trapezoid is a quadrilateral in which one pair of opposite sides is parallel and the other pair is not parallel.

Figure 8.25 represents a *triangle*. The symbol for a triangle is △. A triangle has three vertices and three sides.

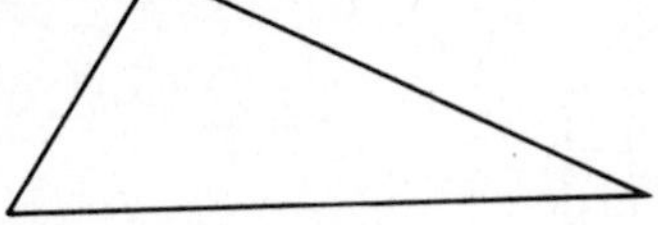

Figure 8.25

Figure 8.26(a) is an illustration of a triangle with three congruent sides. Such a triangle is called an *equilateral triangle*.

Figure 8.26(b) illustrates an *isosceles triangle*. In an isosceles triangle at least two of the sides are congruent.

A triangle of which no two sides are congruent is called a *scalene triangle*. Such a triangle is represented in Figure 8.26(c).

Figure 8.26(d) shows a *right triangle*. In a right triangle one of the angles is a right angle.

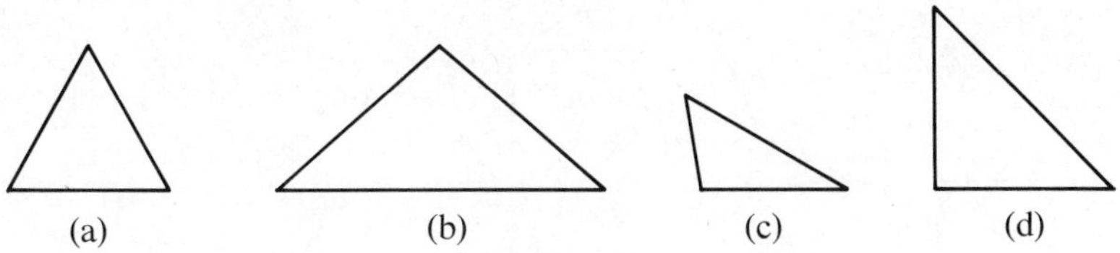

Figure 8.26

Congruent triangles have the same size and the same shape. The fact that the triangles illustrated in Figure 8.27 are congruent is indicated as follows: $\triangle BAC \cong \triangle EDF$.

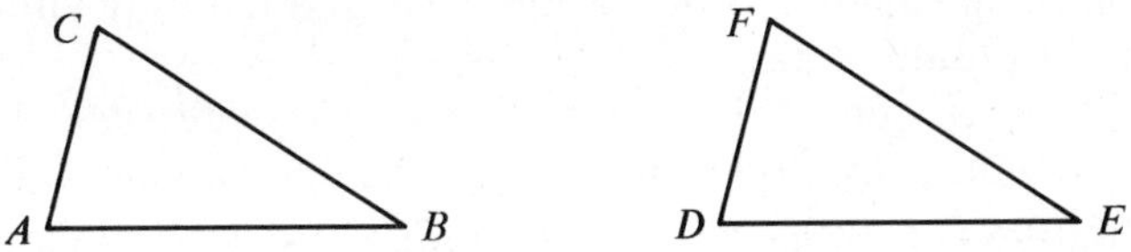

Figure 8.27

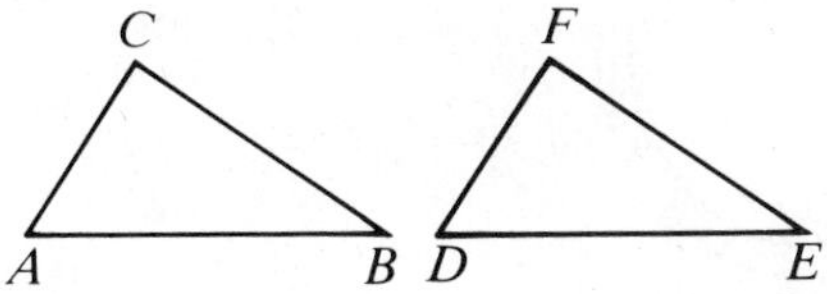

$\triangle\ ABC \cong \triangle\ DEF$

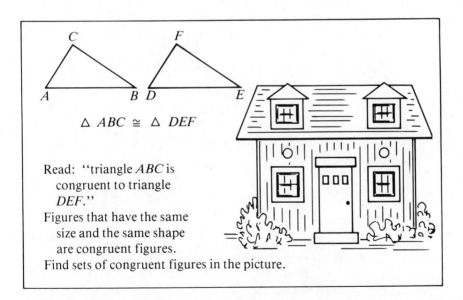

Read: "triangle *ABC* is congruent to triangle *DEF*."
Figures that have the same size and the same shape are congruent figures.
Find sets of congruent figures in the picture.

Circles

A *circle* is a simple closed curve in a given plane, where all the points of the curve are the same distance from a given point called the *center*.

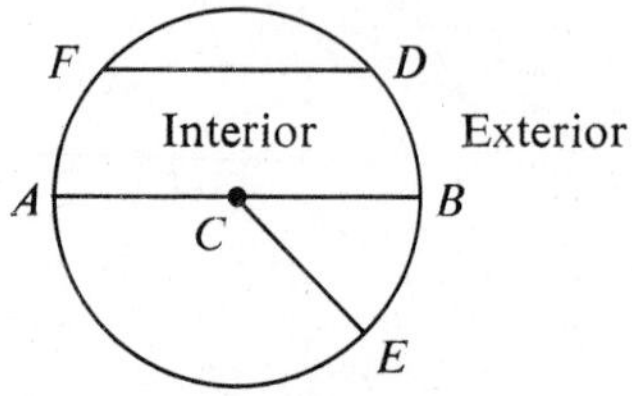

Figure 8.28

Figure 8.28 is an illustration of a circle. Point C is called the center of the circle and the circle is called circle C. A line segment that has both endpoints on the circle is called a *chord* of the circle. $\overline{FD}$ is a chord of circle C. A chord that passes through the center of the circle is a *diameter* of the circle. $\overline{AB}$ is a diamenter of circle C. If one endpoint of a line segment is the center of the circle and the other endpoint is on the circle, the segment is called a *radius* of the circle. $\overline{CE}$ is a radius of circle C. $\overline{CA}$ and $\overline{CB}$ are also radii of circle C.

The distance around a circle is called its *circumference*. In Figure 8.29, The circumference of the circle is divided into two parts. Each part is called an *arc*.

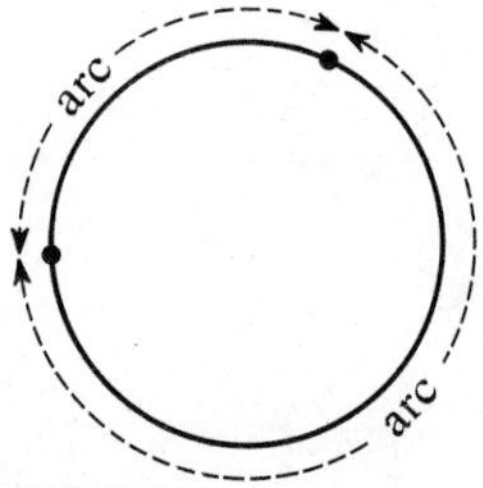

Figure 8.29

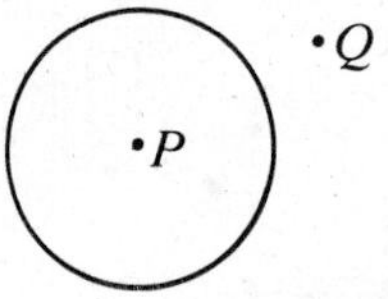

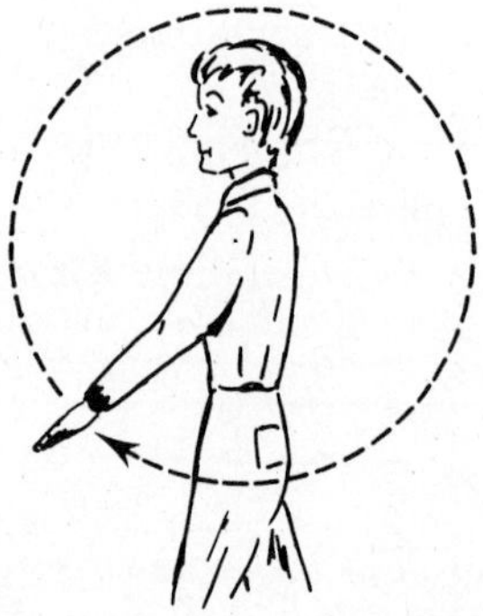

A circle is round.
Point P is in the *interior* (inside).
Point Q is in the *exterior* (outside).

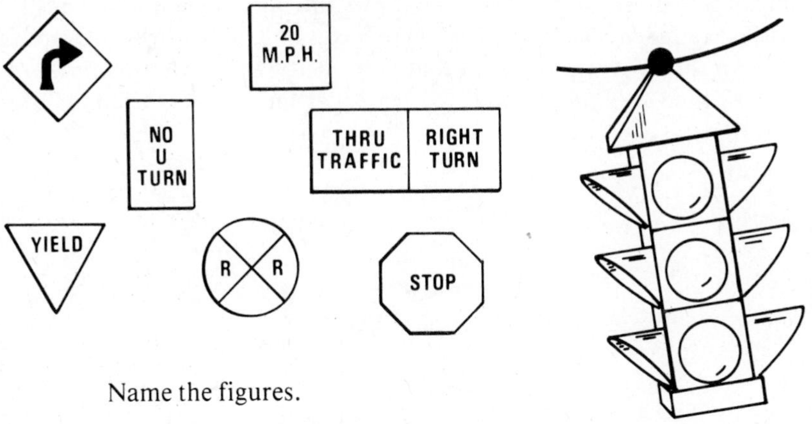

Name the figures.

SPACE FIGURES

All points of a plane figure are in the same plane. When all points of a figure are not in the same plane, the figure is called a *space figure*.

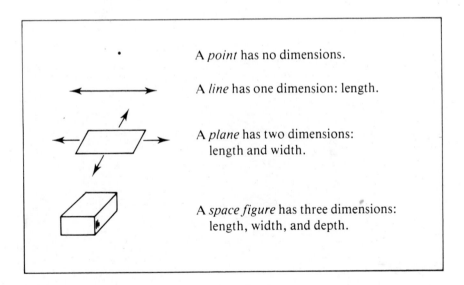

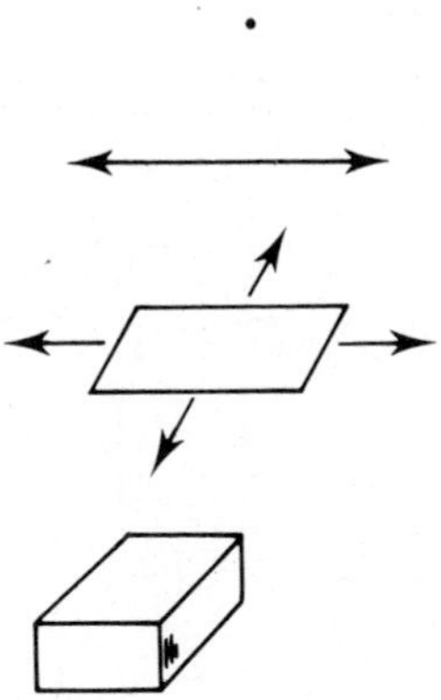

A *point* has no dimensions.

A *line* has one dimension: length.

A *plane* has two dimensions: length and width.

A *space figure* has three dimensions: length, width, and depth.

A space figure is formed by the set of points on the surface of the figure; advanced pupils should realize the difference between the inside of the figure and the figure itself.

Figure 8.30 represents a space figure called a *prism*. The bases are triangular, and the figure is a *triangular prism*. A triangular prism has five surfaces, called *faces*, two of which are *bases* and three of which are *sides* or *lateral faces*. A line segment that is formed by the intersection of two faces is called an *edge*. A point where edges intersect is called a *vertex*.

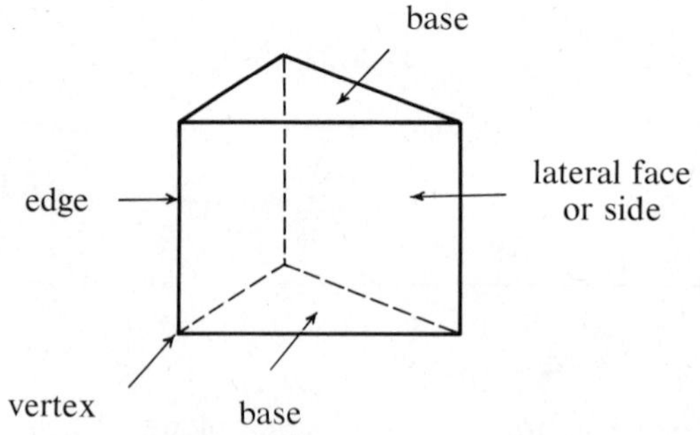

Figure 8.30

Figure 8.31 represents figures with rectangular bases. Figure 8.31(a) pictures a rectangular prism. When the faces are squares, as in Figure 8.31(b), the figure is called a *cube*.

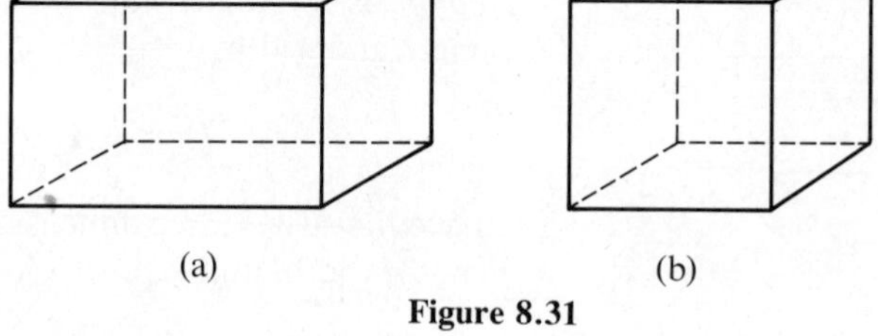

Figure 8.31

Other space figures are pictured in Figure 8.32: a *triangular pyramid* (a), a *rectangular pyramid* (b), a *cylinder* (c), a *cone* (d), and a *sphere* (e).

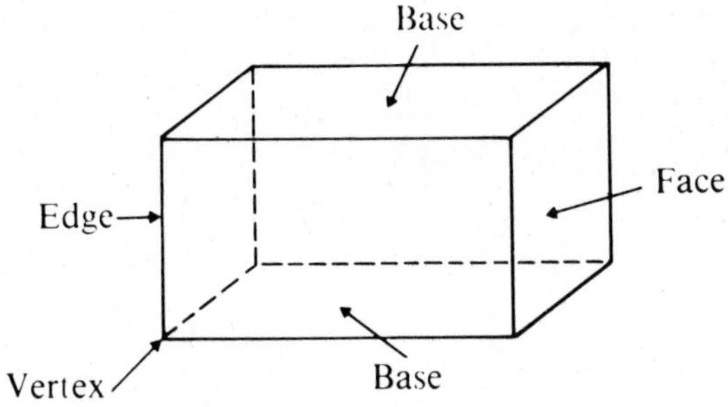

The figure shows a
rectangular prism.
There are 12 edges,
8 vertices, and
6 faces.
Two of the faces are bases.
Point at all edges, vertices, and faces.

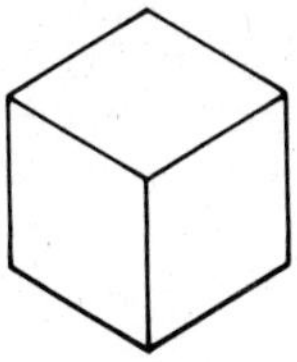

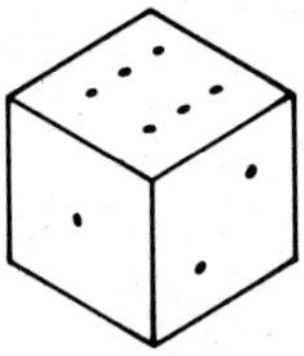

The six faces of the
prism are squares.
The figure is a cube.

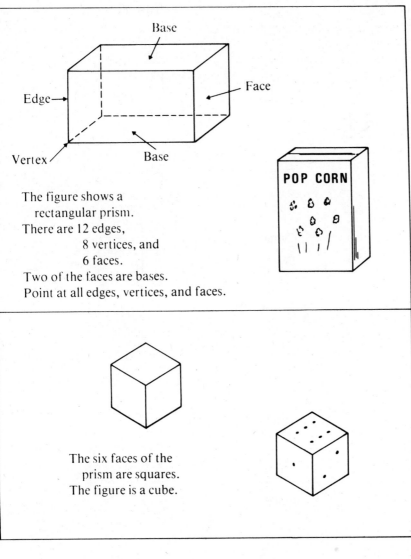

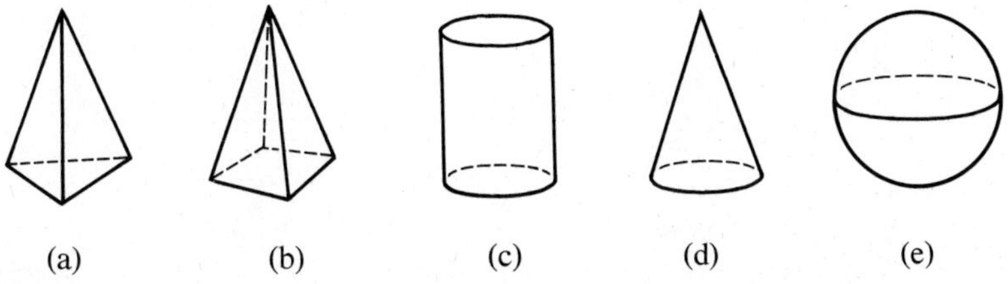

(a) (b) (c) (d) (e)

Figure 8.32

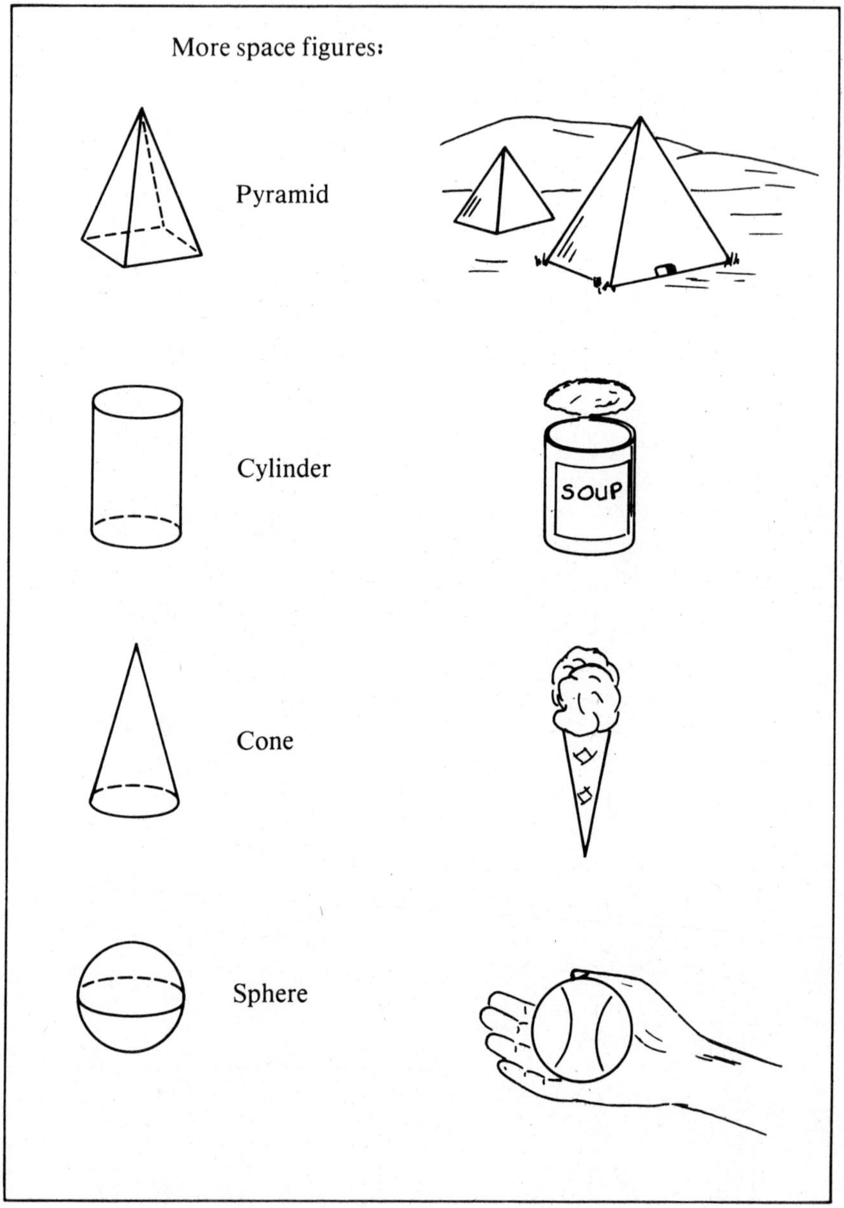
More space figures:
Pyramid
Cylinder
SOUP
Cone
Sphere

GEOMETRIC CONSTRUCTIONS

Drawing a circle with a given diameter

To draw a circle with a diameter of 6 centimeters: Set the compass so that the distance between the needle point and the pencil point is 3 centimeters. The circle that is then drawn has a radius of 3 centimeters and a diameter of 6 centimeters.

Bisecting a line segment

To bisect line segment *AB*:

1. Draw arc *a* with *A* as center. The radius must be greater than half the length of the line segment.

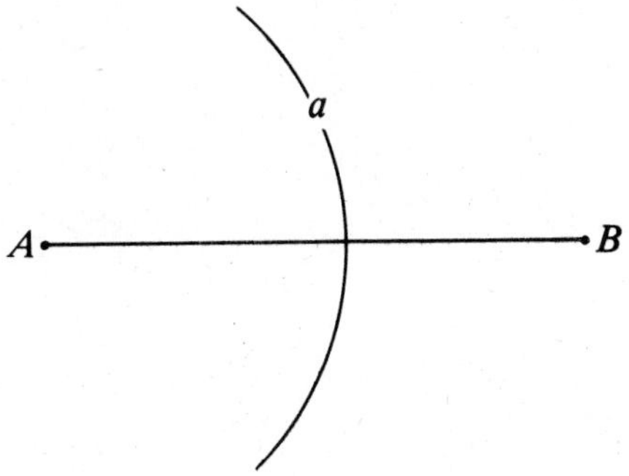

2. Draw arc *b* with *B* as center and a radius congruent to the radius of arc *a*.

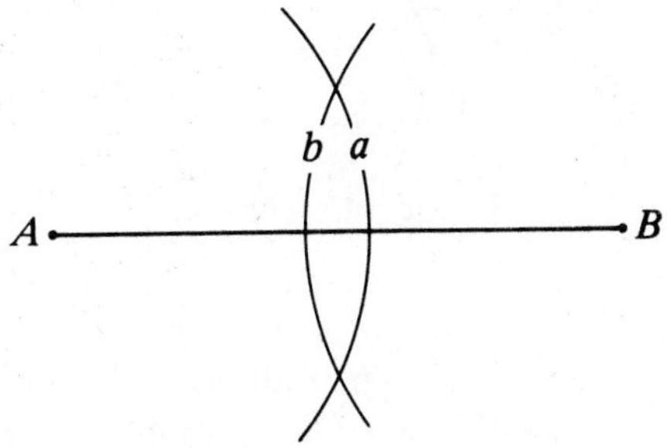

3. Draw line c as shown to bisect line segment AB.

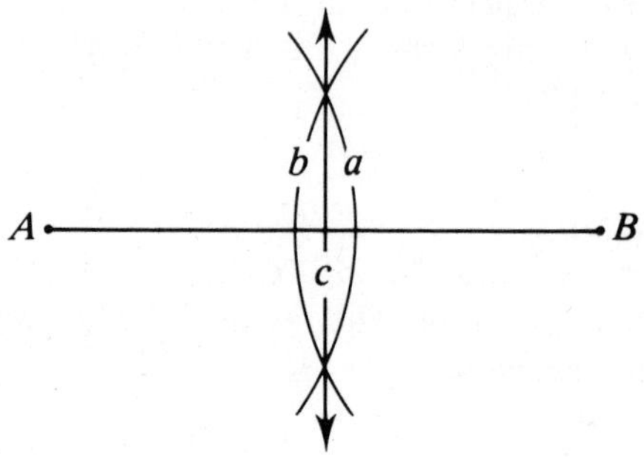

Bisecting an angle To bisect angle A:

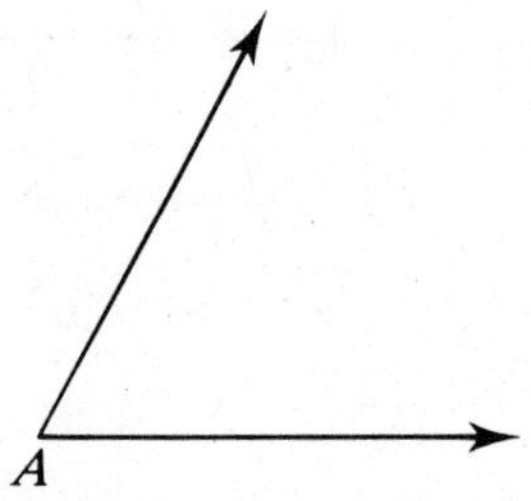

1. Draw arc a with a radius of arbitrary length and with A as center. Label the points of intersection B and C.

   $AB = AC$

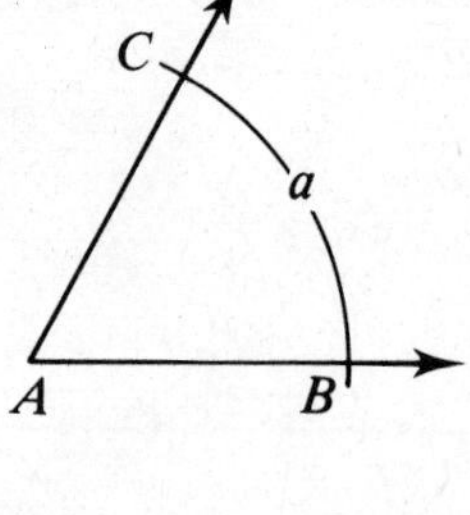

2. Draw arcs b and c with the same radius and with C and B as centers. The length of the radius is arbitrary but must be long enough for the arcs to intersect.

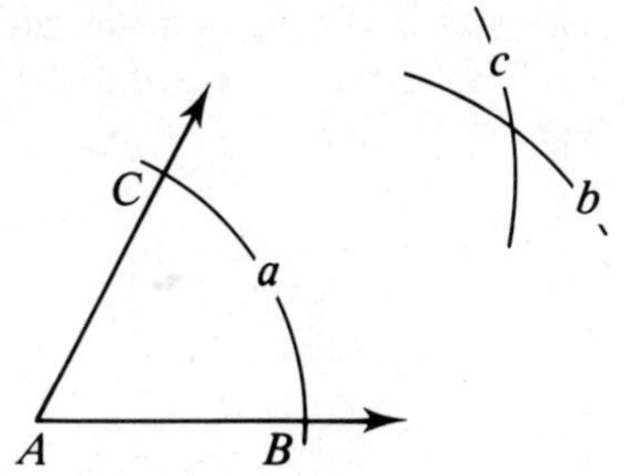

3. Draw a ray from A through the intersection of arcs b and c to bisect the angle.

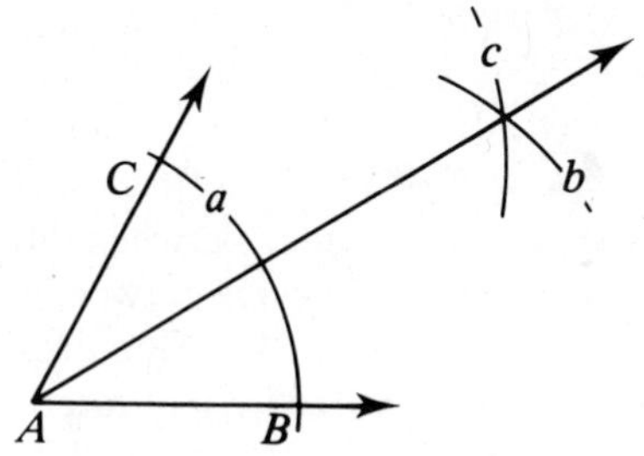

Constructing an angle congruent to a given angle

To construct an angle congruent to angle A:

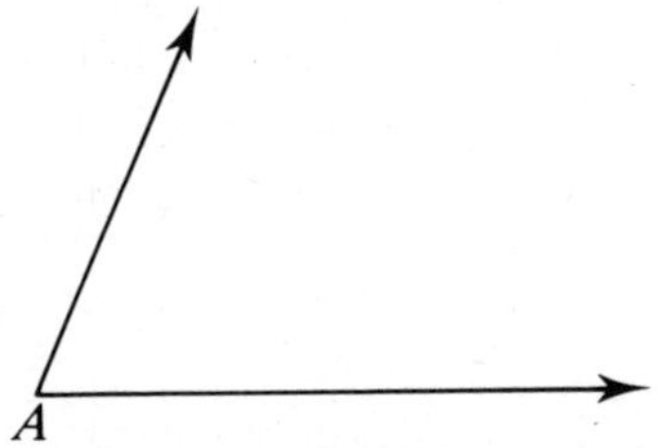

1. Draw arc a with a radius of arbitrary length and with A as center.

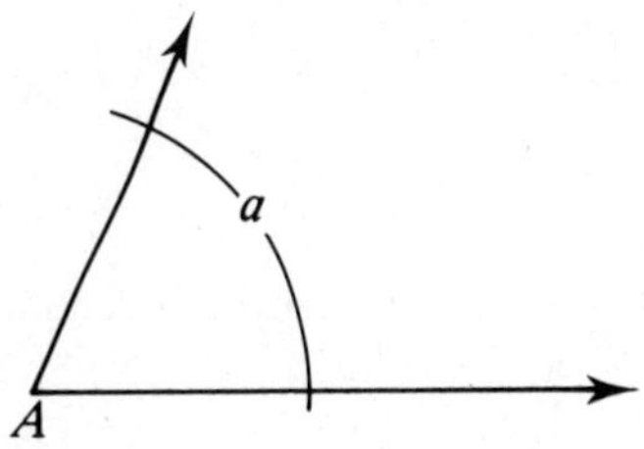

2. Draw a ray. Label its orgin B. Then with B as center, draw arc b with a radius congruent to the radius of arc a. Label the point of intersection of the ray and arc b C.

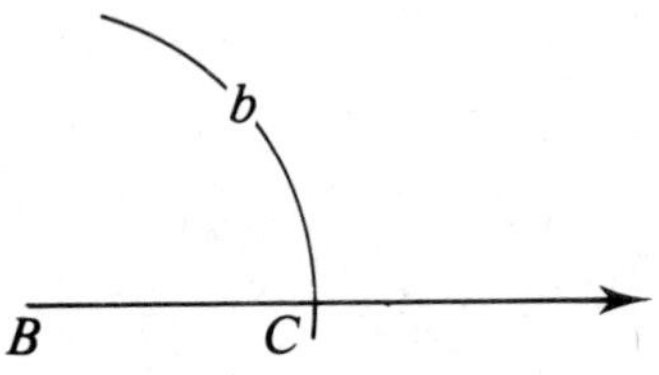

3. Set the compass so that the distance between the needle point and the pencil point is the same as the distance between the points of intersection of ray a and the sides of angle A. Using that compass setting, put the needle point at C and draw arc c that intersects arc b.

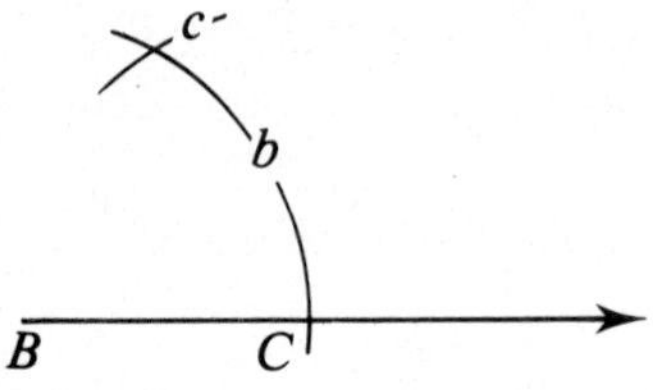

4. Draw a ray from B through the intersection of arcs b and c.

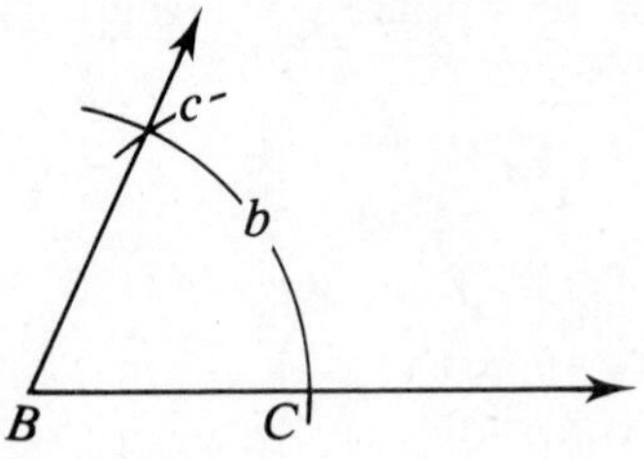

CONGRUENCY AND SIMILARITY

Congruent figures have the same size and the same shape. In such figures the measures of the corresponding angles and of the corresponding sides are equal. Thus if congruent figures are superimposed they coincide. In Figure 8.33 triangles (*a*) and (*b*) are congruent and pentagons (*c*) and (*d*) are congruent.

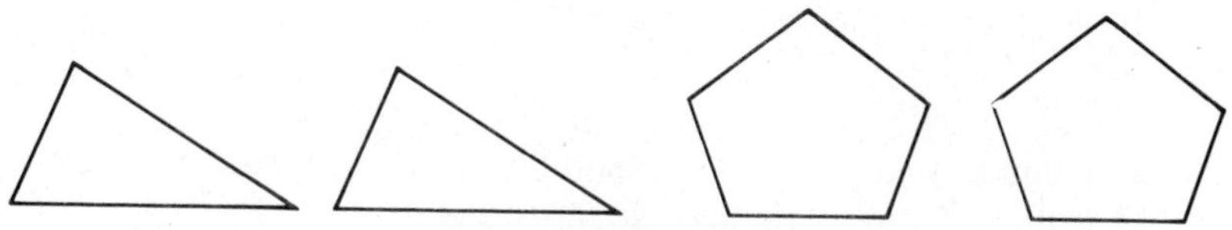

(*a*) (*b*) (*c*) (*d*)

Figure 8.33

Similar figures have the same shape but not necessarily the same size. In such figures corresponding angles are congruent and corresponding line segments are proportional. In Figure 8.34, triangles (*a*) and (*b*) are similar and hexagons (*c*) and (*d*) are similar.

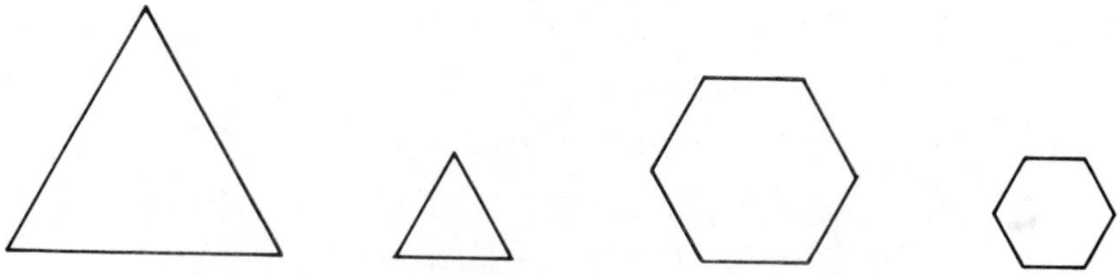

(*a*) (*b*) (*c*) (*d*)

Figure 8.34

Note that in Figure 8.35, square (*a*) is congruent to square (*b*) and that square (*c*) is similar to squares (*a*) and (*b*).

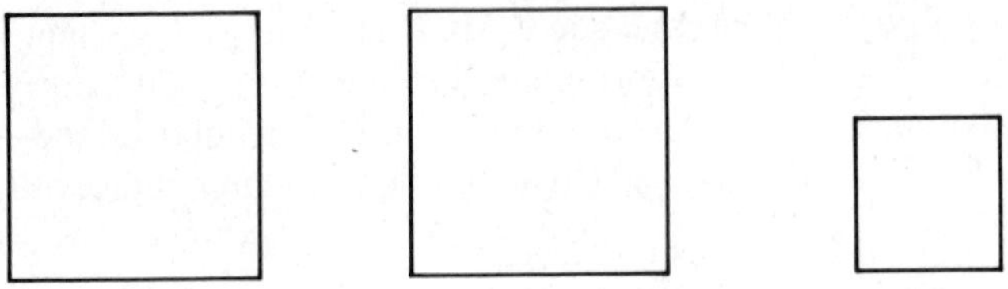

(a) (b) (c)

Figure 8.35

Since in similar figures the corresponding angles are equal, it will be realized that, for example, any two squares are similar.

SYMMETRY Make a copy of the figures shown in Figure 8.36, cut them out, and fold the cutouts along a dotted line.

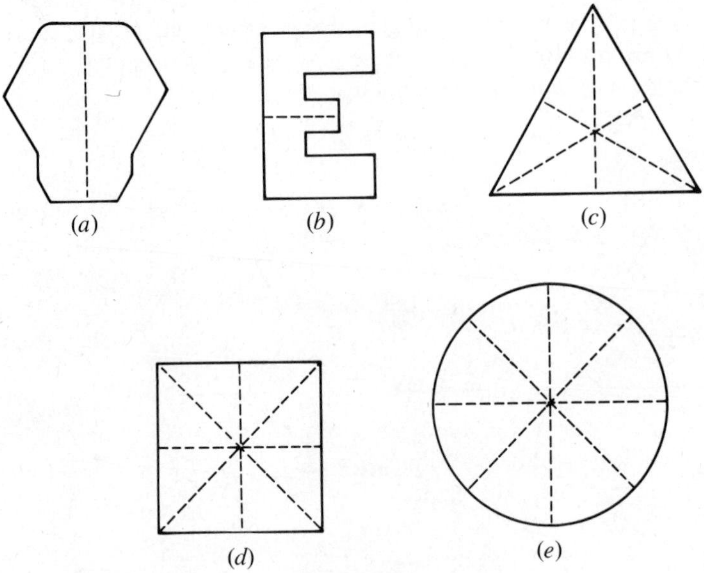

(a) (b) (c) (d) (e)

Figure 8.36

The parts on the opposite sides of a fold coincide, and the figures are called *symmetric* figures. The line of the fold is called an *axis* or a *line of symmetry*.

Note that Figure 8.36 (*a*) has one line of symmetry (vertical) and that Figure 8.36 (*b*) has also one line of symmetry (horizontal). Note also that the equilateral triangle has three lines of symmetry, that the square has four lines of symmetry, and that the circle has an infinite number of lines of symmetry. Thus the equilateral triangle, the square, and the circle can be folded in various ways so that the halves coincide. The pupil may want to predict the possible number of lines of symmetry in a regular pentagon, a regular hexagon, and a regular octagon, and then check the answer.

A symmetric figure has two parts that have the same size and the same shape; thus the two matching parts are congruent. However, if two halves of a figure are congruent, they are not necessarily symmetric. Copy the parallelogram shown in Figure 8.37, cut it out, fold it along the dotted line, and decide whether the dotted line is a line of symmetry.

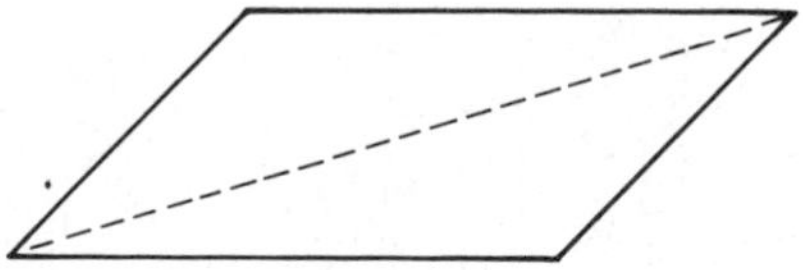

Figure 8.37

TRANSFORMATIONS

The more formal approach to teaching geometry in the elementary school encourages the introduction of simple activities dealing with geometric transformations.

Three motions that change the position of a figure but leave the figure unchanged are a translation (often called a slide), a reflection (called a flip), and a rotation (called a turn).

A *slide* is a motion in a given straight direction over a specified distance. When a checkers player makes a move, he practices a slide. Figure 8.38 portrays the result of a slide, where pentagon $ABCDE$ is the original, $A'B'C'D'E'$ the slide image, and a is the slide arrow showing the direction and the length of the slide. Imagine that line segments were drawn to connect corresponding points AA', BB', CC', DD', and EE'. Such segments would be equal in length and parallel.

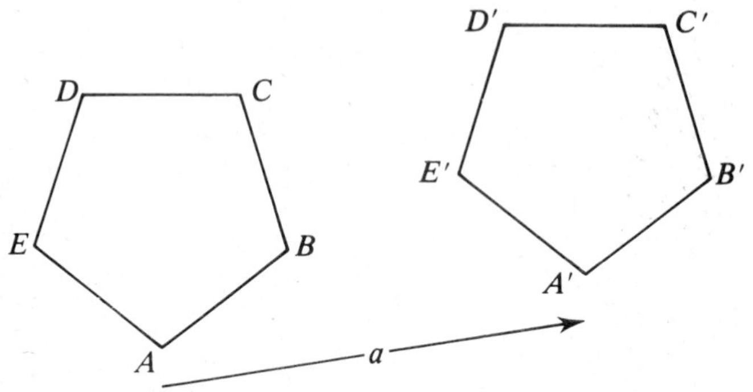

Figure 8.38

A *flip* moves a figure over a line (the flip axis) from its original position through different planes to a position upside down from where it started. In Figure 8.39 the model has been flipped over to the right from the original position *a* to position *b*. We say that *b* is the flip image, or the reflection, of *a*.

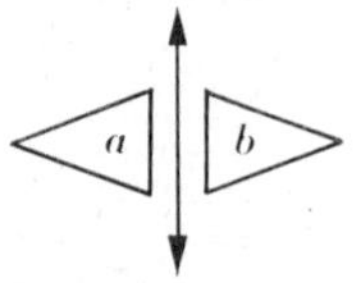

Figure 8.39

Through these activities children can develop the concept of symmetry. As an activity, a mirror can be placed on the line of symmetry.

A *turn* moves a figure a given amount around a fixed point (the center) in a specified direction. A turn occurs in the same plane. In Figure 8.40 the model has been turned from the original position *a* to position *b* around point *P*. The arrow shows the direction and the amount of the turn.

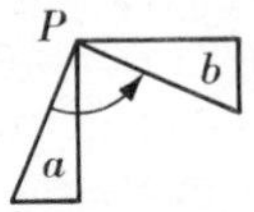

Figure 8.40

Slides, flips, and turns provide opportunities for children to perform hands-on activities and may assist in the development or refinement of such geometric concepts as parallelism, symmetry, and congruency.

TOPOLOGY

Topology deals with geometric properties that do not vary when figures are transformed in a prescribed way. It is not concerned with length, distance, or size. It is sometimes called rubber-sheet geometry, since in topology the figures are allowed to change in shape and in size. A straight line drawn on a rubber sheet may be curved and lengthened by stretching the sheet (Figure 8.41).

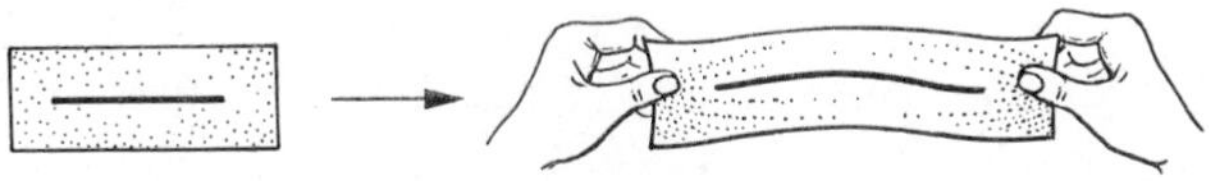

Figure 8.41

A rubber band can be transformed into a circle, a square, a triangle, etc. (Figure 8.42). In topology these figures are treated as equivalent figures. When transformations are made, the rubber must not be torn, for then two originally adjacent points are separated. Nor should two different points be fused into one.

Figure 8.42

Figure 8.43 shows a batch of clay which is transformed into a sphere, then into a cube, and then into a cylinder. In topology the figures are equivalent.

Figure 8.43

Copeland[2], reporting experiments of Piaget, suggests that the first type of geometric activities of children in the nursery, kindergarten, and

2. R. W. Copeland, *How Children Learn Mathematics* (New York: Macmillan Publishing Company, Inc., 1970), chap. VIII.

Grade 1 be topologic in character. As he states, the child can distinguish open forms from closed forms before he can differentiate between such closed forms as a square and a rectangle. He also remarks that, if Piaget is correct, to talk of lines as sets of points is a purely rote exercise in the primary grades.

Children in kindergarten and Grade 1 should engage in experiences that are designed to assist them in the formulation of these topological spacial relations:

Proximity. Example: Objects may be near to or far from a given object.

Separation. Example: Objects may be separated from or attached to a given object.

Order. Example: There is order in a pattern of beads and blocks.

Enclosure. Example: Animals in a pen are enclosed by a fence.

Exercises and activities that should help children acquire concepts of topological relations include: deciding whether an object is near or far from a given object; attaching missing parts to a paper doll; copying a given pattern; placing a piece of yarn around some of several objects and deciding which objects are inside and which are outside the yarn.

It was stated before that, if a figure is transformed into another figure (for example, a circle into an ellipse), the two figures are topologically equivalent. When such a transformation is made, the relations identified above remain constant. This will be observed by performing the following activity:

a. Draw on a rubber sheet figures as shown.

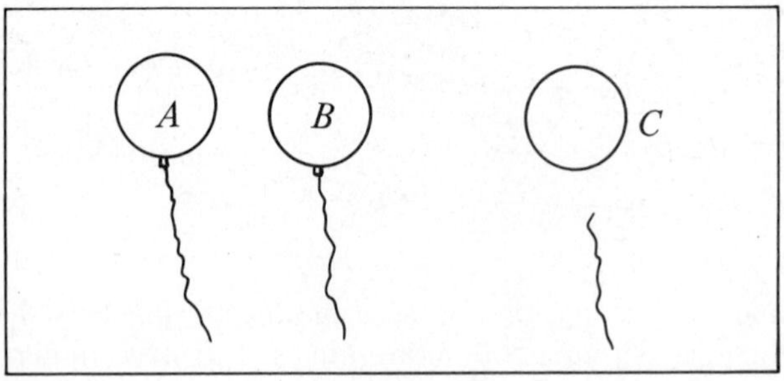

b. Stretch the sheet without tearing it.

c. Observe that—

1. Figure *B*, which was originally closer to *A* than to *C*, is still closer to *A*. Thus the relative position of the figures is maintained.
2. The string, which was originally attached to *A* and to *B*, is still attached to those figures. The string, which was originally separated from figure *C*, is still separated from that figure.
3. The original order of figures *A*, *B*, and *C* has not changed. Thus *B* remains to be between *A* and *C*.
4. The letters *A* and *B*, which were originally inside the figures, are still inside those figures. The letter *C*, which was originally outside the figure at the right side, remains to be outside that figure.

GRAPHING ON THE NUMBER PLANE

Graphing on the number plane can be introduced in games or in situations from daily life. For example, two dice are rolled in sequence and the numbers shown are graphed. Places can be located in a drawing, as in Figure 8.44. The avenue is listed first. The location of the post office at the corner of Fourth Avenue (4) and Opel Street (0) is expressed by (4, 0), and the location of the church by (2, 3).

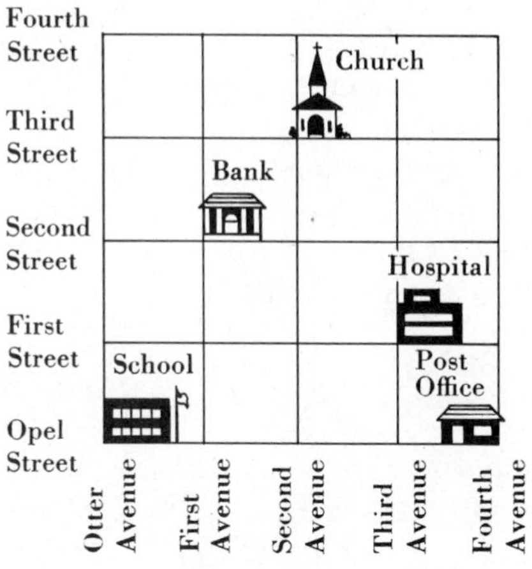

Figure 8.44

The *number plane*, also called the coordinate plane, is formed by two reference lines perpendicular to each other: the horizontal axis, or *x*-axis, and the vertical axis, or y-axis. The axes intersect at the *origin*. The points on the lines that represent successive integers are equally spaced.

In Figure 8.45 the ordered pair $(^+3, {}^+2)$ is graphed and labeled A. The two numbers of the ordered pair are called the *coordinates* of the point.

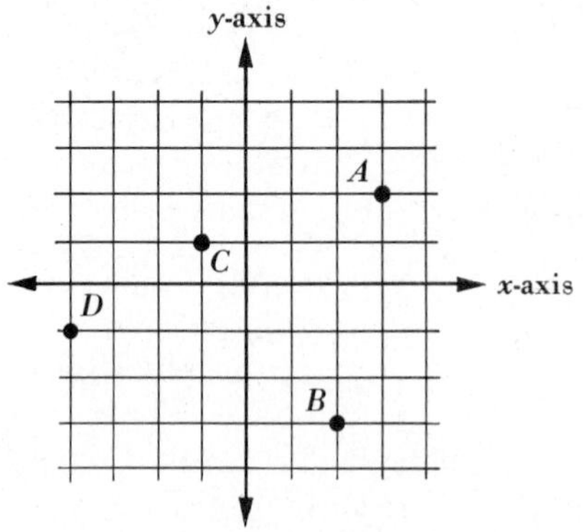

Figure 8.45

In an ordered number pair the order of the numbers cannot be changed without changing the meaning of the expression. The x-axis is the axis for the first component of the ordered pair and the y-axis is the axis for the second component. The student should identify the point corresponding to the ordered pair $(^+3, {}^+2)$.

Three other numbers have been graphed and labeled in Figure 8.45: $B(^+2, {}^-3)$, $C(^-1, {}^+1)$, and $D(^-4, {}^-1)$.

Elementary school mathematics books sometimes include pictures of function machines or function loops which present the rule that must be applied to obtain the second number of a pair. An example is presented under "Selected Activities for Pupils."

SELECTED RESEARCH

The problem in this study[3] was to determine to what extent certain concepts in geometry were satisfactory for children from seven to eleven years old. The content included these concepts: plane figures, nets of figures, symmetry, reflection, rotation, translation, bending and stretching, and networks.

3. S. A. Shah, "Selected Geometric Concepts Taught to Children Ages Seven to Eleven," *The Arithmetic Teacher* (February, 1969), pp. 119–128.

Eleven student teachers taught the specified content to a total of 374 pupils from seven to eleven years old. A test that covered the various elements was administered at the end of two weeks of teaching.

The results showed that the middle test score (50–59) was attained by 50 percent of the youngest children, and that the number of pupils earning this score increased steadily with age.

Observations of the reporter included:

1. The overall mean of about 70 percent indicated that, for the sample used, the content was satisfactory.
2. Performances became better as age increased.
3. Performance by the seven–eight age group was sometimes low.
4. Performance by the eight–eleven age group was, on the whole, satisfactory.

The investigators felt that reactions to the content considered were favorable, though they stressed that teaching techniques played a significant role in the high achievement.

SELECTED ACTIVITIES FOR PUPILS

1. Draw five dots, making them smaller and smaller. Write *A* under the dot that is the closest representation of a point.
2. List names of things that make you think of a point.

   Example

   A needle.
3. What makes you think of a line segment?

   Example

   The edge of a door.
4. What things make you think of a plane?

   Example

   The flat roof of a building.
5. What things make you think of parallel lines?

   Example

   Railroad tracks.

6. Print the capital letters that suggest parallel lines.

   Example

   H.

7. What objects in the room make you think of an angle?
8. Select a picture in one of your books and find several angles in it.
9. Print the capital letters that show right angles.

   Example

   H.

10. What makes you think of a simple closed curve?

    Example

    The path you follow when you ride around a track.

11. Find a picture in one of your books that shows several simple closed curves.
12. Form several different polygons by using a geoboard and rubber bands. Name the figures. If no geoboard is available, objects such as tongue depressors, narrow strips of cardboard, or soda straws can be used.
13. Display pictures that suggest various polygons. Name the figures.

    Examples

    Pictures of traffic signs, pyramids, tanks, silos, honeycombs, snowflakes.

14. If, of three triangles, the first is congruent to the second, and the second is congruent to the third, what statement can you make about the first and the third triangles? Draw three such triangles, label them, and express your statement in mathematical symbols.
15. a. Draw a triangle, a quadrilateral, a pentagon, and a hexagon.
    b. In each polygon draw a diagonal from a given vertex to all nonadjacent vertices.
    c. Complete this table:

Kind of Polygon	*Number of Sides*	*Number of Diagonals from One Vertex*
Triangle	_______	_______
Quadrilateral	_______	_______
Pentagon	_______	_______
Hexagon	_______	_______

    d. Try to formulate a rule.

16. Continue the patterns:
 a. □ △ □ △
 b. ○ △ ⬜ ▱ ○ △
 c. ◺ ○ ○ □ ◺ ○
 d. △ □ ⬠ ○ △ □
 e. □ ⬜ ▱ ▱ ⬜ □

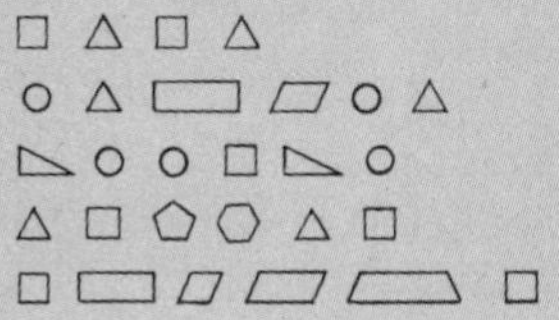

17. Find pictures of road signs that are circular in form. Say what each sign means.

18. Make the five squares shown using toothpicks. Then move three toothpicks to get seven squares.

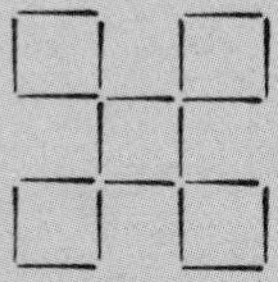

19. a. Find the pattern in the illustration. Then copy it and draw some more rectangles.

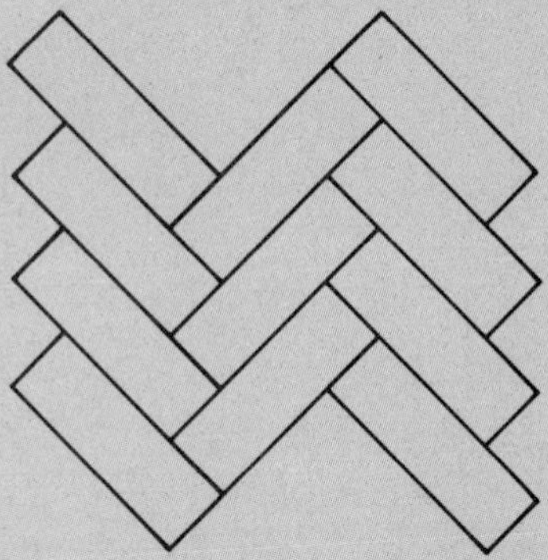

b. Use a template to draw several regular hexagons on sturdy paper. Cut them out and arrange them to produce a pattern.

20. Draw a circle. Draw three line segments which have their endpoints on the circle to get seven parts.

21. Draw a circle. In the circle—
 a. draw a diameter.
 b. draw a radius.
 c. draw a chord.
 d. draw the largest chord possible.
 e. identify the interior or inside of the circle.
 f. identify the exterior or outside of the circle.
 g. mark two points of the circumference, label them, and name two arcs.

22. Display pictures of space figures.

23. Mold clay into different figures and name the figures.

24. a. Find objects that have edges and that cannot roll.
    b. Find objects that have no edges and that can roll.
    c. Find objects that have edges and that can roll.

25. Copy the figures below on sturdy paper and cut them out. Fold the figures where needed and tape the edges together to form the named models. You will understand that you have to tape a base to the cone and two bases to the cylinder.

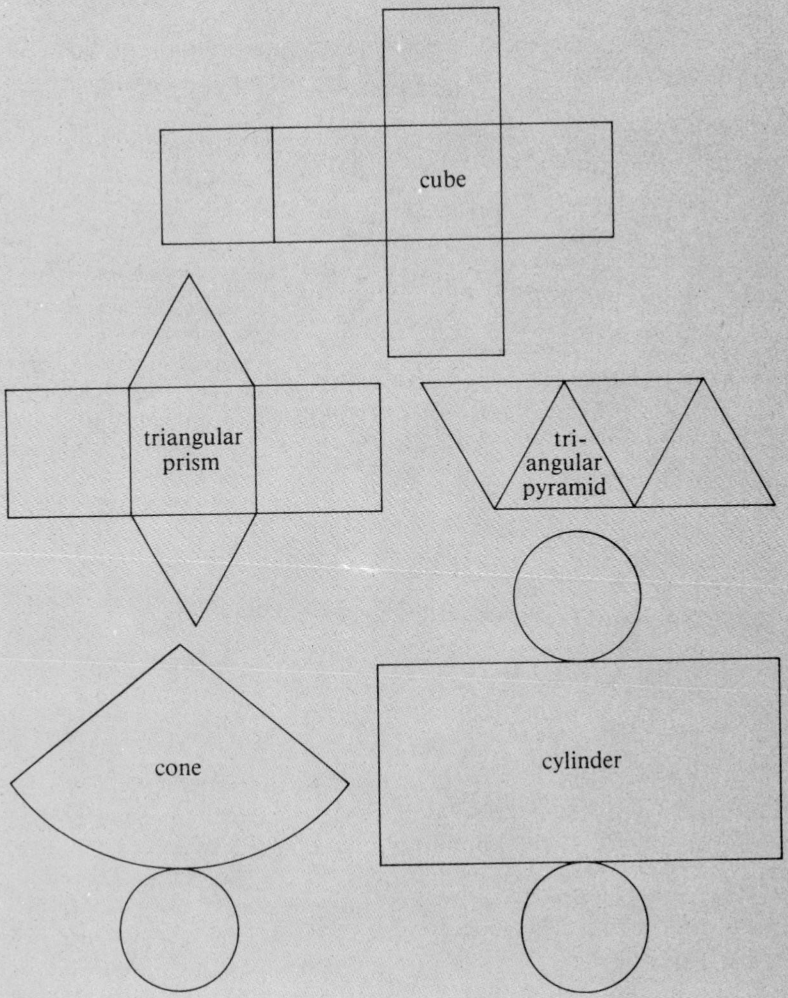

26. Use a compass to draw a figure. Two examples are given.

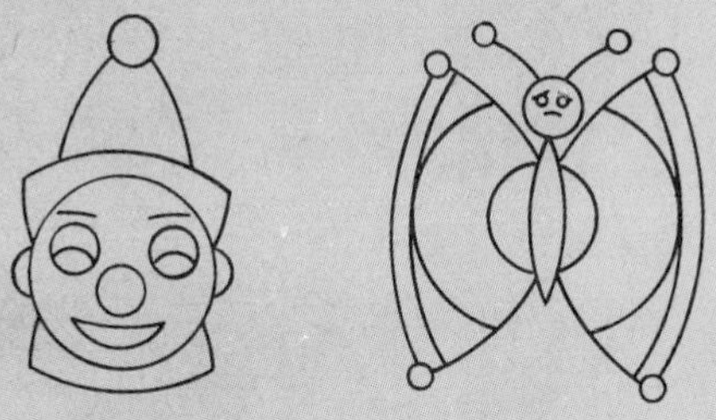

27. Follow the directions to construct a compass.

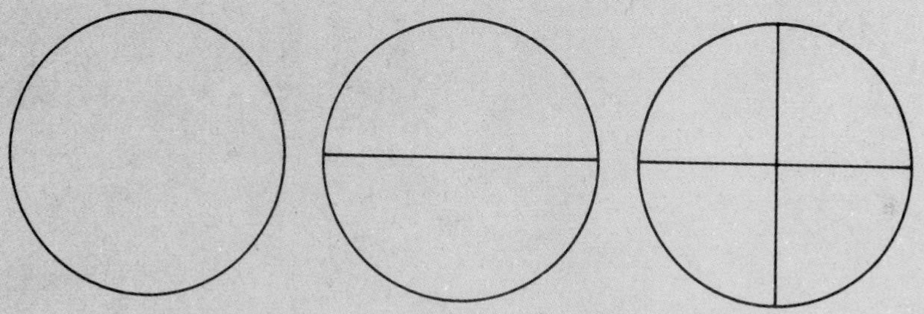

Draw a circle.
Draw a diameter as shown.
Bisect the diameter to get four right angles.

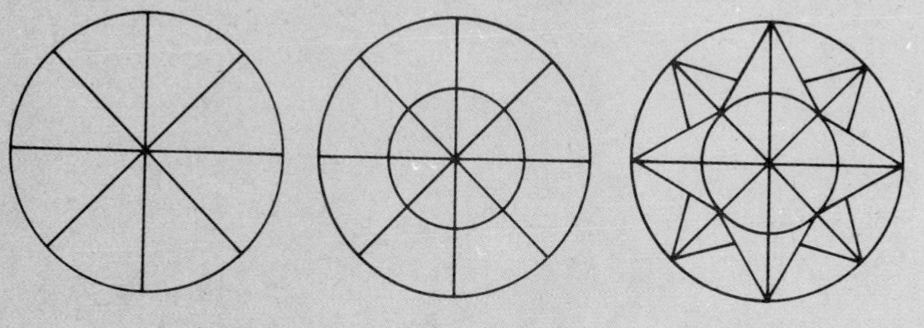

Bisect the four right angles to get 8 congruent angles.
Draw a small circle as shown.
Connect points as shown.

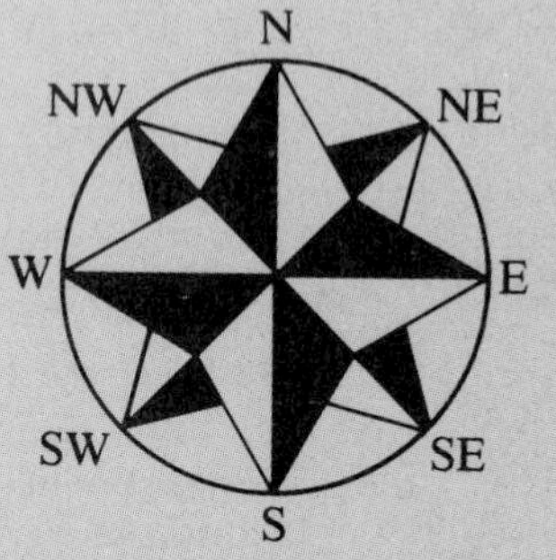

Erase line segments not needed.
Color selected regions.
Write letters for directions.

28. Make two similar triangles on a geoboard by using rubber bands.

29. Make congruent figures on a geoboard by using rubber bands.

30. The examples show that the letters A, B, and H have symmetry. Write other capital letters that have symmetry.

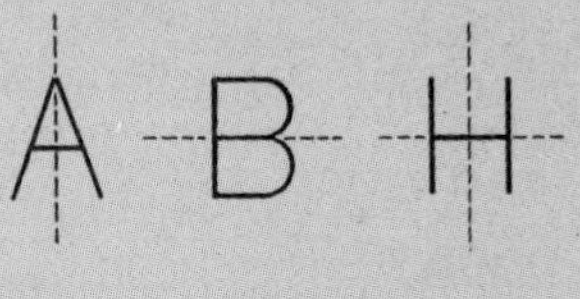

31. In each case, copy the letters and parts of the letters in large print and use a mirror to show the other part of the word.

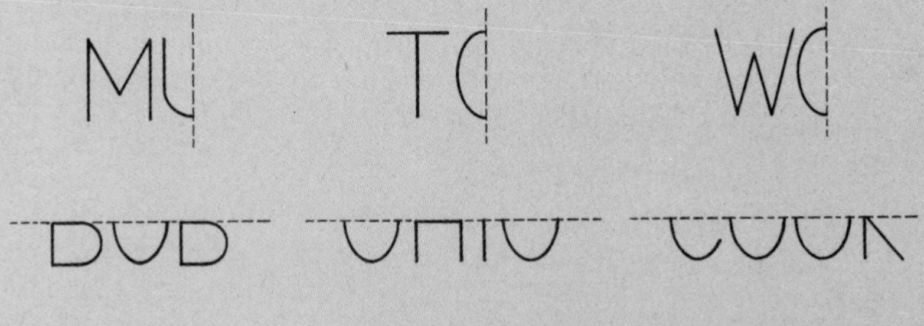

32. Drop a blot of paint on a sheet of paper. Fold the paper in half and press on the paint. Open the paper and draw lines to show symmetry.

33. Write or draw the mirror image.

29314	_____	71860	_____
78941	_____	64201	_____
35709	_____	54321	_____
90528	_____	67124	_____
IMAGE	_____	MIRROR	_____
SYMMETRY	_____	NUMBER	_____

34. a. Cut a long strip of paper.

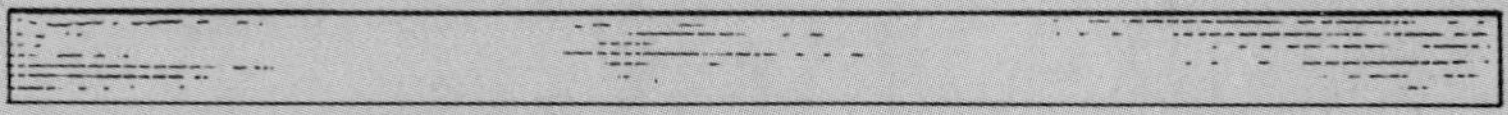

b. Twist the strip once and tape the ends together.

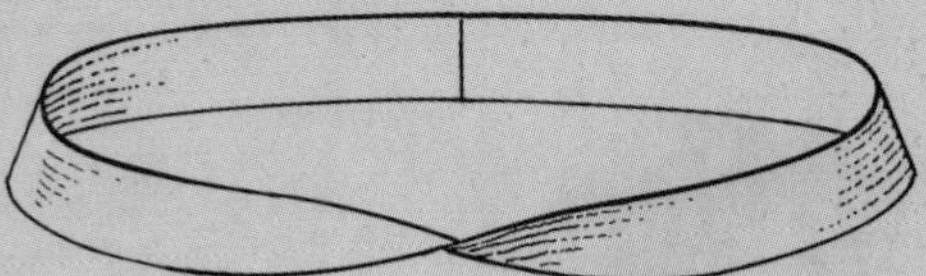

c. Starting at the place where you taped the paper, draw a line on the strip. Keep the pencil point in the middle of the strip. Now look at the whole surface of the strip. Where does the line end? How many sides does the strip have? You have a *Moebius strip*.

35. a. Graph the ordered pairs (0, 0), (3, 0), and (2, 2). Label the points A, B, and C. Draw line segments AB, AC, and BC.
b. Slide triangle ABC 3 units up and 1 unit right. Write the coordinates of the vertices of its slide image.

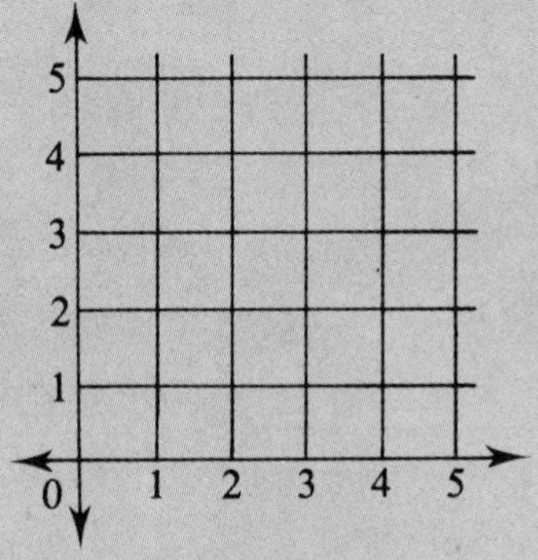

36. Twelve flags are displayed.

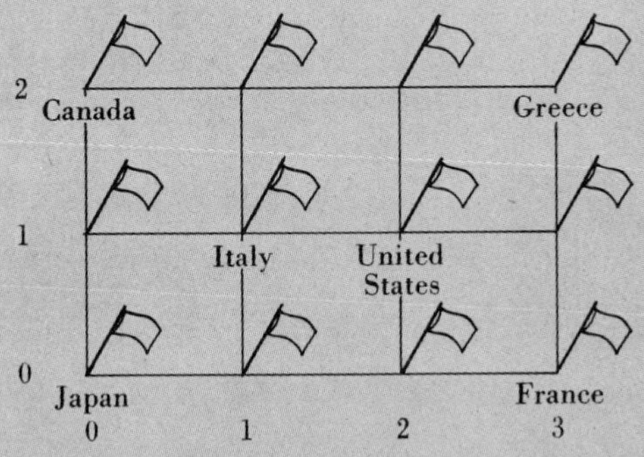

a. Write the ordered pair that describes the location of these flags: Canada ________, United States ________, Greece ________.
b. Write the names of the countries whose flags are placed at these points: (0, 0) ________, (3, 0) ________, (1, 1) ________.
c. The coordinates for flags of other countries are given below. Write the name of the country under its flag.

(0, 1) Belgium
(2, 2) The Netherlands
(2, 0) Sweden
(1, 2) Spain
(3, 1) Denmark
(1, 0) Norway

37. Complete and graph.

(+1)

Input	Output	Coordinates
0	[1]	([0],[1])
1	□	(□,□)
2	□	(□,□)
3	□	(□,□)

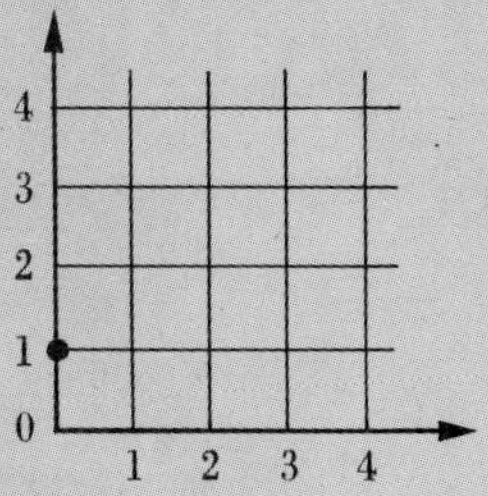

38. a. Copy the grid with its axes and numerals in pencil on an index card or cardboard, but make it much larger.

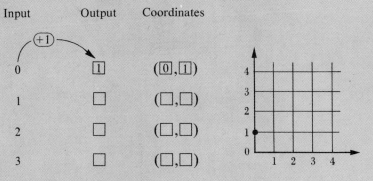

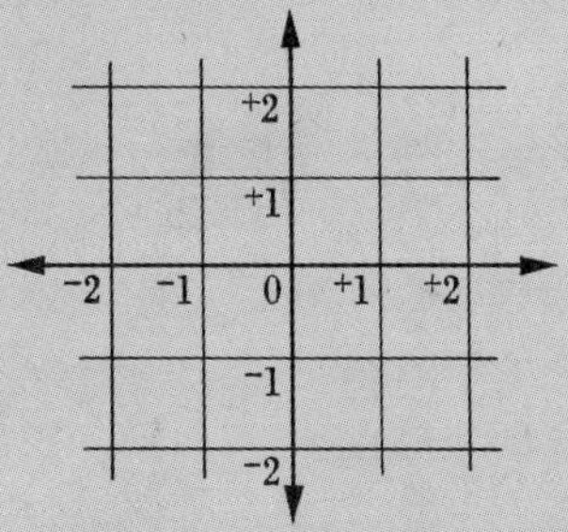

b. Graph the ordered pairs and label the points in pencil.

Ordered Pair	*Label*	*Ordered Pair*	*Label*
(⁻2, ⁺2)	*A*	(⁺2, 0)	*F*
(⁺2, ⁺2)	*B*	(⁻1, ⁻1)	*G*
(⁺2, ⁻2)	*C*	(⁺1, ⁻1)	*H*
(⁻2, ⁻2)	*D*	(⁺1, ⁺1)	*I*
(0, ⁻2)	*E*	(0, 0)	*J*

c. Draw $\overline{AB}$, $\overline{BC}$, $\overline{DC}$, $\overline{DA}$, $\overline{DB}$, $\overline{EF}$, $\overline{IH}$, $\overline{AH}$, and $\overline{GE}$.

d. The figure you have now is a *tangram*. Cut out the seven parts: *AJBA*, *IBFHI*, *JIHJ*, *EFCE*, *GEHJG*, *DEGD*, and *DJAD*.

e. Erase all the pencil marks.
f. Make figures of the pieces of the tangram. Examples are a rectangle, a triangle, a parallelogram, a trapezoid, people, and animals.

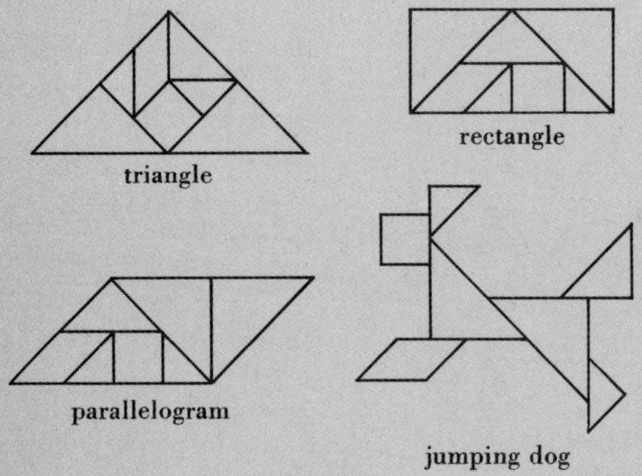

39. Use the code to find the place where the treasure is buried. Here is a map of an island where a treasure is hidden:

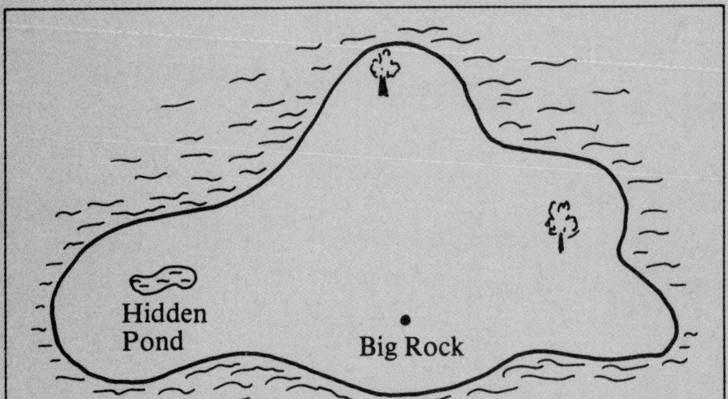

If you can use the given code,
You'll have the clue to find a load
Of silver, diamonds, and gold.
The task you have is to unfold
The message given here.
Let's hope the clue gets clear.
Then you will find the treasure
And money without measure.

Note: The key tells that a distance of 1 centimeter (cm) on the map is 10 kilometers (km) in reality.

This is the message:

[(3, 2) (4, 2) (1, 1) (2, 2) (4, 2)] [(1, 1) (4, 2)] [(2, 1) (5, 5) (5, 3)] [(2, 2) (1, 3) (3, 1) (3, 5)]
[(5, 3) (1, 3)] [(4, 2) (5, 1) (1, 4)] [(3, 5) (1, 5)] [(1, 4) (1, 3) (2, 2) (4, 2) (5, 4)]
[(4, 2) (5, 4) (5, 1) (1, 4)] [(5, 3) (1, 3)] [(4, 2) (3, 4) (5, 1) (1, 4) (4, 2) (2, 3)] [(3, 5) (1, 5)] [(5, 1) (1, 1) (3, 2) (4, 2)]
[(4, 1) (5, 5) (5, 3)] [(4, 2) (5, 4) (5, 1) (2, 2) (5, 1)]
[(2, 3) (1, 3) (4, 3)] [(3, 4) (5, 5) (2, 5) (2, 5)] [(2, 1) (5, 1)] [(2, 2) (5, 5) (3, 1) (5, 4)]

Use this code to find the message:

5	m	l	k	j	i
4	n	x	w	v	h
3	o	y	z	u	g
2	p	r	s	t	f
1	a	b	c	d	e
0	1	2	3	4	5

Mark on the map the place where the treasure is hidden.

EXERCISES

1. a. Make drawings that represent a point, a line segment, a rectangle, and a rectangular prism.
   b. Determine the number of dimensions of each of the figures.
2. Draw, label, and write a symbol for—
   a. a line.
   b. a line segment.
   c. a ray.
   d. an angle.
   e. a triangle.
   f. two congruent triangles.
3. Make five drawings that represent different kinds of quadrilaterals.

4. Explain why a square is a rectangle.
5. Explain why a rectangle is a parallelogram.
6. Draw five polygons—one with three sides, one with four sides, one with five sides, one with six sides, and one with eight sides. Supply the special names of these polygons.
7. Determine the number of bases, sides, edges, and vertices of a cube.
8. Determine how many lines of symmetry a regular hexagon has.
9. Explain why any two circles are similar.
10. Explain: Any two squares are similar but not necessarily congruent.
11. Select a basic mathematics textbook for a grade level that interests you. Examine the topics dealing with geometry. State your opinion on the sequence and methods of presentation.
12. Make an outline of a lesson to teach a topic in geometry to children. Select the topic and the grade level yourself. If possible, teach the lesson to a group of children or, in a simulated situation, to peers.

SOURCES FOR FURTHER READING

Association of Teachers of Mathematics, *Notes on Mathematics in Primary Schools*. London: Cambridge University Press, 1969, Chap. VII.

Brune, I. H., "Geometry in the Grades," *Enrichment Mathematics for the Grades, Twenty-seventh Yearbook*. Washington, D.C.: National Council of Teachers of Mathematics, 1963, pp. 134–147.

Copeland, R. W., *How Children Learn Mathematics,* 2nd ed. New York: Macmillan Publishing Company, Inc., 1974, Chaps. XI–XIII.

Copeland, R. W., *Mathematics and the Elementary Teacher,* 2nd ed. Philadelphia: W. B. Saunders Company, 1972, Chaps. III, IX.

D'Augustine, C. H., *Multiple Methods of Teaching Mathematics in the Elementary School,* 2nd ed. New York: Harper & Row, Publishers, 1973, Chap. XVII.

Heddens, J. W., *Today's Mathematics,* 3d ed. Chicago: Science Research Associates, Inc., 1974, Units XVII, XIX–XXI.

Immerzeel, G., "Geometric Activities for Early Childhood Education," *The Arithmetic Teacher,* October, 1973, pp. 438–443.

Johnson, M. L., "Generating Patterns from Transformations," *The Arithmetic Teacher,* March, 1977, pp. 191–195.

Kennedy, L. M., *Guiding Children to Mathematical Discovery*. 2nd ed. Belmont, California: Wadsworth Publishing Company, Inc., 1975, Chap. XIV.

Liedtke, W., "Geoboard Mathematics," *The Arithmetic Teacher,* April, 1974, pp. 273–277.

Marks, J. L., C. R. Purdy, L. B. Kinney, and A. A. Hiatt, *Teaching Elementary School Mathematics for Understanding,* 4th ed. New York: McGraw-Hill Book Company, 1975, Chap. VI.

McKeeby Phillips, J., and R. E. Zwoyer, *Motion Geometry*. Book 1. *Slides, Flips, and Turns*. New York: Harper & Row, Publishers, 1969.

Morris, J. P., "Investigating Symmetry in the Primary Grades," *The Arithmetic Teacher,* March, 1977, pp. 181–186.

Nuffield Mathematics Project, *Beginnings* 1. London: W. & R. Chambers and John Murray, 1967.

Nuffield Mathematics Project, *Shape and Size* 2, 3, 4. London: W. & R. Chambers and John Murray, 1967.

Robinson, G. E., "Geometry," *Mathematics in Early Childhood, Thirty-seventh Yearbook,* edited by J. N. Payne. Washington, D.C.: National Council of Teachers of Mathematics, 1975, Chap. IX.

Schminke, C. W., N. Maertens, and W. R. Arnold, *Teaching the Child Mathematics*. Hinsdale, Illinois: The Dryden Press, Inc., 1973, Chaps. VI, X.

Underhill, R. G., *Teaching Elementary School Mathematics*. Columbus, Ohio: Charles E. Merrill Publishing Company, 1972, Chap. XVIII.

Walter, M. I., *Boxes, Squares, and Other Things: A Teacher's Guide for a Unit in Informal Geometry*. Washington, D.C.: National Council of Teachers of Mathematics, 1970.

Statistics and Probability 9

In and outside of school children meet situations that involve simple statistics. They examine distributions of grades to find out how they rank, they see graphs, and they study team scores. They also speak about events that may happen; for example, they may state their opinion on what the chances are that a given team will win a game. They may listen to the weather report before going on a trip.

This chapter shows ways to organize and present data, deals with measures of central tendency, and introduces simple activities in probability.

GRAPHS

Graphs are designed to show relationships in such a way that the user can read and interpret the illustrated data easily. Several types of graphs can be used. The type selected depends upon the situation that is to be pictured and the data that are to be summarized.

Line-Segment Graphs

In a line-segment graph, numerical data that tend to fluctuate are shown graphically. The graph in Figure 9.1 shows the results of mathematics tests Jane Brown took during the school year. The highest possible score on each test was 20.

In the graph, two perpendicular lines, the horizontal axis and the vertical axis, serve as the reference lines. On the vertical line the selected units of length have been marked off, and the numerals represent possible

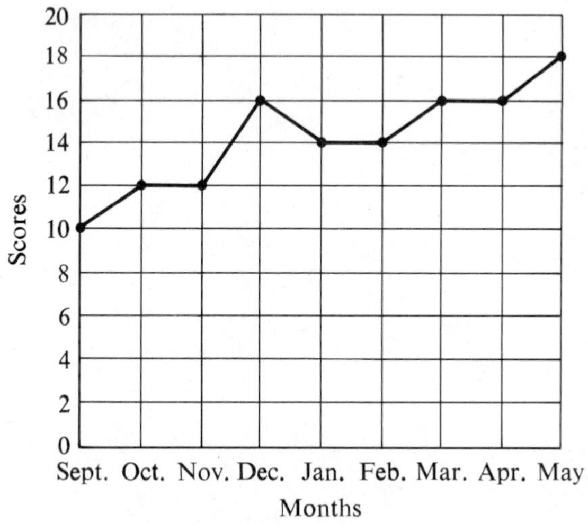

Results of Jane Brown's Mathematics Tests

Figure 9.1

scores. The horizontal axis is the reference line for the nine months during which the tests were taken. Lines drawn parallel to the horizontal axis intersect the vertical axis at points representing the scores. Lines parallel to the vertical axis intersect the horizontal axis at points representing the months. The data have been graphed by plotting points at the appropriate locations. For example, Jane's mathematics score for September was 10; thus the point has been graphed that is the intersection of the horizontal line representing a score of 10 and the vertical line reserved for the September score. The points graphed have been connected by line segments.

A major difficulty in the construction of a graph is the selection of the proper scale. This choice will be influenced by such factors as the amount of data to be graphed, the size of and the difference between the numbers to be pictured, the degree of accuracy required, and the number of units available on the graph paper. These elements should be considered in the class discussion; different plans should be compared and the best one selected.

Bar Graphs Bar graphs show differences among groups of data vividly. For example, a bar graph is an effective means of comparing amounts of money collected for a certain cause by various grades. Either horizontal or vertical bar graphs can be used. In order to avoid a distorted picture of the data, the bars must be of equal width and must be placed equally far apart.

Figure 9.2 allows the reader to compare at a glance the differing amounts of money contributed to the Red Cross by Grades 3, 4, 5, and 6 of Arlington School. From this graph it cannot be determined whether the amounts of money contributed have been rounded to whole dollars.

Parts of dollars can be pictured by extending the bar part of a unit. In this case, the interpreter of the graph must estimate the amount of money pictured.

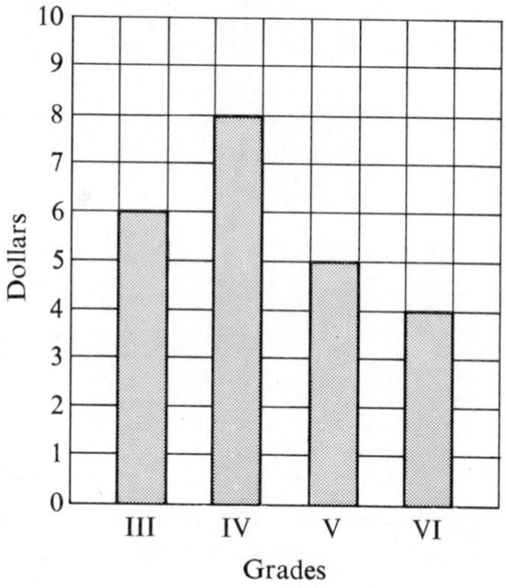

Contributions to the Red Cross by Grades 3–6

Figure 9.2

Pictographs

In a pictograph, pictures are used to represent unit values; for example, the picture of one automobile tire may stand for 1,000,000 tires manufactured. In order to obtain a convenient scale, numbers are usually rounded before they are pictured. This may result in a lack of accuracy. When a part of a unit is shown, the pupil has to estimate the number that that part represents. The graph in Figure 9.3 shows the result of a questionnaire in which 150 sixth-grade pupils told which one of the three subjects, social studies, mathematics, and science, they liked most.

Favorite Subjects of 150 Sixth Graders in Grant School
(Each picture represents 10 pupils)
Figure 9.3

Circle Graphs The comparative sizes of the component parts of a unit or a group can be pictured clearly in a circle graph. The sectors of the circle are in proportion to the sizes of the parts they represent. Thus, when examining a circle graph, the reader can quickly compare the relative sizes of the represented parts.

Before the pupil is introduced to the circle graph, he should be acquainted with the simple characteristics of a circle, with angular measurement, and preferably with percents.

Example

Bill White earned \$50 during his summer vacation. He spent \$25 on a trip, \$10 on books, \$5 on presents, and \$10 on records. Draw a circle graph that shows how Bill spent his money.

Solution: First the pupil prepares a table such as Table 9.1. When the table has been prepared, all the information needed for constructing the circle graph as shown in Figure 9.4 is available. The entire circular region represents Bill's total earnings, and each sector stands for a specific amount of money Bill has spent. The solution can be checked as follows:

$$\frac{1}{2} + \frac{1}{5} + \frac{1}{10} + \frac{1}{5} = \frac{5 + 2 + 1 + 2}{10} = 1$$

The sum of the measures in degrees must equal 360:

$$180° + 72° + 36° + 72° = 360°$$

Table 9.1
How Bill Spent His Money

Money Spent		*Part of Earnings*	*Measure of Sector*
Trip	\$25	$\frac{1}{2}$	$\frac{1}{2} \times 360° = 180°$
Books	10	$\frac{1}{5}$	$\frac{1}{5} \times 360° = 72°$
Presents	5	$\frac{1}{10}$	$\frac{1}{10} \times 360° = 36°$
Records	10	$\frac{1}{5}$	$\frac{1}{5} \times 360° = 72°$

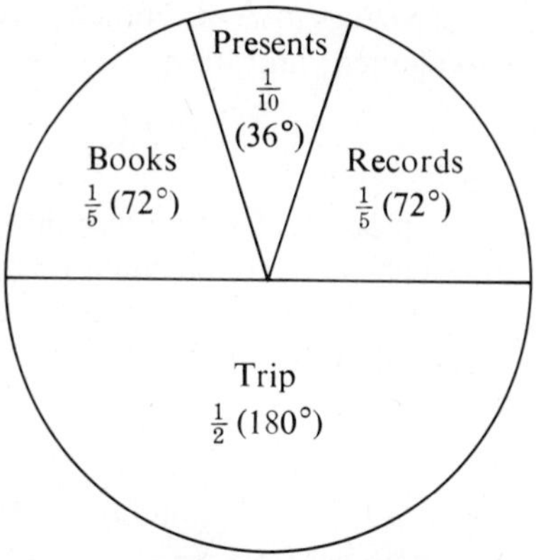

How Bill Spent His $50
Figure 9.4

FREQUENCY DISTRIBUTION

The 21 pupils of a sixth-grade class received the following grades on a 40-item spelling test: 30, 31, 29, 38, 32, 40, 30, 36, 28, 37, 31, 35, 31, 36, 34, 29, 34, 31, 35, 31, 35. The teacher used these scores to introduce and review some statistical terms and concepts.

A frequency distribution was made. The scores were listed in order, a tally was marked for each time a score was earned, and the total number of tallies for each score, or the *frequency distribution*, was recorded. The result is shown in Table 9.2.

Table 9.2
Frequency Distribution of the Scores of 21 Sixth Graders on a 40-Item Spelling Test

Score	*Tally*	*Frequency*
40	|	1
39		0
38	|	1
37	|	1
36	||	2
35	|||	3
34	||	2
33		0
32	|	1
31	~~||||~~	5
30	||	2
29	||	2
28	|	1

The meaning of the term *range*, the difference between the highest and the lowest score, was explained, and the pupils found it to be 12.

MEASURES OF CENTRAL TENDENCY From a set of organized numerical data, numbers that represent the center of the distribution can be derived. Such descriptive statistics are called *measures of central tendency*. There are three common measures of central tendency: the arithmetic mean, usually called the mean, the median, and the mode.

The Mean The *mean* of a set of measures is determined by adding the measures and dividing the sum by the number of observations.

The topic can be introduced as soon as children can divide simple numbers. For example, if, over three days, a child has read respectively 3, 4, and 5 pages, he can find the mean of 3, 4, and 5 by adding the numbers and dividing the sum by 3:

$$\frac{3 + 4 + 5}{3} = \frac{12}{3}$$

or 4. The following diagram illustrates this case.

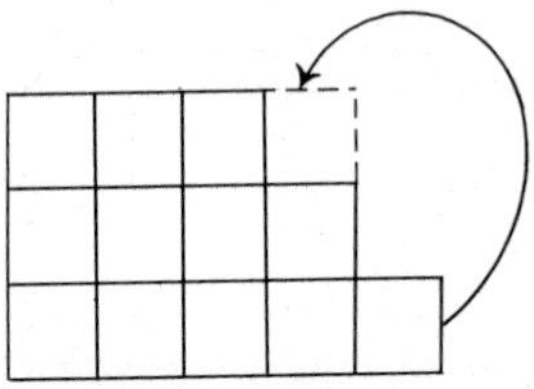

The sixth-grade pupils who prepared Table 9.2 used the data to find the mean of the scores. First the sum of the scores was determined: $(1 \times 40) + (1 \times 38) + (1 \times 37) + (2 \times 36) + (3 \times 35) + (2 \times 34) + (1 \times 32) + (5 \times 31) + (2 \times 30) + (2 \times 29) + (1 \times 28) = 693$. Since 21 pupils took the test, the mean was found by dividing the sum of the scores by 21: $693 \div 21 = 33$.

The Median The *median* of a set of measures arranged in order of size is the middle measure.

If the data in Table 9.2 are used, the pupils are helped to observe that of the 21 scores, the eleventh score (32) is the middle score or the median, since 10 scores are higher than 32 and 10 scores are lower than 32.

The Mode

The mode is the most frequently observed measure in a set of measures.

If, again, the data in Table 9.2 are studied, the teacher's guide questions assist the children to decide that there are five scores of 31 and that no other score has been earned that many times. Then the term *mode* is introduced.

There is no mode if all the scores are different. If two measures occur with the same frequency, the distribution is called *bimodal.*

PROBABILITY

The research study described in this chapter reports that there is evidence that children possess some concepts basic to fundamental notions of probability that have been acquired outside the mathematics class. Such concepts are refined and extended by the teacher in activities that guide the child in predicting events and observing and recording outcomes.

Activities that deal with probability are presented in the following paragraphs. It must be understood that the teacher may have to ask several guide questions to assist the child in his thinking.

Spinning a Spinner

In the primary grades, activities with spinners can serve to introduce simple terms and concepts. When using a spinner as pictured in Figure 9.5(a), the child is led to decide that it is "just as likely" that the spinner will stop at 1 as it is that it will stop at 2. With spinner (b), the terms "least likely" and "most likely" are used.

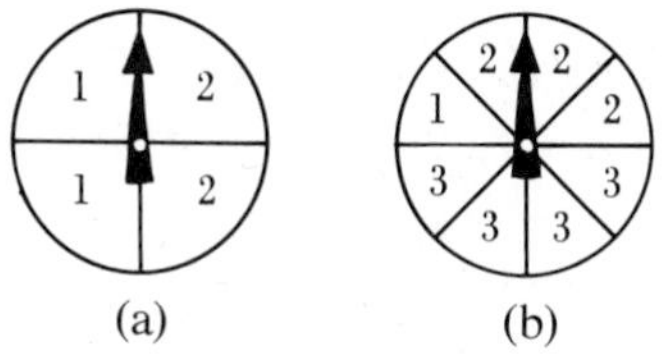

Figure 9.5

Tossing a Coin Once

If you toss a coin, how can it land? (In 1 of 2 ways: heads or tails.) Draw a diagram to show the possible outcomes of tossing a coin.

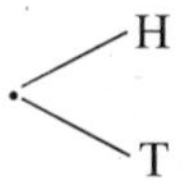

If you toss a coin, what is the chance that it will land heads? (1 out of 2)

What is the chance that it will land tails? (1 out of 2)

With more advanced pupils the teacher will, in a class presentation and discussion, express the probability of getting heads by the ratio $\frac{1}{2}$. He explains that there is one way in which the given event of getting heads can occur and that there are two possible outcomes: heads and tails. Thus the probability that a given event will occur is equal to

$$\frac{\text{Number of ways the event can occur}}{\text{Number of possible outcomes}}$$

Tossing a Coin Twice If you toss a coin twice, how many possible outcomes are there and what are they? (4 outcomes: HH, HT, TH, and TT) Draw a diagram to show the possible outcomes.

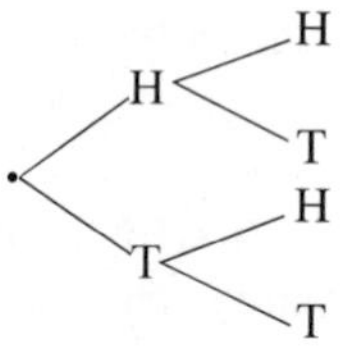

How may ways are there to get two heads? (1)

What is the probability of getting HH? ($\frac{1}{4}$)

In how many ways can you get a head and a tail in any order? (2)

What is the probability of getting either HT or TH? ($\frac{2}{4}$, or $\frac{1}{2}$)

What is the probability of getting first heads and then tails? ($\frac{1}{4}$)

Using Pascal's Triangle Pascal, a French mathematician of three centuries ago, was interested in games of chance and probability. He worked with a number arrangement, called Pascal's triangle (Figure 9.6), that shows the probability of the occurrence of a given event.

Pupils can use the triangle to discover and continue patterns and to determine the possible outcomes of, for example, tossing a coin.

The numbers in row 1 indicate that, when a coin is tossed once, there are 1 + 1, or 2, possible outcomes. (H, T) The numbers in row 2 show that when a coin is tossed twice there are 1 + 2 + 1, or 4, possible outcomes, as shown in Figure 9.6. When a coin is tossed three times, there are 1 + 3 + 3 + 1, or 8, possible outcomes. (HHH, HHT, HTH, HTT, THH, THT, TTH, TTT)

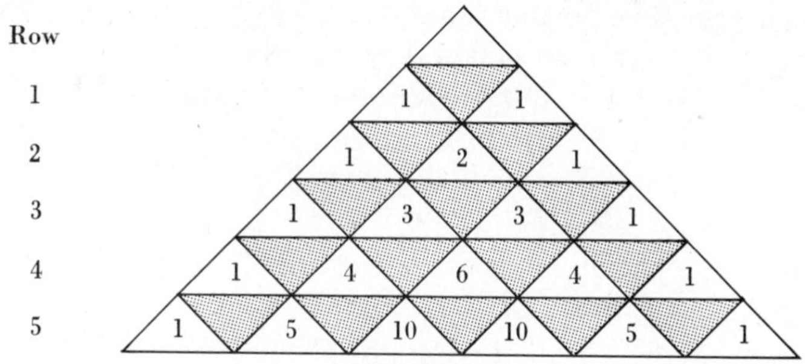

Figure 9.6

Capable pupils should be encouraged to determine and identify the number and form of possible outcomes when a coin is tossed four or five times.

Rolling a Die

If you roll a die, how many possible outcomes are there? (The face of the die will show 1, 2, 3, 4, 5, or 6 dots. There are 6 possible outcomes.)
 What is the probability of getting 6 dots on top? (There is one way in which the die can show 6 dots. There are 6 possible outcomes. The probability of getting 6 dots on top is $\frac{1}{6}$.) What is the probability of getting 4 dots on top? ($\frac{1}{6}$)

Rolling Two Dice

If you roll two dice, the sum of the numbers of dots shown on the tops is one of the numbers 2 through 12. The chart in Figure 9.7 shows all the possible results of rolling two dice.

	•	••	••	::	:•:	:::
•	2	3	4	5	6	7
••	3	4	5	6	7	8
••	4	5	6	7	8	9
::	5	6	7	8	9	10
:•:	6	7	8	9	10	11
:::	7	8	9	10	11	12

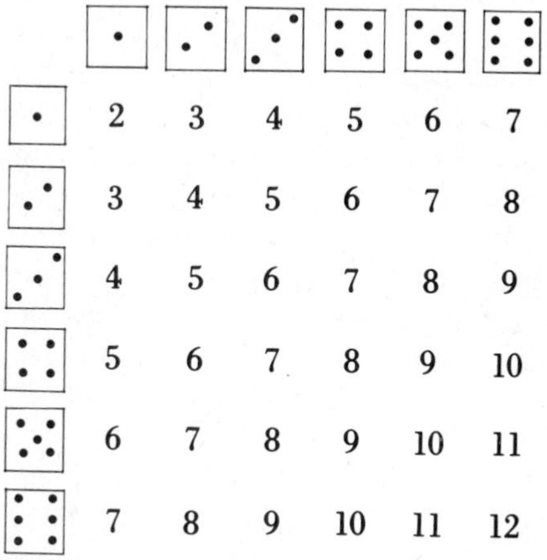

Figure 9.7

1. How many possible outcomes are there? (36)
   How many ways can the sum of 9 occur? (4)
   What is the probability of getting a sum of 9? ($\frac{4}{36}$, or $\frac{1}{9}$)
2. How many ways can a sum of 7 occur? (6)
   What is the probability of getting a sum of 7? ($\frac{6}{36}$, or $\frac{1}{6}$)
3. How many ways can a sum of 12 occur? (1)
   What is the probability of getting a sum of 12? ($\frac{1}{36}$)
4. What sum is most likely to occur? (7)
   What sums are least likely to occur? (2 and 12)
5. What is the probability that the two dice will show the same number of dots on top? (There are 6 ways the event can occur: $1 + 1, 2 + 2, 3 + 3, 4 + 4, 5 + 5, 6 + 6$. Probability is $\frac{6}{36}$, or $\frac{1}{6}$)
6. What is the probability that the sum of the dots will be either 2 or 3? ($\frac{3}{36}$, or $\frac{1}{12}$)

Picking a Coin from a Set of Coins

In a bag are 8 dimes minted in 1940 and 2 dimes minted in 1950. If you take a dime out of the bag without looking, what is the probability of getting—

a. a 1940 dime? ($\frac{8}{10}$, or $\frac{4}{5}$)
b. a 1950 dime? ($\frac{2}{10}$, or $\frac{1}{5}$)
c. either a 1940 or a 1950 dime? ($\frac{10}{10}$, or 1)
d. a 1960 dime? ($\frac{0}{10}$, or 0)

SELECTED RESEARCH

The purpose of this study[1] was to examine the status of three concepts basic to fundamental notions of probability possessed by children in Grades four through seven who had not had any formal learning experiences with topics in probability.

To a sample of 528 children three tests were administered, one for each of the three concepts. The items in the test were designed by the investigator to determine whether the child could apply the concept in a variety of simple experiment and game situations.

1. W. W. Leffin, "A Study of Three Concepts of Probability Possessed by Children in the Fourth, Fifth, Sixth, and Seventh Grades" (Ph.D. thesis, Madison, Wisconsin University, 1971). Available from ERIC Document Reproduction Service (ED 070 657).

Test I contained twelve items on the concept of sample space[2] involving simple counting and simple ideas of combination.

Test II comprised twelve items testing the concept of probability of a simple event. In six items the underlying ideas of sample space involved only simple counting; in six items the underlying ideas of sample space involved combinations.

Test III tested the concept of quantification of probabilities in ten items presenting game situations. The child had to select from two conditions the one that represented the better probability of success for a specified simple event in one trial.

The same tests were administered as written tests to all subjects of Grades four through seven.

The findings showed that the children had acquired considerable knowledge of the three concepts tested and that they could apply these concepts in a variety of situations. Since the children had not received formal training in these areas, their performance must have been a result of their background, experience, and intuition.

The investigator made the observation that, since young children acquire some knowledge of probability outside of school, it seems reasonable to assume that some topics of probability are not too difficult to be included in the elementary school curriculum.

SELECTED ACTIVITIES FOR PUPILS

1. Ask several of your friends which color they like better—orange or green. Make a picture graph to show the results.
2. During one school week record the temperature at nine o'clock every morning on a line graph.
3. Ask several friends which is their favorite football team. Make a bar graph to show the results.
4. a. Write these numbers in order from greatest to least:

   8, 14, 15, 11, 12, 17, 14, 7, 14, 16, 11, 9, 8

   b. Find the difference between the greatest and the least number.
   c. What number is represented the most times?
   d. Suppose these numbers represent scores, and one of them is your score. A number of pupils have a higher score than you do, and the

---

2. A list of all possible outcomes is sometimes called a sample space.

same number of pupils have a lower score than you do, so you have the middle score. What is your score?

e. Find the average of the numbers.

5. When you spin the spinner it will most likely stop on □.

6. When you close your eyes and pick one of the coins, it is least likely that you pick a ________.

7. Flip a coin 30 times. Record the number of times it lands heads and the number of times it lands tails.

8. Write the numerals 2 through 9 on separate slips of paper. Mix the slips and put them in a bag. If you take a slip out of the bag, is it more likely that you will pick a numeral that expresses a prime number or one that expresses a composite number?

9. Number the faces of a sugar cube 5, 5, 5, 5, 6, and 6. Roll the cube 30 times. How many times did the top face show 5? How many times 6?

10. a. Toss a coin twice. The possible outcomes are HH, HT, TH, and TT. What is the probability of getting 2 heads? 2 tails? 2 heads or 2 tails?

b. Two tosses is a trial. Do 30 trials. Record your results on the table.

Results of the trials:	HH	HT	TH	TT
	□	□	□	□

c. How many of the trials were HH? How does this compare with the probability in (a)?

11. Put 3 red marbles and 5 blue marbles in a box. If you, without looking, take one marble out of the box, the chances are 3 out of 8 that you pick a red marble.

a. What are the chances that you get a blue marble?

b. What are the chances that you get a yellow marble?

c. Take a marble out of the box 20 times, record the results and express the results in a bar graph.

12. Play a game.

Mary and Joan played a game. They tossed in turn one coin twice. They decided that the numerical value of heads would be 1 and of tails 2. So, if two heads showed, the score was 2 points, for two tails 4 points, and for one head and one tail 3 points.

Each of them took 20 turns. They recorded the results in the graphs shown.

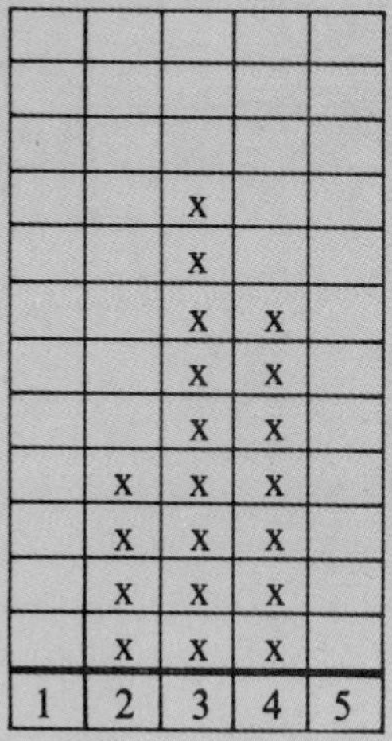

Mary's graph

		X		
		X		
		X	X	
		X	X	
		X	X	
	X	X	X	
	X	X	X	
	X	X	X	
	X	X	X	
1	2	3	4	5

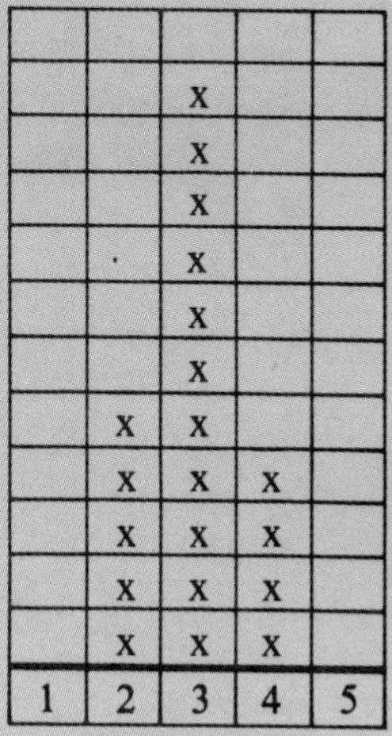

Joan's graph

		X		
		X		
		X		
	·	X		
		X		
		X		
	X	X		
	X	X	X	
	X	X	X	
	X	X	X	
	X	X	X	
1	2	3	4	5

a. Find the total score of each player.
b. Who won the game?
c. Try to explain why two tosses resulted so often in a score of 3.
d. Why are the columns for 1 and 5 not needed?
e. Play the same game with a friend.

EXERCISES

1. Outline a lesson plan for the introduction of a pictograph to a grade level you select.

2. In a 30-problem mathematics test, a fifth grade earned these scores:

23, 20, 30, 26, 22, 25, 28, 19, 21, 29, 28, 24, 27,
24, 23, 24, 27, 20, 28, 26, 22, 26, 29, 24, 30

a. Make a frequency distribution of the scores.
b. Find the range.
c. Find the mean.

d. Find the median.
e. Find the mode.

3. Use Pascal's triangle to determine the possible outcomes when a coin is tossed four times. Then express the probability of obtaining each of the possible outcomes.

SOURCES FOR FURTHER READING

Ball, J., "Finding Averages with Bar Graphs," *The Arithmetic Teacher,* October, 1969, pp. 487–489.

Bruni, J. V., and H. Silverman, "Graphing as a Communication Skill," *The Arithmetic Teacher,* May, 1975, pp. 354–366.

Coppola, J. N., "Graphs Tell a Story," *The Arithmetic Teacher,* April, 1969, pp. 305–306.

Flory, D. W., "What Are the Chances?" *The Arithmetic Teacher,* November, 1969, pp. 581–582.

Heddens, J. W., *Today's Mathematics,* 3d ed. Chicago: Science Research Associates, Inc., 1974, Unit XXII.

Holmann, H. W., and B. M. Ross, "Children's Understanding of Probability Concepts," *Child Development,* March, 1971, pp. 221–236.

Johnson, D. A., and W. H. Glenn, *The World of Statistics.* St. Louis: Webster Publishing Company (McGraw-Hill), 1961.

Kennedy, L. M., *Guiding Children to Mathematical Discovery,* 2nd ed. Belmont, California: Wadsworth Publishing Company, Inc., 1975, Chap. XVI.

Mann, W., et al., *Probability and Statistics.* Columbus: Charles E. Merrill Publishing Company, 1968.

National Council of Teachers of Mathematics, *More Topics in Mathematics for Elementary School Teachers, Thirtieth Yearbook.* Washington, D.C.: The Council, 1969, Bklt. 16.

Niman, J., and R. D. Postman, "Probability on the Geoboard," *The Arithmetic Teacher,* March, 1973, pp. 167–170.

Pierson, R. C., "Elementary Graphing Experiences," *The Arithmetic Teacher,* March, 1969, pp. 199–201.

Pincus, M., and F. Morgenstern, "Graphs in the Primary Grades," *The Arithmetic Teacher,* October, 1970, pp. 499–501.

Riedesel, C. A., *Guiding Discovery in Elementary School Mathematics,* 2nd ed. New York: Prentice-Hall, Inc., 1973, Chap. XV.

Wilkinson, J. D., and O. Nelson, "Probability and Statistics: Trial Teaching in Sixth Grade," *The Arithmetic Teacher,* February, 1966, pp. 100–106.

III

Program for the Development of Basic Mathematics Skills

Beginning Instruction in Mathematics

10

Mathematics is a special language that the children learn by observing their environment and participating in a variety of directed experiences involving number. As children receive proper instruction and mature, they develop an understanding of basic number concepts and mathematical relations. The formation of this understanding is a gradual process that can be fostered but not forced.

Scholars have conducted important research on conceptual thinking in children and have attempted to determine how and when mathematical concepts are formed. They have created devices intended to assist children in the formation of such concepts. Chapter 3 presented current ideas on concept formation in children and some approaches to teaching and learning. This chapter suggests a variety of ideas that can be used to develop and measure mathematical concepts in young children.

THE DEVELOPMENT OF BASIC MATHEMATICAL CONCEPTS

Many of the activities that are presented in this chapter are suitable for kindergarten children, several of them can be presented in Grade 1, and, depending on the children's level, some may have to be introduced or reviewed in Grade 2.

Because of varying levels of difficulty, activities presented under the same heading cannot always be taught in succession. For example, the concept of place value is developed and extended during class periods that are commonly spaced by long periods of time. When selecting activities for the mathematics class, the teacher is guided by the pupils' ability and often by requirements prescribed in the local school curriculum.

Play and Manipulative Experiences

Children's first experiences with number should be the manipulation of objects. Piaget emphasizes that concepts are not derived from the materials themselves, but from the operations performed on the materials. As children manipulate, classify, and rearrange the objects, they observe the transformations and gradually acquire the ability to work the operations mentally and to "think" the transformations. The following activities are suitable for children when they enter school:

Children play with sand, water, blocks, clay, etc.
Containers are filled with water.
Sand pies are made.
Blocks are stacked.
Clay is molded.

Children manipulate and explore objects on a "mathematics table." On such a table various objects are placed; for example, rods, blocks, plastic cubes, disks, beads, balls, tongue depressors, dominoes, containers, measuring cups, spoons, measuring sticks, toy cars, egg cartons, picture books, counting frames, abaci, toy money, a hundred board, a clock, clock faces, geometric figures, templates, a number line, a calendar, a geoboard and colored rubber bands, cutouts representing fractional parts, games, jigsaw puzzles, balance scales, and weights—for example, small bags filled with sand, or bean bags. Usually children do not need much encouragement to play with objects on such a table. While they play, they ask the teacher and each other questions about items and some learning will take place.

On the playground there should be suitable equipment such as sandboxes, plastic balls, and big blocks of wood.

Classifying

In the process of classifying, elements from a given collection are sorted and grouped on the basis of shared characteristics, attributes, or properties.

Young children usually have no trouble during the cleaning-up period putting crayons, pencils, beads, bottle caps, buttons, rulers, clay, etc. in the proper containers. In doing this they sort the materials.

In beginning instruction the teacher talks about things that are alike and belong together. Various activities, in which objects are classified according to such attributes as size, form, color, etc., are undertaken:

Big paper clips are put in one box and small clips in another.
Buttons are sorted according to size.
Crayons are sorted according to color.
Cutouts of geometric figures are sorted according to form.
Toy coins of various denominations are put in different boxes.

Properties of objects are considered—for example: balls can roll all over, juice cans can roll in one direction, cubes cannot roll.

Sorting activities become more difficult when two attributes must be considered, as in the following example in which the child must know the meaning of some simple geometric terms.

Example

> There are two large circles, two small circles, two large squares, and two small squares. One of each set of these two figures is red and the other is blue. The teacher can ask the child to pick up the things that are—
>
> round and red,
> blue and small,
> large and square,
> square and blue, etc.

The sorting activities that were suggested in the preceding paragraphs deal with attributes such as color, shape, and form, which are qualities of objects and which can be observed by children. Number is not a quality of a set of objects but a quantitative idea. Number is abstract and cannot be seen. In most cases it is a difficult process to develop in the child the abstract idea of number. Many school entrants are able to count but do not understand, for example, the "threeness" of three, since they may associate number with the size or with another physical characteristic of the objects under consideration. They may see number not as a quantity but as a quality of things, and may consider it as they do other qualities of an object such as color and shape. Such pupils need many varied experiences with the manipulation of objects to assist them to grasp the idea that the number attached to a group is independent of the physical characteristics of the objects.

Comparing

The teacher displays or points at various sets of objects, and similarities or differences of the sets are identified in class discussions. Statements such as the following are made:

> There are more pencils than crayons.
> There is less water in this bottle than in that one.
> There are fewer coins in this pile than in that one.
> Rick is taller than Jane.
> The book is heavier than the pencil.
> This cube is bigger than that one.
> There are not enough dresses for all the dolls.
> There are as many bats as balls.

When, at a later stage, pupils work with numbers and perform simple operations, numbers are compared and mathematical relations are introduced—for example: 5 is greater than 3, 3 is less than 5, 3 + 2 is equal to 5.

Ordering In beginning instruction in mathematics children need to perform a variety of activities in ordering sets of objects. During such activities terms such as "first," "second," "last," "middle," "before," and "after" are used. The experiences should assist the child when an understanding of the order in the set of counting numbers is being developed.

Examples

Rods of different lengths—for example, Cuisenaire rods—are ordered to make a staircase.
Coins are placed in a row from the smallest to the largest.
Children form a row from the shortest to the tallest child.
On a geoboard steps are made by using rubber bands as in the illustration.

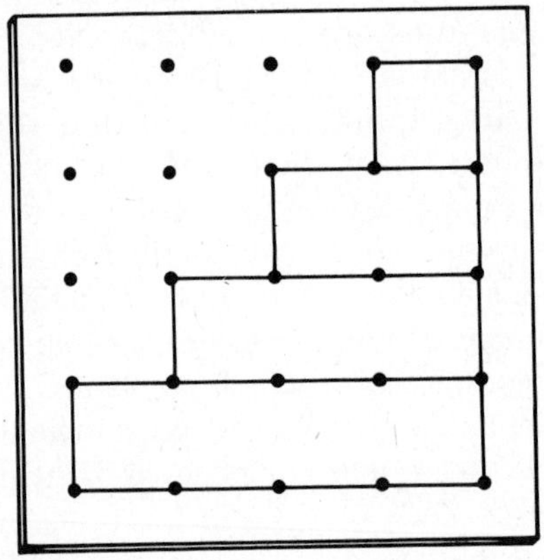

Some toy animals or pictures of animals are placed in a row as illustrated and questions can be presented such as:

Which animal is the first in the row?
Which animal is the second in the row?
Which animal is the last in the row?
Which animal is in the middle of the row?
Which animal is just before the sheep?
Which animal is just behind the dog?

A similar set of animals is placed at random on the table. The child is asked to make a row of animals in the same order as they appear in the teacher's row.

It becomes more difficult when the child has to make a row of animals in which the parade is headed in the opposite direction.

Matching

When children learn to count rationally they must have acquired skill in placing objects in one-to-one correspondence. Young children often have difficulty with such activities if they observe two rows of the same length but with different numbers of objects; they may decide that there are the same number of objects in the rows since they only consider the length. Therefore, the teacher provides experiences in matching when needed. Some suggestions for such activities follow:

Plastic eggs are placed in an egg carton.
Pegs are put in a pegboard.
Dolls are dressed.
Plastic cups and saucers are matched.
Pictures of dogs and doghouses are provided and each dog is matched with a doghouse.

A more advanced activity is playing the game of dominoes. Also, at a later stage, cards are matched, as in the following illustration.

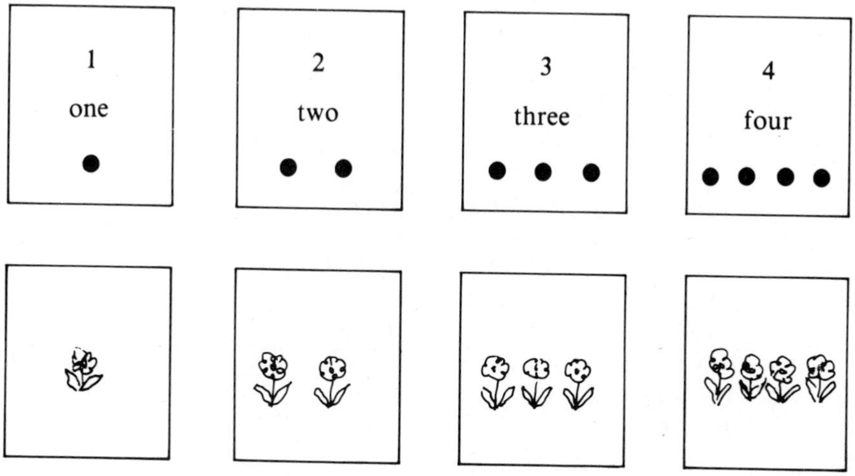

Counting

In *rote counting* the number names are recited in order without referring to objects. For example, the teacher recites number names in order and the children repeat them.

How many?

Rhymes in which number names can be used are memorized. In the example which follows children can perform the suggested actions.

One, two,
Buckle my shoe.
Three, four,
Open the door.
Five, six,
Pick up sticks.
Seven, eight,
Get a plate.
Nine, ten,
Start again.

The purpose of *rational counting* is to determine the cardinal number of a given set of objects or to identify the place that an object under consideration occupies in a series.

Various sets of objects are counted.
Children count off for games.

A song is memorized and acted out. In the following example, ten children are lined up and one pupil points at them in turn while the whole class sings the song.

One little, two little, three little children;
Four little, five little, six little children;
Seven little, eight little, nine little children;
Ten little boys and girls.

Effective counting devices are the counting frame and the hundred board.

A *counting frame* has movable beads on rods. Initially, children work with one rod that has ten beads. Then a frame with two rods of ten beads each is used. Finally a frame with ten rods of ten beads is introduced.

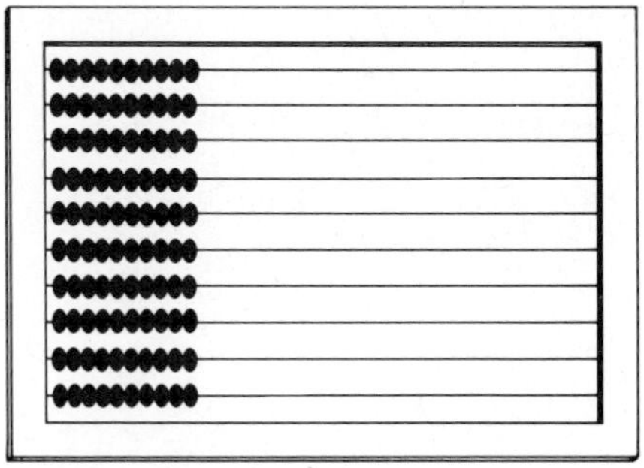

The tool is also used for skip counting; for example, the children count by tens while they move the rows of ten beads one by one successively. At later stages the device is used with addition and subtraction problems, with the introduction of the operations of multiplication and division, and in upper grades with the introduction of bases other than ten if this topic is included in the curriculum.

A *hundred board* is constructed by nailing ten rows of ten brads into a piece of plywood. Disks—for example, price tags—are numbered on one side from 1 to 100. The disks have small holes so that they can be placed on the brads.

The board is used not only for counting, skip counting, and counting backward, but also, in primary and middle grades, for activities such as those described in the following paragraphs.

The teacher places the numerals on the board in order and then turns several of the disks upside down. The child must decide which numerals appear on the other side of the blank disk. This activity is self-corrective.

Only a part of the numbered disks are displayed at the proper places. The remaining disks are put in a pile, and the child must complete the hundred board by putting all the disks on the proper brads.

When, at a later time, multiplication is introduced, the numerals that express multiples of a given number are displayed on the board.

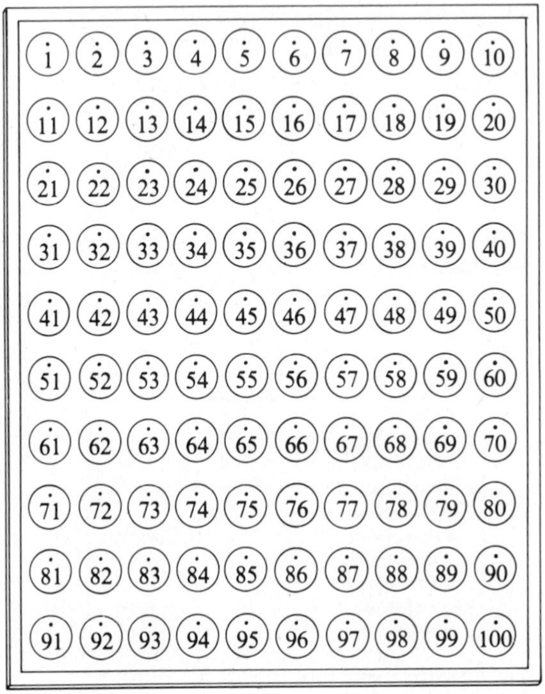

Number patterns are shown on the board. For example, only even numbers are shown, or only odd numbers are displayed, or multiples of 10 are connected by a rubber band, or multiples of 9 through 81 are connected.

The board can be used as a geoboard and the child constructs squares or rectangles by using rubber bands. Then the number of the enclosed small squares is determined.

Working with Sets of Objects

The term *set* is used in early instruction and children gradually become able to use it properly. However, for most young children it is difficult to understand what *subset* means, and it appears that it is better to introduce this term at a later stage. The teacher may also decide to postpone using the expressions "the empty set" and "a set of one object," since this language may confuse many young children.

Hands-on activities are provided and objects are manipulated to develop the idea of number, as suggested in the following paragraphs.

Objects are displayed on the floor, table, flannel board, or magnetic board, and the number of objects in a given set is determined during class discussions. Children also use collections of counters individually and in small groups.

Sets of objects are joined and separated. For example, a set of 3 books and a set of 2 books are joined and the number of the new set is determined; a set of 7 books is separated to form a set of 4 books and a set of 3 books, and the other possible arrangements are found.

Objects are placed on the floor. Some objects are surrounded by a piece of red yarn and the remainder of the objects by a piece of blue yarn. These questions are asked: How many things are in the first set? How many are in the second set? How many things are there in all? How many more are in the second set than in the first set? How many fewer are in the first set than in the second set?

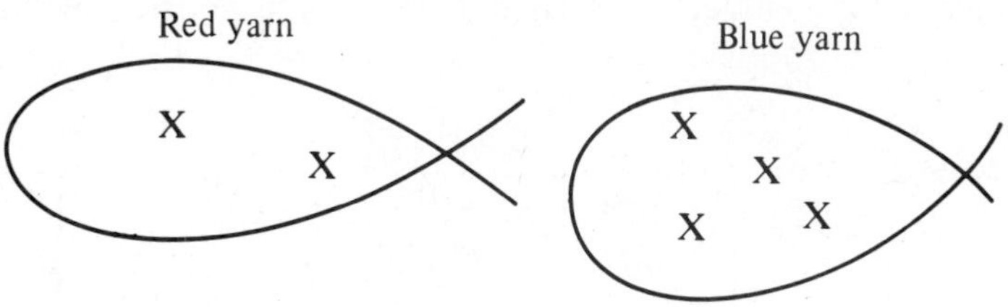

Objects are placed on the floor within two intersecting loops of, for example, red and blue yarn as illustrated. The teacher asks questions such as: How many things are there in all? How many things are within the red yarn? How many are within the blue yarn? How many are within both the red and the blue yarn? How many things are only within the red yarn? Then the arrangement is changed or a different number of objects is used and number questions are presented by the teacher and also by the children. As a variation, children can stand within loops of yarn.

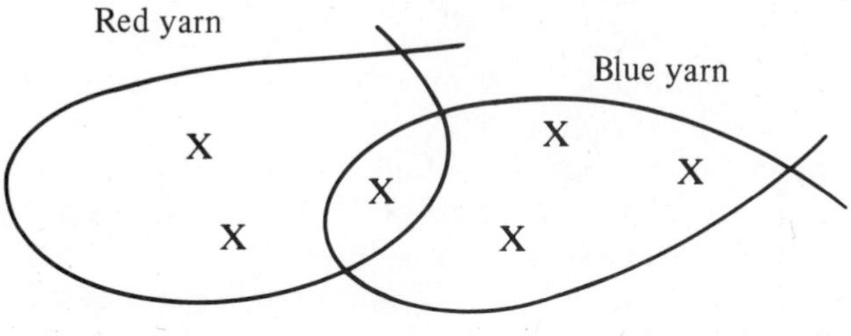

Children should learn to recognize the number of small groups of objects without counting. Cards with 1 through 6 dots are made available. After many experiences in counting the dots, the pupils should become able to say the number of dots without counting. Or a die is rolled and children attempt to say how many dots are shown on the top face without counting.

Counting frames—first with one row of 10 beads and later with 2 rows of 10 beads each—are used. Children isolate a set of beads and find various arrangements of the set.

Recognizing and Writing Numerals Names of displayed numerals are recited by the teacher and repeated by the children.

Numerals cut out of sandpaper are traced by the children.

Children look at a large displayed numeral and write it in the air.

Children make numerals from clay.

Cutout numerals are placed on the bulletin board and accompanied by the printed word and by a corresponding number of pictures.

Children write numerals, assisted by indications concerning the order of the strokes as in the example.

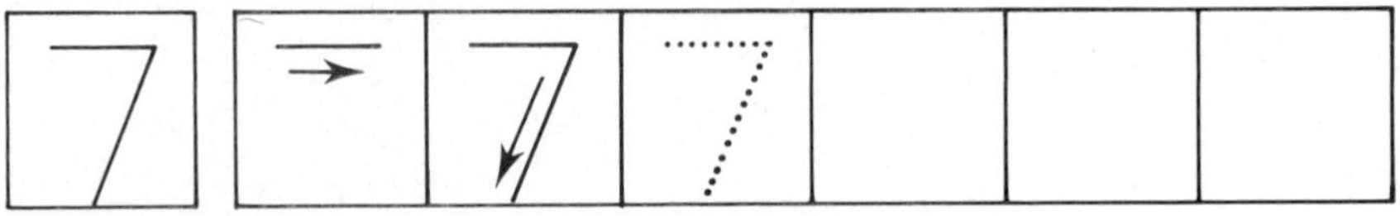

Numerals are read from a calendar.

Children collect and display stamps and read the numerals on the stamps.

Picture books that include large numerals are examined and numerals are identified and read.

Telling Time Several school entrants are somewhat acquainted with the clock and with terms that relate to times of the day. Therefore, activities that deal with the clock and with telling time are new experiences for some children and serve as a review for other pupils.

There should be a clock in each classroom. Also toy clocks, clock faces, short hands, and long hands are needed, and children should be encouraged to play and experiment with these materials.

The terms "morning," "noon," "afternoon," and "evening" are introduced. When children can read numerals to 12, they are introduced to telling time to the hour. The clock is set to show when it is, for example, time to go to school, lunchtime, time to go home, T.V. time, suppertime, time to go to bed.

Commonly in Grade 1 time is told to the half hour; in Grade 2 (and sometimes in Grade 1) to the quarter hour; in Grades 2 and 3 to five-minute and one-minute intervals.

Children who can read numerals do not find it difficult to tell time to the hour and usually can also learn readily to tell time to the half hour. Difficulties often arise when time must be told to the quarter hour and to five-minute intervals. And it becomes greatly confusing to the child when the terms "before" and "to" are used as in "a quarter before ten" or "ten minutes to six."

Clark[1] suggests initial use of a one-handed clock to prepare children for more precise time telling.

Reisman[2] recommends—as a result of conducted research—that instruction begin in telling time to the minute when the child can count to 60, and to have this instruction followed by teaching to tell time by intervals of 5 minutes and of quarter hours.

Using the Calendar

Useful devices for kindergarten and primary-grade children are a regular calendar and a day-to-day calendar that is changed every schoolday to bring it "up-to-date."

On the changeable calendar names of days and months are changed and numerals are placed on brads as required. A simple drawing showing how the weather is—sunny, cloudy, rainy, snowy—can be attached to the calendar. Also the outside temperature, read at the beginning of the schoolday, can be expressed on the calendar in Celsius and Fahrenheit degrees when children are ready for this activity. The illustrated calendar shows Monday, April 7, which is a sunny day with a temperature of 15° Celsius or 59° Fahrenheit.

Terms such as "today," "tomorrow," "yesterday," and "next week" are used in initial instruction, and gradually other terms are introduced, for example, "the day after tomorrow," "next month," and "last year."

First the names of the days of the week are memorized and later the names of the months of the year.

A variety of questions can be asked:

On what days do we go to school?
Do we go to school on Saturday?
When do we have vacation?
Tell me about Christmas.
Tell me about Thanksgiving.

---

1. C. H. Clark, "A One-handed Clock," *The Arithmetic Teacher* (March, 1960), p. 127.
2. F. K. Reisman, "Children's Errors in Telling Time and a Recommended Teaching Sequence," *The Arithmetic Teacher* (March, 1971), pp. 152–155.

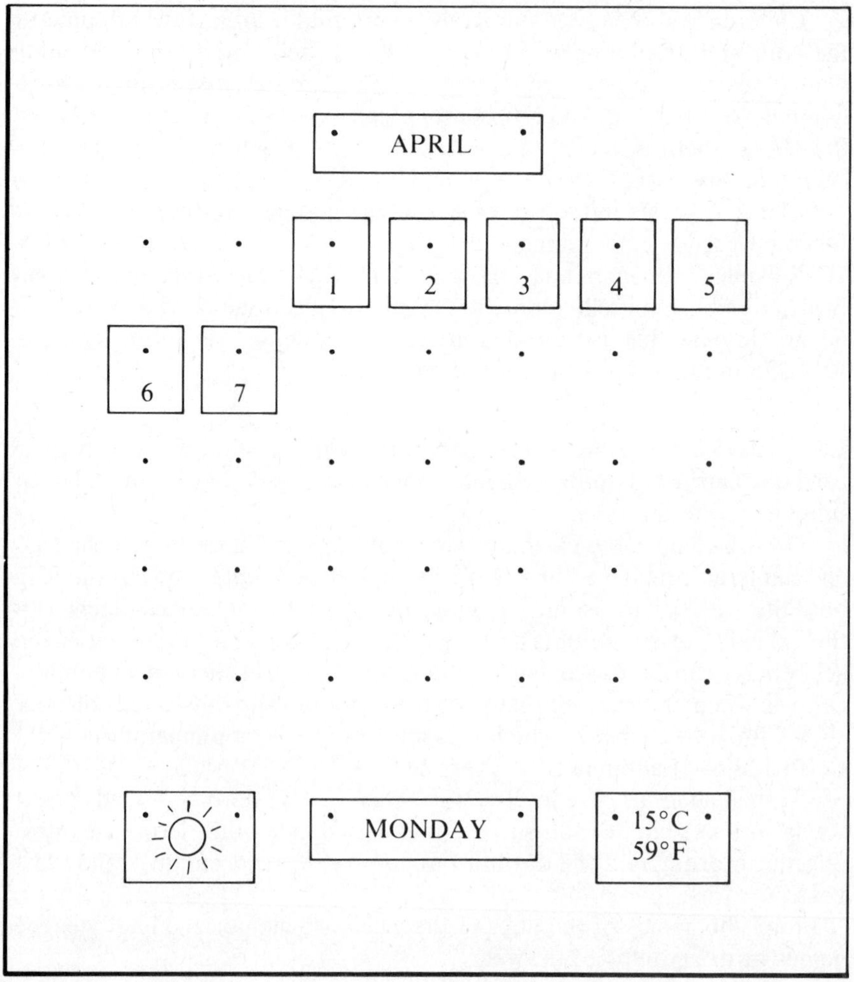

Additional activities include the counting of the number of days the children will have to wait until a special event will occur.

Each schoolday the calendar can be a source for activities even if not all experiences are meaningful to all children. The children will gradually learn to use and interpret this teaching device.

Place Value When children have joined and separated groups of objects and worked addition and subtraction exercises with sums not greater than 10, and also can count rationally beyond 10, the concept of place value is introduced.

Initial instruction in place value deals with the numerals 11 through 19 and is followed by presentations of numerals through 99. Later, numerals of 3 and more digits are considered. In the following paragraphs activities and devices for the development and refinement of the concept of place value are suggested.

A group of, for example, 12 objects, placed on the floor, is counted by the pupils. Following directions of the teacher, the children isolate 10 of them and surround that group by a loop of yarn. The remaining 2 objects are also enclosed by yarn. It is decided that there is 1 group of ten plus 2 ones and the situation is represented on the chalkboard:

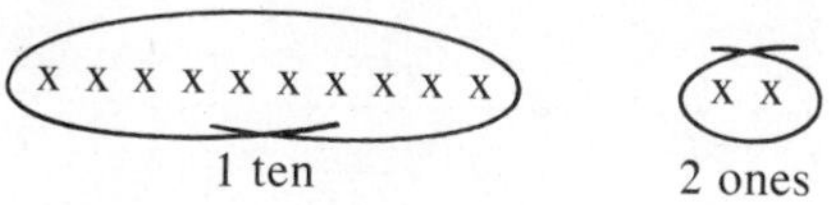

12 = 1 ten 2 ones
12 = 10 + 2

The flannel board, magnetic board, and overhead projector can be used with the whole class. Objects are arranged in groups of 10 each and the remaining 1s are also isolated. On the magnetic board groups of 10 pennies each can be exchanged for 1 dime.

The place-value pocket chart has initially only pockets for tens and ones and is expanded when numerals of more than two digits are considered. In the tens place of the pocket chart bundled groups of 10 objects, for example, tongue depressors or strips of sturdy paper, are inserted to show the number of tens. The illustrated pocket chart shows 3 tens and 4 ones.

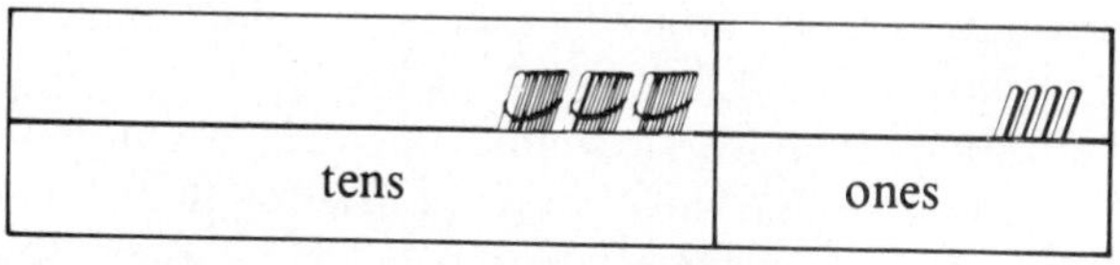

34 = 3 tens 4 ones
34 = 30 + 4

tens	ones
3	4

An abacus is a simple and useful device to assist children in the development of the concept of place value when numerals of three and more digits are considered. An abacus can be constructed by using a block of wood and dowels. Washers or beads with holes can be placed on the rods. In the illustration the number 542 is represented.

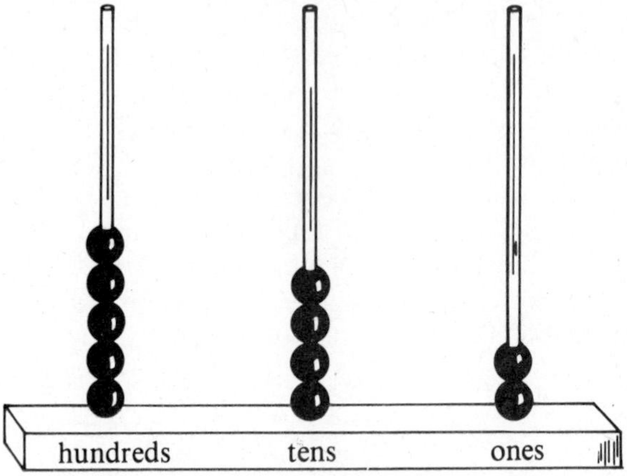

542 = 5 hundreds 4 tens 2 ones

542 = 500 + 40 + 2

Verbal-Problem Solving

Verbal quantitative problems are introduced when children begin to work with numbers. The environment and daily experiences are ideal sources from which problems can be constructed. Also a variety of devices are used for that purpose.

Objects are manipulated and counted to solve problems that are orally presented.

The teacher tells a story involving numbers, presents related verbal problems, and assists children in solving the problems.

Toy money is used to buy and sell articles that have price tags.

Pictures are shown and children are encouraged to ask and solve number questions that can be deduced from the pictures. For example, a picture with three birds, two cats, and four dogs is shown. The children try to find answers to questions such as: How many animals are there in all? How many fewer cats than dogs? How many more birds than cats? How many heads in all? How many legs does a bird have? How many legs does a dog have? How many animals can fly? How many animals cannot fly? How many animals can bark? If each dog will get a doghouse, how many doghouses are needed? How many animals do you think are afraid of the cats? How many animals can get to the top of a tree?

The clock, calendar, and thermometer are used to construct and solve meaningful problems.

Cassettes on which simple word problems are recorded can be used by individual children.

The teacher can give optional assignments such as:

When you go home, count the number of stop signs you see.

Tell me tomorrow how many cars with out-of-state license plates you have seen on your way to school.

Additional Activities

Other activities that are suitable for beginning instruction in mathematics are identified and briefly illustrated in the paragraphs that follow.

Using the Number Line

Example

The numerals 0 through 10 are marked on the floor, about the length of a child's step apart. The child starts at 0 and walks the 10 steps. The concept should be developed that zero is the starting point and that the numeral 1 appears at the end of the first unit.

Measuring

Example 1

The child measures the length of a desk in spans.

Example 2

A trundle wheel with a circumference of 1 meter is used to find the approximate length of the room in meters. The clicks the wheel makes are counted to determine the number of meters.

Example 3

The length of a crayon is measured in centimeters.

Weighing

Example

Five new pencils are placed on one pan of a balance scale and 3 pencils on the other. The child has to determine how many additional pencils must be placed on the second pan or how many must be removed from the first pan to make them balance. The fact that this activity is self-corrective will motivate children.

Finding Properties of Three-dimensional Objects

Example

After explorations it is decided that a ball can roll all over, that a juice can roll in one direction, and that a box cannot roll.

Recognizing Geometric Shapes

Example

The child learns to identify rectangles, squares, and circles and finds examples of such shapes in the room.

Using Fractional Numbers

Example 1

Two children tear a sheet of paper into two parts of the same size and each child gets one part. It is decided that each one has one half of the sheet of paper.

Example 2

Children are asked to pour water into a container so that about half of it is filled.

Example 3

At later stages activities similar to those suggested in examples 1 and 2 are presented but the fractional number one fourth is used.

Finding Patterns

Example 1

The teacher displays in a row a penny, a penny, a nickel, a penny, a penny, a nickel, a penny. The child is asked to examine the row of coins and to tell which coin should come next.

Example 2

The hundred board is used to discover number patterns as described previously in this chapter.

INCIDENTAL EXPERIENCES AND SEQUENTIAL PROGRAMS

The approach to initial mathematics instruction that incorporates the experiences the child meets in daily life has been called by Lovell[3] the *environment approach*. The idea is that incidental experiences that occur during the child's play and class projects make the resultant learning meaningful, since there is a need for it in the situation that is encountered. In such situations, children, individually or in small groups, count, match, combine, separate, compare, measure, and weigh. They engage in ac-

---

3. K. Lovell, *The Growth of Basic Mathematical and Scientific Concepts in Children* (London: University of London Press, Ltd., 1961), pp. 40–45.

tivities they themselves have selected. Exercises with number devices are introduced as the need arises.

Lovell believes that foundations for more complex forms of mental activity are laid during a child's first seven years of play. However, he warns that the flashes of insight or moments of understanding that children get in unstructured (or structured) situations are not always transferred to other more difficult situations, since the child's thinking is still very patchy and uncertain. Thus one may overestimate the quality of the child's thinking.

Most educators doubt the efficiency of an exclusive use of the environmental approach and do not want to rely upon it to form necessary mathematical foundations. In fact, an increasing number of people maintain that basic mathematics facts must be presented in proper sequential order and that such a structured program should be supplemented and reinforced by interesting activities and laboratory situations. The chapters that follow are based upon this premise.

Basic mathematics textbooks and the activities suggested in the first part of this chapter will assist the teacher in planning a structured, sequential mathematics programs.

Commercial devices have also been constructed to provide structured number experiences for the beginning schoolchild. These approaches usually provide some experimental play and then directed work with the materials, so that, from the beginning, the child is aided in abstracting number experiences. The Cuisenaire rods described below are such a device.

The Cuisenaire Rods

The Cuisenaire rods,[4] also known as "Numbers in Color," were devised a few decades ago by George Cuisenaire, a Belgian schoolteacher, in an attempt to provide a new approach to the teaching of the early stages of arithmetic. Dr. Caleb Gattegno, an English mathematician, assisted Cuisenaire later in the further development of the method.

This method of teaching is based on the conviction that it is possible to perceive many mathematical relationships visually or through other sensory experiences. The child manipulates colored wooden rods, compares the resultant patterns, and thereby discovers relations, similarities, and differences. Discoveries of particular relationships are assumed to lead to generalizations and hypotheses whose validity may be directly investigated. The rods are not used for computational purposes. They are

4. The student is referred to J. Davidson, *Using the Cuisenaire Rods—A Photo/Text Guide for Teachers* (New Rochelle, N.Y.: Cuisenaire Company of America, Inc., 1969).

used to provide a basis in experience for understanding the particular facts and general laws of mathematics, and also to investigate, test, or prove mathematical statements.

The materials consist of sets of rods made of wood one square centimeter in cross section and varying in length from one to ten centimeters. Each of the ten different sizes has a characteristic color, and each differently colored rod is represented by a letter symbol, as listed in Table 10.1.

The Cuisenaire rods are introduced in four stages:

1. *The free play stage.* During this stage the pupil makes any arrangement he or she wants to with the rods, and no restrictions are imposed upon the child. Gattegno calls free play a dialogue between the child and the rods, since the rods suggest questions as well as answers. The time allocated for free play depends upon the maturity of the pupils. If the rods are introduced in kindergarten, several months may have to be spent in free play activities. But if they are first introduced in the primary grades, only a few weeks may suffice.

2. *The stage of free play and directed activities without written notation.* During this period the teacher suggests specific arrangements of the rods that bring out basic mathematical ideas and relationships. The child arranges the rods as directed and reports what he or she sees and discovers.

3. *The stage in which written signs and symbols are introduced.* Letter symbols representing the length of the rods are used, and the symbols +, −, ×, ÷, =, and □ are introduced. Sentences such as $r = w + w$, $r - w = w$, and $g - r = w$ are written.

Table 10.1

Length of the Rod	*Color Name*	*Letter Symbol*
1 cm	white	*w*
2 cm	red	*r*
3 cm	light green	*g*
4 cm	purple	*p*
5 cm	yellow	*y*
6 cm	dark green	*d*
7 cm	black	*k*
8 cm	brown	*n*
9 cm	blue	*e*
10 cm	orange	*o*

4. *The stage in which number values are assigned to the rods.* During this stage the pupils treat the rods as models of numbers. Appropriate number values are assigned to each rod and operations are performed. Any rod can be selected as the basic measuring unit. Thus the numerical

value of a rod will change as different rods are selected as basic measuring rods. For example, if the purple rod is the measuring rod and its length is called one, then the red rod is called $\frac{1}{2}$ and the yellow rod $\frac{5}{4}$.

Since any equation made with the rods can be thought of as addition or as subtraction, these two operations are both dealt with at the same time.

Example

The drawing shown below represents an arrangement of black, yellow, and red rods and suggests these sentences:

$$7 = 5 + 2; 7 - 5 = 2; 7 = 2 + 5; 7 - 2 = 5.$$

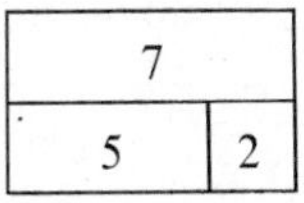

Exercises with the rods have been provided not only for the primary grades, but also for older children.

The Cuisenaire method, if used properly, is an approach that the teacher may use along with other approaches in the teaching of mathematics in kindergarten and the primary grades.

THE MEASUREMENT OF BASIC MATHEMATICAL CONCEPTS

The extensiveness of mathematical skills, as well as the quantity and quality of the number concepts that school entrants have already acquired, varies widely with different children. Concepts and skills are therefore assessed before the teacher plans foundation experiences in mathematics. Though commercial readiness tests are available, the teacher himself can construct an instrument that fits his specific situation.

To assist the teacher in the preparation of such a test, several items are suggested below. Some of these items are to be used in testing skills, and the teacher will need to record the extent to which each pupil has mastered the skill tested. Concepts are tested by means of simple experiments in which the child is to react to situations. When interpreting the responses, the teacher must realize that a correct answer is no guarantee that the concept being tested has been fully acquired. The child who happens to be at an intermediate stage of development may supply the correct response, but may still be very uncertain. Thus if the teacher considers the child's understanding of the situation to be unstable, additional questions should be presented and more experiments that test the same concept should be conducted.

Suggestions for a Number Readiness Test

1. Rote counting to ______.
   Note: The teacher should decide how far the child's counting ability will be tested.
2. Rational counting to ______.
3. Recognition of numerals to ______.
   Note: The numerals presented should be out of sequence.
4. Ability to write numerals to ______.
5. Ability to recognize one-half of an object. ______ (Yes or No).
6. Ability to identify a group of ______ objects.

   Suggested experiment: The teacher presents the child with three cards on which different groups of similar objects are shown—for example, stars. The teacher asks: "On which card are there five stars?" This experiment is repeated with a larger group if the child supplies the correct answer.
7. Ability to reproduce a group of ______ objects.

   Suggested experiment: The teacher shows the child several groups of objects in succession, and asks the child each time to place next to the group shown as many disks as there are objects in the group. The numbers that represent the groups presented should not form a sequence.
8. Awareness of conservation of discontinuous quantities.

   Suggested experiment: The teacher places 24 pennies in two rows of 12 pennies each. The teacher asks the child to match each penny in the first row with one in the second row until all the pennies have been placed in pairs. As a result, the child should agree that there are just as many pennies in the first row as there are in the second. Then the teacher places one of the rows of pennies in a pile and spreads the other row of pennies out so that it becomes longer. By asking carefully worded questions the teacher attempts to determine whether the child is aware of the fact that there is still the same number of pennies in each set.
9. Awareness of conservation of continuous quantities.

   Suggested experiment: Two glasses of the same shape and size are partly filled with water, so that the child readily agrees that there is just as much water in one glass as there is in the other. The teacher then directs the child to pour the water from one of the glasses into a narrower, taller glass. Then the teacher asks questions to determine whether the child is aware of the fact that there is the same amount of water in the two glasses.
10. An understanding of the part-whole relationship.

    Suggested experiment: The teacher shows the child a number of beads—for example, 15—all of which are made of wood and most of which—for example, 12—are white, and the remainder red. The teacher asks: "Are there more white beads or are there more wooden beads?"
11. Capacity for seriation.

Suggested experiment: The child places rods of different lengths in a series, from the shortest to the longest.

12. Ability to use ordinal numbers to ________.

Suggested experiment: The teacher shows the child a set of blocks of different lengths, arranged in the form of a staircase. The teacher points to the bottom step and says: "If this step is number one, point to the step that is number four."

Other experiments may be devised and conducted to appraise the child's concepts of measurement, time, money, and geometry.

SELECTED RESEARCH

The purpose of this study[5] was to determine whether first-grade children at different levels of comprehension of conservation of numerousness perform the same way in other important aspects of the arithmetic curriculum.

A test of twelve items dealing with conservation of numerousness was administered to 341 children at the end of the first grade. The twelve items were subdivided into three parts of four items each. In each part objects were arranged differently: in a rectangle, a line, and a circle. The first three items of each part consisted of a set of six objects and a set of eight objects, whereas the fourth item of each part contained two sets of eight objects each. The results of the test are presented in Table 10.2.

Table 10.2
Frequencies of Correct Responses of 341 Children

Part	*Arrangement*	*Item*			
		1	2	3	4
1	Rectangular	326	333	317	197
2	Linear	227	339	265	128
3	Circular	317	324	289	120

The table indicates that the fourth item, requiring the comparison of sets that contained the same number of elements, was much more

5. L. P. Steffe, "The Relationship of Conservation of Numerousness to Problem-Solving Abilities of First-Grade Children," *The Arithmetic Teacher* (January, 1968), pp. 47–52.

difficult than the first three items. The investigator suggested the following explanation of this phenomenon: A child could score any of the first three items correctly by using no more than a visual inspection of the items, whereas for the fourth item the pupil had to either count or set up a one-to-one correspondence in order to score the item correctly. It was found that if a child missed at least one item of each part, it was practically certain that the fourth item would be among those missed.

As a result of test performance, four levels were designated:

Level 1. Children who had perfect scores on the conservation test ($n = 60$).

Level 2: Children with exactly two parts of the test correct ($n = 69$).

Level 3: Children with exactly one part of the test correct ($n = 84$).

Level 4: Children with at least one item of each part incorrect ($n = 128$).

The investigator also attempted to determine whether children in the levels identified above performed the same way on quantitative word problems and arithmetic facts.

Two tests were administered to the 341 children: one of eighteen addition problems and one of ten addition facts. Of the eighteen addition problems, six had accompanying visual aids, six had accompanying pictorial aids, and six had no aids. Nine of the eighteen problems involved a transformation and nine did not. (Example of a problem involving transformation: There are four jacks in a pile, and four more are put with them. Now how many jacks are in the pile? Example of a problem not involving transformation: There are five cookies on a plate and there are two cookies on another plate. How many cookies are on the plates?)

From each of the four levels of performance a stratified random sample of thirty-three children was taken. These pupils were in the following IQ groups: eleven in the 114–140 groups, eleven in the 101–113 group, eleven in the 78–100 group.

The mean scores to the nearest percent of the thirty-three pupils in each level on the eighteen addition problems were: Level 1, 87; Level 2, 85; Level 3, 82; Level 4, 69. Thus the children in Level 4 performed significantly worse than the children in the first three levels.

Other observations included:

1. The children in Level 4 based their judgments largely on perception instead of bringing to mind procedures (setting up one-to-one correspondence and counting).
2. Problems with physical and pictorial aids appeared to be of about equal difficulty.
3. There was a sharp decline in performance when aids were taken away.
4. The children in Level 4 performed quite modestly on problems with aids and quite poorly on problems without aids.
5. The children in the first three levels performed modestly on the verbal problems but did quite well on the problems with aids.
6. The problems involving transformation appeared to be easier than those that did not involve transformation.

On the test of addition facts, the children in Level 4 also scored significantly lower than the pupils in the other levels.

The investigator stated that these results should not be interpreted to mean that children will do better on problem solving if they are drilled more on addition facts. He suggested that if the problem-solving abilities of Level 4 children can be improved, then their knowledge of addition facts will also improve.

SELECTED ACTIVITIES FOR PUPILS

1. Matching objects.
   Get a cup for each saucer.
2. Ordering sets of objects.
   Put all the long rods in a box.
3. Comparing objects.
   a. Mark the long pencil.

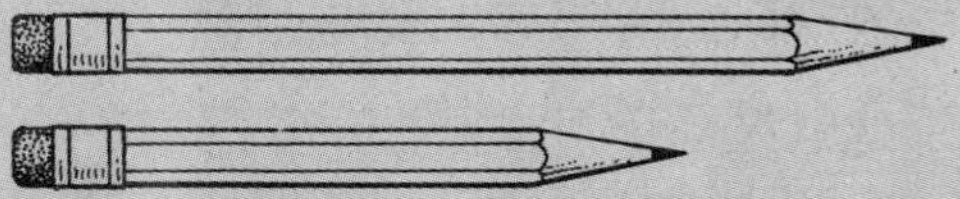

   b. Mark the heavy object.

4. Comparing quantities.
   Mark the set that has more elements.

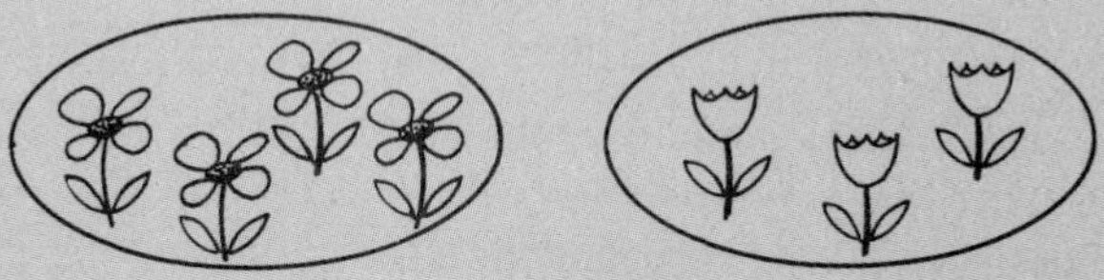

5. Constructing models.
   Build a house from blocks.
6. Arranging objects.
   Put all the rods in order from the shortest to the longest.
7. Changing the form but not the volume of an object.
   Make shapes from modeling clay.
8. Counting.
   Count the beads.

9. Identifying the place that a given element occupies in the series.
   Mark the third flower.

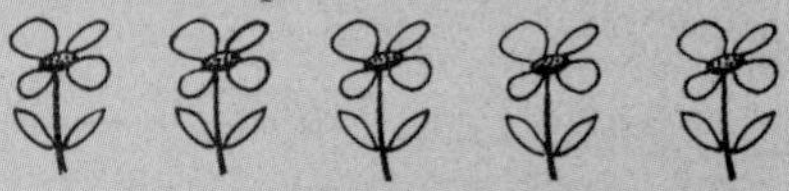

10. Determining how many.
    Color the right numeral.

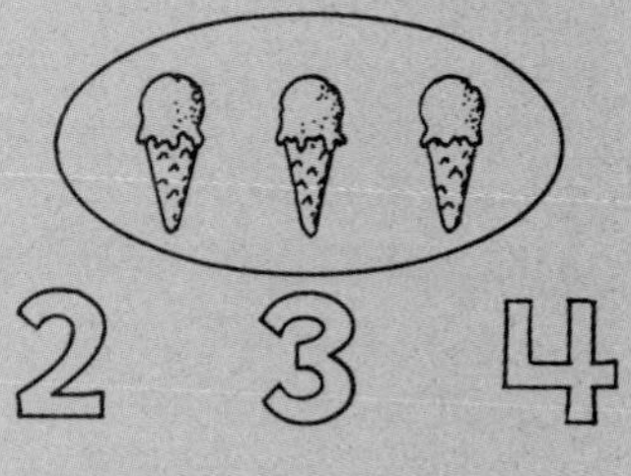

11. Ordering numbers.
    Starting at 1, draw the lines.

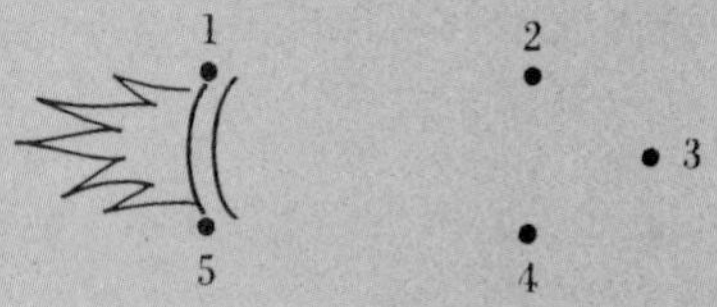

12. Identifying fractional parts.
    Tear a sheet into two parts that are the same size.

13. Recognizing coins.
    Mark the nickel.

14. Measuring length.
    How many paper clips long is the pen?

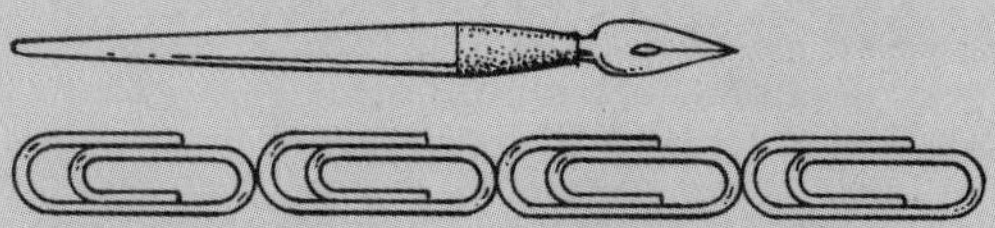

15. Measuring capacity.
    How many spoonfuls of sand are needed to fill a cup?
16. Comparing quantities.
    Cut out the hats.
    Paste them on the heads of the children.

17. Playing games.
    Play the game of dominoes.
18. Using the calendar.
    Tell today's date.
19. Telling time.
    Put the toy clock at the time when school starts.
20. Making a numeral.
    Use clay to make the numeral that tells how old you are.
21. Making shapes.
    Take rubber bands and put them on a geoboard in different shapes.

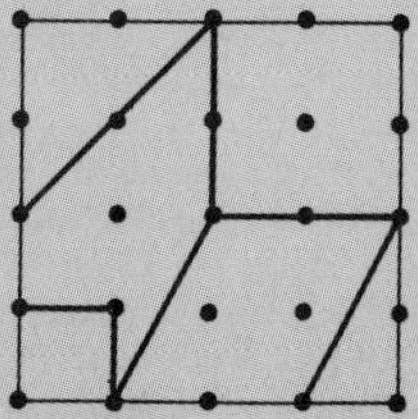

22. Recognizing geometric shapes.
    Color the circle green, the squares blue, the rectangles red, and the triangles orange.

23. Showing shapes.
    Make a circle with your hand.

24. Assigning numbers to parts of a whole.
    Find the number of each part.

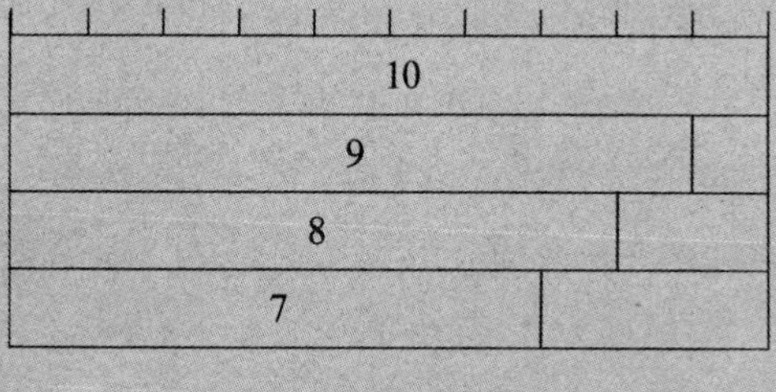

25. Working with money.
    Mark the item that costs more.

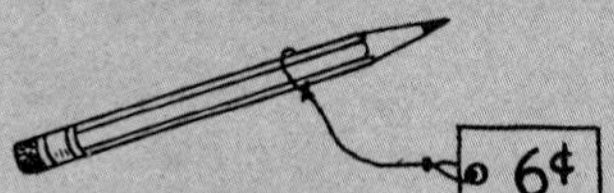

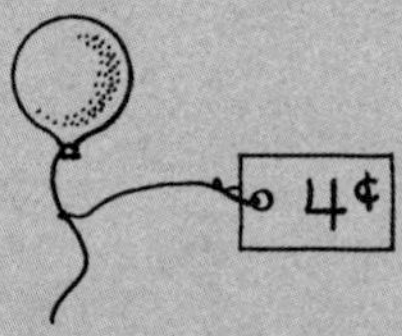

26. Finding patterns.
    Find the patterns and complete the sentences.

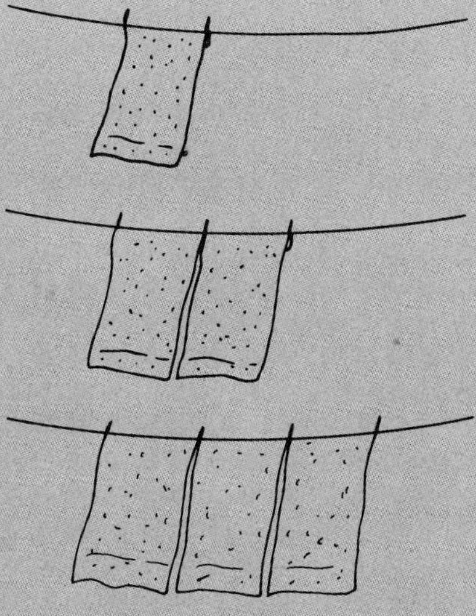

a. I need 2 clothespins to hang 1 towel.
For 2 towels I can use 4 pins, but I really need only 3 pins.
For 3 towels I need only 4 pins.
For 4 towels I need only ______ pins.
For 6 towels I need only ______ pins.
For 10 towels I need only ______ pins.

b. In a row of houses there is 1 tree between 2 houses.

When there are 3 houses there are 2 trees.

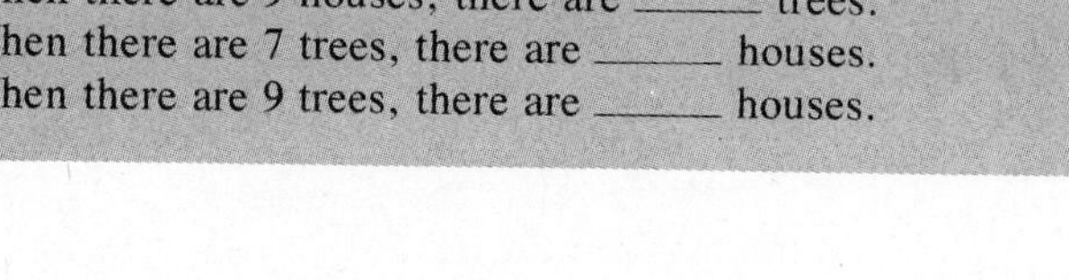

When there are 5 houses, there are ______ trees.
When there are 9 houses, there are ______ trees.
When there are 7 trees, there are ______ houses.
When there are 9 trees, there are ______ houses.

27. Interpreting and making graphs.

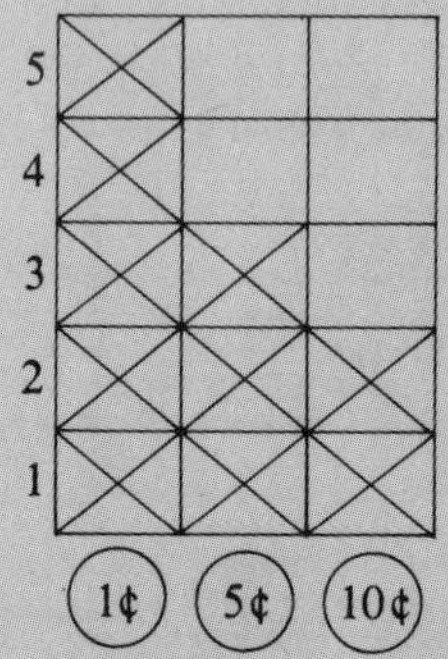

a. Lois made this graph to show how many pennies, nickels, and dimes she had. For each coin she had she marked one box. Lois had ______ pennies, ______ nickels, and ______ dimes.
b. Ray had 4 pennies, 2 nickels, and 3 dimes. Make a graph that shows how many pennies, nickels, and dimes Ray had.

28. Playing games.
Two children play this game.
They draw a number line up to 6 and need a die.
The first one rolls the die.
Suppose 4 dots are shown on the top surface.
The first player draws a mark *above* the 4 on the number line as shown.

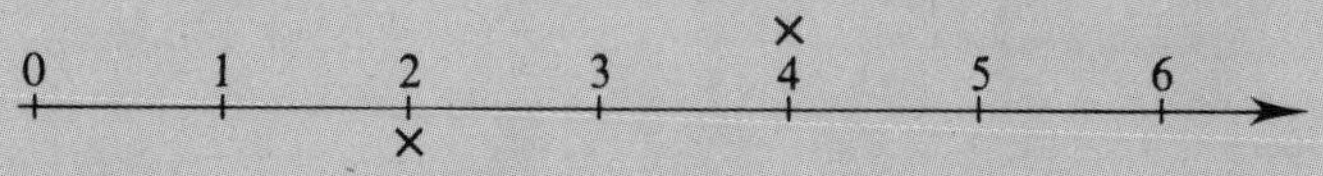

Then the second player rolls the die.
If 2 dots are shown, the player draws a mark *under* the 2 on the number line as shown.
If a player rolls a number that he or she has already marked, that player passes.
The first player who has marked all numbers 1 through 6 is the winner.

29. Coloring part of a whole.
Color one half.

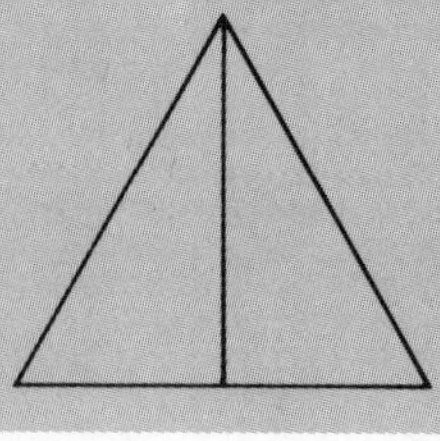

30. Giving information.
    Answer as many of the following questions as you can.
    How old are you?
    What is your birthday?
    What is your address?
    What is your telephone number?
    How tall are you in feet and inches?
    How tall are you in centimeters?
    How many pounds do you weigh?
    How many kilograms do you weigh?

EXERCISES

1. React to this statement: "Concepts are not derived from the materials themselves, but from the operations performed on the materials."
2. Select or design activities to test children's ability to—
   a. classify objects.
   b. compare objects.
   c. order objects.
   d. match objects.
3. Explain the difference between rote counting and rational counting.
4. Identify devices suitable for introducing the concept of place value and describe how you would use them.
5. Draw a picture you would use with young children for the purpose of constructing and solving simple verbal quantitative problems.
6. Explain why many children experience difficulties in telling time.
7. Explain and illustrate how these devices can be used:
   a. Counting frame.
   b. Abacus.
   c. Pocket chart.
   d. Flannel board.
   e. Hundred board.
   f. Clock.
   g. Calendar.
   h. Geoboard.
8. Describe activities in which young children—
   a. use the number line.
   b. measure.
   c. weigh.
   d. use geometric shapes.
9. Contrast the environmental approach and the structured approach in teaching mathematics. State which approach you want to emphasize and defend your statement.
10. Describe the important characteristics of the Cuisenaire rods.
11. Outline a demonstration lesson with the Cuisenaire rods.

SOURCES FOR FURTHER READING

Biggs, E. E., and J. R. MacLean, *Freedom to Learn*. Don Mills, Ontario: Addison-Wesley (Canada), Ltd., 1969.

Bruni, J. V., and H. J. Silverman, "Developing Intuitive Ideas about Time," *The Arithmetic Teacher,* December, 1976, pp. 582–591.

Copeland, R. W., *How Children Learn Mathematics,* 2nd ed. New York: Macmillan Publishing Company, Inc., 1974, Chap. VI.

Copeland, R. W., *Mathematics and the Elementary School Teacher,* 2nd ed. Philadelphia: W. B. Saunders Company, 1972, Chap. IV.

Fennema, E. H., "Models and Mathematics," *The Arithmetic Teacher,* December, 1972, pp. 635–640.

Hollister, G. E., and A. G. Gunderson, *Teaching Arithmetic in the Primary Grades*. Lexington, Mass.: D. C. Heath & Company, 1964.

Kennedy, L. M., *Guiding Children to Mathematical Discovery,* 2nd ed. Belmont, California: Wadsworth Publishing Company, Inc., 1975, Chap. IV.

Lee, J. J., *Suggestions for Teaching Arithmetic in Infant Classes*. Wellington: Department of Education, 1963.

Liedtke, W. W., and L. D. Nelson, "Activities in Mathematics for Preschool Children," *The Arithmetic Teacher,* November, 1973, pp. 536–541.

Liedtke, W. W., "Experiences with Blocks in Kindergarten," *The Arithmetic Teacher,* May, 1975, pp. 406–412.

Lovell, K., *The Growth of Basic Mathematical and Scientific Concepts in Children*. London: University of London Press, Ltd., 1961.

Lucow, W. H., "Testing the Cuisenaire Method," *The Arithmetic Teacher,* November, 1963, pp. 435–438.

Marks, J. L., C. R. Purdy, L. B. Kinney, and A. A. Hiatt, *Teaching Elementary School Mathematics for Understanding,* 4th ed. New York: McGraw-Hill Book Company, 1975, Chap. III.

O'Brien, T. C., "Interviews to Assess Number Knowledge," *The Arithmetic Teacher,* May, 1971, pp. 322–326.

Randolph, W., and V. G. Jeffers, "A New Look for the Hundreds Chart," *The Arithmetic Teacher,* March, 1974, pp. 203–208.

Schminke, C. W., N. Maertens, and W. R. Arnold, *Teaching the Child Mathematics*. Hinsdale, Illinois: The Dryden Press, Inc., 1973, Chap. IV.

Stern, C., and M. B. Stern, *Children Discover Mathematics: An Introduction to Structural Arithmetic*. New York: Harper & Row, Publishers, 1971, Chap. II.

Underhill, R. G., *Teaching Elementary School Mathematics*. Columbus, Ohio: Charles E. Merrill Publishing Company, 1972, Chap. VII.

Addition 11

Before systematic teaching of addition and subtraction can be undertaken, the pupil must have acquired the simple concepts, knowledge, and skills that are prerequisites for such instruction. Chapter 10 suggested ways the teacher could assess the child's mathematical maturity and presented activities designed to build the background required before the pupil can profit from instruction in addition and subtraction.

This chapter deals with addition of whole numbers and addition involving negative integers. It suggests methods and materials that can be used to make instruction meaningful and techniques that can be employed to assist the child in retaining acquired knowledge and skills.

SKILLS TEST[1]

1. Add and check by subtracting one of the addends from the sum.

438	850	294	772	481
89	333	98	293	185

2. Add and check.

8424	2749	5003	6644	1243
1516	2994	4870	2895	1111
3005	411	2210	6739	5812
452	7014	3563	4414	3033

1. The student is referred to the preface of this book for a statement of the purpose of the skills tests.

3. Find the answers.

$5 + {}^{-}2 =$	$6 + {}^{-}1 =$	${}^{-}1 + {}^{-}8 =$
$8 + {}^{-}3 =$	$7 + {}^{-}3 =$	${}^{-}5 + {}^{-}6 =$
$6 + {}^{-}2 =$	$3 + {}^{-}6 =$	${}^{-}4 + {}^{-}7 =$
$4 + {}^{-}4 =$	$2 + {}^{-}9 =$	${}^{-}2 + {}^{-}1 =$

MEANING AND TERMS

Addition is an operation on two numbers resulting in a single number called the *sum*. In $7 + 5 = 12$, 7 and 5 are the *addends* and 12 is the *sum*. The operation is *binary* in nature because only two numbers are added at a time. If there are three or more addends, first two of these are added, then the third is added to the result of the first operation, etc.

In set language, addition of whole numbers can be described as the operation by which the cardinal number of a single set of objects is determined when that set contains two disjoint subsets of which the cardinal numbers are known. Hence, if the cardinal numbers of the disjoint sets A and B are 2 and 3, the cardinal number of the set $A \cup B$ is the sum of 2 and 3, which is 5. It should be emphasized that this result is obtained only when the sets are disjoint, so that $A \cap B$ is empty. In the operation described, the union of set A and set B—not of the cardinal numbers—is formed, and the cardinal numbers—not the sets—are added.

Example

If A = [○, □] and B = [△, ⬡, ▭], then $A \cup B$ = [○, □, △, ⬡, ▭]. The cardinal number of A is 2 and that of B is 3, and A and B are disjoint sets. Thus the cardinal number of $A \cup B$ is $2 + 3 = 5$, or $n(A \cup B) = 5$.

If two sets are not disjoint sets, the cardinal numbers of the sets cannot be added to find the cardinal number of the union of the sets. This is shown in the following example.

Example

If A = [Sun, Moon, Venus] and B = [Sun, Moon, Mars, Earth], then $A \cup B$ = [Sun, Moon, Venus, Mars, Earth]. The cardinal number of $A \cup B$ is 5, not 7. The operation can be illustrated in a Venn diagram. The diagram also shows that $A \cap B$ = [Sun, Moon].

The meaning of the equal sign in a mathematical sentence such as $3 + 2 = 5$ should be clearly understood. The sign indicates that the total of the numbers expressed by the symbols to its left equals the number expressed by the symbol to its right. Consequently, before the operation of addition takes place, two specific groups are considered, and after the operation has taken place, a single group is considered, the cardinal number of which is the total of those of the two original groups.

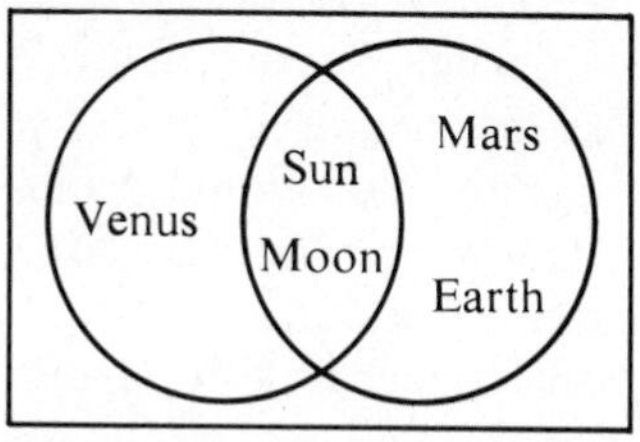

PROPERTIES

Basic properties that apply to the addition of whole numbers are:

1. *Commutative property of addition.* In adding two whole numbers, the order of the addends can be changed without affecting the sum. Thus, if a and b are whole numbers, then $a + b = b + a$.

Example

$5 + 4 = 4 + 5$

2. *Associative property of addition.* In adding more than two whole numbers, the way in which the addends are grouped does not affect the sum. Thus, if a, b, and c are whole numbers, then $(a + b) + c = a + (b + c)$.

Example

$(8 + 9) + 1 = 8 + (9 + 1)$

3. *Closure property of addition.* The result of the addition of any two whole numbers is a whole number. We say that the set of whole numbers is closed with respect to addition. Thus, if a and b are whole numbers, then $a + b$ is a whole number.

Example

$8 + 4 = 12$

4. *Identity element for addition.* If zero is added to any whole number, the result is the same number. Zero is the identity element for addition. Thus, if a is a whole number, then $a + 0 = a$.

Example

$5 + 0 = 5$

THE KEY ADDITION FACTS

The *key addition facts,* also called the *basic* addition facts, comprise all the two-term addition facts that can be formed using all the one-digit addends. A *fact* includes the sum. If the sum is not given, the addition pair is called a *combination*. There are one hundred key addition facts.

The length of the readiness program preceding the introduction of the key addition facts depends on the maturity of the pupil and the number sense he or she has acquired. As described in the preceding chapter, such readiness activities should include matching, counting, grouping, combining, separating, and exercises to acquaint the pupil with the necessary vocabulary and symbols.

There is no agreement concerning the order in which the key facts should be presented, nor is there a definite rule as to whether a key subtraction fact should be presented immediately after the related addition fact has been introduced. In some textbooks the key addition facts and the key subtraction facts are presented simultaneously, whereas in others the presentation of a few addition facts is followed by the introduction of the related subtraction facts. Some authorities advocate presentation of the so-called "easy" addition facts (those that have a sum of ten or less) first, and the so-called "hard" facts later. There are other authors[2] who present the facts in stages, according to assumed degree of difficulty.

The key facts in which zero is added, called *zero facts,* are also treated differently. In some books the zero facts are omitted and are taught later as a generalization in situations requiring addition of two-digit numbers. In other books zero facts are introduced together with the other key addition facts. The latter method seems to be preferable. Occasionally situations arise in Grade 1 in which zero must be added—for example, if the total number of pupils absent during the morning and afternoon periods of a schoolday has to be determined when two pupils were absent during the morning and none during the afternoon. Moreover, since children are to develop the idea that the operation of subtraction is the inverse of addition, and since there are several situations resulting in a fact such as $4 - 4 = 0$, children should be able to write the following sentence: Since $4 - 4 = 0$, $0 + 4 = 4$. The zero facts may cause some difficulty for pupils just beginning the study of the key addition facts. It is therefore recommended that the zero facts be introduced only after some of the other facts have been presented.

The following sequence for the study of addition facts is suggested:

1. The facts with sums of 2, 3, 4, and 5 consecutively.
2. The zero facts with sums of 0, 1, 2, 3, 4, and 5.

---

2. E. H. Taylor and C. N. Mills, *Arithmetic for Teacher-Training Classes* (New York: Holt, Rinehart and Winston, Inc., 1955), pp. 41–42.

3. The facts with sums of 6, 7, 8, 9, and 10 consecutively.
4. A thorough study of the component parts of 10—for example, 4 + □ = 10, 10 = 7 + □. This will prepare the pupils for addition of facts with sums greater than 10 when the second number must be renamed as the sum of two numbers, one being the complement of the first addend. For example,

$$\begin{aligned} 7 + 5 &= 7 + (3 + 2) \\ &= (7 + 3) + 2 \\ &= 10 + 2 \\ &= 12 \end{aligned}$$

5. A presentation of related facts such as 10 + 1 = 11, 10 + 2 = 12, etc. An understanding of these facts will help the pupils to work exercises such as 7 + 5 = □, illustrated above.
6. The basic facts with sums of 11, 12, 13, 14, 15, 16, 17, and 18 consecutively.
7. Related facts in which a one-digit number is added to 11 through 20, the sum being not greater than 20.

Example

12 + 6 = 18.

It is recommended that the key subtraction facts with minuends of 2, 3, 4, and 5 be introduced after the key addition facts with sums of 2, 3, 4, and 5 are understood. The presentation of each key subtraction fact with a minuend greater than 5 should, in like manner, follow the related addition fact. This sequence will enable the children to understand that the operation of subtraction is the inverse[3] of addition, and it will contribute toward an understanding of the so-called "number families."

INTRODUCING THE KEY ADDITION FACTS

When the pupils have acquired the basic concepts of addition and subtraction and have obtained some skill in finding answers to easy basic number questions meaningfully, the key addition facts are introduced in sequential order. This is often done in number families. The number family of six, for example, comprises all the addition facts with sums of 6 and all the subtraction facts with minuends of 6. The complete family of six consists of the following facts:

---

3. *See* glossary.

$6 + 0 = 6$	$6 - 0 = 6$
$5 + 1 = 6$	$6 - 1 = 5$
$4 + 2 = 6$	$6 - 2 = 4$
$3 + 3 = 6$	$6 - 3 = 3$
$2 + 4 = 6$	$6 - 4 = 2$
$1 + 5 = 6$	$6 - 5 = 1$
$0 + 6 = 6$	$6 - 6 = 0$

When a new family is introduced, the pupils should have sufficient opportunity to discover the facts and to form their own generalizations. The teacher assumes an active role in this process by asking proper guide questions and by encouraging pupils to engage in activities leading to formation of the desired concepts.

Many activities can be suggested for a meaningful introduction of the facts and families. The teacher may want to include in the program several of the activities described below. The selection will depend on the background and ability of the pupils.

1. Pupils who still need to work with concrete materials are encouraged to manipulate objects such as counters, blocks, and beads on a counting frame. When the family of seven is introduced, the children form as many different groups as possible using 7 objects. They are led to decide that a group of 7 beads can be separated into a group of 5 beads and one of 2 beads, or into a group of 4 beads and one of 3 beads, etc. The Cuisenaire rods and the Stern blocks are useful for this purpose.
2. The facts are developed by the teacher on the flannel board or the magnetic board while he or she leads the class discussion. The group under consideration is separated into component parts, and number questions and number facts are presented. A board illustrating the family of three in addition is depicted in Figure 11.1.

★ ★ ★
3 stars

★		★ ★		★ ★ ★
1	+	2	=	3
★ ★		★		★ ★ ★
2	+	1	=	3
$1 + 2 = \square$		$1 + \square = 3$		$3 = \square + 1$
$2 + 1 = \square$		$\square + 2 = 3$		$3 = 1 + \square$
		$1 + 2 = 2 + 1$		

Figure 11.1

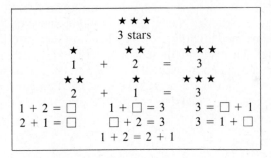

The counting frame and the number line are useful devices in the teaching and learning of mathematics.

3. Cards with dots, pictures, or stars showing the possible component parts of the group under consideration can be prepared by the teacher, or, if time allows, by the children. These cards can be prepared as in Figure 11.2 in order to suggest the commutative property. For the family of six there are four cards: (1) for 6 + 0 and 0 + 6, (2) for 5 + 1 and 1 + 5, (3) for 4 + 2 and 2 + 4, and (4) for 3 + 3.

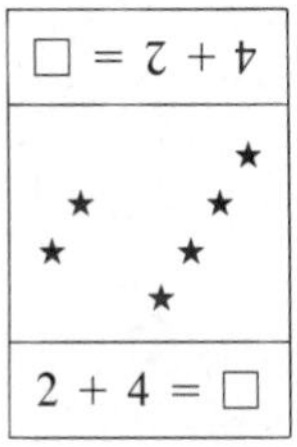

Figure 11.2

4. The pupils draw circles on a line representing beads on a rod, and write number sentences that can be derived from such a pattern:

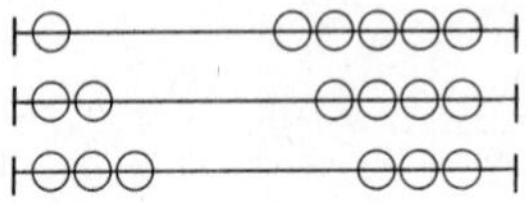

$$
\begin{array}{lcl}
1 + 5 = 6 & \text{and} & 6 = 1 + 5. \\
2 + 4 = 6 & \text{and} & 6 = 2 + 4. \\
3 + 3 = 6 & \text{and} & 6 = 3 + 3.
\end{array}
$$

After some number families have been introduced and the patterns have been properly discussed, the pupils are guided toward the discovery of similarities. The teacher's questions should stimulate the children to form these important generalizations:

1. If 1 is added to a given number, the answer is the next larger number.
2. If zero is added to a number, the answer is the same number.
3. Changing the order of two addends does not change the sum.

Before the addition facts with sums of more than ten are introduced, the teacher should: (1) ascertain that the pupils can find the different component parts of 10, (2) make sure that the children understand the concept of place value, and (3) introduce the case in which ones are added to 10, as in $10 + 5 = 15$. These skills assist the children when adding, for example, $8 + 7$:

$$
\begin{aligned}
8 + 7 &= 8 + (2 + 5) \\
&= (8 + 2) + 5 \\
&= 10 + 5 \\
&= 15
\end{aligned}
$$

The operations can be illustrated on the number line:

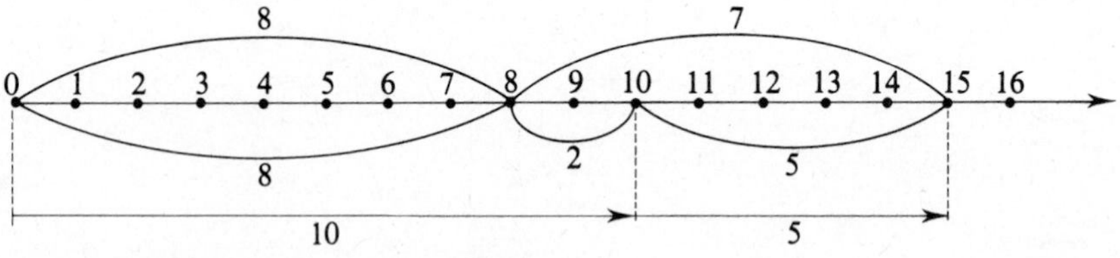

An understanding of the concept of place value is essential for meaningful addition of ones to 10. If this concept is understood, the pupils will be able to complete sentences such as these:

$$12 = 10 + \square$$
$$12 = \square + 2$$
$$10 + 2 = \square$$
$$10 + \square = 12$$
$$\square + 2 = 12$$

Here the number line may be useful:

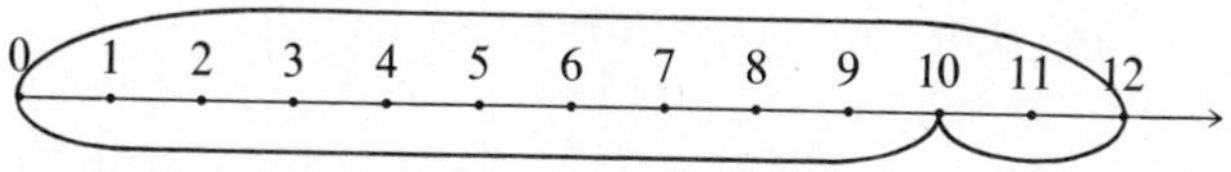

If the pupils can add a one-digit number to 10, they will not encounter much difficulty later when adding a one-digit number to a multiple of 10, as in 30 + 5 = 35.

DEVELOPING AND ANCHORING SKILLS

The sequential nature of mathematics requires that skills be developed and anchored after a process has been understood. Therefore, during and after the activities described above, the teacher should continuously strive to improve the pupils' skill in supplying answers to addition questions. The final goal should be that the pupils master the facts to perfection. Presentation of various kinds of exercises and of carefully selected devices will reduce the chance of the children's losing interest. Descriptions of several exercises and devices from which a selection can be made are presented below.

1. Exercises presented in the pupil's textbook and workbook and those provided by the teacher, including:
   a. Finding doubles.

   Example

   $\square + \square = 4.$

   The same shape of the frames in this example suggests that the missing addends are identical.
   b. Finding several different facts with the same sum.

Example

□ + △ = 10.

The different shapes of the frames suggest that the addends are different.

c. Working exercises that involve the concept of place value.

Example

For 13 pennies you can buy the same amount as you can for 1 dime and □ pennies. So 13 = 1 ten and □ ones, or 13 = 10 + □.

d. Finding different names for the number 10.

e. Drawing a picture to fit a given number sentence.

Example

Draw a picture of a set that shows that 3 + 2 = 5.

2. Different presentations of number questions.

a.

10 =		
6	+	□
□	+	8
3	+	□
□	+	1

b.

How much?	
6	
4	
3	
1	

c.

Just as much:	
4 + 2	3 + □

d.

The total should be 12:	
8 + □	3 + □

e.

Add 3:	
14	□
9	□
10	□
12	□

f.

Make each column equal 10.
The first one has been done.

4	5	7	9	2	3	8
6						

g. Count the number of boxes. Decide how many are shaded. Then write the addition facts. The first one has been done.

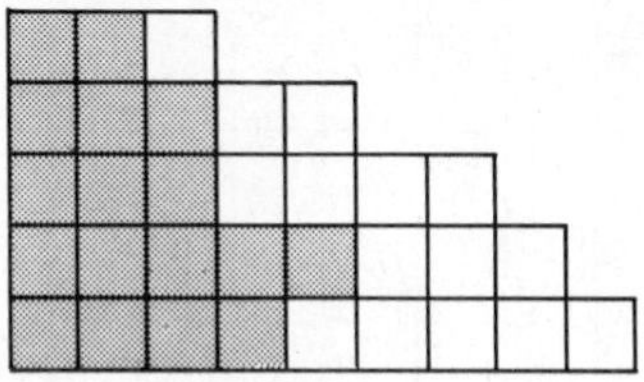

2 + 1 = 3

h. Draw the missing stars and write the numeral:

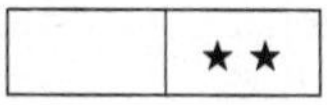

□ + 2 = 5

i. Write the answers. The first one has been done.

	6	3	9	10	2	13	11
+4	10						

3. The reading and writing of addition facts from illustrations on number lines.

Example

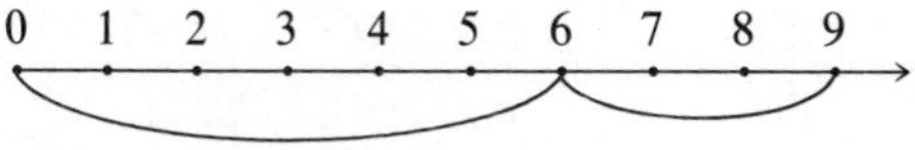

6 + 3 = 9

4. The preparation of an addition table. The numbers named in the left column are added to those in the top row or vice versa. Two examples have been given.

+	0	1	2	3	4	5	6	7	8	9
0										
1										
2										
3			5							
4										
5					9					
6										
7										
8										
9										

For addition facts with sums not greater than 10, only a part of the table is needed:

+	0	1	2	3	4	5	6	7	8	9	10
0											
1											
2											
3											
4											
5											
6											
7											
8											
9											
10											

The addition facts can also be presented in similar tables in which the addends are not arranged in numerical order. The teacher may supply such exercises to pupils who need extra practice.

5. Exercises with flashcards. On one side of an addition flashcard the number question is presented, and on the other side the fact is given so that the pupils can check their answers. In individual use, cards to which incorrect responses are given are put aside for restudy. Since horizontal presentation of mathematical sentences is important, the questions and the facts are presented on the flashcards in horizontal form, as shown in the following example. They are presented vertically on a different set of flashcards in order to prepare the pupils for column addition.

6. Exercises with the addition wheel. The addition wheel is illustrated below. One of the addends is presented on a rectangular piece of oak tag which is hung in the center on a bolt. This part can be removed and replaced by other pieces showing different numerals. The second addend appears through a window in the front board. Other addends appear in turn when the back board is rotated. This device presents the addition questions in horizontal form.

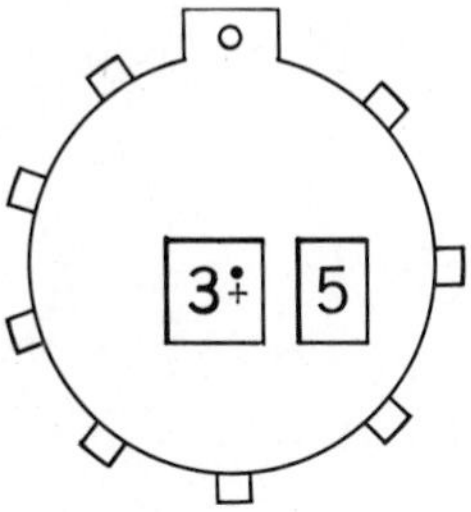

7. Writing sentences such as 6 + 0 = 5 + 1 = 4 + 2, etc. (for pupils of at least average ability). These pupils are also encouraged to complete number sentences by supplying the symbol =, >, or < in sentences of the following kind:

$$6 + 0 \bigcirc 4 + 2$$
$$4 + 1 \bigcirc 2 + 2$$
$$4 + 1 \bigcirc 3 + 3$$

8. Writing and memorizing facts.
9. Devising and solving verbal problems to fit given open mathematical sentences.
10. Finding a missing addend. Young children often experience difficulties closing sentences such as $3 + \square = 5$, $\square + 2 = 5$, $5 = 3 + \square$, and $5 = \square + 2$. Some diagrams and illustrations that can be used to help children in finding missing addends follow. The drawings can easily be interpreted and expanded by the teacher.
    a. Using parts of egg cartons.

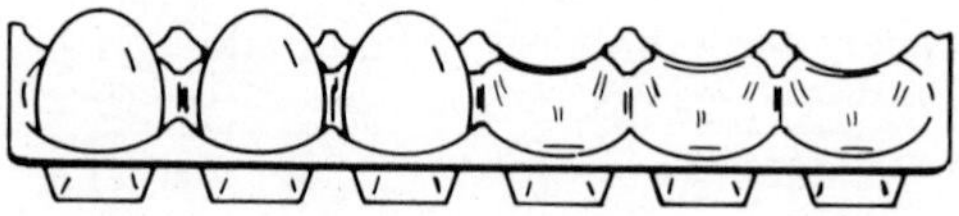

    b. Using beads on a rod.

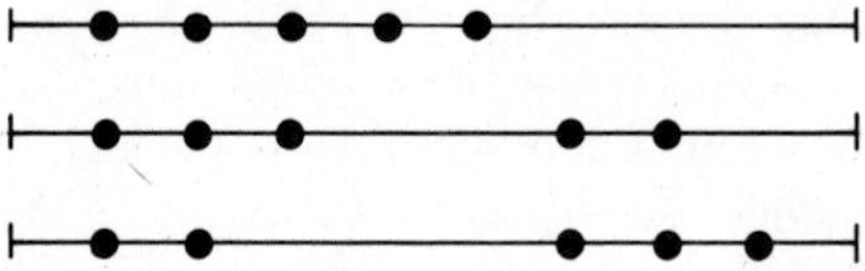

    c. Using toy money.

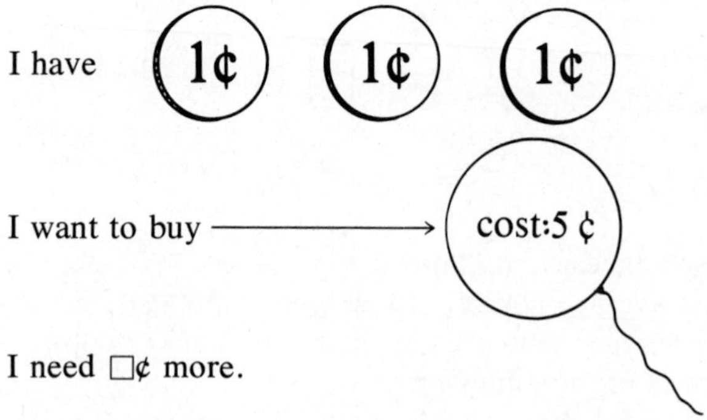

    d. Using the folded paper model.

$5 = 3 + \square$ $\quad\quad$ $\square + 2 = 5$

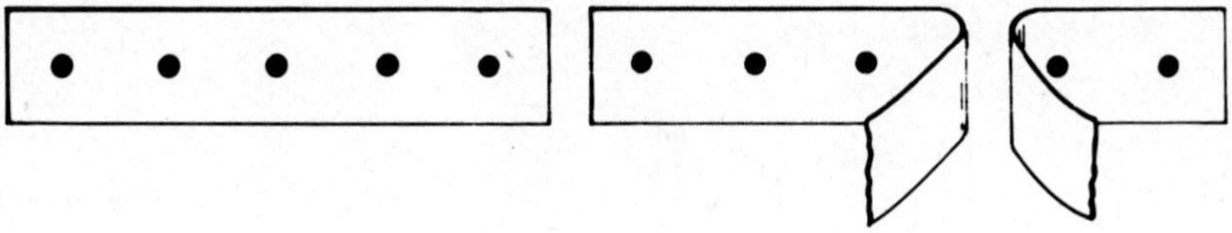

e. Using the number line.

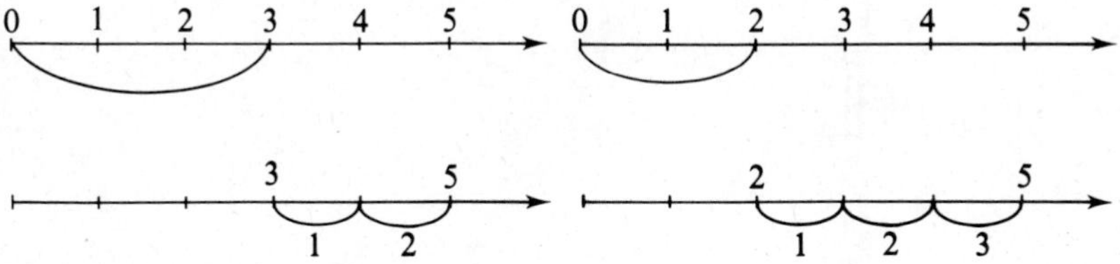

f. Displaying mobiles.

One side
3 + 2 = 5
Other side
3 + ☐ = 5

g. Making cards.

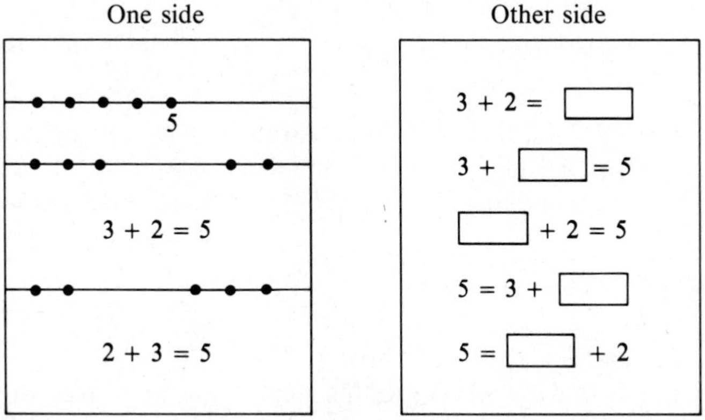
One side
5
3 + 2 = 5
2 + 3 = 5
Other side
3 + 2 = ☐
3 + ☐ = 5
☐ + 2 = 5
5 = 3 + ☐
5 = ☐ + 2

h. Using paper clips.

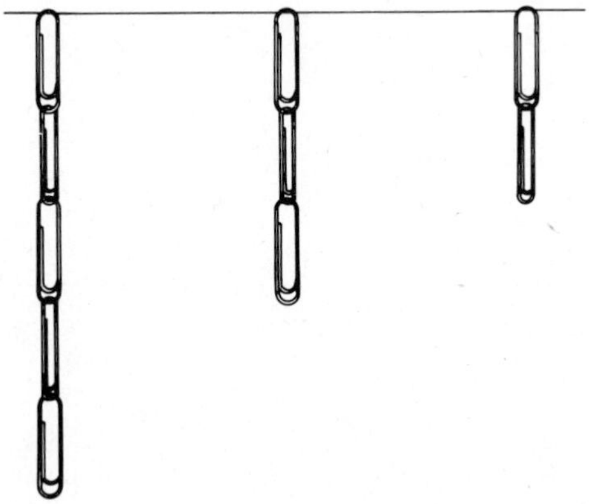

How many more needed to get 5 clips in the second row?
How many more needed to get 5 clips in the third row?

i. Using a balance.

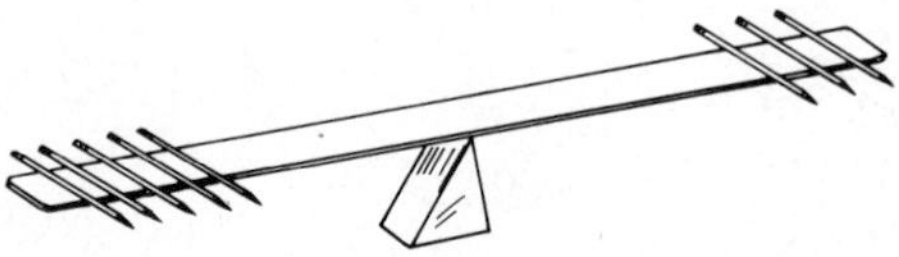

How many pencils are needed to make it balance?
How many pencils must be taken away to make it balance?

ADDITION OF MORE THAN TWO ONE-DIGIT NUMBERS

When the key addition facts with sums through 10 have been developed, additions of three and more one-digit numbers should be introduced. In such additions no combinations are included that have not yet been presented.

Example

$4 + 3 + 2 = \square$.

When the pupils find the answer to this number question, they do not see the numeral that represents the sum of 4 and 3. If this causes difficulties, the teacher encourages the children to work several exercises in two steps, as follows: $4 + 3 = 7$ and $7 + 2 = 9$. The number line can be used to illustrate the process and to allow the pupils to see the numeral that represents the sum of the first two addends:

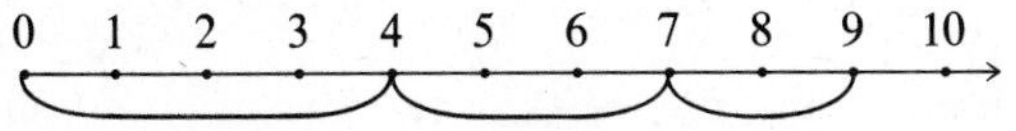

When illustrating $3 + 2 + 1 = 6$ on the flannel board or on the magnetic board, the teacher presents the objects in different groupings and has the children determine the sum. After several exercises have been illustrated, the pupils should discover that a different grouping of the addends does not change the sum (associative property). Then the pupils will do exercises such as

$$\begin{array}{ll} (3+2)+1= & \quad 3+(2+1)= \\ \bigcirc+1=\square & \quad 3+\triangle=\square \end{array}$$

and finally they will write

$$(3 + 2) + 1 = 5 + 1 = 6$$

and

$$3 + (2 + 1) = 3 + 3 = 6$$

so

$$(3 + 2) + 1 = 3 + (2 + 1)$$

The associative property is applied frequently in later stages when exercises are presented in which pairs of addends total 10 or a multiple of 10.

Examples

$3 + 6 + 4 = 3 + (6 + 4) = 3 + 10 = 13.$
$9 + 1 + 7 + 3 = (9 + 1) + (7 + 3) = 10 + 10 = 20.$

After they understand the equation form, the pupils will rapidly acquire skill in adding one-digit numbers presented in a vertical arrangement. These column additions are checked by adding in the direction opposite to the original one. Both the commutative and the associative properties are applied when column addition that was originally added up is checked by adding down:

$$\begin{array}{r} 4 \\ 5 \\ +6 \\ \hline 15 \end{array}$$

When adding up, the order is: $6 + 5 + 4 = 15$.
When adding down, the order is: $4 + 5 + 6 = 15$.

This can be justified as follows:

$(6 + 5) + 4$	$= 4 + (6 + 5)$	commutative property
	$= 4 + (5 + 6)$	commutative property
	$= (4 + 5) + 6$	associative property

As in horizontal addition of more than two one-digit numbers, in column addition the case of the unseen sum and addend presents itself. In the example shown, the addition of 5 to 4 results in the unseen sum 9, which is an addend in the next addition question $9 + 6 = \square$. The number 9 is not expressed on paper, so it must be remembered. If pupils have received proper instruction in horizontal addition of more than two one-digit numbers and have been encouraged to illustrate the process on the number line, they should not experience much difficulty with simple column additions. If difficulties arise, the children should be encouraged to work additional exercises in horizontal form, as illustrated above.

Addition exercises with more than two one-digit numbers include those in which a missing addend must be found.

Examples

$5 + \square + 2 = 9$

$\square + 1 + 1 = 6$

$9 = 6 + 1 + \square$

$$\begin{array}{r} 5 \\ 1 \\ +\square \\ \hline 8 \end{array}$$

At a later stage, additions consisting of more than two one-digit numbers with sums greater than 10 are introduced. Although the pupils are then supposed to know the key addition facts involved, they continue to work exercises using the component parts of 10.

Example

$4 + 7 = 4 + \square + 1 = \bigcirc + 1 = \triangle.$

SUGGESTED SEQUENCE FOR ADDITION CASES

Theoretically a child can add any two numbers if he or she has mastered the key facts and knows how to regroup in addition. However, leading the pupil with a minimum of practice from the stage of the key facts to the stage in which multi-digit numbers presented in a column are to be added would not enable the pupil to develop an understanding of the mathematical processes involved. Instead, the different cases that can be distinguished in addition must be presented in a logical sequence, while previously taught skills are utilized and practiced. This will gradually develop a deeper understanding of the processes.

A new case should be presented in equation form, so that the pupil is encouraged to find the answer by mental computation. If the addition question is too difficult to be computed mentally, or if there are too many addends, the numerals can be arranged vertically.

One possible sequence for the introduction of the addition cases with sums not greater than 100 is as follows:

1. The key addition facts, interrupted by the case in which ones are added to 10, as previously described. Addition of three or more one-digit numbers is undertaken simultaneously or after the key facts have been developed.
2. Addition of multiples of 10 with sums not greater than 100.

   Example

   20 + 10 = □.
3. Addition of a multiple of 10 and ones.

   Example

   30 + 5 = □.
4. Addition of a two-digit number and a one-digit number without regrouping.

   Example

   45 + 2 = □.
5. Addition of a two-digit number to a multiple of 10.

   Example

   20 + 15 = □.
6. Addition of a multiple of 10 to a two-digit number.

   Example

   35 + 10 = □.
7. Addition of two two-digit numbers without regrouping.

   Example

   35 + 12 = □.
8. Addition of a two-digit number and a one-digit number with regrouping.

   Example

   45 + 7 = □.
9. Addition of two two-digit numbers with regrouping.

   Example

   35 + 17 = □.

The grade placement of addition cases with sums greater than 100 should also be based on a logical sequence. Cases that can precede addition of two two-digit numbers with regrouping are: (1) addition of multiples of 10 with sums greater than 100, (2) addition of multiples of 100 with sums not greater than 1,000, and (3) addition of a one-, two-, or three-digit number to a three-digit number without regrouping. Simple exercises with more than two addends are included. Of great importance are the exercises in which a multiple of ten and ones must be added to 100 or to a multiple of 100, as in $200 + 40 + 5 = \square$.

ADDITION OF MULTIPLES OF 10

In teaching addition of multiples of 10, previously acquired knowledge and skills are utilized. If, as is recommended, this case immediately follows the addition exercises with sums through 20, the pupils will already have added 10 to 10 by using counters, beads, or the number line. They can count by tens to 100, they are acquainted with the place of the tens on the hundred board, and they should be able to handle the key addition facts. Consequently, the addition of multiples of 10 with sums not greater than 100 is a comparatively easy case. Several procedures can be followed in the introduction of this case of addition. The teacher should select the procedures that are most suitable for the pupils.

Example

Dave had 30 baseball cards. He got 20 cards from his friend. Then how many cards did Dave have in all?

Number question: $30 + 20 = \square$.

Solutions:

1. Multiple counting:

20 = 2 tens. Count two tens after 30: 30 40 50.

$$30 + 20 = 50$$

Note: When pupils compute the answer, they work with numbers. Thus, when the equation has been solved, the answer must be interpreted. The interpretation of the answer in the example under consideration is: Dave had 50 cards in all. In many examples in this volume the interpretation of the answer has been left out.

2. Using the tens blocks:

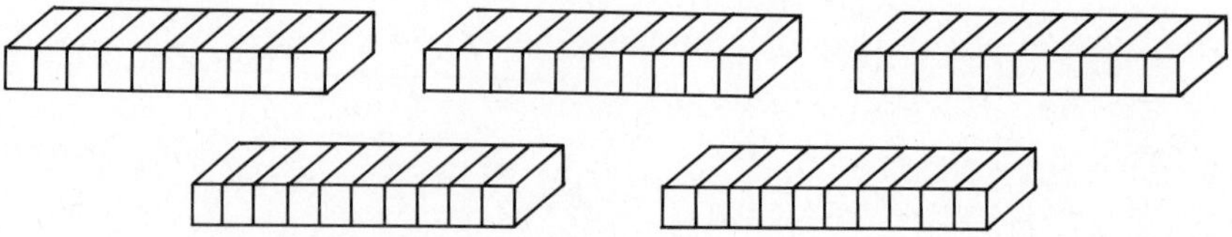

The pupils reason as follows:
3 + 2 = 5, and 3 tens + 2 tens = 5 tens.
Thus 30 + 20 = 3 tens + 2 tens = 5 tens = 50. 30 + 20 = 50.
3 + 2 = 5 and 30 + 20 = 50 are called *related facts*.
At a later stage the pupils will learn additional facts that are related to basic facts such as 3 + 2 = 5:

$$
\begin{aligned}
3 + 2 &= 5\\
30 + 20 &= 50\\
300 + 200 &= 500\\
3{,}000 + 2{,}000 &= 5{,}000
\end{aligned}
$$
etc.

3. Using the hundred board:

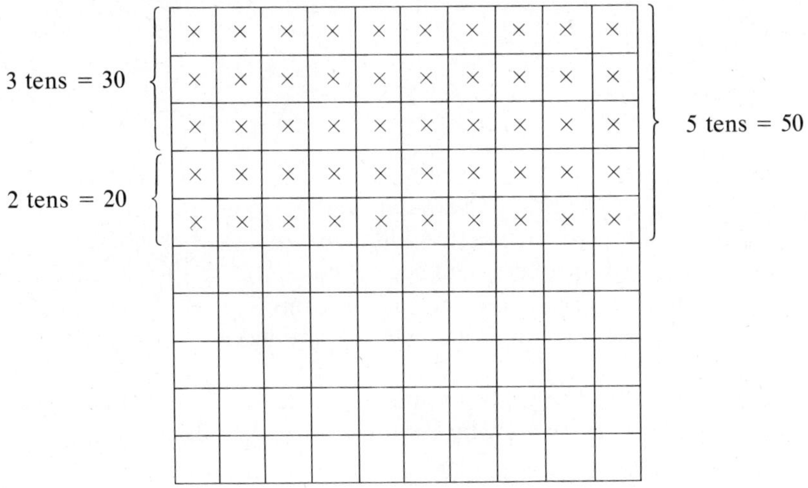

30 + 20 = 50

4. Using the number line:

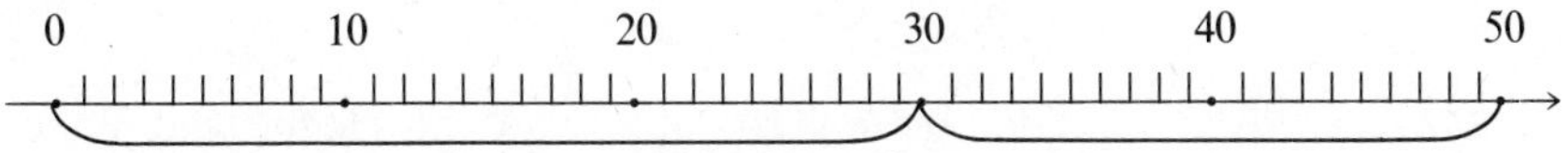

30 + 20 = 50

Exercises in which three or more multiples of 10 are added and those in which a missing addend is found follow the kind presented above.

Examples

20 + 20 + 10 = □
30 + 10 + □ = 70
100 = 50 + 20 + □

40 + □ = 70
□ + 20 = 60
100 = 70 + □

ADDITION OF A MULTIPLE OF 10 AND A ONE-DIGIT NUMBER

Addition of multiples of 10 and one-digit numbers is performed meaningfully if the principle of place value is understood Therefore, pertinent exercises must be presented and discussed. These exercises are intended to develop the ability to answer such number questions as 20 + 7 = □.

Examples

27 = □ tens and ○ ones
2 tens and 7 ones = 20 + □
2 tens + 7 ones = 20 + 7 = □
27 = 20 + □
27 = □ + 7
20 + 7 = □

It is recommended that the number line or the hundred board with movable disks be used by those pupils who need additional help.

When a multiple of 10 must be added to a one-digit number, as in 7 + 20, the commutative property can be applied: 7 + 20 = 20 + 7 = 27. When the pupils have worked several similar exercises, they will not consciously apply the commutative property any more, but will supply the answer automatically.

These exercises are also presented in vertical arrangement. The identity element is then stressed by demonstrating the addition of zero to a number:

$$\begin{array}{r} 20 \\ +4 \\ \hline 24 \end{array} \qquad \begin{array}{r} 4 \\ +20 \\ \hline 24 \end{array}$$

DECADE ADDITION

A decade addition combination consists of a two-digit addend and a one-digit addend. There are two types of combinations: (1) those that result in a sum that is in the same decade as the two-digit addend, for example, 24 + 5, and (2) those that require bridging the decade, for example, 24 + 9. In the second example, the two-digit addend is in the third decade and the sum is in the fourth decade.

Decade addition that does not involve bridging presents no special difficulty for pupils who have mastered the key addition facts. The teacher should present several related facts such as

$$\begin{aligned} 3 + 2 &= 5 \\ 13 + 2 &= 15 \\ 23 + 2 &= 25 \\ 33 + 2 &= 35 \end{aligned}$$

and should guide the pupils to see that, in all these examples, the key fact $3 + 2 = 5$ is applied. After a sufficient amount of practice, the children should know the answer to such a question immediately when it is presented. This way of adding is commonly called *adding by endings*.

Exercises involving bridging are more difficult and are introduced at a later stage. When finding the answer to a question such as $27 + 8 = \square$, some pupils may think: $7 + 8 = 15$ and $20 + 15 = 35$. A more mature procedure is to add enough to 27 to get 30, and then to add the remainder to 30, as follows:

$$\begin{aligned} 27 + 8 &= 27 + (3 + 5) \\ &= (27 + 3) + 5 \\ &= 30 + 5 \\ &= 35 \end{aligned}$$

This procedure can be shown on the number line:

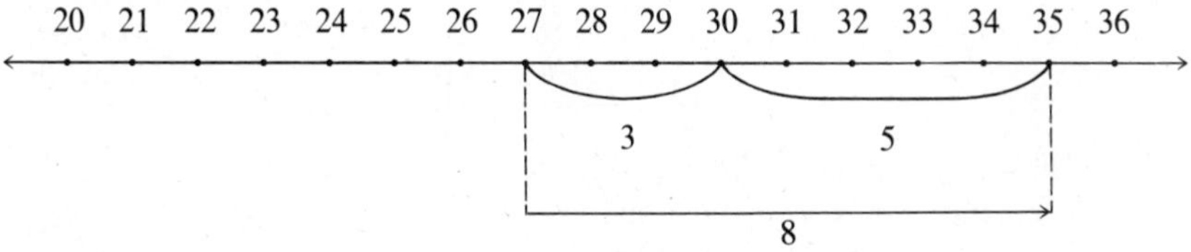

This method is especially recommended as a foundation for mental computation. The final goal is for pupils to say the answer almost immediately whenever they look at a question. To reach this goal, most children will have to do a great deal of practice in decade addition, including oral exercises.

ADDITION OF A TWO-DIGIT NUMBER TO A MULTIPLE OF 10

Example

Ted had 20 baseball cards. He got 12 more cards. How many cards did Ted have in all?

Number question: $20 + 12 = \square$.

Solutions:

1. If the previously discussed cases have been understood, the pupils will be able to solve this number question as follows:

$$
\begin{aligned}
12 &= 10 + 2 \\
20 + 12 &= 20 + (10 + 2) \\
&= (20 + 10) + 2 \\
&= 30 + 2 \\
&= 32
\end{aligned}
$$

These steps can be illustrated on the number line:

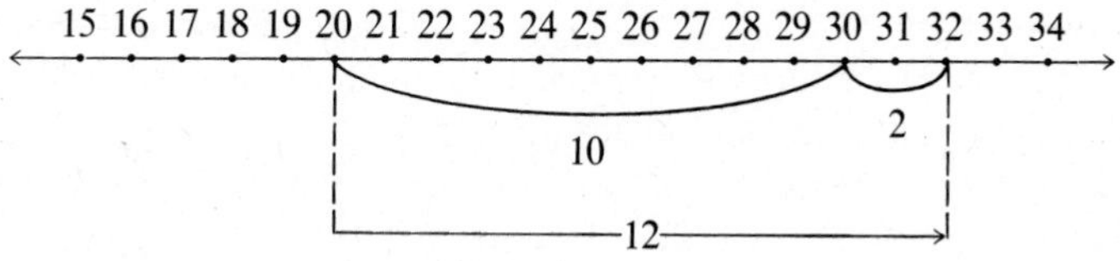

2. The process is illustrated on an abacus with 9 beads on each rod:

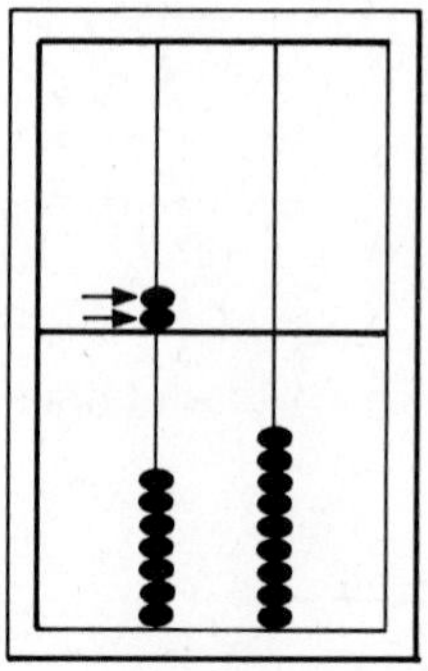

The abacus shows 2 tens.
1 ten and 2 ones are moved up.

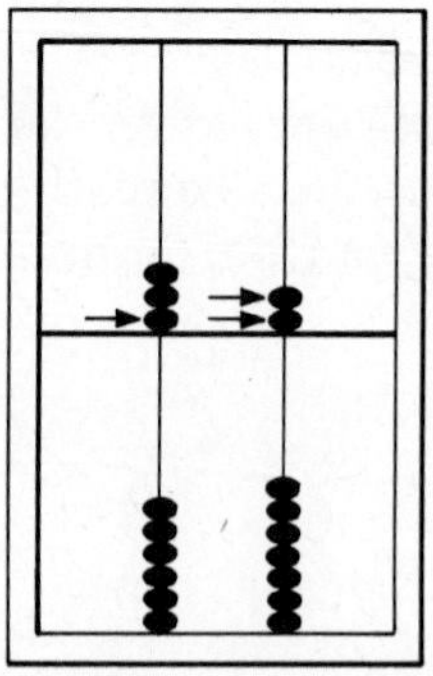

The abacus shows 3 tens and 2 ones, or 32.

3. On a hundred board with movable disks, 2 rows of 10 are turned over. Then 1 row of 10 and 2 ones are turned over, and it is decided that a total of 3 rows of 10 and 2 ones have been turned over. 3 tens + 2 ones = 32.

4. Vertical addition should follow the meaningful presentations described above.

Example

ADDITION OF A MULTIPLE OF 10 TO A TWO-DIGIT NUMBER

Linda had 22 cards. She got 20 more cards. How many cards did Linda have in all?

Number question: $22 + 20 = \square$.

Solutions:

1. The answer is found by applying the commutative property:

$$\begin{aligned} 22 + 20 &= 20 + 22 \\ 20 + 22 &= 20 + (20 + 2) \\ &= (20 + 20) + 2 \\ &= 40 + 2 \\ &= 42 \end{aligned}$$

   In this solution, use is made of a previous case in which a two-digit number was added to a multiple of 10. The two-digit number 22 is renamed 20 + 2. The associative property is applied. First 20 is added to 20, and then 2 is added to 40.
2. Previously learned cases are applied. The pupil is led to reason as follows: Since 20 + 20 = 40, 22 + 20 = 42.
3. The addends are written in a vertical arrangement and expressed in expanded notation. Then vertical addition takes place:

$$\begin{array}{rl} 22 = & \text{2 tens and 2 ones} = 20 + 2 \\ +20 = & \text{2 tens} \qquad\qquad\quad = 20 \\ \hline & \text{4 tens and 2 ones} = 40 + 2 = 42 \end{array}$$

$$22 + 20 = 42.$$

4. The number question is solved using the standard algorism:

$$\begin{array}{r} 22 \\ +20 \\ \hline 42 \end{array}$$

Example

ADDITION OF TWO TWO-DIGIT NUMBERS WITHOUT REGROUPING

Joan sold 32 Christmas cards on Monday and 23 on Tuesday. How many cards did Joan sell in all?

Number question: $32 + 23 = \square$.

Solutions:

1. This case is considered an extension of the case in which a multiple of 10 is added to a two-digit number, as in 32 + 20. The extension is that 3 ones are added to the obtained sum. Twenty-three is renamed as follows: 23 = 20 + 3. Then 20 is added to 32 and 3 is added to that sum:

$$\begin{aligned} 32 + 23 &= 32 + (20 + 3) \\ &= (32 + 20) + 3 \\ &= 52 + 3 \\ &= 55 \end{aligned}$$

The process should be illustrated on the number line.

2. The tens and ones are isolated and then added: 32 + 23 = (30 + 20) + (2 + 3) = 50 + 5 = 55. The mathematical justification for this procedure is presented later in this chapter.
3. The answer to the number question is found by using the abacus. First, 3 tens and 2 ones are isolated. Then 2 tens and 3 ones are moved up. Finally the total is determined.
4. The answer is found by vertical addition. This presentation should follow the equation form. The pupils will then be able to perform the operation meaningfully as follows:

$$\begin{array}{rl} 32 & \\ +23 & \\ \hline 50 & (30 + 20 = 50) \\ +5 & (2 + 3 = 5) \\ \hline 55 & \end{array} \qquad \text{or} \qquad \begin{array}{rl} 32 & \\ +23 & \\ \hline 5 & (2 + 3 = 5) \\ +50 & (30 + 20 = 50) \\ \hline 55 & \end{array}$$

When this process is understood, the teacher suggests writing the final answer immediately, without first writing the sum of the ones and the sum of the tens separately:

$$\begin{array}{r} 32 \\ +23 \\ \hline 55 \end{array}$$

ADDITION OF TWO TWO-DIGIT NUMBERS WITH REGROUPING

Example

Ray had 28 postcards from foreign countries. During his vacation he collected 23 more cards. How many cards did Ray have in all?

Number question: 28 + 23 = □.

Solutions:

1. The process involved in this addition is a combination of two cases previously learned: (1) addition of a multiple of 10 to a two-digit number, and (2) addition of a one-digit number to a two-digit number involving bridging. Therefore, to solve the number question, 23 is renamed as follows: 23 = 20 + 3. First, 20 is added to 28, then 3 is added to the obtained sum:

$$\begin{aligned} 28 + 23 &= 28 + (20 + 3) \\ &= (28 + 20) + 3 \\ &= 48 + 3 \\ &= 51 \end{aligned}$$

The following sequence of exercises is recommended for leading the pupils to this method of solution:

18 + 10 = □, and 28 + 7 = □, so 18 + 17 = □.

2. The tens and the ones in each of the two addends are isolated and added separately:

$$28 + 23 = (20 + 20) + (8 + 3) = 40 + 11 = 51$$

3. The place-value pocket chart—which was introduced in the previous chapter—can be used to illustrate the process. For addition the use of a chart with three pockets is recommended.
   a. Two bundles of 10 markers and 8 single markers are placed in the top pocket. Two bundles of 10 and 3 ones are placed in the second pocket.

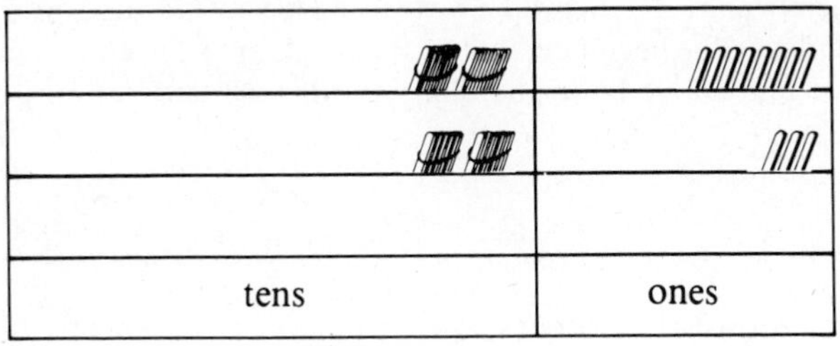

28 = 20 + 8

23 = 20 + 3

   b. The 2 tens from the top pocket and the 2 tens from the second pocket are placed in the third pocket.

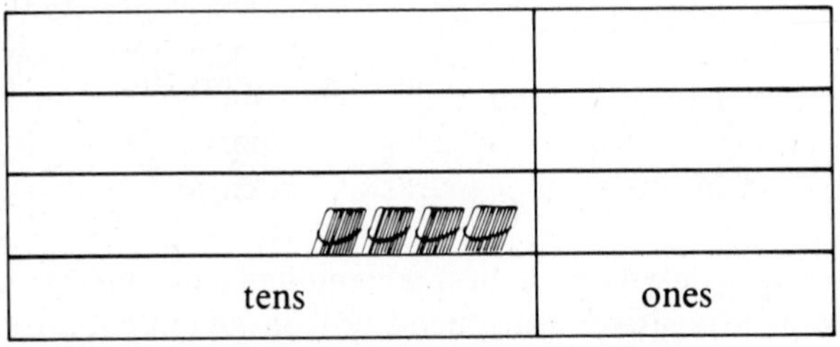

20 + 20 = 40

   c. From the 11 ones in the two top pockets, 10 are isolated, bundled, and placed in the tens place of the third pocket. The remaining one is placed in the ones place of the third pocket.

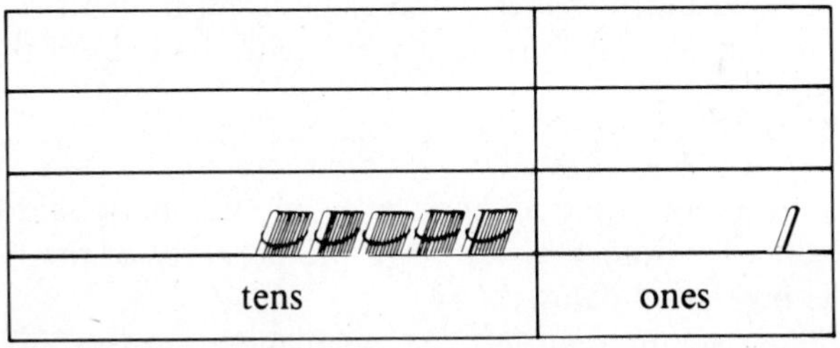

28 + 23 = 51

4. After the process of adding 28 and 23 has been developed meaningfully as described above, the addends are presented in vertical arrangement.

Step 1: 28 and 23 are written in expanded notation and the addition is performed:

$$\begin{array}{r} 28 = 20 + \ 8 \\ +23 = 20 + \ 3 \\ \hline 40 + 11 \end{array} = 51$$

Step 2: The pupils determine that in

$$\begin{array}{r} 28 \\ \underline{+23}, \end{array} \qquad 3 + 8 = 11$$

which equals 1 ten and 1 one. They write down the 1 one and remember the 1 ten, which is then added to the total of the tens column. In the beginning stages, the pupils are allowed to write the 1 (for 1 ten) above the digits that stand for the tens:

$$\begin{array}{r} \scriptstyle 1 \quad \\ 28 \\ +23 \\ \hline 51 \end{array}$$

Addition of multi-digit numbers and columns with several addends should not be started before the pupils clearly understand the process of regrouping. Much practice is necessary before the children can perform column additions with several addends accurately.

ADDITION INVOLVING NEGATIVE INTEGERS

Occasionally the elementary school child meets situations that involve negative numbers—for example, in weather reports. Such situations should be utilized when the number line is extended to include negative integers.

Addition exercises in which the first addend has a negative value and the second addend a positive value need not be difficult for pupils of average ability. Exercises in which the second addend has a negative value, thus resulting in an answer less than the first addend, may prove to be quite difficult for many children. The teacher may want to introduce this case to rapid learners.

It is recommended that the thermometer be used in initial exercises and that, later on, simple problems be worked with the help of the horizontal number line.

Properties and Terms

The properties that apply to the addition of whole numbers hold for the addition of integers. The integers also have the property of the additive inverse, which is presented below.

If a number line extends both left and right, the points on the line to the right of zero—which is called the origin—represent by convention *positive numbers* and their names are preceded by a *positive sign,* whereas the points on the line to the left of zero represent *negative numbers* and their names are preceded by a *negative sign.* Such numbers are called *directed* or *signed numbers.* With the exception of zero, an integer is either positive or negative. Mathematicians have agreed that a numeral that does not have a positive or negative sign is considered to represent a positive number.

The marks on the number line shown below represent integers. The set of all integers is tabulated as follows:

$$\{\cdots, {}^-3, {}^-2, {}^-1, 0, {}^+1, {}^+2, {}^+3, \cdots\}$$

The symbol $^+1$ is read "positive one," the symbol $^-2$ "negative 2," etc. Since the number line extends in opposite directions from zero, each integer except zero has an opposite or an additive inverse. That is, to each positive or negative integer there corresponds a second integer such that the sum of the two integers is zero. For example, the *additive inverse* of $^+1$ is $^-1$, since $^+1 + {}^-1 = 0$; the *opposite* of $^-5$ is $^+5$, since $^-5 + {}^+5 = 0$, etc.

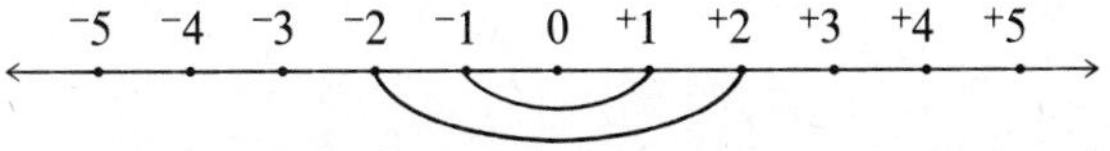

Examples of addition exercises in which the second addend is a negative integer are presented below.

Example 1

$5 + {}^-2 = \square.$

Solutions:

1.

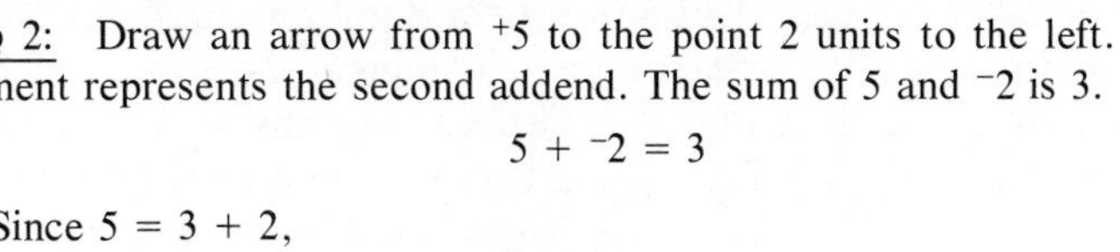

<u>Step 1:</u> Draw an arrow from 0 to $^+5$ (we draw the arrows above or below the number line). This line segment represents the first addend.

<u>Step 2:</u> Draw an arrow from $^+5$ to the point 2 units to the left. This line segment represents the second addend. The sum of 5 and $^-2$ is 3.

$$5 + {}^-2 = 3$$

2. Since $5 = 3 + 2$,

$5 + {}^-2$	$= (3 + 2) + {}^-2$	renaming
	$= 3 + (2 + {}^-2)$	associative property
	$= 3 + 0$	additive inverse property
	$= 3$	identity element for addition

Example 2

4 + $^{-}6$ = □.

Solution:

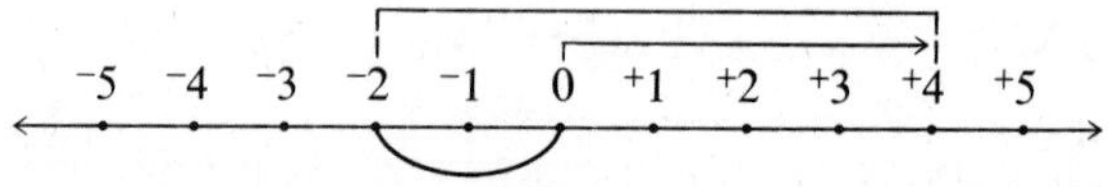

Step 1: Draw an arrow from 0 to $^{+}4$. This line segment represents the first addend.

Step 2: Draw an arrow from $^{+}4$ to the point 6 units to the left. This line segment represents the second addend. The sum of 4 and $^{-}6$ equals $^{-}2$.

$$4 + {}^{-}6 = {}^{-}2$$

Example 3

$^{-}4$ + $^{-}2$ = □.

Solution:

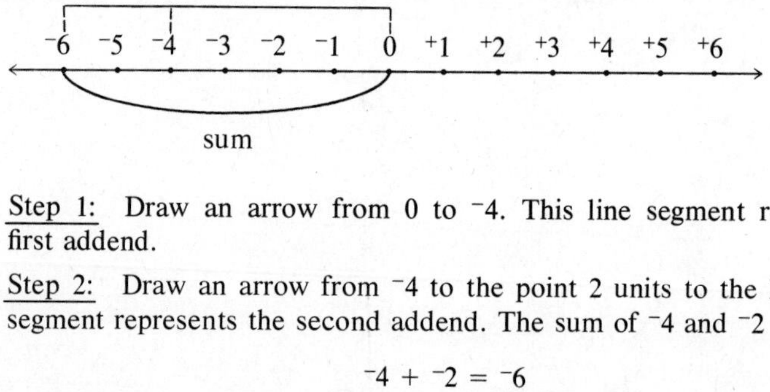

Step 1: Draw an arrow from 0 to $^{-}4$. This line segment represents the first addend.

Step 2: Draw an arrow from $^{-}4$ to the point 2 units to the left. This line segment represents the second addend. The sum of $^{-}4$ and $^{-}2$ is $^{-}6$.

$${}^{-}4 + {}^{-}2 = {}^{-}6$$

MISCELLANEOUS PRACTICE EXERCISES

The pupils' textbook and the accompanying workbook usually provide a sufficient number of exercises in vertical addition. In many cases the teacher will have to provide extra practice in horizontal and oral addition, and sometimes in vertical addition. The teacher may also have to supply enrichment exercises for the rapid learners. Several books with enrichment exercises are available. The following exercises for oral and written work may be considered for grade levels to be determined by the teacher according to the mathematical maturity of the pupils.

1. Counting by multiples.

Examples

Counting by 11s, 12s, 13s, etc.

2. Adding numbers according to a specified pattern.

Example

1—2—4—7—, etc. In this example each successive addend is 1 more than the immediately preceding one. (The difference between 2 and 1 is 1; between 4 and 2 it is 2; between 7 and 4 it is 3; etc.)

3. Adding numbers called out by the teacher mentally.
4. Adding numbers expressed in columns, as illustrated below.

Example

	$48 + 27 = 48 + (20 + 7) = (48 + 20) + 7$
45	$= 68 + 7 = 75$
36	$75 + 36 = 75 + (30 + 6) = (75 + 30) + 6$
27	$= 105 + 6 = 111$
+48	$111 + 45 = 111 + (40 + 5) = (111 + 40) + 5$
	$= 151 + 5 = 156$

5. Adding in a ring. The teacher writes several numerals in a ring on the chalkboard. The pupils have to add the numbers expressed by the numerals he points to. An example of such a ring is shown below. An exercise might be: 5 + 2 + 1 + 3 + 7 + 5, etc.

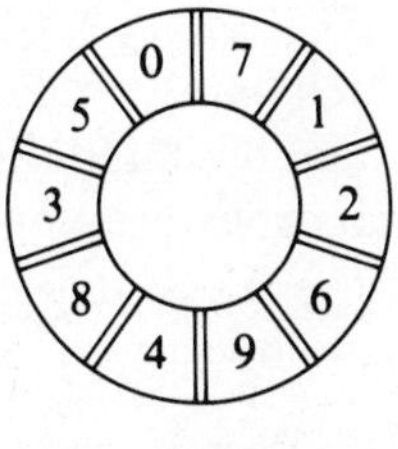

6. Adding the numbers named in a magic square.

Example

In the magic square shown below, the sum of the numbers named in each row, column, and long diagonal equals 12:

1	6	5
8	4	0
3	2	7

1 + 6 + 5 = 12, 1 + 8 + 3 = 12, 1 + 4 + 7 = 12, etc.

7. Adding in rows and columns. The teacher selects numbers to put in the boxes. Then the pupils add the rows and the columns. Practice is provided in both horizontal and vertical addition. The grand total expressed in the bottom box at the right must be the total of both the sums of the columns and the sums of the rows.

Example

25	16	9	14	
30	21	13	8	
16	9	5	10	

8. Adding a given set of numbers—for example, the odd numbers from 5 through 25, or the even numbers from 10 through 40.
9. Adding with dollars and cents, both by mental and written computation.
10. Playing "follow me" in mental computation.

Example

Start with 5, add 3, add 10, add 2, add 8, add 4, add 9. Write the last answer.

MATHEMATICAL JUSTIFICATION OF A SELECTED PROCEDURE

When working an exercise such as 32 + 24, the pupil may decide to add first the tens, then the ones, and then find the total of these sums. In this simple procedure several properties are applied. Young children should not be required to show all the steps and state all the properties. They simply work the exercise as follows:

$$32 + 24 = (30 + 20) + (2 + 4) = 50 + 6 = 56$$

Pupils who are more mature mathematically can understand the mathematical justification of the procedure presented below.

$$\begin{aligned}
32 + 24 &= (30 + 2) + (20 + 4) && \text{renaming}\\
&= [(30 + 2) + 20] + 4 && \text{associative property}\\
&= [30 + (2 + 20)] + 4 && \text{associative property}\\
&= [30 + (20 + 2)] + 4 && \text{commutative property}\\
&= [(30 + 20) + 2] + 4 && \text{associative property}\\
&= (30 + 20) + (2 + 4) && \text{associative property}\\
&= 50 + 6 && \text{addition}\\
&= 56 && \text{addition}
\end{aligned}$$

CHECKING THE SUM

Several methods are available to test the accuracy of the sum of an addition. The procedures used should be simple enough for the children to understand. Some ways of checking addition are presented below.

1. The order in which the addends were originally added is reversed. If, in column addition, the sum was found by adding up, the check is made by adding down.

   Example

   $$\begin{array}{r} 6 \\ 7 \\ 5 \\ +9 \\ \hline 27 \end{array}$$

   When adding up, the order is: 9 + 5 + 7 + 6.
   When adding down, the order is: 6 + 7 + 5 + 9.
   Though different combinations are encountered, the result must be the same.

2. The rule of compensation is used.

   Example

   25 + 19 = 44.

   Check: (25 − 1) + (19 + 1) = 24 + 20 = 44.

3. Another method of adding is used.

   Example

   27 + 24 = 27 + (20 + 4) = (27 + 20) + 4 = 47 + 4 = 51.

   Check: 27 + 24 = (20 + 20) + (7 + 4) = 40 + 11 = 51.

4. One of the two addends is subtracted from the sum and it is determined whether the difference equals the other addend. This check can be made only when there are just two addends.

   Examples

   25 + 12 = 37.

   Check: 37 − 12 = 25.
   37 − 25 = 12.

   $$\begin{array}{r} 579 \\ +386 \\ \hline 965 \end{array}$$

   Check: $\begin{array}{r} 965 \\ -579 \\ \hline 386 \end{array}$ or $\begin{array}{r} 965 \\ -386 \\ \hline 579 \end{array}$

5. Columns consisting of several addends are sometimes divided into smaller groups of addends. Then each group is added and the total of the sums of the groups is determined. This total must equal the original sum.

Example

$$
\begin{array}{r}
14 \\
25 \\
19 \\
36 \\
28 \\
30 \\
18 \\
+45 \\
\hline
215
\end{array}
$$

Check:

$$
\begin{array}{r}
14 \\
25 \\
19 \\
+36 \\
\hline
94
\end{array}
\qquad
\begin{array}{r}
28 \\
30 \\
18 \\
+45 \\
\hline
121
\end{array}
\qquad
\begin{array}{r}
94 \\
+121 \\
\hline
215
\end{array}
$$

6. The check of nines is used. When a whole number has been divided by 9, the remainder is 0, 1, 2, 3, 4, 5, 6, 7, or 8. This remainder is called the excess of nines in that number. In our decimal system, the excess of nines in a given number equals the excess of nines in the sum of the digits.

Example

If 763 is divided by 9, the remainder is 7. The sum of the digits of 763 is $7 + 6 + 3 = 16$. If 16 is divided by 9, the remainder is also 7. The equality of the remainders of 763 and of the sum of the digits 7, 6, and 3 can be demonstrated as follows:

$$
\begin{aligned}
763 &= (7 \times 100) + (6 \times 10) + 3 \\
&= 7 \times (99 + 1) + 6 \times (9 + 1) + 3 \\
&= (7 \times 99) + 7 + (6 \times 9) + 6 + 3 \\
&= (7 \times 99) + (6 \times 9) + 7 + 6 + 3
\end{aligned}
$$

Since both 7×99 and 6×9 are multiples of 9, the remainders of 763 and of the sum of 7, 6, and 3 must be equal.

When the accuracy of an addition is tested by using the check of nines, the sum of the digits of each addend is determined. If the sum of the digits is more than 8, the excess of nines is found. The total of the excesses of nines in the addends must equal the excess of nines in the sum of the addition. In the example below, this procedure has been followed.

Example

	Sum of the digits:	Excess of nines:
4,567	22	4
1,234	10	1
+1,002	3	+3
6,803	17	8

Since the excesses of nines in the addends total 8 and the excess of nines in 6,803 is also 8, it can be stated that the answer is probably correct.

Errors that will not be detected by the check of nines are: (1) an error of 9 or a multiple of 9, (2) a faulty omission of a zero, and (3) an error in the order of the digits.

7. The answer is checked by estimation. The reasonableness of the sum in 149 + 22 = 171 or in

$$\begin{array}{r} 149 \\ +22 \\ \hline 171 \end{array}$$

can be determined quickly by adding 150 and 20 mentally. In order to develop the pupil's ability to approximate answers, the teacher should ask the pupil repeatedly to decide whether an answer makes sense, and should assist in finding proper techniques for rounding numbers and estimating answers.

MENTAL COMPUTATION

In the solution of addition sentences in this chapter the horizontal method was frequently used. This method of solution promotes the use of mental computation.

Exercises in mental addition where the sums are greater than 100 can be patterned after cases previously presented. To assist the teacher in this task, several examples are presented below.

Example 1

70 + 70 = □.

Think: How much do I add to 70 to get 100? The answer is 30. Since 70 = 30 + 40, first add 30 to 70 and then add 40 to the sum:

$$\begin{aligned} 70 + 70 &= 70 + (30 + 40) \\ &= (70 + 30) + 40 \\ &= 100 + 40 \\ &= 140 \end{aligned}$$

Example 2

$75 + 77 = \square$.

a. *Think:* $77 = 70 + 7$. First add 70 to 75 and then add 7 to the sum:

$$\begin{aligned} 75 + 77 &= 75 + (70 + 7) \\ &= (75 + 70) + 7 \\ &= 145 + 7 \\ &= 152 \end{aligned}$$

b. Rename 75 as $70 + 5$ and 77 as $70 + 7$. Add the tens, add the ones, and then find the total of the sums:

$$\begin{aligned} 75 + 77 &= (70 + 70) + (5 + 7) \\ &= 140 + 12 \\ &= 152 \end{aligned}$$

Example 3

$420 + 170 = \square$.

a. *Think:* $170 = 100 + 70$. First add 100 to 420 and then add 70 to the sum:

$$\begin{aligned} 420 + 170 &= 420 + (100 + 70) \\ &= (420 + 100) + 70 \\ &= 520 + 70 \\ &= 590 \end{aligned}$$

b. Rename 420 as $400 + 20$ and 170 as $100 + 70$. Add the hundreds, add the tens, and then find the total of the sums:

$$\begin{aligned} 420 + 170 &= (400 + 100) + (20 + 70) \\ &= 500 + 90 \\ &= 590 \end{aligned}$$

Example 4

$97 + 8 = \square$.

Think: How much do I add to 97 to get 100? The answer is 3. Since $8 = 3 + 5$, first add 3 to 97 and then add 5 to the sum:

$$\begin{aligned} 97 + 8 &= 97 + (3 + 5) \\ &= (97 + 3) + 5 \\ &= 100 + 5 \\ &= 105 \end{aligned}$$

Example 5

$65 + 98 = \square$.

Think: 98 is 2 less than 100. Since $65 + 100 = 165$, $65 + 98 = 163$.

Example 6

$243 + 104 = \square$.

Think: $104 = 100 + 4$. First add 100 to 243 and then add 4 to the sum:

$$\begin{aligned} 243 + 104 &= 243 + (100 + 4) \\ &= (243 + 100) + 4 \\ &= 343 + 4 \\ &= 347 \end{aligned}$$

Example 7

$125 + 49 = \square$.

Think: 49 is 1 less than 50. Since $125 + 50 = 175$, $125 + 49 = 174$.

DIAGNOSIS OF MISTAKES

An important task of the teacher is to analyze the pupils' daily work in order to identify faulty reasoning. Too often a simple error goes undetected and becomes persistent when it could have been prevented by a little help. The Selected Research that follows deals with diagnosis of mistakes.

SELECTED RESEARCH

This study[4] was mainly concerned with the problem of how systematic errors that relate to addition and subtraction of whole numbers can be detected.

Cox identifies three kinds of computational errors: systematic, random, and careless errors.

Systematic errors are those computational errors that occur in at least three out of five problems for a specific algorithmic computation. They show a pattern of incorrect responses.

Random errors occur in at least three out of five problems but contain no discernible pattern. Thus they are difficult to remediate.

Careless errors occur in one or two out of five problems. The errors may be due to distractions, boredom, or a lapse in attention.

The investigator lists the following set of systematic errors in addition and subtraction of whole numbers that were taken from children's papers.

$$1.\quad \begin{array}{r} 476 \\ +\ 17 \\ \hline 25 \end{array} \qquad \begin{array}{r} 205 \\ +\ 86 \\ \hline 21 \end{array} \qquad \begin{array}{r} 754 \\ +\ 28 \\ \hline 26 \end{array} \qquad\qquad 2.\quad \begin{array}{r} 519 \\ +\ 82 \\ \hline 511 \end{array} \qquad \begin{array}{r} 345 \\ +\ 76 \\ \hline 511 \end{array} \qquad \begin{array}{r} 483 \\ +\ 57 \\ \hline 711 \end{array}$$

4. L. S. Cox, "Diagnosing and Remediating Systematic Errors in Addition and Subtraction Computations," Using Research in Teaching, ed. R. E. Reys, *The Arithmetic Teacher* (February, 1975), pp. 151–157.

3.	46 + 3 43	21 + 8 13	15 + 2 13
4.	46 + 3 79	21 + 8 109	15 + 2 37
5.	48 + 3 411	79 + 9 718	26 + 7 213
6.	37 − 4 23	43 − 1 32	85 − 3 72
7.	32 − 6 34	50 − 8 58	24 − 5 21
8.	3 19 ~~49~~ −11 218	1 18 ~~28~~ −16 12	7 13 ~~83~~ −32 411
9.	53 −14 49	72 −56 26	45 −19 36
10.	5 13 4~~93~~ − 45 418	2 16 3~~76~~ − 58 338	3 15 2~~65~~ − 39 206

The errors are described by Cox as follows:

1. Adds each digit separately disregarding columns.

   (476 + 17 = 4 + 7 + 6 + 1 + 7 = 25)

2. The digits in the sum were reversed. The ones digits were renamed instead of the tens digits.

   30
   483
   + 57

   The "carried" numerals were not shown on the child's paper.
3. Subtracts instead of adds.
4. Adds single-digit addend to both digits of the other addend.
5. Did not rename the sum of the ones column. This is placed in the answer and the digit in the tens column is placed to the left of the ones column.
6. "Borrowed" from the tens column when it was unnecessary.
7. Did not regroup the minuend. Subtracted in the ones column the smaller number from the larger number.
8. Renamed the minuend when it was unnecessary. The difference in the ones column is a two-digit number. The two-digit number is placed in the answer.
9. Renamed the minuend and correctly subtracted in the ones column. No renaming or borrowing was performed in the tens column.

10. Incorrectly renamed the minuend. The renamed number in the tens column is obtained by subtracting the smaller digit from the larger digit in the tens column. Subtraction in the tens column is then performed with this renamed number; for example, the renamed ten of 493 − 45 is obtained by subtracting 9 − 4 = 5. Five is the renamed number.

The investigator states that research has shown that, if pupils make systematic errors without proper intervention, a significant number of children continue to make these errors a year later. She also suggests that, since research tells us little regarding the most appropriate methods for handling such errors, teachers continue to use their own judgment in selecting remedial activities.

SELECTED ACTIVITIES FOR PUPILS

1. Show on the number line that 9 + 4 = 13.
2. Write 1, 3, 5, 7, 9, and 11 on the sides of a sugar cube. You and a friend take turns rolling the cube. Keep a record of the numbers you roll. Add your own numbers and check your friend's. The first one to reach a sum of 50 or more is the winner.

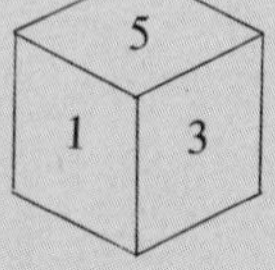

3. Use your mathematics book. On what pages is the sum of the digits of the page numbers equal to 9?
4. I have 6 coins worth a total of 32¢. What coins do I have?
5. What different sets of coins can you use to pay a debt of 21¢?
6. Copy and replace the frames with the correct digits.

1○○3	○82○	7777	○○○○
+○72○	+1○79	+○○○○	+3781
699○	72○5	9332	8332

7. JEREMIAH DECODER assigned a number to each letter in this way: A—1, B—2, C—3, to Z—26. He said the number code for his first name

was 69. Was he right? What is the number code for Jeremiah's last name? Find the number codes for your names.

8. Code: A—1, B—2, C—3, D—4, E—5, F—6, G—7, H—8, I—9, J—10, K—20, L—30, M—40, N—50, O—60, P—70, Q—80, R—90, S—100, T—200, U—300, V—400, W—500, X—600, Y—700, Z—800.
What is the number code of your teacher's last name?
What is the number code of the city or town where you live?
What is the number code of WIZZARD?

9. Study the dart board. In how many different ways can you score 21 with 2 darts? 24 with 3 darts? 18 with 4 darts? 24 with 8 darts? (Of course you may hit the same section more than once.)

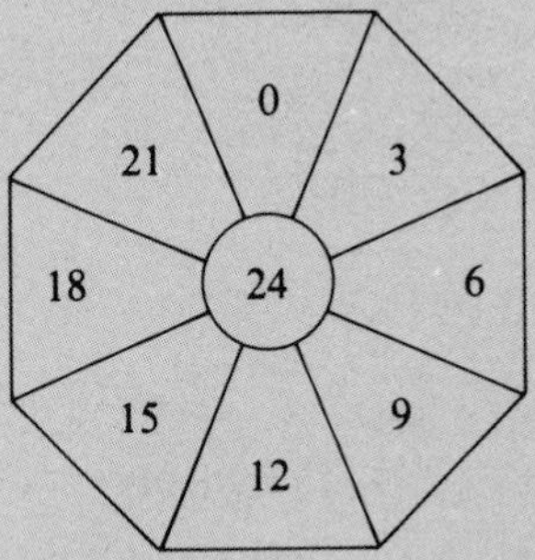

10. This dart board also uses negative numbers. Rex hits $^{+}3$, $^{-}3$, $^{-}2$, $^{+}4$, 0, and $^{+}1$. What is his score? Make up some problems yourself and solve them.

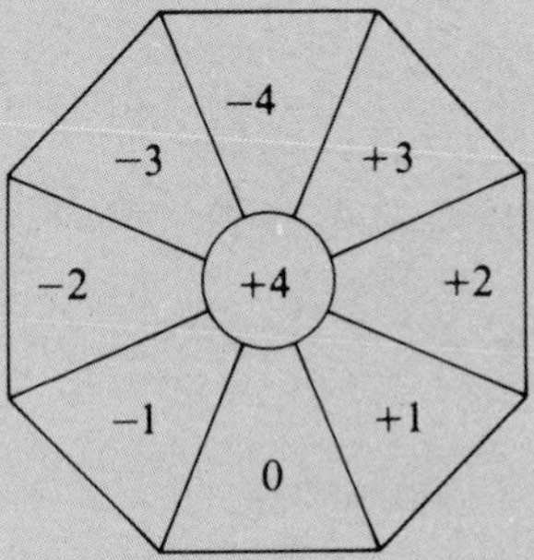

11. Place punctuation marks in the following:

The farmers of the Northern land
Have ten fingers on each hand
Five and twenty on hands and feet
Tell me how to count them, Pete!

Solution: Place a comma after "fingers" and one after "five."

12. Work the magic square.

  a. Find the sum of the numbers expressed in the square:

202	1212	1010
1616	808	0
606	404	1414

left-right →	up-down ↓	corner-corner ⤡
202 + 1212 + 1010 =	202 + 1616 + 606 =	202 + 808 + 1414 =
1616 + 808 + 0 =	1212 + 808 + 404 =	606 + 808 + 1010 =
606 + 404 + 1414 =	1010 + 0 + 1414 =	

  b. In each addition in (a), the sum is ______.
  The square is a magic number square.

  c. Add 15 to each number in the square.
  Then add the sums in the order that you followed in (a).
  Is the square a magic square?

  d. Try to make other magic squares.
  Add any number you want.

13. Find a sum without adding.

Example

Directions:	Example:
Ask a friend to write a 2-digit number.	61
You write 38.	38
Let your friend write again a 2-digit number.	52
You write 47.	47
Without adding you write the sum.	198

  a. Explain why the sum is always 198.

  Hint: Find the sum of 61 and 38 and also of 52 and 47.
  Add these sums.

  b. Follow the same procedure using 3-digit numbers.
  Try to explain why the sum is always 1,998.

14. A *palindrome* is a word, phrase, or sentence that reads the same backward and forward. Examples are the words BOB and DAD. You can get palindromic numbers by writing a number, reversing the digits, and adding the two numbers. If regrouping is necessary, the process must be repeated until a palindromic number is obtained.

Example 1

Directions:	Example:
Write a number.	134
Reverse the digits.	431
Add.	565

Explain why the sum reads the same backward and forward.

Example 2

Directions:	Example:
Write a number.	379
Reverse the digits.	973
Add.	1,352
Reverse the digits.	2,531
Add.	3,883

Explain why the process had to be repeated.

Do some similar activities starting with different numbers.

EXERCISES

1. Explain and illustrate three properties of addition.
2. Write all the facts belonging to the family of 7.
3. Write 5 mathematical sentences, each expressing an inequality.
4. Enumerate some techniques that should serve to anchor skill in the key addition facts.
5. Prepare an addition table for facts with sums not greater than 6.
6. Give the mathematical justification of the following sentence:

$$25 + 31 = (20 + 30) + (5 + 1) = 50 + 6 = 56.$$

7. A column addition is often added down and checked by adding up. Justify this.
8. Write an illustrative lesson on the addition of two 2-digit numbers with regrouping.
9. Report on the selected research described in this chapter.
10. Diagnose the persistent mistake in each of the following sets of additions.

a.

75	28	62	55	16
+19	+13	+29	+37	+16
84	31	81	82	22

b.

205	601	502	402	303
+394	+137	+262	+296	+454
509	708	704	608	707

c.

85	68	24	49	38
+77	+84	73	56	38
117	116	+95	+34	38
		120	121	+38
				134

11. Add four 5-digit numbers. Check the answer by using the check of nines.

SOURCES FOR FURTHER READING

Ashlock, R. B., *Error Patterns in Computation.* Columbus: Charles E. Merrill Publishing Company, 1972.

Bidwell, J. K., "Learning Structures for Arithmetic," *The Arithmetic Teacher,* April, 1969, pp. 263–268.

D'Augustine, C. H., *Multiple Methods of Teaching Mathematics in the Elementary School,* 2nd ed. New York: Harper & Row, Publishers, 1973, Chaps. VI, XVI.

Edmonds, G. F., "Discovering Patterns in Addition," *The Arithmetic Teacher,* April, 1969, pp. 245–248.

Granito, D., "Number Patterns and the Addition Operation," *The Arithmetic Teacher,* October, 1976, pp. 432–434.

Heddens, J. W., *Today's Mathematics,* 3d ed. Chicago: Science Research Associates, Inc., 1974, Units VII, XVI.

Kennedy, L. M., *Guiding Children to Mathematical Discovery,* 2nd ed. Belmont, California: Wadsworth Publishing Company, Inc., 1975, Chaps. VI, VII.

Marks, J. L., C. R. Purdy, L. B. Kinney, and A. A. Hiatt, *Teaching Elementary School Mathematics for Understanding,* 4th ed. New York: McGraw-Hill Book Company, 1975, Chap. IV.

Moon, L., Jr., and S. P. Moon, "Mystic Squares for Primary Pupils," *The Arithmetic Teacher,* December, 1976, pp. 592–595.

Murray, P. J., "Addition Practice through Partitioning of Sets of Numbers," *The Arithmetic Teacher,* October, 1976, pp. 430–431.

National Council of Teachers of Mathematics, *Topics in Mathematics, Twenty-ninth Yearbook.* Washington, D.C.: The Council, 1964, Bklt. 2.

Schminke, C. W., N. Maertens, and W. R. Arnold, *Teaching the Child Mathematics.* Hinsdale, Illinois: The Dryden Press, Inc., 1973, Chaps. IV, VII.

Spitzer, H. F., *Teaching Elementary School Mathematics.* Boston: Houghton Mifflin Company, 1967, Chap. IV.

Subtraction 12

During the early stages of mathematics study the pupils should discover that addition and subtraction are inverse operations. This is best achieved when these operations are presented concurrently.

In this volume addition and subtraction are considered in separate chapters for purposes of organization. The present chapter is mainly concerned with the teaching of the subtraction of whole numbers and deals in a few paragraphs with subtraction involving negative integers.

SKILLS TEST

1. Subtract and check by adding the difference and the subtrahend.

456	258	4,045	3,404	25,001
389	107	2,147	1,675	17,345

2. Subtract and check.

6,065	9,007	5,100	62,789	40,708
3,405	8,888	1,203	31,999	27,785

3. Find the answers.

$3 - {}^{-}1 =$	${}^{-}3 - {}^{-}2 =$	$7 - {}^{+}2 =$	${}^{-}4 - {}^{-}6 =$
$6 - {}^{-}4 =$	${}^{-}6 - {}^{-}3 =$	$9 - {}^{+}5 =$	${}^{-}5 - {}^{-}9 =$
$8 - {}^{-}2 =$	${}^{-}4 - {}^{-}3 =$	$8 - {}^{+}7 =$	${}^{-}7 - {}^{-}8 =$

MEANING AND TERMS

Subtraction "undoes" what addition "does" and is called the inverse operation of addition. For example, in $4 + 3 = 7$, 3 has been added to 4 to get 7, whereas in $7 - 3 = 4$, 3 has been subtracted from 7 to get the original number 4. Thus

$$4 + 3 = 7$$

and

$$(4 + 3) - 3 = 4$$

Subtraction can be defined as the operation by which the missing addend is found when the other addend and the sum are known. When finding the answer to $5 - 3 = \square$, the question can be asked: What number do I add to 3 to get 5? The given sum (5) is called the *minuend,* the given addend (3) the *subtrahend,* and the missing addend the *difference* or *remainder*. In general, it can be stated that if a, b, and c represent whole numbers such that $a + b = c$, then $a = c - b$ and $b = c - a$. Subtraction is a binary operation because it is performed on two numbers at a time.

Subtraction can also be thought of in terms of sets and subsets, as illustrated in the following situations.

Example 1

From set A (containing five members), subset B (containing two members) is removed, and the number of members in the remainder set C must be determined.

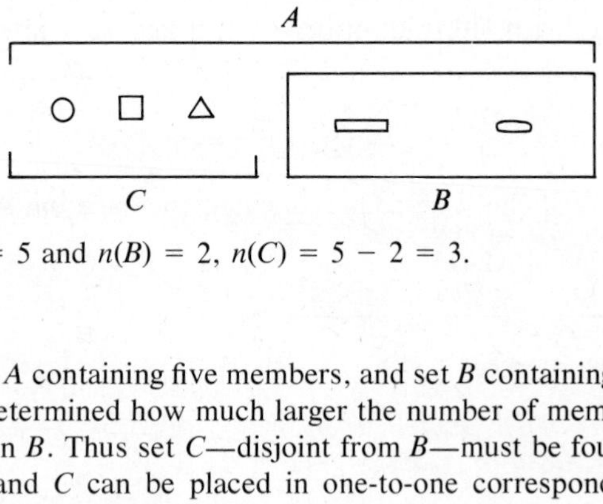

Since $n(A) = 5$ and $n(B) = 2$, $n(C) = 5 - 2 = 3$.

Example 2

Consider set A containing five members, and set B containing three members. It must be determined how much larger the number of members in A is than the number in B. Thus set C—disjoint from B—must be found such that the union of B and C can be placed in one-to-one correspondence with A. It appears that C must contain two members. Thus $n(C) = 2$ and $5 = 3 + 2$, or $5 - 3 = 2$.

PROPERTIES

The commutative property does not apply to subtraction of whole numbers.

Example

$3 - 2 \neq 2 - 3.$

The associative property does not apply to subtraction of whole numbers.

Example

$(8 - 5) - 2 \neq 8 - (5 - 2).$

The set of whole numbers is not closed with respect to subtraction.

Example

In $3 - 5 = \square$, the difference is not a whole number.

The pupils should acquire functional knowledge of several rules used in subtraction:

1. The difference between two numbers can be found by renaming both the minuend and the subtrahend as the sum of two numbers, subtracting each part of the subtrahend from a part of the minuend, and adding the obtained differences.

   Example

   $$\begin{aligned} 45 - 21 &= (40 + 5) - (20 + 1) \\ &= (40 - 20) + (5 - 1) \\ &= 20 + 4 = 24 \end{aligned}$$

2. The difference between the minuend and the subtrahend remains unchanged if both the minuend and the subtrahend are increased or decreased by the same number. This rule, called the *rule of compensation,* is applied in the equal-additions method of subtraction and sometimes in mental computation.

   Examples

   $46 - 19 = (46 + 1) - (19 + 1) = 47 - 20 = 27.$
   $41 - 12 = (41 - 1) - (12 - 1) = 40 - 11 = 29.$

3. A number is decreased by the sum of two numbers if that number is first decreased by one of the addends and the obtained difference is decreased by the other addend.

   Example

   $48 - (10 + 9) = (48 - 10) - 9 = 38 - 9 = 29.$

4. A number is decreased by the difference between two numbers if the number is increased by the subtrahend and the obtained sum is decreased by the minuend.

Example

$56 - (25 - 9) = (56 + 9) - 25 = 65 - 25 = 40.$

THE KEY SUBTRACTION FACTS

In the preceding chapter the 100 key addition facts were identified. Since the operation of subtraction is the inverse of addition, there are 100 key subtraction facts (also called basic subtraction facts). The key addition facts comprise all the possible two-term addition facts that can be formed by using the figures 0 through 9. Thus the key subtraction facts are obtained when the numbers 0 through 9 are subtracted from the numbers 0 through 18, provided that the difference is less than 10. A subtraction fact includes the difference.

Usually the key subtraction facts are arbitrarily divided into two groups: (1) the so-called "easy" facts, with minuends of 10 or less, and (2) the "hard" facts, the minuends of which are greater than 10.

READING A SUBTRACTION FACT

A subtraction fact may be read in different ways. For example, $9 - 4 = 5$ may be read as "nine minus four equals five," and "four from nine is five." It is advisable that the pupils in the primary grades become well acquainted with the particular phrase they will use when they advance in mathematics: Nine minus four equals five. It is the teacher's responsibility to attempt to prevent mere verbalism by ascertaining that the pupils understand the meaning of all phrases and words used.

METHODS OF SUBTRACTION

Two methods can be used to find the answer to a subtraction question—for example, finding the difference between 15 and 4:

1. *The additive method.* In determining the answer by the additive method, the question "How much do I add to 4 to get 15?" is asked. This question can be translated into the mathematical sentence $4 + \square = 15$. Then the missing addend is found.

2. *The subtractive method.* In finding the answer by the subtractive method, the question "How much is 15 minus 4?" is asked. The number sentence is expressed as $15 - 4 = \square$.

Whereas several decades ago the additive method was popular in this country, at present the subtractive method is generally used as the initial method of subtraction. The additive approach has the advantage that its terminology is closely related to that of addition. The subtractive method, however, seems to be easier for elementary school pupils to understand. Therefore it is recommended that, in initial teaching of subtraction, the subtractive method be used, and that the additive method be presented at higher grade levels as a reintroduction of subtraction and as an enrichment activity.

$$\begin{array}{r} 42 \\ -17 \\ \hline \end{array}$$

In the subtraction question shown above, the digit 7 represents a larger number than the corresponding digit in the minuend. Since there is no whole number that satisfies the equation $2 - 7 = \square$, a technique must be used to subtract 7. Various methods are available:

1. *The decomposition*[1] *method*. In this method, 1 ten is regrouped into 10 ones (a process often incorrectly called "borrowing"), the 10 ones are added to the 2 ones, and the difference between the ones and between the tens is determined by one of the two previously described methods:

$$\begin{array}{r} {\scriptstyle 3\,12} \\ \not{4}\,\not{2} \\ -1\;7 \\ \hline \end{array}$$

a. *The subtractive method,* by which 7 ones are subtracted from 12 ones, and 1 ten from 3 tens.
b. *The additive method,* by which it is determined what number must be added to 7 to get 12 and how many tens must be added to 1 ten to get 3 tens.

2. *The equal-additions method.* In this method, the reasoning is as follows: Since 7 cannot be subtracted from 2, add 10 ones to the 2 ones in the minuend. In order to keep the difference between the minuend and the subtrahend equal, add 1 ten to the 1 ten in the subtrahend. The answer can then be determined by one of the two basic methods: the subtractive method or the additive method.

$$\begin{array}{r} {\scriptstyle 12} \\ 4\,\not{2} \\ {\scriptstyle 2}\;\; \\ -\not{1}\,7 \\ \hline \end{array}$$

Of the different methods of subtraction presented, the subtractive-decomposition method seems to be the most promising. As stated above, the subtractive approach appears to be easier to understand than the additive method if it is introduced in concrete situations. Brownell and Moser[2] found that the decomposition method, when taught meaningfully, was more successful than the equal-additions method.

---

1. The verb "decompose" means to separate a substance into its elements.
2. A résumé of this study is presented at the end of this chapter.

TYPES OF SUBTRACTION SITUATIONS

Three types of subtraction situations can be identified:

1. *The "how many left" or "remainder" type.*

Example

Bill had 5 marbles. He gave 2 marbles to his friend. How many marbles did Bill have left?

Number question: 5 − 2 = □.

Interpretation: In this subtraction situation it must be determined how many marbles are left after the operation has taken place, and thus the cardinal number of the remainder set must be found. The situation can be represented easily on paper:

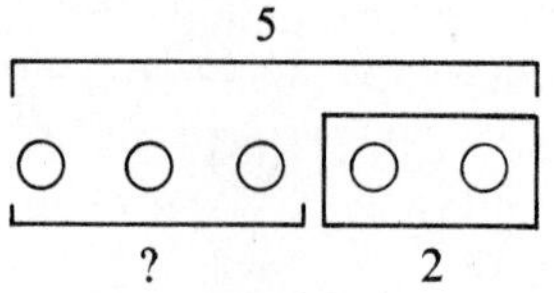

2. *The "how many more" or "difference" type.*

Example

Tom has 5 marbles and Ray has 3 marbles. How many more marbles does Tom have than Ray?

Number question: 5 − 3 = □ or 5 = 3 + □.

Interpretation: It must be determined how many more marbles there are in Tom's set than in Ray's:

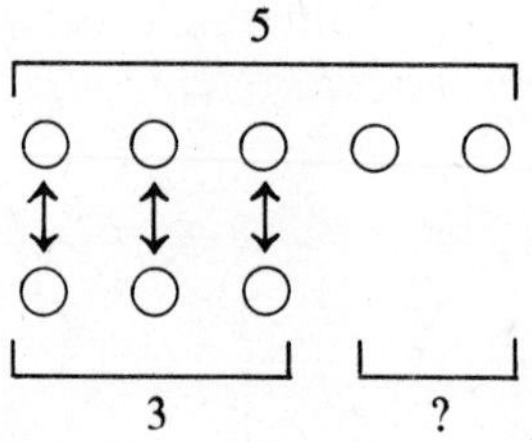

3. *The "how many (much) more needed" type.*

Example

Ed has 3 marbles. He needs 5 marbles to play a game. How many more marbles does Ed need?

Number question: 3 + □ = 5.

Interpretation: One addend and the sum are known, and the missing addend must be found. The situation can be represented on paper by drawing 5 marbles, identifying 3 of them, and determining how many are needed to get 5. This is, in reality, an addition situation.

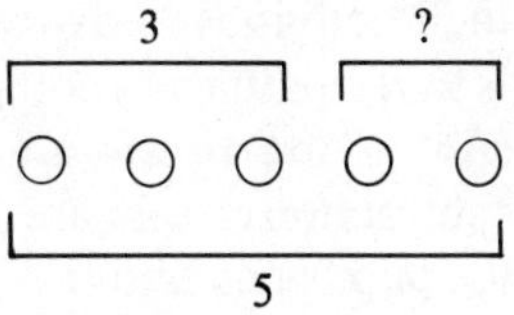

INTRODUCING THE KEY SUBTRACTION FACTS

Subtraction is the inverse operation of addition, and some of the techniques suggested in Chapter 11 for the teaching of the key addition facts can be adapted and used when the key subtraction facts are introduced. The relation between addition and subtraction can be illustrated when given key subtraction facts are presented together with or subsequent to the presentation of the corresponding key addition facts.

Activities for a meaningful introduction of the key subtraction facts are suggested below. The teacher's selection of techniques should depend on the background and ability of the pupils.

1. Concrete materials such as objects, disks, counters, beads, Cuisenaire rods, and Stern blocks are manipulated. From the group of objects under consideration, a predetermined number of objects are removed and the appropriate number sentence is stated and written.
2. The subtraction fact to be studied is represented on the flannel board or the magnetic board. The corresponding number sentences are presented under the illustration.
3. Cards with pictures, dots, or stars illustrating the number fact are used. The number fact is printed at the bottom of the card. If the sentence is covered, the child, after constructing the fact from the illustration, can check the answer.
4. The pupils illustrate a fact by drawing circles on a line to represent beads on a rod. Then the corresponding number sentences are written:

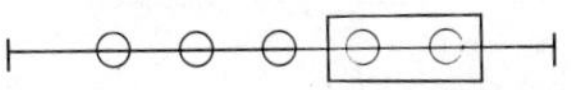

$5 = 3 + 2$
$5 - 2 = 3$

5. Facts are illustrated on the number line:

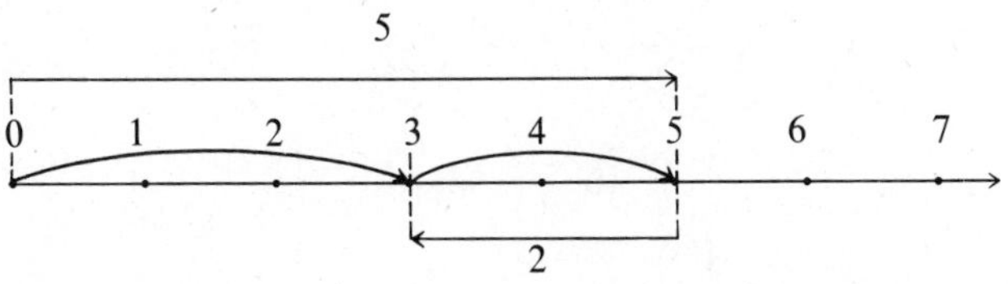

$5 = 3 + 2$
$5 - 2 = 3$

By pursuing several such activities and working a great many exercises, the pupils should discover patterns and form generalizations, such as the generalization for subtracting 1 from a given number.

Before the "hard" subtraction facts are introduced, the teacher should: (1) ascertain that the pupils can find the different component parts of 10, (2) review the concept of place value, and (3) introduce the case in which ones are subtracted from 11 through 19 to get a difference of 10, as in $13 - 3 = 10$. Such skills will assist the pupils in working an exercise such as $13 - 7 = \square$ in parts:

$$\begin{aligned} 13 - 7 &= 13 - (3 + 4) \\ &= (13 - 3) - 4 \\ &= 10 - 4 \\ &= 6 \end{aligned}$$

A useful device to assist the child in "first going to 10" is the folded paper model illustrated in Figure 12.1. To solve, for example, $13 - 7 = \square$, 13 dots (shown as $10 + 3$) are made on a strip of paper. The child follows this procedure:

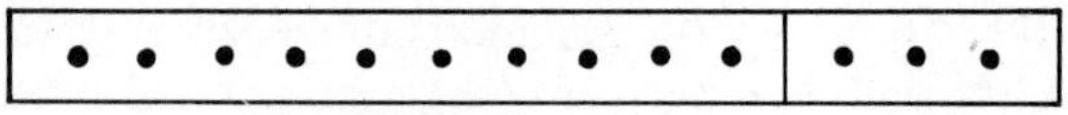

Figure 12.1 (a)

What number do I subtract from 13 to get 10? The answer is 3, and 3 dots are covered.

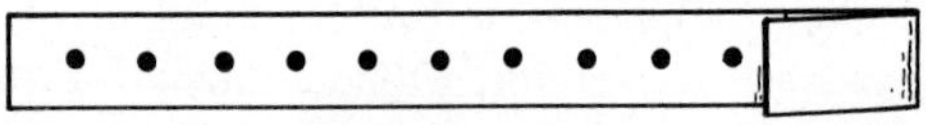

$13 - 3 = 10$

Figure 12.1 (b)

How much more do I have to subtract? Since $7 = 3 + 4$, I must subtract 4 more. Four more dots are covered.

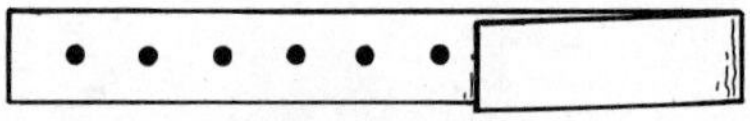

$10 - 4 = 6$

Figure 12.1 (c)

Thus

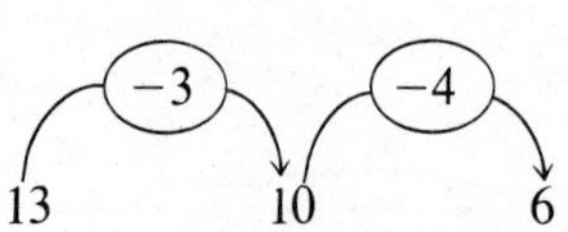

$13 - 7 = 6$

DEVELOPING AND ANCHORING SKILLS

Gradually the pupils should become so well acquainted with the basic subtraction facts that they readily know the answer to a question when it is presented. In the study for mastery, the facts should be used meaningfully in exercises of various kinds so that the pupils see a need for memorizing them. Proper devices should be used to develop and anchor the facts. Because of the great importance of these skills in computation, the final aim should be complete mastery.

Many of the techniques described in Chapter 11 for anchoring the key addition facts can be modified to fit subtraction. Some of these modified techniques and additional ones are presented below.

1. Exercises presented in the textbook and workbook and those provided by the teacher, including the following:
   a. Finding the relationship between addition and subtraction.

   Example

   $3 + 2 = 5, 5 - 2 = \square.$

   b. Finding the minuend or the subtrahend.

   Example

   $\square - 3 = 6; \quad 8 - \square = 5.$

   c. Subtracting in parts.

   Example

   $16 - 9 = 16 - 6 - \square = \bigcirc.$

   d. Deciding which operation has been performed by supplying the symbol + or −.

   Example

   $10 \square 4 = 6; \quad 7 \square 2 = 9.$

   e. Subtracting two or more one-digit numbers.

   Example

   $10 - 3 - 2 = \square.$

   When the children find the answer to this number question, they do not see the numeral that names the difference between 10 and 3. If this presents a difficulty, the teacher should encourage the pupils to work several exercises in two steps, as follows: $10 - 3 = 7$, and $7 - 2 = 5$. The number line can also be used to illustrate the process and to allow the pupils to see the numeral that names the difference between the minuend and the first subtrahend:

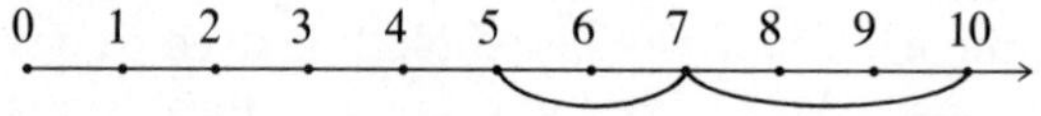

2. Different presentations of number questions.

a.

10 =		
15	−	□
□	−	3
17	−	□
□	−	7

b.

16 in all:	
□	7
□	3
□	9
□	12

c.

Subtract 5:	
16	□
9	□
12	□
7	□

d.

Just as much:	
11 − 4	9 − □
15 − 7	10 − □
18 − 9	14 − □
11 − 5	9 − □

e.

Write the answers. The first one has been done.							
	16	8	14	7	15	9	10
−7	9						

3. The construction of a table of the following kind.

0	1	2	3	4	5	6	7	8	9
9−9 8−8	10−9 9−8	11−9 10−8	12−9 11−8	13−9 12−8	14−9 13−8	15−9 14−8	16−9 15−8	17−9 16−8	18−9 17−8

etc.

4. The use of flashcards by small groups of pupils and by individual children. Different sets of flashcards should be used: one set on which the questions and facts are presented horizontally, and another set on which they are presented vertically.
5. Exercises with the subtraction wheel. The addition wheel described in Chapter 11 can be modified for use with the subtraction questions.
6. The completion of number sentences by pupils of at least average ability by supplying the symbol =, >, or <.

   Example

   15 − 7 □ 12 − 5.
7. Writing and memorizing facts.

SUGGESTED SEQUENCE FOR SUBTRACTION CASES

A possible sequence for the presentation of the cases with minuends not greater than 100 is as follows:

1. The key subtraction facts, interrupted by exercises such as 13 − 3 = □ in which ones are subtracted from 11 through 19 to get a difference of 10. Subtraction of two or more one-digit numbers is undertaken simultaneously and continued after the key facts have been developed.
2. Subtraction of multiples of 10.

   Example

   70 − 40 = □.
3. Subtraction of a one-digit number from a two-digit number resulting in a multiple of 10.

   Example

   35 − 5 = □.
4. Subtraction of a one-digit number from a two-digit number without regrouping.

   Example

   35 − 2 = □.
5. Subtraction of a multiple of 10 from a two-digit number.

   Example

   45 − 10 = □.

6. Subtraction with two two-digit numbers without regrouping.

   Example

   45 − 12 = □.

7. Subtraction of a one-digit number from a multiple of 10.

   Example

   30 − 2 = □.

8. Subtraction of a two-digit number from a multiple of 10.

   Example

   70 − 42 = □.

9. Subtraction of a one-digit number from a two-digit number with regrouping.

   Example

   35 − 7 = □.

10. Subtraction with two two-digit numbers with regrouping.

    Example

    45 − 17 = □.

The grade placement of subtraction cases with minuends greater than 100 should be based on a logical sequence. Before the introduction of the case in which a two-digit number is subtracted from a two-digit number with regrouping, easy cases with minuends greater than 100 can be presented, such as those suggested for the corresponding cases of addition.

Example

180 − 60 = □; 500 − 300 = □.

In the sections below, suggestions are presented for the teaching of subtraction cases with minuends not greater than 100. Since subtraction is the inverse operation of addition, the student is also referred to corresponding addition cases in Chapter 11. Many of the procedures described there can be modified and used for subtraction. For this reason, some of the presentations below have been condensed.

SUBTRACTION OF MULTIPLES OF 10

Example

Dan gave 20 of his 40 baseball cards to his friends. How many cards did Dan have left?

Number question: 40 − 20 = □.

Solutions:

1. Multiple counting. 20 = 2 tens. Count 2 tens backward:

   40 30 20

2. Using the tens blocks. The pupil reasons as follows:

   40 = 4 tens, and 20 = 2 tens
   Since 4 − 2 = 2, 4 tens − 2 tens = 20.

3. Using illustrations such as the one shown below.

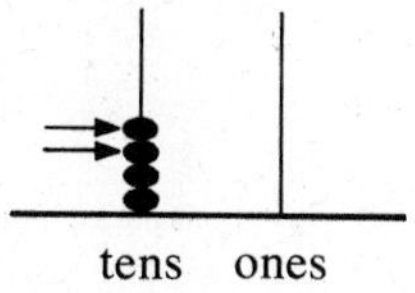

4. Using the hundred board.
5. Using the number line.

This case is followed by exercises of the following kind:

$$100 - 20 = \square$$
$$100 - \square = 60$$
$$\square - 30 = 50$$

SUBTRACTION OF A ONE-DIGIT NUMBER FROM A TWO DIGIT NUMBER RESULTING IN A MULTIPLE OF 10

This case is best introduced by reviewing the concept of place value:

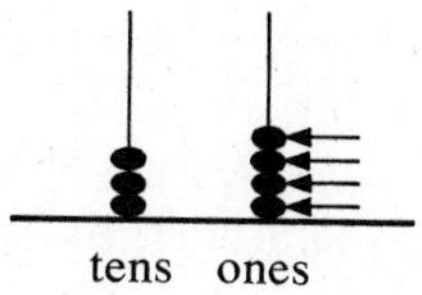

$$34 = \square \text{ tens and } \bigcirc \text{ ones}$$
$$3 \text{ tens and } 4 \text{ ones} - 4 \text{ ones} = \square \text{ tens}$$
$$34 - 4 = \square$$

SUBTRACTION OF A ONE-DIGIT NUMBER FROM A TWO-DIGIT NUMBER WITHOUT REGROUPING

Example

35 − 2 = □.

Solution: *Think:* Since 5 − 2 = 3, 35 − 2 = 33.

SUBTRACTION OF A MULTIPLE OF 10 FROM A TWO-DIGIT NUMBER

Example

43 − 10 = □.

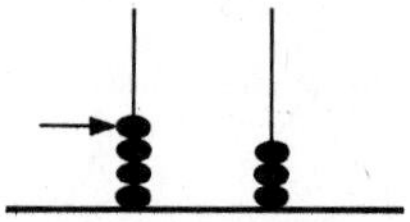

Solution: 43 − 10 = 4 tens and 3 ones − 1 ten = 3 tens and 3 ones = 33. Or, since 40 − 10 = 30, 43 − 10 = 33.

SUBTRACTION WITH TWO TWO-DIGIT NUMBERS WITHOUT REGROUPING

Example

45 − 12 = □.

Solutions:

1. Since 12 = 10 + 2, first subtract 10 from 45, and then subtract 2 from the obtained difference:

$$\begin{aligned} 45 - 12 &= 45 - (10 + 2) \\ &= (45 - 10) - 2 \\ &= 35 - 2 \\ &= 33 \end{aligned}$$

   This process can be illustrated on the number line:

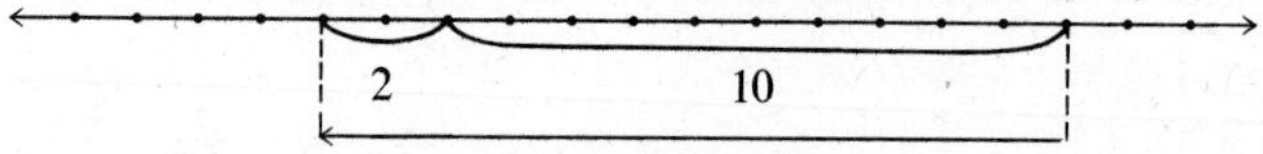

2. The number question is solved by using illustrations or devices such as the counting frame, the hundred board, and the abacus.

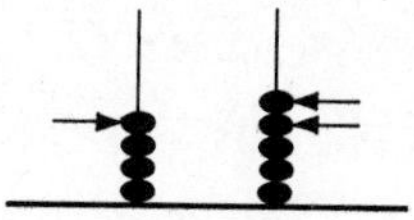

3. The answer is found by using the algorism in common use:

$$\begin{array}{r} 45 \\ -12 \\ \hline 33 \end{array}$$

SUBTRACTION OF A ONE-DIGIT NUMBER FROM A MULTIPLE OF 10

Example

$30 - 5 = \square$.

Solutions:

1. The process is illustrated on an abacus:

Step 1:

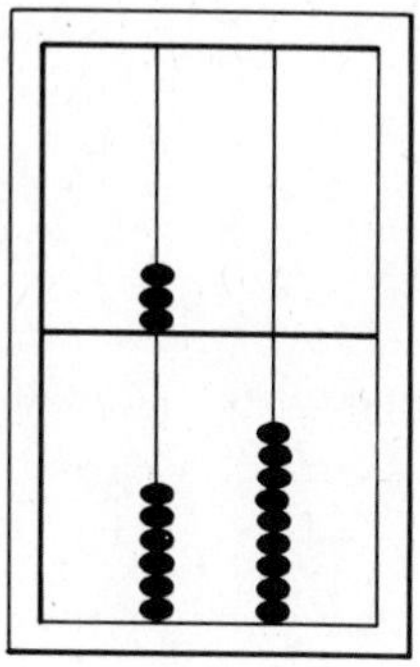

tens ones

3 tens are isolated.

5 ones must be subtracted.
1 ten is moved down. Since we have to subtract only 5 ones (and not 1 ten), 5 ones are moved up.

Step 2:

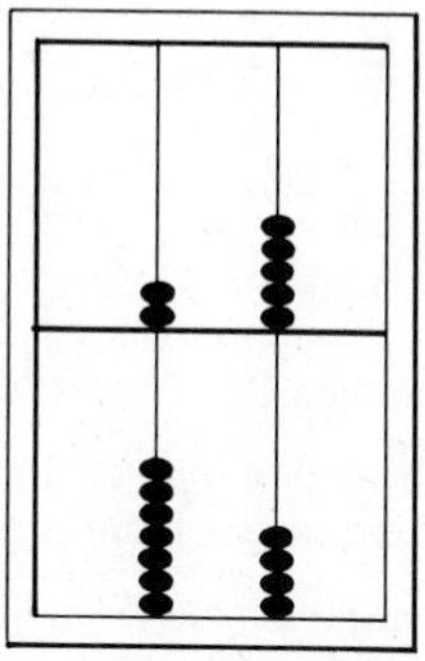

tens ones

The top part of the abacus now shows 2 tens and 5 ones, or 25.

2. The process can be expressed as follows: 3 tens − 5 ones = 2 tens and 10 ones − 5 ones = 2 tens and 5 ones = 25, or, vertically,

$$\begin{array}{rcrcl} 30 & = & 20 & + & 10 \\ -5 & = & & & 5 \\ \hline & & 20 & + & 5 = 25 \end{array}$$

3. After the process of regrouping has been clearly illustrated, the algorism in common use is presented. Initially, the pupils are often allowed to use crutches.

$$\begin{array}{r} {}^{2}\,{}^{10} \\ \not{3}\,\not{0} \\ -\;5 \\ \hline 2\;5 \end{array}$$

SUBTRACTION OF A ONE-DIGIT NUMBER FROM A TWO-DIGIT NUMBER WITH REGROUPING

Example

Ted gave 7 of his 35 foreign postage stamps to his brother. How many stamps did Ted have left?

Number question: $35 - 7 = \square$.

Solutions:

1. First enough is subtracted from 35 to get 30: $35 - 5 = 30$. Since $7 = 5 + 2$, 2 is subtracted from 30: $30 - 2 = 28$.

$$\begin{aligned} 35 - 7 &= 35 - (5 + 2) \\ &= (35 - 5) - 2 \\ &= 30 - 2 \\ &= 28 \end{aligned}$$

This process can be illustrated on the number line:

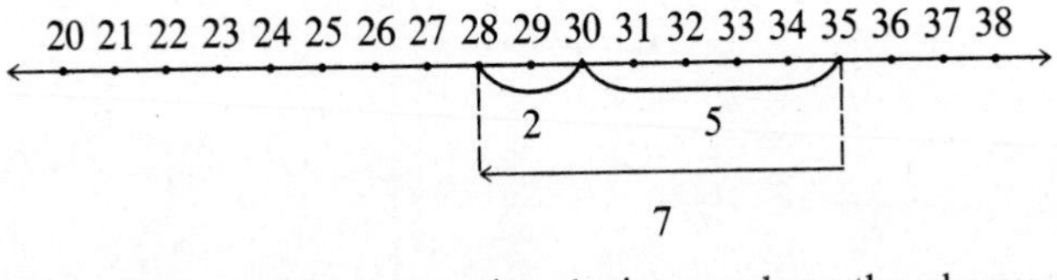

2. The answer is found by using devices such as the abacus, the counting frame, and the hundred board.
3. The teacher creates a situation that is expressed by the sentence $35¢ - 7¢ = \square$. Toy money is used, and a dime is exchanged for 10 pennies.
4. After the process of regrouping has been illustrated by the use of a device, the number question is written in vertical arrangement and solved with the help of crutches.

$$\begin{array}{r} {}^{2}\,{}^{15} \\ \not{3}\,\not{5} \\ -\;7 \\ \hline 2\;8 \end{array}$$

SUBTRACTION WITH TWO TWO-DIGIT NUMBERS WITH REGROUPING

Example

Dick had 42 birthday cards that he wanted to sell. He sold 18 of them. How many cards did Dick have left?

Number question: $42 - 18 = \square$.

Solutions:

1. Since $18 = 10 + 8$, first 10 is subtracted from 42, and then 8 is subtracted from the difference:

$$\begin{aligned} 42 - 18 &= 42 - (10 + 8) \\ &= (42 - 10) - 8 \\ &= 32 - 8 \\ &= 24 \end{aligned}$$

This process can be illustrated on the number line:

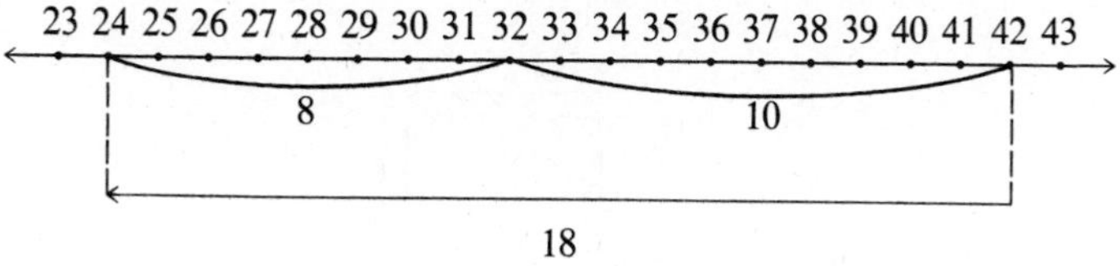

2. The process can be illustrated on an abacus:

Step 1:

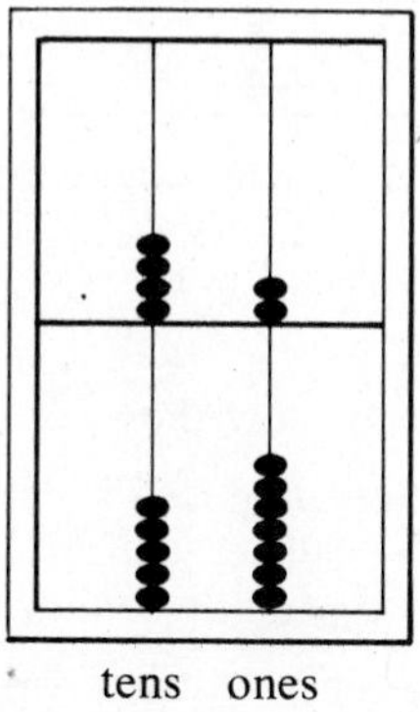

4 tens and 2 ones are isolated.

$18 = 10 + 8$, or 1 ten and 8 ones.
First 8 ones are subtracted.
There are only 2 beads on the top part of the ones rod, thus 1 ten is moved down. Since only 8 ones must be subtracted, 2 ones beads are moved up.

Step 2:

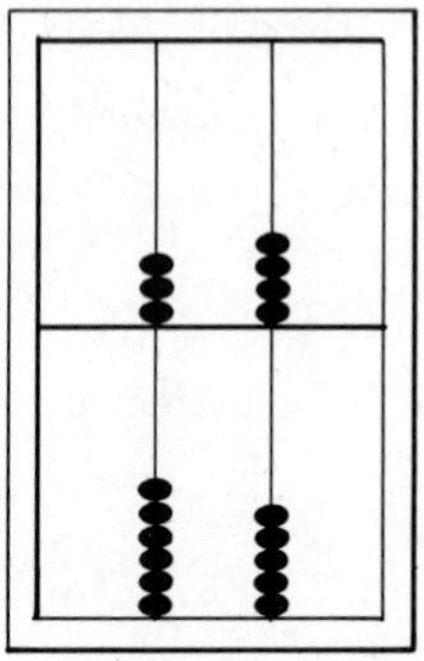

tens ones

The top part of the abacus shows 3 tens and 4 ones, or 34.

Step 3:

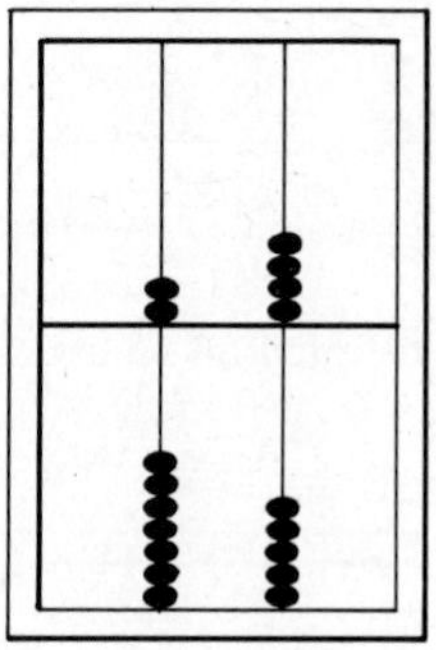

tens ones

Finally 1 ten must be subtracted (18 = 10 + 8). Thus 1 ten is moved down. The top part of the abacus now shows 2 tens and 4 ones, or 24.

3. Toy money is used. A situation is created in which 1 dime and 8 pennies must be taken away from 4 dimes and 2 pennies. Since this is impossible, 1 dime is exchanged for 10 pennies.
4. The place-value pocket chart is used. In a class discussion the teacher attempts to guide the children toward the understanding of the following algorism by using a place-value pocket chart.

$$\begin{array}{r} 42 = 40 + 2 = 30 + 12 \\ -18 = 10 + 8 = 10 + 8 \\ \hline 20 + 4 = 24 \end{array}$$

   a. Four bundles of 10 markers each and 2 single markers are placed in the proper pockets of the chart:

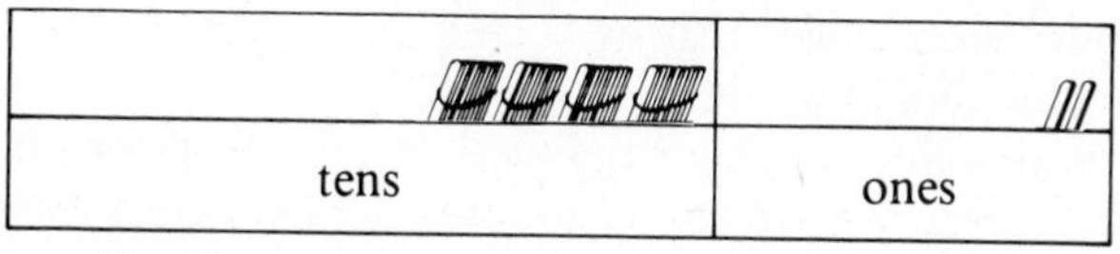

42 = 40 + 2

b. One ten and 8 ones must be taken away. First the ones are considered. Since 8 ones must be taken and there are only 2 ones in the ones pocket, one bundle is taken from the tens pocket, the string or tape is removed, and the 10 ones are placed in the ones pocket:

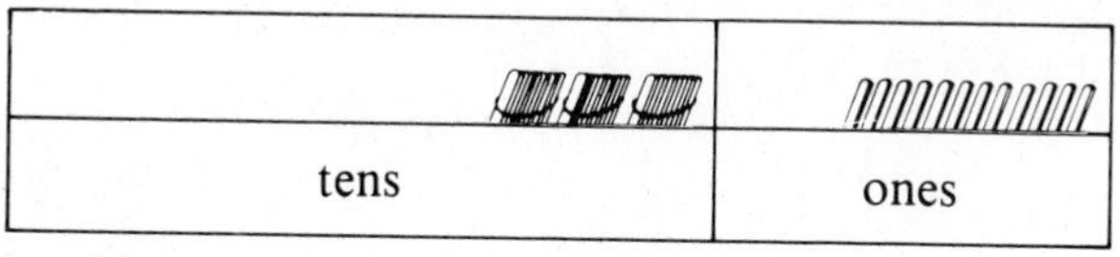

42 = 30 + 12

c. The pocket chart contains now 3 tens and 12 ones. Eight ones are removed. Then 1 ten is removed. Two tens and 4 ones, or 24 remain:

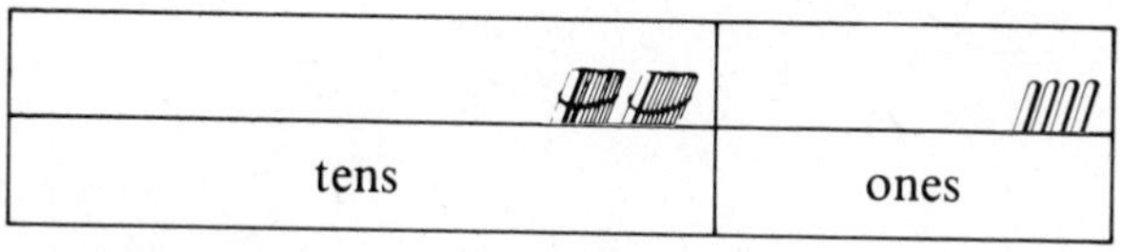

2 tens 4 ones = 24

5. The common algorism is presented. Since, in the set of whole numbers, 8 cannot be subtracted from 2, 42 is renamed 3 tens and 12 ones. 12 ones − 8 ones = 4 ones, and 3 tens − 1 ten = 2 tens.

$$\begin{array}{r} {\scriptstyle 3\ 12} \\ \not{4}\,\not{2} \\ -\,1\,8 \\ \hline 2\,4 \end{array}$$

Before this method is introduced, the pupils should understand the process of regrouping as described above.

The student should study carefully the presented sequence of the cases in subtraction. In each case, either a new step is introduced or two cases previously considered separately are combined. For example, in 45 − 10 = □, one new step is presented; in 45 − 12 = □, two previously introduced cases are combined: 45 − 10 = □ and 35 − 2 = □. The author considers this sequence and also the initial presentations of the subtraction questions in horizontal form to be important for a meaningful development of the subtraction concepts and for a proper development of ability in mental computation.

The form of solution using expanded notation and renaming may be new to some students. Therefore, additional examples are provided below.

Example 2

$53 - 27 = \square.$

Solution:

$$\begin{array}{r} 53 = 50 + 3 = 40 + 13 \\ -27 = 20 + 7 = 20 + 7 \\ \hline 20 + 6 = 26 \end{array}$$

Example 3

$87 - 59 = \square.$

Solution:

$$\begin{array}{r} 87 = 80 + 7 = 70 + 17 \\ -59 = 50 + 9 = 50 + 9 \\ \hline 20 + 8 = 28 \end{array}$$

ZEROS IN THE MINUEND

The presence of a zero in the minuend, as in 407 − 178, may cause difficulty for some pupils. It is recommended that the "40" in 407 be thought of as 40 tens. One ten is then exchanged for 10 ones, resulting in 39 tens and 17 ones. Before this process is suggested, the pupil should be thoroughly acquainted with the process of using a ten to obtain more ones and of using a hundred to obtain more tens.

$$\begin{array}{r} {\scriptstyle 3\;9\;17} \\ \cancel{4}\,\cancel{0}\,\cancel{7} \\ -1\,7\,8 \\ \hline \end{array}$$

USE OF THE CRUTCH IN SUBTRACTION

In the example shown below, a crutch is used to help the child understand the process of regrouping. The introduction of this crutch should be preceded by meaningful presentations of the regrouping process.

$$\begin{array}{r} {\scriptstyle 7\;11} \\ \cancel{8}\,\cancel{1} \\ -1\,6 \\ \hline \end{array}$$

Some teachers are hesitant to introduce such a crutch for fear that the pupil may never abandon the device. Yet there is some evidence that the dangers of teaching the crutch in subtraction have been greatly overrated. Brownell, Moser, and others[3] found that it facilitated learning in the initial stages. They reported that most children abandoned the crutch when a shorter form of solution was taught. Other children had to be encouraged by the teacher to discontinue its use.

It is recommended that the teacher introduce the crutch in subtraction, since it helps the pupil move from subtraction without regrouping to subtraction with regrouping. Its use should be discouraged as soon as the pupil is ready for a more mature process.

SUBTRACTION INVOLVING NEGATIVE INTEGERS

The set of whole numbers is not closed with respect to subtraction. For example, in the set of whole numbers there is no member that satisfies the equation $2 - 3 = \square$. To solve such problems we need the set of integers, which is expressed as $\{\cdots, {}^{-}3, {}^{-}2, {}^{-}1, 0, {}^{+}1, {}^{+}2, {}^{+}3, \cdots\}$. The set of integers is closed with respect to subtraction. This means that for any integers a and b, there is an integer c such that $a - b = c$.

Simple cases of subtraction involving negative integers do not seem to be too difficult for the child of average ability. More difficult cases should probably be presented as enrichment exercises.

Example 1

$5 - {}^{-}3 = \square$.

Solution: When working the exercise $8 - 5 = \square$, the number must be found that, when added to 5, gives 8 as the sum. $8 - 5 = 3$, since $5 + 3 = 8$. Similarly, when determining the answer to $5 - {}^{-}3$, the number must be found that, when added to ${}^{-}3$, gives 5 as the sum. The answer can be determined by using the number line.

Think: What number do I add to ${}^{-}3$ to get 5? First go from ${}^{-}3$ to 0, and then from 0 to 5:

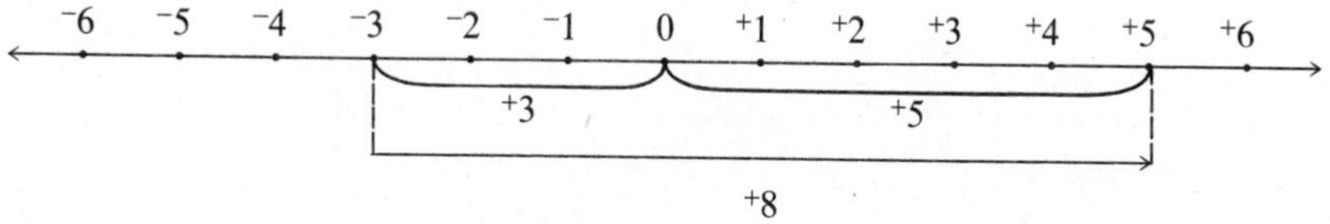

$5 - {}^{-}3 = 8$

Example 2

${}^{-}7 - {}^{-}3 = \square$.

3. A résumé of this study is presented near the end of this chapter.

Solution: What number do I add to $^{-}3$ to get $^{-}7$? Go from $^{-}3$ to $^{-}7$.

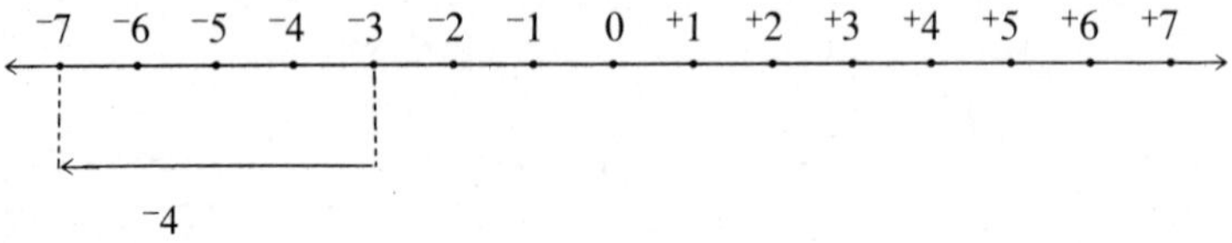

$$^{-}7 - {}^{-}3 = {}^{-}4$$

Example 3

$5 - {}^{+}7 = \square$.

Solution: What number do I add to 7 to get 5? Go from 7 to 5.

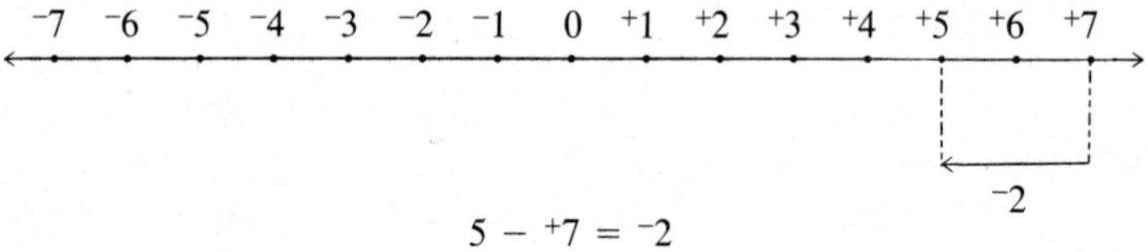

$$5 - {}^{+}7 = {}^{-}2$$

Example 4

$^{-}3 - {}^{-}5 = \square$.

Solution: What number do I add to $^{-}5$ to get $^{-}3$? Go from $^{-}5$ to $^{-}3$.

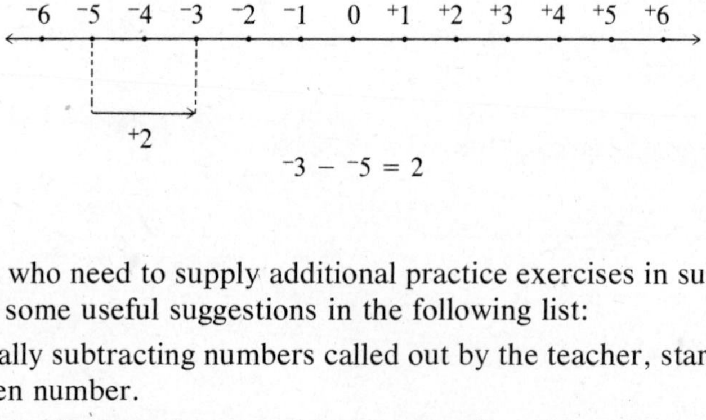

$$^{-}3 - {}^{-}5 = 2$$

MISCELLANEOUS PRACTICE EXERCISES

Teachers who need to supply additional practice exercises in subtraction may find some useful suggestions in the following list:

1. Mentally subtracting numbers called out by the teacher, starting with a given number.
2. Counting backward by equal groups, starting with a given number.
3. Performing various exercises in subtraction by mental compuation.
4. Subtracting dollars and cents, both by written and mental computation.
5. Practicing making change in money situations.

6. Using a different method of subtraction—for example, the equal-additions method.
7. Finding the complement of a number.

CHECKING SUBTRACTION

One of the objectives in mathematics instruction is the development of the pupil's skill in checking the correctness of obtained computational results. Thus the teacher should introduce methods of checking subtraction that fit the ability level of the pupils. Some ways of checking subtraction are presented below.

1. The most frequently used check for subtraction is based on the fact that the operation of subtraction is the inverse of addition. Since the difference plus the subtrahend equals the minuend, it can be determined whether a sentence such as $51 - 13 = 38$ is true or false by adding the difference and the subtrahend: $38 + 13 = 51$. In vertical subtraction the procedure shown below can be followed, so that the numeral that expresses the difference need not be rewritten.

$$\begin{array}{r} 547 \\ -159 \\ \hline 388 \\ +159 \\ \hline 547 \end{array}$$

   A variation of this method is based on the fact that the minuend minus the difference equals the subtrahend. Thus $51 - 13 = 38$ can be checked by subtracting 38 from 51, which must yield 13 as a result.

2. The check of nines in subtraction is based on the same principles as the check of nines in addition, and the limitations of the two checks are also the same.

Example

	Sum of the digits:	Excess of nines:
4,578	24	6
−1,784	20	−2
2,794	22	4

Since the difference between the excesses of nines in the minuend and the subtrahend is equal to the excess of nines in the difference, it may be concluded that the answer is probably correct.

It may happen that the excess of nines in the minuend is smaller than that in the subtrahend. In that case the excess of nines in the minuend is increased by 9.

3. The pupils should become skillful in checking an answer to a subtraction by approximation. The reasonableness of the obtained difference in the example below can be determined quickly by subtracting 300 from 500 by mental computation.

$$\begin{array}{r} 503 \\ -298 \\ \hline 205 \end{array}$$

MENTAL COMPUTATION In this chapter several mental-computation exercises involving subtraction were presented. To assist the teacher further in teaching this important mathematical skill, some additional examples follow.

Example 1

$150 - 80 = \square$.

Think: How much do I subtract from 150 to get 100? The answer is 50. Since $80 = 50 + 30$, first subtract 50 from 150, and then subtract 30 from the difference:

$$\begin{aligned} 150 - 80 &= 150 - (50 + 30) \\ &= (150 - 50) - 30 \\ &= 100 - 30 \\ &= 70 \end{aligned}$$

Example 2

$120 - 73 = \square$.

Think: $73 = 70 + 3$. First subtract 70 from 120, and then subtract 3 from the difference:

$$\begin{aligned} 120 - 73 &= 120 - (70 + 3) \\ &= (120 - 70) - 3 \\ &= 50 - 3 \\ &= 47 \end{aligned}$$

Example 3

$125 - 60 = \square$.

Think: Since $120 - 60 = 60$, $125 - 60 = 65$.

Example 4

$125 - 61 = \square$.

Think: $61 = 60 + 1$. First subtract 60 from 125, and then subtract 1 from the difference:

$$\begin{aligned}125 - 61 &= 125 - (60 + 1)\\ &= (125 - 60) - 1\\ &= 65 - 1\\ &= 64\end{aligned}$$

Example 5

$133 - 48 = \square$.

Think: $48 = 40 + 8$. First subtract 40 from 133, and then subtract 8 from the difference:

$$\begin{aligned}133 - 48 &= 133 - (40 + 8)\\ &= (133 - 40) - 8\\ &= 93 - 8\\ &= 85\end{aligned}$$

Example 6

$1{,}000 - 345 = \square$.

Think: $345 = 300 + 40 + 5$. Subtract these numbers consecutively:

$$\begin{aligned}1{,}000 - 345 &= [(1000 - 300) - 40] - 5\\ &= (700 - 40) - 5\\ &= 660 - 5\\ &= 655\end{aligned}$$

Example 7

$510 - 130 = \square$.

Think: $130 = 100 + 30$. First subtract 100 from 510, and then subtract 30 from the difference:

$$\begin{aligned}510 - 130 &= 510 - (100 + 30)\\ &= (510 - 100) - 30\\ &= 410 - 30\\ &= 380\end{aligned}$$

Example 8

$105 - 8 = \square$.

Think: First subtract enough from 105 to get 100: $105 - 5 = 100$. Since $8 = 5 + 3$, subtract 3 more: $100 - 3 = 97$.

$$\begin{aligned}105 - 8 &= 105 - (5 + 3)\\ &= (105 - 5) - 3\\ &= 100 - 3\\ &= 97\end{aligned}$$

Example 9

337 − 103 = □.

Think: 103 = 100 + 3. First subtract 100 from 337, and then subtract 3 from the difference:

$$\begin{aligned} 337 - 103 &= 337 - (100 + 3) \\ &= (337 - 100) - 3 \\ &= 237 - 3 \\ &= 234 \end{aligned}$$

Example 10

425 − 97 = □.

Think: 97 = 100 − 3. First subtract 100 from 425, and then add 3 to the difference:

$$\begin{aligned} 425 - 97 &= 425 - (100 - 3) \\ &= (425 - 100) + 3 \\ &= 325 + 3 \\ &= 328 \end{aligned}$$

SELECTED RESEARCH

In this study,[4] the results of teaching several methods of subtraction were compared. Approximately 1,400 third-graders from 41 classrooms in four school systems were placed in four equivalent experimental groups. Half the classes were taught to borrow—regroup—by the decomposition method, and half by the equal-additions method. Each of these two groups was divided again; one part was taught the process meaningfully (rationally), and one mechanically. This resulted in four groups: decomposition—mechanically, decomposition—rationally, equal additions—mechanically, and equal additions—rationally. The study was carried on for a period of 15 schooldays.

Of the reported results, the following are presented:

1. The meaningfully taught sections were quite consistently superior in performance to the mechanically taught sections.

---

4. W. A. Brownell, H. E. Moser et al., *Meaningful Versus Mechanical Learning: A Study of Grade III Subtraction,* Duke University Research Studies in Eduction, no. 8 (Durham, N.C.: Duke University Press, 1949).

2. The section to which the decomposition method was taught rationally produced better results than the section to which the equal-additions method was taught rationally.
3. This study substantiated the claim that the extra time needed for meaningful instruction, as compared with mechanical learning, is not lost. The record of the section to which the decomposition method was taught rationally shows that the acquired understanding facilitated later learning.
4. The crutch, which was used as a device in the teaching of the regrouping process in subtraction, facilitated learning.

SELECTED ACTIVITIES FOR PUPILS

1. Show on the number line that $12 - 7 = 5$.
2. Find the numbers. The same frame stands for the same number.

   $\square + \triangle = 9$ and $\square - \triangle = 5$
3. Complete:

   $24 - 9 = \square - 10$ $82 - 19 = 83 - \square$ $265 - 99 = \square - 100$
4. Copy and replace the frames with the correct numerals.

   $\begin{array}{r} 777 \\ -\square\triangle\triangledown \\ \hline 345 \end{array} \quad \begin{array}{r} \square\triangle\triangledown \\ -111 \\ \hline 789 \end{array} \quad \begin{array}{r} 7\square4 \\ -23\triangle \\ \hline 553 \end{array} \quad \begin{array}{r} \square2\triangledown \\ -1\triangle3 \\ \hline 216 \end{array}$
5. Write four addition and (or) subtraction sentences using the numbers 16, 14, and 30.
6. Copy and complete.

−	38	60	93	100
12	26			
31				
28				

−	100	300	410	1000
75	25			
81				
99				

7. Check the answer.

   Example

   $32 - 15 = 17$.

<u>Check:</u> $17 + 15 = 32$.

$101 - 24 = 77$ $\quad 971 - 225 = 746$ $\quad 2051 - 894 = 1157$

8. Write the integers from least to greater.

$$0,\ {}^{+}5,\ {}^{-}6,\ {}^{+}2,\ {}^{+}1,\ {}^{-}8,\ {}^{-}4$$

9. Draw a number line with the numerals from $^{-}10$ to 10. Mark on the line $^{-}4$, $^{+}3$, $^{-}9$, $^{+}10$, and $^{-}6$.

10. Start at 100. Subtract 1, then 2, then 3, then 4, and so on through 13. What is your final answer? If you added to your final answer the sum of the numbers you have subtracted, what would be the sum?

11. Find the answer to subtraction problems using the complementary method.

    The *complement* of a number is the difference between that number and the next higher power of ten. The complement of 7 is 3, since $10 - 7 = 3$; 25 is the complement of 75, since $100 - 75 = 25$; and 350 is the complement of 650.

    To find the difference between 7 and 4, first add the complement of 4 to 7 and then subtract the next power of ten after 7:

$$7 - 4 = (7 + 6) - 10 = 3 \qquad \text{or} \qquad \begin{array}{r} 7 \\ \underline{-4} \end{array} \rightarrow \begin{array}{r} 7 \\ \underline{+6} \\ \not{1}3 \end{array}$$

Examples

$$\begin{array}{r} 74 \\ \underline{-17} \end{array} \rightarrow \begin{array}{r} 74 \\ \underline{+83} \\ \not{1}57 \end{array} \qquad \begin{array}{r} 654 \\ \underline{-281} \end{array} \rightarrow \begin{array}{r} 654 \\ \underline{+719} \\ \not{1}373 \end{array}$$

12. Give examples of situations in which negative numbers are used.

13. Toss a dime, a nickel, and a penny. Starting at zero, when the dime shows heads, add $^{+}10$; when the dime shows tails, add $^{-}10$; when the nickel shows heads, add $^{+}5$; when the nickel shows tails, add $^{-}5$; etc. Find the sum after 10 tosses.

EXERCISES

1. Describe how you would teach the case in which a two-digit number is subtracted from a two-digit number with regrouping.
2. Explain and illustrate why subtraction is called the inverse operation of addition.
3. Describe some teaching techniques that can be used to anchor skills in subtraction.
4. Solve the subtraction question $65 - 18 = \square$ by both the additive and the subtractive method.
5. Solve the subtraction question $131 - 74 = \square$ by both the decomposition and the equal-additions method.
6. State and illustrate the rule that is applied when equal amounts are added to the minuend and the subtrahend in the equal-additions method of subtraction.
7. Give examples of the three types of subtraction situations, write the corresponding number questions, and illustrate each situation in a diagram.
8. Illustrate the number sentence $22 - 5 = 17$ on the number line.
9. Find the answer to the exercise $75 - 19 = \square$ by using an abacus.
10. Describe the difficulty that a zero in a minuend may cause a pupil.
11. Find the answer to the exercise $60 - 12 = \square$ by using a device.
12. Prepare an illustrative lesson on the teaching of subtraction involving negative integers.
13. Report on a piece of research pertaining to the subtraction of whole numbers.
14. If, in applying the check of nines in subtraction, the difference between the excesses of nines in the minuend and the subtrahend is equal to the excess of nines in the difference, it is concluded that the answer is probably correct. Explain why the word "probably" is included.
15. The sum of two numbers is 15 and their difference is 9. Why does $15 + 9$ equal twice the larger number? Why does $15 - 9$ equal twice the smaller number?
16. Diagnose the persistent mistake in each of the following sets of subtractions.

a.

200	154	901	222	900
17	27	83	78	56
193	137	828	154	854

b.

408	502	909	608	207
74	231	666	13	94
404	301	303	605	203

c.

648	531	818	996	777
171	128	545	693	191
537	417	333	363	626

SOURCES FOR FURTHER READING

Ashlock, R. B., *Error Patterns in Computation.* Columbus: Charles E. Merrill Publishing Company, 1972.

Bachrach, B., "Using Money to Clarify the Decomposition Subtraction Algorithm," *The Arithmetic Teacher,* April, 1976, pp. 244–246.

Bennett, A. B., Jr., and G. L. Musser, "A Concrete Approach to Integer Addition and Subtraction," *The Arithmetic Teacher,* May, 1976, pp. 332–336.

Burns, M., "Ideas," *The Arithmetic Teacher,* January, 1975, pp. 34–46.

D'Augustine, C. H., *Multiple Methods of Teaching Mathematics in the Elementary School,* 2nd ed. New York: Harper & Row, Publishers, 1973, Chaps. VII, XVI.

Heddens, J. W., *Today's Mathematics,* 3d ed. Chicago: Science Research Associates, Inc., 1974, Units VII, XVI.

Hutchings, B., "Using Research in Teaching," (R. E. Reys, ed.) "Low-stress Subtraction," *The Arithmetic Teacher,* March, 1975, pp. 226–232.

Kennedy, L. M., *Guiding Children to Mathematical Discovery,* 2nd ed. Belmont, California: Wadsworth Publishing Company, Inc., 1975, Chaps. VI, VII.

Marks, J. L., C. R. Purdy, L. B. Kinney, and A. A. Hiatt, *Teaching Elementary School Mathematics for Understanding,* 4th ed. New York: McGraw-Hill Book Company, 1975, Chap. IV.

National Council of Teachers of Mathematics, *Topics in Mathematics, Twenty-ninth Yearbook.* Washington, D.C.: The Council, 1964, Bklt. 2.

Schminke, C. W., N. Maertens, and W. R. Arnold, *Teaching the Child Mathematics.* Hinsdale, Illinois: The Dryden Press, Inc., 1973, Chaps. IV, VII.

Silvey, I. M., "Fourth Graders Develop Their Own Subtraction Algorithm," *The Arithmetic Teacher,* March, 1970, pp. 233–236.

Spitzer, H. F., *Teaching Elementary School Mathematics.* Boston: Houghton Mifflin Company, 1967, Chap. V.

Werner, M., "The Case for a More Universal Number-Line Model of Subtraction," *The Arithmetic Teacher,* January, 1973, pp. 61–64.

West, T. A., "Diagnosing Pupil Errors: Looking for Patterns," *The Arithmetic Teacher,* November, 1971, pp. 467–469.

Multiplication 13

When children have acquired an understanding of addition and subtraction of equal numbers and some skill in performing these operations, they can be introduced to the operations of multiplication and division. This chapter is concerned with the instruction to be given in the multiplication of whole numbers. It deals with the meaning of multiplication, presents a variety of methods and procedures that can be used to introduce multiplication, and suggests activities that can be used to develop and refine needed concepts.

Beginning instruction in multiplication is made meaningful when it is related to addition, as this chapter illustrates. Then when children are ready to learn to work more advanced problems, they can be introduced to various algorisms which will assist them in the formation of proper concepts.

SKILLS TEST

1. Multiply and check each answer by dividing the product by one of the factors.

33 × 75 =	66 × 93 =	22 × 64 =	39 × 49 =
20 × 64 =	47 × 51 =	80 × 93 =	65 × 75 =

2. Multiply and check each answer by multiplying the factors in reverse order.

13 × 175 =	96 × 671 =	87 × 103 =	23 × 177 =
32 × 105 =	25 × 525 =	80 × 705 =	54 × 652 =

3. Multiply and check.

12 × 25 =	50 × 44 =	125 × 64 =	76 × 50 =
74 × 50 =	25 × 88 =	250 × 56 =	52 × 25 =

4. Multiply and check.

157 × 346 =	779 × 304 =	1,654 × 9,480 =	6,510 × 4,444 =
902 × 257 =	205 × 106 =	7,002 × 9,540 =	2,509 × 1,009 =

MEANING AND TERMS

Multiplication is an operation on two numbers resulting in a single number, called the *product*. Since only two numbers are involved at a time, the operation is binary in nature. In the number sentence 5 × 7 = 35, 7 is the *multiplicand,* 5 is the *multiplier,* and 35 is the *product*. The sentence is usually read "5 times 7 equals 35." Both the multiplicand and the multiplier are called *factors* of the product.

The operation of multiplication may be used as a short way of adding equal addends. For example, the answer to 5 × 3 = □ can be found by adding 3 five times: 3 + 3 + 3 + 3 + 3 = 15. The addition of these equal groups can be illustrated on the number line:

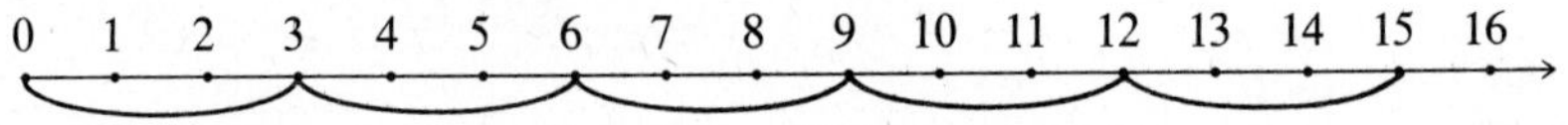

Multiplication may be interpreted as finding the Cartesian product of two sets. If set *A* = {John, Bill, Tom} and set *B* = {Dick, Al}, the elements of the sets can be paired as follows: {(John, Dick), (John, Al), (Bill, Dick), (Bill, Al), (Tom, Dick), (Tom, Al)}. The set made up of all the ordered pairs that can be formed by pairing each element of *A* with each element of *B* is called the *Cartesian product* of *A* and *B*. The pairings can be placed in an array:

	Dick	Al
John	(John, Dick)	(John, Al)
Bill	(Bill, Dick)	(Bill, Al)
Tom	(Tom, Dick)	(Tom, Al)

The product of the cardinal numbers of *A* and *B* can be determined by counting the pairings in the array. There are 3 rows of 2 each, or a total of 6 pairings. 3 × 2 = 6.

Example

Joan has 3 dolls and 5 dresses for the dolls. How many pairings of dolls and dresses can she make?

Solution: The following array expresses the possible number of pairings:

```
        5
   ___________
  | * * * * *
3 | * * * * *
  | * * * * *
```

There are 3 rows of 5 each, or a total of 15. $3 \times 5 = 15$.

PROPERTIES

Basic properties that apply to the multiplication of whole numbers are:

1. *Commutative property of multiplication.* In multiplying two whole numbers, the order of the factors can be changed without affecting the product. Thus, if a and b are whole numbers, then $a \times b = b \times a$.

Example

$3 \times 5 = 5 \times 3$.

2. *Associative property of multiplication.* In multiplying more than two whole numbers, the way in which the factors are grouped does not affect the product. Thus, if a, b, and c are whole numbers, then $(a \times b) \times c = a \times (b \times c)$.

Example

$(3 \times 4) \times 5 = 3 \times (4 \times 5)$.

3. *Distributive property of multiplication with respect to addition.* When the sum of two whole numbers is to be multiplied by a given number, it is proper to multiply each addend by the given number and to add the products. Thus, if a, b, and c are whole numbers then $a \times (b + c) = (a \times b) + (a \times c)$.

Example

$3 \times (4 + 5) = (3 \times 4) + (3 \times 5) = 12 + 15 = 17$.

4. *Closure property of multiplication.* The result of the multiplication of any two whole numbers is a whole number. We say that the set of whole numbers is closed with respect to multiplication. Thus, if a and b are whole numbers, then $a \times b$ is a whole number.

Example

$7 \times 3 = 21$

FOUNDATION ACTIVITIES FOR MULTIPLICATION

Before the multiplication facts are introduced, the pupils engage in foundation activities designed to prepare them for formal instruction in multiplication. Average and above-average children could begin direct instruction in multiplication sooner than they do currently in the traditional mathematics program. When pupils know that 2 threes equal 6, they can also be taught to interpret the equation $2 \times 3 = 6$.

Foundation experiences for multiplication of whole numbers may include the following:

1. Counting objects by twos, threes, etc.
2. Joining groups of objects.
3. Adding groups of beads on the counting frame.
4. Multiple rote counting.
5. Manipulating blocks of related sizes, such as Cuisenaire rods, Stern blocks, and the blocks of the fraction board.
6. Interpreting arrays, such as 3 groups of 4 elements each.
7. Marking equal intervals on the number line.
8. Finding doubles of numbers.
9. Adding equal addends.
10. Studying examples of arrays, such as egg cartons and rows and sheets of trading stamps.

THE KEY MULTIPLICATION FACTS

The key multiplication facts (also called the basic multiplication facts) comprise all the two-factor multiplication facts that can be formed by using the figures 0 through 9. There are a total of 100 key multiplication facts.

It is suggested that the case in which a number is multiplied by 10 be introduced together with the key facts or immediately after their presentation.

INTRODUCING THE KEY FACTS

A key fact should be introduced in a meaningful situation. This makes it possible for the children to consider the problem in a concrete setting in which they can use previously acquired knowledge to arrive at the answer. If pupils have successfully pursued a meaningful mathematics program in addition, they will be acquainted with exercises such as $3 + 3 = \square$, $2 + 2 + 2 = \square$, $4 + 4 + 4 + 4 = \square$, etc. The interpretations and presentations of the teacher should lead the children toward the standard form of expressing a multiplication question.

Example 1

How many pennies equal 3 nickels?

Solutions: Several solutions may be presented or suggested by the pupils:

1. The use of toy money: exchanging 3 nickels for pennies and determining the number of pennies.
2. The use of counters or cutouts on the flannel board.
3. Horizontal addition.
4. Vertical addition.
5. The use of the number line.
6. The use of diagrams or arrays.

The teacher guides the class discussion, during which the pupils evaluate and refine suggested procedures. The teacher then commends solutions that lead to the correct answer, introduces the standard forms of expressing a multiplication fact as $3 \times 5 = 15$ and

$$\begin{array}{r} 5 \\ \times 3 \\ \hline 15 \end{array}$$

and suggests that these sentences be read as "Three times five equals fifteen." The sentence $3 \times 5 = 15$ is illustrated in an array and on the number line as follows:

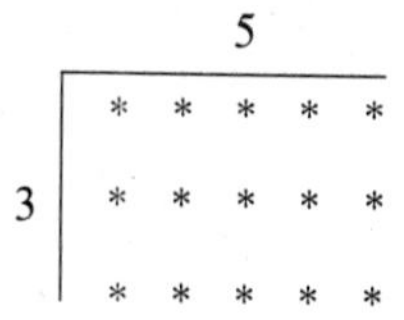

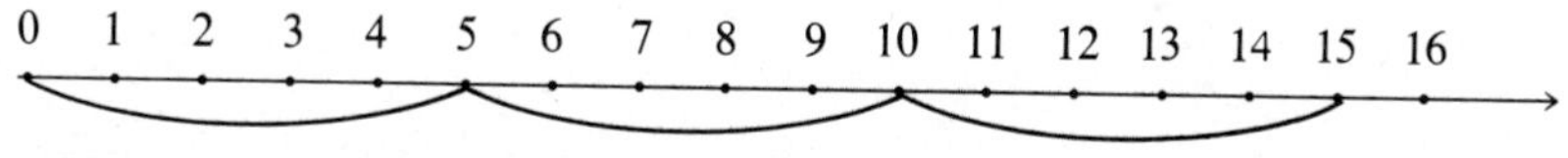

Example 2

Three bikes have how many wheels?

Solution: While solving the problem with the class, the teacher may present the following on the chalkboard:

There are 3 sets of 2 wheels.

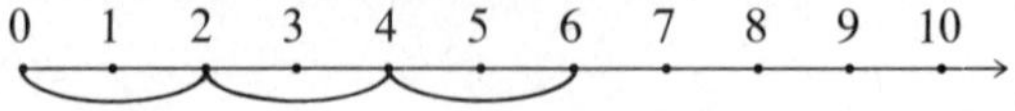

$$2 + 2 + 2 = 6$$

Two has been added 3 times. We can write $3 \times 2 = 6$ or

$$\begin{array}{r} 2 \\ \times 3 \\ \hline 6 \end{array}$$

We read: "Three times two equals six." $3 \times 2 = 6$ is a *multiplication sentence*. We multiply 2 by 3 to get 6. Six is the *product* of 2 and 3.

The pupils are also introduced to the commutative property of multiplication. The lesson could be developed in this way:

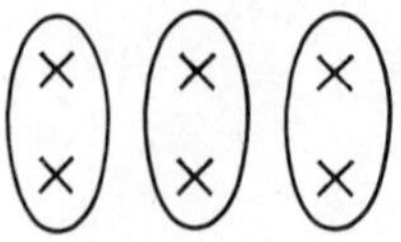

3 sets of 2
$2 + 2 + 2 = 6$
$3 \times 2 = 6$

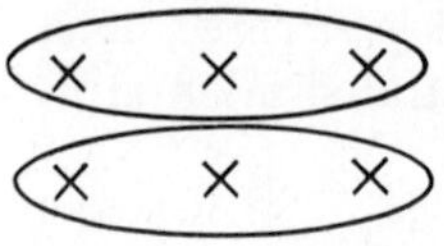

2 sets of 3
$3 + 3 = 6$
$2 \times 3 + 6$
$3 \times 2 = 6$ and $2 \times 3 = 6$

3×2 and 2×3 name the same number:

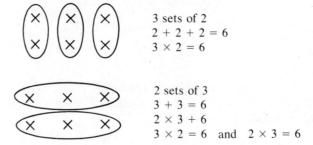

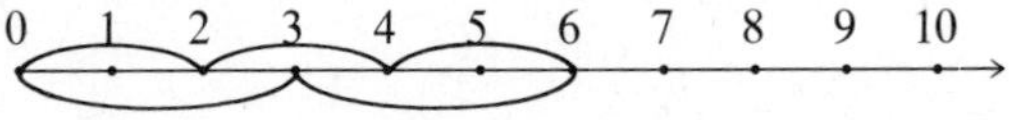

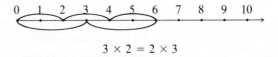

$$3 \times 2 = 2 \times 3$$

DEVELOPING AND ANCHORING SKILLS

After a meaningful introduction of the facts, the children are led to see the usefulness of memorizing the key facts. They must realize that it takes too much time to find the answer by serial addition or by using the number line, a diagram, or an array.

Various techniques are available for developing and anchoring skill in the key multiplication facts, including the following:

1. Exercises in the pupils' textbook and workbook and those provided by the teacher, such as:

a. Finding a missing factor.

Examples

3 × □ = 12; △ × 4 = 12.

b. Expressing one of the factors as the product of two factors.

Example

6 × 3 = 3 × □ × 3.

c. Expressing a number as the product of two factors.

Examples

10 = △ × ○; 9 = □ × □.

d. Expressing a number as the product of different pairs of factors.

Example

12 = □ × 2 = 3 × ○ = 12 × △.

e. Applying the commutative property.

Example

4 × 5 = 5 × □.

2. Different forms of presentation:

a.

12 =		
6	×	□
□	×	3
1	×	□

b.

Just as much:	
4 × 4	□ × ○
6 × 2	□ × ○
2 × 10	□ × ○

c.

The total must be 16:
3 × □ + 1
5 × □ + 1
7 × □ + 2

d.

Find the missing numbers:
4 × 4 = 3 × 4 + □
6 × 2 = 4 × 2 + □
7 × 3 = 5 × 3 + □

e.

Write the products. The first one has been done.									
	7	9	2	1	5	8	3	6	4
3 ×	21								

3. The construction of a multiplication table. The numbers named in the top row are to be multiplied by those named in the left column. Some examples have been given:

×	0	1	2	3	4	5	6	7	8	9	10
0											
1											
2				6							
3						15					
4									32		
5											
6											
7											
8											
9											
10											

4. Reading and writing multiplication facts from illustrations on the number line.

Example

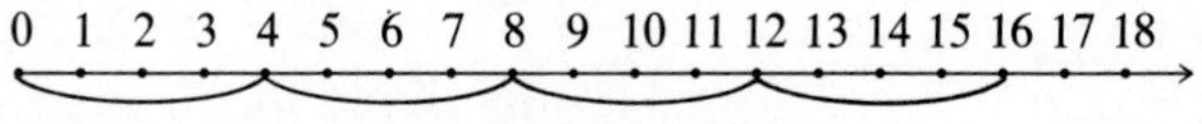

4 × 4 = 16

5. Exercises with flashcards on which the questions are presented in horizontal form.

6. Exercises with flashcards on which the questions are presented in vertical form.
7. Writing and memorizing facts.
8. Writing, checking, and memorizing the tables of multiplication.
9. Exercises with the multiplication wheel. The addition wheel described in Chapter 11 can be modified for use with the multiplication facts.
10. Completing number sentences by supplying the symbol =, >, or <.

    Examples

    $5 \times 3 \square 2 \times 7$; $6 \times 4 \square 5 \times 5$; $9 \times 2 \square 3 \times 6$.

11. Finding or suggesting patterns in the products of the multiplication tables and exploring the reasons for these patterns.

    Examples

    Table of 2: The ones digit is always an even number.
    Table of 3: The sum of the digits is always evenly divisible by 3.
    Table of 4: There is a regular sequence in the ones digits:

    4–8–2–6–0–4–8, etc.

    Table of 5: The ones digit is either a 5 or a 0.
    Table of 6: There is a regular sequence in the ones digits:

    6–2–8–4–0–6–2–8–, etc.

    Table of 7: Each digit occurs once in the ones place:

    7–4–1–8–5–2–9–6–3–0.

    Table of 8: The ones digits are even numbers that occur in descending order:

    8–6–4–2–0–8–6–4–2–0, etc.

    Table of 9: (1) the sum of the digits is evenly divisible by 9, and (2) the ones digits occur in descending order, and the tens digits in ascending order.

12. Verifying statements such as:
    The product of two even numbers is always an even number.
    The product of two odd numbers is always an odd number.
    The product of an even number and an odd number is always an even number.

13. Brief daily reviews of the basic multiplication facts until all the facts have been mastered.

THE ONES FACTS AND THE ZERO FACTS

The ones facts and the zero facts are best introduced after several other multiplication facts have been presented and understood. The teacher may present meaningful situations that introduce questions such as 5 × 1 = □ and 5 × 0 = □. Such introductions should be followed by practice exercises.

Example 1

Ron and Tom sold baseball cards for 1¢ each. If they sold 4 cards, how many pennies did they receive?

Number question: 4 × 1 = □.

Example 2

In a guessing game a score of 1 was given for each correct guess. Bill got 5 turns and missed each guess. What was Bill's score?

Number question: 5 × 0 = □.

The answer to questions such as 1 × 5 = □ and 0 × 5 = □ may be determined by applying the commutative property.

The pupils are finally guided to form these generalizations:

Any number times 1 equals that number.
1 times any number equals that number.
Any number times 0 equals 0.
0 times any number equals 0.

FINDING THE PRODUCT OF THREE ONE-DIGIT NUMBERS

Example

In a set of blocks there are 2 rows of 4 blocks on the bottom layer. If there are 3 layers, how many blocks are there in the set?

Number question: 3 × 2 × 4 = □.

Solution: The pupils are guided to discover that any two factors may be multiplied first. This associative property is demonstrated with a set of blocks. It can also be illustrated on the number line.

MULTIPLYING WITH A POWER OF 10

Example

If there are 10 rows of 12 chairs each in a room, how many chairs are there in all?

Number question: $10 \times 12 = \square$.

Solution: The pupils find the answer to this number question by adding 12 ten times. After working several similar exercises, they are guided to discover the rule for multiplying a number by 10 inductively. After the rule has been stated, it is applied deductively.

The answer to a number question such as $12 \times 10 = \square$ can be found by applying the commutative property: $10 \times 12 = 12 \times 10$. The answer is checked by adding 10 twelve times.

When the pupils know how to multiply a number by 10, the development of rules for multiplying a number by higher powers of 10 will not cause much difficulty.

MULTIPLYING A MULTIPLE OF 10 AND A ONE-DIGIT NUMBER

Example

If there are 30 trading stamps on one page of a stamp book, how many stamps are there on 5 pages?

Number question: $5 \times 30 = \square$.

Solution: Since 5×3 ones = 15 ones, 5×3 tens = 15 tens, or $5 \times 30 = 150$. After several exercises of the same kind have been worked and discussed, the vertical form is presented:

$$\begin{array}{r} 30 \\ \times 5 \\ \hline 150 \end{array}$$

The answer can also be found by using the following procedure:

$$\begin{aligned} 5 \times 30 &= 5 \times (3 \times 10) && \text{renaming} \\ &= (5 \times 3) \times 10 && \text{associative property} \\ &= 15 \times 10 && \text{multiplication} \\ &= 150 && \text{multiplication} \end{aligned}$$

The number question $30 \times 5 = \square$ can be solved by using the commutative property: $30 \times 5 = 5 \times 30 = 150$. Or the pupils may reason:

$$\begin{aligned} 30 \times 5 &= (10 \times 3) \times 5 \\ &= 10 \times (3 \times 5) \\ &= 10 \times 15 \\ &= 150 \end{aligned}$$

MULTIPLYING MULTIPLES OF 10

Example

Each of the 20 pupils in Grade 4 sold 30 tickets for the school play. How many tickets did they sell in all?

Number question: $20 \times 30 = \square$.

Solution: $20 \times 30 = (10 \times 2) \times 30$ renaming
$= 10 \times (2 \times 30)$ associative property
$= 10 \times 60$ multiplication
$= 600$ multiplication

After working several similar exercises, the pupils are led to discover that two zeros are annexed to the product of 2 and 3, and to reason as follows: Since $2 \times 3 = 6$, $20 \times 30 = 600$. Thus the answer is found by mental computation.

MULTIPLYING A TWO-DIGIT NUMBER BY A ONE-DIGIT NUMBER WITHOUT REGROUPING

The pupil prepares for vertical multiplication by pursuing several meaningful steps in horizontal multiplication. The pupil uses previously acquired knowledge and is guided from the horizontal form to the vertical form. The multiplicand in the vertical arrangement is first presented in expanded notation. In the following example these steps are shown.

Example

How many months are there in 3 years?

Number question: $3 \times 12 = \square$.

Solutions:

1. $3 \times 12 = 3 \times (10 + 2)$ renaming
$= (3 \times 10) + (3 \times 2)$ distributive property
$= 30 + 6$ multiplication
$= 36$ addition

2. $\begin{array}{r} 12 \\ \underline{\times 3} \end{array} = \begin{array}{r} 10 + 2 \\ \underline{\times 3} \\ 30 + 6 \end{array} = 36$

3. $\begin{array}{r} 12 \\ \underline{\times 3} \\ 36 \end{array}$ 3×2 ones $= 6$ ones; write 6 in the ones place.
3×1 ten $= 3$ tens; write 3 in the tens place.

MULTIPLYING A TWO-DIGIT NUMBER BY A ONE-DIGIT NUMBER WITH REGROUPING

Example

How many eggs are there in 7 dozen?

Number question: $7 \times 12 = \square$.

Solutions:

1. $7 \times 12 = 7 \times (10 + 2)$ renaming
$= (7 \times 10) + (7 \times 2)$ distributive property
$= 70 + 14$ multiplication
$= 84$ addition

2. $\begin{array}{r} 12 \\ \times 7 \\ \hline \end{array} = \begin{array}{r} 10 + 2 \\ \times 7 \\ \hline 70 + 14 \end{array} = 84$

3. A useful device for illustrating the process of regrouping is the counting frame, which has 10 rows of 10 beads each. Seven groups of 10 beads each and 7 groups of 2 beads each are isolated on the frame, and the 7 groups of 2 beads each are regrouped to form one group of 10 beads and one group of 4 beads.

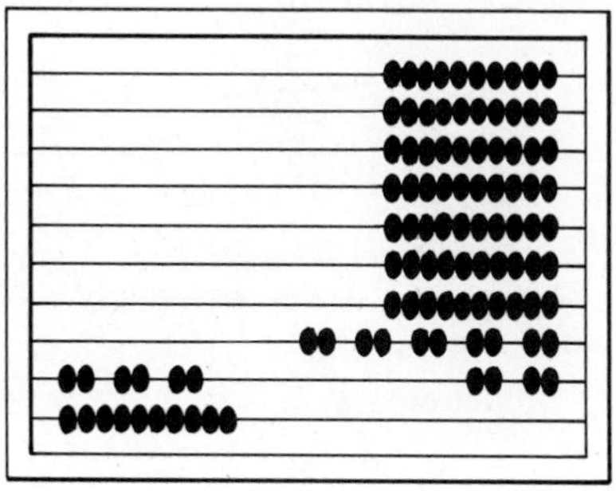

After regrouping, it is evident that 7 × 12 results in 8 tens and 4 ones, or 84.

4. The standard algorism is used. The child is guided to think as follows:

12	7 × 2 ones = 14 ones; write 4 in the ones place and remember 1 ten.
×7	7 × 1 ten = 7 tens; 7 tens + 1 ten = 8 tens; write 8 in the tens place.
84	

MULTIPLYING A MULTI-DIGIT NUMBER BY A ONE-DIGIT NUMBER

Example 1

The teacher has 2 boxes of pencils. If there are 144 pencils in each box, how many pencils are there in all?

Number question: 2 × 144 = □.

Solutions:

1.

2 × 144	= 2 × (100 + 40 + 4)	renaming
	= (2 × 100) + (2 × 40) + (2 × 4)	distributive property
	= 200 + 80 + 8	multiplication
	= 288	addition

2.

1 hundred, 4 tens, 4 ones	144	
×2	×2	
2 hundreds, 8 tens, 8 ones	200	(2 × 100)
	80	(2 × 40)
	8	(2 × 4)
	288	

3. If first the ones are multiplied, then the tens, and finally the hundreds, the multiplication is written as follows:

$$\begin{array}{r} 144 \\ \times 2 \\ \hline 8 \\ 80 \\ 200 \\ \hline 288 \end{array} \qquad \text{or} \qquad \begin{array}{rl} 144 & \\ \times 2 & \\ \hline 8 & \text{(ones)} \\ 8 & \text{(tens)} \\ 2 & \text{(hundreds)} \\ \hline 288 & \end{array}$$

4. From the preceding presentation the standard algorism is derived.

$$\begin{array}{r} 144 \\ \times 2 \\ \hline 288 \end{array}$$

The child is guided to think as follows:
2×4 ones $=$ 8 ones; write 8 in the ones place.
2×4 tens $=$ 8 tens; write 8 in the tens place.
2×1 hundred $=$ 2 hundreds; write 2 in the hundreds place.

Example 2

Tom has 8 scrapbooks filled with pictures. If there are 192 pictures in each book, how many pictures does Tom have in all?

Number question: $8 \times 192 = \square$.

Solutions:

1.
$$\begin{aligned} 8 \times 192 &= 8 \times (100 + 90 + 2) && \text{renaming} \\ &= (8 \times 100) + (8 \times 90) + (8 \times 2) && \text{distributive property} \\ &= 800 + 720 + 16 && \text{multiplication} \\ &= 1{,}536 && \text{addition} \end{aligned}$$

2.
$$\begin{array}{rr} & 192 \\ & \times 8 \\ \hline 8 \times 2 = & 16 \\ 8 \times 90 = & 720 \\ 8 \times 100 = & 800 \\ \hline & 1{,}536 \end{array}$$

3. With the help of the previous presentations and the interpretations of the teacher, pupils develop the standard algorism.

$$\begin{array}{r} 192 \\ \times 8 \\ \hline 1{,}536 \end{array}$$

8×2 ones $=$ 16 ones; write 6 in the ones place and remember 1 ten.
8×9 tens $=$ 72 tens; 72 tens $+$ 1 ten $=$ 73 tens; write 3 in the tens place and remember 7 hundreds.
8×1 hundred $=$ 8 hundreds; 8 hundreds $+$ 7 hundreds $=$ 15 hundreds; write 5 in the hundreds place and 1 in the thousands place.

MULTIPLYING TWO TWO-DIGIT NUMBERS

Example 1

How many eggs are there in 20 dozen?

Number question: $20 \times 12 = \square$.

Solutions:

1. $$\begin{aligned} 20 \times 12 &= (10 \times 2) \times 12 \\ &= 10 \times (2 \times 12) \\ &= 10 \times 24 \\ &= 240 \end{aligned}$$

2. $$\begin{array}{r} 12 \\ \times 20 \\ \hline \end{array} = \begin{array}{r} 10 + 2 \\ \times 20 \\ \hline 200 + 40 \end{array} = 240$$

3. $$\begin{array}{rr} & 12 \\ & \times 20 \\ \hline 20 \times 2 = & 40 \\ 20 \times 10 = & 200 \\ \hline & 240 \end{array}$$

4. When using the short form of multiplication, the pupil learns to reason as follows: If 12 is multiplied by 2, the product is 24. If 12 is multiplied by 20, a zero is annexed to 24, making the product 240. Thus 12 can be multiplied by 20 by first writing the zero, and then writing the product of 12 and 2 to the left of the zero.

$$\begin{array}{r} 12 \\ \times 20 \\ \hline 240 \end{array}$$

Example 2

One day a farmer sold 13 dozen eggs. How many eggs did he sell that day?

Number question: $13 \times 12 = \square$.

Solutions:

1. $$\begin{aligned} 13 \times 12 &= (10 + 3) \times 12 \\ &= (10 \times 12) + (3 \times 12) \\ &= 120 + 36 \\ &= 156 \end{aligned}$$

2. The horizontal presentation of the multiplication can be expressed vertically. The product of 3 and 12 can be written as the first partial product:

$$\begin{array}{r} 12 \\ \times 13 \\ \hline 36 \\ 120 \\ \hline 156 \end{array}$$

3. When multiplying vertically, the steps can be recorded as follows:

$$\begin{array}{rr} & 12 \\ & \times 13 \\ \hline 3 \times 2 \text{ ones} = & 6 \\ 3 \times 1 \text{ ten} = & 30 \\ 1 \text{ ten} \times 2 = & 20 \\ 1 \text{ ten} \times 1 \text{ ten} = & 100 \\ \hline & 156 \end{array}$$

4. In the final step the standard algorism is developed:

$$\begin{array}{r} 12 \\ \times 13 \\ \hline 36 \\ 12 \\ \hline 156 \end{array}$$

The teacher explains that the zero in 120 is usually omitted, since the places that the digits occupy indicate their positional value.

Example 3

A grocer bought 36 boxes of apples. If there were 48 apples in each box, how many apples did he buy?

Number question: $36 \times 48 = \square$.

Solutions:

1. First the horizontal form of solution is developed. (Many pupils may have to find the answers to partial products by vertical multiplication and add the partial products in a column.)

$$\begin{aligned} 36 \times 48 &= (30 + 6) \times 48 \\ &= (30 \times 48) + (6 \times 48) \\ &= 1{,}440 + 288 \\ &= 1{,}728 \end{aligned}$$

2. The partial products found by the first method of solution are written vertically:

$$\begin{array}{rr} & 48 \\ & \times 36 \\ \hline 6 \times 48 = & 288 \\ 30 \times 48 = & 1{,}440 \\ \hline & 1{,}728 \end{array}$$

3. The standard algorism is developed.

$$\begin{array}{r} 48 \\ \times 36 \\ \hline 288 \\ 144 \\ \hline 1{,}728 \end{array}$$

The pupil is guided to reason as follows:
$6 \times 8 = 48$; write 8 in the ones place and remember the 4 tens.
6×4 tens $= 24$ tens; 24 tens + 4 tens = 28 tens; write 8 in the tens place and 2 in the hundreds place.
3 tens $\times 8 = 24$ tens; write 4 in the tens place and remember 2 hundreds.
3 tens $\times$ 4 tens = 12 hundreds; 12 hundreds + 2 hundreds = 14 hundreds; write 4 in the hundreds place and 1 in the thousands place. Finally the partial products are added.

MULTIPLYING TWO MULTI-DIGIT NUMBERS

Example 1

Multiply 337 by 242.

Number question: $242 \times 337 = \square$.

Solution:

1. The multiplication is worked horizontally:

$$\begin{aligned} 242 \times 337 &= (200 + 40 + 2) \times 337 \\ &= (200 \times 337) + (40 \times 337) + (2 \times 337) \\ &= 67{,}400 + 13{,}480 + 674 \\ &= 81{,}554 \end{aligned}$$

2. The horizontal form of solution is written vertically:

$$\begin{array}{rr} & 337 \\ & \times 242 \\ \hline 200 \times 337 = & 67{,}400 \\ 40 \times 337 = & 13{,}480 \\ 2 \times 337 = & 674 \\ \hline & 81{,}554 \end{array} \qquad \text{or} \qquad \begin{array}{rr} & 337 \\ & \times 242 \\ \hline 2 \times 337 = & 674 \\ 40 \times 337 = & 13{,}480 \\ 200 \times 337 = & 67{,}400 \\ \hline & 81{,}554 \end{array}$$

3. The algorism in common use is developed as in the immediately preceding example.

$$\begin{array}{r} 337 \\ \times 242 \\ \hline 674 \\ 1348 \\ 674 \\ \hline 81{,}554 \end{array}$$

Example 2

Multiply 406 by 307.

Number question: $307 \times 406 = \square$.

Solutions:

1. The difficulty that presents itself in this example is the zero in the multiplier. The pupil must realize that $307 = 300 + 7$, and that 406 is multiplied by 7 and by 300:

$$\begin{aligned}307 \times 406 &= (300 + 7) \times 406\\ &= (300 \times 406) + (7 \times 406)\\ &= 121{,}800 + 2{,}842\\ &= 124{,}642\end{aligned}$$

2. The solution in (1) is written as follows:

$$\begin{array}{rr} & 406\\ & \times 307\\ \hline 300 \times 406 = & 121{,}800\\ 7 \times 406 = & 2{,}842\\ \hline & 124{,}642\end{array} \quad \text{or} \quad \begin{array}{rr} & 406\\ & \times 307\\ \hline 7 \times 406 = & 2{,}842\\ 300 \times 406 = & 121{,}800\\ \hline & 124{,}642\end{array}$$

3. The standard algorism is developed. The pupil should understand by now that the second partial product shown represents hundreds and that the two zeros in that partial product are not usually written.

$$\begin{array}{r} 406\\ \times 307\\ \hline 2\ 842\\ 121\ 8\\ \hline 124{,}642\end{array}$$

CHECKING THE PRODUCT

Various methods can be applied to check the product of a multiplication. The method selected will depend upon the mathematical maturity of the pupils.

1. *Dividing the product by one of the factors*. When the product of a multiplication is divided by one of the factors, the quotient must equal the other factor.

Example

$5 \times 13 = 65$, and $65 \div 13 = 5$, or $65 \div 5 = 13$.

2. *Multiplying the factors in reverse order.*

Example

The sentence $17 \times 38 = 646$ can be checked by finding the answer to $38 \times 17 = \square$.

3. *Applying the rule of compensation.*

Example

The mathematical sentence $24 \times 25 = 600$ can be checked by dividing one factor and multiplying the other factor by the same number:

$$24 \times 25 = 12 \times 50 = 6 \times 100 = 600.$$

4. *Writing the steps in horizontal form.*

Example

The mathematical sentence $15 \times 22 = 330$ can be checked by multiplying 22 first by 10, then by 5, and adding the products:

$$\begin{aligned} 15 \times 22 &= (10 + 5) \times 22 \\ &= (10 \times 22) + (5 \times 22) \\ &= 220 + 110 \\ &= 330 \end{aligned}$$

5. *Approximating.* When an approximate answer is sufficient, the numbers can be rounded and then multiplied by mental computation.

Example

The reasonableness of the answer in the mathematical sentence $38 \times 61 = 2{,}318$ can be checked by multiplying 60 by 40. Since $60 \times 40 = 2{,}400$, 2,318 appears to be a reasonable answer for $38 \times 61 = \square$.

6. *Applying the check of nines.* In the upper grades, pupils of at least average ability can learn to check the product of a multiplication by applying the check of nines. The excesses of nines in each of the two factors are multiplied, and the excess of nines in this product must equal the excess of nines in the product of the original multiplication.

Example

125	excess of nines in the multiplicand:	8
17	excess of nines in the multiplier:	×8
875	product of 8 and 8:	64
125	excess of nines in 64:	1
2,125	excess of nines in 2,125:	1

Since the excesses of nines in 64 and 2,125 are equal, it may be stated that the answer is probably correct.

The limitations of the check of nines have been presented in the chapter on addition.

MENTAL COMPUTATION

In the preceding paragraphs the importance of mental computation in the introduction of a new multiplication case was illustrated. For the benefit of the teacher who is not yet sufficiently familiar with techniques used in mental computation, the following summary is presented.

1. $10 \times 16 = \square$.
   A number is multiplied by 10 by annexing a zero to the numeral that stands for the number. Thus $10 \times 16 = 160$.

2. $100 \times 175 = \square$.
A number is multiplied by 100 by annexing two zeros to the numeral that stands for the number. Thus $100 \times 175 = 17{,}500$.
3. $1{,}000 \times 28 = \square$.
A number is multiplied by 1,000 by annexing three zeros to the numeral that stands for the number. Thus, $1{,}000 \times 28 = 28{,}000$.
4. $6 \times 12 = \square$.
Think:

$$\begin{aligned} 6 \times 12 &= 6 \times (10 + 2) \\ &= (6 \times 10) + (6 \times 2) \\ &= 60 + 12 \\ &= 72 \end{aligned}$$

5. $9 \times 12 = \square$.
Think:

$$\begin{aligned} 9 \times 12 &= (10 - 1) \times 12 \\ &= (10 \times 12) - (1 \times 12) \\ &= 120 - 12 \\ &= 108 \end{aligned}$$

6. $7 \times 125 = \square$.
Think:

$$\begin{aligned} 7 \times 125 &= 7 \times (100 + 20 + 5) \\ &= (7 \times 100) + (7 \times 20) + (7 \times 5) \\ &= 700 + 140 + 35 \\ &= 875 \end{aligned}$$

7. $20 \times 36 = \square$.
Think:

$$\begin{aligned} 20 \times 36 &= (2 \times 10) \times 36 \\ &= 2 \times (10 \times 36) \\ &= 2 \times 360 \\ &= 720 \end{aligned}$$

Or: Since $2 \times 36 = 72$, $20 \times 36 = 720$.

8. $15 \times 42 = \square$.
Think: $15 = 10 + 5$ and $5 = \frac{1}{2} \times 10$.

$$\begin{aligned} 15 \times 42 &= (10 + 5) \times 42 \\ &= (10 \times 42) + (5 \times 42) \\ &= 420 + (\tfrac{1}{2} \times 420) \\ &= 420 + 210 \\ &= 630 \end{aligned}$$

9. $4 \times 17 \times 25 = \square$.

   Think: Since the product of 4 and 25 is 100, these numbers are multiplied first:

$$\begin{aligned}(4 \times 17) \times 25 &= (17 \times 4) \times 25\\ &= 17 \times (4 \times 25)\\ &= 17 \times 100\\ &= 1{,}700\end{aligned}$$

10. $32 \times 50 = \square$.

    Think: The product of a multiplication remains unchanged if one of the factors is divided by a number, provided that the other factor is multiplied by the same number. Thus, $32 \times 50 = 16 \times 100 = 1{,}600$.

SELECTED RESEARCH

The investigator's purpose[1] was to determine (1) how well third-grade pupils can learn to use the distributive property of multiplication over addition expressed in horizontal form, as in $3 \times 5 = (3 \times 3) + (3 \times 2)$, (2) the approximate number of lessons needed to learn this procedure reasonably well, and (3) any differences in this respect between high and low achievers.

Nine lessons were constructed using the facts from $1 \times 1 = 1$ through $9 \times 5 = 45$. They were taught to 198 pupils in nine classes. The first five lessons dealt with the basic facts, lessons six and seven with the property, and lessons eight and nine reviewed the previous learnings. A 41-item test was administered on the tenth day. The last 14 items tested knowledge of the distributive property.

On the basis of the results, three conclusions were presented:

1. Third-grade pupils can learn to use the property in two introductory lessons and a review lesson, though they may not perform as well as they do on learning basic multiplication facts.
2. The items dealing with the distributive property were significantly more difficult than the other items.
3. For low-scoring pupils the distributive property items were decidedly more difficult than the other items; for high-scoring pupils performance on both types of items was about the same.

---

1. L. M. Schell, "Learning the Distributive Property by Third Graders," *School Science and Mathematics* (January, 1968), pp. 28–32.

SELECTED ACTIVITIES FOR PUPILS

1. Show on the number line that $3 \times 5 = 15$.
2. Complete.

   $4 \times 5 = 2 \times \square$ $\quad 6 \times 8 = 3 \times \square$ $\quad 5 \times 12 = 10 \times \square$

3. $9 \times 24 = (10 - 1) \times 24$
   $= (10 \times 24) - (1 \times 24)$
   $= 240 - 24$
   $= 216$

   Follow the same procedure in these exercises:

   $9 \times 18 = \square$ $\quad 9 \times 77 = \square$ $\quad 9 \times 89 = \square$

4. $11 \times 34 = (10 + 1) \times 34$
   $= (10 \times 34) + (1 \times 34)$
   $= 340 + 34$
   $= 374$

   Follow the same procedure in these exercises:

   $11 \times 15 = \square$ $\quad 11 \times 26 = \square$ $\quad 11 \times 42 = \square$

5. Find the numbers. The same frame stands for the same number.

   $\square + \triangle = 500$ and $\square \times \triangle = 60{,}000$

6. What two numbers have a sum of 11 and a product of 30?
7.
   $\div 2$
   $12 \times 50 = 6 \times 100 = 600$
   $\times 2$

   Follow the same procedure in these exercises:

   $18 \times 500 = \square$ $\quad 24 \times 25 = \square$ $\quad 12 \times 250 = \square$

8. Complete:

×	10	5	18
3	30		
5			
7			

×	20	2	22
4			
6			
8			

9. Study the presentation. Multiply other numbers by 11. Then find the pattern.

```
     4 2
   × 1 1
     4 2      4 + 2 = 6
   4 2
   4 6 2
```

10. Study the presentation. Multiply other two-digit numbers by 101. Then find the pattern.

```
      2 3
  × 1 0 1
      2 3
  2 3
  2 3 2 3
```

11. Explain how the distributive property for multiplication with respect to addition is used below.

```
      5 4
    × 3 2
    1 0 8
  1 6 2
  1,7 2 8
```

12. Write the missing digits. You may want to check your answers by using a minicalculator if there is one available.

59	□7	432	852
×□3	×□7	×□□□	×36□
□□□	□1□	3024	□□□□
□□8	□□4	864	□□□□
□,□□□	□,□□□	432	□□□□
		□□,□□□	314,388

13. Ray can read 5 pages in 25 minutes.
    Lois can read three times as fast.
    How many minutes does it take Lois to read 30 pages?

14. Which two numbers have a sum of 20 and a product of 64?

EXERCISES

1. Explain and illustrate different interpretations of multiplication.
2. State what is meant by the commutative and the associative properties of multiplication and give illustrations.

3. Describe several foundation activities for multiplication.
4. Describe various activities designed to anchor the key multiplication facts.
5. Write an illustrative lesson dealing with the case in which a number is multiplied by 10.
6. Explain and illustrate the distributive property of multiplication with respect to addition.
7. Describe the steps you would take when introducing the multiplication case in which a three-digit number is multiplied by a one-digit number.
8. Write and justify the steps involved in solving the number question 30 × 23 = □ by horizontal multiplication.
9. Show the steps you would take in introducing the multiplication case in which a two-digit number is multiplied by a two-digit number.
10. Describe various methods that can be used to check the product of a multiplication.
11. Explain the use of the check of nines to check an answer to a multiplication.
12. Report on the research described in this chapter.
13. Diagnose the persistent mistake in each of the following sets of multiplications:

a.	302	430	1012	2200	601
	×3	×2	×4	×3	×2
	936	862	4448	6633	1222

b.	33	25	69	88	57
	×4	×5	×2	×3	×7
	162	205	148	304	639

c.	25	63	33	27	80
	×34	×12	×21	×23	×15
	75	63	66	54	80
	100	126	33	81	400
	175	189	99	135	480

SOURCES FOR FURTHER READING

Ando, M., and H. Ikeda, "Learning Multiplication Facts—More than a Drill," *The Arithmetic Teacher,* October, 1971, pp. 366–369.

Ashlock, R. B., *Error Patterns in Computation*. Columbus: Charles E. Merrill Publishing Company, 1972.

Boykin, W. E., "The Russian-Peasant Algorithm: Rediscovery and Extension," *The Arithmetic Teacher,* January, 1973, pp. 29–32.

Brown, S. I., "A New Multiplication Algorithm: On the Complexity of Simplicity," *The Arithmetic Teacher,* November, 1975, pp. 546–554.

Bruni, J. V., and H. J. Silverman, "The Multiplication Facts: Once More, with Understanding," *The Arithmetic Teacher,* October, 1976, pp. 402–409.

Callahan, L. C., "A Romantic Excursion into the Multiplication Table," *The Arithmetic Teacher,* December, 1969, pp. 609–613.

D'Augustine, C. H., *Multiple Methods of Teaching Mathematics in the Elementary School,* 2nd ed. New York: Harper & Row, Publishers, 1973, Chap. VIII.

Davis, R. B., "Algebra in Grades Four, Five, and Six," *Grade Teacher,* April, 1962, pp. 57, 106–109.

Heddens, J. W., *Today's Mathematics,* 3d ed. Chicago: Science Research Associates, Inc., 1974, Unit VIII.

Kennedy, L. M., *Guiding Children to Mathematical Discovery,* 2nd ed. Belmont, California: Wadsworth Publishing Company, Inc., 1975, Chaps. VIII, IX.

Marks, J. L., C. R. Purdy, L. B. Kinney, and A. A. Hiatt, *Teaching Elementary School Mathematics for Understanding,* 4th ed. New York: McGraw-Hill Book Company, 1975, Chap. V.

National Council of Teachers of Mathematics, *Topics in Mathematics, Twenty-ninth Yearbook.* Washington, D.C.: The Council, 1964, Bklt. 2.

Reardin, C. R., Jr., "Understanding the Russian Peasant," *The Arithmetic Teacher,* January, 1973, pp. 33–35.

Schminke, C. W., N. Maertens, and W. R. Arnold, *Teaching the Child Mathematics.* Hinsdale, Illinois: The Dryden Press, Inc., 1973, Chap. IV.

Spitzer, H. F., *Teaching Elementary School Mathematics.* Boston: Houghton Mifflin Company, 1967, Chap. VI.

Division 14

The previous chapters considered the operations of addition, subtraction, and multiplication. The operation of division is presented in this chapter.

In beginning instruction, division can be effectively related to multiplication and to subtraction, as will be illustrated. It should be realized that the solution of a division problem that results in a multi-digit quotient requires the use of multiplication, subtraction, and—when regrouping is involved—addition. It is therefore only logical that instruction in division be undertaken subsequent to the introduction of the other operations.

SKILLS TEST

1. Divide and check by multiplying the quotient and the divisor:

   $806 \div 62 =$ $2{,}044 \div 28 =$ $5{,}069 \div 137 =$ $26{,}832 \div 258 =$
   $495 \div 11 =$ $1{,}932 \div 23 =$ $6{,}032 \div 104 =$ $84{,}436 \div 404 =$

2. Divide and check:

   $4{,}560{,}792 \div 3{,}714 =$ $11{,}111{,}100 \div 2{,}002 =$ $1{,}720{,}546 \div 263 =$

3. Determine whether the quotients are correct by using the following check: quotient × divisor + remainder = dividend.

   $197 \div 15 = 13$ r. 2 $845 \div 25 = 33$ r. 10 $26{,}134 \div 125 = 209$ r. 9

MEANING AND TERMS

Division "undoes" what multiplication "does," and is called the inverse operation of multiplication. For example, in $2 \times 3 = 6$, 3 has been multiplied by 2 to get 6, whereas in $6 \div 2 = 3$, 6 has been divided by 2 to get the original number 3. Thus

$$2 \times 3 = 6$$

and

$$(2 \times 3) \div 2 = 3$$

When finding the answer to $15 \div 5 = \square$ the question can be asked: By what number do I multiply 5 to get 15? The operation of division is thus used to find the missing factor in a multiplication situation where one of the two factors and the product are known. It is binary in nature because only two numbers are involved at a time.

Example

If $n \times 4 = 12$, then $n = 12 \div 4 = 3$. This situation is illustrated in the following array:

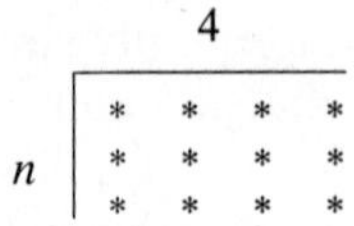

There are 12 elements in the array.

Division may be illustrated by subtracting equal groups successively. For example, the answer to $25 \div 5 = \square$ can be found by subtracting 5 successively: $25 - 5 = 20$ (1), $20 - 5 = 15$ (2), $15 - 5 = 10$ (3), $10 - 5 = 5$ (4) $5 - 5 = 0$ (5). Thus 5 fives equal 25, and $25 \div 5 = 5$.

There are several ways to indicate division. For example, $12 \div 4$, $4\overline{)12}$, and $\frac{12}{4}$ each indicate division.

The *dividend* is divided by the *divisor* to obtain the *quotient*. At present the divisor is often called the *known factor* and the quotient the *missing factor* of the *product*.

PROPERTIES

The *commutative property* does not apply to the division of whole numbers.

Example

$12 \div 4 \neq 4 \div 12$.

The *associative property* does not apply to the division of whole numbers.

Example

$(24 \div 4) \div 2 \neq 24 \div (4 \div 2)$.

The set of whole numbers is not closed under division. For example, in $15 \div 2$, the quotient is not a whole number.

The rule of *compensation* applies in division. In a division the dividend and the divisor can both be multiplied or divided by the same number (the number not being zero) without affecting the quotient.

Examples

$12 \div 6 = 24 \div 12$; $12 \div 6 = 4 \div 2$.

This rule is often used in mental computation.

Examples

$625 \div 25 = 1{,}250 \div 50 = 2{,}500 \div 100 = 25$.
$72 \div 18 = 36 \div 9 = 4$.

ZERO IN DIVISION

1. $0 \div 2 = \square$.
   Zero can be used as a dividend. Since the operation of division is the inverse of multiplication, zero divided by any number (the number not being zero) is equal to zero. $0 \div 2 = 0$, since $= 0 \times 2 = 0$.
2. $0 \div 0 = \square$.
   Any number multiplied by zero yields zero as the product. Hence, $0 \div 0$ cannot be uniquely defined.
3. $2 \div 0 = \square$.
   Since any number multiplied by zero yields zero as the product, $2 \div 0$ is undefined.

TWO DIVISION SITUATIONS

The multiplication situation 3×4 apples $= 12$ apples can be inversed to two different division questions:

1. If 12 apples are put into boxes so that each box holds 4 apples, how many boxes are filled?
2. If 12 apples are divided into 3 equal groups, how many apples will there be in each group?

In the first situation the number of equal groups must be found. This kind of division is called *measurement division.*

In the second situation the size of the share must be determined. This kind of division is called *partition division.*

The two situations are described below for the benefit of the teacher. There does not seem to be much need for the pupil to learn to make the distinction.

Measurement Division In measurement division it must be determined how many groups of a given size are contained in the dividend. The question is: How many times the one equals the other?

Example

We have 12 children working on committees. There are 4 children on each committee. How many committees are there?

Solution: $12 \div 4 = 3$. There are 3 committees.

This division situation is shown graphically as follows:

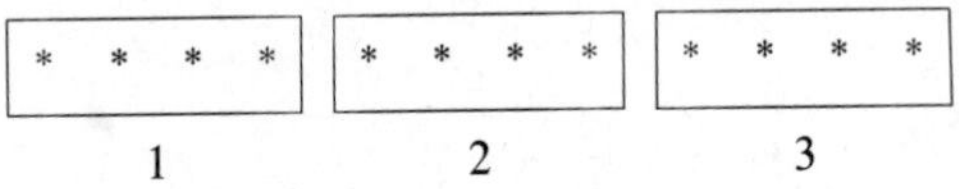

The number line can also be used to illustrate the problem:

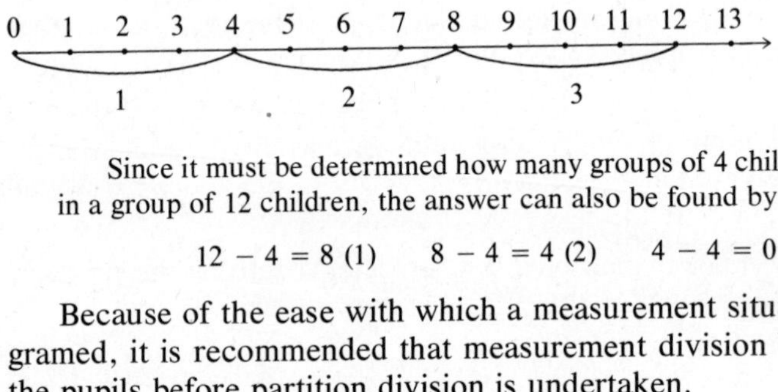

Since it must be determined how many groups of 4 children are contained in a group of 12 children, the answer can also be found by serial subtraction:

$$12 - 4 = 8\ (1) \qquad 8 - 4 = 4\ (2) \qquad 4 - 4 = 0\ (3)$$

Because of the ease with which a measurement situation can be diagramed, it is recommended that measurement division be introduced to the pupils before partition division is undertaken.

Partition Division In partition division the number of groups is known and the size of the share must be determined.

Example

Twelve apples are equally divided among 3 boys. How many apples does each boy get?

Solution: 12 ÷ 3 = 4. Each boy gets 4 apples.

This situation is not as easy to show graphically as the measurement situation:

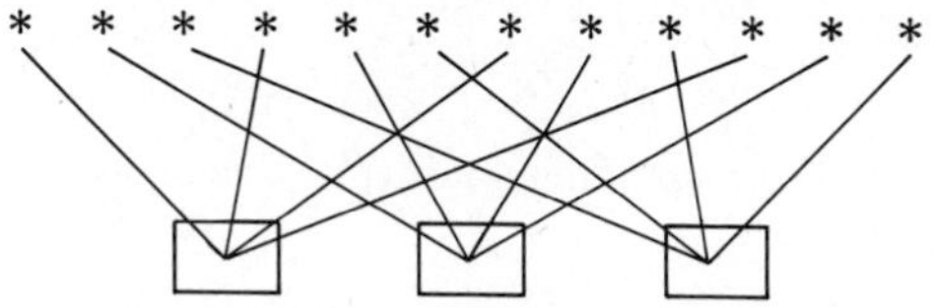

The partition situation can be changed into a measurement situation by dividing the 12 apples into groups of 3 apples each. In each group of 3 apples there is 1 apple for each boy. Each boy gets as many apples as there are groups of 3 apples. This process can be illustrated on the number line:

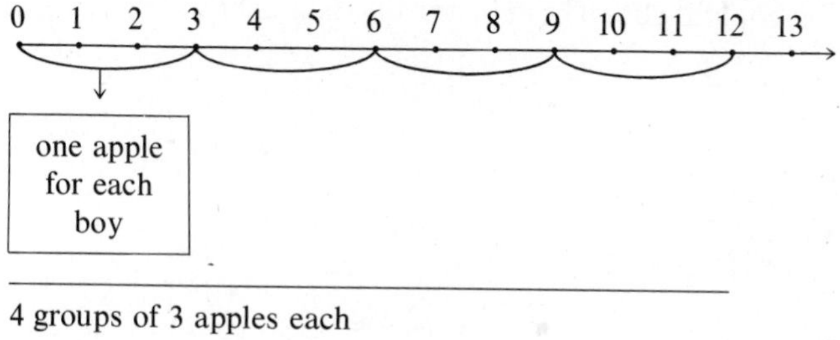

FOUNDATION ACTIVITIES FOR DIVISION

The key division facts—presented elsewhere in this chapter—are usually not introduced in the primary grades. However, foundation experiences in these grades can prepare children for direct and thoroughly planned instruction in division.

The introduction of easy division facts could probably be undertaken sooner than is the practice now. If children can answer the question "How many fours equal eight?" and can understand the meaning of the division symbol, it seems logical to present the division question 8 ÷ 4 = □.

Foundation experiences for division of whole numbers include the following activities:

1. *Counting objects by twos, threes, etc.* Although counting objects by twos, threes, etc. is first of all a preparation for multiplication, these exercises can also be considered foundation activities for division.

2. *Working with blocks.* Manipulating blocks of related sizes such as those of the fraction board, the Cuisenaire rods, or the Stern blocks is a recommended foundation activity for division. Through this activity chil-

dren will begin to see that the size of a certain block is one-half the size of another, that four selected blocks when put together equal the length of another block, etc.

3. *Separating a collection of objects into smaller groups.*

Example

Draw a line around a group of four stars. Make as many groups of four as you can.

* * * * * * * * * *
* * * * * * * * * *

4. *Multiple counting*. Based on the pupils' level in arithmetic, counting by twos, threes, etc. without referring to objects is undertaken to develop the children's skill in determining answers to questions such as: How many twos equal eight? The number line is a useful device in developing this skill.

Example

Count by twos to 10. Show the steps on the number line.

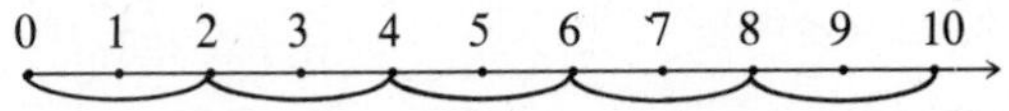

5. *Doubles, etc.* Exercises such as 6 = □ + □ and 9 = □ + □ + □ develop skill in renaming a number. The number line is used here also:

6. *Serial subtraction*. With serial subtraction the question is: Starting at 8, how many twos can I subtract?

7. *Teaching the concepts of "part" and "whole" and their relationship.*

8. *Teaching the concept of one-half.*

THE KEY DIVISION FACTS

The key division facts (also called the basic division facts) are the inverse of the basic multiplication facts. Since there are no facts in which a number is divided by zero, there are only 90 basic division facts.

INTRODUCING THE KEY FACTS

The children should understand that the operation of division is the inverse of multiplication, or that division "undoes" what multiplication "does." It is therefore recommended that the key division facts be introduced together with or immediately after the presentation of the corresponding multiplication facts. When the pupils know that 2 fours equal 8, the teacher should guide them to see that 8 divided by 2 equals 4. Then the multiplication and division sentences are written and compared, and the necessary vocabulary is introduced.

In introducing the first basic division facts, meaningful situations must be used. An exercise such as $8 \div 2 = \square$ deals with abstract numbers, but a word problem resulting in this number question gives the child something concrete to think about.

Example

Ann pastes 8 pictures in her scrapbook. She puts only 2 pictures on a page. How many pages does Ann fill?

Solutions: Several ways of solving this problem are available.

1. The most meaningful way is actually to use 8 pictures and put 2 on a page until all 8 are used. The child finds out that 4 groups of 2 pictures each are contained in 8 pictures. Following this, counters, such as disks or beads on a counting frame, may be used to give the pupil practice in separating the collection into groups of two each and counting the groups.
2. The situation can be shown in a diagram:

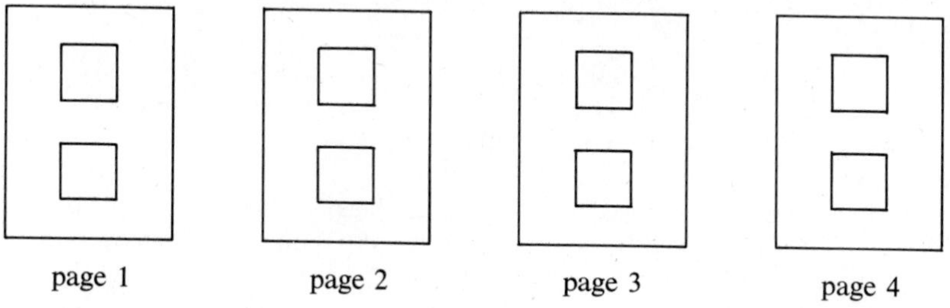

In order to put 8 pictures in the scrapbook, 4 pages are needed if 2 pictures are put on one page.

3. The answer is found by repeated subtraction: $8 - 2 = 6$ (1), $6 - 2 = 4$ (2), $4 - 2 = 2$ (3), $2 - 2 = 0$ (4).
4. The problem can be solved by using the number line:

We can rename 8 as 4 twos.

5. The answer can be found by relating the division situation to the corresponding multiplication situation: Since 4 twos equal 8, 4 groups of 2 each are contained in 8. The relation can be shown in an array:

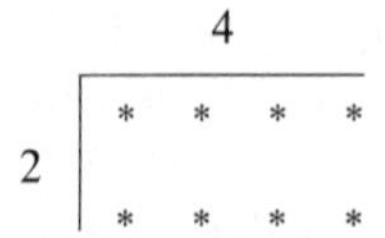

After the division process has been developed meaningfully in ways such as those presented above, the division symbolism is introduced and arithmetic symbols are substituted for language symbols. The division sentence $8 \div 2 = 4$ is then presented, and the new vocabulary is stressed in the teaching that follows.

When the process of division is understood by the pupils and several word problems have been solved, the presentation of exercises of the following kind is recommended:

$$4 \times 3 = \square \qquad 12 = \square \times 3 \qquad 12 \div 3 = \square \qquad 12 \div \square = 4$$
$$\text{Since } 3 \times 4 = 12,\ 12 \div 4 = \square.$$

Partition division is introduced only after several measurement divisions have been discussed and are understood by the children.

Example

Twelve marbles are divided among 3 boys. How many marbles does each boy receive?

Solution: The most meaningful way to solve this problem is to have 12 marbles actually divided among 3 boys, each boy receiving 1 marble at a time until all 12 marbles have been divided. Then a diagram is made, illustrating what has been done.

The teacher can also show that 3 marbles are needed if each boy is to receive 1 marble, and he can then ask the question: How many groups of 3 marbles are there in 12 marbles? When the partition situation has thus been changed to a measurement division, the number line can be used and serial subtraction can be employed.

When the form $\begin{array}{r}4\\3\overline{)12}\end{array}$ is presented, it is stressed that 4 means 4 ones, and that the numeral 4 is written above the 2 in 12, which also represents ones.

DEVELOPING AND ANCHORING SKILLS

It is not sufficient for pupils to have an understanding of the division process and to know how to find the answer to a division question. After an understanding of the basic division facts has been acquired, the children must practice in order to master the facts and anchor the skills. The final goal is that the children know the answer to a basic division question instantly when it is presented. When teachers are satisfied with understanding only, the skills will not be well enough fixed; this means that at higher grade levels teachers will have to do too much review work in the basic facts.

Several techniques, such as the following, can be employed by the resourceful teacher to assure mastery of the basic facts. Some of these have been explained in previous chapters.

1. Flashcards, including those on which the question is presented in horizontal form.
2. The division wheel, which is a modification of the addition wheel.
3. The construction of a division table, which is a modification of the multiplication table.
4. Division card games.
5. The supplying of missing factors.
6. The writing, checking, and memorizing of the tables of facts.
7. Graphical illustrations on the number line.
8. Brief daily reviews of the facts.

The multiplication board may be used as a division board, since division is the inverse operation of multiplication.

DIVISION WITH A REMAINDER

Division with remainders must be introduced in word problems, since the answer to the problem depends on the situation. For example, the division question $10 \div 3 = \square$ has different answers, depending on the situation it represents:

1. Ten inches of ribbon is divided into 3 equal parts. How long is each part?
   The number sentence is $10 \div 3 = 3\frac{1}{3}$. Each part is $3\frac{1}{3}$ inch.
2. Jim has 10¢. He buys chocolate bars for 3¢ apiece. How many bars can Jim buy, and how many pennies does he have left?
   The number sentence is $10 \div 3 = 3$, remainder 1. Jim can buy 3 bars, and has 1¢ left. Thus $10 \div 3 = 3$ r. 1.
3. If the price of 3 apples is 10¢, how much does 1 apple cost? Since we cannot pay $3\frac{1}{3}$¢, the grocer will charge 4¢. Hence, the answer is 4¢.
4. How much interest does a bank pay on \$5.00 at 2% per year in 4 months? In 1 year, the bank pays $2 \times \$.05 = \$.10$, or 10¢. In 4 months the interest is $\frac{1}{3}$ of 10¢. Since $10 \div 3 = 3\frac{1}{3}$, the bank pays 3¢.

DIVIDING BY A ONE-DIGIT DIVISOR

Division of a multi-digit dividend by a one-digit divisor is introduced with cases in which there is no regrouping and no remainder.

Example

Four boys divided 48 baseball cards equally among themselves. How many cards did each boy get?

Number question: $4\overline{)48}$, or $48 \div 4 = \square$.

Solution: At this stage the pupils already know that 4 tens divided by 4 equals 1 ten, or that 40 divided by 4 equals 10. They also know the fact $8 \div 4 = 2$. Hence

$$\begin{aligned} 48 \div 4 &= (40 + 8) \div 4 \\ &= (40 \div 4) + (8 \div 4) \\ &= 10 + 2 \\ &= 12 \end{aligned}$$

After the problem has been worked with reference to objects, the common method of division is developed. The following steps are discussed:

1. How many fours equal 40? Ten fours equal 40. The 1 (for 1 ten) is written in the tens column, above the 4 in 48. Ten fours are subtracted from 48.

$$\begin{array}{r} 1 \\ 4\overline{)48} \\ \underline{40} \\ 8 \end{array}$$

2. How many fours equal 8? Two fours equal 8. The numeral 2 is written above the 8 in 48, and 8 is subtracted from the partial dividend 8.

$$\begin{array}{r} 12 \\ 4\overline{)48} \\ \underline{40} \\ 8 \\ \underline{8} \\ 0 \end{array}$$

3. The teacher again emphasizes that $48 = 40 + 8$, and that first 40 and then 8 has been divided by 4, resulting in $10 + 2 = 12$.
4. The answer may be checked by multiplying the quotient and the divisor: $4 \times 12 = 48$. Through proper guide questions, the pupils are again led to conclude that the operation of division is the inverse of multiplication, or that division "undoes" what multiplication "does."
5. In the class discussion it is pointed out that the zero in 40 is usually not written, but understood, and that the division is written as follows:

$$\begin{array}{r} 12 \\ 4\overline{)48} \\ \underline{4} \\ 8 \\ \underline{8} \\ 0 \end{array}$$

A more difficult case to be presented is a division such as $91 \div 7 = \square$. Through the use of devices such as beads, children should understand that 70 and 21 are divided by 7, and that the two quotients are added. This is excellent preparation for mental computation.

When divisions with three-digit quotients are introduced, special attention should be paid to those exercises that call for a zero in the quotient. These exercises are very difficult for some children, because after a figure is brought down from the dividend, the divisor is larger than the partial dividend then under consideration. It is recommended that an exercise such as $525 \div 5 = \square$ be worked first horizontally, as follows:

$$\begin{aligned} 525 \div 5 &= (500 + 25) \div 5 \\ &= (500 \div 5) + (25 \div 5) \\ &= 100 + 5 \\ &= 105 \end{aligned}$$

and that the pupils find out why there is a zero in the quotient.

VARIOUS ALGORISMS

A different procedure for performing division is the subtractive method. To determine the number of sixes that equal 42, the pupil can subtract 6 repeatedly. Or, if he knows that $3 \times 6 = 18$, he may subtract 3×6 or 18, again 3×6 or 18, and finally 1×6 or 6.

$$\begin{array}{r|l} 6\overline{)42} & \\ \underline{6} & 1 \\ 36 & \\ \underline{6} & 1 \\ 30 & \\ \underline{6} & 1 \\ 24 & \\ \underline{6} & 1 \\ 18 & \\ \underline{6} & 1 \\ 12 & \\ \underline{6} & 1 \\ 6 & \\ \underline{6} & \underline{1} \\ 0 & 7 \end{array} \qquad \begin{array}{r|l} 6\overline{)42} & \\ \underline{18} & 3 \\ 24 & \\ \underline{18} & 3 \\ 6 & \\ \underline{6} & \underline{1} \\ 0 & 7 \end{array}$$

An example with a larger dividend is shown below. Pupils estimate the number of times the divisor can be taken from the dividend or from the partial dividend. After a sufficient amount of practice, they will become more accurate in their estimations and consequently the form will be shortened.

4)172	
40	10
132	
40	10
92	
40	10
52	
40	10
12	
12	3
0	43

Two additional examples are represented below.

75)2400	
1500	20
900	
750	10
150	
150	2
0	32

58)8874	
5800	100
3074	
2320	40
754	
580	10
174	
174	3
0	153

The length of the procedure is often said to be a disadvantage, but it should be realized that pupils learn to shorten the process as their proficiency increases. Some teachers introduce this form as initial work in division, then change to the conventional form after the process is well understood.

The subtractive method of division can likewise be introduced at higher grade levels as an enrichment activity or as a reintroduction of division.

Another expanded form of division is shown below.

$$\left.\begin{array}{r}3\\40\end{array}\right\}43$$

```
 4)172
   160
    12
    12
     0
```

The value of each digit in the quotient is shown. This method should be introduced in initial work in long division and used extensively later, when more difficult cases of division by mental computation are taught. An example of such a mental computation exercise follows.

$$\begin{aligned} 172 \div 4 &= (160 + 12) \div 4 \\ &= (160 \div 4) + (12 \div 4) \\ &= 40 + 3 \\ &= 43 \end{aligned}$$

When both the horizontal and vertical forms of division are used, the pupil has a better opportunity to understand the process.

DIVIDING BY TWO- AND THREE-DIGIT DIVISORS

Division with two-digit divisors is introduced in problems in which divisors and dividends are multiples of 10. These situations should be related to multiplication: Since $4 \times 20 = 80$, $80 \div 20 = 4$. Then the long form is written and discussed. The pupils should try to explain why, in

$$\begin{array}{r} 4 \\ 20\overline{)80} \\ \underline{80} \\ 0 \end{array}$$

the quotient is 4. The leading questions are: How many twos are there in 8? So, how many 20s are there in 80? What number times 20 equals 80?

Other examples, such as $150 \div 30 = \square$, follow, and the pupils are led to discover that the quotient can be found by asking: How many threes are there in 15? This leads to: How many 3 tens are there in 15 tens? Or: How many 30s are there in 150?

After these cases have been mastered, division exercises with remainders are presented, such as $183 \div 30 = \square$, and soon those with a two-digit quotient, such as $630 \div 30 = \square$, can be introduced.

Three-digit divisors do not present much more difficulty when the estimated quotient figure is the true quotient figure, as in $800 \div 200$. The difficulties appear when the estimated quotient figure is not the true quotient figure.

ESTIMATING A QUOTIENT FIGURE

In exercises such as $28\overline{)140}$, various methods for estimating the quotient can be used:

1. *The one-rule, round-down method.* The pupil rounds 28 to 20, and decides that there are 7 twos in 14, but $7 \times 28 = 196$, so the pupil tries 6×28. $6 \times 28 = 168$, and 168 is still too large to be subtracted from 140. After trying 5×28, the pupil decides that 5 is the true quotient. The pupil has tried three times and has erred twice. It should be noticed that in

working the exercise 140 ÷ 21 = □ by this method there will be two trials and one error.

2. *The one-rule, round-up method.* The pupil rounds 28 to 30, and decides that there are 4 threes in 14. Since 4 × 28 = 112, the pupil tries 5 × 28, and finds 5 to be the true quotient. The pupil has tried twice and erred once. When working the exercise 140 ÷ 21 by this method, the pupil will try three times and err twice.

3. *The two-rule method.*

   a. *Round down* when the ones figure is 1, 2, 3, or 4.
   b. *Round up* when the ones figure is 5, 6, 7, 8, or 9.

After working some division exercises, the reader will discover that the two-rule method eliminates work for the pupil, since the estimated quotient figure is more often the true quotient figure with this method than with the one-rule methods.

Although the two-rule method results in fewer corrections of the estimated quotient figure, the pupils have to decide whether the first digit in the divisor should be rounded up or down. During the process of determining the true quotient figure, the estimated quotient may have to be either increased or decreased. This places an extra burden on the pupil. For this reason and for other reasons presented below (which make the round-up method inferior to the round-down method), the author does not recommend the use of the two-rule method in initial teaching of this case.

Of the two one-rule methods, the one-rule, round-down method seems to be the better. Pupils are accustomed to working with the given divisor when they start division with two-digit divisors. Moreover, the one-rule, round-down method paves the way better for the mature method of estimating the quotient by inspection. When 156 must be divided by 26, mature pupils should see 156 as 120 + 36. They will work with 20s, and not with 30s.

The one-rule, round-up method has still another disadvantage. Pupils who have not yet had much experience in dividing by a two-digit divisor do not always identify a case in which the estimated quotient must be increased. As a result, they may work an exercise in the manner shown below.

$$\begin{array}{r} 41 \\ 28\overline{)140} \\ \underline{112} \\ 28 \\ \underline{28} \\ 0 \end{array}$$

4. *Estimation of the quotient figure by inspection,* for pupils more ma-

ture in mathematics. They should use their knowledge of the number system and rename the divisior and the dividend as sums of tens and ones (when the divisor is a two-digit number), then decide upon a reasonable estimate and check it. These pupils will make use of the distributive property of multiplication with respect to addition.

Example

272 ÷ 34 = □. The quotient must be less than 10, since 10 × 34 = 340. If the pupil estimates the quotient to be 7, he will think 7 × 34 = (7 × 30) + (7 × 4) = 210 + 28 = 238. Then he will try 8 as quotient: 8 × 34 = (8 × 30) + (8 × 4) = 240 + 32 = 272.

CHECKING THE QUOTIENT

Various methods can be applied for checking the quotient. The method selected will depend on the mathematical maturity of the pupil.

1. *Application of the relation between the terms*. The check is based on the fact that the product of the quotient and the divisor plus the remainder equals the dividend.

Examples

35 ÷ 7 = 5, and 5 × 7 = 35;
36 ÷ 7 = 5, remainder 1, and 5 × 7 + 1 = 36;
1,325 ÷ 49 = 27, remainder 2, and 27 × 49 + 2 = 1,325.

2. *Approximation*. When an approximate answer is sufficient, the dividend and the divisor may be rounded, and an approximate answer can sometimes be found easily by mental computation.

Example

The reasonableness of the quotient in 1,323 ÷ 49 = 27 can be checked by dividing 1,300 by 50.

3. *The check of nines*. In the upper grades, pupils of at least average ability can learn to check a quotient by applying the check of nines. The excess of nines is determined in the quotient, the divisor, and the remainder. The excesses of nines in the divisor and the quotient are multiplied, and to this product the excess of nines in the remainder (if any) is added. This sum (or the excess of nines in this sum) must equal the excess of nines in the dividend.

Example

23	Excess of nines in the quotient:	5
434)9,988	Excess of nines in the divisor:	×2
8 68	Product:	10
1,308	Excess of nines in the remainder:	+6
1,302	Total:	16, or 7
6	Excess of nines in the dividend:	7

The limitations of the check of nines have already been presented in Chapter 11.

SHORT AND LONG DIVISION

In long division the complete process of division is shown, as in the example below:

$$\begin{array}{r} 9 \\ 5\overline{)47} \\ \underline{45} \\ 2 \end{array}$$

In short division the computation is left out, as in $\begin{array}{r} 9\frac{2}{5} \\ 5\overline{)47} \end{array}$.

There is a need for both the long and the short forms of division. As was stated previously, an ideal way to introduce the basic division facts is to show the relation between a division fact and the corresponding multiplication fact. For example, since $5 \times 2 = 10$, $10 \div 2 = 5$. This is the short form of division, which is introduced as one of the first steps. The same division fact is then shown in the long form, for example,

$$\begin{array}{r} 5 \\ 2\overline{)10} \\ \underline{10} \\ 0 \end{array} \quad \text{or} \quad \begin{array}{r} 10 \div 2 = 5 \\ \underline{10} \quad\quad\quad \\ 0 \quad\quad\quad \end{array}$$

in order to prepare the pupils for more difficult division problems.

Thorpe writes:

> When pupils have mastered the division facts and have learned the simple algorism, $\begin{array}{r} 2 \\ 3\overline{)6} \end{array}$, as meaning how many 3's in 6, they are using short division, not long division, as in $\begin{array}{r} 2 \\ 3\overline{)6} \\ \underline{6} \end{array}$. A logical next step is $3\overline{)60}$. This implies how many 3's in 6 tens, or how many 3's in 60, and the answer is 20, shown as $\begin{array}{r} 20 \\ 3\overline{)60} \end{array}$. This is still short division form.[1]

It seems logical to recommend that pupils do as much short division as their ability allows, provided that it is done meaningfully. Pupils should be taught how to rename numbers mentally, divide each part, and add the quotients.

---

1. C. B. Thorpe, *Teaching Elementary Arithmetic* (New York: Harper & Row, Publishers, 1962), p. 152.

MENTAL COMPUTATION

The teaching of mental computation in division according to a well-defined, sequential plan should result in a better understanding of the number properties and in proficiency in mentally computing simple division problems.

Example 1

$$\begin{aligned} 42 \div 3 &= (30 + 12) \div 3 \\ &= (30 \div 3) + (12 \div 3) \\ &= 10 + 4 \\ &= 14 \end{aligned}$$

In this example, 30 is selected as one of the addends, since it equals 10×3.

Example 2

$$\begin{aligned} 84 \div 4 &= (80 + 4) \div 4 \\ &= (80 \div 4) + (4 \div 4) \\ &= 20 + 1 \\ &= 21 \end{aligned}$$

Since $80 = 20 \times 4$, this number is selected as one of the addends of the sum that renames 84.

Example 3

$$\begin{aligned} 468 \div 9 &= (450 + 18) \div 9 \\ &= (450 \div 9) + (18 \div 9) \\ &= 50 + 2 \\ &= 52 \end{aligned}$$

It is clear why 450, equalling 50×9, is selected as one of the addends.

Example 4

$$\begin{aligned} 396 \div 4 &= (400 - 4) \div 4 \\ &= (400 \div 4) - (4 \div 4) \\ &= 100 - 1 \\ &= 99 \end{aligned}$$

396 is written as $400 - 4$, since it is easy first to divide 400 by 4, then 4 by 4, and then to subtract the quotients.

Example 5

Through inductive teaching, the pupils should be led to discover the rules for dividing a number by 10, 100, etc.

The rule of compensation should be found inductively by using simple exercises. Then the rule can be applied in more difficult situations.

$$\begin{aligned} 650 \div 25 &= 1{,}300 \div 50 \\ &= 2{,}600 \div 100 \\ &= 26 \end{aligned}$$

SELECTED RESEARCH

The conductors of this study[2] attempted to find answers to questions dealing with division involving zero. Findings gathered from paper-and-pencil tests of more than seven hundred pupils in fourth, sixth, and eighth grades from schools in four school districts were analyzed and implications were discussed. Selected parts of the article are summarized in the following paragraphs.

The study was conducted over three consecutive days. On the first day a pre-test was administered. On the second day instruction on division was given and practice exercises were completed and discussed. On the third day the pupils took a post-test, which was a form parallel to the pre-test. Immediately following the post-test, four pupils from each class were individually interviewed to obtain in-depth information about how children thought about division examples that were similar to those on the post-test. Six weeks after the post-test, a retention test, which was parallel in form to the pre-test and the post-test, was administered.

These instructional approaches were used: The division-multiplication (D-M) approach and the multiplication-division (M-D) approach. The approach used with each class was determined by random assignment so that in each school district and at each grade level the same number of classes received each of the instructional treatments.

In the D-M lesson, a sentence like $15 \div 3 = \square$ was presented and a related multiplication sentence was found; namely, $3 \times \square = 15$. After working with several pairs of examples, the children were led to generalize the inverse pattern. At that point, division examples involving zero as either a dividend or a divisor were introduced. It was concluded that division by zero is undefined because the related multiplication sentence has no solution. Similarly, zero in the dividend was found to lead to zero quotient. The case $0 \div 0$ was not presented. The balance of the time was devoted to working and discussing examples.

In the M-D lesson the multiplication sentence ($10 \times \square = 20$) was presented first and then the related division sentence ($20 \div 10 = \square$) was written. During the practice period the emphasis was always on working with a multiplication sentence first.

---

2. D. A. Grouws and R. E. Reys, "Division Involving Zero: An Experimental Study and Its Implications," *The Arithmetic Teacher* (January, 1975), pp. 74–80.

The post-test was composed of the following items. (The different ways of writing a division example had been reviewed initially.)

$15\overline{)0}$	$4\overline{)0}$	$6\overline{)18}$	$7 \div 0 =$	$\frac{8}{0} =$	$0 \div 16 =$
$24 \div 6 =$	$0 \div 6 =$	$\frac{14}{0} =$	$\frac{6}{2} =$	$8 \div 2 =$	$0\overline{)12} =$
$\frac{15}{3} =$	$12 \div 0 =$	$0\overline{)6} =$	$\frac{0}{5} =$	$\frac{0}{10} =$	$3\overline{)9} =$

The findings included:

1. The mean number of correct responses on the pre-test was 10.4 and the mean score on the post-test was 11.9. The difference was statistically significant.
2. The mean post-test scores for the D-M group was 12.4 and for the M-D group 11.4. Thus the D-M lesson was associated with significantly higher post-test scores than was the M-D lesson.
3. Although the mean pre-test score for sixth-grade pupils was lower than that for fourth-grade pupils, the initial difference was more than made up on the post-test results.
4. The mean retention score across all pupils was 11.2. Thus children did not do as well six weeks after the division lesson as they did on the day following the lesson.
5. On the retention test there was no significant different in the performances of the pupils in the D-M group and the pupils in the M-D group. Thus the pupils in the D-M group regressed more than those in the M-D group.
6. On the pre-test children scored on the average less than one item correct on the six items that had zero as the divisor, on the post-test the average score was 3, and on the retention test the average score was 2.46 on such items.
7. On the pre-test children scored on the average 4.79 correct on the six items that had zero as the dividend, whereas the average scores on the post-test and the retention test were 3.20 and 3.16 consecutively for such items.

Of the implications for teaching that the authors suggest, the following are noted:

1. The method of instruction chosen by the teacher can make a difference in pupil achievement.

2. A good instructional approach to teaching division involving zero might first focus on the division sentence to be solved and then on writing the related multiplication sentence.
3. Practice and review are necessary in connection with this mathematical topic as well as with others.
4. Children tend to over-generalize. Many pupils evidently generalized that because division by zero does not result in a numerical answer, whenever zero is found in a division problem there is no answer.

SELECTED ACTIVITIES FOR PUPILS

1. Show on the number line that $12 \div 2 = 6$.
2. Write four number sentences using the numbers 15, 3, and 5.
3. $18 \div 6 = 9 \div \square$ $\quad 36 \div 4 = 18 \div \square$ $\quad 48 \div 8 = 24 \div \square$
4. $\overset{(\div 2)}{\overbrace{72 \div 18 = 36}} \div 9$, $\quad 72 \div \underset{(\div 2)}{\underbrace{18 = 36 \div 9}}$

   Follow the same procedure in working these exercises:

   $84 \div 14 = \square \div 7$ $\quad 24 \div 12 = 12 \div \square$ $\quad 90 \div 18 = \square \div 9$
5. $$\begin{aligned} 108 \div 9 &= (90 + 18) \div 9 \\ &= (90 \div 9) + (18 \div 9) \\ &= 10 + 2 \\ &= 12 \end{aligned}$$

   Follow the same procedure in working these exercises:

   $65 \div 5 = \square$ $\quad 68 \div 4 = \square$ $\quad 105 \div 7 = \square$
6. $$\begin{aligned} 291 \div 3 &= (300 - 9) \div 3 \\ &= (300 \div 3) - (9 \div 3) \\ &= 100 - 3 \\ &= 97 \end{aligned}$$

   Follow the same procedure in working these exercises:

   $490 \div 5 = \square$ $\quad 392 \div 4 = \square$ $\quad 693 \div 7 = \square$

7. Find the quotient.

÷	48	24	96
6	8		
4			
8			

÷	48	96	144
12			
16			
24			

8. Complete.

	(×4)	(÷4)
6	24	6
5	□	□
9	□	□
10	□	□

	(×12)	(÷12)
3	36	3
8	□	□
2	□	□
4	□	□

9. Complete:

If 6 × 8 = 48, then 48 ÷ 8 = □.
If 5 × 120 = 600, then 600 ÷ 5 = □.
If 17 × 28 = 476, then 476 ÷ 28 = □.

10. Check the answer. An example has been given.

38 ÷ 7 = 5, r. 3.

Check: (5 × 7) + 3 = 38.

65 ÷ 12 = 5, r. 5 73 ÷ 4 = 18, r. 1 97 ÷ 15 = 6, r. 7

11. Supply the missing numerals in this mathematical sentence:

62,500 ÷ 25 = □ ÷ 50 = △ ÷ 100 = ○.

12. Work the crossnumber puzzle.

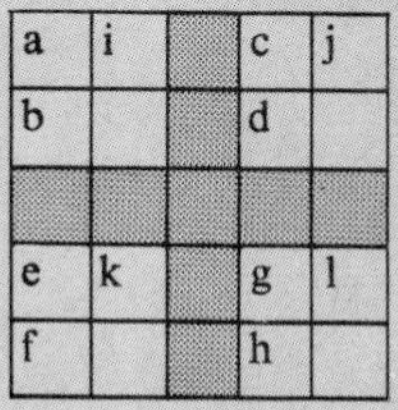

left-right
a) 15 + 10 =
b) 3 × 9 =
c) 30 − 12 =
d) 100 ÷ 10 =
e) 25 − 9 =
f) 8 × 8 =
g) 50 − 13 =
h) 6 × 4 =

up-down
a) 2 × 11 =
i) 60 − 3 =
c) 20 − 9 =
j) 4 × 20 =
e) 4 × 4 =
k) 70 − 6 =
g) 16 + 16 =
l) 100 − 26 =

13. Write different numerals on the six sides of two sugar cubes. (The exposed numbers vary according to the level of the class.) The two cubes are rolled, and the numbers expressed on the top faces are considered. Various assignments can be made:

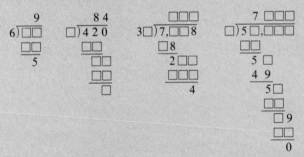

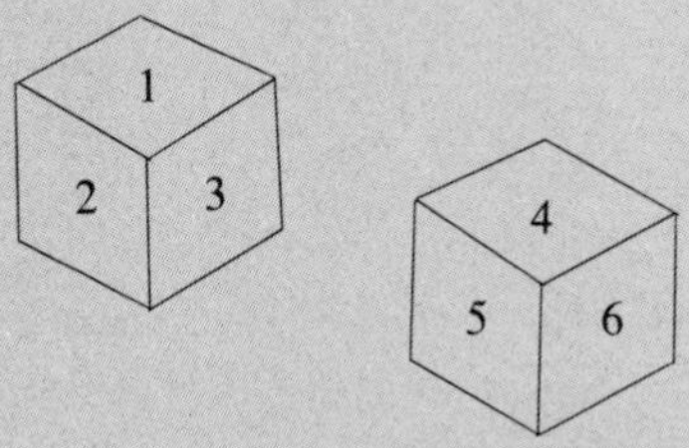

a. Add the numbers.
b. Subtract the smaller number from the larger one.
c. Multiply the numbers.
d. Divide the larger number by the smaller one.
e. Subtract the larger number from the smaller one.

14. Write the missing digits. Check your answers by using a minicalculator if one is available.

```
     9           8 4            □□□            7 □□□
 6)□□        □)4 2 0     3□)7,□□8       □)5□,□□□
   □□          □□           □8            □□
    5           □□           2□□            5 □
                □□           □□□            4 9
                 □              4            5□
                                             □□
                                              □9
                                              □□
                                               0
```

15. Farmer Berry has 64 animals.
One half of the number of animals have four feet.
One fourth of the four-footed animals are black.
One half of the four-footed black animals can bark.
How many of the four-footed black animals can bark?

16. Ron has 6 nickels.
He also has: four times as many pennies as nickels,
half as many dimes as pennies.
half as many quarters as dimes.
If Ron were to exchange his nickels, dimes, and quarters for pennies, how many pennies would he have?

EXERCISES

1. Explain and illustrate the difference between measurement division and partition division.
2. Give an example of the rule of compensation in division.
3. Explain why a zero in a quotient may be difficult for pupils who are beginning their study of division.
4. Describe some activities for the primary grades that are designed to develop the concept of division.
5. Should pupils memorize the basic division facts? Defend your answer.
6. Describe and illustrate how you would introduce division with a remainder.
7. Explain and illustrate the difference between the subtractive method and the traditional method of division.
8. Describe a device that can be used by pupils studying to master the division facts.
9. Describe the different methods for estimating a quotient figure. What is, in your opinion, the best method? Why?
10. Describe the check of nines in division.
11. Report on a piece of research pertaining to division of whole numbers.
12. Write an illustrative lesson on the division of a three-digit number by a two-digit number, where the first estimated quotient figure is not the true quotient figure.
13. Diagnose the persistent mistake made in each of the following sets of divisions.

a.	1,206 ÷ 6 = 21	1,806 ÷ 2 = 93
	2,505 ÷ 5 = 51	2,409 ÷ 3 = 83
b.	844 ÷ 4 = 112	287 ÷ 7 = 14
	682 ÷ 2 = 143	364 ÷ 4 = 19
c.	63 ÷ 6 = 12	1,628 ÷ 4 = 422
	42 ÷ 4 = 12	3,515 ÷ 5 = 751

SOURCES FOR FURTHER READING

Ashlock, R. B. *Error Patterns in Computation*. Columbus: Charles E. Merrill Publishing Company, 1972.

Connelly, R., and J. Heddens, "'Remainders' That Shouldn't Remain," *The Arithmetic Teacher*, October, 1971, pp. 379–380.

D'Augustine, C. H., *Multiple Methods of Teaching Mathematics in the Elementary School*, 2nd ed. New York: Harper & Row, Publishers, 1973, Chap. IX.

Heddens, J. W., *Today's Mathematics,* 3d ed. Chicago: Science Research Associates, Inc., 1974, Unit VIII.

Heddens, J. W., and B. Lazerick, "So 3 'Guzinta' 5 Once! So What!!" *The Arithmetic Teacher,* November, 1975, pp. 576–578.

Kennedy, L. M., *Guiding Children to Mathematical Discovery,* 2nd ed. Belmont, California: Wadsworth Publishing Company, Inc., 1975, Chaps. VIII, IX.

Marks, J. L., C. R. Purdy, L. B. Kinney, and A. A. Hiatt, *Teaching Elementary School Mathematics for Understanding,* 4th ed. New York: McGraw-Hill Book Company, 1975, Chap. V.

National Council of Teachers of Mathematics, *Topics in Mathematics, Twenty-ninth Yearbook*. Washington, D.C.: The Council, 1964, Bklt. 2.

Schminke, C. W., N. Maertens, and W. R. Arnold, *Teaching the Child Mathematics*. Hinsdale, Illinois: The Dryden Press, Inc., 1973, Chap. IV.

Scott, R., "A Study of Teaching Division through the Use of Two Algorisms," *School Science and Mathematics,* December, 1963, pp. 739–752.

Spitzer, H. F., "Measurement or Partition Division for Introducing Study of the Division Operation," *The Arithmetic Teacher,* May, 1967, pp. 369–372.

Spitzer, H. F., *Teaching Elementary School Mathematics*. Boston: Houghton Mifflin Company, 1967, Chap. XIV.

Thorpe, C. B., *Teaching Elementary Arithmetic*. New York: Harper & Row, Publishers, 1962, Chap. XIV.

Van Engen, H., "Teach Fundamental Operations through Problem Solving," *Grade Teacher,* April, 1962, pp. 58–59.

Zweng, M. J., "The Fourth Operation Is Not Fundamental," *The Arithmetic Teacher,* December, 1972, pp. 623–627.

Fractions 15

In the set of integers there is no element that can replace n in the equation $1 \div 2 = n$ and make the statement true. Moreover, if we have only the integers to work with, the result of a measurement must be expressed by a measure that is an integer, whereas greater accuracy is often required. Thus, the need for an extension of the number system that comprises the set of integers is evident. This extended number system is called the *rational number system*.

In the following chapters a subset of the rational numbers called the fractional numbers is considered. Fractional numbers can be expressed in different ways. This chapter is concerned with common fractions, Chapter 16 deals with decimals and Chapter 17 introduces percents.

SKILLS TEST

1.	$12\frac{5}{8} + 7\frac{2}{3} =$	$19\frac{1}{2} + 16\frac{3}{5} =$	$24\frac{5}{6} + 5\frac{3}{4} =$	$3\frac{1}{5} + 2\frac{9}{10} =$
2.	$10\frac{1}{7} - 3\frac{1}{2} =$	$20\frac{1}{4} - 5\frac{4}{5} =$	$60\frac{1}{3} - 4\frac{1}{2} =$	$9\frac{3}{5} - \frac{7}{8} =$
3.	$\frac{1}{3}$ of 21 =	$\frac{1}{5}$ of 55 =	$\frac{1}{8}$ of 104 =	$\frac{1}{4}$ of 72 =
4.	$\frac{2}{3}$ of 12 =	$\frac{3}{8}$ of 24 =	$\frac{5}{7}$ of 77 =	$\frac{3}{10}$ of 120 =
5.	$\frac{3}{5} = \frac{\square}{20}$	$\frac{5}{9} = \frac{\square}{27}$	$\frac{2}{3} = \frac{\square}{21}$	$\frac{7}{8} = \frac{\square}{56}$

6. $\frac{5}{6} = \frac{15}{\square}$ $\frac{2}{3} = \frac{20}{\square}$ $\frac{7}{8} = \frac{77}{\square}$ $\frac{4}{5} = \frac{48}{\square}$

7. $5 \times 1\frac{2}{5} =$ $9 \times 3\frac{3}{4} =$ $4\frac{1}{2} \times 6\frac{1}{3} =$ $\frac{3}{7} \times \frac{7}{12} =$

8. 16 is $\frac{4}{5}$ of ______. 35 is $\frac{7}{8}$ of ______.

9. Find the reciprocal of:

   5; $\frac{1}{4}$; $\frac{5}{6}$; $\frac{8}{5}$.

10. Find the answers by using the common denominator method.

    $6 \div 1\frac{1}{2} =$ $12\frac{1}{2} \div 1\frac{1}{4} =$ $4\frac{1}{5} \div 3\frac{1}{2} =$ $\frac{7}{10} \div \frac{2}{5} =$

11. Find the answers by using the inversion method.

    $8 \div 1\frac{3}{5} =$ $2\frac{2}{5} \div \frac{3}{10} =$ $3\frac{1}{3} \div 1\frac{8}{9} =$ $1\frac{1}{5} \div \frac{3}{10} =$

12. $(2\frac{1}{2} \times 1\frac{2}{5}) + (1\frac{3}{4} \div 3\frac{1}{2}) =$ $(3\frac{1}{5} \times 2\frac{1}{2}) - (\frac{3}{4} \div \frac{1}{2}) =$

MEANING AND TERMS

A *rational number* is a number that can be expressed as the quotient of an integer and a nonzero integer. It should be understood that integers are included in the set of rational numbers ($5 = \frac{5}{1}$, $^{-}3 = \frac{^{-}3}{1}$).

The subset of the rational numbers consisting of 0 and the positive rational numbers we shall call the *fractional numbers*. In this chapter, fractional numbers are expressed as *fractions* that take the form $\frac{a}{b}$, in which a stands for a whole number and b for a natural number. These fractions are also called *common fractions*.

The fraction $\frac{1}{2}$ can replace n in the equation $1 \div 2 = n$ and make the statement true. The statement $1 \div 2 = \frac{1}{2}$ expresses the division of a unit into congruent subunits (subunits that have the same measure), each of which equals $\frac{1}{2}$ of the original unit. In general, if a unit is divided into n congruent subunits, the measure of each subunit is $1/n$ of the original unit.

On the number line that follows, the same point is named by the fractions $\frac{1}{2}$, $\frac{2}{4}$, and $\frac{4}{8}$. Since these fractions are associated with the same point on the line, they are different expressions of the same idea. These fractions are called *equivalent fractions*. A test of the equivalence of fractions a/b and c/d is whether or not $a \times d = b \times c$. Thus $\frac{1}{2} = \frac{2}{4}$, since $1 \times 4 = 2 \times 2$; and $\frac{2}{4} = \frac{4}{8}$, since $2 \times 8 = 4 \times 4$. The simplest name—sometimes called the standard form—for the fractional number here under consideration is $\frac{1}{2}$. In this fraction the lowest possible terms are used.

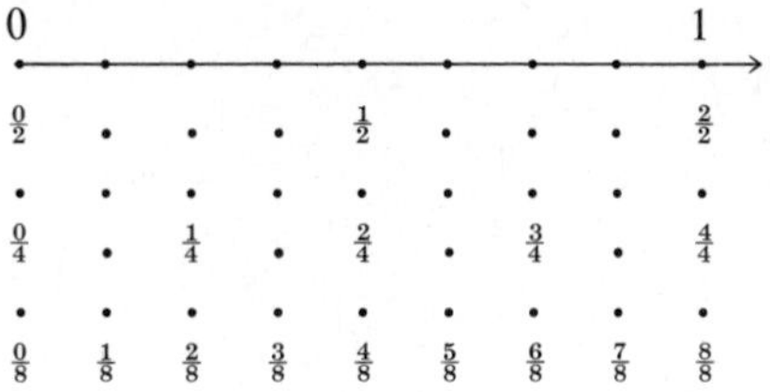

Many more fractions—each representing the same point on the line and thus the same fractional number—could be written, for example, under the point on the line identified by $\frac{1}{2}$, $\frac{2}{4}$, and $\frac{4}{8}$. Indeed, an infinite number of fractions represent that same point on the line, and therefore the same fractional number.

Fractions may represent different situations:

1. A fraction may express one or more equal parts of a whole.

   Examples

   The trip took $\frac{1}{2}$ hour. We ate $\frac{3}{4}$ of a cake.

2. A fraction may express one of the equal parts of a group of units.

   Example

   When 5 boys divide 2 apples equally, each boy will get $\frac{2}{5}$ of an apple.

3. A fraction may indicate the division of a whole number by a natural number.

   Example

   $\frac{3}{4} = 3 \div 4$.

In a fraction such as $\frac{2}{3}$, 2 represents the *numerator,* and 3 the *denominator*. The denominator is the "namer" of the number of congruent subunits into which the original unit or group is divided. The word denominator is derived from the Latin word *nomen,* which means "name." The numerator of a fraction is the "numberer" or the "counter" of the subunits expressed by the denominator. For example, the fraction $\frac{2}{3}$ indicates that the original unit has been divided into three subunits and that two of these subunits are considered. The denominator and the numerator are called the *terms* of the fraction.

A *mixed fraction* contains a numeral naming a natural number and a fraction.

Examples

$1\frac{1}{2}$; $3\frac{1}{4}$; $5\frac{3}{4}$.

The mixed fraction $1\frac{1}{2}$ is a name for $1 + \frac{1}{2}$.

A *proper fraction* represents a number less than 1.

Examples

$\frac{7}{8}$; $\frac{3}{4}$; $\frac{12}{15}$.

An *improper fraction* represents a number equal to or greater than 1.

Examples

$\frac{5}{5}$; $\frac{7}{5}$; $\frac{12}{8}$.

A *unit fraction* has 1 as its numerator.

Examples

$\frac{1}{2}$; $\frac{1}{4}$; $\frac{1}{12}$.

A *multipart fraction* has a numerator greater than 1.

Examples

$\frac{2}{3}$; $\frac{4}{5}$; $\frac{7}{3}$.

Like fractions or similar fractions have the same denominator.

Examples

$\frac{3}{4}$ and $\frac{1}{4}$; $\frac{1}{9}$ and $\frac{8}{9}$; $\frac{3}{5}$ and $\frac{2}{5}$.

Unlike fractions or dissimilar fractions have different denominators.

Examples

$\frac{3}{4}$ and $\frac{3}{5}$; $\frac{1}{3}$ and $\frac{1}{2}$; $\frac{4}{7}$ and $\frac{2}{9}$.

Two numbers are said to be *reciprocals* or *multiplicative inverses* if their product is 1.

Examples

The reciprocal of $\frac{2}{3}$ is $\frac{3}{2}$, since $\frac{2}{3} \times \frac{3}{2} = 1$. The reciprocal of $\frac{5}{6}$ is $\frac{6}{5}$, since $\frac{5}{6} \times \frac{6}{5} = 1$.

SOME IMPORTANT PROPERTIES OF FRACTIONAL NUMBERS

The following properties apply to fractional numbers:

1. *Commutative property of addition and multiplication.*

Examples

$\frac{1}{2} + \frac{1}{4} = \frac{1}{4} + \frac{1}{2}$; $\frac{1}{2} \times \frac{1}{4} = \frac{1}{4} \times \frac{1}{2}$.

2. *Associative property of addition and multiplication.*

Examples

$(\frac{1}{2} + \frac{1}{4}) + \frac{1}{3} = \frac{1}{2} + (\frac{1}{4} + \frac{1}{3})$; $(\frac{1}{2} \times \frac{1}{4}) \times \frac{1}{3} = \frac{1}{2} \times (\frac{1}{4} \times \frac{1}{3})$.

3. *Distributive property of multiplication and division with respect to addition.*

Examples

$\frac{2}{3} \times (\frac{6}{11} + \frac{3}{11}) = (\frac{2}{3} \times \frac{6}{11}) + (\frac{2}{3} \times \frac{3}{11}) = \frac{4}{11} + \frac{2}{11} = \frac{6}{11}$;

$(\frac{1}{9} + \frac{1}{12}) \div \frac{1}{3} = (\frac{1}{9} \div \frac{1}{3}) + (\frac{1}{12} \div \frac{1}{3}) = \frac{1}{3} + \frac{1}{4} = \frac{7}{12}$.

4. *Closure property of addition, multiplication, and division—division by zero excepted.*

Examples

$\frac{1}{5} + \frac{2}{5} = \frac{3}{5}$; $\frac{1}{5} \times \frac{2}{5} = \frac{2}{25}$; $\frac{1}{5} \div \frac{2}{3} = \frac{3}{10}$.

5. *Identity element for addition.* A fractional number remains unchanged if zero is added to it.

(*Note:* $0 = \frac{0}{1} = \frac{0}{2} = \frac{0}{3}$, etc.)

Example

$\frac{3}{4} + 0 = \frac{3}{4}$.

6. *Identity element for multiplication.* A fractional number remains unchanged if it is multiplied by 1.

(*Note:* $1 = \frac{1}{1} = \frac{2}{2} = \frac{3}{3}$, etc.)

Example

$1 \times \frac{3}{4} = \frac{3}{4}$.

7. *Reciprocal property.* The product of a fractional number and its reciprocal is 1. This property is also called the *multiplicative inverse property.*

Example

$\frac{5}{8} \times \frac{8}{5} = 1$.

RULES

The following rules should be noted:

1. Multiplying both terms of a fraction by the same natural number does not change the value of the fraction.

Example

$$\frac{1}{2} = \frac{2 \times 1}{2 \times 2} = \frac{2}{4}$$

If $\frac{1}{2}$ is written as $\frac{2}{4}$, it has been renamed or changed to higher terms, but its value has not changed. $\frac{1}{2}$ and $\frac{2}{4}$ are equivalent fractions and are only different names for the same fractional number.

2. Dividing both terms of a fraction by the same natural number does not change the value of the fraction.

Example

$$\frac{3}{9} = \frac{3 \div 3}{9 \div 3} = \frac{1}{3}.$$

If $\frac{3}{9}$ is written as $\frac{1}{3}$, it has been renamed or changed to its lowest terms, but its value has not changed. $\frac{3}{9}$ and $\frac{1}{3}$ are different names for the same fractional number.

3. Multiplying the numerator of a fraction by a natural number multiplies the value of the fraction by that number.

Example

Multiplying the numerator of the fraction $\frac{2}{5}$ by 2 results in the number expressed by the fraction $\frac{4}{5}$, the value of which is twice as large as the value of the original fraction $\frac{2}{5}$.

4. Multiplying the denominator of a fraction by a natural number divides the value of the fraction by that number.

Example

Multiplying the denominator of the fraction $\frac{3}{4}$ by 2 results in the number expressed by the fraction $\frac{3}{8}$, the value of which is half as large as that of the original fraction $\frac{3}{4}$.

5. Dividing the numerator of a fraction by a natural number divides the value of the fraction by that number.

Example

Dividing the numerator of the fraction $\frac{4}{5}$ by 2 results in the number expressed by the fraction $\frac{2}{5}$, the value of which is half as large as that of the original fraction $\frac{4}{5}$.

6. Dividing the denominator of a fraction by a natural number multiplies the value of the fraction by that number.

Example

Dividing the denominator of the fraction $\frac{3}{8}$ by 2 results in the number expressed by the fraction $\frac{3}{4}$, the value of which is twice as large as that of the original fraction $\frac{3}{8}$.

FOUNDATION ACTIVITIES

Mathematics books for the primary grades deal with the development of concepts of fractional numbers. Simple operations on these numbers are often introduced as early as Grade 3. In the middle grades, operations on fractional numbers are emphasized.

At the time of entering school, many children have already acquired some ideas of fractional parts. They may have used expressions such as "half a glass of milk," "half an apple," and "half an hour." The teacher needs to provide a rich environment in which such concepts are extended, other concepts are built, and the needed vocabulary and symbols are introduced.

For kindergarten pupils, cooperative activities are recommended. If, for example, a cake is baked under the direction of the teacher, the children use fractional parts as they try to read the recipe, weigh and measure the ingredients, decide that the baking time is half an hour, and finally cut the cake into parts. The best learning takes place in the performing of such activities.

Suggested foundation activities for the primary grades are—

1. folding, tearing, or cutting a sheet of paper into two or more parts.
2. dividing a group, say of six blocks, into two equivalent groups.
3. comparing parts of circular and rectangular cutouts and answering questions of the following kind:
   a. How many halves equal one whole?
   b. Which is larger, $\frac{1}{2}$ or $\frac{1}{4}$?
   c. How many fourths equal one-half?
4. measuring the length of an object by using a foot ruler graduated in half inches.
5. measuring different amounts of various materials by using measuring cups, measuring spoons, cartons of various sizes, and other common containers.
6. manipulating rods of different lengths in free and directed activities.
7. weighing objects on scales. Labeled bags filled with sand weighing 1 pound, $\frac{1}{2}$ pound, $\frac{1}{4}$ pound, etc. can be used as weights.

After initial work, the use of unit fractions as a part of a whole and as a part of a group is extended to include smaller fractions. When the pupils have acquired the concept of division, they are introduced to exercises such as $\frac{1}{4}$ of 20; they should be able to interpret $\frac{1}{4}$ of 20 as $20 \div 4$.

DIFFERENT FRACTIONS EXPRESSING THE SAME FRACTIONAL NUMBER

Prerequisites for performing operations involving fractional numbers are a knowledge of multipart fractions and the understanding that the same fractional number may be named by an endless number of fractions. Specific instruction in changing a fraction to another equivalent fraction is essential.

Whole Numbers and Improper Fractions

Circular disks divided into halves, fourths, eighths, etc., as in Figure 15.1, illustrate the equivalence of 1, $\frac{2}{2}$, $\frac{4}{4}$, $\frac{8}{8}$, etc.

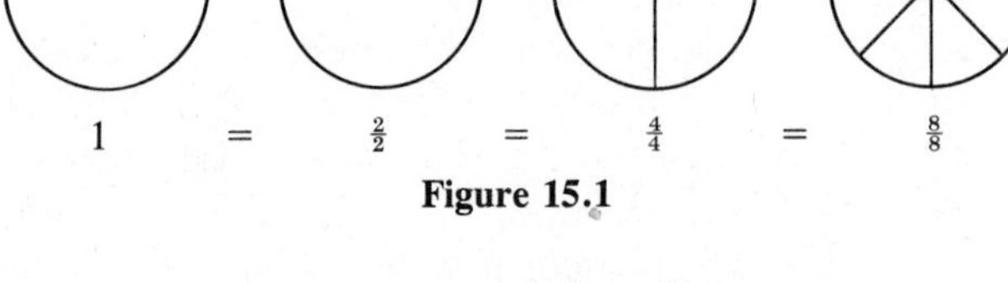

Figure 15.1

This can also be shown on the number line:

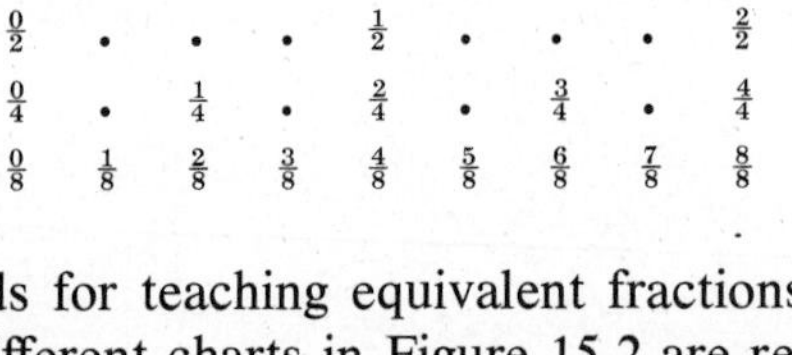

Other useful aids for teaching equivalent fractions are the fraction charts. The three different charts in Figure 15.2 are recommended. The first one illustrates one whole, two halves, four fourths, etc. On the second one, the unit has been divided into thirds, sixths, and twelfths. The third one represents one whole, two halves, three thirds, etc.

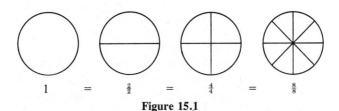

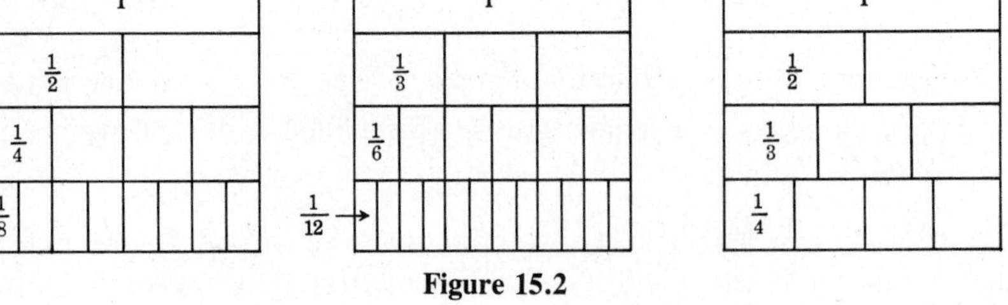

Figure 15.2

The study of these charts is followed by related exercises and by meaningful manipulation of the fraction board, which resembles the fraction chart but which has movable pieces that fit in grooves.

Mixed Fractions and Improper Fractions

Mixed fractions are easily illustrated with circular cutouts. The pupil will have no trouble identifying $1\frac{1}{2}$ circles. When the whole circle is replaced by two halves, as in Figure 15.3, it is shown that $1\frac{1}{2} = \frac{3}{2}$.

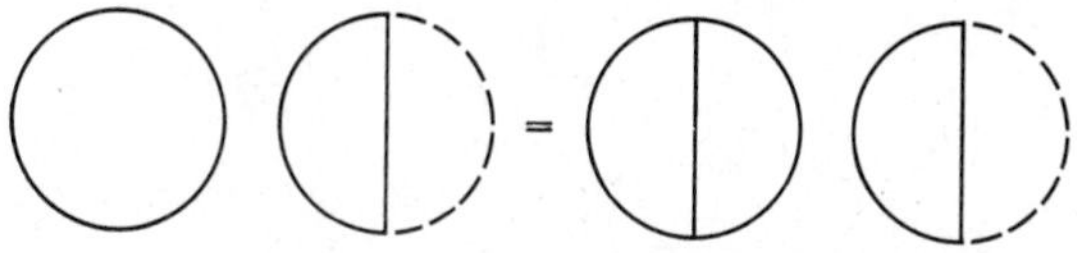

$1\frac{1}{2} \quad = \quad \frac{3}{2}$

Figure 15.3

Fourths are similarly illustrated in Figure 15.4.

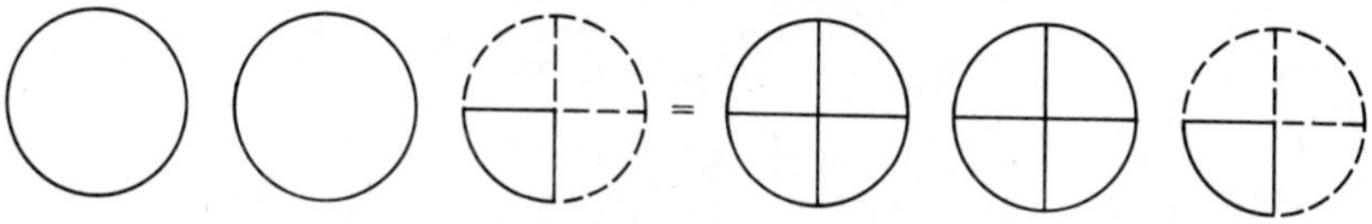

$2\frac{1}{4} \quad = \quad \frac{9}{4}$

Figure 15.4

These presentations are followed by illustrations of equivalent fractions on the number line:

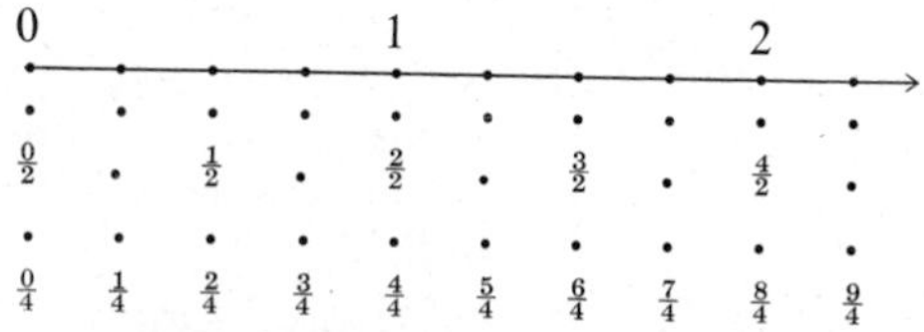

The teacher may supply the pupils with a sheet on which number lines like the foregoing are provided. With the initial help of these number lines, the children change mixed fractions to improper fractions, and vice versa. For example,

$$2\tfrac{1}{4} = \frac{4}{4} + \frac{4}{4} + \frac{1}{4} = \frac{4+4+1}{4} = \frac{9}{4}$$

$$2\tfrac{1}{4} = \frac{(2 \times 4) + 1}{4} = \frac{9}{4}$$

$$\frac{9}{4} = 9 \div 4 = 2\tfrac{1}{4}$$

Changing a Fraction to One with Higher or Lower Terms

Cutouts (Figure 15.5), diagrams, and number lines are also useful to illustrate that the same fractional number can be expressed by different fractions.

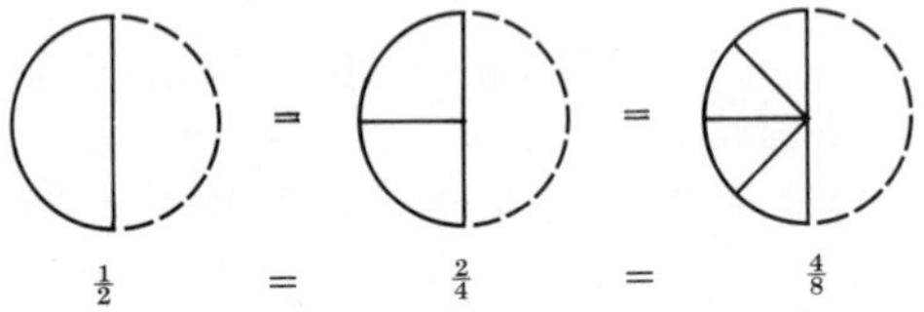

Figure 15.5

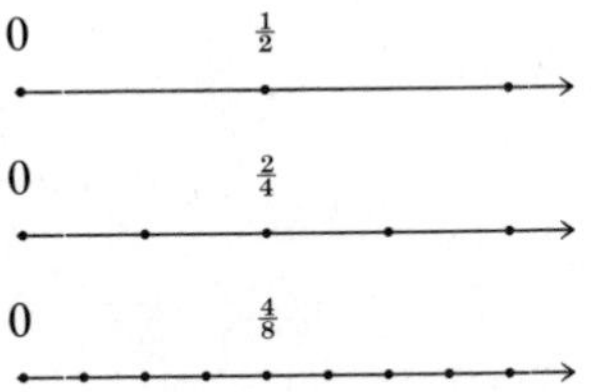

The children interpret such presentations and are guided to write:

$$\tfrac{1}{2} = \tfrac{2}{4} \text{ and } \tfrac{2}{4} = \tfrac{1}{2}$$
$$\tfrac{1}{2} = \tfrac{4}{8} \text{ and } \tfrac{4}{8} = \tfrac{1}{2}$$
$$\tfrac{1}{4} = \tfrac{2}{8} \text{ and } \tfrac{2}{8} = \tfrac{1}{4}$$

At this stage the pupils should practice with the rules that state that the terms of a fraction can be multiplied or divided by the same number without changing the value.

To change $\frac{6}{12}$ to its lowest terms, the children should determine by inspection that 6 is the largest number by which both 6 and 12 can be evenly divided, and divide the terms of the fraction by that number:

$$\frac{6}{12} = \frac{6 \div 6}{12 \div 6} = \frac{1}{2}$$

The fraction $\frac{1}{3}$ is changed to sixths by writing the number question $\frac{1}{3} = \frac{\square}{6}$ or $\frac{1}{3} = \frac{n}{6}$ and thinking: Since the denominator of $\frac{1}{3}$ is multiplied by 2 to get 6, the numerator must also be multiplied by 2.

$$\frac{1}{3} = \frac{2 \times 1}{2 \times 3} = \frac{2}{6}$$

ADDITION WITH FRACTIONS

In addition with fractions, four main types are distinguished:

1. Fractions with like denominators.

2. Fractions with unlike denominators, where the smallest common denominator is one of the given denominators.
3. Fractions with unlike denominators, where the smallest common denominator is the product of the given denominators.
4. Fractions with unlike denominators, where the smallest common denominator is larger than any of the given denominators but smaller than the product of the given denominators.

Illustrations of possible methods of solution of selected cases follow.

Example 1

One week Ted spent $\frac{1}{3}$ of his allowance on supplies and $\frac{1}{3}$ on stamps for his collection. What part of his allowance did Ted spend on supplies and stamps together?

Number question: $\frac{1}{3} + \frac{1}{3} = \square$.

Solutions:

1. The exercise is illustrated on the flannel board or on the magnetic board:

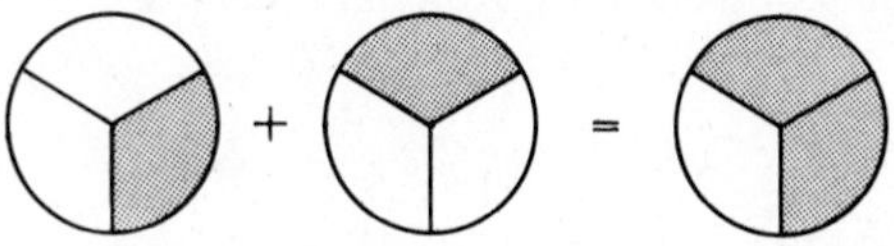

$\frac{1}{3} \quad + \quad \frac{1}{3} \quad = \quad \frac{2}{3}$

2. The process is shown on the number line:

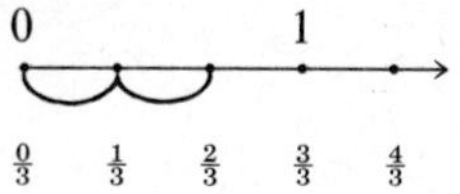

$$\frac{1}{3} + \frac{1}{3} = \frac{1+1}{3} = \frac{2}{3}$$

3. The pupils reason: 1 third + 1 third = 2 thirds, so $\frac{1}{3} + \frac{1}{3} = \frac{2}{3}$. Ted spent $\frac{2}{3}$ of this allowance on supplies and stamps together.

Example 2

From Janet's house to school is $\frac{1}{4}$ mile. How far is it from home to school and back?

Number question: $\frac{1}{4} + \frac{1}{4} = \square$.

Solutions:

1. Cutouts:

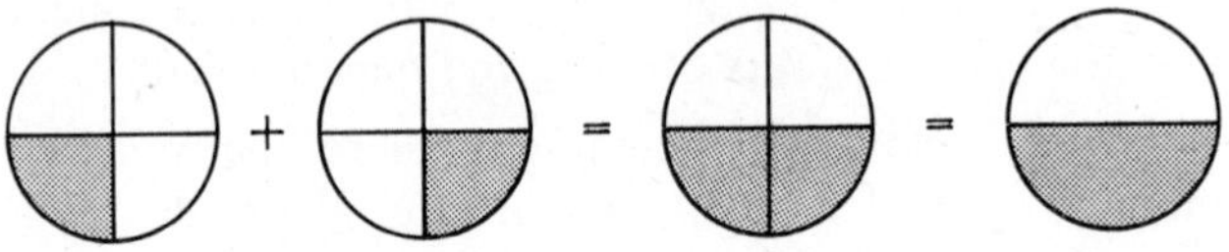

$\frac{1}{4} + \frac{1}{4} = \frac{2}{4} = \frac{1}{2}$

2. Number line:

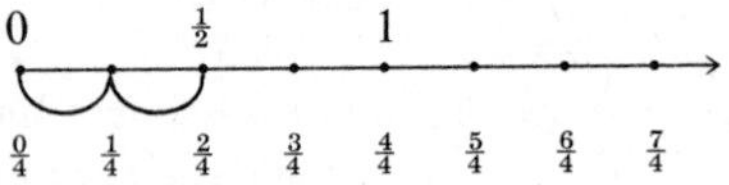

$$\frac{1}{4} + \frac{1}{4} = \frac{1+1}{4} = \frac{2}{4} = \frac{1}{2}$$

3. The pupils reason: 1 fourth + 1 fourth = 2 fourths, so $\frac{1}{4} + \frac{1}{4} = \frac{2}{4} = \frac{1}{2}$. From Janet's house to school and back is $\frac{1}{2}$ mile.

Example 3

Sue buys $\frac{3}{4}$ pound of ham and $\frac{1}{4}$ pound of salami. How much meat does Sue buy in all?

Number question: $\frac{3}{4} + \frac{1}{4} = \square$.

Solutions:

1. Cutouts:

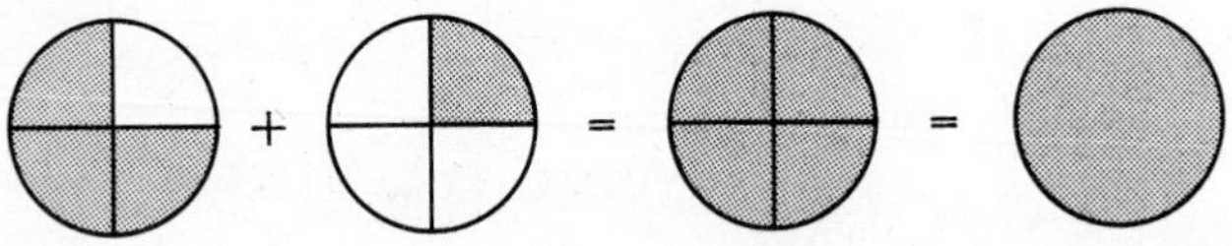

$\frac{3}{4} + \frac{1}{4} = \frac{4}{4} = 1$

2. Number line:

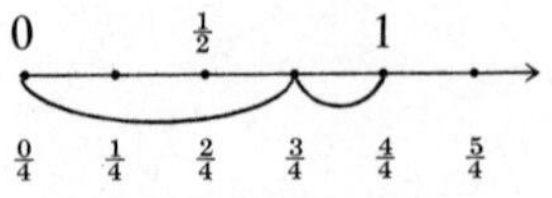

$$\frac{3}{4} + \frac{1}{4} = \frac{3+1}{4} = \frac{4}{4} = 1$$

3. The pupils reason: 3 fourths + 1 fourth = 4 fourths, so $\frac{3}{4} + \frac{1}{4} = \frac{4}{4} = 1$. Sue buys 1 pound of meat.

Example 4

Sam walked $2\frac{3}{4}$ kilometers in the morning and $1\frac{3}{4}$ kilometers in the afternoon. How many kilometers did Sam walk in all?

<u>Number question:</u> $2\frac{3}{4} + 1\frac{3}{4} = \square$.

Solutions:

1. Cutouts:

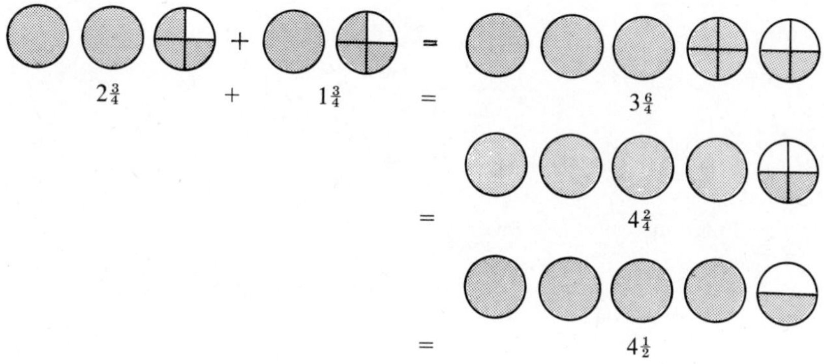

2. Number line:

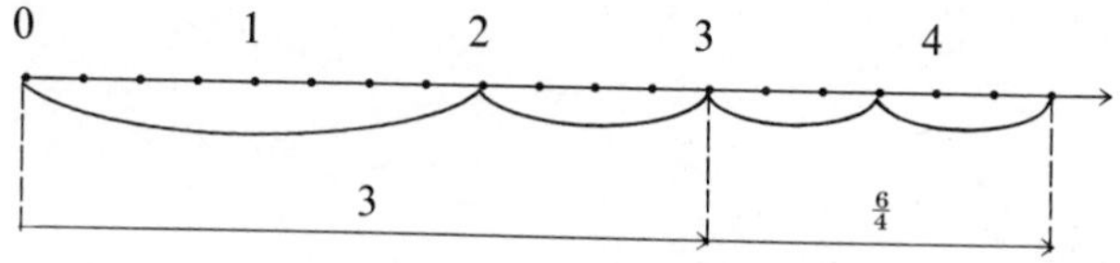

$$2\tfrac{3}{4} + 1\tfrac{3}{4} = (2 + 1) + (\tfrac{3}{4} + \tfrac{3}{4}) = 3 + \tfrac{6}{4} = 4\tfrac{2}{4} = 4\tfrac{1}{2}$$

3. Vertical form of solution:

$$\begin{array}{r} 2\frac{3}{4} \\ +1\frac{3}{4} \\ \hline 4\frac{2}{4} = 4\frac{1}{2} \end{array}$$

Think: $\frac{3}{4} + \frac{3}{4} = \frac{6}{4} = 1\frac{2}{4}$. Write the $\frac{2}{4}$ and remember the 1. $1 + 1 + 2 = 4$. Write the 4. Express $4\frac{2}{4}$ in its simplest form.

Sam walked $4\frac{1}{2}$ kilometers.

Example 5

If one letter weighs $\frac{1}{2}$ ounce and another $\frac{1}{4}$ ounce, how much do the two letters weigh together?

<u>Number question:</u> $\frac{1}{2} + \frac{1}{4} = \square$.

Note: From previous work, the pupils know that the numerators of like fractions are added to find the sum of the fractions. Thus, the fractions $\frac{1}{2}$ and $\frac{1}{4}$ must first be expressed as a pair of like fractions.

Solutions:

1. Cutouts:

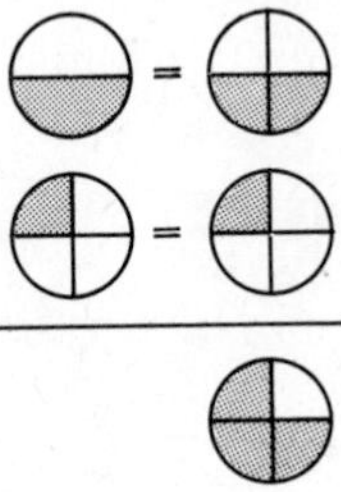

$\frac{1}{2} = \frac{2}{4}$

$\frac{1}{4} = \frac{1}{4}$

$\frac{3}{4}$

2. Fraction board:

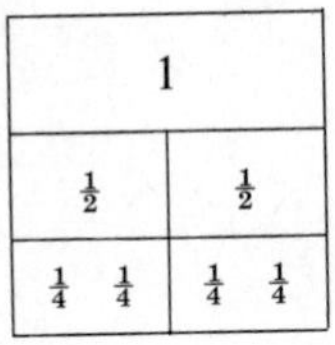

$\frac{1}{2} = \frac{2}{4}$

So $\frac{1}{2} + \frac{1}{4} = \frac{2}{4} + \frac{1}{4} = \frac{3}{4}$

3. Number line:

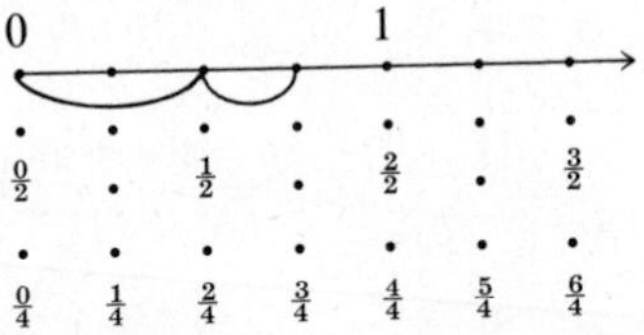

$\frac{1}{2} + \frac{1}{4} = \frac{3}{4}$

The two letters weigh $\frac{3}{4}$ ounce.

Example 6

Helen eats $\frac{1}{2}$ of a chocolate bar and Linda eats $\frac{1}{3}$ of it. What part of the bar is eaten?

Number question: $\frac{1}{2} + \frac{1}{3} = \square$.

Solutions:

1. The larger denominator of $\frac{1}{2}$ and $\frac{1}{3}$ is not a common denominator of the two fractions. By studying a fraction chart, the pupils decide that the smallest common denominator of the fractions is 6:

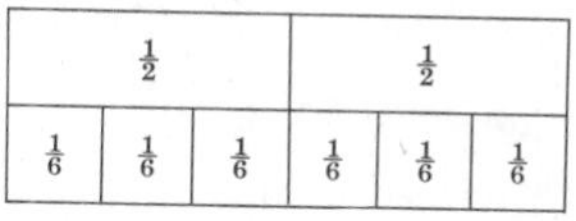

$\frac{1}{2} = \frac{3}{6}$

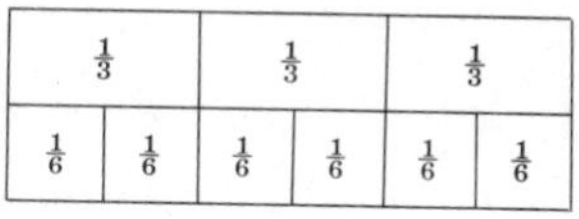

$\frac{1}{3} = \frac{2}{6}$

Then the fractions are expressed as like fractions and added:

$$\frac{1}{2} + \frac{1}{3} = \frac{3}{6} + \frac{2}{6} = \frac{5}{6} \quad \text{or} \quad \begin{array}{r} \frac{1}{2} = \frac{3}{6} \\ +\frac{1}{3} = \frac{2}{6} \\ \hline \frac{5}{6} \end{array}$$

2. Number line:

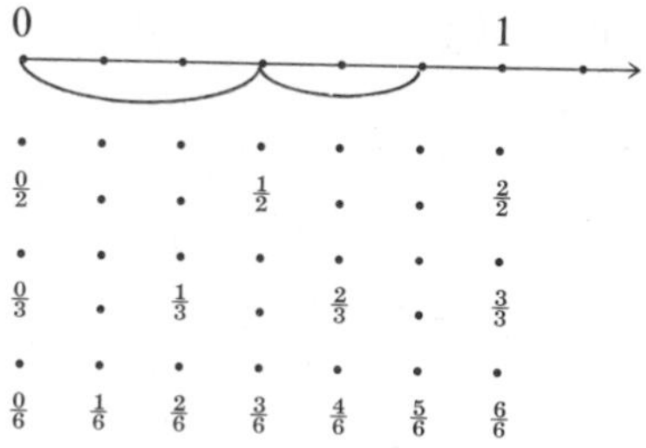

$$\frac{1}{2} + \frac{1}{3} = \frac{3}{6} + \frac{2}{6} = \frac{5}{6}$$

$\frac{5}{6}$ of the bar is eaten.

Who said that teaching fractions is easy?

Example 7

Larry spent $\frac{3}{4}$ hour painting and $\frac{5}{6}$ hour mowing. How long did Larry work?

Number question: $\frac{3}{4} + \frac{5}{6} = \square$.

Solution: To find the smallest common denominator of the given fractions, the pupils are guided to follow this procedure:

Step 1: Determine whether the larger denominator (6) is a common denominator of the fractions under consideration. The larger denominator cannot be evenly divided by 4, and is therefore not a common denominator.

Step 2: Multiply the larger denominator (6) by 2: $2 \times 6 = 12$. Twelve can be evenly divided by both 4 and 6, so 12 is the smallest common denominator. (If 12 were not a multiple of the given denominators, the next step would be to multiply 6 by 3, etc.)
Thus

$$\frac{3}{4} + \frac{5}{6} = \frac{9}{12} + \frac{10}{12} = \frac{19}{12} = 1\frac{7}{12} \quad \text{or} \quad \begin{array}{r} \frac{3}{4} = \frac{9}{12} \\ +\frac{5}{6} = \frac{10}{12} \\ \hline \frac{19}{12} = 1\frac{7}{12}. \end{array}$$

Larry worked $1\frac{7}{12}$ hours.

Example 8

Sally has to add these numbers: $1\frac{3}{4} + 2\frac{1}{6}$, $3\frac{9}{15}$, and $1\frac{4}{25}$. Find the answer for her.

Number question: $1\frac{3}{4} + 2\frac{1}{6} + 3\frac{9}{15} + 1\frac{4}{25} = \square$.

Solution: The technique described in Example 7 above for finding the smallest common denominator is too cumbersome to use in solving a problem such as the one under consideration. Therefore, the pupils find the least common multiple (LCM) of the denominators by the technique described in Chapter 6. Since 300 is the LCM of 4, 6, 15, and 25, and is thus the smallest common denominator of the fractions, each fraction is expressed with a denominator of 300, and the sum of the addends is found:

$$\begin{array}{r} 1\frac{3}{4} = 1\frac{225}{300} \\ 2\frac{1}{6} = 2\frac{50}{300} \\ 3\frac{9}{15} = 3\frac{180}{300} \\ 1\frac{4}{25} = 1\frac{48}{300} \\ \hline 7\frac{503}{300} = 8\frac{203}{300} \end{array}$$

SUBTRACTION WITH FRACTIONS The different types of subtraction with fractions are introduced in order of difficulty. In general, the guidelines presented for addition with fractions can be followed. The student is urged to outline the types of subtraction problems in order of difficulty and to determine whether this sequence is in agreement with the order of presentation in some of the widely used pupils' textbooks.

Illustrations of possible solutions of selected cases follow.

Example 1

Barbara has $\frac{1}{2}$ dozen eggs. She eats $\frac{1}{4}$ dozen. She now has □ dozen eggs left.

Number question: $\frac{1}{2} - \frac{1}{4} = \square$.

Solutions:

1. Fraction chart:

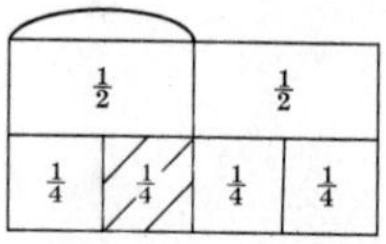

$\frac{1}{2} - \frac{1}{4} = \frac{2}{4} - \frac{1}{4} = \frac{1}{4}$

2. Cutouts:

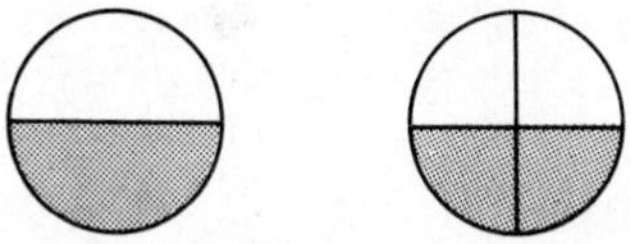

$\frac{1}{2} \quad = \quad \frac{2}{4}$

How much is left if one-fourth is subtracted from two-fourths?

$$\frac{1}{2} - \frac{1}{4} = \frac{2}{4} - \frac{1}{4} = \frac{2-1}{4} = \frac{1}{4}$$

3. Number line:

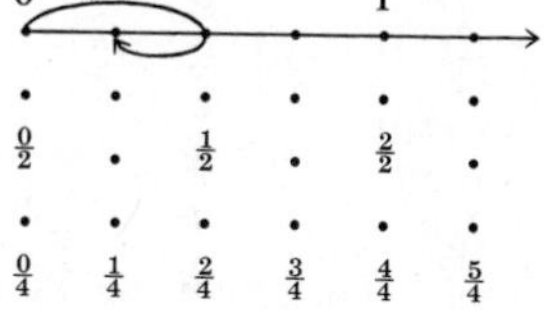

$$\frac{1}{2} - \frac{1}{4} = \frac{2}{4} - \frac{1}{4} = \frac{2-1}{4} = \frac{1}{4}$$

Barbara has $\frac{1}{4}$ dozen eggs left.

Example 2

Ed has $\frac{3}{5}$ meter of copper wire. He used $\frac{1}{4}$ meter. Ed has □ meter of wire left.

Number question: $\frac{3}{5} - \frac{1}{4} = \square$.

Solution:

Think: The smallest number into which 4 and 5 can be evenly divided is 20. Thus 20 is the smallest common denominator of the fractions $\frac{3}{5}$ and $\frac{1}{4}$. The fractions are therefore changed to fractions with a denominator of 20:

$$\frac{3}{5} - \frac{1}{4} = \frac{12}{20} - \frac{5}{20} = \frac{7}{20} \quad \text{or} \quad \begin{array}{r} \frac{3}{5} = \frac{12}{20} \\ -\frac{1}{4} = \frac{5}{20} \\ \hline \frac{7}{20} \end{array}$$

Ed has $\frac{7}{20}$ meter of wire left.

Example 3

Of a road $3\frac{1}{6}$ miles long, $1\frac{3}{4}$ miles are paved. How many miles are not paved?

Number question: $3\frac{1}{6} - 1\frac{3}{4} = \square$.

Solution:

Think: The smallest number into which both 4 and 6 can be evenly divided is 12. Thus 12 is the smallest common denominator of the fractions $\frac{1}{6}$ and $\frac{3}{4}$. The fractions are therefore changed to fractions with a denominator of 12: $3\frac{1}{6} - 1\frac{3}{4} = 3\frac{2}{12} - 1\frac{9}{12}$. Since $\frac{9}{12}$ cannot be subtracted from $\frac{2}{12}$, one whole in the minuend is changed to $\frac{12}{12}$ and added to $\frac{2}{12}$. Then the fractions are subtracted.

$$3\frac{2}{12} - 1\frac{9}{12} = 2\frac{14}{12} - 1\frac{9}{12} = 1\frac{5}{12} \quad \text{or} \quad \begin{array}{r} 3\frac{1}{6} = 3\frac{2}{12} = 2\frac{14}{12} \\ -1\frac{3}{4} = 1\frac{9}{12} = 1\frac{9}{12} \\ \hline 1\frac{5}{12} \end{array}$$

$1\frac{5}{12}$ miles are not paved.

MULTIPLICATION WITH FRACTIONS

In the following presentation of multiplication with fractions, six main types will be considered:

Type I: $5 \times \frac{2}{3} = \square$
Type II: $\frac{3}{4} \times 12 = \square$
Type III: $\frac{1}{3} \times \frac{1}{4} = \square$
Type IV: $3 \times 1\frac{3}{5} = \square$
Type V: $2\frac{1}{3} \times 9 = \square$
Type VI: $1\frac{1}{2} \times 1\frac{1}{4} = \square$

Illustrations of possible methods of solution are presented below.

Type I

Example 1

The space between lines on a sheet of ruled paper is $\frac{1}{4}$ inch. What is the total width of 3 spaces:

Number question: $3 \times \frac{1}{4} = \square$.

Solution: The answer to $3 \times \frac{1}{4} = \square$ can be found by adding $\frac{1}{4}$ three times:

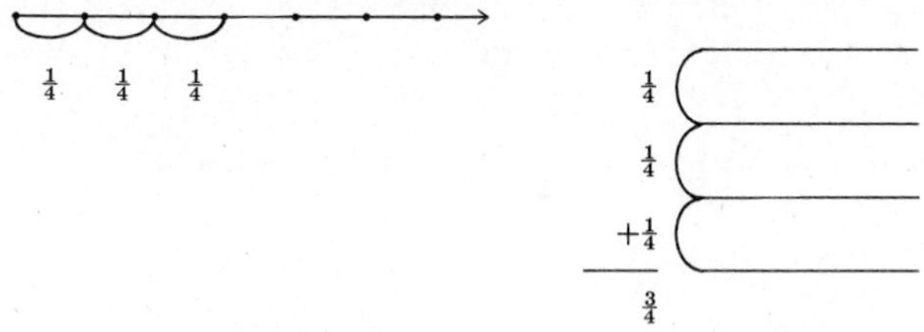

The illustrations indicate that $3 \times \frac{1}{4} = \frac{1}{4} + \frac{1}{4} + \frac{1}{4} = \frac{3}{4}$. This can also be expressed as $3 \times \dfrac{1}{4} = \dfrac{3 \times 1}{4} = \dfrac{3}{4}$. The total width of 3 spaces is $\frac{3}{4}$ inch.

After working several similar exercises, the pupils are guided to formulate the rule: Multiplying the numerator of a fraction by a number multiplies the value of the fraction by that number.

Example 2

The space between lines on ruled paper is $\frac{1}{4}$ inch. What is the total width of 6 spaces?

Number question: $6 \times \frac{1}{4} = \square$.

Solution: The answer to $6 \times \frac{1}{4}$ can be found by adding $\frac{1}{4}$ six times. The answer is then written in its simplest form.

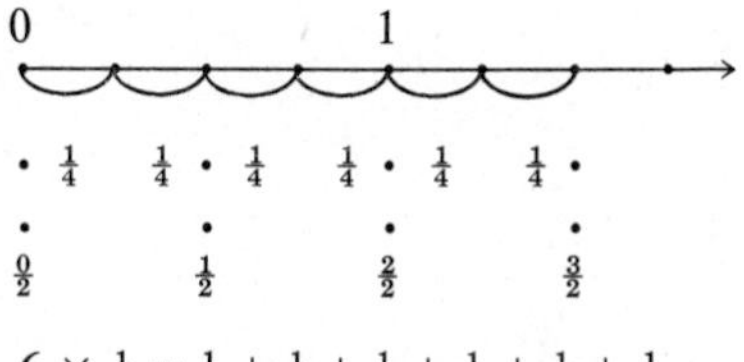

$6 \times \frac{1}{4} = \frac{1}{4} + \frac{1}{4} + \frac{1}{4} + \frac{1}{4} + \frac{1}{4} + \frac{1}{4}$
$= \frac{6}{4} = 1\frac{2}{4} = 1\frac{1}{2}$

or

$$6 \times \frac{1}{4} = \frac{6 \times 1}{4} = \frac{6}{4} = 1\tfrac{2}{4} = 1\tfrac{1}{2}$$

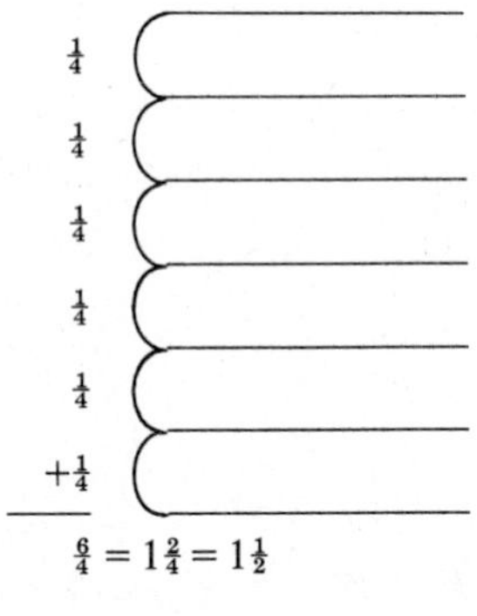

The total width of 6 spaces is $1\frac{1}{2}$ inches.

Type II

Example 1

Ann and Linda sold 9 magazine subscriptions. Ann sold $\frac{2}{3}$ of them and Linda the remainder. How many subscriptions did Ann sell?

Number question: $\frac{2}{3} \times 9 = \square$.

Solution: When this case is presented, the pupils have already worked such exercises as $\frac{1}{2}$ of $6 = 6 \div 2 = 3$, and $\frac{1}{3}$ of $9 = 9 \div 3 = 3$. Since $\frac{2}{3} \times 9$ means 2 out of the 3 equal parts of 9, the product is $2 \times (9 \div 3) = 2 \times 3 = 6$. Ann sold 6 subscriptions.

Assignment: The student should find another method of solution in which the commutative property is used.

Example 2

If it costs 5¢ to use an electric iron for one hour, how much does it cost to use it for $\frac{3}{4}$ hour?

Number question: $\frac{3}{4} \times 5 = \square$.

Solution: Since 5 cannot be evenly divided by 4, another procedure is followed when finding the answer to this number question: $\frac{3}{4} \times 5$ means 3 of the 4 equal parts of 5. Thus $\frac{3}{4} \times 5 = 3 \times \frac{5}{4}$ or $\frac{3 \times 5}{4} = \frac{15}{4} = 3\frac{3}{4}$. It costs $3\frac{3}{4}$¢ to use the electric iron for $\frac{3}{4}$ hour.

Assignment: The student should find an alternative method of solution in which the commutative property is used.

Type III **Example 1**

Mrs. Black bought $\frac{1}{2}$ pound of cheese. She used $\frac{1}{2}$ of the amount she bought for a recipe. What fractional part of a pound did Mrs. Black use?

Number question: $\frac{1}{2} \times \frac{1}{2} = \square$.

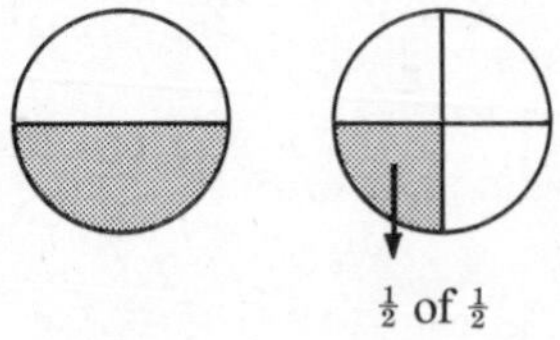

(a) (b)

Solution: In (a), $\frac{1}{2}$ of the circle has been shaded. In (b), a vertical line divides the circle into fourths. One-half of the shaded part of circle (a) equals one-fourth of the whole circle. Thus $\frac{1}{2}$ of $\frac{1}{2} = \frac{1}{4}$, or $\frac{1}{2} \times \frac{1}{2} = \frac{1}{4}$. Mrs. Black used $\frac{1}{4}$ pound of cheese.

It should be observed that the number of equal parts (1) has not changed, but that the size of the parts has become half as large:

$$\frac{1}{2} \times \frac{1}{2} \times \frac{1 \times 1}{2 \times 2} = \frac{1}{4}$$

The number of parts remains the same, since the numerator is multiplied by 1.

The size of the parts becomes half as large, since the denominator is multiplied by 2.

It is important that the pupils understand that multiplying by a number that is less than 1 results in a product that is smaller than the multiplicand.

Example 2

Mr. Farmer has $\frac{3}{4}$ acres of land. He uses $\frac{2}{3}$ of it for a vegetable garden. What fractional part of an acre is Mr. Farmer's vegetable garden?

Number question: $\frac{2}{3} \times \frac{3}{4} = \square$.

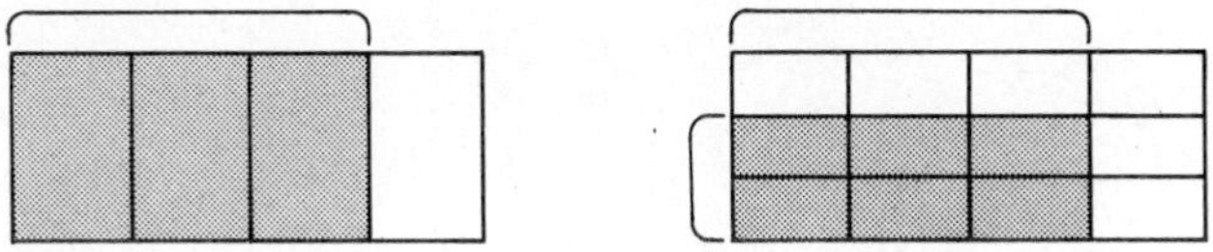

$\frac{2}{3}$ of $\frac{3}{4}$

(a) (b)

Solution: In (a), $\frac{3}{4}$ of the unit is shaded. In (b), the unit has been divided by horizontal lines into three equal parts, resulting in 12 small rectangles. Three-fourths of the unit equals 9 small rectangles, and $\frac{2}{3} \times 9$ small rectangles = 6 small rectangles, or $\frac{6}{12}$ of the unit. Thus $\frac{2}{3}$ of $\frac{3}{4} = \frac{6}{12} = \frac{1}{2}$. Mr. Farmer's vegetable garden is $\frac{6}{12}$ acre, or $\frac{1}{2}$ acre.

After working several similar exercises, the pupils are guided to formulate the rule for this case: Multiply the numerators and the denominators and, if necessary, write the answer in its simplest form. This leads to the common algorism: $\frac{2}{3} \times \frac{3}{4} = \frac{2 \times 3}{3 \times 4} = \frac{6}{12} = \frac{1}{2}$.

Example **Type IV**

Jane wanted to make 6 earrings for a craft project. Each ring would take $2\frac{3}{4}$ inches of copper metal strip. How many inches of copper metal strip did Jane have to buy?

Number question: $6 \times 2\frac{3}{4} = \square$.

Solutions:

1. Number line:

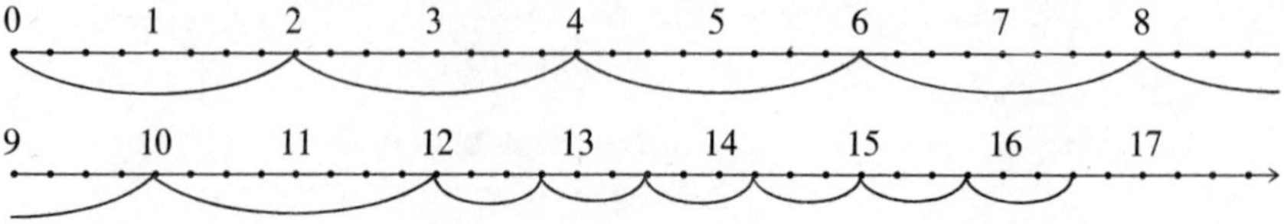

$$2\tfrac{3}{4} + 2\tfrac{3}{4} + 2\tfrac{3}{4} + 2\tfrac{3}{4} + 2\tfrac{3}{4} + 2\tfrac{3}{4} = 12\tfrac{18}{4} = 16\tfrac{2}{4} = 16\tfrac{1}{2}$$

2. Horizontal form:

   Think: $2\frac{3}{4} = 2 + \frac{3}{4}$. Thus

   $6 \times 2\frac{3}{4} = 6 \times (2 + \frac{3}{4}) = (6 \times 2) + (6 \times \frac{3}{4}) = 12 + \frac{18}{4} = 16\frac{2}{4} = 16\frac{1}{2}$.

3. Vertical form:

$$\begin{array}{r} 2\frac{3}{4} \\ \times 6 \\ \hline 12\frac{18}{4} \end{array} = 16\tfrac{2}{4} = 16\tfrac{1}{2}.$$

4. Using improper fractions:

$$6 \times 2\tfrac{3}{4} = 6 \times \frac{11}{4} = \frac{6}{1} \times \frac{11}{4} = \frac{6 \times 11}{1 \times 4} = \frac{66}{4} = 16\tfrac{2}{4} = 16\tfrac{1}{2}.$$

Jane had to buy $16\frac{1}{2}$ inches of copper metal strip.

Type V **Example**

Dave went on a $1\frac{1}{2}$-hour hike. He walked an average of 4 miles per hour. How many miles did Dave walk?

Number question: $1\frac{1}{2} \times 4 = \square$.

Solutions:

1. Horizontal form:

   Think: $1\frac{1}{2} = 1 + \frac{1}{2}$. Thus

$$1\tfrac{1}{2} \times 4 = (1 + \tfrac{1}{2}) \times 4 = (1 \times 4) + (\tfrac{1}{2} \times 4) = 4 + 2 = 6.$$

2. Using improper fractions:

$$1\tfrac{1}{2} \times 4 = \frac{3}{2} \times \frac{4}{1} = \frac{3 \times 4}{2 \times 1} = \frac{12}{2} = 6.$$

3. Using the commutative property:

   Think:

   $1\frac{1}{2} \times 4 = 4 \times 1\frac{1}{2} = 4 \times (1 + \frac{1}{2}) = (4 \times 1) + (4 \times \frac{1}{2}) = 4 + 2 = 6.$

Dave walked 6 miles.

Type VI

Example

Ronald went on a $3\frac{1}{2}$-hour hike. He averaged $3\frac{1}{4}$ miles per hour. How many miles did Ronald hike?

Number question: $3\frac{1}{2} \times 3\frac{1}{4} = \square$.

Solution:

Think: $3\frac{1}{2} = \frac{7}{2}$ and $3\frac{1}{4} = \frac{13}{4}$. Thus

$$3\tfrac{1}{2} \times 3\tfrac{1}{4} = \frac{7}{2} \times \frac{13}{4} = \frac{7 \times 13}{2 \times 4} = \frac{91}{8} = 11\tfrac{3}{8}.$$

Ronald hiked $11\frac{3}{8}$ miles.

Dividing before Multiplying

The process of multiplying with fractions can sometimes be shortened by dividing out factors common to both a numerator and a denominator of the fractions before multiplying.

Examples

$$\frac{4}{7} \times \frac{1}{8} = \frac{4 \times 1}{7 \times 8} = \frac{\overset{1}{\cancel{4}} \times 1}{7 \times \underset{1}{\cancel{4}} \times 2} = \frac{1}{14}$$

$$\frac{\overset{1}{\cancel{3}}}{\underset{1}{\cancel{5}}} \times \frac{\overset{1}{\cancel{5}}}{\underset{4}{\cancel{12}}} = \frac{1}{4} \qquad \frac{1}{\underset{1}{\cancel{4}}} \times \frac{\overset{2}{\cancel{8}}}{\underset{3}{\cancel{9}}} \times \frac{\overset{1}{\cancel{3}}}{5} = \frac{2}{15}$$

This process is often called *cancellation*. Since this term is misleading, it is better to use the expression *dividing before multiplying*.

DIVISION WITH FRACTIONS

In division with fractions, six main types will be considered:

Type I: $2 \div \frac{1}{4} = \square$
Type II: $\frac{1}{4} \div 2 = \square$
Type III: $\frac{1}{2} \div \frac{1}{3} = \square$
Type IV: $18 \div 2\frac{1}{2} = \square$
Type V: $7\frac{2}{3} \div 2 = \square$
Type VI: $3\frac{1}{2} \div 1\frac{1}{2} = \square$

Illustrations of possible methods of solution follow.

Type I

Example 1

Two acres of land is divided into building lots of $\frac{1}{2}$ acre each. How many lots can be sold?

Number question: $2 \div \frac{1}{2} = \square$.

Solutions: In this situation, a measurement division is involved. Various methods of solution are available:

1. Serial subtraction:
   The pupils determine by serial subtraction how many times $\frac{1}{2}$ is contained in 2. Since 4 halves equal 2, $2 \div \frac{1}{2} = 4$. Four lots can be sold.

$$\begin{array}{rl} 2 & \\ -\frac{1}{2} & (1) \\ \hline 1\frac{1}{2} & \\ -\frac{1}{2} & (2) \\ \hline 1 & \\ -\frac{1}{2} & (3) \\ \hline \frac{1}{2} & \\ -\frac{1}{2} & (4) \\ \hline 0 & \end{array}$$

2. Diagrams:

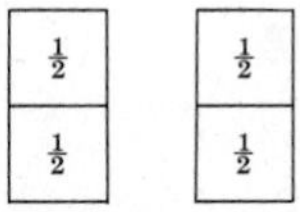

   The diagrams illustrate that 2 halves equal 1 whole. Thus, 4 halves equal 2 wholes.

$$2 \div \tfrac{1}{2} = 4$$

3. Number line:

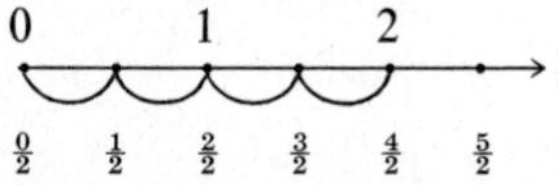

   By counting the spaces it is determined that 4 halves equal 2.
4. Common demoninator method:

$$2 \div \frac{1}{2} = \frac{4}{2} \div \frac{1}{2} = \frac{4 \div 1}{2 \div 2} = \frac{4}{1} = 4.$$

   Two is changed to an improper fraction with the same denominator as the fraction $\frac{1}{2}$. Since the quotient of the denominators is 1, the answer to the division question is the quotient of the numerators ($4 \div 1 = 4$).
5. Inversion method:
   The dividend is multiplied by the reciprocal of the divisor. Therefore the pupils should first learn to find the reciprocal of a number. (The term "reciprocal" was introduced previously in this chapter.)

   For a meaningful development of the inversion method, the number line can be used. To solve the number question under consideration, halves are marked on the line and the mathematical sentence stating that $2 \div \frac{1}{2}$ equals 2 times 2 halves is written:

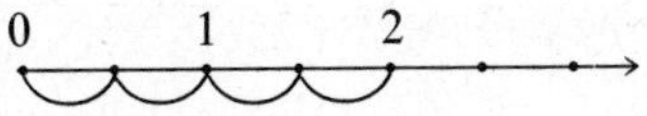

$$2 \div \tfrac{1}{2} = 2 \times 2 = 4$$

The teacher points out that 2 can be written as $\frac{2}{1}$ and asks whether the following sentence is true:

$$2 \div \frac{1}{2} = \frac{2}{1} \times \frac{2}{1} = \frac{2 \times 2}{1 \times 1} = \frac{4}{1} = 4$$

Several other exercises are then presented, including those that have multipart fractions as divisors, as in the following example.

Example 2

Three acres of land was divided into building lots of $\frac{3}{4}$ acre each. How many building lots could be sold?

Number question: $3 \div \frac{3}{4} = \square$.

Solution: The answer to this number question can be found in ways similar to those used in the immediately preceding example. The inversion method is developed below.

The number line or a diagram can be used to show how many fourths are contained in 3:

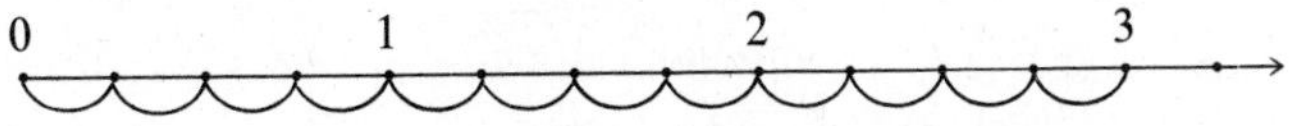

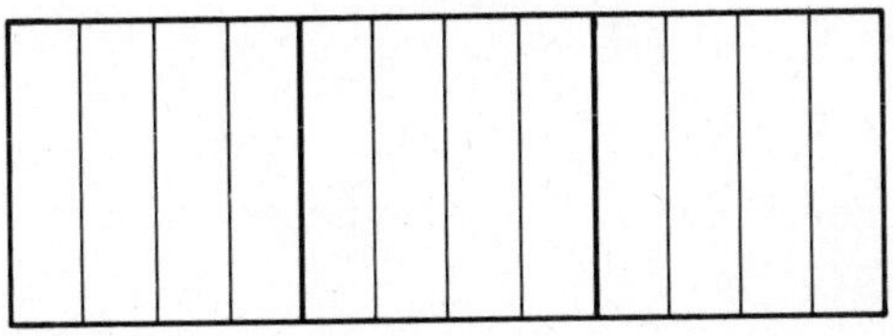

Twelve fourths equal 3. Thus

$$3 \div \frac{1}{4} = \frac{3}{1} \times \frac{4}{1} = \frac{3 \times 4}{1 \times 1} = \frac{12}{1} = 12.$$

What happens to the number of parts if the 3 acres are not divided into parts of $\frac{1}{4}$ acre, but into parts of $\frac{3}{4}$ acre each? Since the *size* of the parts becomes 3 times as large, the *number* of parts becomes 3 times as small. Instead of 12 lots, there are now only 4 lots available. Thus

$$3 \div \frac{3}{4} = \frac{3 \times 4}{3} = \frac{12}{3} = 4.$$

↑ ————The number of parts becomes 3 times as small.

This sentence can be written as:

$$3 \div \frac{3}{4} = \frac{3}{1} \times \frac{4}{3} = \frac{3 \times 4}{1 \times 3} = \frac{12}{3} = 4.$$

A great deal of class discussion and much practice should precede the rule: When dividing by a number expressed as a fraction, multiply the dividend by the reciprocal of the divisor.

Though probably only the brightest pupils will understand the rationale of the inversion method, the teacher should put forth efforts to present the process clearly, and certainly should be able to explain the method as well.

The inversion method can be justified as follows:

$3 \div \frac{3}{4} = \frac{3}{\frac{3}{4}}$ The division is expressed in a different way.

$= \frac{3 \times \frac{4}{3}}{\frac{3}{4} \times \frac{4}{3}}$ Multiplying the dividend and the divisor of a division by the same number does not change the quotient.

$= \frac{3 \times \frac{4}{3}}{1}$ $\frac{3}{4} \times \frac{4}{3} = 1$

$= 3 \times \frac{4}{3}$ If the divisor is 1, the quotient is equal to the dividend.

Type II **Example**

If $\frac{1}{2}$ pound of cheese is equally divided between 2 boys, what fraction of a pound does each boy get?

Number question: $\frac{1}{2} \div 2 = \square$.

Solutions:

1. Diagram:

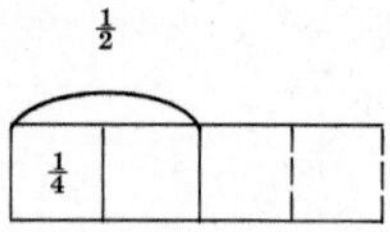

$\frac{1}{2} \div 2 = \frac{1}{4}$

2. Number line:

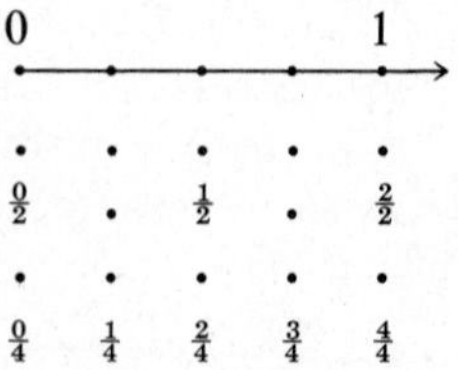

$\frac{1}{2} \div 2 = \frac{1}{4}$

3. Common denominator method:

$$\frac{1}{2} \div 2 = \frac{1}{2} \div \frac{4}{2} = \frac{1 \div 4}{2 \div 2} = \frac{\frac{1}{4}}{1} = \frac{1}{4}.$$

4. Inversion method:

$$\frac{1}{2} \div 2 = \frac{1}{2} \div \frac{2}{1} = \frac{1}{2} \times \frac{1}{2} = \frac{1 \times 1}{2 \times 2} = \frac{1}{4}.$$

Each boy gets $\frac{1}{4}$ pound of cheese.

Example **Type III**

A contractor has to pave a $\frac{1}{2}$-mile road. He can pave $\frac{1}{4}$ mile per day. How many days will it take him to pave the road?

Number question: $\frac{1}{2} \div \frac{1}{4} = \square$.

Solutions:

1. Common denominator method:

$$\frac{1}{2} \div \frac{1}{4} = \frac{2}{4} \div \frac{1}{4} = \frac{2 \div 1}{4 \div 4} = \frac{2}{1} = 2.$$

2. Inversion method:

$$\frac{1}{2} \div \frac{1}{4} = \frac{1}{2} \times \frac{4}{1} = \frac{1 \times \overset{2}{\cancel{4}}}{\underset{1}{\cancel{2}} \times 1} = \frac{2}{1} = 2.$$

It will take the contractor 2 days to pave the road.

Remark: It is recommended that the pupils use the inversion method as the regular method for working division exercises involving fractions. The common denominator method and other applicable methods of solution should be used from time to time to check the correctness of an answer.

Example **Type IV**

Ray took a 14-mile hike. He walked an average of $3\frac{1}{2}$ miles per hour. How long did the hike take?

Number question: $14 \div 3\frac{1}{2} = \square$.

Solution: $14 \div 3\frac{1}{2} = \frac{14}{1} \div \frac{7}{2} = \frac{\overset{2}{\cancel{14}}}{1} \times \frac{2}{\underset{1}{\cancel{7}}} = \frac{2 \times 2}{1 \times 1} = \frac{4}{1} = 4.$

The hike took 4 hours.

Check: $14 \div 3\frac{1}{2} = \frac{28}{2} \div \frac{7}{2} = \frac{28 \div 7}{2 \div 2} = \frac{4}{1} = 4.$

Type V **Example**

$5\frac{3}{4}$ yards of ribbon is divided into 2 equal parts. How long is each part?

Number question: $5\frac{3}{4} \div 2 = \square$.

Solution: $5\frac{3}{4} \div 2 = \frac{23}{4} \div \frac{2}{1} = \frac{23}{4} \times \frac{1}{2} = \frac{23 \times 1}{4 \times 2} = \frac{23}{8} = 2\frac{7}{8}$.

Each part is $2\frac{7}{8}$ yards.

Check: $5\frac{3}{4} \div 2 = \frac{23}{4} \div \frac{8}{4} = \frac{23 \div 8}{4 \div 4} = \frac{\frac{23}{8}}{1} = \frac{23}{8} = 2\frac{7}{8}$.

Type VI **Example**

Rex walked $12\frac{1}{4}$ miles. He averaged $3\frac{1}{2}$ miles per hour. How long did it take him to walk the $12\frac{1}{4}$ miles?

Number question: $12\frac{1}{4} \div 3\frac{1}{2} = \square$.

Solution: $12\frac{1}{4} \div 3\frac{1}{2} = \frac{49}{4} \div \frac{7}{2} = \frac{\overset{7}{\cancel{49}}}{\underset{2}{\cancel{4}}} \times \frac{\overset{1}{\cancel{2}}}{\underset{1}{\cancel{7}}} = \frac{7 \times 1}{2 \times 1} = \frac{7}{2} = 3\frac{1}{2}$.

It took Rex $3\frac{1}{2}$ hours to walk $12\frac{1}{4}$ miles.

Check: $12\frac{1}{4} \div 3\frac{1}{2} = \frac{49}{4} \div \frac{7}{2} = \frac{49}{4} \div \frac{14}{4} = \frac{49 \div 14}{4 \div 4} = \frac{\frac{49}{14}}{1} = \frac{49}{14} = 3\frac{7}{14} = 3\frac{1}{2}$.

SELECTED RESEARCH

This study[1] was concerned with difficulties in multiplication with fractions that result from teaching division with fractions by the common denominator method.

The sample consisted of twenty sixth-grade classes. The instructional period lasted three weeks. A pre-test, a post-test, and a test three weeks after the close of the instructional period were administered.

The following findings were reported:

1. With reference to the ability to multiply with fractions immediately after instruction, the inversion method of teaching divi-

---

1. L. R. Capps, "Division of Fractions," *The Arithmetic Teacher* (January, 1962), pp. 10–16.

sion with fractions yielded significantly better results than the common denominator method.

2. With reference to the ability to multiply with fractions three weeks after the close of the instructional period, the groups showed significant differences in favor of the inversion method.
3. During the three-week retention period without review of fraction processes, the common denominator group gained significantly in the ability to multiply with fractions. In the same period, the inversion group showed no significant change.

The investigator concluded that many facets of the two methods need further investigation before either can be condemned or commended.

SELECTED ACTIVITIES FOR PUPILS

1. Show on the number line: $\frac{5}{8} + \frac{3}{8} = 1$.
2. Show on the number line: $1 - \frac{3}{4} = \frac{1}{4}$.
3. Show on the number line: $5 \times \frac{2}{3} = 3\frac{1}{3}$.
4. Show on the number line: $2 \div \frac{1}{2} = 4$.
5. Write on the six faces of a sugar cube $\frac{1}{2}$, $\frac{1}{4}$, $\frac{3}{8}$, 1, $1\frac{1}{2}$, and 5, and, on another cube, $\frac{2}{3}$, $\frac{3}{4}$, 2, $\frac{1}{8}$, $\frac{7}{8}$, and 3. Roll the two cubes. Find the sum of the numbers expressed on the top faces. Repeat the activity several times.
6. Repeat Activity 5. Now subtract the smaller number from the larger number.
7. Repeat Activity 5. Now find the product of the numbers.
8. Repeat Activity 5. Now find the quotient of the numbers. Let the larger number be the dividend.
9. Let A stand for $\frac{1}{2}$, B for $\frac{2}{2}$, C for $\frac{3}{2}$, D for $\frac{4}{2}$ and so on, with Z being $\frac{26}{2}$. Write all the letters with the corresponding numerals under them.
   a. Which letter stands for a fraction that expresses a number less than 1?
   b. Which letters stand for fractions that can be renamed as whole numbers?
   c. Which letters stand for fractions that can be renamed as mixed fractions?

d. Write the fractions for the following letters and perform the indicated computations. Write the answers in simplest terms.

A + C E ÷ A I − E G × Y

10. $3\frac{1}{3} \times 30 = (3 \times 30) + (\frac{1}{3} \times 30)$
$= 90 + 10$
$= 100$

Use the same procedure to work these exercises:

$5\frac{1}{5} \times 15 = \square$ $7\frac{1}{2} \times 40 = \square$ $6\frac{1}{9} \times 90 = \square$

11. Write in order from the least to the greatest.

$1\frac{1}{2}$ $\frac{9}{8}$ $1\frac{3}{4}$ $1\frac{2}{3}$ $\frac{7}{4}$

12. Explain why these shortcuts work for adding and subtracting with unit fractions:

$$\frac{1}{2} + \frac{1}{3} = \frac{2+3}{2 \times 3} = \frac{5}{6} \qquad \frac{1}{2} - \frac{1}{3} = \frac{3-2}{2 \times 3} = \frac{1}{6}$$

13. Write =, <, or > to make a true statement.

$10 - 2\frac{1}{2} \bigcirc 5 \times 1\frac{1}{2}$ $2\frac{1}{2} + 1\frac{1}{2} \bigcirc 4 \times \frac{3}{4}$ $3 - \frac{1}{4} \bigcirc 15 - 2\frac{1}{4}$

EXERCISES

1. Distinguish between fractional numbers and fractions.
2. Give an example of—
   a. a mixed fraction.
   b. an improper fraction.
   c. a unit fraction.
   d. a proper fraction.
   e. a pair of equivalent fractions.
3. Name and give examples of several properties of fractional numbers.
4. List some activities that a first-grade teacher might select for the purpose of developing the concept of fractional numbers.
5. Suggest two possible methods of solution for the following number question: $1\frac{3}{5} \div 2\frac{1}{2} = \square$.
6. Explain and illustrate how you would teach children to find the lowest common denominator of the fractions $\frac{5}{6}$ and $\frac{4}{9}$.
7. Find the LCM of the denominators of the fractions $\frac{1}{6}$, $\frac{5}{8}$, $\frac{2}{15}$, and $\frac{7}{20}$.
8. Write an illustrative lesson dealing with the case in which a whole number is multiplied by a fractional number.
9. Justify the inversion method.

10. Report on a piece of research on the teaching of fractions.
11. Diagnose the mistakes made in the following presentations.

$$\frac{1}{4}+\frac{1}{4}=\frac{2}{8} \quad \frac{3}{5}-\frac{1}{2}=\frac{2}{3} \quad \frac{2}{5}\times\frac{2}{5}=\frac{4}{5} \quad \frac{8}{9}\div\frac{2}{9}=\frac{4}{9}$$

SOURCES FOR FURTHER READING

Ashlock, R. B., *Error Patterns in Computation.* Columbus: Charles E. Merrill Publishing Company, 1972.

Bruni, J. V., and H. Silverman, "An Introduction to Fractions," *The Arithmetic Teacher,* November, 1975, pp. 538–545.

D'Augustine, C. H., *Multiple Methods of Teaching Mathematics in the Elementary School,* 2nd ed. New York: Harper & Row, Publishers, 1973, Chaps. X–XII.

Duquette, R. J., "Some Thoughts on Piaget's Findings and the Teaching of Fractions," *The Arithmetic Teacher,* April, 1972, pp. 273–275.

Green, G. F., Jr., "A Model for Teaching Multiplication of Fractional Numbers," *The Arithmetic Teacher,* January, 1973, pp. 5–9.

Heddens, J. W., *Today's Mathematics,* 3d ed. Chicago: Science Research Associates, Inc., 1974, Units XII–XIV.

Kennedy, L. M., *Guiding Children to Mathematical Discovery,* 2nd ed. Belmont, California: Wadsworth Publishing Company, Inc., 1975, Chaps. XI, XII.

Marks, J. L., C. R. Purdy, L. B. Kinney, and A. A. Hiatt, *Teaching Elementary School Mathematics for Understanding,* 4th ed. New York: McGraw-Hill Book Company, 1975, Chap. VII.

National Council of Teachers of Mathematics, *Topics in Mathematics, Twenty-ninth Yearbook.* Washington, D.C.: The Council, 1964, Bklt. 6.

Schminke, C. W., N. Maertens, and W. R. Arnold, *Teaching the Child Mathematics.* Hinsdale, Illinois: The Dryden Press, Inc., 1973, Chap. IX.

Sowder, L., "Criteria for Concrete Models," *The Arithmetic Teacher,* October, 1976, pp. 468–470.

Spitzer, H. F., *Teaching Elementary School Mathematics.* Boston: Houghton Mifflin Company, 1967, Chaps. IX, X.

Decimals 16

In the preceding chapter, common fractions were presented as a form in which fractional numbers can be expressed. In this chapter, another form of expressing such numbers will be considered—namely *decimals,* also called *decimal fractions*.

The use of decimals instead of common fractions facilitates considerably the computation and comparison of fractional numbers, since the understood denominator of decimals is a power of ten. For example, it is easier to add or compare .75 and .72 than $\frac{3}{4}$ and $\frac{18}{25}$.

Decimals are widely used in daily life, and almost exclusively in scientific and technical work. Also, the inclusion of the metric system in the curriculum and the use of the hand-held calculator will result in an earlier introduction and increased use of decimals. The elementary-school pupil should therefore develop an understanding of decimals and reasonable skill in working with them.

SKILLS TEST

1. 4.6 + 7.9 + 4.2 = 104.06 + 2.26 + 3.8 =
   21.33 + 25 + 49.6 = 200.003 + 1.65 + 9.9 =
2. \$150.20 + \$13 + \$16.36 = \$900.41 + \$1.26 + \$.06 =
   \$16 + \$.33 + \$1.10 = \$19.96 + \$1.70 + \$2 =
3. 46.25 − 19.77 = 50.56 − 6.9 = 71 − 1.19 =
   70.02 − 69.65 = 290.04 − 13.136 = 80 − 15.6 =

4. $100 − $3.75 = $60.80 − $50.90 = $11 − $.73 =
   $10 − $6.84 = $700.04 − $555.55 = $24 − $5.86 =
5. 6 × .9 = .9 × .8 = 1.2 × 3.65 = .18 × 9.4 =
   .7 × 8 = .06 × .4 = .17 × .77 = 1.31 × 6.1 =
6. 5 × $3.73 = 13 × $2.57 = 29 × $.75 = 66 × $15.20 =
   9 × $9.04 = 17 × $1.06 = 44 × $.19 = 78 × $10.42 =
7. 12.5 ÷ 5 = 2.5 ÷ 5 = 38 ÷ 7.6 = 46.2 ÷ 6.6 =
   78.4 ÷ 7 = 3.69 ÷ 9 = 47 ÷ 9.4 = 77.4 ÷ 8.6 =
8. 328.7 ÷ 17.3 = $47.70 ÷ 9 = $1,102.20 ÷ 15 =
   543.4 ÷ 24.7 = $120.40 ÷ 7 = $1,531.35 ÷ 45 =
9. What decimal part of 24 is 6? What decimal part of 45 is 9?
10. Round to the nearest tenth:

    16.66 25.94 18.47 16.251 6.922

11. Round to the nearest dollar:

    $15.49 $6.50 $8.71 $20.29 $8.62

12. Round to the nearest cent:

    $1.555 $2.375 $6.008 $9.104 $2.906

13. Change these fractions to decimals:

    $\frac{5}{8}$ $\frac{3}{4}$ $\frac{5}{16}$ $\frac{7}{25}$ $\frac{3}{5}$ $\frac{9}{10}$

14. Change these decimals to fractions, and express the fractions in lowest terms:

    .15 .255 .8 .875 .175 .27

15. Write in figures:
    a. five hundred and three thousandths
    b. five hundred three thousandths
    c. fifty-five and fifty-five thousandths
    d. five and five thousandths

MEANING, TERMS, AND NOTATION

The fractions $\frac{4}{10}$, $\frac{16}{100}$, and $\frac{125}{1000}$ can be rewritten as *decimals* in this way: .4, .16, and .125. Thus, in decimals, the positional-value system is extended to places to the right of the ones place, which is identified by the decimal point.

Terminating and Repeating Decimals

Some fractions can be expressed as terminating decimals, others as repeating decimals. The denominators of fractions such as $\frac{2}{5}$, $\frac{7}{20}$, and $\frac{9}{50}$ have only those prime factors that are prime factors of 10 (2 and 5), and the fractions are expressed in simplest form. If the division indicated by such a fraction is performed, the process terminates, and the result is called a *terminating decimal.*

Examples

$$
\begin{array}{r}
.4 \\
5\overline{)2.0} \\
\underline{2\,0} \\
0
\end{array}
\qquad
\begin{array}{r}
.35 \\
20\overline{)7.00} \\
\underline{6\,0} \\
1\,00 \\
\underline{1\,00} \\
0
\end{array}
\qquad
\begin{array}{r}
.18 \\
50\overline{)9.00} \\
\underline{5\,0} \\
4\,00 \\
\underline{4\,00} \\
0
\end{array}
$$

$\frac{2}{5} = .4$ $\quad$ $\frac{7}{20} = .35$ $\quad$ $\frac{9}{50} = .18$

The denominators of fractions such as $\frac{1}{9}$ and $\frac{1}{6}$ have prime factors other than 2 and 5, and the fractions are expressed in simplest form. If the division indicated by such fractions is performed, the process does not terminate, but a repeating pattern is observed in the quotient. The result is called a *repeating decimal.*

Examples

$$
\begin{array}{r}
.11\overline{1}\cdots \\
9\overline{)1.000\cdots} \\
\underline{9} \\
10 \\
\underline{9} \\
10 \\
\underline{9} \\
1
\end{array}
\qquad
\begin{array}{r}
.166\overline{6}\cdots \\
6\overline{)1.0000\cdots} \\
\underline{6} \\
40 \\
\underline{36} \\
40 \\
\underline{36} \\
40 \\
\underline{36} \\
4
\end{array}
$$

$\frac{1}{9} = .11\overline{1}\cdots$ $\quad$ $\frac{1}{6} = .166\overline{6}\cdots$

In a repeating decimal a bar is sometimes drawn over the cycle that repeats, or both a bar and three dots are used.

Examples

$\frac{1}{3} = .\overline{3}$; $\quad$ $\frac{5}{11} = .45\overline{45}$; $\quad$ $\frac{1}{9} = .11\overline{1}$ or $.11\overline{1}\cdots$

It is interesting to observe how a fraction such as $\frac{1}{9}$ can be expressed as the sum of a set of fractions that have denominators that are powers of 10:

$$\frac{1}{9} = \frac{10}{90} = \frac{9}{90} + \frac{1}{90} = \boxed{\frac{1}{10}} + \frac{1}{90}$$

and

$$\frac{1}{90} = \frac{10}{900} = \frac{9}{900} + \frac{1}{900} = \boxed{\frac{1}{100}} + \frac{1}{900}$$

and

$$\frac{1}{900} = \frac{10}{9000} = \frac{9}{9000} + \frac{1}{9000} = \boxed{\frac{1}{1000}} + \frac{1}{9000}, \text{ etc.}$$

Thus

$$\frac{1}{9} = \frac{1}{10} + \frac{1}{100} + \frac{1}{1000} + \cdots$$

or

$$\frac{1}{9} = .1 + .01 + .001 + \cdots = .11\overline{1}\cdots.$$

Notation The decimal point is only a device to indicate the ones place. The ones place is the center in our system of notation, as can be inferred from Figure 16.1. The tens are located one place to the left of the ones, and the tenths place is one step to the right of the ones. The hundreds are

1,000	100	10	1	.1	.01	.001
10^3	10^2	10^1	10^0	10^{-1}	10^{-2}	10^{-3}
thousands	hundreds	tens	ones	tenths	hundredths	thousandths
1	1	1	1	1	1	1

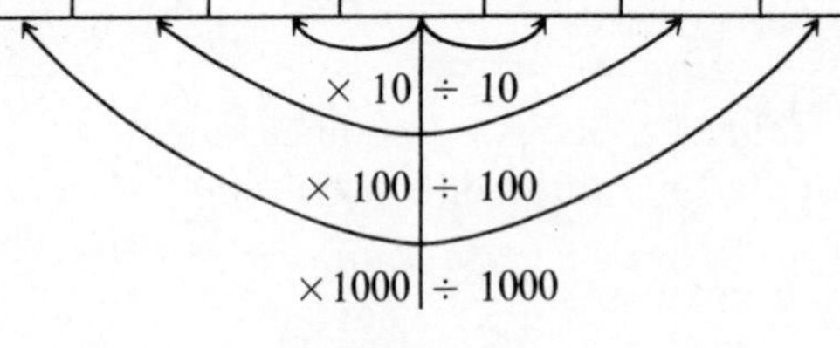

Figure 16.1

located two places to the left of the ones, and the hundredths place is two steps to the right of the ones, etc.

From Figure 16.1, the following statement can be derived:

$$\begin{aligned} 1{,}111.111 &= 1(10^3) + 1(10^2) + 1(10^1) + 1(10^0) \\ &= 1(10^{-1}) + 1(10^{-2}) + 1(10^{-3}) \\ &= 1{,}000 + 100 + 10 + 1 + \tfrac{1}{10} + \tfrac{1}{100} + \tfrac{1}{1000} \\ &= 1{,}000 + 100 + 10 + 1 + .1 + .01 + .001 \\ &= 1{,}111.111 \end{aligned}$$

In Figure 16.2, the positional value of each of the digits in the numeral 2,222.222 is shown.

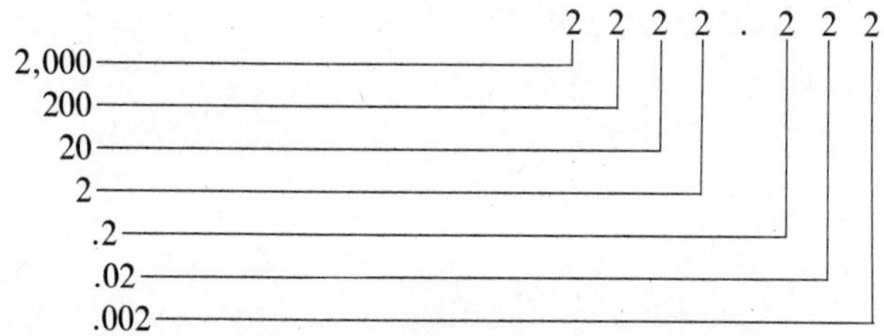

$$2{,}222.222 = 2(1{,}000) + 2(100) + 2(10) + 2(1) + 2(.1) + 2(.01) + 2(.001)$$

Figure 16.2

EQUIVALENTS

Numerals that express the same number are called *equivalents*. Thus the fraction $\frac{1}{10}$ and the decimal .1 are equivalents.

In the preceding chapter we decided that $\frac{5}{10} = \frac{50}{100} = \frac{500}{1000}$, etc. Since $\frac{5}{10} = .5$, $\frac{50}{100} = .50$, and $\frac{500}{1000} = .500$, we may write $.5 = .50 = .500$. It will not be difficult to decide why $.500 = .50 = .5$. We call .5, .50, and .500 *equivalent decimals*. Thus we may annex as many zeros to the end of a decimal or take as many zeros from the end of a decimal as we wish.

Changing a Fraction to an Equivalent Decimal

Example 1

Write $\frac{3}{5}$ as a decimal.

Solution:

Step 1: Rename $\frac{3}{5}$ to get a fraction with a denominator of a power of ten:

$$\frac{3}{5} = \frac{2 \times 3}{2 \times 5} = \frac{6}{10}$$

Step 2: Write $\frac{6}{10}$ as a decimal: $\frac{6}{10} = .6$.

$$\frac{3}{5} = \frac{6}{10} = .6$$

Example 2

Write $\frac{3}{4}$ as a decimal.

Solution:

Step 1: Rename $\frac{3}{4}$ to get a fraction with a denominator of a power of 10. Four is not a factor of 10, but it is a factor of 100. Thus the new fraction will have 100 as denominator:

$$\frac{3}{4} = \frac{25 \times 3}{25 \times 4} = \frac{75}{100}$$

Step 2: Write $\frac{75}{100}$ as a decimal: $\frac{75}{100} = .75$.

$$\frac{3}{4} = \frac{75}{100} = .75$$

Example 3

Write $\frac{7}{8}$ as a decimal.

Solution:

Step 1: Rename $\frac{7}{8}$ to get a fraction with a denominator of a power of 10. Eight is not a factor of 10, and it is not a factor of 100, but it is a factor of 1,000. Thus the new fraction will have 1,000 as denominator:

$$\frac{7}{8} = \frac{125 \times 7}{125 \times 8} = \frac{875}{1{,}000}$$

Step 2: Write $\frac{875}{1000}$ as a decimal:

$$\frac{7}{8} = \frac{875}{1000} = .875$$

The decimal equivalent of a fraction can also be obtained by performing the division indicated by the fraction, as shown previously.

Note: The decimal equivalent of $\frac{7}{8}$ is expressed as .875 and not as $.87\frac{1}{2}$. Similarly, $\frac{1}{8} = .125$ and not $.12\frac{1}{2}$. Notations such as $.12\frac{1}{2}$, $87\frac{1}{2}$, and $.33\frac{1}{3}$ are not decimals and may build faulty concepts.

Changing a Decimal to an Equivalent Fraction

When a decimal is being changed to an equivalent fraction, the decimal can be written first in fraction form in the way it is pronounced. Then, if necessary, the fraction is expressed in simplest terms.

Example 1

Write .9 as a fraction.

Solution: .9 = nine tenths = $\frac{9}{10}$.

Example 2

Write .675 as a fraction.

Solution: .675 = six hundred seventy-five thousandths = $\frac{675}{1000} = \frac{27}{40}$.

Changing a Repeating Decimal to a Fraction

Example

Write $.66\overline{6} \cdots$ as a fraction.

Solution:

Step 1: Represent the unknown fraction by n:

$$n = .66\overline{6} \cdots$$

Step 2: We need to find a multiple of $.66\overline{6} \cdots$ such that the difference between this multiple and $.66\overline{6} \cdots$ is a whole number. Since $6.66\overline{6} \cdots$ satisfies this condition, we multiply both members of the equation $n = .66\overline{6} \cdots$ by 10: $10n = 6.66\overline{6} \cdots$.

Note: If the repeating cycle consists of two or more digits, both members of the equation must be multiplied by a higher power of 10.

Step 3: Find the difference between $10n$ and n:

$$\begin{aligned} 10n &= 6.66\overline{6} \cdots \\ -n &= .66\overline{6} \cdots \\ \hline 9n &= 6 \end{aligned}$$

Step 4: Find n: Since $9n = 6$, $n = \frac{6}{9} = \frac{2}{3}$. Thus $.66\overline{6} \cdots = \frac{2}{3}$.

INTRODUCING DECIMALS

In the primary grades, readiness activities for the teaching of decimals are presented. When specific instruction in decimals is undertaken, the pupils are already acquainted with the decimal point from experiences with money situations. They have used the decimal point to indicate the digits that stand for dollars. They have also performed operations involving money and are supposed to know that decimal points must be aligned in vertical addition and subtraction. Such experiences have prepared the children for formal instruction in decimals.

For the introduction of decimals the teacher has several devices available.

Odometer

The car odometer shows the numerals that represent the tenths in a contrasting color. In the following illustration, the square reserved for the tenths is shaded. After a complete rotation of the tenths dial, a numeral appears in the ones dial that represents the number that is one unit larger than the preceding number in the ones dial.

0	0	1	2	3	5

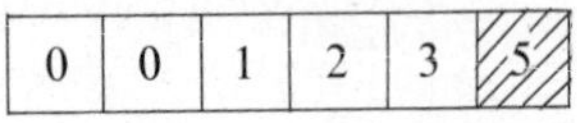

Number Line The units on the number line that is used to introduce decimals are subdivided into tenths. The marks on the line representing the tenths are labeled with both fractions and decimals:

0										1	
.0	.1	.2	.3	.4	.5	.6	.7	.8	.9	1.0	1.1
$\frac{0}{10}$	$\frac{1}{10}$	$\frac{2}{10}$	$\frac{3}{10}$	$\frac{4}{10}$	$\frac{5}{10}$	$\frac{6}{10}$	$\frac{7}{10}$	$\frac{8}{10}$	$\frac{9}{10}$	$\frac{10}{10}$	$1\frac{1}{10}$

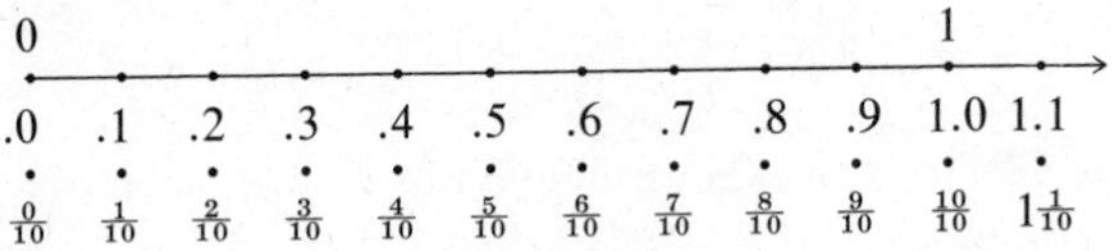

Ruler and Tape An engineer's ruler and a surveyor's tape, both graduated in inches and tenths of inches, and metric rulers are used by the pupils to measure lengths and distances.

Diagrams Diagrams on graph paper and worksheets with mimeographed squares and divided squares can be used effectively to introduce the meaning of decimals and to illustrate simple operations involving decimals. In Figure 16.3 an empty square represents a unit of one, a square divided into ten strips the tenths, and a hundred square the hundredths.

1 unit $\frac{1}{10} = .1$ $\frac{1}{100} = .01$

 1 unit $= \frac{10}{10}$ 1 unit $= \frac{10}{10} = \frac{100}{100}$

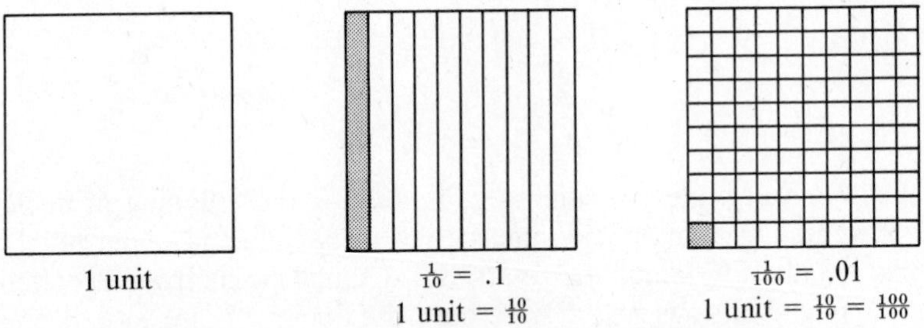

Figure 16.3

If the pupils understand the meaning of decimals and can work with tenths and hundredths, it will probably not be necessary to introduce thousandths in the way tenths and hundredths have been presented. The child will usually be able to extend the decimals to thousandths by applying the knowledge he has already acquired. If there is a need to introduce thousandths separately, the graduation of the meter in decimeters, centimeters, and millimeters is recommended as a device, provided that the pupils have already been introduced to the metric system of measures. Another device that can be used is the micrometer, which measures the width of small objects in thousandths of an inch.

READING DECIMALS

In learning to read decimals, the pupils must realize that the ones digit is the center of our system of notation. Thus, in 45.6, the 5 stands for ones, the 4 for tens, and the 6 for tenths. A diagram on the chalkboard will be helpful to emphasize that the decimal point is only a device to indicate the ones place.

In reading a decimal, we must determine its denominator. Starting with the first digit to the right of the decimal point, we assign names to each position (tenths, hundredths, etc.), and the name of the position of the last digit agrees with the denominator of the decimal.

The rule reserving the conjunction "and" for the decimal point in a mixed decimal has become widely accepted.

Examples

4,578	—	four thousand, five hundred, seventy-eight
.7	—	seven tenths
.07	—	seven hundredths
.007	—	seven thousandths
.77	—	seventy-seven hundredths
.777	—	seven hundred seventy-seven thousandths
6.6	—	six and six tenths
66.66	—	sixty-six and sixty-six hundredths

The decimal point is sometimes read as "point":

5.3—five point three.

WRITING DECIMALS

Instruction in the writing as well as the reading of decimals is a necessary part of the program. The tenths are introduced first, in both decimal and fraction form. When smaller decimals are introduced, the pupils are guided to discover that hundredths are expressed by two digits to the right of the decimal point, and thousandths by three digits to the right of that point. Thus, in the decimal .005, the zeros hold the places for the tenths and the hundredths, and, consequently, .5, .05, and .005 express different numbers. In introductory exercises the number is expressed in words, in fraction form, and in decimal form.

Examples

one and three tenths = $1\frac{3}{10}$ = 1.3
fourteen and seventeen hundredths = $14\frac{17}{100}$ = 14.17
nine and one hundredth = $9\frac{1}{100}$ = 9.01
seven and eleven thousandths = $7\frac{11}{1000}$ = 7.011
five thousandths = $\frac{5}{1000}$ = .005

THE FUNDAMENTAL OPERATIONS WITH DECIMALS

Several examples of exercises involving decimals and possible ways of working those exercises are presented in the following paragraphs. Methods of solution include mental computation, horizontal addition, the standard algorism or vertical addition, substituting fraction equivalents (thus applying already acquired knowledge), and working with devices or aids such as the number line, rulers graduated in inches and tenths of an inch or in decimeters and centimeters, and divided squares. Since various methods of solution are usually available, the teacher will have to select those that fit the program of instruction best. In initial exercises the obtained answer can be checked easily by substituting fractions for decimals and then performing the indicated operations. For more difficult problems, methods of checking presented in the chapters dealing with the fundamental operations involving whole numbers are easier to use.

ADDITION WITH DECIMALS

The first exercises are derived from easy problem situations and usually make use only of tenths. The types presented increase gradually in difficulty through the inclusion of more addends, mixed decimals, and so-called ragged decimals. *Ragged decimals* have denominators that express different powers of 10, as in 6.5 + .45 + 3.664.

Example 1

It is .3 mile from Jack's home to school. How far is it from his home to school and back?

Number question: .3 + .3 = □.

Solutions:

1. Fractions:

$$.3 + .3 = \frac{3}{10} + \frac{3}{10} = \frac{3+3}{10} = \frac{6}{10} = .6$$

2. Horizontal addition:

   Since 3 tenths + 3 tenths = 6 tenths, .3 + .3 = .6.

3. Number line:

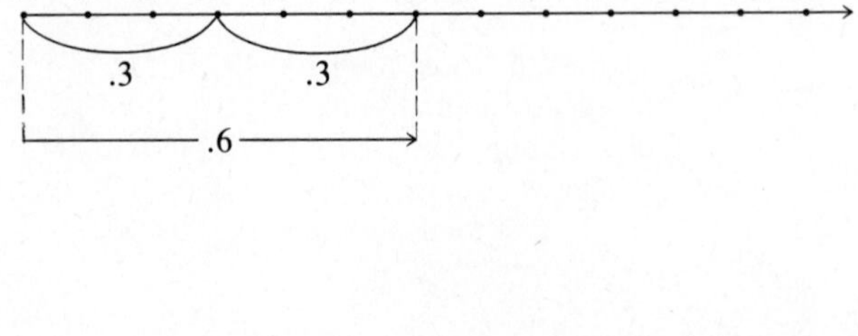

4. Diagram:

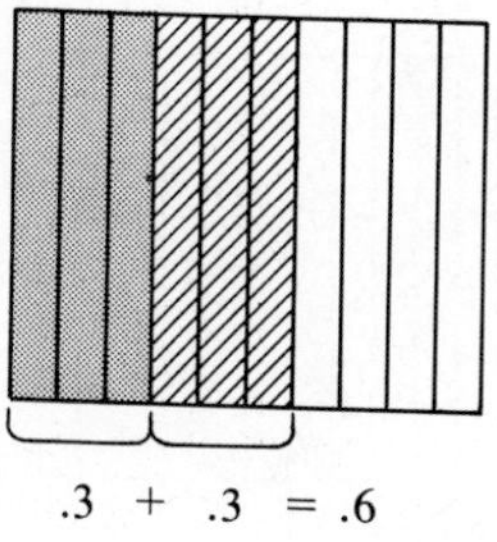

5. Vertical addition:

3 tenths	.3
+3 tenths	+.3
6 tenths	.6

The distance from Jack's home to school and back is .6 mile.

Example 2

Add 1.7 and .5.

Number question: 1.7 + .5 = □.

Solutions:

1. Horizontal addition:

Think: How much do I add to 1.7 to get 2? The answer is .3. If .3 is added, then .2 more must be added, because .5 = .3 + .2. 1.7 + .3 = 2, and 2 + .2 = 2.2, so 1.7 + .5 = 2.2.

1.7 + .5 = (1 + .7) + .5	renaming
= 1 + (.7 + .5)	associative property
= 1 + 1.2	addition
= 2.2	addition

2. Number line:

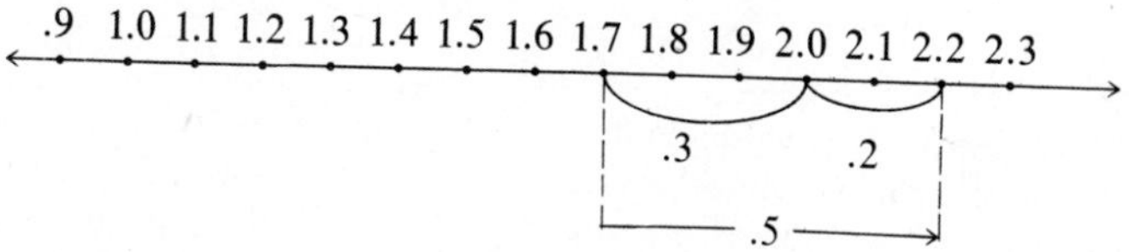

3. Diagrams:

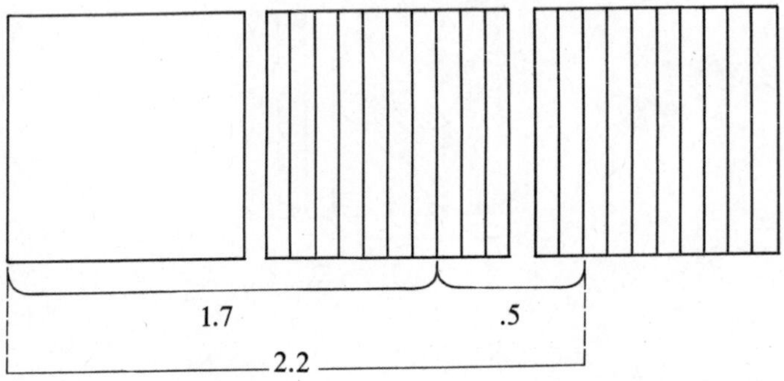

4. Vertical addition:

$$\begin{array}{r} 1.7 \\ +\ .5 \\ \hline 2.2 \end{array}$$

7 tenths + 5 tenths = 12 tenths.
Ten tenths equal 1 one. Thus 12 tenths = 1.2.
The 1 one in 1.2 is added to the unit in the ones column.

Check: $1.7 + .5 = 1\frac{7}{10} + \frac{5}{10} = 1\frac{12}{10} = 2\frac{2}{10} = 2.2.$

Example 3

Add 2.5, 17.55, and 3.7.

Number question: $2.5 + 17.55 + 3.7 = \square$, or $\begin{array}{r} 2.5 \\ 17.55 \\ +3.7 \\ \hline \end{array}$

Solutions:

1. The addends are expressed in expanded notation and then added:

$$\begin{array}{rcrrrr} 2.5 & = & & 2\ + & .5 & \\ 17.55 & = & 10\ + & 7\ + & .5\ + & .05 \\ +3.7 & = & & 3\ + & .7 & \\ \hline & & 10\ + & 12\ + & 1.7\ + & .05 \end{array} = 10 + 12 + 1 + .7 + .05 = 23.75$$

2. Standard algorism:

$$\begin{array}{rcr} 2.5 & = & 2.50 \\ 17.55 & = & 17.55 \\ +3.7 & = & 3.70 \\ \hline & & 23.75 \end{array}$$

Procedure: Rewrite the addends so that they have like denominators. For this purpose zeros are annexed where necessary. In the exercise under consideration, enough zeros are annexed to each addend to make it a two-place decimal. Add as whole numbers are added. Place the decimal point.

Note: The pupils must realize why the decimal points are aligned.

Check: $2.5 + 17.55 + 3.7 = 2\frac{50}{100} + 17\frac{55}{100} + 3\frac{70}{100}$
$= 22\frac{175}{100} = 23\frac{75}{100} = 23.75$

SUBTRACTION WITH DECIMALS

Example 1

Subtract .3 from .7.

Number question: $.7 - .3 = \square$.

Solutions:

1. Horizontal subtraction:

   7 tenths − 3 tenths = 4 tenths, so $.7 - .3 = .4$.

2. Number line:

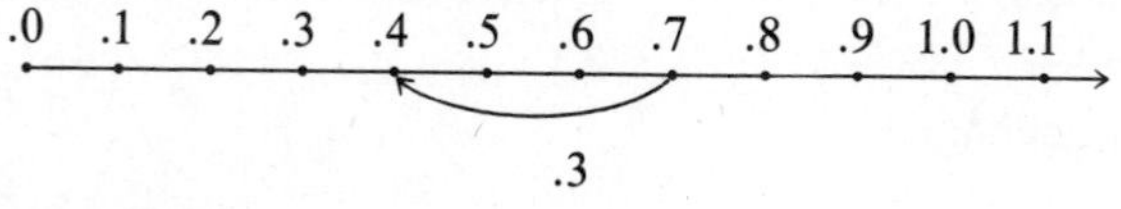

3. Vertical subtraction:
   Subtract as whole numbers are subtracted. Then place the decimal point.

$$\begin{array}{r} .7 \\ -.3 \\ \hline .4 \end{array}$$

Check: $.7 - .3 = \frac{7}{10} - \frac{3}{10} = \frac{4}{10} = .4$.

Example 2

From Mary's home to school is 1.3 miles. From Jane's home to school is .8 mile. What is the difference in distance?

Number question: $1.3 - .8 = \square$.

Solutions:

1. Horizontal subtraction:
   First subtract enough from 1.3 to get 1: $1.3 - .3 = 1$. Since $.8 = .3 + .5$, .5 more must be subtracted: $1 - .5 = .5$. Thus $1.3 - .8 = 1.3 - (.3 + .5) = (1.3 - .3) - .5 = 1 - .5 = .5$.

2. Number line:

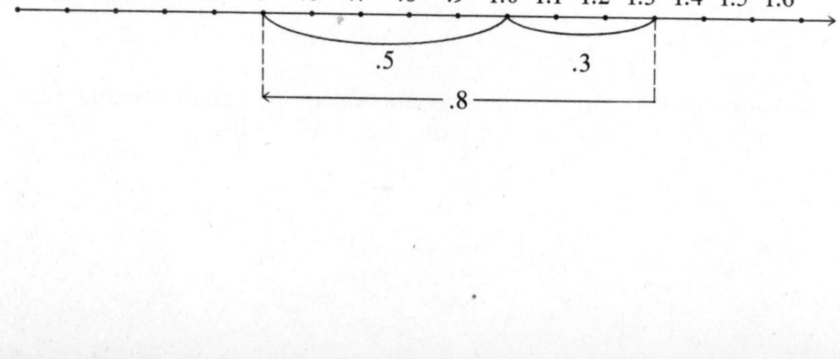

3. Vertical subtraction:

$$\begin{array}{rl} 1.3 = & 1 \text{ one, } 3 \text{ tenths} = 13 \text{ tenths} \\ -.8 = & \qquad\qquad\qquad\quad 8 \text{ tenths} \\ \hline & \qquad\qquad\qquad\quad 5 \text{ tenths} = .5 \end{array}$$

Or subtract as whole numbers are subtracted. Then place the decimal point:

$$\begin{array}{r} 1.3 \\ -\ .8 \\ \hline .5 \end{array}$$

The difference in distance is .5 miles.

Check: $1.3 - .8 = 1\frac{3}{10} - \frac{8}{10} = \frac{5}{10} = .5.$

Example 3

Helen planned to walk 4 miles. After she had walked 2.7 miles, how much farther did she have to go?

Number question: $4 - 2.7 = \square.$

Solutions:

1. Horizontal form:
   Subtract 2 ones from 4 ones, and then .7 from the remainder.

$$\begin{aligned} 4 - 2.7 &= 4 - (2 + .7) \\ &= (4 - 2) - .7 \\ &= 2 - .7 \\ &= 1.3 \end{aligned}$$

2. Expanded notation:

$$\begin{array}{rl} 4 \quad = & 3 + 1.0 \\ -2.7 = & 2 + \ \ .7 \\ \hline & 1 + \ \ .3 = 1.3 \end{array}$$

3. Standard algorism:
   Write 4 as 4.0. Subtract as whole numbers are subtracted. Place the decimal point.

$$\begin{array}{r} 4.0 \\ -2.7 \\ \hline 1.3 \end{array}$$

Helen had 1.3 miles to go.

Check: $4 - 2.7 = 3\frac{10}{10} - 2\frac{7}{10} = 1\frac{3}{10} = 1.3.$

MULTIPLICATION WITH DECIMALS Multiplication with decimals is best introduced in examples that can be solved by serial addition and by using the number line.

Example 1

When training for track, Jim ran 4 times around the school building. The distance around the building was .4 miles. How many miles did Jim run?

Number question: 4 × .4 = □.

Solutions:

1. Number line:

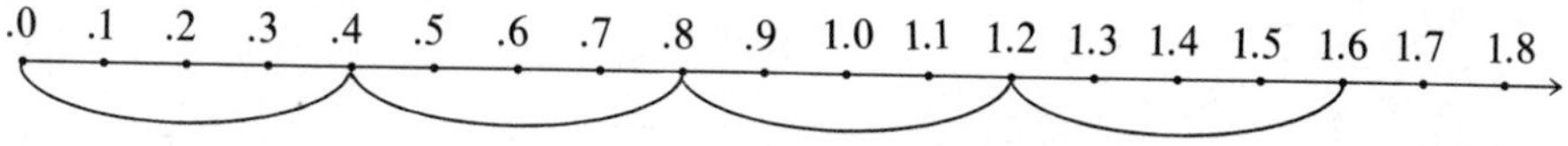

2. Horizontal form:

 4 tenths + 4 tenths + 4 tenths + 4 tenths = 16 tenths = 1.6
 4 × 4 tenths = 16 tenths = 1.6
 4 × .4 = 1.6

3. Vertical form:
 From the previous solutions, the pupils know that the answer is 1.6. The class then discusses why the answer cannot be 16. In such easy examples, the place of the decimal point is determined by inspection and by using common sense in deciding what the answer should be.

$$\begin{array}{r} .4 \\ \times 4 \\ \hline 1.6 \end{array}$$

Jim ran 1.6 miles.

Check: $4 \times .4 = 4 \times \frac{4}{10} = \frac{16}{10} = 1.6$.

The next step is to develop the rule: When multiplying with decimals, point off as many places in the product as there are decimal places in the two factors together. It is recommended that this rule be arrived at inductively by working several exercises in which fractions are substituted for decimals.

Example 2

$.2 \times .4 = \frac{2}{10} \times \frac{4}{10} = \frac{2 \times 4}{10 \times 10} = \frac{8}{100} = .08$: multiplication of tenths by tenths yields hundredths.

$.2 \times .04 = \frac{2}{10} \times \frac{4}{100} = \frac{2 \times 4}{10 \times 100} = \frac{8}{1{,}000} = .008$: multiplication of hundredths by tenths yields thousandths.

$.04 \times .2 = \frac{4}{100} \times \frac{2}{10} = \frac{4 \times 2}{100 \times 10} = \frac{8}{1{,}000} = .008$: multiplication of tenths by hundredths yields thousandths.

Example 3

Find the product of 1.4 and 3.65.

Number question: 1.4 × 3.65 = □.

Solution: Multiply as whole numbers are multiplied. First decide where the decimal point should be placed by comparing the product with the product of the whole numbers 3 and 1. Then find the total number of decimal places in the factors. Starting at the right, count off the same number of decimal places in the product and place the decimal point.

$$\begin{array}{r} 3.65 \\ \times 1.4 \\ \hline 1460 \\ 365 \\ \hline 5.110 \end{array}$$

DIVISION WITH DECIMALS In the following presentation of division with decimals, four main types will be considered:

Type I:	5.6 ÷ 4 = □
Type II:	4 ÷ 5 = □
Type III:	27 ÷ 4.5 = □
Type IV:	8.5 ÷ 3.4 = □

Illustrations of possible methods of solution are presented below.

Type I **Example 1**

Ted walked 9.6 miles in 3 hours. What was his average speed in miles per hour?

Number question: 9.6 ÷ 3 = □.

Solution: The procedure is to divide as whole numbers are divided and place the decimal point in the quotient. The pupils should learn to decide where to place the decimal point in the quotient by using several meaningful methods such as the following:

1. Inspection:
   After the division has been worked without considering the decimal point, the class reasons as follows: Since 9.6 expresses a number between 9 (which equals 3 × 3) and 12 (which equals 4 × 3), the quotient of 9.6 ÷ 3 must be a number between 3 and 4. Thus the decimal point must be placed between the 3 and the 2, and the quotient is 3.2.
2. Changing the dividend to tenths:
   Since 9.6 = 96 tenths, 9.6 ÷ 3 = 96 tenths ÷ 3 = 32 tenths, or 3.2.

3. Using fractions:

$$9.6 \div 3 = 9\tfrac{6}{10} \div 3 = \frac{96}{10} \div 3 = \frac{96 \div 3}{10} = \frac{32}{10} = 3\tfrac{2}{10} = 3.2$$

Ted's average speed was 3.2 miles per hour.

Several examples should be worked in various ways. These examples should include dividends with hundredths and thousandths. Then the pupils conclude that there are as many decimal places in the quotient as there are in the dividend. (Note that the divisor is a whole number.)

Example 2

Divide 6.2 by 5.

Number question: $6.2 \div 5 = \square$.

Solution: In the type of division under consideration, the division is not finished when all the digits in the dividend have been brought down. Thus zeros are annexed to the dividend in order to continue the dividing. In the exercise $6.2 \div 5 = \square$, one zero needs to be annexed during the division process. Since this results in two decimal places in the dividend, there will also be two decimal places in the quotient:

```
   1.24
5)6.20
  5
  12
  10
   20
   20
    0
```

Check: $6.2 \div 5 = 6\tfrac{2}{10} \div 5 = \frac{62}{10} \times \frac{1}{5} = \frac{62 \times 1}{10 \times 5} = \frac{62}{50} = 1\tfrac{12}{50} = 1\tfrac{24}{100} = 1.24.$

Example 3

Divide 1.5 by 3.

Number question: $1.5 \div 3 = \square$.

Solution: Since the quotient of $1.5 \div 3$ is not a whole number, 1.5 is changed to 15 tenths and then divided by 3: 15 tenths $\div$ 3 = 5 tenths = .5. Thus $1.5 \div 3 = .5$. The sentence $1.5 \div 3 = .5$ can be illustrated on graph paper and on the number line.

Check: $1.5 \div 3 = 1\tfrac{5}{10} \div 3 = \frac{15}{10} \div 3 = \frac{15 \div 3}{10} = \frac{5}{10} = .5.$

The pupils should first estimate the quotient of a division problem. By using common sense, they will decide that the answer to $1.5 \div 3 = \square$ cannot be 5. Checking the answer by determining whether the product of the quotient and the divisor equals the dividend will also assist them in placing the decimal point correctly.

Example 4

Divide .15 by 3.

Number question: $.15 \div 3 = \square$.

Solution: 15 hundredths ÷ 3 = 5 hundredths. Thus $.15 \div 3 = .05$. The use of the zero in the quotient often causes difficulties. It is recommended that graph paper be used to illustrate why the quotient is .05, and not .5. The necessity of using the zero as a placeholder in the tenths place is also emphasized by working the exercise with common fractions:

$$.15 \div 3 = \frac{15}{100} \div 3 = \frac{15 \div 3}{100} = \frac{5}{100} = .05$$

After the pupils have worked several exercises and understand what it is that they are doing, they are guided to reason as follows:

a. There are no ones in the dividend. Thus a decimal point is placed in the quotient.

$$\begin{array}{r} . \\ 3\overline{).15} \end{array}$$

b. There is only 1 tenth in the dividend. Thus a zero is placed in the tenths place of the quotient.

$$\begin{array}{r} .0 \\ 3\overline{).15} \end{array}$$

c. There are 15 hundredths in the dividend. 15 hundredths ÷ 3 = 5 hundredths. Thus a 5 is placed in the hundredths place of the quotient and the division is completed.

$$\begin{array}{r} .05 \\ 3\overline{).15} \\ \underline{15} \\ 0 \end{array}$$

Check: The answer is checked by working the exercise with fractions, as shown above, or by multiplying the quotient and the divisor: $3 \times .05 = .15$.

Example 5

Divide 25.1 by 3.

Number question: $25.1 \div 3 = \square$.

Solution: When the division indicated by 25.1 ÷ 3 is performed, the process does not terminate. The quotient can be expressed as a repeating decimal:

$$
\begin{array}{r}
8.36\overline{6}\ \cdots,\ \text{or } 8.3\overline{6} \\
3\overline{)25.100} \\
\underline{24} \\
1\,1 \\
\underline{9} \\
20 \\
\underline{18} \\
20 \\
\underline{18}
\end{array}
$$

A repeating decimal is usually rounded to the nearest one, tenth, hundredth, etc. When rounding a decimal to the nearest one—

a. round *down* if the tenths digit is 1, 2, 3, or 4.
b. round *up* if the tenths digit is 5, 6, 7, 8, or 9.

Similar rules can be formulated for rounding a decimal to the nearest tenth, hundredth, or thousandth.

If the quotient of 25.1 ÷ 3 is rounded to the nearest tenth, the answer is 8.4.

Example **Type II**

Change the fraction $\frac{3}{4}$ to a decimal fraction.

Number question: 3 ÷ 4 = □.

Solution: Since the divisor is larger than the dividend, a decimal point is placed to the right of the 3, and zeros are annexed as necessary to continue the dividing:

$$
\begin{array}{r}
.75 \\
4\overline{)3.00} \\
\underline{2\,8} \\
20 \\
\underline{20} \\
0
\end{array}
$$

Example **Type III**

Divide 14 by 3.5.

Number question: 14 ÷ 3.5 = □.

Solutions: The decimal point in the divisor presents a new difficulty. Therefore, the answer is first found by using previously learned methods:

1. Serial subtraction. (In order to use serial subtraction, the verbal problem under consideration should be a type of measurement division.)

   $14 - 3.5 = 10.5(1)$, $10.5 - 3.5 = 7(2)$, $7 - 3.5 = 3.5(3)$, $3.5 - 3.5 = 0(4)$

   Thus four 3.5s equal 14.

2. Number line:

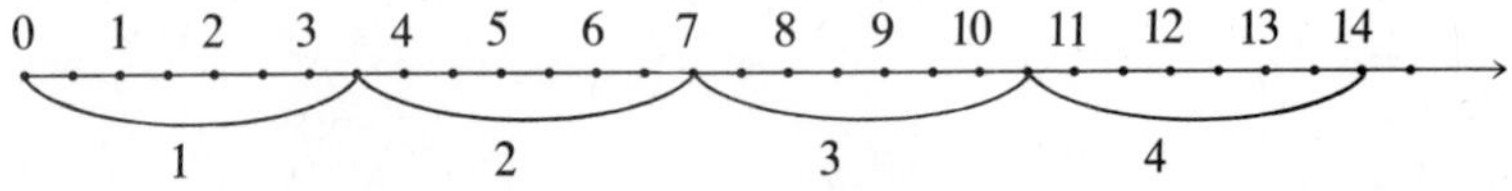

3. Fractions:

$$14 \div 3.5 = 14 \div 3\frac{5}{10} = \frac{14}{1} \div \frac{35}{10} = \frac{\overset{2}{\cancel{14}}}{1} \times \frac{10}{\underset{5}{\cancel{35}}} = \frac{20}{5} = 4$$

In order to arrive at the method in common use, the teacher suggests that it would be more convenient if the divisor were a whole number. It is decided that the divisor (3.5) must be multiplied by 10 to get 35. This leads to the rule that states that multiplying the dividend and the divisor by the same natural number does not change the quotient. Examples such as the following are presented:

Sentence:	$10 \div 5 = 2$
Dividend and divisor are multiplied by 2:	$20 \div 10 = 2$
Dividend and divisor are multiplied by 5:	$50 \div 25 = 2$
Dividend and divisor are multipied by 10:	$100 \div 50 = 2$

After the rule has been understood and tested, the pupils multiply both the dividend and the divisor in $14 \div 3.5$ by 10 and perform the division:

$$\underline{3.5\overline{)14}}$$

$$\begin{array}{r} 4 \\ 35\overline{)140} \\ \underline{140} \\ 0 \end{array}$$

Type IV Example

A rope 10.5 feet long is cut into pieces of 3.5 feet each. How many pieces of 3.5 feet are there?

Number question: $10.5 \div 3.5 = \square$.

Solution:

a. Write the division question.
b. Draw a line under the exercise.

$$\underline{3.5\overline{)10.5}}$$

c. Decide by which power of ten 3.5 must be multiplied to get 35.
d. Multiply both the dividend and the divisor by 10 and rewrite the division question.
e. Proceed with the division.

$$\begin{array}{r} 3 \\ 35\overline{)105} \\ \underline{105} \\ 0 \end{array}$$

There are 3 pieces of 3.5 feet each.
Check: 3 × 3.5 = 10.5.

Note: A decimal divisor is multiplied by the power of 10 needed to get a whole number as divisor. The dividend is then multiplied by the same power of 10.

MULTIPLYING AND DIVIDING BY POWERS OF 10

The multiplication and division of numbers expressed as decimals by powers of 10 is an extension of the cases in which whole numbers are multiplied and divided by those powers. Such cases should be presented early in the study of decimals. In fact, the pupils will already have worked with sentences such as 10 × $.25 = $2.50 in preceding grades. The rules should be arrived at inductively. They are then extended to cover other powers of 10. The rules are applied extensively in mental computation.

SELECTED RESEARCH

The purpose of the study[1] was to compare two methods used to locate the decimal point in the quotient: making the divisor a whole number by multiplying by a power of 10 and then multiplying the dividend by the same number (Method I), and subtracting the number of decimal places in the divisor from the number of decimal places in the dividend (Method II).

Three sixth-grade classes with a total of seventy-one pupils used Method I, and three sixth grades with a total of sixty-six pupils used Method II. The median grade-level arithmetic achievement for each of the two groups was 5.8.

At the end of the period of instruction, a test that measured computation and understanding of the method was administered.

Of the investigator's conclusions, the following are presented:

1. F. Flournoy, "A Consideration of Pupils' Success with Two Methods for Placing the Decimal Point in the Quotient," *School Science and Mathematics* (June, 1959), pp. 445–460.

1. In general, pupils taught Method I placed the decimal point in the quotient correctly more often than pupils who were taught Method II.
2. For the below-average arithmetic achievers Method II was decidely more difficult than Method I.
3. The nature of Method II seems to provide more opportunity for error in placing the decimal point in the quotient than that of Method I.

SELECTED ACTIVITIES FOR PUPILS

1. Complete.
   .5, 1, 5, ______, ______, ______, ______, ______.
   .9, 1.8, 2.7, ______, ______, ______, ______, ______.
2. Write in order from the least to the greatest:

   2.06, 2.12, 2.084, 2.111, 2.009.
3. Connie wrote 19.72 instead of 1.972. Find the difference between the numbers.
4. Put the decimal point in the numeral below in the sensible place.
   Ron paid $8725 for his bike.
5. Write the numeral that expresses the larger number in each pair.
   $1\frac{3}{4}$ and 1.7 $2\frac{7}{8}$ and 2.8 $\frac{7}{25}$ and .26
6. Complete:

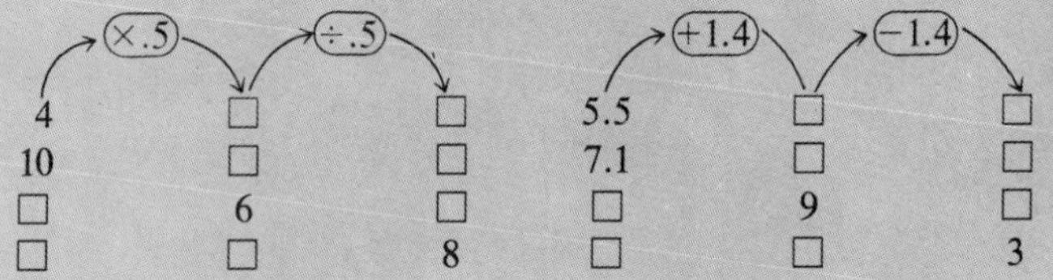

7. Estimate the sum of 5.9, 7.2, 9.14, and 3.88. Then compute the sum. What is the difference between the computed answer and your estimated answer?
8. Write 2.4, 24, 4.8, 48, 9.6, and 96 on the six faces of a sugar cube. Write .1, .2, .3, .4, .6, and .8 on another cube. Roll the two cubes. Divide the larger of the two numbers rolled by the smaller one. Repeat the activity several times.
9. Check the quotient.

Example

15 ÷ .5 = 30.

Check: 30 × .5 = 15.

60 ÷ .4 = 150 22.5 ÷ 7.5 = 3 8 ÷ 40 = .2

10. Which is greater: fifty-five thousandths or six hundredths?

11. Work the magic square.
    a. Find the sum of the numbers expressed in the square:

.223	.728	.627
.930	.526	.122
.425	.324	.829

left-right	up-down	corner-corner
.223 + .728 + .627 =	.223 + .930 + .425 =	.223 + .526 + .829 =
.930 + .526 + .122 =	.728 + .526 + .324 =	.425 + .526 + .627 =
.425 + .324 + .829 =	.627 + .122 + .829 =	

    b. In each addition in (a), the sum is ______. The square is a magic number square.
    c. Make another magic square by adding the same number to all the numbers expressed in the square above. Check to see if the square is really a magic square.
    d. Make another magic square by subtracting the same number from all the numbers expressed in the square.
    e. Make another magic square by multiplying each number expressed in the square by the same number.

12. Find the pattern and write the missing numerals.

.35						
.35	.35					
.35	.7	.35				
.35	1.05	1.05	.35			
.35	1.4					

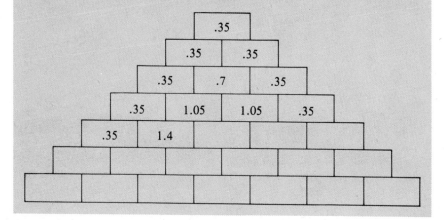

EXERCISES

1. Give two examples of—
   a. a terminating decimal.
   b. a repeating decimal.
2. Solve .3 + .9 = □ by using—
   a. the number line.
   b. squares divided into ten strips each.
   c. fractions.
   d. mental computation.
3. Solve 3 × .28 by using—
   a. the number line.
   b. squares divided into 100 small squares.
   c. fractions.
   d. mental computation.
4. Show .15 on graph paper or on a square divided into 100 small squares.
5. Solve 15.3 ÷ .9 = □ in the way suggested in this chapter.
6. What is the positional value of each digit in the numeral 504.39?
7. In the numeral 126.45, how much more is the positional value of the 1 than that of the 5?
8. Read these decimals:

   15.704 .064 15.015 1,400.14 3,333.333
9. Give examples of the four main types of problems in division with decimals.
10. Explain what is meant by ragged decimals.
11. Write out what you would say and do to teach the multiplication of two numbers expressed as decimals.
12. Report on a piece of research pertaining to the teaching of decimals.
13. Diagnose the mistakes made in the following presentations.

$$\begin{array}{r} .7 \\ +.5 \\ \hline .12 \end{array} \qquad \begin{array}{r} 2.3 \\ \times 6 \\ \hline 1.38 \end{array} \qquad \begin{array}{r} 3.3 \\ .5\overline{)10.5} \\ 9 \\ \hline 15 \\ 15 \\ \hline 0 \end{array}$$

SOURCES FOR FURTHER READING

Ashlock, R. B., *Error Patterns in Computation.* Columbus: Charles E. Merrill Publishing Company, 1972.

D'Augustine, C. H., *Multiple Methods of Teaching Mathematics in the Elementary School,* 2nd ed. New York: Harper & Row, Publishers, 1973, Chap. XIV.

Heddens, J. W., *Today's Mathematics,* 3d ed. Chicago: Science Research Associates, Inc., 1974, Unit XV.

Henry, B., "Do We Need Separate Rules to Compute in Decimal Notation?" *The Arithmetic Teacher,* January, 1971, pp. 40–42.

Kennedy, L. M., *Guiding Children to Mathematical Discovery,* 2nd ed. Belmont, California: Wadsworth Publishing Company, Inc., 1975, Chap. XIII.

Marks, J. L., C. R. Purdy, L. B. Kinney, and A. A. Hiatt, *Teaching Elementary School Mathematics for Understanding,* 4th ed. New York: McGraw-Hill Book Company, 1975, Chap. VIII.

Prielipp, R. W., "Decimals," *The Arithmetic Teacher,* April, 1976, pp. 285–288.

Schminke, C. W., N. Maertens, and W. R. Arnold, *Teaching the Child Mathematics*. Hinsdale, Illinois: The Dryden Press, Inc., 1973, Chap. IX.

Spitzer, H. F., *Teaching Elementary School Mathematics*. Boston: Houghton Mifflin Company, 1967, Chap. XI.

Winzenread, M. R., "Repeating Decimals," *The Arithmetic Teacher,* December, 1973, pp. 678–682.

Percents 17

Situations involving percents are frequently encountered by elementary-school children in daily life and in their reading materials. Upper-grade pupils, as well as adults, are at a loss on many occasions if they do not understand the language of percent. The teaching of this part of the mathematics curriculum is therefore essential.

A common fraction can have any natural number as a denominator. The denominators of decimal fractions are always powers of ten. As we shall see in this chapter, in percents there is an understood denominator of one hundred.

SKILLS TEST

1. Change the decimals to percents:

.04	.36	.09	.15
.74	1.15	.99	2.50

2. Change the fractions to percents:

$\frac{1}{2}$	$\frac{3}{10}$	$\frac{3}{4}$	$\frac{3}{8}$
$\frac{1}{4}$	$\frac{2}{5}$	$\frac{1}{20}$	$\frac{3}{50}$

3. Change the percents to decimals:

22%	3%	17%	1%
49%	8%	60%	9%

4. Change the percents to fractions:

10%	50%	90%	5%
15%	75%	60%	25%

5. Find the answers to the following exercises by using the fraction method:

10% of 60 =	75% of 20 =	80% of 25 =	$37\frac{1}{2}$% of 40 =
5% of 40 =	$12\frac{1}{2}$% of 32 =	$33\frac{1}{3}$% of 15 =	$87\frac{1}{2}$% of 16 =

6. Find the answers to the following exercises:

6% of 240 =	12 = ______% of 40	8 = 40% of ______
28% of 1250 =	150 = ______% of 200	63 = 21% of ______

7. Find the interest on $200 at 5% for 3 months.
8. A school team won 12 of the 20 games played. What percent of the games played did the team win?
9. A salesman sold a vacuum cleaner for $60 and made a profit of $15. What was the percent of profit on the selling price?
10. How much money must be invested at 4% to earn a yearly income of $200?

MEANING AND TERMS

The term *percent* comes from the Latin words *per centum,* which mean "for each hundred." A percent expresses a ratio between a given number and 100. Nine percent of 200 means 9 per 100, or 18.

In the example 9% of 200 = 18, the *rate* is 9% (which can be expressed by the decimal .09), the *base* is 200, and the *percentage* is 18. The difference between the percent (9) and the percentage (18) should be noted.

A percent can easily be shown as a fraction with a denominator of 100. For example, 5% of 200 = $\frac{5}{100}$ of 200, or .05 of 200. Since percents express the ratio between the given number and 100, they can be compared easily. It is easier to compare 14% and 15% than $\frac{7}{50}$ and $\frac{3}{20}$.

The concepts of ratio and proportion are often used in the teaching of percents. In a *ratio* two numbers are compared. For example, the ratio of the number 5 to the number 8 is written as 5 to 8, or 5:8, or $\frac{5}{8}$. A *proportion* expresses the equality of two ratios. An example of a proportion is 3:6 = 12:24, or $\frac{3}{6} = \frac{12}{24}$.

INTRODUCING PERCENT

The meaning of percent can be introduced effectively by using a hundred board, as shown in Figure 17.1. This board consists of 10 rows of 10 movable disks or squares. All the squares have a certain color on one side and another color on the other side. Thus, when the squares are turned over, they show a color different from that exposed by the remaining squares on the board. The total of 100 small squares represents 100%, so each small square is .01 or 1% of the total area. When the pupils understand the relationship between 100% and 1% of the board, they are encouraged to do exercises such as (1) turning over the number of squares that corresponds to a given percent, (2) telling what percent of all the squares have been turned over, (3) illustrating on the board expressions such as "one out of every ten," and (4) completing sentences such as "1 out of every 10 squares on the hundred board gives a total of □ squares."

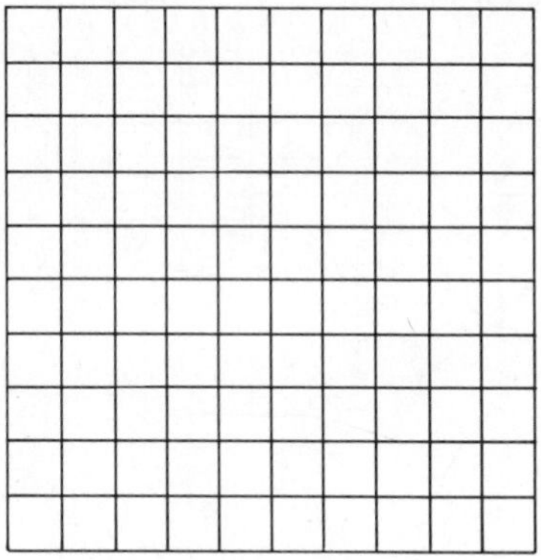

Figure 17.1

The pupils can work individually on worksheets with squares consisting of 10 rows of 10 small squares each. They are directed to write what percent of a given square has been shaded or to shade a given percent of a square, as in the following examples.

Example 1

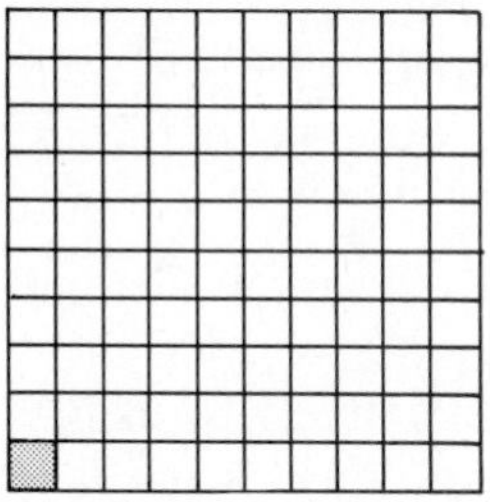

1 small square is shaded.
$\frac{1}{100}$ of the large square is shaded.
.01 of the large square is shaded.
□% of the large square is shaded.

Example 2

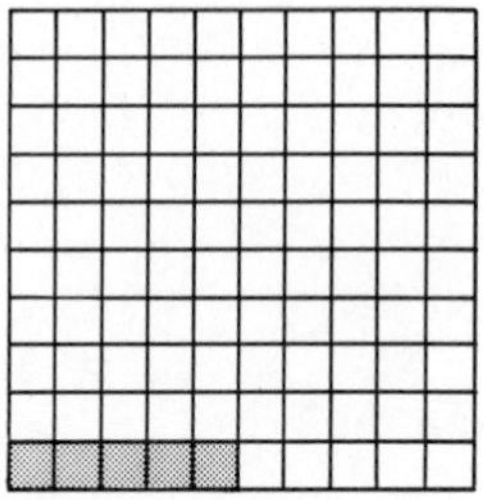

5 small squares are shaded.
$\frac{5}{100}$ of the large square is shaded.
.05 of the large square is shaded.
□% of the large square is shaded.

Example 3

What percent of each of the following squares is shaded?

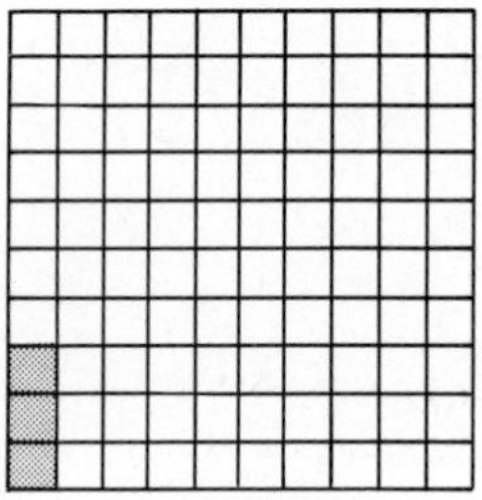

□%

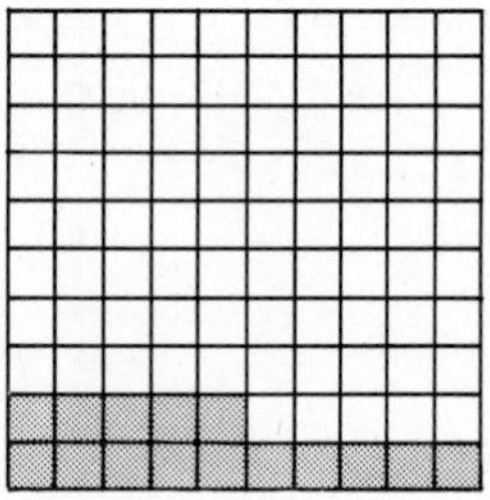

□%

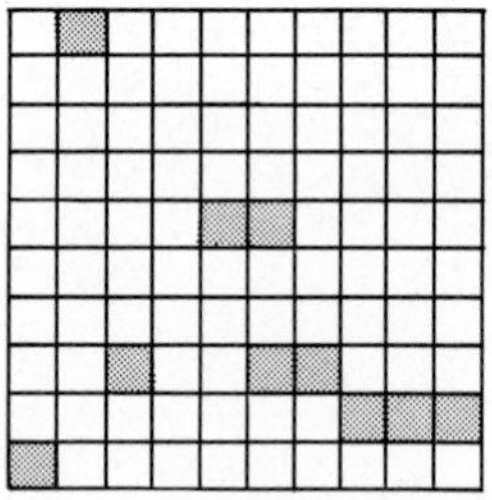

□%

Example 4

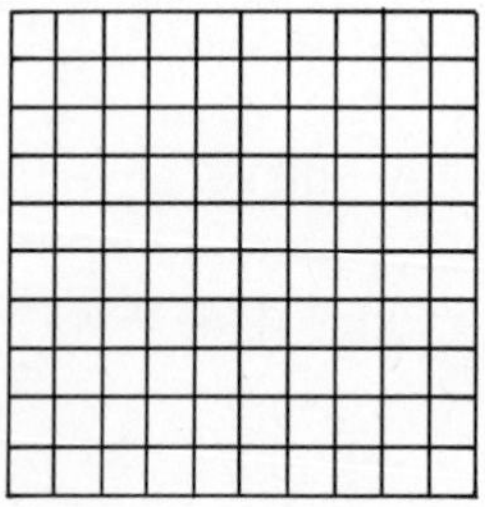

Shade 27% of the square.

Example 5

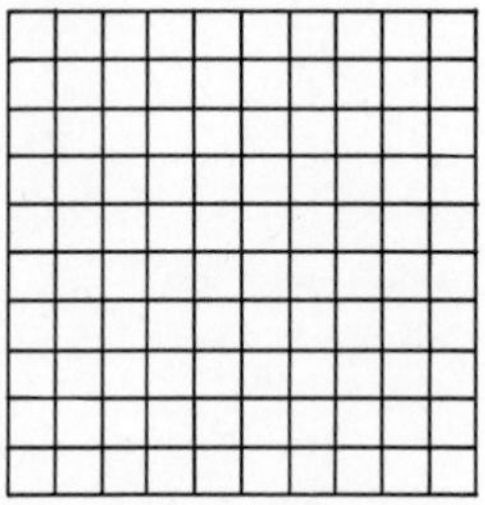

Shade $\frac{1}{2}$ of the square.

$\frac{1}{2} = \frac{\square}{100}$.

$\frac{1}{2} = \square\%$.

Example 6

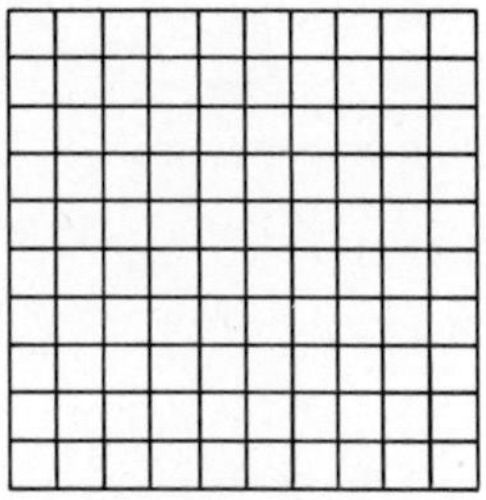

Shade $\frac{1}{5}$ of the square.

$\frac{1}{5} = \frac{\square}{100}.$

$\frac{1}{5} = \square\%.$

Divided figures are used to illustrate the fact that the total of the component parts of a unit equals 100%. They also suggest the relation between fractions and percents.

Example 1

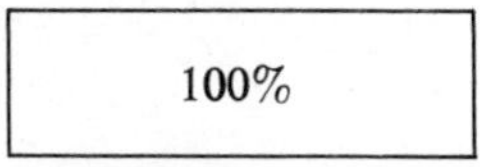

The whole bar represents 100%.

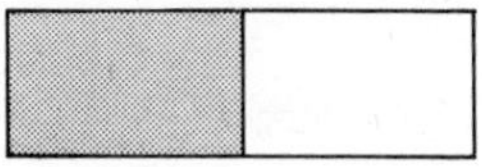

$\frac{1}{2}$ of the bar represents $\square\%$.

Example 2

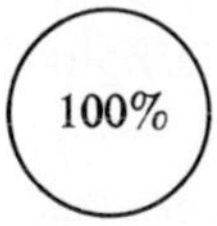

The whole circle represents $\square\%$.

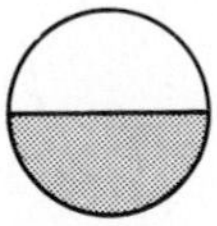

$\frac{1}{2}$ of the circle represents $\square\%$.

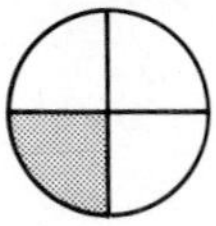

$\frac{1}{4}$ of the circle represents $\square\%$.

EQUIVALENTS

The number line is an effective aid for showing relationships among fractions, decimals, and percents:

0										1
$\frac{0}{10}$	$\frac{1}{10}$	$\frac{2}{10}$	$\frac{3}{10}$	$\frac{4}{10}$	$\frac{5}{10}$	$\frac{6}{10}$	$\frac{7}{10}$	$\frac{8}{10}$	$\frac{9}{10}$	$\frac{10}{10}$
$\frac{0}{100}$	$\frac{10}{100}$	$\frac{20}{100}$	$\frac{30}{100}$	$\frac{40}{100}$	$\frac{50}{100}$	$\frac{60}{100}$	$\frac{70}{100}$	$\frac{80}{100}$	$\frac{90}{100}$	$\frac{100}{100}$
.0	.1	.2	.3	.4	.5	.6	.7	.8	.9	1.0
.00	.10	.20	.30	.40	.50	.60	.70	.80	.90	1.00
0%	10%	20%	30%	40%	50%	60%	70%	80%	90%	100%

The pupils can also construct such number lines themselves and write sentences such as $\frac{1}{2} = .5 = 50\%$. When they understand the relationships among fractions, decimals, and percents, they are ready to formulate these rules with the help of the teacher:

1. A decimal is converted to a percent by moving the decimal point two places to the right and annexing the percent sign.

   Examples

   $.17 = 17\%$ $.5 = .50 = 50\%$ $.03 = 3\%$

2. A fraction is converted to a percent by changing the fraction to a decimal and then changing the decimal to a percent.

   Examples

   $\frac{1}{5} = .2 = 20\%$ $\frac{1}{10} = .1 = 10\%$ $\frac{3}{8} = .375 = 37.5\%$

   A fraction can often be changed to a percent more meaningfully by thinking: Since the whole equals 100%, $\frac{1}{2} = 50\%$, $\frac{1}{4} = 25\%$, etc.

3. A percent is changed to a decimal by dropping the percent sign and moving the decimal point two places to the left.

   Examples

   $35\% = .35$ $50\% = .50 = .5$ $8\% = .08$

   $25.5\% = .255$ $100\% = 1.00 = 1$ $250\% = 2.50 = 2.5$

4. A percent is changed to a fraction by expressing the percent as a fraction with a denominator of 100 and, if necessary, writing the fraction in simplest terms.

   Examples

   $50\% = \frac{50}{100} = \frac{1}{2}$ $15\% = \frac{15}{100} = \frac{3}{20}$

   $\frac{1}{5}\% = \frac{\frac{1}{5}}{100} = \frac{5 \times \frac{1}{5}}{5 \times 100} = \frac{1}{500}$ $61\% = \frac{61}{100}$

A recommended exercise is the preparation of a table presenting important equivalent fractions, decimals, and percents. These equivalents should be memorized in order to facilitate future computations with percents and to enable pupils to interpret immediately common expressions such as "12½% off" that frequently appear on price tags and in advertisements in newspapers.

METHODS OF TEACHING

There are three cases or types of percent problems:

Case I. Finding a percent of a number.

Example

5% of 800 = □.

Case II. Finding what percent one number is of another number.

Example

6 = □% of 24.

Case III. Finding a number when a percent of it is given.

Example

8 = 2% of □.

These types of problems can be solved by any of several methods. Some methods are more promising than others and are more commonly taught. The presentation in this chapter deals with:

I. Formula method
II. Equation method
III. Unitary analysis method

Formula Method

The formulas are developed after pupils know the meaning of percent and have had experience in solving simple percent problems by using fractions and decimals or by working with the hundred board and the number line. Two examples follow.

Example 1

Find 10% of $400. The number line shown previously indicates that 10% = .1. Thus, 10% of $400 = .1 × $400 = $40.

Example 2

Twenty-five percent of $16 is found by taking ¼ of $16, since 25% = ¼.

After the pupils have learned to identify the *rate, base,* and *percentage,* the letters *r, b,* and *p* are substituted for these terms and the formula is developed:

$$5\% \text{ of } 700 = .05 \times 700 = 35$$
$$r \times b = p$$

The formulas for Cases II and III are derived from the formula for Case I. Problem situations are of the type where the pupils already know the answers or where the answers can easily be found.

From the exercise presented above, the pupils know that 5% of 700 = 35. In Case II the rate must be found, and the formula is derived as follows:

$$\square\% \text{ of } 700 = 35$$
$$5\% \text{ of } 700 = 35$$
$$.05 \times 700 = 35$$
$$.05 = \frac{35}{700}$$
$$r = \frac{p}{b}$$

In Case III the base is the unknown. The formula is derived in a similar way:

$$5\% \text{ of } \square = 35$$
$$5\% \text{ of } 700 = 35$$
$$.05 \times 700 = 35$$
$$700 = \frac{35}{.05}$$
$$b = \frac{p}{r}$$

Example of Case I

On a snowy day the teacher said that 15% of the 400 pupils enrolled in school were absent. How many pupils were absent?

Number question: 15% of 400 = □.

Formula: $p = r \times b$.

Solution: $b = 400$
$r = 15\%$, which must be expressed as .15.
$p = .15 \times 400$
$p = 60$
There were 60 pupils absent.

Example of Case II

In a spelling test of 50 words, Bill spelled 10 words incorrectly. What percent of the words did he spell incorrectly?

Number question: 10 = □% of 50.

Formula: $r = \frac{p}{b}$.

Solution: $p = 10$
$b = 50$
$r = \frac{10}{50} = .20$
$r = 20\%$
Bill spelled 20% of the words incorrectly.

Example of Case III

Tom received a commission of 25% for selling Christmas cards. If Tom earned $10, how much money did he collect from the customers in all?

Number question: 10 is 25% of □.

Formula: $b = \frac{p}{r}$.

Solution: $p = 10$
$r = 25\%$, which must be expressed as .25.
$b = \frac{10}{.25} = 40$
The amount of Tom's sales was $40.

Equation Method

The equation method presented below uses a *proportion,* a statement expressing the equality of two ratios.

A percent expresses the ratio of a number to 100. Therefore, one of the ratios in the proportion is always $\frac{\text{number of percents}}{\text{one hundred}}$. The other part of the equation expresses the ratio between the percentage and the base. Thus the equation is expressed as $\frac{\text{number of percents}}{\text{one hundred}} = \frac{\text{percentage}}{\text{base}}$, in which the number of percents, the percentage, or the base is the missing number.

In Case I, the percentage must be found, and the equation is written as:

$$\frac{\text{number of percents}}{100} = \frac{n}{\text{base}}$$

In Case II, the number of percents must be found. This is expressed as:

$$\frac{n}{100} = \frac{\text{percentage}}{\text{base}}$$

In Case III, the base is the unknown shown in the equation:

$$\frac{\text{number of percents}}{100} = \frac{\text{percentage}}{n}$$

When a percent problem is being solved by the equation method, the pupils do not need to identify the case to which it belongs. Yet, for the purpose of organization, the different problem situations will be discussed in the traditional order of the cases.

Example of Case I

A salesman earned 5% commission on a sale of \$300. How much commission did he receive?

Number question: 5% of 300 = □, or 5% of 300 = n.

Solution: Equation: $\frac{5}{100} = \frac{n}{300}$. In initial exercises the pupils are guided to reason as follows: I multiply 100 by 3 to get 300, so I multiply 5 by 3 to find the missing number. This process is expressed as follows:

$$\frac{5}{100} = \frac{3 \times 5}{3 \times 100} = \frac{15}{300}$$

Since the missing number is 15, 5% of 300 = 15. (Of course, other approaches can be selected, for example: 5 to 100 = n to 300.) The salesman received \$15.

It is not always possible to multiply a given number by a whole number and get 100. Therefore, at a more advanced stage, the children are taught to solve the problem by applying the principle that the cross products of a proportion are equal. The missing number is then found in this way:

$$\frac{5}{100} = \frac{n}{300}$$
$$100 \times n = 5 \times 300$$
$$100n = 1500$$
$$n = 15$$

The equality of the cross products of a proportion is demonstrated by using an example involving simple computations:

$\frac{2}{3} = \frac{4}{6}$ multiply both $\frac{2}{3}$ and $\frac{4}{6}$ by 6

$$\frac{6 \times 2}{3} = \frac{6 \times 4}{6}$$

$\frac{6 \times 2}{3} = 4$ multiply both $\frac{6 \times 2}{3}$ and 4 by 3

$$\frac{3 \times 6 \times 2}{3} = 3 \times 4$$

$$6 \times 2 = 3 \times 4$$

Example of Case II

When selling Christmas cards, Ted collected \$20. If he was allowed to keep \$4, what was the rate of his commission?

Number question: 4 is □% of 20.

Solutions:

1. Equation: $\frac{n}{100} = \frac{4}{20}$, or $\frac{4}{20} = \frac{n}{100}$. Since 20 is multiplied by 5 to get 100, 4 must also be multiplied by 5 to find the missing number: $5 \times 4 = 20$. Thus $n = 20$. Ted received a commission of 20%.
2. Equation: $\frac{n}{100} = \frac{4}{20}$
$$20n = 400$$
$$n = 20$$

Example of Case III

Judy has \$10 in her bank. If this is 20% of the money she has, how much money does she have in all?

Number question: 10 is 20% of □.

Solutions:

1. Equation: $\frac{20}{100} = \frac{10}{n}$. Since 20 is divided by 2 to get 10, 100 must be divided by 2 to find the missing number: $100 \div 2 = 50$. Thus $n = 50$. Judy has \$50 in all.
2. Equation: $\frac{20}{100} = \frac{10}{n}$
$$20n = 1000$$
$$n = 50$$

Unitary Analysis Method

The unitary analysis method, also called the *unit method,* is easy to understand and apply. When solving a percent problem, the pupils do not have to determine to which case it belongs. Problems can often be solved by mental computation.

Example of Case I

One day 3% of the 800 pupils of Jefferson School were absent. How many pupils were absent that day?

Number question: 3% of 800 = □.

Solution:

a. Find 1% of the given base: 1% of 800 = 8.
b. Find 3% of 800: 3% of 800 = 3 × 8 = 24.
c. There were 24 pupils absent.

Example of Case II

One day 8 of the 400 pupils of Grant School were absent. What percent of the pupils were absent that day?

Number question: 8 is □% of 400.

Solution:

a. Find 1% of the given base: 1% of 400 = 4.
b. Determine what percent 8 is of 400: Since 4 = 1% of 400, 8 = 2% of 400.
c. 2% of the pupils were absent.

Example of Case III

Twenty percent of the pupils of Washington School are members of the choir. If the choir has 40 members, how many pupils are enrolled in Washington School?

Number question: 40 is 20% of □.

Solution:

a. Find 1% of the base: Since 20% of the base = 40, 1% of the base = 40 ÷ 20 = 2.
b. Find 100%: Since 1% of the base = 2, 100% of the base = 100 × 2 = 200.
c. There are 200 pupils enrolled in Washington School.

The unitary analysis method of teaching percentage appears to be a very logical method. The pupils first find 1% of the base. Then they decide what must be found and compute the answer.

In cases where the percent is an aliquot part of 100, it is simpler to use the method sometimes called the *fraction method.*

Examples

10% of $400 = \frac{1}{10} \times 400 = 40$.
$12\frac{1}{2}\%$ of $24 = \frac{1}{8} \times 24 = 3$.
75% of $80 = \frac{3}{4} \times 80 = 60$.

SELECTED RESEARCH

In this study[1] percentage was taught to three groups of seventh-grade pupils, a total of 475 pupils. An effort was made to balance the ability

1. R. A. Kenney and J. D. Stockton, "An Experimental Study in Teaching Percentage," *The Arithmetic Teacher* (December, 1958), pp. 294–303.

of the groups. Three methods or approaches were used:

1. Drill procedures were emphasized, with reliance on rules and repetition. No explanations were given, and no aids were used.
2. Understanding and mathematical reasoning were emphasized. The *why* and *how* were stressed. No rules were taught as such. All kinds of aids were used.
3. A combination of the first two methods were used: Procedures were employed to develop understanding, and drill was used to fix and facilitate learning.

A pre-test, post-test, and follow-up test, all of equal difficulty, were administered.

Athough the results were not conclusive, the combination method appeared to be the best of the three approaches used. One of the clear findings was that the upper three-quarters of all three groups made significant progress during the experimental period. Small gains were made by the lowest level.

SELECTED ACTIVITIES FOR PUPILS

1. Find the answers to the exercises by mental computation.

   10% of 50 = □   20% of 40 = □   25% of 80 = □   50% of 10 = □

2. Complete.

   Sale—10% off on all items

Items	*Regular price*	*Sale price*
Shoes	\$15.00	_____
Coat	32.00	_____
Socks	.80	_____
Tie	3.50	_____

3. Write =, <, or > to make a true statement.

   60% ○ $\frac{3}{5}$ $\frac{7}{8}$ ○ 90%   .4 ○ 30%   70% ○ .91

4. Complete.

Fraction	$\frac{1}{10}$	$\frac{2}{10}$	$\frac{3}{10}$	$\frac{4}{10}$	$\frac{5}{10}$	$\frac{6}{10}$	$\frac{7}{10}$	$\frac{8}{10}$	$\frac{9}{10}$	$\frac{10}{10}$
Decimal	.1	.2								
Percent	10		30							

5. Complete.

Fraction	$\frac{1}{2}$	$\frac{1}{3}$	$\frac{1}{4}$	$\frac{1}{5}$	$\frac{1}{6}$	$\frac{1}{7}$	$\frac{1}{8}$	$\frac{1}{9}$	$\frac{1}{10}$
Percent	50								

6. Complete.

Fraction	$\frac{1}{2}$			$\frac{9}{10}$		
Decimal	.5	.75			.4	
Percent	50		25			80

7. Roll a wooden disk until it completes one rotation. Measure the length of circumference (C) and diameter (d). Find the ratio of the two measures.

Note: You should have found a ratio of a little more than 3 to 1. The first number of the ratio is expressed by the symbol π (read "pi"). Approximations of π are 3.14 and $3\frac{1}{7}$.

EXERCISES

1. Explain the meaning of *percent*.
2. Write a percent problem, find the answer to it, and identify the rate, the base, and the percentage.
3. Without consulting the text, express in words the proportion used in the equation method presented in this chapter.

4. Construct a problem for each of the three cases in the text dealing with percents. Solve each problem by a method you select.
5. What visual aids can help in the teaching of the meaning of percent?
6. Write an illustrative lesson for sixth-grade pupils in which one of the three types of percent problems is taught by any one of the methods presented in this chapter.
7. Report on an important piece of research dealing with the teaching of percent.

SOURCES FOR FURTHER READING

Brousseau, R. L., T. A. Brown, and P. J. Johnson, "Introduction to Ratio and Proportion," *The Arithmetic Teacher,* February, 1969, pp. 89–90.

Cole, B. L., and H. S. Weissenfluh, "An Analysis of Teaching Percentages," *The Arithmetic Teacher,* March, 1974, pp. 226–228.

Crumley, R. D., "Teaching Rate and Ratio in Middle Grades," *School Science and Mathematics,* February, 1960, pp. 143–150.

D'Augustine, C. H., *Multiple Methods of Teaching Mathematics in the Elementary School,* 2nd ed. New York: Harper & Row, Publishers, 1973, Chap. XIV.

Kennedy, L. M., *Guiding Children to Mathematical Discovery,* 2nd ed. Belmont, California: Wadsworth Publishing Company, Inc., 1975, Chap. XIII.

Marks, J. L., C. R. Purdy, L. B. Kinney, and A. A. Hiatt, *Teaching Elementary School Mathematics for Understanding,* 4th ed. New York: McGraw-Hill Book Company, 1975, Chap. VIII.

Riedesel, C. A., *Guiding Discovery in Elementary School Mathematics.* New York: Appleton-Century-Crofts, 1967, Chap. X.

Schminke, C. W., N. Maertens, and W. R. Arnold, *Teaching the Child Mathematics.* Hinsdale, Illinois: The Dryden Press, Inc., 1973, Chap. IX.

Spitzer, H. F., *Teaching Elementary School Mathematics.* Boston: Houghton Mifflin Company, 1967, Chap. XI.

Tredway, D. C., and G. E. Hollister, "An Experimental Study of Two Approaches to Teaching Percentage," *The Arithmetic Teacher,* December, 1963, pp. 491–495.

Van Engen, H., "Rate Pairs, Fractions, and Rational Numbers," *The Arithmetic Teacher,* December, 1960, pp. 389–399.

Measurement 18

Measurement is an important topic in the elementary school mathematics program because of its extensive use in life and because of the numerous occasions when children are faced with measurement situations both in and out of school.

In Canada and in the United States metric units are gradually replacing "English" units of measure. However, it is obvious that for several years English units will still be used on many occasions. Therefore, this chapter deals with the English system, and the Metric System of Measures and Weights (SI) is introduced in Chapter 19.

In the primary grades, the teacher introduces the meaning and the needed terms of measurement, acquaints the children with the important units of measure, and directs their efforts to use the common tools. As pupils move up in the grades, the teacher refines the acquired concepts, extends the vocabulary, and leads the children from crude comparisons to more refined measurements.[1] The teacher must, therefore, be acquainted with the main principles of measurement and with their applications.

SKILLS TEST

1. 1 ft. 8 in. + 1 ft. 7 in. = 	3 × 3 ft. 5 in. =
   6 lb. 5 oz. − 2 lb. 7 oz. = 	7 bu. 2 pk. ÷ 3 =

---

1. The student is referred to E. M. Churchill, *Counting and Measuring* (Toronto: University of Toronto Press, 1961), chap. VII.

2. 2 lb. 11 oz. + 3 lb. 8 oz. = 3 × 3 gal. 2 qt. =
   3 mi. 600 ft. − 1 mi. 900 ft. = 2 hr. 40 min. ÷ 4 =
3. 52 oz. = ______ lb. ______ oz. 1 cu. ft. − 200 cu. in. = ______ cu. in.
   205 sq. in. = ______ sq. ft. ______ sq. in. 1 cu. yd. − 1 cu. ft. = ______ cu. ft.
4. 6,000 ft. = ______ mi. ______ ft. 2 cu. ft. + 1 cu. yd. = ______ cu. ft.
   1,280 acres = ______ sq. mi. 1 cu. ft. − 500 cu. in. = ______ cu. in.
5. The sides of a triangle measure $1\frac{1}{2}$ yd., 7 ft., and 60 in. What is the perimeter of the triangle in feet?
6. What is the circumference in inches of a circle with a radius of 1 ft.?
7. How many tiles 9 inches square are needed to cover a floor 12 ft. by 15 ft.?
8. The base of a parallelogram measures 7 yd. and its altitude $3\frac{1}{2}$ yd. What is its area in square feet?
9. Find the area in square inches of a triangle with a base of 10 in. and an altitude of $8\frac{1}{2}$ in.
10. The bases of a trapezoid measure $1\frac{1}{2}$ ft. and $12\frac{1}{2}$ in., and its altitude is 8 in. What is the area in square inches of the trapezoid?
11. Find the area in square inches of a circle with a diameter of 5 in.
12. The excavation for the basement of a house that is to be constructed is 39 ft. long, 33 ft. wide, and $7\frac{1}{2}$ ft. deep. Find the number of cubic yards of earth that have been removed to make the excavation.
13. The volume of a cube is 64 cubic in. What is the surface area of each of its bases?
14. A cylindrical tank is $2\frac{1}{2}$ ft. in diameter and 6 ft. long. How many gallons of water will the tank hold? (1 cu. ft. = $7\frac{1}{2}$ gal.)
15. What is the total surface area of a cube with an edge of 8 in.?

MEANING In measurement, the ratio between a magnitude—which is a property of an object that is measurable, such as length or weight—and a given *standard unit* of the same nature is expressed by a number. Such a reference unit must necessarily be accurately defined.

When the number of beads in a group is determined, the beads are counted. In this activity a group that consists of *discrete* or separate elements is measured and its cardinal number is determined.

When the length of an object is measured, or the measure of a distance is determined, a *continuous property* is considered, and the length of the object or the distance is compared with a continuous scale. A standard unit of the same nature, such as the inch, is selected, and it is decided how many of the selected units approximately equal the length of the object or the distance to be measured. The number that expresses the length of the object in standard units is called a *measure* of the object. Such a measurement cannot be performed exactly—not even by scientists who use refined tools—and the measure decided upon expresses an approximation.

The term *measuring* is used when a continuous property is involved. The term *counting* refers to the activity in which the cardinal number of a set is determined.

SOME HISTORY OF MEASUREMENT

In primitive society there was not much need for specific units of measure, since crude comparisons were sufficient. An object under consideration was compared with a known object; for example, an animal was described as being larger or smaller than a deer. When the need for more accurate descriptions arose, man established units of measure for common use. Such units were related to parts of the body, to conspicuous objects, or to natural phenomena, and therefore were not standardized. The different positions of the sun and the moon suggested units of time. Lengths were expressed by referring to dimensions of certain parts of the human body, such as *girth,* the length around the waist; *cubit,* from the elbow to the tip of the middle finger; *palm,* the width of the hand; *span,* from the tip of the thumb to the tip of the little finger when the hand is spread out; *digit,* the width of the finger; *ell,* from the tip of the middle finger on an outstretched arm to the middle of the body; and *fathom,* from the tip of one middle finger to the tip of the other when the arms are outstretched. Common units for measuring distances were *foot, step,* and *pace* (a double step). Longer distances were compared with an arrow's flight or a day's journey. The Romans called a distance of 1,000 paces a *mille passum,* which equaled approximately 5,000 feet.[2]

Unstandardized units of measure were employed for a long time, and some are still in use. For example, it is common to refer to a handful of sand, a pinch of salt, and an armful of firewood, but such measures are not reliable, since they vary with different people and on different occasions. Thus the need for standardized units of measure arose. People gradually

---

2. For a study of the origin of units of measure the student is referred to a more extensive treatment of the topic—for example, to H. G. Wheat, *How to Teach Arithmetic* (New York: Harper & Row, Publishers, 1956), chap. XII.

became more specific in their descriptions until, finally, governments defined standard units of measure by law.

DIRECT AND INDIRECT MEASUREMENT

In direct measurement the selected standard unit is applied directly to the object under consideration. For example, determining the length of a table by using a foot ruler is direct measurement.

In indirect measurement the standard unit is not applied directly to the object to be measured. The altitude of a mountain top, for instance, is measured indirectly by application of a proper formula.

PRECISION IN MEASUREMENT

The measurement of a continuous magnitude results in a measure that expresses the ratio between the considered magnitude of the object and the selected unit. Such a number expresses an approximation of that ratio and, since it names the selected unit of measure, it is usually called a *denominate number*.

A measurement is assumed to be precise to the smallest unit reported. If the length of an object is reported to be 9.6 inches, the last significant digit indicates tenths, and it is assumed that the measure of the length has been reported to the nearest tenth of an inch. Thus 9.6 expresses an approximate number and may represent any number from 9.55 to 9.65. If the length is given as 9.75 inches, the last significant digit indicates hundredths, and it is assumed that the measure of the length has been rounded to the nearest hundredth of an inch. Thus 9.75 may represent any number from 9.745 to 9.755. Since the number in the first example has been rounded to the nearest tenth, the error may be as much as .05 inch, whereas in the second example the *maximum error* is .005.

FOUNDATION EXPERIENCES

The primary-grade teacher who wants to provide suitable activities for the pupils will first determine the quantity and the quality of the concepts of measurement the children have already acquired. The teacher may administer a self-made test and record each pupil's knowledge and abilities on a checksheet. With this information, the teacher will then attempt to help the children refine concepts they already possess, develop new ones, and extend their measurement vocabulary.

Many exercises in the pupil's textbook and workbook will serve the teacher in providing proper experiences in measurement. Yet it will often be necessary to supply additional activities. Several foundation experiences from which the teacher may make a selection have been suggested in Chapter 10.

In beginning instruction, unstandardized units of measure should be used. A few examples of such activities are presented in the following paragraphs.

1. Measure the length of your pencil by using your thumb. How many thumbs long is the pencil?

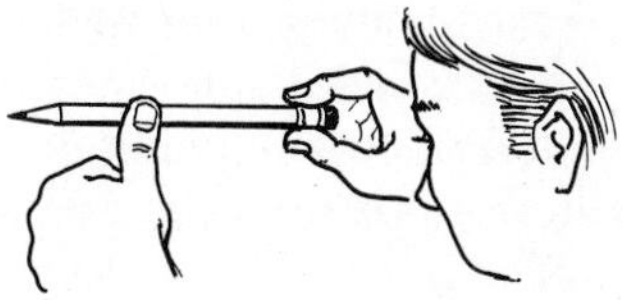

2. How many paper clips fit around your waist? Guess first, then check your answer.

3. Get a book, a crayon, and a ruler. How many paper clips long is the book? How many paper clips long is the crayon? How many paper clips long is the ruler?

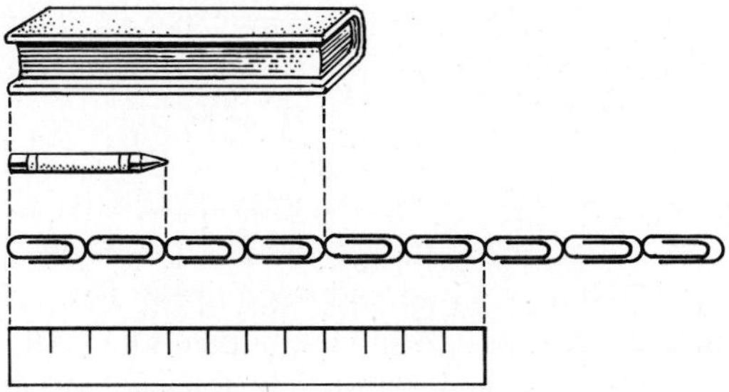

4. How many steps do you have to take to walk from the door to the window? First guess, then check your answer.

LINEAR MEASURES

A rich program in foundation experiences will gradually lead the child from unstandardized units to the meaningful use of standard units. Foot rulers, yardsticks, and tape measures are used, and lengths and distances are expressed in increasingly smaller units. The following are examples of some activities:

Comparing lengths and distances.
Comparing line segments.
Identifying various measuring instruments and comparing them.
Measuring the dimensions of the schoolroom and of objects in the room.
Measuring the distance that a pupil can jump.
Determining the growth of a plant during a period of time.
Measuring the heights of pupils and comparing the answers.
Estimating the length of an object and verifying the result.
Selecting the appropriate unit of measure to be used for measuring the lengths of small and large objects.
Measuring the length of the school building by using a tape measure or a rope of a given length.
Drawing a line segment of a given length.
Measuring the length of a line segment.
Estimating the length of a line segment and verifying the result.
Drawing a line segment of a given length without using a foot ruler and verifying the result.
Performing computations with linear measures.
Working with simple fractional units of measure.
Translating one unit of measure into another.
Rounding reported measures.

Through frequent use of common measuring tools the children will become well enough acquainted with equivalents such as 1 foot = 12 inches, 1 yard = 3 feet, and 1 yard = 36 inches to construct their own table of measures. Such equivalents as 1 mile = 5,280 feet are provided by the teacher.

Perimeters

The perimeter of a polygon equals the sum of the measures of its sides. Thus if the letters l and w stand for the measures of the length and the width of a rectangle, the formula for its perimeter can be expressed as $P = l + w + l + w$. The pupil should develop the formula $P = 2l + 2w$. Since a square is a quadrilateral with four congruent sides, the formula for its perimeter is written as $P = 4s$.

Circumference of a Circle

After the teacher has introduced or reviewed the common terms such as circumference, diameter, and radius by presenting and discussing an illustration like Figure 18.1, the pupils are directed to find the measure of the circumferences of cans, baskets, or wooden disks by using a tape measure. The answers are pooled and compared, and the ratio of the circumference to the diameter is approximated. It is suggested that a reasonable approximation of the number that expresses the ratio of the circumference to the diameter of a circle is 3.14 or $3\frac{1}{7}$. The teacher tells the pupils that the exact ratio is expressed by the symbol π (read "pi") but that in computations the approximation 3.14 or $3\frac{1}{7}$ may be used. The formula is then written as $C = \pi d$ or $C = \pi 2r$.

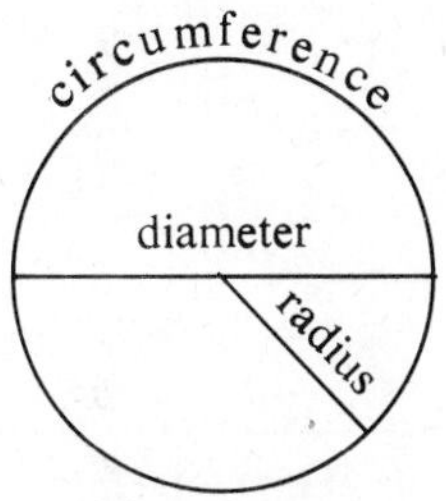

Figure 18.1

AREA

The area of a surface is found by determining how many of the selected units of measure are needed to cover that surface. In initial teaching unstandardized units are used—the child determines how many books will cover the surface of a desk, how many squares of a certain size it takes to cover the surface of a book, or how many tiles are needed to cover the surface of a certain part of the floor. After these exercises the teacher directs the class discussion so that the need for standard units of area becomes apparent. The square inch—a square region with sides measuring one inch each—and the square foot are introduced. The pupil manipulates these units and determines, for example, how many units of one square inch it takes to cover the surface of a book, or how many units of one square foot are needed to cover the surface of a table top. Such activities prepare the child for a meaningful development of the needed formulas. The square yard is usually introduced at a later time.

Rectangle

The area of the rectangle[3] illustrated in Figure 18.2 is first determined by covering its surface with models measuring one square unit and counting the number of units needed. The pupil is then led to the shorter way, in

---

3. When reference is made to the area of a plane figure, the plane figure and its interior are meant.

which the number of units in one row is multiplied by the number of rows: 3×4 square units = 12 square units, or 4×3 square units = 12 square units. This leads to the development of the formula: Area = length × width ($A = l \times w$).

It should be understood that when the formula $A = l \times w$ is applied, the *number* of square units in a row is multiplied by the *number* of rows in the width to find the *number* of square units in the area.

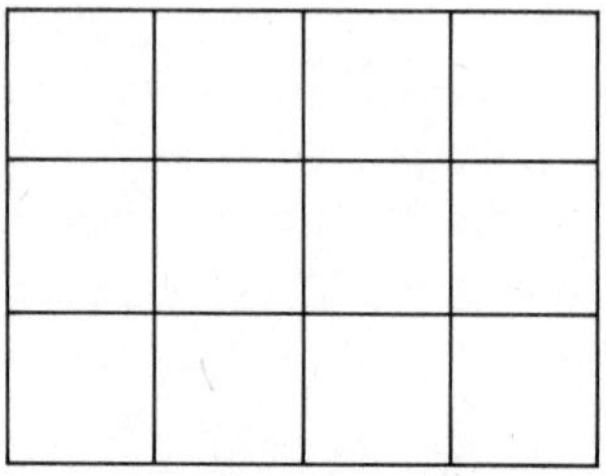

Figure 18.2

Square A square is a rectangle with congruent sides. Therefore, when its area is determined by finding how many selected square units it takes to cover its surface, there prove to be as many rows as there are columns. This leads to the formula: Area = side × side ($A = s \times s$ or $A = s^2$).

Parallelogram The nonrectangular parallelogram shown in Figure 18.3 can be converted into a rectangle with the same amount of surface. This is done by moving

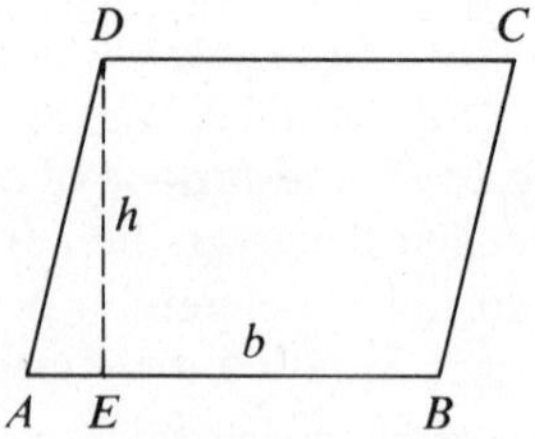

Figure 18.3

triangle *AED* to the right of the parallelogram to form triangle *BFC*, as illustrated in Figure 18.4. The parallelogram *ABCD* has been converted into rectangle *EFCD* with the same area. Thus the formula for the area of a parallelogram can be written as Area = base × height (or altitude), or $A = b \times h$.

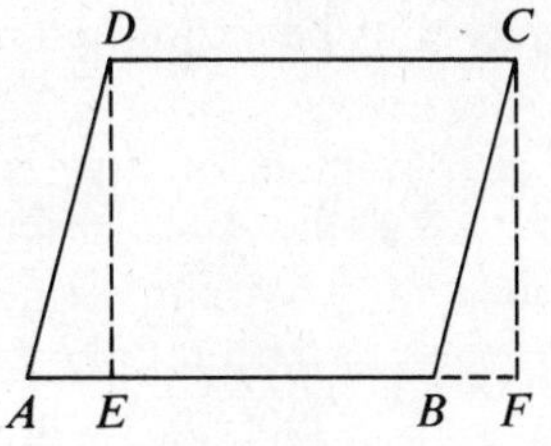

Figure 18.4

Triangle

The parallelogram *ABCD* shown in Figure 18.5 is divided into two congruent triangles by the diagonal *BD*. The pupils verify that the area of triangle *ABD* is equal to one-half of the area of parallelogram *ABCD*. Since the formula for the area of a parallelogram can be expressed as $A = b \times h$, the formula for the area of a triangle can be written as $A = \frac{b \times h}{2}$, or as $A = \frac{1}{2} \times b \times h$.

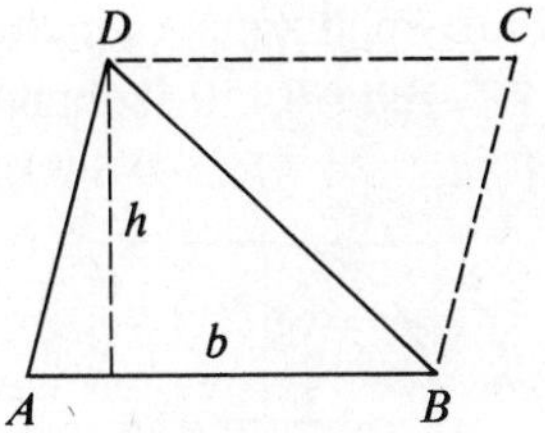

Figure 18.5

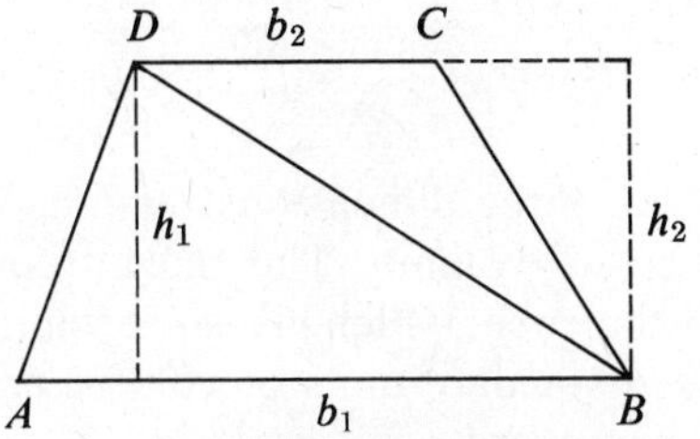

Figure 18.6

Trapezoid

In the illustration in Figure 18.6, trapezoid *ABCD* has been divided into two triangles, *ABD* and *DCB*, with the bases b_1 and b_2, respectively. The base of triangle *DCB* (b_2) has been extended, and h_2 represents the altitude of that triangle. Since the opposite sides *AB* and *DC* are parallel, $h_1 = h_2$.

The area of a trapezoid may thus be expressed as the sum of the areas of two triangles:

$$\text{Area of triangle } ABD\text{: } \frac{b_1 \times h}{2}$$

$$\text{Area of triangle } DCB\text{: } \frac{b_2 \times h}{2}$$

$$+$$

$$\text{Area of trapezoid } ABCD\text{: } \frac{(b_1 + b_2) \times h}{2}$$

Circle The formula for the area of a circle is πr^2. The reasonableness of this formula may be illustrated by a circle inscribed in a square, as in Figure 18.7. The area of one-fourth of the square is expressed as r^2. By comparing the area of the circle with that of the square, the pupils are led to see that the total area of three small squares ($3r^2$) is not enough to cover the area of the circle. (If necessary, this can be illustrated more accurately on graph paper by making a count of the small square units needed to cover the area of the circle and of those needed to cover the area of the square.) Since it is obvious that four small squares include much more area than the circle, $3.14 \times r^2$, or πr^2, appears to be a sensible formula.

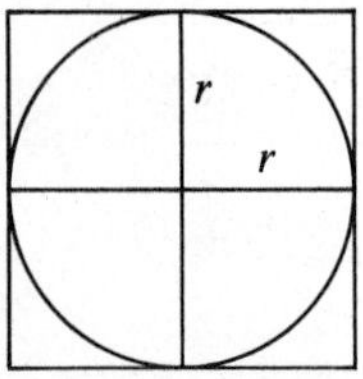

Figure 18.7

VOLUME A solid is a figure with three dimensions: length, width, and height. A measure of a solid is its volume. The most frequently used unit for measuring volume is the cube, which is a solid with six congruent square faces. Commonly used standard units of volume are the cubic inch, the cubic foot, and the cubic yard.

When the concept of volume is introduced, the pupils engage in such activities as filling various boxes with units, and are led to conclude that the volume of a solid is determined by finding how many of the selected units are needed to fill the box. The differences in the various units used suggest the need for standard units of measure, and the cubic inch, the cubic foot, and the cubic yard are introduced. If time permits, the pupils should construct some of these units from cardboard or construction paper.

Terms such as rectangular prism, cylinder, cone, pyramid, and sphere are reviewed or introduced as needed.

Rectangular Solid

The volume of a box is initially determined as in Figure 18.8 by counting the number of cubic-inch blocks it takes to fill the box. After several similar activities, the rule for finding the volume of a rectangular solid is developed by the pupils or suggested by the teacher in the following steps:

1. The number of cubic-unit blocks (for example, cubic-inch blocks) in the bottom layer is determined by multiplying the number of cubes in one row by the number of rows. (Base = length × width. This is abbreviated as $B = l \times w$.)

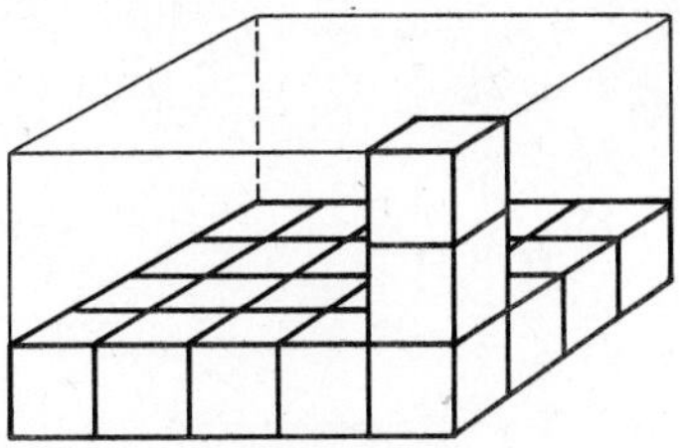

Figure 18.8

2. The number of cubes in the bottom layer is multiplied by the number of layers (height × base).
3. The volume (V) of a rectangular solid can then be expressed as: $V = l \times w \times h$, or $V = B \times h$.

Cube

Experiments in filling a cubical box or frame with cubic-inch blocks lead to the formula for the volume of a cube: $V = s^3$.

If enough cubic-inch blocks are available, the pupils can discover that 1,728 cubic inches are contained in a cubic foot: 12 × 12 cubic-inch blocks constitute the bottom layer, and there are 12 such layers. Similarly, it is determined that a cubic yard equals 27 cubic feet: 3 layers of 9 cubic-foot blocks are placed in a frame that measures one cubic yard.

MEASURES OF CAPACITY

In the United States, the basic unit for liquid measure is the gallon. Other liquid measures are the quart ($\frac{1}{4}$ gallon), the pint ($\frac{1}{2}$ quart), and the cup ($\frac{1}{2}$ pint). The capacity of bottles or cans is often expressed in fluid ounces; a fluid ounce equals $\frac{1}{16}$ of a pint.

Our basic unit for dry measure is the bushel. Other dry measures are the peck ($\frac{1}{4}$ bushel), the quart ($\frac{1}{8}$ peck), and the pint ($\frac{1}{2}$ quart).

In the English System there is still much confusion concerning various measures. A liquid quart is less than a dry quart, and several types of bushels are in use. Attempts to define the bushel by weight have resulted in various definitions in different states. A universal use of metric units will bring an end to these undesirable situations.

The young child frequently comes into contact with units of liquid measure. As early as the primary grades children manipulate gallons, quarts, and pints, fill containers with water, and observe simple relationships between the units.

Although children have little need for units of dry measure, they should be acquainted with the bushel basket, quart, and peck. Only in some rural areas may there be a need for more extensive computations involving such units.

As enrichment exercises, interested pupils may study the history of the development of units of measure of capacity; they may also investigate the origin and meaning of less frequently used terms, such as barrel and hogshead.

MEASURES OF WEIGHT

The avoirdupois pound, which is the standard pound in common use in the United States, is divided into 16 ounces of 437.5 grains each.

The hundredweight, which equals 100 pounds, is used for weighing heavy commodities, such as livestock. The ton of 2,000 pounds, which is the legal ton, is used for weighing goods sold in large bulk—coal, for instance. It is sometimes called the short ton to distinguish it from the British long ton of 2,240 pounds.

The modern teacher engages pupils in activities in which they perform measurements and verify the obtained answers. For this purpose the following activities are suggested:

Weighing objects.
Comparing the weights of objects.
Estimating the weight of an object and verifying the answer by weighing.
Filling bags with sand to weigh 1 pound, 2 pounds, 5 pounds, $\frac{1}{2}$ pound, etc., and labeling the bags.
Investigating and reporting which articles are sold by the pound, in a bag of 10 pounds, etc.

Comparing and using different types of weighing instruments.
Keeping a record of one's weight.

MEASURES OF TIME

The three main units of time are the year (the period of time needed for one revolution of the earth around the sun), the month (the period of time needed for one revolution of the moon around the earth), and the day (the period of time needed for one rotation of the earth on its axis). The fact that not one of these units can be expressed as an integral part of another has created great difficulties for the makers of calendars all through the centuries. Though the presently used Gregorian calendar has some weaknesses, it is quite usable. Scientists favor the adoption of the "World Calendar," which would be an improvement on the Gregorian calendar.[4]

Time has been determined in the past by observing the position of the sun in the sky, by measuring the lengths of shadows, and by using instruments such as sundials, water clocks, and sandglasses. Clocks were first run by weights and pendulums; later springs and balance wheels were invented. Clocks and watches were gradually improved and equipped with an hour hand, a minute hand, and often a second hand.

In the present system of measuring time, the following units are in common use:

1 century	= 100 years
1 common year	= 365 days
1 leap year	= 366 days
1 common year	= 52 weeks and 1 day
1 year	= 12 calendar months
1 calendar month	= 28, 29, 30, or 31 days
1 week	= 7 days
1 day	= 24 hours
1 hour	= 60 minutes
1 minute	= 60 seconds
1 solar year	= 365 days, 5 hours, 48 minutes, and 46 seconds

Elementary-school pupils receive systematic instruction in reading the calendar and in telling and measuring time by consulting the clock. They must develop concepts of commonly used units of time and become acquainted with the common vocabulary.

The hour hand of the clock revolves twice during the period of one

---

4. The student is referred to H. F. Spitzer, *The Teaching of Arithmetic* (Boston: Houghton Mifflin Company, 1961), pp. 238–242.

day. One set of 12 hours is designated as A.M. (ante meridiem), and the other set as P.M. (post meridiem). In the armed forces of the United States and in some foreign countries, the 24-hour clock is used. On this clock the hours and minutes lapsed since midnight are registered by a four-figure numeral. The first two figures indicate the hour, and the last two the minutes. Thus midnight is indicated as 2400, 6:30 P.M. as 1830, 2 A.M. as 0200, etc.

Other topics of interest related to time are time zones, conversion of units of longitude into units of time, and the history of the development of calendars and time pieces.

SELECTED RESEARCH

This study[5] attempted to determine the nature and extent of the functional knowledge of measures of fifth-grade and sixth-grade pupils by having them estimate and measure the following quantities:

1. The weight of a bar of plumber's lead ($4\frac{1}{2}$ pounds).
2. The weight of a blackboard eraser (2 ounces).
3. The weight of a block of wood (8 ounces).
4. The length of a piece of rope (16 feet).
5. The thickness of a lead pencil ($\frac{5}{16}$ inch).
6. The circumference of a basketball (30 inches).
7. The room temperature.
8. The outdoor temperature.
9. The time required for sand to run through an egg timer (3 minutes).
10. The amount of water in a half-filled pail (6 quarts).

The sample consisted of 108 sixth-graders and 39 fifth-graders. The children estimated each quantity during an individual interview after having been allowed to manipulate objects, use aids or devices, or assist themselves as they saw fit. After the estimates had been completed, each child selected from a table a measuring device that he thought suitable for each measuring task assigned to him.

---

5. C. G. Corle, "A Study of the Quantitative Values of Fifth and Sixth Grade Pupils," *The Arithmetic Teacher* (November, 1960), pp. 333–340.

The index of estimate error and of measurement error was determined by dividing the amount of error by the actual measure of the quantity. Thus, if a block of lead weighing $3\frac{1}{2}$ pounds was estimated to be $10\frac{1}{2}$ pounds, the error of 7 pounds yielded an index of $7 \div 3\frac{1}{2} = 2$. Percents of estimate error and measurement error were also computed.

Of the presented findings, the following are reported:

1. Boys estimated more accurately than girls.
2. Sixth-grade pupils were more effective in estimating and in measuring quantities than were fifth-graders.
3. Fifth-graders missed the correct estimate by approximately 6 times and sixth-graders by almost $1\frac{1}{2}$ times the actual values.
4. Errors in measurement averaged 2.39 times the actual values for fifth-graders, and .78 of the actual values for sixth-graders.
5. When the gross error in the index of measurement was reduced to percents not exceeding 100, there was still substantial evidence that the pupils were unable to work effectively with common measuring tools.
6. The smallest discrepancy in estimating and in measuring occurred in temperature, the greatest in weighing.
7. Pupils appeared to be more accurate in estimating linear distance than in measuring it.

The findings reveal that fifth-graders and sixth-graders make a great number of errors both in estimating and in actually measuring quantities. Many common quantitative concepts needed to work certain textbook problems successfully have not been acquired by the pupils. Teachers appear to have made a limited use of common measuring tools in the teaching of practical applications of measures; this results in the lack of functional knowledge of measures among the pupils. However, the better performance of sixth-graders in estimating and measuring quantities indicates that the pupils' ability in these skills increases during the school year.

SELECTED ACTIVITIES FOR PUPILS

1. Use a balance scale to determine the number of paper clips needed to balance a pencil.

2. How many hands high is your desk?
3. How many paper clips long is your desk?
4. How does your paper-clip measure compare with an inch measure?
5. Which is heavier, a pound of marbles or a pound of feathers?
6. The scale balances. What is the missing number?

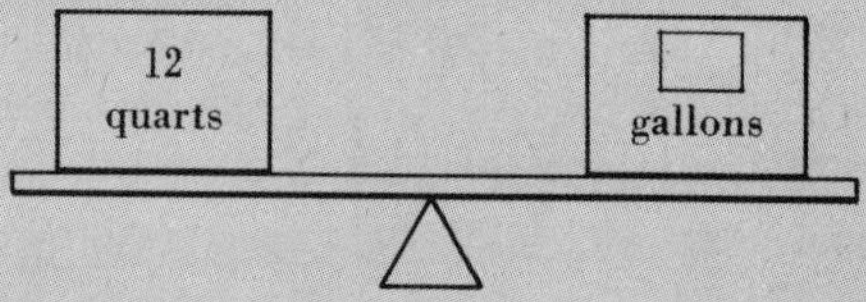

7. Cut a piece of string as long as your foot. Use it to measure the width of a door. Ask a friend to do the same. If the answers are not the same, why are they different?
8. The scale balances. What is the weight of object *a* in ounces?

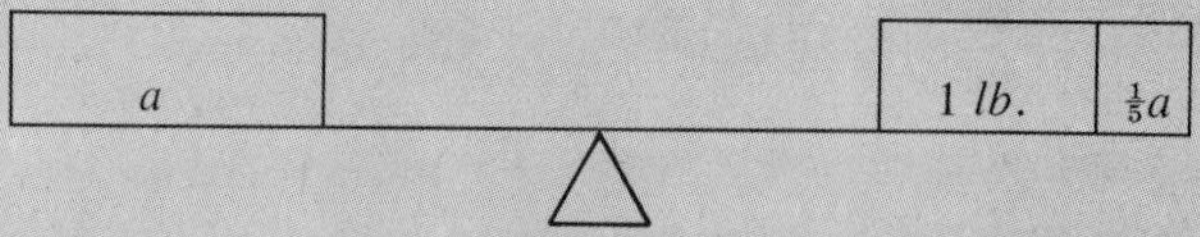

9. Use a trundle wheel to measure the length of the hall in your school.
10. It is 10 o'clock. What time will it be a hundred hours from now?
11. It is now March 17. What date will it be seventeen days from now?
12. Jean divided a cube of cheese into seven pieces in only three cuts. How did she do it?
13. Farmer Nichol's corral has only three sides that are the same length. He wants to make the corral twice as large by moving one side and adding another side of the same length. Make a drawing to show how he can do this.

14. First estimate the answers to the following questions. Then check your estimate by performing the needed measurements or computations.
    a. How tall are you in inches?
    b. How many pounds do you weigh?
    c. How old are you in months?
    d. How many quarts of milk do you drink in a week?
    e. How long will it take you to count to five hundred?
    f. Close your eyes and open them after you think one minute has passed. Find out how many seconds you are off.
    g. How many yards long is your building?
    h. How far is it from your home to your school?
    i. How many steps do you have to take to walk across the room?
    j. How many hours do you sleep during a week?
    k. How many square feet is the chalkboard area in your classroom?
    l. If new tiles with sides that are one foot long have to be put on the floor of your classroom, how many tiles would be needed?
    m. About how many times do you breathe in a minute?
    n. About how many inches long is a dollar bill?
    o. Get a cup. About how many tablespoons of water are needed to fill the cup?
    p. About how many pennies are there in a pile of pennies that is one inch high?
15. How many pennies can be put edge to edge on a board that is two feet long and one and a half feet wide?
    a. Estimate the number.
    b. Compute the answer by using this procedure:
        (1) Fit pennies along the length of a foot ruler and count them.
        (2) Decide how many pennies will fit along the length of the board.
        (3) Determine how many rows will fit on the board.
        (4) Compute the answer.

EXERCISES

1. Explain and illustrate what is meant by a unit of measure and a standard unit of measure.
2. Explain and illustrate the difference between direct and indirect measurement.
3. Suggest some activities in linear measurement for kindergarten and the primary grades.
4. Describe how you would develop with your pupils the formulas for the perimeter of a rectangle and for the circumference of a circle.
5. Develop the formulas for the areas of a rectangle, a square, a parallelogram, a triangle, a trapezoid, and a circle.

6. Develop the formulas for the volume of a rectangular soiid and a cube.
7. List the basic standard units of measure for measuring time, capacity, weight, and volume.
8. Preview some filmstrips or films on the teaching of measurement in the elementary school and list their strengths and weaknesses.
9. Report on a piece of research pertaining to the teaching of measurement in the elementary school.

SOURCES FOR FURTHER READING

Beamer, J. E., "The Tale of a Kite," *The Arithmetic Teacher,* May, 1975, pp. 382–386.

Churchill, E. M., *Counting and Measuring*. Toronto: University of Toronto Press, 1961, Chap. VII.

Heddens, J. W., *Today's Mathematics,* 3d ed. Chicago: Science Research Associates, Inc., 1974, Unit XVIII.

Kennedy, L. M., *Guiding Children to Mathematical Discovery,* 2nd ed. Belmont, California: Wadsworth Publishing Company, Inc., 1975, Chap. XV.

Marks, J. L., C. R. Purdy, L. B. Kinney, and A. A. Hiatt, *Teaching Elementary School Mathematics for Understanding,* 4th ed. New York: McGraw-Hill Book Company, 1975, Chap. IX.

Patterson, W., Jr., "A Device for Indirect Measurements: An Entertaining Individual Project," *The Arithmetic Teacher,* February, 1973, pp. 124–127.

Schminke, C. W., N. Maertens, and W. R. Arnold, *Teaching the Child Mathematics*. Hinsdale, Illinois: The Dryden Press, Inc., 1973, Chap. X.

Spitzer H. F., *Teaching Elementary School Mathematics*. Boston: Houghton Mifflin Company, 1967, Chap. XIII.

Steffe, L. P., "Thinking about Measurement," *The Arithmetic Teacher,* May, 1971, pp. 332–338.

Strangman, K. B., "The Sands of Time—A Sandglass Approach to Telling Time," *The Arithmetic Teacher,* February, 1972, pp. 123–125.

Walter, M., "A Common Misconception about Area," *The Arithmetic Teacher,* April, 1970, pp. 286–289.

19 The Metric System of Measures and Weights (SI)

Recent developments in Canada and in the United States have made the teaching of the metric system in the schools mandatory. This chapter presents basic concepts of the metric system and offers suggestions for teaching it to elementary school children.

SOME HISTORY

The metric system is the official system of measures and weights in almost all the important countries of the world. Introduced in France at the end of the eighteenth century, it was gradually adopted in other countries. In 1965 England changed to the metric system, followed by Canada and Australia.

By about the year 1800, statesmen such as George Washington, Thomas Jefferson, and John Quincy Adams had advocated the establishment of a decimal system of measures and weights in the United States.

The metric system became legal, but not mandatory, in the United States in 1866. Scientists in Canada and in the United States began to use it, and gradually measures of several articles such as drugs, films, and guns were reported in metric units. In recent times the use of the system has been increasing. Several manufacturing companies have begun to "go metric." Road signs that name distances in kilometers are being erected. The liter bottle is becoming common. Sewing patterns give measures in both English and metric units. On juice cans the amount of liquid is reported in both fluid ounces and milliliters.

In 1975 the United States Metric Bill was passed in both houses of Congress and signed into law by President Ford. The bill declares that the policy of the United States shall be to coordinate and plan the increasing use of the metric system in the country. It also provides for the establishment of a 17-member United States metric board to coordinate the voluntary conversion to the metric system.

CHARACTERISTICS

The superiority of the metric system to the English system is assured by two main characteristics:

1. *Subdivisions of base units are decimally related.* Multiples and submultiples of units are based on powers of ten, and prefixes express such powers of ten. In Table 19.1 the prefixes from kilo to milli are listed in order. There are additional prefixes that are not important for elementary school children.

Table 19.1

Prefix	*Meaning*		*Symbol*
Kilo	1 000	(10^3)	k
Hecto	100	(10^2)	h
Deka	10	(10^1)	da
Deci	0.1	(10^{-1})	d
Centi	0.01	(10^{-2})	c
Milli	0.001	(10^{-3})	m

2. *Units of different quantities are connected.* Liter is another name for cubic decimeter. Also, in the original system the gram was defined as the weight of one cubic centimeter of pure water at a specified temperature.

THE INTERNATIONAL SYSTEM OF UNITS (SI)

Changes have been made in the original metric system. In 1960, the General Conference of Weights and Measures—an international body—adopted the Système International d'Unités (SI) or the International System of Units.

SI uses the prefixes kilo and milli with basic units and suggests the use of the prefix centi in centimeter. A working knowledge of the remaining prefixes will enhance the student's appreciation of the regularity of the system and will result in a better understanding of the way in which various units are connected.

At present, SI is built up from seven base units. These base units and two supplementary units are listed in Table 19.2. There are also derived units. For example, the square meter and the cubic meter are derived from the meter.

This chapter deals only with base units of length, mass, and temperature, and with derived units that cover area and volume. The SI base unit of time needs no introduction to teachers. Base units for additional quantities identified in Table 19.2 do not fall in the realm of elementary school mathematics.

Table 19.2

Quantity	*Name of Unit*	*Symbol*
Length	Meter	m
Mass	Kilogram	kg
Temperature	Kelvin	K
Time	Second	s
Electric current	Ampere	A
Luminous intensity	Candela	cd
Amount of substance	Mole	mol
Plane angle	Radian*	rad
Solid angle	Steradian*	sr

*Supplementary unit

Since SI is an international system, spelling and punctuation rules had to be made:

1. Symbols for units are the same in all metric countries.
2. Symbols for units are not followed by a period except at the end of a sentence.
3. Space is left between a numeral and a symbol for a metric unit (as in 6 m).
4. In decimal numerals expressing numbers less than one the decimal point is preceded by a zero (as in 0.8 km).
5. No comma is used to separate groups of three digits in numerals. Instead, space is left between the groups of digits (as in 250 000 m). The reason is that in several countries a comma is used to indicate the place of the ones in a numeral as is done by our decimal point.

CONTENT, METHODS, AND ACTIVITIES

Length

The meter (also spelled *metre*) is the SI base unit of length. A meter is 39.37 inches. Table 19.3 presents multiples and submultiples of the meter.

Table 19.3

Equivalents	*Symbols*
1 kilometer = 1000 meters	1 km = 1000 m
1 hectometer = 100 meters	1 hm = 100 m
1 dekameter = 10 meters	1 dam = 10 m
1 decimeter = 0.1 meter	1 dm = 0.1 m
1 centimeter = 0.01 meter	1 cm = 0.01 m
1 millimeter = 0.001 meter	1 mm = 0.001 m

Frequently used units are the meter, millimeter, centimeter, and kilometer. The decimeter is used on occasion.

To form an idea of the length of these units, consider the following comparisons:

1. The diameter of the wire of a small paper clip is about one millimeter.
2. The diameter of a small thumbtack is about one centimeter.
3. The width of a 6″ by 4″ index card is about one decimeter.
4. A meter is a little longer than a yard.
5. A kilometer is a little longer than half a mile.

To show the order and the regularity of the metric system, in Figure 19.1 all the prefixes from kilo to milli are combined with the meter. The student who is acquainted with the prefixes can find the relation between units. Each unit is ten times the next smaller unit and is one one-tenth of the next larger unit.

To solve 1 m = □ cm, start at m, determine that cm is two steps up, and decide that 1 m = 10 × 10 cm, or 100 cm. To solve 1 mm = □ dm, start at mm, determine that dm is two steps down, and decide that 1 mm = 0.1 × 0.1 dm, or 0.01 dm.

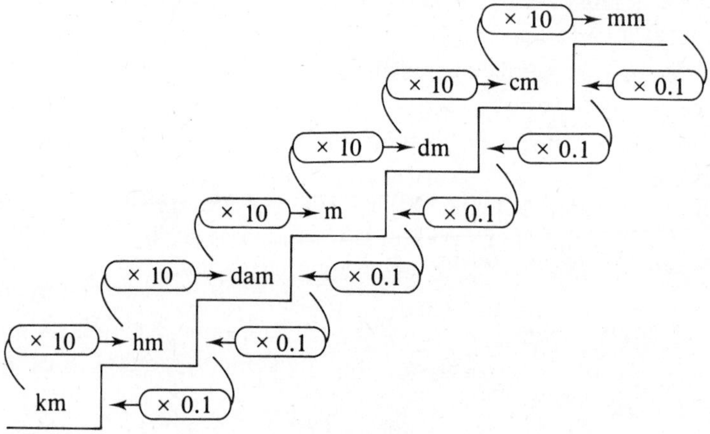

Figure 19.1

Example 1

1 255 m = □ km.
Since 1 m = 0.1 × 0.1 × 0.1 km = 0.001 km, multiply 1 255 by 0.001 or divide 1 255 by 1 000.
0.001 × 1 255 = 1.255 or 1 255 ÷ 1 000 = 1.255.
1 255 m = 1.255 km.

Example 2

8 dm = □ mm
Since 1 dm = 10 × 10 mm = 100 mm, multiply 8 by 100.
100 × 8 = 800
8 dm = 800 mm

Example 3

The measures of the sides of a triangle are 1.26 m, 95 cm, and 80 cm. Find the measure of the perimeter in meters.

$$\begin{array}{rcl} 1.26\text{ m} & = & 1.26\text{ m} \\ 94\text{ cm} & = & 0.94\text{ m} \\ +80\text{ cm} & = & 0.80\text{ m} \\ \hline & & 3.00\text{ m} \end{array}$$

The perimeter is 3 m.

Example 4

From 1.1 m of copper wire a piece of 95.5 cm is cut off. What is the length of the remaining piece of wire in millimeters?

$$\begin{array}{rcr} 1.1\text{ m} & = & 1\,100\text{ mm} \\ -95.5\text{ cm} & = & 955\text{ mm} \\ \hline & & 145\text{ mm} \end{array}$$

145 mm of wire is left.

Example 5

Jim rides his bike four times around a circular track, which has a diameter of 175 m. How many kilometers is Jim's trip? Round the answer to the nearest tenth of a kilometer. (Use $\pi = 3.14$.)

$$3.14 \times 175 = 549.5$$

One trip around the track is 549.5 m.
4 × 549.5 m = 2198 m or 2.198 km. This measure is rounded to 2.2 km. In four trips Jim rides 2.2 km.

Example 6

A rope that is 4.5 m long is cut into five pieces of the same length. How long is each of the five pieces of rope in centimeters?

$$4.5\text{ m} = 450\text{ cm}$$
$$450 \div 5 = 90$$

Each piece of rope is 90 cm.

Equivalents.

Table 19.4 lists approximate equivalents for common English and metric units of length.

Table 19.4

1 mile =	1.6 kilometers
1 yard =	0.9 meter
1 foot =	0.3 meter
1 inch =	2.5 centimeters
1 kilometer =	0.6 mile
1 meter =	1.1 yards
1 meter =	39 inches
1 centimeter =	0.4 inch

EXERCISES: Length

1. 5 km = _____ m
   0.4 cm = _____ mm
   2 m = _____ dm
   888 mm = _____ m
2. 655 m = _____ km
   2.6 mm = _____ cm
   50 cm = _____ dm
   15 dm = _____ m
3. 1 m + 1 cm + 1 mm = _____ mm
   2 m + 20 cm + 80 mm = _____ m
   2 km + 500 m = _____ m
   0.5 km + 200 m = _____ m
4. 1 m − 30 cm = _____ cm
   8 cm − 20 mm = _____ cm
   1.8 m − 8 dm = _____ m
   1.3 cm − 5 mm = _____ mm
5. 4 × 25 cm = _____ m
   8 × 1.5 mm = _____ cm
   10 × 0.5 dm = _____ m
   6 × 400 m = _____ km
6. 1 m ÷ 2 = _____ cm
   2.4 cm ÷ 4 = _____ mm
   1.8 dm ÷ 10 = _____ cm
   1.5 km ÷ 5 = _____ m
7. The length of a rectangle is 60 cm and its width is 40 cm. The perimeter of the rectangle is _____ m.
8. The perimeter of a square is 1.24 m. A side of the square is _____ cm.
9. The circumference of the head of a thumbtack is 3.14 cm. The radius of the circular region is _____ mm.
10. The speed limit is 50 mi. per hour. You are traveling 70 km per hour. About how many kilometers are you traveling above or below the speed limit?
11. True or false:
    a. A piece of string that is 5 m long is shorter than a piece of string that is 6 yd. long. _____.
    b. A ruler that is 30 cm long is longer than a ruler that is 10 in. long. _____.

SELECTED ACTIVITIES FOR PUPILS
Length

1. How many centimeters long is each object?

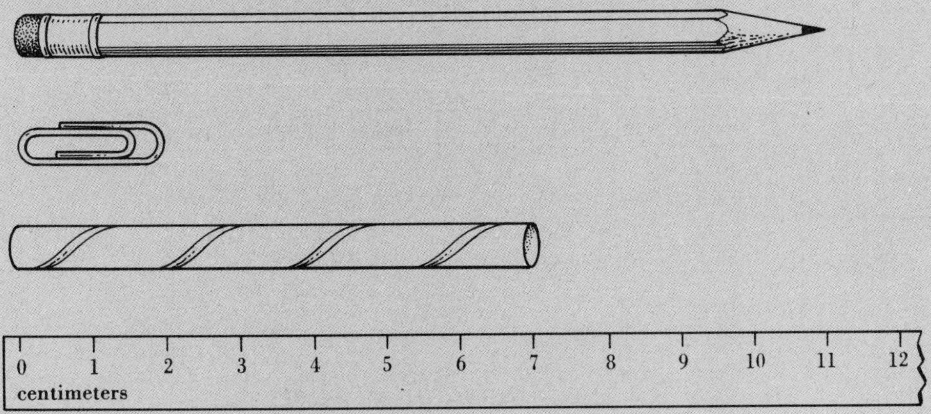

2. Find the length of your desk in number of paper clips and in centimeters.
3. Show the length of a centimeter as a distance between your thumb and index finger. Try to do the same for a millimeter.
4. Make a centimeter ruler 20 cm long. About how many inches long is the ruler?
5. Make a strip of cardboard 1 m long and graduate it in decimeters and centimeters.
6. Without using a meter stick, hold your hand against the wall 1 m from the floor. Then check your estimate.
7. What is your height in centimeters?
8. Do you think that the schoolroom is more or less than 10 m long? Check to see if you are correct.
9. If you walked a kilometer from your school, about where would you be?
10. Get a sheet of paper. First estimate and then measure its length and its width in centimeters.
11. Estimate the thickness of a nickel in millimeters. Then make a pile of several nickels, measure the total thickness, and divide the measure by the number of nickels you used.
12. Put on a bulletin board objects that are: 1 mm thick, 1 cm long, 1 dm long, and 1 m long. Label the objects.
13. Find a report of the Olympic games and discuss it.

Area The square meter is used for measuring area. It is derived from the meter which is the SI base unit of length. Table 19.5 presents units of area. Prefixes designate multiples and submultiples of the square meter. An alternate name for the square hectometer is the *hectare,* which is a unit of land measure. Another unit of land measure is the *are,* which is an alternate name for the square dekameter.

Table 19.5

Unit	*Alternate Name*	*Equivalents and Symbols*
Square kilometer		$1\ km^2 = 1\,000\,000\ m^2$
Square hectometer	Hectare	$1\ ha = 10\,000\ m^2$
Square dekameter	Are	$1\ a = 100\ m^2$
Square meter		
Square decimeter		$1\ dm^2 = 0.01\ m^2$
Square centimeter		$1\ cm^2 = 0.000\,1\ m^2$
Square millimeter		$1\ mm^2 = 0.000\,001\ m^2$

Consider these comparisons:

1. If you circumscribe a square around a dot made by a typewriter, the area of the square would be about one square millimeter.
2. If you draw the largest possible square on the nail of your thumb, the area of the square would be approximately one square centimeter.
3. If you cut a 6″ by 4″ index card to make a square with a side of four inches, the area of the piece you cut is about one square decimeter.
4. A square meter is about one fifth larger than a square yard.

Figure 19.2 shows relations between metric units of area. Each unit equals one hundred times the next smaller unit and is one one-hundredth part of the next larger unit.

Use Figure 19.2 to check these statements:

$1\ km^2 = 100 \times 100 \times 100\ m^2 = 1\,000\,000\ km^2$
$1\ m^2 = 0.01 \times 0.01 \times 0.01\ km^2 = 0.000\,001\ km^2$
$1\ m^2 = 100 \times 100 \times 100\ mm^2 = 1\,000\,000\ mm^2$
$1\ mm^2 = 0.01 \times 0.01 \times 0.01\ m^2 = 0.000\,001\ m^2$
$1\ m^2 = 100 \times 100\ cm^2 = 10\,000\ cm^2$
$1\ cm^2 = 0.01 \times 0.01\ m^2 = 0.000\,1\ m^2$
$1\ cm^2 = 100\ mm^2$
$1\ mm^2 = 0.01\ cm^2$
$1\ ha = 100\ a$
$1\ a = 0.01\ ha$
$1\ a = 100\ m^2$

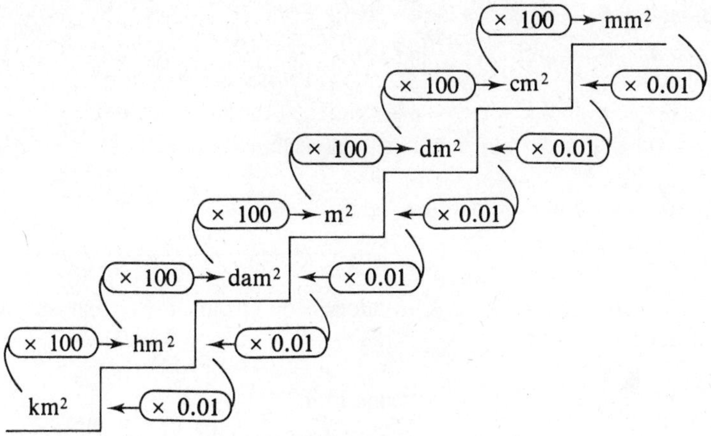

Figure 19.2

Example 1

Mr. Gates has two plots of land. One plot is 60 m long and 50 m wide and the other is 80 m long and 30 m wide. What is the total area of the plots in ares?

$$\begin{array}{r} 50 \times 60 \text{ m}^2 = 3\ 000 \text{ m}^2 \\ +\ 30 \times 80 \text{ m}^2 = 2\ 400 \text{ m}^2 \\ \hline 5\ 400 \text{ m}^2 \end{array}$$

The total area is 5 400 m² or 54 ares.

Example 2

From a plot of land with an area of 1 ha, 45 a are sold. What is the area of the remaining plot in ares?

$$\begin{array}{r} 1 \text{ ha} = 100 \text{ a} \\ -\quad 45 \text{ a} \\ \hline 55 \text{ a} \end{array}$$

The area of the remaining plot is 55 a.

Example 3

A floor that is 6.3 m long and 4.5 m wide is tiled. Square tiles with sides of 30 cm are used. How many tiles are needed?
The area of the floor is $4.5 \times 6.3 \text{ m}^2 = 28.35 \text{ m}^2$ or $283\ 500 \text{ cm}^2$.
The area of a tile is $30 \times 30 \text{ cm}^2 = 900 \text{ cm}^2$.

$$283\ 500 \div 900 = 315$$

315 tiles are needed.

Example 4

A rectangular plot of land is 400 m long and 150 m wide. What is its area in hectares?

$$150 \times 400 \text{ m}^2 = 60\,000 \text{ m}^2 \text{ or } 6 \text{ ha.}$$

The area of the plot of land is 6 ha.

Equivalents.

Table 19.6 lists approximate equivalents for common English and metric units of area.

Table 19.6

1 square mile =	2.6 square kilometers
1 square yard =	0.8 square meter
1 square inch =	6.5 square centimeters
1 acre =	0.4 hectare
1 square kilometer =	0.4 square mile
1 square meter =	1.2 square yards
1 square centimeter =	0.16 square inch
1 hectare =	2.5 acres

EXERCISES: Area

1. 3 m² = ______ cm²
   0.6 cm² = ______ mm²
   300 000 m² = ______ km²
   0.8 km² = ______ m²

2. 500 mm² = ______ cm²
   2.4 m² = ______ dm²
   1.2 km² = ______ m²
   5 000 cm² = ______ m²

3. 800 000 mm² = ______ m²
   24 000 cm² = ______ m²
   100 dm² = ______ m²
   1.5 m² = ______ dm²

4. 0.5 ha = ______ a
   2.4 a = ______ m²
   125 a = ______ ha
   100 m² = ______ a

5. 1 cm² + 100 mm² = ______ cm²
   1 m² + 4 000 cm² = ______ cm²
   6 × 4 000 cm² = ______ m²
   1 km² ÷ 2 = ______ m²

6. 75 a + 25 a = ______ ha
   1 ha − 60 a = ______ a
   4 × 50 a = ______ ha
   1 a ÷ 4 = ______ m²

7. Rectangle. Length: 125 cm. Width: 80 cm. Area: ______ m².

8. Triangle. Base: 2 cm. Height 15 mm. Area: ______ cm².

9. True or false:
   a. A square mile is more than 2 square kilometers. ______.
   b. A square inch is less than 5 square centimeters. ______.
   c. An acre is more than 1 hectare. ______.

SELECTED ACTIVITIES FOR PUPILS
Area

1. a. Cut a square piece of index card with sides of 1 cm to get a model of a square centimeter.
   b. Cut a square piece of index card with sides of 10 cm to get a model of a square decimeter.
   c. Label your models and put them on a bulletin board.
2. a. Cut four pieces of yarn each 1 m long.
   b. Tape them on the chalkboard to get a model of a square meter.
   c. Label the model.
3. a. Draw a rectangle that is 4 cm long and 3 cm wide.
   b. Cut from an index card several models of a square centimeter.
   c. Place rows of square centimeter models on the rectangular region to cover it.
   d. Find the number of square centimeters in the bottom row.
   e. Find the number of rows.
   f. Decide what the area of the rectangle is in square centimeters.
4. Estimate the area of a sheet of paper in square centimeters. Check your estimate in this way:
   a. Measure the length of the sheet in centimeters. (You may round the measures of the length and the width to whole numbers.)
   b. Measure the width of the sheet in centimeters.
   c. Multiply the measures (area = length × width).
   d. Find the difference between your estimated measure and the computed measure.
5. Estimate the area of a room in square meters. Check your estimate by following the steps listed in Activity 4.
6. Get a postage stamp. Estimate its area in square millimeters. Check your estimate by following the steps listed in Activity 4.
7. Use an atlas or an almanac to find the area of your state in square kilometers. If the area is only given in square miles, convert the measure into square kilometers.
8. Get centimeter grid paper. Draw on it some geometric shapes and find the area of each figure in square centimeters.

9. Find and write the area of each figure in square centimeters.

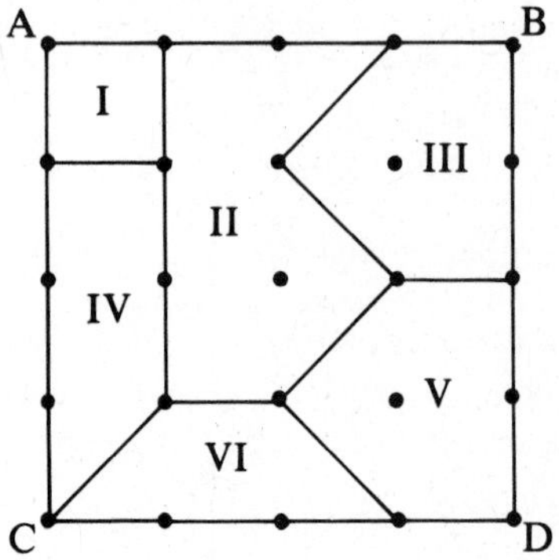

I 1 cm²
II ___ cm²
III ___ cm²
IV ___ cm²
V ___ cm²
VI ___ cm²
Total ___ cm²

The length of each side of square ABCD is ______ cm.
The area of ABCD is ______ × ______ cm² = ______ cm².
How can you check to see if you made a mistake?

10. Solve the metric crossnumber puzzle.

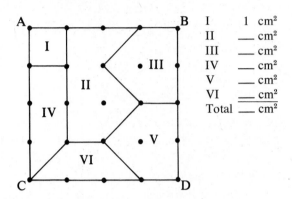

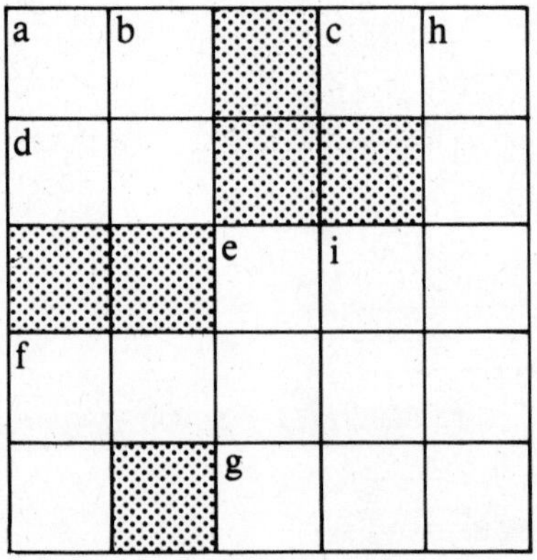

Left–right

a) $0.25\ cm^2 =$ ______ mm^2
c) $1\ 200\ mm^2 =$ ______ cm^2
d) $5\ 500\ m^2 =$ ______ a
e) $2.5\ m^2 =$ ______ dm^2
f) $1\ m^2 =$ ______ cm^2
g) $1\ cm^2 =$ ______ mm^2

Up–down

a) $1\ m^2 \div 4 =$ ______ dm^2
b) $1\ a - 45\ m^2 =$ ______ m^2
h) $0.02\ km^2 =$ ______ m^2
e) 2.01 ha = ______ a
i) $1\ m^2 \div 20 =$ ______ cm^2
f) $1\ cm^2 \div 10 =$ ______ mm^2

Volume and Capacity Volume is the amount of space that a three-dimensional object occupies or encloses.

The cubic meter is used for measuring volume. It is derived from the meter which is the SI base unit of length. Table 19.7 lists submultiples of the cubic meter.

Table 19.7

Unit	*Symbol*
Cubic meter	m^3
Cubic decimeter	dm^3
Cubic centimeter	cm^3
Cubic millimeter	mm^3

Consider the following comparisons:

1. A model of the cubic centimeter is the smallest unit in the set of Cuisenaire rods, which is a cube that is one centimeter long, one centimeter wide, and one centimeter high.
2. The cubic millimeter is a very small unit of volume. Try to imagine a tiny cube that is one thousandth part of a cubic centimeter.
3. A cubic decimeter is ten centimeters long, ten centimeters wide, and ten centimeters high.
4. A cubic meter is about one third larger than a cubic yard.

Figure 19.3 shows relations between metric units of volume. Each unit equals one thousand times the next smaller unit and is one one-thousandth part of the next larger unit.

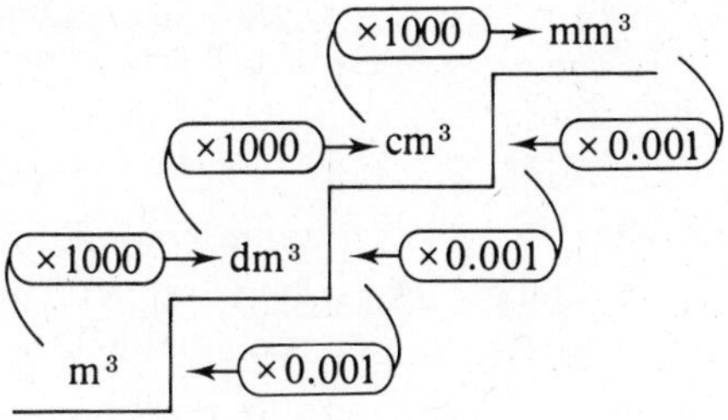

Figure 19.3

Use Figure 19.3 to check these statements:

$1\ m^3 = 1\ 000 \times 1\ 000\ cm^3 = 1\ 000\ 000\ cm^3$
$1\ mm^3 = 0.001\ cm^3$
$1\ m^3 = 1\ 000\ dm^3$
$1\ cm^3 = 0.001 \times 0.001\ m^3 = 0.000\ 001\ m^3$

Alternate Names for Units of Volume.

Another name for cubic decimeter is *liter* (also spelled *litre*). Commonly the liter and milliliter, and on occasion the kiloliter are used to express the capacity of containers and the volume of liquids. These units and other multiples and submultiples of the liter are presented in Table 19.8.

Table 19.8

Prefix and Meaning		*Equivalents*		*Symbols*	
Kilo	= 1 000 (10^3)	1 kiloliter	= 1 000 liters	1 kl	= 1 000 l
Hecto	= 100 (10^2)	1 hectoliter	= 100 liters	1 hl	= 100 l
Deka	= 10 (10^1)	1 dekaliter	= 10 liters	1 dal	= 10 l
Deci	= 0.1 (10^{-1})	1 deciliter	= 0.1 liter	1 dl	= 0.1 l
Centi	= 0.01 (10^{-2})	1 centiliter	= 0.01 liter	1 cl	= 0.01 l
Milli	= 0.001 (10^{-3})	1 milliliter	= 0.001 liter	1 ml	= 0.001 l

Table 19.9 lists three important units of volume and their alternate names.

Table 19.9

Unit	*Alternate Name*	*Equivalents*
Cubic meter	Kiloliter	1 m^3 = 1 kl
Cubic decimeter	Liter	1 dm^3 = 1 l
Cubic centimeter	Milliliter	1 cm^3 = 1 ml

SI uses the liter, milliliter, and kiloliter. To get an idea of the capacity of these containers, consider the following comparisons:

1. A liter is a little less than a United States quart and a little more than a British quart.
2. A milliliter is another name for a cubic centimeter. Think of a container that is one centimeter long, one centimeter wide, and one centimeter high. The capacity of such a container is one milliliter.
3. A kiloliter is a large unit of capacity. If you can imagine a barrel that has a diameter of one meter and a height of one meter and twenty-seven centimeters, you have formed an idea of a container with a capacity of approximately one kiloliter.

Figure 19.4 shows relations between metric units of capacity. Each unit equals ten times the next smaller unit and is one one-tenth part of the next larger unit.

Use Figure 19.4 to check these statements:

1 l = 0.1 × 0.1 × 0.1 kl = 0.001 kl
1 kl = 10 × 10 × 10 l = 1 000 l
1 ml = 0.1 × 0.1 × 0.1 l = 0.001 l
1 l = 10 × 10 × 10 l = 1 000 ml

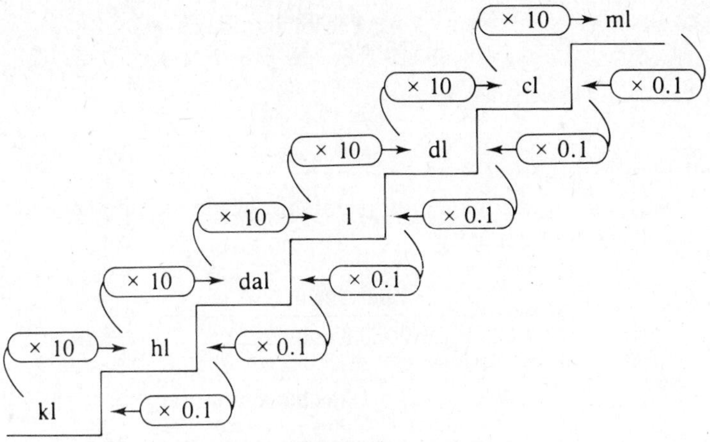

Figure 19.4

Example 1

Suppose that the edges of a sugar cube are 13 mm long. Find its volume in cubic centimeters. Round the answer to the nearest tenth of a unit.
The volume of the cube is $13 \times 13 \times 13\ \text{mm}^3 = 2\,197\ \text{mm}^3$.
$2\,197\ \text{mm}^3 = 2.197\ \text{cm}^3$. The rounded measure is $2.2\ \text{cm}^3$.

Example 2

A sandbox on the inside is 2.5 m long, 1.5 m wide, and 50 cm high. Compute the number of cubic meters of sand that are needed to fill the box up to 10 cm from the top edges.
The sand will reach a height of 40 cm, or 0.4 m.
$2.5 \times 1.5 \times 0.4\ \text{m}^3 = 1.5\ \text{m}^3$.
$1.5\ \text{m}^3$ of sand are needed.

Example 3

A water storage tank that is cylindrical in form is 60 cm in diameter and 71 cm high. About how many liters of water can the tank hold?
Since 1 liter = 1 cubic decimeter, express the measures in decimeters: the diameter is 6 dm, the radius is 3 dm, and the height is 7.1 dm.
Use the formula: Volume = $\pi r^2 h$.
$3.14 \times 3 \times 3 \times 7.1 = 200.646$.
The volume of the tank is $200.646\ \text{dm}^3$.
The tank can hold about 200 l of water.

Example 4

How many persons can you serve from 9 l of milk, if each person gets 225 ml of milk?

$$9\ l = 9\ 000\ ml$$
$$9\ 000 \div 225 = 40$$

You can serve 40 persons.

Equivalents.

Table 19.10 lists approximate equivalents for common English and metric units of volume and capacity.

Table 19.10

1 cubic yard	=	0.8 cubic meter
1 cubic inch	=	16 cubic centimeters
1 cubic meter	=	1.3 cubic yards
1 cubic centimeter	=	0.06 cubic inch
1 U.S. gallon	=	3.8 liters
1 Canadian gallon	=	4.5 liters
1 U.S. liquid quart	=	0.9 liter
1 Canadian quart	=	1.1 liters
1 liter	=	0.26 U.S. gallon
1 liter	=	0.22 Canadian gallon
1 liter	=	1.06 U.S. liquid quarts
1 liter	=	0.88 Canadian quart

EXERCISES: Volume and Capacity

1. $1\ cm^3 =$ ______ mm^3
   $1\ mm^3 =$ ______ cm^3
   $1\ m^3 =$ ______ dm^3
2. $3\ 000\ mm^3 =$ ______ cm^3
   $1.2\ m^3 =$ ______ dm^3
   $0.5\ cm^3 =$ ______ mm^3
3. 1 l = ______ dm^3
   1 kl = ______ l
   1 ml = ______ l
4. 600 l = ______ kl
   4 000 ml = ______ l
   2.5 kl = ______ l
5. A rectangular solid is 1.6 m long, 1.5 m wide, and 75 cm high. Find its volume in cubic meters.
6. The total surface area of a cube is 54 cm^2. What is the volume of the cube in cubic centimeters?
7. The diameter of the base of a circular container is 14 cm and the height of the container is 19.5 cm. Find the capacity of the container in liters. Round the answer to the nearest whole number.
8. If you have 3.5 liters of juice, how many persons can you serve if each serving is 175 milliliters?
9. True or false:
   a. A U.S. liquid quart is more than a liter. ______.
   b. A Canadian gallon is more than four liters. ______.
   c. A cubic meter is more than a cubic yard. ______.

SELECTED ACTIVITIES FOR PUPILS
Volume and Capacity

1. a. Copy the figure on a piece of sturdy paper. Be sure that the sides of the squares are 1 cm long.

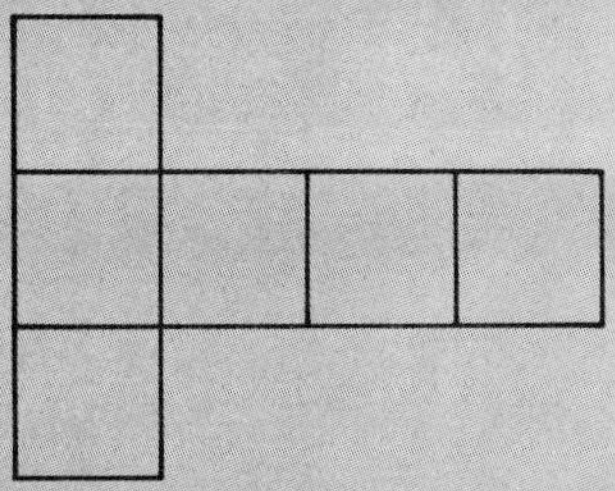

   b. Cut out the figure, fold it to get a cube, and tape the edges together. You have a model of a cubic centimeter.
   c. Label your model.

2. a. Draw on a large piece of sturdy paper a figure similar to the one in Activity 1, but make each side of the squares 10 cm long.
   b. Make a cube of the figure. You have a model of a cubic decimeter.
   c. Label your model.

3. a. Cut from a sheet of construction paper a piece that is 25 cm long and 20 cm wide.
   b. Tape the edges together to form a tube that is 20 cm high.
   c. Cut from an index card a circular piece with a radius of 4 cm. Tape it to the tube to give it a base.
   d. Compute the capacity of the container to determine if it is about one liter.

4. Get a cardboard box. First estimate and then compute its volume in cubic centimeters.

5. Get a die. First estimate and then compute its volume in cubic millimeters.

6. First estimate and then compute the volume of a room in cubic meters.

7. Fill a quart bottle with water. Find out if you can pour all the water into a liter container. Then decide which is more, a liter of water or a quart of water.

8. Get a cup or a glass. First estimate and then find the actual capacity of the container in milliliters.

9. a. Get a glass container that shows a scale graduated in milliliters. [Answers to exercises (b), (d), and (e) will be approximations.]
   b. Fill the glass partly with water and note how many ml of water it contains.

c. Place a rock in the container.
d. Use the scale to decide how much the water has risen.
e. Express the volume of the rock in cm^3.

10. Solve the metric crossnumber puzzle.

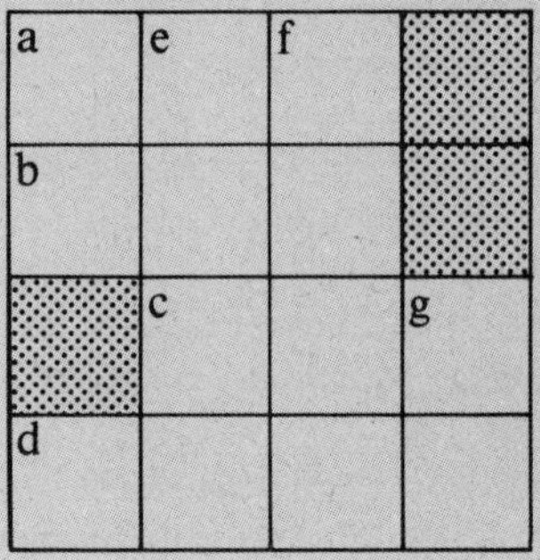

Left–right
a) 0.125 l = ______ ml
b) 0.15 kl = ______ l
c) Cube. Edge: 5 cm. Volume: ______ cm^3.
d) 6 cm^3 = ______ mm^3

Up–down
a) 11 l = ______ dm^3
e) 2.51 l = ______ ml
f) 5.02 m^3 = ______ dm^3
g) 50 dm^3 = ______ l

Weight The weight of an object is the gravitational pull that the earth or another planet exerts on the object. The mass of an object is a measure of the amount of matter of the object. An object weighs more on the earth than on the moon, but its mass is the same in different locations. In every-day use, the term *weight* commonly means mass. Therefore, since the distinction between mass and weight is rarely made, the term *weight* is used in the following paragraphs.

The kilogram is the SI base unit of weight. It is the only SI base unit that has a prefix.

A kilogram is equal to one thousand grams. Multiples and submultiples of the gram are presented in Table 19.11. Of the listed units only the kilogram, gram, and milligram need to be emphasized. Another important unit is the metric ton (t), which is equal to one thousand kilograms.

Table 19.11

Unit	*Symbol*	*Equivalents*
Kilogram	kg	1 kg = 1000 g
Hectogram	hg	1 hg = 100 g
Dekagram	dag	1 dag = 10 g
Gram	g	1 g = 1 g
Decigram	dg	1 dg = 0.1 g
Centigram	cg	1 cg = 0.01 g
Milligram	mg	1 mg = 0.001 g

Consider the following comparisons:

1. A kilogram is about ten percent more than two pounds. Think of a pound of butter that comes in a package of four sticks. Nine of such sticks weigh a little more than one kilogram.
2. Two thumbtacks with heads that have a diameter of one centimeter weigh about one gram.
3. Cut from a piece ditto paper a square with an edge of five millimeters. The weight of such a small piece of paper is about one milligram.
4. A small Volkswagen weighs about one metric ton.

Figure 19.5 shows relations between metric units of weight. Each unit equals ten times the next smaller unit and is one one-tenth part of the next larger unit.

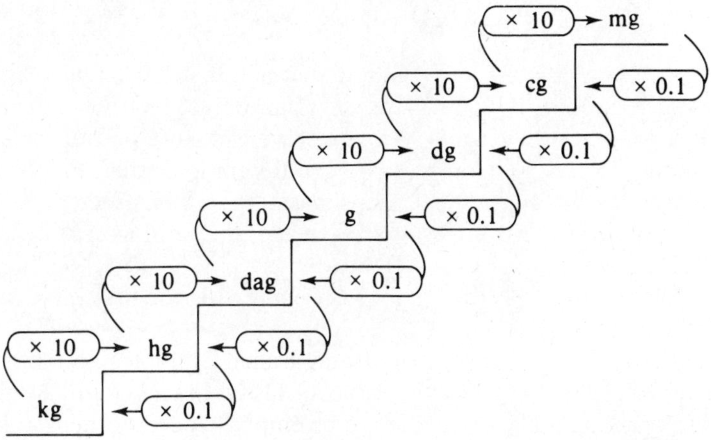

Figure 19.5

Use Figure 19.5 to check these statements:

$1 \text{ kg} = 10 \times 10 \times 10 \text{ g} = 1\,000 \text{ g}$
$1 \text{ g} = 10 \times 10 \times 10 \text{ mg} = 1\,000 \text{ mg}$
$1 \text{ g} = 0.1 \times 0.1 \times 0.1 \text{ kg} = 0.001 \text{ kg}$
$1 \text{ mg} = 0.1 \times 0.1 \times 0.1 \text{ g} = 0.001 \text{ g}$

Example 1

Mrs. Johnson buys 1.9 kg of T-bone steak, 400 g of hamburger, and 300 g of luncheon meat. How many kilograms of meat does Mrs. Johnson buy in all?

$$\begin{array}{rl} 1.9 \text{ kg} & = 1.9 \text{ kg} \\ 400 \text{ g} & = 0.4 \text{ kg} \\ +\ 300 \text{ g} & = 0.3 \text{ kg} \\ \hline & \ 2.6 \text{ kg} \end{array}$$

Mrs. Johnson buys 2.6 kg of meat.

Example 2

Mr. Smith has 1 metric ton of potatoes. He sells 150 bags containing 4 kg of potatoes each. How many kilograms of potatoes does he have left?
Mr. Smith has 1 metric ton or 1 000 kg of potatoes.
He sells 150 × 4 kg, or 600 kg.
He has 1 000 kg − 600 kg, or 400 kg of potatoes left.

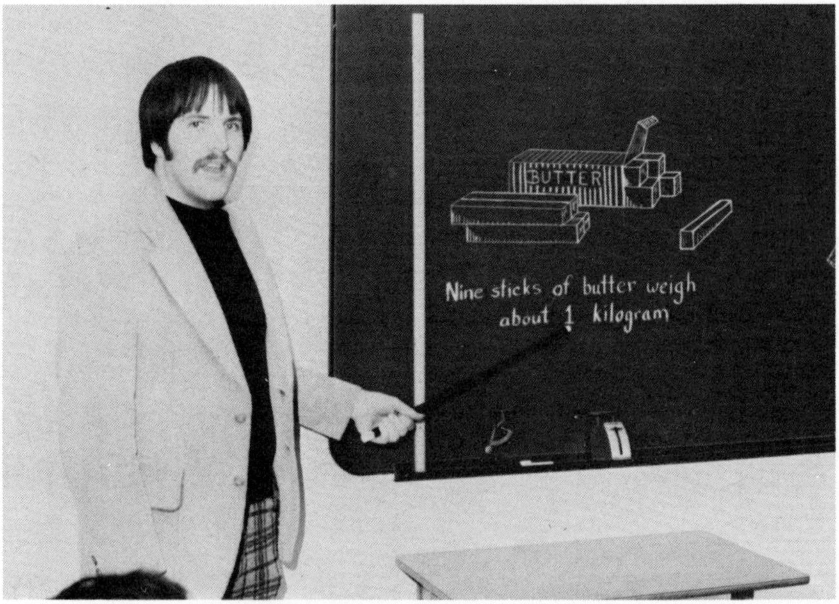

How much is a kilogram of butter?

Example 3

If one thumbtack weighs 500 mg, how many grams do 100 thumbtacks weigh?
100 × 500 mg = 50 000 mg, or 50 g.
100 thumbtacks weigh 50 g.

Example 4

If a strip of 200 paper staples weighs 8 g, how many milligrams does one staple weigh?
8 g = 8 000 mg.
8 000 mg ÷ 200 = 40 mg.
One paper staple weighs 40 mg.

Equivalents.

Table 19.12 lists approximate equivalents for common English and metric units of weight.

Table 19.12

1 ounce	=	28 grams
1 pound	=	454 grams
1 short ton	=	0.9 metric ton
1 kilogram	=	2.2 pounds
1 metric ton	=	2,200 pounds
1 metric ton	=	1.1 short tons

EXERCISES: Weight

1. 1 g = ______ mg
   1 g = ______ kg
   1 mg = ______ g
   1 kg = ______ g
2. 4 000 g = ______ kg
   1.5 kg = ______ g
   500 mg = ______ g
   2.5 g = ______ mg
3. 1 g + 400 mg = ______ g
   1 kg − 100 g = ______ g
   5 × 400 mg = ______ g
   1 g ÷ 5 = ______ mg
4. 2 kg + 500 g = ______ kg
   2 g − 600 mg = ______ g
   8 × 250 g = ______ kg
   2.5 kg ÷ 5 = ______ g
5. If a brick weighs 400 g, how many bricks are there in a metric ton of bricks?
6. If cheese contains 8 percent of fat, how many grams of fat are there in 1.5 kg of cheese?
7. If a drug tablet contains 2 mg of an antibiotic, how many grams of the antibiotic are in 600 such tablets?
8. True or false:
   a. A kilogram is more than 2 pounds. ______.

b. A pound is more than 500 grams. ______.
c. A metric ton is equal to 1 000 kilograms. ______.

9. A person weighs 160 pounds, or about ______ kilograms.

10. Round the answers to whole numbers.

a. 10 kg = ______ lbs. b. 100 lbs. = ______ kg
c. 140 g = ______ oz. d. 0.5 oz. = ______ g

SELECTED ACTIVITIES FOR PUPILS
Weight

1. Find the weight in grams of—
   a. two thumbtacks with heads that have diameters of 1 cm.
   b. a dime.
   c. a nickel.
   d. a new pencil.
2. Find the weight of a toothpick in milligrams. You can weigh several toothpicks and divide the total weight by the number of toothpicks.
3. Make a balance scale by using a soda straw, two paper cups, and string. Weigh several small objects. As weight artifacts you can use objects whose weights you determined in Activities 1 and 2.
4. Get a big book. First estimate and then find its actual weight in kilograms.
5. Get an envelope and several sheets of paper. First estimate and then determine how many sheets of paper you can put in the envelope so that the total weight is not more than 28 grams.
6. a. Get an empty container.
   b. First estimate and then find its actual weight in grams.
   c. Estimate how many grams or kilograms of water it can hold.
   d. Fill the container with water and find the total weight.
   e. Find the weight of the water.
7. Find objects that weigh approximately: 1 g, 5 g, 10 g, 50 g, 100 g, 500 g, and 1 kg. Attach the objects to the bulletin board and label them to show their weight.
8. Get ten books. First estimate and then find their total actual weight in kilograms.
9. Find your weight in kilograms. If no scale that is graduated in kilograms is available, convert from pounds to kilograms. A simple way to do this is: subtract 10 percent from the number of pounds you weigh and divide the remainder by 2.

   [Example: A person who weighs 110 pounds weighs approximately (110 − 11) ÷ 2 = 49.5 kilograms.]

10. Solve the metric crossnumber puzzle.

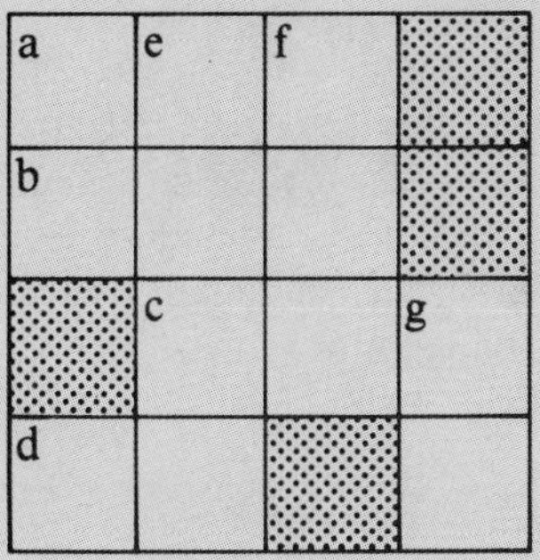

Left-right
a) 0.315 kg = _____ g
b) 0.7 g = _____ mg
c) 1 kg ÷ 8 = _____ g
d) 40 × 500 g = _____ kg

Up-down
a) 1 g − 963 mg = _____ mg
e) 1 kg + 10 g = _____ g
f) 0.5 kg + 2 g = _____ g
g) 1 g ÷ 20 = _____ mg

Temperature

The SI base unit for measuring temperature is the *kelvin*. Since the Kelvin scale is not used by the layman, there is no need to introduce it in the elementary school.

In SI the use of the Celsius (C) scale is acceptable. It is also called *Centigrade scale,* but the use of the term *Celsius scale* is recommended.

The Celsius scale is gradually replacing the Fahrenheit (F) scale in the United States and in Canada.

In Figure 19.6 some temperatures are expressed in both degrees Celsius (°C) and in degrees Fahrenheit (°F). Note that on the Celsius scale the freezing point of water is designated as 0° and the boiling point as 100°, whereas on the Fahrenheit scale the freezing point of water is 32° and the boiling point 212°.

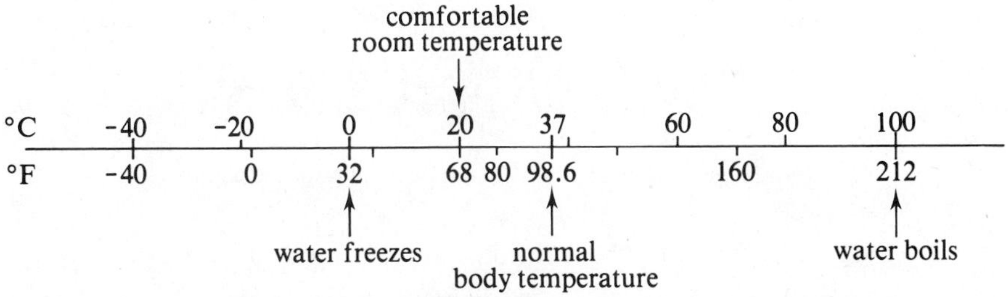

Figure 19.6

On the Fahrenheit scale the freezing point of water is designated as 32° and there are 180 degrees between the freezing point and the boiling point. On the Celsius scale the freezing point of water is 0° and there are 100 degrees between the freezing point and the boiling point. Thus the formula $F - 32 = \frac{9}{5}C$ or $F = \frac{9}{5}C + 32$ can be used to convert a temperature reading from one scale to the other.

Children should read and record daily the inside and outside temperature. A thermometer showing both the Fahrenheit and the Celsius scale should be available in the classroom so that temperature readings on these scales can be compared by children who already have some knowledge of the Fahrenheit scale. The use of the conversion formula can be reserved for pupils in higher grade levels, if it will be required at all.

Examples of Conversion

1. $98.6°F = \square°C$
   $F - 32 = \frac{9}{5}C$
   $66.6 = \frac{9}{5}C$
   $C = \frac{5}{9} \times 66.6 = 37$
   $98.6°F = 37°C$

2. $14°F = \square°C$
   $F - 32 = \frac{9}{5}C$
   $^{-}18 = \frac{9}{5}C$
   $C = \frac{5}{9} \times {}^{-}18 = {}^{-}10$
   $14°F = {}^{-}10°C$

3. $20°C = \square°F$
   $F = \frac{9}{5}C + 32$
   $F = 36 + 32$
   $F = 68$
   $20°C = 68°F$

4. $^{-}20C = \square°F$
   $F = \frac{9}{5}C + 32$
   $F = (\frac{9}{5} \times {}^{-}20) + 32$
   $F = {}^{-}4$
   $^{-}20°C = {}^{-}4°F$

EXERCISES: Temperature

1. 77°F = _____ °C
   100.4°F = _____ °C
   71.6°F = _____ °C
   $^{-}40$°F = _____ °C

2. 10°C = _____ °F
   24°C = _____ °F
   15°C = _____ °F
   $^{-}12$°C = _____ °F

SELECTED ACTIVITIES FOR PUPILS
Temperature

1. First estimate and then check the temperature in the room in degrees Celsius.
2. First estimate and then check the outside temperature in degrees Celsius.
3. Put some luke-warm water in a container. Put your hand in the water and estimate its temperature in degrees Celsius. Then place a Celsius thermometer in the water for a few minutes and check your estimate.
4. Put ice cubes in a glass and place a Celsius thermometer in it. Read the temperature after a few minutes.

5. Read the outside temperature each morning at the same time from Monday through Friday. Use a Celsius scale. Make a graph to show the readings.
6. Make a mobile. Use the different parts to express on them, in degrees Celsius, such temperatures as—
   a. the freezing point of water.
   b. the boiling point of water.
   c. normal human body temperature.
   d. a comfortable room temperature.
   e. a nice temperature to go skating.
   f. water temperature in a swimming pool that you like when you use the pool.
   g. a temperature on a very hot day in the place where you live.

EXERCISES

1. State the advantages of the universal use of the metric system of measures and weights.
2. Explain in what respects the metric system is superior to the English system of measures and weights.
3. Explain the decimal nature of the metric system.
4. Prepare an illustrative lesson on the metric system for a grade level you select.
5. If possible, prepare some overhead transparencies that will assist in the teaching of the metric system.
6. Examine a mathematics book for a grade level you select and determine which concepts of the metric system are presented in it.
7. Make an outline of a talk to parents on the metric system.

SOURCES FOR FURTHER READING

Bitter, G. G., J. L. Mikesell, and K. Maurdeff, *Activities Handbook for Teaching the Metric System.* Boston: Allyn and Bacon., Inc., 1976.

Dubisch, R., "Some Comments on Teaching the Metric System," *The Arithmetic Teacher,* February, 1976, pp. 106–107.

Edson, L., "Metrication: New Dimensions for Practically Everything," *American Education,* April, 1972, pp. 10–14.

Glaser, A., *Neater by the Meter.* Southampton, Pennsylvania: Anton Glaser, 1974.

Higgins, J. L. (ed.), *A Metric Handbook for Teachers.* Reston, Virginia: National Council of Teachers of Mathematics, 1974.

Izzi, J., *Metrication, American Style.* Bloomington, Indiana: Phi Delta Kappa Educational Foundation, 1974.

Kendig, F., "Coming of the Metric System," *Saturday Review, Science,* December, 1972, pp. 40–44.

Leffin, W. W., *Going Metric.* Reston, Virginia: National Council of Teachers of Mathematics, 1975.

Michigan Council of Teachers of Mathematics, *Metric Measurement Activity Cards.* Birmingham, Michigan: The Council, 1974.

National Bureau of Standards, *International System of Units (SI).* Washington, D.C.: U.S. Printing Office, 1972.

Odom, J. V., *A History and Overview of Metrication and Its Impact on Education.* Washington, D.C.: Metric Information Office, National Bureau of Standards, 1972.

Odom, J. V. (ed.), *Successful Experiences in Teaching Metric.* Washington, D.C.: Metric Information Office, National Bureau of Standards, 1976.

Prigge, G. (ed.), *Metric Measurement.* Grand Forks, North Dakota: University of North Dakota Mathematics Department, 1975.

Shapiro, A. T., *Le Système Métrique.* Ottawa: Les Éditions La Presse, 1974.

Shumway, R. J., and L. Sachs, "Don't just Think Metric—Live Metric," *The Arithmetic Teacher,* February, 1975, pp. 103–110.

Smart, J. R., *Metric Math: The Modernized Metric System (SI).* Monterey, California: Brooks/Cole Publishing Company, 1974.

20 *Verbal-Problem Solving*

One of the main objectives in the teaching of elementary-school mathematics is the development of the ability to solve verbal problems. The child meets such problems in school and in daily life and, growing older, encounters numerous additional situations in which this ability is required. Thus the modern teacher should be acquainted with promising techniques for improving the child's ability to solve verbal problems. This chapter includes the presentation of several techniques which should be considered as suggestions and not as prescriptions.

TERMS

A problem has been described by John Dewey as anything that perplexes and challenges the mind so that it makes belief uncertain. The individual faced with a problem must analyze the situation, gather facts that point toward a solution, decide which of the facts are pertinent to the problem, and then, by reasoning logically with the data at hand, make an intelligent choice to terminate the confusion.

A quantitative problem may be expressed as a number question, the answer to which cannot be given by a habitual response of the individual who faces the problem. Depending on the mathematical maturity of the person who is confronted with a quantitative situation, a number question is an enigma, a problem, or an exercise. The number question $4 + 3 = \square$ is an enigma to the typical three-year-old child, since the question has no meaning for him or her. To the first-grade pupil who understands the situation but cannot supply an automatic response, it is a problem. To a fourth-grade pupil who can give the answer immediately, it is an exercise.

A verbal quantitative problem is considered to be a described situation that involves a quantitative question for which the individual has no ready answer. In this chapter a verbal quantitative problem is called a verbal problem or a word problem.

THE PROCESS OF VERBAL-PROBLEM SOLVING

Though a definite pattern in the process of verbal-problem solving has not been discerned, some steps in the process can be identified. First the problem is recognized and a goal is set. This presumes the realization of a difficulty, since the existence of a problem excludes an automatic response. A problem can be compared with a situation in which an individual has to unlock a door without readily knowing which key to use. The person starts the process of deliberation and tries to decide which key must be used to open the door and reach the goal. In the drill method, the teacher furnishes the key and urges the pupil to practice opening the door until it can be done automatically. The teacher who uses the meaning method encourages the pupil to size up the situation, gather and analyze the data available, perceive the relations, and decide on a possible solution or hypothesis. Again in comparison with the situation of the locked door, the pupil is to use all the available information and select with discrimination the key he or she thinks might fit the door. When a key has been selected, the tentative solution is tested and either accepted or rejected. If it is rejected, another solution or hypothesis must be formulated and tested.

When the pupil has unlocked the problem and found the correct solution, a meaningful learning process has been pursued. It is expected that in future problems similarities or common relations will be perceived. Ideally, the pupil should repeat the meaningful process by unlocking various problems to develop skill in organizing data, identifying relations, and testing tentative solutions.

THE IMPORTANCE OF THE TEACHING OF VERBAL-PROBLEM SOLVING

Teaching pupils to solve verbal problems is an integral part of a good mathematics curriculum and is to be emphasized for several reasons:

1. Situations in which verbal problems must be solved arise frequently in daily life, and ability to cope with them is often crucial. An individual's success in a chosen occupation may well depend on skill in this area. Adults' performance in solving verbal problems is to a great extent related to the thoroughness of the mathematics instruction they received in school.
2. Verbal problems arise repeatedly in subjects other than mathematics that pupils pursue in school. Success in interpreting quantitative situa-

tions presented in subjects such as science and social studies depends on their skill in problem solving. Verbal problems also occur frequently in various school activities in which children are engaged. In such situations dividends are gathered from a sound investment in the mathematics program.

3. The verbal problem may show the child the importance of a skill introduced in the problem and the need for this skill, and thereby provide the motivation to learn it.
4. Verbal problems provide meaningful practice in computational skills.

SUGGESTED PROCEDURES IN THE SOLVING OF VERBAL PROBLEMS

When the word problem is presented for solution, the pupil needs a sufficient amount of time to read it. The pupil must identify the number question and proceed to find, check, and interpret the answer. This procedure is illustrated in the following example.

Example

Jim gave 7 of his 25 marbles to his friend. How many marbles did Jim have left?

Number question: $25 - 7 = \square$.

Solution: $25 - 7 = 18$.

Check: $18 + 7 = 25$.

Interpretation: Jim had 18 marbles left.

If the problem presented is an application of a learned process or a review of a previously mastered skill, the pupil should have no difficulty in finding the answer to a correctly stated number question. The difficulty for some pupils is the identification of the number question itself. Even this difficulty is reduced to a minimum in one-step problems, such as the one presented above, in which the numerals and the word "left" suggest that 7 must be subtracted from 25. Techniques for removing such cues from the statement of a problem are described elsewhere in this chapter.

Multi-step problems are situations that must be interpreted by finding the relationship between what is given and what is to be found. A definite pattern for solving such problems can hardly be prescribed, since children seem to find the relationships in different ways, and conditions in word problems differ. Consequently, the procedure for teaching verbal-problem solving by directing the child to pursue a series of prescribed steps is not an all-purpose one. However, the teacher may want to design a systematic procedural plan for the benefit of pupils who experience difficulties. The following suggestions for such a plan of attack should serve as a guideline rather than as a definite prescription. Ideally, the pupil is assisted in the development of an ability to solve word problems by the presentation of examples that illustrate how it can be done, and by being encouraged to find and use various methods of solution. The pupil is stimulated to think out loud so that the teacher can assist him or her by asking proper guide questions. The teacher's interpretations, aided by diagrams presented on the chalkboard, will help the pupil to discover relationships in the problem situation.

The following procedure for solving multi-step verbal problems may assist the pupil who encounters difficulties:

1. Reading the problem.
2. Identifying what is given.
3. Deciding what is asked.
4. Deliberating, if necessary with the help of diagrams, in order to find the relationship between what is given and what is asked, and to determine which operations must be performed.
5. Writing the number question—also called the open mathematical sentence.
6. Finding the answer.

The best learning takes place when pupils are actively engaged in the learning process.

7. Checking the answer.
8. Interpreting the answer.

The following example illustrates the suggested procedure:

Example

Mr. Ames owns $1\frac{3}{4}$ acres of land. He keeps $\frac{1}{2}$ acre and sells the remainder in lots of $\frac{1}{8}$ acre each. How many lots does Mr. Ames sell?

Solution:

Reading the problem: The pupil reads the problem carefully. The teacher may ask the pupil to interpret the situation in his or her own words.

Identifying what is given: Of his $1\frac{3}{4}$ acres of land, Mr. Ames keeps $\frac{1}{2}$ acre and sells what is left in lots of $\frac{1}{8}$ acre each.

Deciding what is asked: How many lots does Mr. Ames sell?

Deliberating: First, $\frac{1}{2}$ acre must be subtracted from $1\frac{3}{4}$ acres. Then it must be determined how many lots of $\frac{1}{8}$ acre each are contained in the remainder.

Writing the number question: $(1\frac{3}{4} - \frac{1}{2}) \div \frac{1}{8} = \square$.

Finding the answer:

$$(1\tfrac{3}{4} - \tfrac{1}{2}) \div \frac{1}{8} = 1\tfrac{1}{4} \div \frac{1}{8} = \frac{5}{4} \div \frac{1}{8} = \frac{5 \times \overset{2}{\cancel{8}}}{\underset{1}{\cancel{4}} \times 1} = \frac{10}{1} = 10.$$

Checking the answer: $10 \times \frac{1}{8} = \frac{10}{8} = 1\frac{2}{8} = 1\frac{1}{4}$; $1\frac{1}{4} + \frac{1}{2} = 1\frac{3}{4}$.

Interpretation: The pupil computes the answer by working with numbers. Thus, when the equation has been solved, the answer is interpreted: Mr. Ames sells 10 lots of $\frac{1}{8}$ acre each.

POSSIBLE CAUSES OF POOR PERFORMANCE IN THE SOLVING OF VERBAL PROBLEMS

Elementary school teachers often complain about the poor performance of their pupils in verbal-problem solving. Frequently discrepancies are evident between the pupils' proficiency in computation and their ability to solve word problems as measured by standardized tests and as observed by the teacher in regular classwork. Many pupils have acquired computational skills that they cannot apply promptly in verbal situations. On the other hand, there are pupils who display an understanding of verbal quantitative problems but who are unable to perform the required computations. The causes of such deficiencies should be determined, and effective techniques should be applied to improve the pupils' proficiency.

The following possible causes of poor performance in verbal-problem solving are suggested for the teacher's consideration:

1. *The teacher overemphasizes computation at the expense of problem solving.* The importance of considerable practice in problem solving is not always realized, and the time allotted to it is frequently insufficient. More than mere knowledge of numbers is needed for the solving of word problems. Pupils may master mathematical skills without being able to apply them because of their inability to understand the meaning of the fundamental operations and the interrelationships among those operations. Such deficiencies may be the result of a lack of experience in applying mathematical knowledge and skills in situations. It seems logical to assume that practice in problem solving will result in more proficiency in this area. Pace[1] concluded that understanding the fundamental operations is a vital factor in the improvement of problem-solving ability and that consequently the teacher should provide for the development of understanding of the fundamental operations.

2. *The wording of many verbal problems in textbooks does not encourage analytical thinking, and these books do not suggest enough promising techniques for problem solving.* The way in which some word problems are stated in textbooks allows the pupils to determine at a glance—or just by skimming the sentences—which operation is to be performed on which numbers. Such word problems are not much more than computation exercises. Preferably, word problems should be stated so that the child is forced to analyze the situation presented. Spitzer and Flournoy[2] suggest that the typical textbook program for improving or developing problem-solving ability be supplemented by more promising techniques.

3. *The pupils lack skills needed to read and interpret word problems.* The children whose reading ability is below average are at a disadvantage when they must read and solve word problems. In fact, interpreting quantitative situations requires skills beyond those needed for reading sentences in stories. Children must be able to locate within the problem the information that is pertinent, discard the data that are irrelevant, and thus discriminate between expressions that are essential to solving the problem and those that are not. Children must be thoroughly acquainted with the mathematical vocabulary presented so that they can decide which operations are inferred by clue words in expressions such as the *total* of 5 and 9, the *product* of 4 and 13, 5 *percent* of 300, $\frac{3}{4}$ *of* 8, etc. If children are deficient in such skills, they cannot be expected to perform well in solving verbal problems.

---

1. A résumé of this study is presented near the end of the chapter.
2. H. F. Spitzer and F. Flournoy, "Developing Facility in Solving Verbal Problems," *The Arithmetic Teacher* (November, 1956), pp. 177–182.

4. *The time allotted for children to solve a verbal problem presented in class is insufficient.* The solving of a problem requires time for analyzing the situation, deliberating on the steps that should be followed, identifying the number question, and computing the answer. Striving to cover a specified amount of subject matter in too little time and evaluating the children's progress by quantity covered instead of quality of work accomplished are, at best, questionable techniques. The teacher must take time to encourage the pupils to think out loud, to show a visual representation of the situation, and to correct faulty thinking.

5. *The pupils lack knowledge of mathematical vocabulary.* Treacy[3] showed that pupils who are well acquainted with the special vocabulary of mathematics do better in solving verbal problems than the pupils to whom these words convey little meaning or an inappropriate meaning. Johnson[4] concluded that vocabulary instructional materials should be used regularly and systematically as an integral part of the classroom procedure.

6. *The pupils cannot perform simple computations mentally.* Children who are completely dependent on paper and pencil for the solving of common problems involving small numbers do not show evidence that they understand the processes. Flournoy[5] found that intermediate-grade pupils who had finished a program in mental computation had made significant gains both in mental computation and in problem solving.

7. *The pupils lack ability to perform the required computations.* With the exception of word problems used to introduce a new skill, verbal problems should not involve computations that have not yet been taught, so that the pupils are free to concentrate on the problem situation.

8. *The situations presented in the word problems are not appealing to the age level for which they are intended.* Children should have at least some interest in the situations that are presented so that they will be motivated for their tasks. This does not mean that all the verbal problems must be real situations. Banks,[6] reporting on a study conducted by Welch, presented evidence showing that pupils prefer fantasy problems to problems describing real-life situations. Even ridiculous situations were not

---

3. J. P. Treacy, "The Relationship of Reading Skills to the Ability to Solve Arithmetic Problems," *Journal of Educational Research* (October, 1944), pp. 86–96.

4. H. C. Johnson, "The Effect of Instruction in Mathematical Vocabulary upon Problem Solving in Arithmetic," *Journal of Educational Research* (October, 1944), pp. 97–110.

5. M. F. Flournoy, "The Effectiveness of Instruction in Mental Arithmetic," *The Elementary School Journal* (November, 1954), pp. 148–153.

6. J. H. Banks, *Learning and Teaching Arithmetic,* 2nd ed. (Boston: Allyn and Bacon, Inc., 1964), p. 407.

found to be a distraction. Pupils performed as well on the unreal problems as they did on the real problems.

9. *The classroom climate is not conducive to a proper learning situation.* The way in which the teacher directs the class discussions may be of a nature such that the child hesitates to volunteer an answer for fear of making a mistake. In such a situation the teacher has not succeeded in establishing a relaxed atmosphere in which the child's thinking is stimulated and constructively corrected. The master teacher strives toward the ideal situation, where each child engages actively in the learning process, volunteers answers, challenges solutions, and experiences some degree of success. The teacher who understands and likes mathematics and who attempts to stimulate the children's thinking will motivate the pupils.

TECHNIQUES FOR IMPROVING PROBLEM-SOLVING SKILLS

Several techniques are available for the improvement of problem-solving skills. The degree of success with which pupils use each of these will depend on the kind of problems used, the ability and enthusiasm of the teacher, and the mathematical maturity and motivation of the pupils. The following techniques are suggested:

1. *Applying the method of analysis.* The procedure followed in solving verbal problems by the analysis method has been described elsewhere in this chapter.

2. *Applying the method of analogy.* After a pupil has worked a problem that makes use of easy numbers, a more difficult problem, containing cumbersome numbers but requiring use of the same operations, can be attacked. This technique allows the pupil to concentrate on the relationship between the numbers in the problem without being hampered by unwieldy computations. After the relationships have been detected and the pupil has ascertained that the solution of the easier problem is correct, the more difficult problem is solved by applying the same principles.

Example

In a spelling test Judy spelled $12\frac{1}{2}\%$ of the 56 words incorrectly. How many words did she spell correctly?

Simpler problem: In a spelling test Judy spelled $\frac{1}{10}$ of the 60 words incorrectly. How many words did she spell correctly?

3. *Devising problems by interpreting pictures.* In the primary grades pictures illustrating simple numerical data are interpreted and translated into number questions.

4. *Solving verbal problems with the help of visual representations.*

Number lines and diagrams may assist the pupils in visualizing the problem situation.

Example 1

Linda has 11 coins. She has only pennies and nickels. If she has 8 pennies, how many nickels does she have?

The mathematical sentence $11 = 8 + \square$ or $11 = 8 + n$ can be illustrated on the number line:

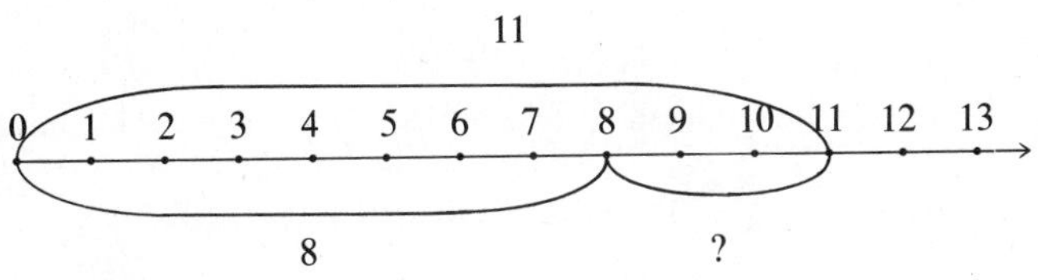

Example 2

Mr. Right sold $1\frac{1}{4}$ of his 2 acres of land. How much land did Mr. Right have left?

The situation can be represented in a diagram:

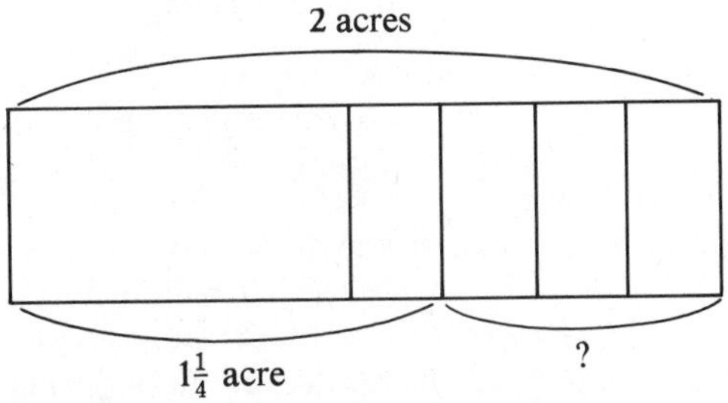

5. *Solving simple problems by mental computation.* Most quantitative problems that arise in daily life and classroom activities are common problems, and the computations required for their solution are usually simple. The pupil should acquire skill in solving such easy problems without the use of paper and pencil. His experiences with simple situations will deepen his understanding of the relationships involved, and the success he experiences will motivate him to attack problems requiring written computations.

The results of research conducted in this area point clearly to the need for a systematic program in mental computation in the elementary school. Flournoy[7] stated that mental arithmetic seems to be more prevalent than written computation in daily life.

7. F. Flournoy, "Providing Mental Arithmetic Experiences," *The Arithmetic Teacher* (April, 1959), pp. 133–139.

Because of the great importance of mental computation in the modern mathematics curriculum, provision should be made for a sequential program that presents both mental computation exercises and verbal problems in all the grades at levels that become gradually more difficult.

In the teaching of mental computation, number properties are applied when feasible, and mathematical sentences are pictured on the number line or by arrays. The pupil should discover how the application of number properties can simplify difficult mathematical sentences.

Example 1

Tom added 13 rocks to his collection of 49 rocks. How many rocks did Tom have in all?

Number question: $49 + 13 = \square$.

Solution:

1. $49 + 13 = 49 + (10 + 3) = (49 + 10) + 3 = 59 + 3 = 62$. Tom had 62 rocks in all.

Mathematical justification:

$49 + 13$	$= 49 + (10 + 3)$	renaming
	$= (49 + 10) + 3$	associative property
	$= 59 + 3$	addition
	$= 62$	addition

2. $49 + 13 = (40 + 10) + (9 + 3) = 50 + 12 = 62$. The mathematical justification for this procedure was presented in Chapter 11.

Example 2

Mrs. House bought 4 dozen eggs. How many eggs did she buy?

Number question: $4 \times 12 = \square$.

Solution: $4 \times 12 = 4 \times (10 + 2) = (4 \times 10) + (4 \times 2) = 40 + 8 = 48$. Mrs. House bought 48 eggs.

Mathematical justification:

4×12	$= 4 \times (10 + 2)$	renaming
	$= (4 \times 10) + (4 \times 2)$	distributive property
	$= 40 + 8$	multiplication
	$= 48$	addition

Example 3

Rex read 78 pages in his reader in 6 days. How many pages did he read on an average per day?

Solution: $78 \div 6 = (60 + 18) \div 6 = (60 \div 6) + (18 \div 6) = 10 + 3 = 13$. On an average, Rex read 13 pages per day.

Mathematical justification:

$78 \div 6 = (60 + 18) \div 6$	renaming
$= (60 \div 6) + (18 \div 6)$	distributive property
$= 10 + 3$	division
$= 13$	addition

Example 4

On 3 different days, the Johnson family traveled 165 miles, 159 miles, and 41 miles, respectively. How many miles did the family travel in all?

Number question: $165 + 159 + 41 = \square$.

Solution: $165 + 159 + 41 = 165 + (159 + 41) = 165 + 200 = 365$. The Johnson family traveled 365 miles in all.

Mathematical justification:

$165 + 159 + 41 = 165 + (159 + 41)$	associative property
$= 165 + 200$	addition
$= 365$	addition

6. *Estimating answers to verbal problems*. Estimating the answer to a problem requires mental computation with rounded numbers. The sum of 29, 71, and 42 is estimated by adding 30, 70, and 40. The product of 48 and $7\frac{1}{2}$ is estimated by multiplying 50 by 7. Skill in estimating answers is a help to the pupil in checking the reasonableness of an answer to a problem, and applying this skill may prevent the pupil from supplying answers that are not sensible. Many textbooks do not include a sufficient number of exercises in estimation. Thus the teacher may have to provide additional word problems constructed for the specific purpose of developing the child's ability in this area.

Example

On a trip of 196 miles, Mr. Green's car traveled, on an average, 20 miles on one gallon of gasoline. Approximately how many gallons of gasoline were needed for the trip?

7. *Formulating questions to fit given quantitative situations*. A serious limitation of many verbal problems in textbooks is the presence of strong cue words that practically tell the pupil what operation to use. Such cues allow the child to find the answer to the problem without reading it carefully. Consider the following problem: Dave worked 36 arithmetic exercises in the morning and 15 in the afternoon. How many exercises did Dave work that day in all? The answer can be found by skimming the sentences, noticing the numerals 36 and 15 and the words "in all," and then adding 15 to 36. Thus the problem has been reduced to a mere

computational exercise. The technique of omitting the question and having the pupil formulate it forces the child to read the problem carefully.

Example

Ken had 45 customers on his paper route. He got 16 new customers.

Solution: The child formulates a question such as "How many customers did Ken then have in all?" and he proceeds to find the answer.

8. *Identifying superfluous data in given problems.* The inclusion of superfluous information in the problem requires the pupil to read it carefully and to select the pertinent data.

Example

Mr. Red estimated that he had to spend $2,500 on house improvements and a new garage. He figures that the improvements on his house would cost $1,800, and he had $1,300 in his bank account. What was his estimate of the cost of the garage?

Solution: The pupil who understands the problem situation realizes that the amount of money in Mr. Red's bank account need not be considered when the problem is solved. The identification of the superfluous information is a guarantee that the pupil has isolated the relevant data.

9. *Identifying the kind of additional data needed.* When situations are presented that lack data needed to answer the number question, the pupil must identify the additional information needed. He can do this only if he understands the problem, and thus he is required to analyze the situation.

Example

Mr. Brown bought a radio. He paid $25 down and the remainder in monthly payments of $10 each. What was the total cost of the radio?

Solution: The pupil must realize that the number of monthly payments is not given. If he or she has spotted this lack of information then the problem situation has been understood.

10. *Working with problems in which no numbers are used.* In the lower grades such problems are simple, one-step situations. The pupil is to identify the operation that must be performed.

Example 1

Ted knows how many baseball cards he has and how many his brother has. How can Ted find out how many he will have if he gets all his brother's cards?

In the middle grades the problems become more difficult and involve more than one step.

Example 2

Mary wants to buy as many rings as she can with the money she has in her purse. How can she find out how many rings she can buy and how much money she will have left?

In the upper grades the problems involve several steps.

Example 3

Mr. Grant wants to estimate the cost of the gasoline needed to drive his car from New York to Chicago. What must Mr. Grant know and do to arrive at a reasonable estimate of the cost?

Solution: The pupil is expected to list three steps:

a. Find out how many miles it is from New York to Chicago.
b. Find out how many miles Mr. Grant's car travels on one gallon of gasoline.
c. Determine how many times the number of miles Mr. Grant's car travels on one gallon of gasoline is contained in the total number of miles traveled.
d. Estimate the average price of a gallon of gasoline.
e. Estimate the total cost of the gasoline by multiplying the average price of one gallon by the number of gallons needed.

After these steps have been outlined, the pupil supplies numbers in the problem situation and finds the answer. The problem may be rewritten as follows:

Mr. Grant plans to drive from New York to Chicago, a distance of approximately 832 miles. His car travels about 16 miles on one gallon of gasoline and the average cost of one gallon of gasoline is estimated to be 59¢. Find the approximate cost of all the gasoline needed for the trip.

11. *Translating the given problem situation into a mathematical sentence.* The basic difficulty encountered in the solving of a verbal problem is the translation of the situation into a number question—also called an open mathematical sentence. Several examples are presented in Chapter 7.

12. *Devising verbal problems to fit given mathematical sentences.* Composing a verbal problem that is a description of a situation expressed in a given mathematical sentence forces the pupil to study the meaning of the abstract symbols and to translate the mathematical idea into a concrete situation. Thus the pupil moves from number operations to problems of daily life. Such activities are expected to deepen the child's understanding of the abstract symbols and to help when the child must express a verbal problem in symbolic form.

Example

$85 - \square = 60.$

Solution: Ann had to read an 85-page book. After she had read for a while, she discovered that there were 60 pages left to read. How many pages had Ann read?

13. *Providing brain teasers for capable pupils.* Rapid learners often finish their assigned work in less than the allotted time. These pupils need additional assignments that are interesting and stimulating. Most children like enrichment exercises called brain teasers. Such problems are designed to improve skill in reasoning.

Example

Ray had a square piece of cardboard with a side measuring half a yard. Ron had a piece with an area of half a square yard. Which boy had the larger piece of cardboard?

14. *Teaching reading skills that are essential in the solving of verbal problems.* The nature of verbal problems requires that ideas included therein be expressed accurately and exactly. This can often be accomplished only by using sentences that are somewhat complicated in structure. The interpretation of such sentences requires skill in analytical reading, which includes locating pertinent information given, classifying concepts presented, drawing inferences, and retaining data. Treacy[8] conducted a study on the relationship of reading skills to the ability to solve verbal problems in arithmetic. He stated that his findings suggest that the development of reading skills is of help in the improvement of problem-solving ability. He also concluded that help that enriches pupils' understanding of their reading may have a beneficial effect on their performance in problem solving.

15. *Devising various questions to fit a given quantitative situation.* Sometimes several questions can be derived from a quantitative situation. The pupil tries to frame as many questions as he can.

Example

Ted spelled 20 out of 30 words correctly in a spelling test. Ray took the same test and made 5 mistakes.

Solution:

a. How many words did Ray spell correctly?
b. How many mistakes did Ted make?
c. How many more mistakes did Ted make than Ray?
d. What was the total number of mistakes Ted and Ray made?
e. What fractional part of the total number of words did Ted spell correctly?

---

8. J. P. Treacy, "The Relationship of Reading Skills to the Ability to Solve Arithmetic Problems," *Journal of Educational Research* (October, 1944), pp. 86–96.

SELECTED RESEARCH

The investigator's purpose[9] was to determine the effect of the level of understanding of the fundamental operations upon problem-solving ability in arithmetic.

The sample comprised two groups of children from the fourth grade of a training school: Group I, the control group, and Group II, the experimental group. The exact size of the sample was not reported. The groups were equally divided with respect to chronological age, mental ability, and performance in arithmetic reasoning and computation.

During the experimental period of eight weeks, systematic instruction in understanding of processes in arithmetic was provided for Group II only. Twenty-four sets of problems—three sets for each week—were used as a basis for discussions. Each set contained two one-step verbal problems for each of the operations, addition, subtraction, multiplication, and division. The children in the experimental group had to read each problem, tell how it was to be solved, and defend their choice of operation. The children in the control group merely solved the problems without any discussion of the work. At the end of the experimental period, an equivalent form of the arithmetic reasoning test that had been used as pre-test was administered. The scores earned on these equivalent tests were compared and the gains determined. Added information was obtained by administering to both groups four special problem tests constructed for use at spaced intervals during the experimental period. Each test contained ten problems of the conventional variety and five problems with distorted cues. The administration of these tests was accompanied by individual interviews with the children to determine how children solve problems and what effect understanding has upon the ability to solve problems.

Of the results reported by the investigator, the following are presented:

1. The gains in performance on the arithmetic reasoning test administered at the end of the experimental period, as compared with performance on the equivalent form used initially, were negligible for Group I, but were statistically significant for Group II.

---

9. A. Pace, "Understanding and the Ability to Solve Problems," *The Arithmetic Teacher* (May, 1961), pp. 226–233.

2. On the problem tests both groups showed improvement from Test I to Test IV in the number of correct methods of solution used to solve both the conventional problems and the problems with distorted cues. Group II showed greater improvement than Group I.

The implications of the study presented by the investigator are summarized as follows:

1. Children should be given many opportunities to solve problems.
2. Children should be allowed to solve problems in various ways, since there is more than one correct way of solving a problem. Pupils should be led gradually to use more mature and efficient processes.
3. The teacher should provide for the development of understanding of the four fundamental operations, since this is a vital factor in improving problem solving. Development of understanding is a gradual process; it takes place as the fundamental operations are presented and as problems are solved.

In another study on problem solving,[10] the goal was to determine whether pupils are as successful in solving problems in which numerical data are not given in the order in which they are needed to solve the problems as they are in solving problems in which such data are given in the order in which they are used to solve the problems.

Four fifth-grade classes—a total of 95 pupils ranging in IQ from 81 to 137 with a mean IQ of 113—took part in the experiment. The range in terms of composite arithmetic achievement was 3.4 to 9.1 in grade equivalent.

An arithmetic problem-solving test consisting of ten pairs of problems was constructed. The problems in each pair were similar in terms of vocabulary and numerical difficulty, but differed in the order in which the numerical data were presented. The pairs were split and placed in a test booklet in random order.

The results showed that 38 pupils scored higher on the proper-order type of problems, 29 scored higher on the mixed-order type, and 28 earned the same score on the two types. Of the 950 possible

---

10. P. C. Burns and J. L. Yonally, "Does the Order of Presentation of Numerical Data in Multi-Step Arithmetic Problems Affect Their Difficulty?" *School Science and Mathematics* (April, 1964), pp. 267–270.

correct answers for each test for all the pupils, there were 678 correct answers for the proper-order type problems and 645 for the mixed-order type. This difference was not statistically significant. (In the study the 5 percent level of confidence was used.)

When the achievement of pupils grouped according to IQ as measured by the *Otis Intelligence Test, Beta Form* was studied, it was found that the 26 pupils in the bottom 27 percent as well as those in the upper 27 percent scored higher on the proper-order type problems, but the differences were not statistically significant.

When pupils were grouped according to reasoning ability as measured by the *SRA Achievement Series,* a study of their achievement showed that the bottom 27 percent did significantly better on the proper-order type problems. The upper 27 percent did better on the mixed-order type problems, but the difference was not statistically significant.

The investigators felt that especially pupils who are low in arithmetic reasoning ability would profit from having greater experience with proper-order type problems before beginning instruction with multi-step problems. They also suggest that, since reasoning ability and the ability to solve problems seem to be related, ways of increasing arithmetic ability should be explored in order to improve the pupils' ability to solve both types of problems.

The third part of this section deals with the National Assessment of Educational Progress (NAEP).[11]

The paragraphs that follow contain a part of an article[12] in which the NAEP mathematics assessment was examined. The selected part deals with a word problem involving whole numbers.

The following word problem exercise was given to 25,000 nine-year-olds and 30,000 thirteen-year-olds:

> A rocket was directed at a target 525 miles south of its launching point. It landed 624 miles south of its launching point. By how many miles did it miss its target?
>
> Answer ______

---

11. For additional information the student is referred to the Selected Research presented in Chapter 1.

12. T. P. Carpenter, T. G. Coburn, R. E. Reys, and J. W. Wilson, "Results and Implications of the NAEP Mathematics Assessment: Elementary School," *The Arithmetic Teacher* (October, 1975), pp. 438–450.

The distribution of various responses expressed in percents follows:

Response	Age 9	Age 13
Correct answer	22	72
Correct number sentence but no answer or wrong answer	10	9
Attempt to add	8	4
Borrowing error in subtraction	1	0
Reversal error in subtraction	14	5
Other unacceptable response	29	7
"I don't know"	15	2
No response	2	1

The authors make these interesting observations:

The pupils' performance on this exercise was not very good. Do the data suggest why? First, although difficulties in reading the problem were presumably minimized by the tape-recorded administration, in which the pupils could hear as well as see the entire text, this procedure does not guarantee understanding. Some 9-year-olds may have had difficulty with *launching point, target, rocket,* or the distance concepts. The key to solving the problem is understanding the relative location of the points. Evidence for some lack of understanding is that 17 percent of the 9-year-olds and 3 percent of the 13-year-olds failed to attempt the exercise (giving either no response or a response of "I don't know"). Another reason for this failure, particularly for 9-year-olds, may have been an unfamiliarity with word problems. Nearly all of the 13-year-olds attempted the problem.

When they attempted the problem, did the pupils select the right operation? Usually they did. A few pupils in each age group attempted to add 525 and 624. But at least 47 percent of the 9-year-olds and 86 percent of the 13-year-olds used or tried to use subtraction. Also, many of the "other unacceptable" responses are likely to have been a consequence of numerical errors in subtraction.

These observations are reinforced and complemented by the data from other word problem exercises. The 9-year-olds tended to perform at a lower level than the 13-year-olds, were more likely to respond "I don't know," and made more errors in selecting the operation, doing the computations, and recalling number facts. In both age groups, the performance on word problem exercises tended to be slightly lower than the corresponding performance on computation exercises requiring the same operations.

The data suggest, indirectly, that the pupils seldom checked to see whether their answers to the word problems were correct or reasonable. For example, at least 14 percent of the 9-year-olds gave the answer of 101 to the word problem just discussed. The simple computation $101 + 525 = 626$ could have alerted them to their error.

Systematic development of the habit of checking one's results after doing a computation or working a problem should reduce dramatically the frequency of "careless" errors, and may even help overcome misunderstandings of arithmetic operations. The digit reversal error disappears with an increased understanding of subtraction, and checking subtraction problems by addition should reinforce the idea that addition and subtraction are inverse operations.

Learning to solve word problems is notoriously difficult. Yet the assessment data suggest that when pupils understand the related mathematical concepts, a large percentage can analyze a simple word problem correctly. If they are not completely familiar with the concepts, or if the problem is complex, then errors in the analysis of the problem (selection of the wrong operation, and so on) tend to occur.

Teachers may be able to improve pupils' performance beyond the levels shown in the assessment by providing instruction and practice to develop the pupils' skill in translating from a verbal sentence to a number sentence, their ability to analyze a problem situation, and their appreciation of the value of checking the reasonableness of a result.

SELECTED ACTIVITIES FOR PUPILS

1. If it takes $1\frac{1}{2}$ minutes to toast one slice of bread, how long will it take to toast 16 slices? (In a discussion the pupils should decide that answers will vary. The number of slices that can be toasted at the same time is not given.)
2. How many coins can you get in exchange for a quarter? (The class lists all possible answers: 25 pennies, 1 dime and 15 pennies, 2 dimes and 5 pennies, 1 dime and 3 nickels, 1 nickel and 20 pennies, etc.)
3. How much does a three-minute telephone call cost? (The pupils find the cost of calls to different locations and for various situations: a local call, a call to a selected city, a call to a selected foreign country, a night call, a weekend call, a collect call, an operator-assisted call, etc.)
4. Suppose you have only two jars, one holding 3 quarts and the other holding 5 quarts, and a pail filled with water. How would you get 1 quart of water?
5. A certain number of dogs and a certain number of birds together have 5 heads and 14 legs. How many of the animals can bark? How many wings are there?
6. If there are 2 people, 1 handshake can take place. If there are 3 people, 3 different handshakes can take place. If there are 4 people, 6 handshakes can take place. How many handshakes can there be with 5 people? With 6 people? Find the pattern.
7. Two people (A and B) can stand in a different order in 2 ways: AB and BA ($1 \times 2 = 2$). Three people (A, B, and C) in 6 ways: ABC, ACB, BAC,

BCA, CBA, and CAB ($1 \times 2 \times 3 = 6$). Find the number of ways 4 people can stand. What is the pattern?

8. If you know how much Mr. Red earns per month and how much his yearly expenses are, how do you find the amount he saves each year?
9. Open a reading book at any page. Estimate the number of words on the page. Check your estimate.
10. Find out what time it is now in New York, in Chicago, in Denver, and in San Francisco.
11. Find out how much postage is needed on a letter that weighs 20 grams if it is mailed to New York City, to Toronto, and to London, England.
12. In order to pay a debt of 49 cents with the fewest number of coins, what coins do you use?
13. Determine about how many pints of milk you drink in a week, in a month, and in a year. About how many quarts of milk do you drink in a month? About how many gallons in a year?
14. Find the names of five cities that have more than 500,000 people.
15. Get a newspaper that gives the rate of the advertisements. Select an advertisement and figure out how much it would cost.
16. Get a map. Select two cities and find the distance between the cities in miles. Then try to figure out the distance in kilometers.
17. Larry is younger than Mary. Sue is younger than Mark. Larry is older than Mark. Who is the oldest of the four?
18. Eight bananas have the same weight as 6 pears. Two apples have the same weight as 3 pears. How many apples have the same weight as 12 bananas?
19. Hank's weight is 5 kilograms less than Carol's weight. Carol's weight is 3 kilograms less than Ann's weight. Ann's weight is 6 kilograms less than Fred's weight. Hank's weight is 42 kilograms. How many kilograms does Fred weigh?
20. Ann has two coins with a total value of 15 cents. One of the coins is not a nickel. What coins does Ann have?

    Hint: If one of the coins is not a nickel, what is it?
21. The train "The Golden Express" leaves Rank City with the destination Copper City at 8 o'clock in the morning. It travels at an average speed of 60 miles per hour. The train "The Silver Arrow" leaves Copper City also at 8 o'clock in the morning with the destination Rank City and travels at an average speed of 70 miles per hour. Which train is nearer to Rank City when they pass?

    Hint: Consider the last word of the problem.

EXERCISES

1. Explain these terms: problem, quantitative problem, verbal quantitative problem, exercise, enigma.
2. Describe the steps that you think can be identified in the process of problem solving.
3. Describe the way in which a verbal problem can be used in the introduction of a new case in elementary school mathematics.
4. React to this statement: In elementary school mathematics generalizations should be formed inductively and applied deductively.
5. Why should the teaching of problem solving receive major attention in the mathematics curriculum of the elementary school?
6. Construct a one-step verbal problem and present a question, a solution, a check, and an interpretation of the answer.
7. Construct a multi-step verbal problem and solve it by pursuing the several steps presented in this chapter.
8. What, in your opinion, are five major causes of poor performance in the solving of verbal problems?
9. Translate each of the following verbal problems into an open mathematical sentence:
   a. After Ronald bought 30 postage stamps, he had a total of 150 stamps. How many stamps did Ronald have before he bought the 30 stamps?
   b. Mr. Nelson had $350 in his checking account. After he paid a debt by check he had $310 left. For what amount did Mr. Nelson write the check?
   c. Mary filled 8 pages in her scrapbook with pictures. She pasted the same number of pictures on each page. If she put a total of 48 pictures in her book, how many pictures did she paste on each page?
   d. A number of baseball cards were divided equally among 8 boys. If each boy got 7 cards, how many cards were there to be divided?
   e. Ed owned 35 books. After he received some more books he had a total of 42 books. How many books did Ed receive?
   f. Ken bought a bag of potato chips for 29¢. He paid 1¢ sales tax. How much change did Ken receive from a half dollar?

10. In this chapter several techniques were presented for improving problem solving. Describe and illustrate the following methods:
    a. The method of analogy.
    b. The method in which the pupil formulates a question to fit the situation presented.
    c. The method in which superfluous data must be identified.
    d. The method of presenting insufficient data.
    e. The method of using verbal problems without numbers.
    f. The method in which verbal problems are solved with the help of visual representations.

g. The method in which verbal problems that fit a given mathematical sentence are devised.

11. Explain how organized instruction in mental computation could improve the pupils' ability to solve verbal problems.
12. Select an important piece of research dealing with problem solving and report on it.
13. Suppose that you are responsible for the improvement of the mathematics curriculum in a typical elementary school. Assume that achievement test scores indicate that most pupils are not performing as well in problem solving as might be expected. Describe in detail what you would do to correct the situation.
14. Criticize the construction of several verbal problems in a randomly selected elementary school mathematics book. Offer suggestions for improvement.

SOURCES FOR FURTHER READING

Buswell, G. T., "Solving Problems in Arithmetic," *Education,* January, 1959, pp. 287–290.

D'Augustine, C. H., *Multiple Methods of Teaching Mathematics in the Elementary School,* 2nd ed. New York: Harper & Row, Publishers, 1973, Chap. IV.

Dewey, J., *How We Think.* Lexington, Mass.: D. C. Heath & Company, 1933, Chap. I.

Grossman, R., "Problem-Solving Activities Observed in British Primary Schools," *The Arithmetic Teacher,* January, 1969, pp. 34–38.

Henney, M., "Improving Mathematics Verbal Problem-Solving Ability through Reading Instruction," *The Arithmetic Teacher,* April, 1971, pp. 223–229.

Kennedy, L. M., *Guiding Children to Mathematical Discovery,* 2nd ed. Belmont, California: Wadsworth Publishing Company, Inc., 1975, Chap. XVII.

Koenker, R. H., "Twenty Methods for Improving Problem Solving," *The Arithmetic Teacher,* March, 1958, pp. 74–78.

Polya, G., *How to Solve It.* Garden City, N.Y.: Doubleday & Company, Inc., 1957.

Riedesel, C. A., "Problem Solving: Some Suggestions from Research," *The Arithmetic Teacher,* January, 1969, pp. 54–58.

Steffe, L. P., and D. C. Johnson, "Problem-Solving Performances of First-Grade Children," *Journal for Research in Mathematics Education,* January, 1971, pp. 50–64.

Trueblood, C. R., "Promoting Problem-Solving Skills through Nonverbal Problems," *The Arithmetic Teacher,* January, 1969, pp. 7–9.

Glossary[1]

Acute Angle. An angle whose measure is greater than 0° but less than 90°.

Addend. In $5 + 4 = 9$, five and four are the addends.

Addition. An operation on two numbers resulting in a single number, which is called the *sum*.

Additive Inverses (Opposites). To each positive or negative integer there corresponds a second integer such that the sum of these integers is zero. Thus each integer except zero has an opposite or additive inverse. Examples: The additive inverse of $^+2$ is $^-2$, since $^+2 + ^-2 = 0$; the opposite of $^-9$ is $^+9$, since $^-9 + ^+9 = 0$.

Algorism (Algorithm). A procedural pattern followed in finding the answer to a number question.

Aliquot Part. An aliquot part of a number is an exact divisor of that number. Example: Aliquot parts of 100 include 10, 25, and 50.

Angle. The union of two rays that have a common point of origin.

Area. A measure of a plane region.

Array. An arrangement of elements in rows and columns.

Associative Property of Addition. In the addition of more than two numbers, the way in which the addends are grouped does not affect the sum. Thus $(a + b) + c = a + (b + c)$. Example: $(15 + 17) + 13 = 15 + (17 + 13)$.

Associative Property of Multiplication. In the multiplication of more than two numbers, the way in which the factors are grouped does not affect the product. Thus $(a \times b) \times c = a \times (b \times c)$. Example: $(9 \times 5) \times 8 = 9 \times (5 \times 8)$.

Base. (1) *Number base:* The first collection in the number series. The base of the decimal system is ten. (2) *Of a geometric figure:* A side or a face of the figure.

---

1. The terms and expressions included in this glossary are explained or illustrated by definition, description, example, or by a combination of these.

(3) *In exponential notation:* In 2^3, the base is 2. (4) *In relation to percents:* In 6% of 400 = 24, the base is 400.

Binary Number Operation. An operation on two numbers.

Cardinal Number. A cardinal number indicates how many objects are being considered. Example: This book has 92 pages.

Cartesian Product. The Cartesian product of sets A and B is the set made up of all the ordered pairs that can be formed by pairing each element of A with each element of B.

Chord of a Circle. A line segment that has both endpoints on a given circle.

Circle. A simple closed curve in a given plane, all the points of which are the same distance from the center.

Circumference of a Circle. The perimeter of the circle.

Closed Mathematical Sentence. A mathematical sentence that is true or that is false. Examples $7 + 2 = 9$; $7 + 2 = 8$.

Closure. If an operation on any members of a set results in a member of that set, the operation is said to have the property of closure. Example: The sum of any two whole numbers is a whole number. Thus the set of whole numbers is closed with respect to addition.

Commutative Property of Addition. In the addition of two numbers, the order of the addends can be changed without affecting the sum. Thus $a + b = b + a$. Example: $5 + 6 = 6 + 5$.

Commutative Property of Multiplication. In the multiplication of two numbers, the order of the factors can be changed without affecting the product. Thus $a \times b = b \times a$. Example: $5 \times 6 = 6 \times 5$.

Complement of a Number. A complement of a number is the difference between that number and the next greater power of ten. Examples: The complement of 8 is 2; the complement of 76 is 24.

Composite Numbers. Integers greater than one that have integral factors other than the number itself and one. Example: 6.

Concurrent Lines. Lines that have one single point of intersection.

Congruency. Congruent line segments have the same length. Congruent angles have the same measure. Congruent triangles have the same size and the same shape.

Counting Numbers. The set of counting numbers is expressed as $\{1, 2, 3, \cdots\}$.

Cube. A solid with six congruent square faces.

Curve. A curve is thought of as a continuous set of points passed through in going from one point to another.

Decimal. A numeral in which the positional-value system is extended to places to the right of the ones. Examples: 1.3; .34; .345.

Denominator of a Fraction. The "namer" of the number of congruent subunits into which the original unit or group is divided. Example: In $\frac{2}{3}$, three is the denominator.

Diameter. A line segment that has both endpoints on a given circle and that passes through the center of the circle. A diameter of a circle is the largest possible chord of that circle.

Difference. In $9 - 5 = 4$, four is the difference.

Digits. In the decimal system, ten digits or symbols are used for writing numerals: 0, 1, 2, 3, 4, 5, 6, 7, 8, 9.

Directed Numbers (Signed Numbers). Numbers whose numerals are preceded by a positive sign ($^+$) or a negative sign ($^-$).

Direct Measurement. In direct measurement the selected standard unit is applied to the object under consideration. For example, the length of a table is determined by using a foot ruler.

Disjoint Sets. Two sets are disjoint sets if the intersection of the two sets is the empty set.

Dissimilar Fractions. *See* Unlike Fractions.

Distributive Property of Multiplication with Respect to Addition. When the sum of two numbers is to be multiplied by a given number, it is proper to multiply each addend by the given number and to add the products. Thus $a \times (b + c) = (a \times b) + (a \times c)$. Example: $6 \times (10 + 4) = (6 \times 10) + (6 \times 4) = 60 + 24 = 84$.

Dividend. In $12 \div 4 = 3$, twelve is the dividend.

Division. An operation used to find the missing factor in a multiplication situation where one of the two factors and the product are known.

Divisor. In $12 \div 4 = 3$, four is the divisor.

Domain. *See* Replacement Set.

Elements (Members) of a Set. The items that make up a set.

Empty Set (Null Set). The set that has no members.

Equal (Identical) Sets. Sets that have precisely the same members.

Equation. A sentence that asserts an equality between two expressions. The symbol = is used to express an equality. Example: $8 + 5 = 10 + 3$.

Equilateral Triangle. A triangle with three congruent sides.

Equivalent Fractions. Fractions that name the same fractional number. Example: $\frac{1}{2}$ and $\frac{2}{4}$.

Equivalent Sets. Sets whose elements can be placed in one-to-one correspondence. Example: If $A = \{1, 2, 3\}$ and $B = \{7, 8, 9\}$, then $A \leftrightarrow B$.

Even Number. A whole number that is evenly divisible by 2.

Expanded Notation. In $325 = 300 + 20 + 5$, 325 has been expressed in expanded notation. Note that the positional value of each digit is shown.

Exponent. In 2^3, the superscript 3 is the exponent and indicates the number of times the base 2 is used as a factor.

Exponential Notation. If 100 is written as 10^2, it is expressed in exponential notation.

Factor. Any of two or more numbers that are multiplied to form a product is a factor of that product. Example: In $2 \times 4 = 8$, 2 and 4 are factors of the product 8.

Finite Set. A set that has a limited number of elements.

Flip. *See* Reflection.

Fractional Numbers. The positive rational numbers and zero.

Function. A set of ordered pairs in which each pair has a different first element.

Fundamental Theorem of Arithmetic. A composite number can be expressed as a product of primes in a unique way.

Greatest Common Divisor (GCD). The GCD of two or more numbers is the largest of all the common divisors of the numbers. Example: The GCD of 12 and 30 is 6.

Hexagon. A six-sided polygon.

Highest Common Factor (HCF). *See* Greatest Common Divisor.

Identical Sets. *See* Equal Sets.

Identity Element for Addition. The identity element for addition is zero. Thus $a + 0 = a$. Example: $5 + 0 = 5$.

Identity Element for Multiplication. The identity element for multiplication is one. Thus $1 \times a = a$. Example: $1 \times 5 = 5$.

Indirect Measurement. In indirect measurement the standard unit of measure is not applied directly to the object under consideration. For example, the altitude of a mountain top is measured indirectly by application of the proper formula.

Inequality. A sentence that asserts that one expression is greater than, less than, or not equal to another expression. Examples: $5 \neq 6$; $6 > 5$; $5 < 6$.

Infinite Set. A set that is not finite.

Integers. The set of integers is expressed as $\{\cdots, {}^-3, {}^-2, {}^-1, 0, {}^+1, {}^+2, {}^+3, \cdots\}$.

Intersection of Two Sets. The intersection of two sets is another set that contains the members that are common to both sets. Example: If $A = \{1, 2, 3\}$ and $B = \{2, 3, 4\}$, then $A \cap B = \{2, 3\}$.

Inverse Operations. Addition and subtraction are inverse operations: $(5 + 2) - 2 = 5$. Multiplication and division are inverse operations: $(4 \times 5) \div 4 = 5$. Note that in inverse operations one operation "undoes" what the other one "does."

Irrational Number. A number that cannot be expressed as the quotient of an integer and a nonzero integer.

Isosceles Triangle. A triangle that has at least two congruent sides.

Least (Lowest) Common Multiple (LCM). The LCM of two or more numbers is the smallest number that is evenly divisible by each of these numbers. Example: The LCM of 6 and 15 is 30.

Like Fractions (Similar Fractions). Fractions that have the same denominator. Example: $\frac{1}{4}$ and $\frac{3}{4}$.

Line. A line is a mathematical idea; it is thought of as a one-dimensional figure that extends without end in two directions.

Line Segment. A set of points whose members are two given points and all points on the straight line between these two points.

Matching Sets. Sets whose elements can be placed in one-to-one correspondence. (*See also* Equivalent Sets.)

Mathematical Expression. A mathematical phrase. It does not tell or ask anything by itself. Example: $5 + 3$.

Mathematical Sentence. A group of mathematical symbols that tells or asks something by itself. Example: $5 > 3$.

Mean. The mean of, for example, 3 numbers is determined by adding the numbers and dividing the obtained sum by 3. Example: The mean of 4, 5, and 6 is

$$\frac{4 + 5 + 6}{3} = \frac{15}{3} = 5.$$

Measure. A number that expresses some aspect of an object in standard units. Example: The measure of the length of an object may be expressed as five inches.

Median. The median of a set of measures arranged in order of size is the middle measure. Example: The median of 7, 8, 9, 12, 15, 16, and 19 is 12.

Members of an Equation. The expressions to the left and the right of the equal sign in an equation.

Members of a Set. *See* Elements of a Set.

Minuend. In $9 - 5 = 4$, nine is the minuend.

Mixed Fraction. A fraction that contains a numeral naming a whole number and a fraction. Example: $3\frac{1}{2}$.

Mode. The most frequently observed measure in a set of measures. Example: If the scores on a test are 35, 37, 38, 37, 41, 33, 43, 35, 37, 39, 41, and 39, the mode is 37.

Multipart Fraction. A fraction that has a numerator greater than 1. Example: $\frac{3}{4}$.

Multiple. A multiple of a number is any number of which the given number is a factor.

Multiplicand. In $5 \times 9 = 45$, nine is the multiplicand.

Multiplication. An operation on two numbers resulting in a single number, which is called the *product*.

Multiplicative Inverses. *See* Reciprocals.

Multiplier. In $5 \times 9 = 45$, five is the multiplier.

Natural Numbers. The numbers that are used in the counting series are usually called the natural numbers. The set of natural numbers is expressed as $\{1, 2, 3, \cdots\}$.

Negative Number. A number that is less than zero. The numeral for such a number is preceded by the negative sign, as in $^-5$.

Notation System. A system of writing numbers.

Null Set. *See* Empty Set.

Numeral. A symbol for a number.

Numeration System. A system of expressing numbers by words and of reading numerals.

Numerator of a Fraction. The "numberer" or "counter" of the subunits expressed by the denominator of the fraction. Example: In $\frac{2}{3}$, two is the numerator.

Obtuse Angle. An angle whose measure is greater than 90° and less than 180°.

Odd Number. A whole number that when divided by 2 leaves a remainder of 1.

One-to-One Correspondence. Sets A and B are said to be in one-to-one correspondence if their elements can be matched so that to each element in set A there corresponds one and only one element in set B, and vice versa.

Open Mathematical Sentence. A mathematical sentence that contains an unknown and that cannot be said to be either true or false. Example: $4 + \square = 7$.

Opposites. *See* Additive Inverses.

Ordered Number Pair. In an ordered pair of numbers the numbers occur in a special order.

Ordinal Number. An ordinal number tells which place an object occupies in a series. Example: Turn to the second page.

Parallel Lines. Lines that are in the same plane and that have no point in common.

Parallelogram. A quadrilateral whose pairs of opposite sides are parallel and congruent.

Pentagon. A five-sided polygon.

Percent. Percent means per hundred. Example: 6% means 6 per hundred. Thus 6% of 400 = 24.

Percentage. In 6% of 400 = 24, the percentage is 24.

Perimeter of a Polygon. The sum of the measures of the sides.

Perpendicular Lines. Lines that intersect at right angles.

Placeholder. A symbol in an open mathematical sentence that holds the place for a numeral. Example: $6 + \square = 10$. Note that the zero in a numeral such as 304 is considered to be a placeholder, since it holds the place of the tens.

Place Value. In our system of notation the place value or positional value of a digit depends on the place it occupies in the numeral. In 45, the place value or positional value of the 4 is 40, since it represents 4 tens.

Plane. A plane is a set of points that can be thought of as a flat surface, such as an extended table top. A plane is unlimited in extent.

Point. A geometric point is a mathematical idea; it is thought of as an exact location in space.

Polygon. A simple closed curve that is the union of line segments.

Positional Value. *See* Place Value.

Positive Number. A number that is greater than zero.

Power. Since $100 = 10^2$, 100 is the second power of 10. The exponent (the superscript) expresses the power.

Precision in Measurement. A measurement is assumed to be precise to the smallest unit reported. For example, if a measure is reported as 15 inches (rounded to the nearest inch) and another measure is reported as 6 inches (also rounded to the nearest inch), the objects have been measured with the same precision.

Prime Numbers. Integers greater than one that have exactly two integral factors: the number itself and one. Example: 5.

Product. In $9 \times 5 = 45$, 45 is the product.

Proportion. A proportion expresses the equality of two ratios. Example: 3:5 = 6:10, or $\frac{3}{5} = \frac{6}{10}$.

Quadrilateral. A four-sided polygon.

Quotient. In $12 \div 4 = 3$, the quotient is 3.

Radius (Plural: Radii). A radius of a circle is a line segment with one endpoint at the center of the circle and the other endpoint on the circle.

Ratio. A comparison between two numbers. Example: The ratio of the number 4 to the number 5 is expressed as 4 to 5, or 4:5, or $\frac{4}{5}$.

Rational Number. A number that can be expressed as the quotient of an integer and a nonzero integer.

Ray. A set of points containing the point of origin and all the points on the (straight) line extending in one direction from that point.

Real Numbers. The real numbers comprise the rational and the irrational numbers.

Reciprocals. Two numbers are said to be reciprocals or multiplicative inverses if their product is one. Example: $\frac{1}{2}$ and 2.

Rectangle. A quadrilateral having four right angles. The opposite sides of a rectangle are congruent.

Reflection. A reflection moves a figure over a line from its original position through different planes to a position upside down from where it started. In the classroom it is usually called a flip.

Remainder. In the division $\begin{array}{r} 3 \\ 3\overline{)10} \\ \underline{9} \\ 1 \end{array}$, the remainder is 1.

Renaming. 25 can be renamed as 20 + 5, $1\frac{1}{2}$ as $\frac{3}{2}$, $\frac{6}{8}$ as $\frac{3}{4}$.

Repeating Decimal. When the division indicated by a fraction is performed and the division process does not terminate, but a repeating pattern is observed in the quotient, the result is called a repeating decimal. Example: $\frac{1}{9} = .11\overline{1} \cdots$ or $.\overline{1}$.

Replacement Set (Domain). The set of objects that can be used as replacements in a condition.

Rhombus. A quadrilateral with four congruent sides.

Right Angle. An angle that has a measure of 90°.

Right Triangle. A triangle in which one of the angles is a right angle.

Rotation. A rotation moves a figure a given amount around a fixed point in a specified direction. In the classroom it is usually called a turn.

Scalene Triangle. A triangle in which no two sides are congruent.

Set. A collection of concrete or abstract entities.

Signed Numbers. *See* Directed Numbers.

Similar Fractions. *See* Like Fractions.

Similarity. Similar figures have the same shape but not necessarily the same size. In such figures corresponding angles are congruent and corresponding line segments are proportional.

Simple Closed Curve. A curve that begins and ends at the same point and that does not cross itself.

Slide. *See* Translation.

Solid. A three-dimensional figure.

Solution Set (Truth Set). The set containing all members that will make a given open mathematical sentence true. Example: If $D = \{0, 1, 2, 3, \cdots\}$ and the condition is $5 + \square < 10$, the solution set is $\{0, 1, 2, 3, 4\}$.

Space. The set of all points.
Square. A rectangle with four congruent sides.
Straight Angle. An angle that has a measure of 180°.
Subset. If set A is contained in set U, it is called a subset of set U. Example: If set $U = \{1, 2, 3, \cdots\}$ and set $A = \{2, 4, 6, \cdots\}$, then A is a subset of U.
Subtraction. An operation used to find the missing addend if one of the two addends and the sum are known.
Subtrahend. In $9 - 5 = 4$, five is the subtrahend.
Sum. In $5 + 4 = 9$, nine is the sum.
Supplementary Angles. Two angles, the sum of whose measures is 180°.

Terminating Decimal. When the division indicated by a fraction is performed and the division process ends, the result is called a terminating decimal. Example: $\frac{5}{20} = .25$.
Topology. Topology deals with geometric properties that do not vary when figures are transformed in a prescribed way.
Translation. A motion in a given straight direction over a specified distance. In the classroom it is usually called a slide.
Trapezoid. A quadrilateral in which one pair of opposite sides is parallel and the other pair is not parallel.
Triangle. A three-sided polygon.
Truth Set. *See* Solution Set.
Turn. *See* Rotation.

Union of Two Sets. The union of two sets is the set whose members belong to one set, to the other set, or to both sets. Example: If $A = \{1, 2\}$ and $B = \{2, 3\}$, then $A \cup B = \{1, 2, 3\}$.
Unit Fraction. A fraction that has one as numerator. Example: $\frac{1}{4}$.
Universal Set. A specified set from which other sets (subsets) are derived.
Unlike Fractions (Dissimilar Fractions). Fractions that have different denominators. Example: $\frac{1}{2}$ and $\frac{1}{4}$.

Venn Diagram. A graphical representation of operations on sets and relations between them.
Vertex (Plural: Vertices). The point of intersection of two rays or of two sides of a polygon.
Volume. A measure of a solid.

Whole Numbers. The set of whole numbers is expressed as $\{0, 1, 2, 3, \cdots\}$.

Important Symbols in Elementary School Mathematics

Symbol	Meaning or Description
$+$	plus, add; positive
$-$	minus, subtract; negative
$\times$	times, multiply
$\div$	divide (by)
$\overline{)\ }$	division
$\sqrt{}$	square root of
$\cup$	union
$\cap$	intersection
$=$	is equal to
$\neq$	is not equal to
$>$	is greater than, is more than
$<$	is less than
$\leftrightarrow$	is equivalent to
$\not\leftrightarrow$	is not equivalent to
$\subset$	is a subset of
2^3	$2 \times 2 \times 2$ (2 is the base, 3 is the exponent)
π	pi
%	percent
$.166\overline{6} \cdots$ or $.1\overline{6}$	showing repeating decimal
:	to (ratio)
( )	parentheses
[ ]	brackets
{ }	braces
(3, 4)	the ordered pair 3, 4
$\varnothing$ or { }	null set, empty set
{3, 4, 5}	the set whose members are 3, 4, 5
$\{n \mid n < 5\}$	the set whose members are all n that satisfy the condition that n be less than 5

$\overleftrightarrow{AB}$	line AB
$\overline{AB}$	line segment AB
$\overrightarrow{AB}$	ray AB
$\overline{AB} \cong \overline{CD}$	line segment AB is congruent to line segment CD
$\angle BAC$	angle BAC
$\triangle ABC$	triangle ABC
$90°$	90 degrees

Answers to Selected Exercises

CHAPTER 4

11.

17	1,610
29	100,101
467	13
11	4
103	21
2,001	10

CHAPTER 5

7. no yes
8. False. True. True. False.
9. 32
10. {1, 3, 5, 7 9} {5}
11. $\{a, b, c, d\}$ $\{b, c, d\}$ $\{a, b, d\}$
$\{b\}$ { } $\{d\}$
12. {7, 8, 9, 10, 11, 12} {9, 10}
13. a. infinite
b. infinite
c. finite
14. 5

CHAPTER 6

8. $252 = 2^2 \times 3^2 \times 7$
$540 = 2^2 \times 3^3 \times 5$

$375 = 3 \times 5^3$
$3{,}150 = 2 \times 3^2 \times 5^2 \times 7$
$2{,}112 = 2^6 \times 3 \times 11$

9. 30

10. 2,100

11. 7

12. GCD is 6
LCM is 270

13. $2^2 \times 3^2 \times 5^3$

CHAPTER 7

5.

11	12	5
35	9	15

6. a. $n \div 9$ or $\frac{n}{9}$
b. $4 \times (10 + 15)$
c. $3n - 9$

7. 12

8. 17 dimes and 12 quarters

9. {3}
{1, 2, 3, 4, 5}
{1, 2}

CHAPTER 9

2. b. 11 c. 25 d. 25 e. 24

3. Sixteen possible outcomes:

HHHH	HHHT	HHTT	TTTH	TTTT
	HHTH	HTTH	TTHT	
	HTHH	THTH	THTT	
	THHH	TTHH	HTTT	
		HTHT		
		THHT		

Probability:

4H: $\frac{1}{16}$
3H and 1T in any order: $\frac{4}{16}$, or $\frac{1}{4}$
2H and 2T in any order: $\frac{6}{16}$, or $\frac{3}{8}$
3T and 1H in any order: $\frac{4}{16}$, or $\frac{1}{4}$
4T: $\frac{1}{16}$

CHAPTER 19

Exercises: Length

1. 5 000
4
20
0.888

2. 0.655
0.26
5
1.5

3. 1 011
2.28
2 500
700

4. 70
6
1
8

5. 1
   1.2
   0.5
   2.4
6. 50
   6
   1.8
   300
7. 2
8. 31
9. 5
10. 10 below
11. a. True.
    b. True.

Exercises: Area

1. 30 000
   60
   0.3
   800 000
2. 5
   240
   1 200 000
   0.5
3. 0.8
   2.4
   1
   150
4. 50
   240
   1.25
   1
5. 2
   14 000
   2.4
   500 000
6. 1
   40
   2
   25
7. 1
8. 1.5
9. a. True.
   b. False.
   c. False.

Exercises: Volume and Capacity

1. 1 000
   0.001
   1 000
2. 3
   1 200
   500
3. 1
   1 000
   0.001
4. 0.6
   4
   2 500
5. 1.8
6. 27
7. 3
8. 20
9. a. False.
   b. True.
   c. True.

Exercises: Weight

1. 1 000
   0.001
   0.001
   1 000
2. 4
   1 500
   0.5
   2 500

3. 1.4
900
2
200

4. 2.5
1.4
2
500

5. 2 500

6. 120

7. 1.2

8. a. True.
b. False.
c. True.

9. 72

10. a. 22
b. 45
c. 5
d. 14

Exercises: Temperature

1. 25
38
22
⁻40

2. 50
75.2
59
10.4

Answers to Skills Tests

CHAPTER 11

1.	527	1,183	392	1,065	666
2.	13,397	13,168	15,646	20,692	11,199
3.	3	5	$^{-}9$		
	5	4	$^{-}11$		
	4	$^{-}3$	$^{-}11$		
	0	$^{-}7$	$^{-}3$		

CHAPTER 12

1.	67	151	1,898	1,729	7,656
2.	2,660	119	3,897	30,790	12,923
3.	$^{+}4$	$^{-}1$	$^{+}5$	$^{+}2$	
	$^{+}10$	$^{-}3$	$^{+}4$	$^{+}4$	
	$^{+}10$	$^{-}1$	$^{+}1$	$^{+}1$	

CHAPTER 13

1.	2,475	6,138	1,408	1,911
	1,280	2,397	7,440	4,875
2.	2,275	64,416	8,961	4,071
	3,360	13,125	56,400	35,208
3.	300	2,200	8,000	3,800
	3,700	2,200	14,000	1,300
4.	54,322	236,816	15,679,920	28,930,440
	231,814	21,730	66,799,080	2,531,581

CHAPTER 14

1. 13 73 37 104
45 84 58 209
2. 1,228 5,550 6,542
3. $13 \times 15 + 2 = 197$ $33 \times 25 + 10 = 835$ $209 \times 125 + 9 = 26{,}134$

CHAPTER 15

1. $20\frac{7}{24}$ $36\frac{1}{10}$ $30\frac{7}{12}$ $6\frac{1}{10}$
2. $6\frac{9}{14}$ $14\frac{9}{20}$ $55\frac{5}{6}$ $8\frac{29}{40}$
3. 7 11 13 18
4. 8 9 55 36
5. 12 15 14 49
6. 18 30 88 60
7. 7 $33\frac{3}{4}$ $28\frac{1}{2}$ $\frac{1}{4}$
8. 20 40
9. $\frac{1}{5}$ 4 $\frac{6}{5}$ $\frac{5}{8}$
10. 4 10 $1\frac{1}{5}$ $1\frac{3}{4}$
11. 5 8 $1\frac{13}{17}$ 4
12. 4 $6\frac{1}{2}$

CHAPTER 16

1. 16.7 110.12
95.93 211.553
2. $179.56 $901.73
$17.43 $23.66
3. 26.48 43.66 69.81
.37 276.904 64.4
4. $96.25 $9.90 $10.27
$3.16 $144.49 $18.14
5. 5.4 .72 4.38 1.692
5.6 .024 .1309 7.991
6. $18.65 $33.41 $21.75 $1003.20
$81.36 $18.02 $8.36 $812.76
7. 2.5 .5 5 7
11.2 .41 5 9
8. 19 $5.30 $73.48
22 $17.20 $34.03
9. .25 .2
10. 16.7 25.9 18.5 16.3 6.9
11. $15 $7 $9 $20 $9
12. $1.56 $2.38 $6.01 $9.10 $2.91
13. .625 .75 .3125 .28 .6 .9
14. $\frac{3}{20}$ $\frac{51}{200}$ $\frac{4}{5}$ $\frac{7}{8}$ $\frac{7}{40}$ $\frac{27}{100}$
15. a. 500.003 b. .503 c. 55.055 d. 5.005

CHAPTER 17

1. 4% 36% 9% 15%
74% 115% 99% 250%

2.	50%	30%	75%	$37\frac{1}{2}$%
	25%	40%	5%	6%
3.	.22	.03	.17	.01
	.49	.08	.60	.09
4.	$\frac{1}{10}$	$\frac{1}{2}$	$\frac{9}{10}$	$\frac{1}{20}$
	$\frac{3}{20}$	$\frac{3}{4}$	$\frac{3}{5}$	$\frac{1}{4}$
5.	6	15	20	15
	2	4	5	14
6.	14.4	30	20	
	350	75	300	

7. $2.50
8. 60%
9. 25%
10. $5,000

CHAPTER 18

1.	3 ft. 3 in.	3 yd. 1 ft. 3 in.
	3 lb. 14 oz.	2 bu. 2 pk.
2.	6 lb. 3 oz.	10 gal. 2 qt.
	1 mi. 4980 ft.	40 min.
3.	3 lbs. 4 oz.	1528 cu. in.
	1 sq. ft. 61 sq. in.	26 cu. ft.
4.	1 mi. 720 ft.	29 cu. ft.
	2 sq. mi.	1228 cu. in.

5. $16\frac{1}{2}$ ft.
6. 75.36 in.
7. 320 tiles
8. 220.5 sq. ft.
9. $42\frac{1}{2}$ sq. in.
10. 122 sq. in.
11. 19.625 sq. in.
12. $357\frac{1}{2}$ cu. yd.
13. 16 sq. in.
14. 220.8 gal.
15. 384 sq. in.

Index

NATIONAL UNIVERSITY
LIBRARY

NAL UNIVER
LIBRARY

QA 135.5 K7 1978 c.2

Kramer, Klaas

VISTA

Teaching elementary school mathematics

DATE DUE

DEC 14 1981			
AUG 03 1982	AUG 20 2002		
SEP 05 1983			
NOV 24 1983			
NOV 23 1983 AUG 22 1984			
Sep 4			
OCT 07 1986			
SEP 14 1987			

019912